Blacks in the New World

Edited by August Meier and John H. Bracey

A list of books in the series appears at the end of this book.

LOCAL PEOPLE

JOHN DITTMER

LOCAL
PEOPLE

The Struggle
for Civil Rights
in Mississippi

UNIVERSITY OF ILLINOIS PRESS
Urbana and Chicago

Publication of this book was supported by a grant from DePauw
University, Greencastle, Indiana.

This book is printed on acid-free paper.

Library of Congress Cataloging-in-Publication Data

Dittmer, John, 1939–
    Local people : the struggle for civil rights in Mississippi / John
Dittmer.
        p.   cm. — (Blacks in the New World)
    ISBN 0-252-02102-9 (cloth : acid-free paper)
    1. Afro-Americans—Mississippi—Politics and government.
2. Afro-Americans—Mississippi—Suffrage. 3. Civil rights
movements—Mississippi—History—20th century.
4. Mississippi—Race relations. 5. Mississippi—Politics and
government—1865–1950. 6. Mississippi—Politics and
government—1951–   . I. Title. II. Series
E185.93.M6D58   1994
323.1'1960730762—dc20   93-39632
                                                              CIP

For Julie, Dave, and Ellen

Contents

1   We Return Fighting   1

2   Rising Expectations, 1946–54   19

3   The Magnolia Jungle   41

4   Toward a New Beginning   70

5   Outside Agitators   90

6   Into the Delta   116

7   Greenwood and Jackson   143

8   Organizing Mississippi   170

9   Conflicting Strategies   194

10 Freedom Days   215

11 That Summer   242

12 The Mississippi Freedom Democratic Party
    and the Atlantic City Challenge   272

13 Aftermath in McComb   303

14 Battle Fatigue   315

15 The Collapse of the COFO Coalition   338

16 CDGM and the Politics of Poverty   363

17 The Last March   389
18 A New Mississippi?   408
    Afterword   431
    Acknowledgments   435
    Notes   439
    Index   513

Illustrations follow pages 142 and 314

1

We Return Fighting

We return from the slavery of the uniform which the
world's madness demanded us to don to the freedom of
civilian garb. . . . We sing: This country of ours, despite all
its better souls have done and dreamed, is yet a shameful
land. It *lynches*. . . . It *disfranchises* its own citizens. . . . It
encourages *ignorance*. . . . It steals from us. . . . It insults
us. . . . We *return*. We *return from fighting*. We *return
fighting*.
—W. E. B. Du Bois, *Crisis*, 19 (May 1919), 13–14

On July 2, 1946, Medgar Wylie Evers celebrated his twenty-first birthday by leading a group of World War II veterans, including his brother Charles, through the nearly abandoned streets
of Decatur, Mississippi. Their destination was the county courthouse, where they intended to vote in the Democratic primary election. Medgar had seen combat in both France and Germany, but
he and the other GIs were unprepared for the scene that greeted
them in their hometown. When the group arrived at the courthouse,
"some 15 or 20 armed white men surged in behind us, men I had
grown up with, had played with. . . . We stood there for a minute.
We were bluffing. We knew we weren't going to get by this mob."
As the veterans retreated down the street, Evers looked up to see a
black Ford cruising alongside, and "a guy leaned out with a shotgun, keeping a bead on us all the time."[1]

Angered and humiliated, the men went home and returned with
their guns. Leaving the weapons hidden in their car, they again attempted to enter the polling place, but once more the mob turned

them away. After that, "We didn't pursue it. We drove back." Years later Medgar Evers, now the Mississippi NAACP state field secretary, ruefully observed that "I was born in Decatur, was raised there, but I never in my life was permitted to vote there."[2]

The 1946 election was the first statewide Mississippi contest since *Smith* v. *Allwright*, the 1944 U.S. Supreme Court decision that had outlawed the white primary. (The Democratic primary was the only election of importance in the Deep South.) National attention had focused on the Magnolia State, for Theodore "The Man" Bilbo was seeking a third U.S. Senate term in a hotly contested race. A political force in Mississippi for four decades, Bilbo was the champion of the state's poor whites and an ardent white supremacist. His solution to the nation's race problems was to deport black Americans to Africa. Along with his Mississippi colleague Senator James O. Eastland, Bilbo had fought the repeal of the poll tax, antilynching legislation, and a bill to establish a permanent Fair Employment Practices Committee (FEPC). In this reelection campaign, however, he focused on the immediate threat posed by *Smith* v. *Allwright*.

In towns and hamlets across the state, Bilbo urged his white audiences to prevent blacks from voting in the primary, predicting that "if you let a handful go to the polls in July there will be two handfuls in 1947, and from there on it will grow into a mighty surge." He warned that "the white people of Mississippi are sleeping on a volcano, and it is left up to you red-blooded men to do something about it." Then, dramatically lowering his voice, the senator would confide, "But you and I know what's the best way to keep the nigger from voting. You do it the night before the election. I don't have to tell you any more than that. Red-blooded men know what I mean." Bilbo was not alone in his determination to keep blacks from the polls. The *Jackson Daily News* gave this advice to Negro voters under the headline "DON'T TRY IT!": "Don't attempt to participate in the Democratic primaries anywhere in Mississippi on July 2nd. Staying away from the polls on that date will be the best way to prevent unhealthy and unhappy results."[3] Nevertheless, on primary day several thousand blacks turned out to vote, among them the Reverend William Albert Bender.

A chaplain at Tougaloo College, the sixty-year-old Bender had been the leading spiritual force at that American Missionary Association school, founded in the aftermath of the Civil War on a cotton plantation just north of the state capital at Jackson. Proud, cou-

rageous, and combative, Bender embodied the democratic principles set forth in the college's charter and transmitted to generations
of black Mississippi students trapped along the color line. On primary day Bender enlisted two Tougaloo students to drive him to
his voting precinct in Ridgeland, a small community a few miles
from the campus. As he approached the schoolhouse where the voting was underway, three white men stopped him, bluntly stating
that they were not permitting blacks to vote. When Bender replied
that he was registered and asked what right they had to "prevent a
citizen from voting," one of the whites retorted, "This is a Democratic primary, this is a white man's primary, and niggers haven't
any business voting in a Democratic primary." The Tougaloo chaplain calmly told the men, "I came here to vote, and I guess I will
attend to my business." As he pushed past them and climbed the
steps he found his path blocked by a deputy sheriff who, with his
pistol drawn, cursed Bender and dared him to enter the polls. Bender
called to the two students to come over and act as witnesses. Terrified, they remained in the car. A short time later the minister rejoined the students, assuring them that "we will have a chance to
come back in the next election." On returning home Bender filed a
complaint with U.S. Attorney General Tom Clark. It was futile.
Later, a cross burned on the Tougaloo campus.[4] The experiences
of William Bender and Medgar Evers were typical on that election
day.

Bilbo easily won the primary. Of 5,000 black registrants, approximately half were permitted to cast their ballots. Even if all registered blacks had voted against Bilbo, the results would have been
the same. But these figures beg the question. Almost 350,000 black
Mississippians were of voting age in 1946, and blacks believed that
Bilbo's intimidating speeches frightened away thousands of potential registrants. On September 19, fifty Mississippians (including
several whites) filed a complaint with the U.S. Senate Committee
to Investigate Campaign Expenditures, claiming that Bilbo had subjected blacks to a "reign of terror" during the campaign and urging the full Senate to impeach Bilbo and remove him from office.
Leading the anti-Bilbo campaign were local NAACP branches and
the Progressive Voters' League, a new middle-class black civic organization that had chapters in several cities and towns.[5]

Although the committee agreed to hold hearings in Jackson during the first week in December, the deck was already stacked against

the petitioners. Three of the five senators on the committee—Democrats Burnett Maybank of South Carolina, Elmer Thomas of Oklahoma, and Chairman Allen Ellender of Louisiana—represented states with long histories of discrimination against black voters. The two Republican members, Styles Bridges of New Hampshire and Burton Hickenlooper of Iowa, were conservatives not known for their advocacy of civil rights. Ellender, a close friend of Bilbo, rejected a request that NAACP lawyers serve as formal counsel for the witnesses; declined to subpoena blacks to testify, thereby leaving "volunteer" witnesses more vulnerable to reprisal; and refused to summon reporters covering the campaign to verify their stories describing Bilbo's inflamatory rhetoric. Blacks received some support from the national office of the NAACP and from attorney Emanuel Bloch of the leftist Civil Rights Congress. Still, few observers believed that blacks would turn out to testify in significant numbers. NAACP attorney Charles Houston reported from Jackson that "everybody on our side was afraid that only a few witnesses would show up," and Senator Ellender told the press that he expected only about twenty-five people to agree to testify under oath.[6]

When the hearings opened at the Federal Building courtroom in Jackson on December 2, nearly 200 blacks from all parts of the state were packing the corridors, registering to testify. Included in the group were farmers, day laborers, doctors, ministers, and college students. A majority were World War II veterans. Ellender was not the only person "taken aback by the numbers who appeared." Although civil rights attorneys had counseled a few key people, they had not met with most of the witnesses, a failure Houston immediately regretted. To begin with, there was no mistaking the fact that the deliberations were taking place deep in the Jim Crow South. The federal courtroom was strictly segregated, with the first seventeen of the twenty rows of seats reserved for white spectators. Court officials at first refused attorney Houston admittance to the chamber and then denied him a seat with the other attorneys inside the bar. At the end of each day's session, a court attendant stationed himself at the huge rear door to make sure that all white spectators had cleared the hall before blacks were permitted to leave.[7]

Chairman Ellender made his biases clear early on. He stated that the election officials were within their legal rights in barring black voters from the white primary. In his view, *Smith* v. *Allwright,* a Texas case, was not binding on Mississippi. He charged that the

entire challenge had developed through the machinations of outsiders from New York. Throughout the four days of the hearings
Ellender acted informally as Bilbo's counsel, badgering witnesses,
anticipating and asking questions handed up by Bilbo's attorneys,
and exchanging winks with the senator as black victims testified.
Ellender made no effort to mask his sympathies for Bilbo's position. "You know, I am sure," he lectured one black witness, "that
only white folks should vote in the Democratic primaries."[8]

Still, despite their inadequate briefing, the partisanship of the
committee's Democratic majority, and the intimidating presence of
several hundred unfriendly white Mississippians in the audience, the
witnesses acquitted themselves admirably. Victor Bernstein of *PM*
newspaper, one of about twenty reporters on the scene, recorded
his impressions of the first day of the hearing: "More than a score
of Negro witnesses, dressed carefully in their Sunday best, dignified in manner but by no means servile, calmly laid bare some of
the less appetizing aspects of American democracy." Their testimony
revealed a pattern of discrimination throughout the state, ranging
from paternalistic coercion to kidnapping and beating, all designed
to prevent blacks from voting in the Democratic primary, the only
election that counted.[9]

Among those giving testimony was Vernando R. Collier, a thirty-
six-year-old army veteran and president of the NAACP's Gulfport
branch. On primary day he and his wife, a local schoolteacher, arrived at city hall to vote. A police officer accompanied them into
the building, and as they approached the polls "about fifteen poor-
looking white men" blocked their way. Collier told the Senate investigators what happened next: "They knocked me down, dragged
me to the front of the porch and threw me out—and at the same
time assaulted and struck my wife, who was constantly screaming
and pleading to the officer to stop them from beating me. The officer ignored us completely and kept walking as though nothing had
happened." The Colliers fled city hall, and after receiving treatment
from a local black physician, V. R. Collier called the FBI in Jackson, requesting federal protection so that he might return to cast
his ballot. The FBI agent's reply would become a familiar litany to
civil rights workers over the next two decades: "It is not our job
to give protection, only to investigate." Collier next called the U.S.
attorney in Jackson, who said that this was the FBI's jurisdiction.
The Colliers did not vote in the primary.[10]

Etoy Fletcher of Rankin County testified as one of the hundreds of thousands of unregistered black voters in Mississippi. Fletcher told the committee that shortly after his army discharge he had unsuccessfully attempted to get his name on the books, and as he was waiting for a bus, four white men abducted him, took him to a woods four miles away, forced him to strip, and then flogged him with large cable wire.[11]

Such acts of violence created the climate of fear that intimidated potential black voters, but subtler methods often achieved the same results. Perhaps the most bizarre story to come out of the hearings was that of J. D. Collins, a black businessman from the Delta town of Greenwood and third district chairman of the Progressive Voters' League. In the spring of 1946 Collins had encouraged black veterans to register for the primary, but shortly before the election the mayor and several white businessmen advised him to contact the veterans and tell them not to vote Although Collins protested that he "didn't want the job," he and another black man made the rounds and persuaded the veterans to stay at home on election day. For performing their civic duty each man was paid twenty-five dollars. A bemused Senator Hickenlooper observed that "usually up our way it costs money to get the vote out. Here it apparently costs money to keep the vote away."[12]

The most effective way to keep blacks from voting had been to prevent them from registering in the first place. Mississippi's two-year residency requirement and two-dollar poll tax were the most exacting in the South. Beyond that, registrars administered the law selectively, as was made clear during the Bilbo hearings. The Mississippi voting statute was the product of the 1890 constitutional convention, which was called for the express purpose of eliminating the Negro vote. Residency requirements and the poll tax were written into the constitution, but the heart of the electoral provision was the "understanding clause," which stated that a prospective voter must be able to read any section of the constitution, *or,* as an alternative, be able to understand it when read to him, *or* to give "a reasonable interpretation of it." The registrar (the circuit clerk) usually insisted that black applicants be able to read *and* interpret the constitution. So widespread was this practice that some registrars might even have believed it to be valid. When committee counsel reminded Leflore County circuit clerk C. E. Cocke that "it is not necessary to question a man on the constitution if that man is able to read," Cocke innocently replied, "Doesn't it go further to state that he must understand the Constitution when read to him?"[13]

In choosing questions for black applicants, registrars often looked beyond the state constitution. Nathaniel Lewis, a black veteran from McComb, told the committee that after he had correctly answered all questions, the Pike County circuit clerk asked him to describe what was on the ballot. Because he had had no opportunity to see the ballot, he could not answer the question, whereupon the clerk dismissed him with "You brush up on your civics and come back." When the clerk in question, Wendell Holmes, later took the stand and was asked whether he had in fact required Lewis to describe the ballot, Holmes replied, "I am sure I did." An incredulous Senator Bridges then inquired whether Holmes believed he could "make up questions at your own convenience . . . rather than confining yourself to the Constitution?" "Well, I thought I was following the procedure of the law," Holmes responded. When another circuit clerk was asked why he made it more difficult for blacks to register than for whites, he truthfully answered, "I have no other reason than that they were colored."[14]

Witnesses recounted other examples of intimidation and fraud, including the common practice of challenging black ballots at the polls. The election official might place the ballot in an envelope, telling the voter that the election commission would decide later whether to count the ballot. Although black voters faced little harassment in a few communities, such as Greenville and Jackson, and in the all-black town of Mound Bayou, the testimony demonstrated a pervasive pattern of unlawful behavior.[15]

However, the issue before the Senate investigating committee was whether *Bilbo* was responsible for the election-day travesty, an allegation that proved more difficult to substantiate. Although politically sophisticated witnesses like Reverend Bender made the connection between black intimidation and Bilbo's campaign rhetoric, others were less successful. Here Chairman Ellender was most effective, leading witnesses into admitting that Bilbo's speeches had not deterred *them* from going to the polls and hammering home the point that the vast majority of white Mississippians shared Bilbo's obsession that blacks should not vote. There is truth in the Senate investigators' conclusion that blacks would have faced the same obstacles attempting to vote in the primary "regardless of who the senatorial candidates may have been, and what they may have said in campaign speeches."[16] The larger point, that Mississippi was making a mockery of the Fifteenth Amendment, was largely ignored by the politicians and press.

On the fourth and final day of the hearings Bilbo himself took the stand, playing to a packed house of white supporters. Although still sporting his flashy tie and diamond horseshoe stickpin, Bilbo looked old and ill as he read his prepared statement. But the senator was not at all chastened by the preceding testimony. (A *Pittsburgh Courier* reporter calculated that Bilbo had used the word *nigger* no fewer than seventy-nine times during his appearance.) Bilbo's defense was simply to deny all charges of wrongdoing. Although he admitted that the newspaper and magazine accounts of his speeches were essentially accurate, he noted one important exception: every time the press made reference to his call for whites to use "every means" to keep blacks from the polls on July 2, reporters had omitted his use of the word *lawful*. He had never advocated illegal methods to prevent blacks from voting. To accept this explanation stretches the limits of credulity; whether they represented the *New York Times* or Mississippi's white supremacist press, reporters to a person failed to pick up the word *lawful* in any of his speeches. As to his oft-repeated observation that "the best way to keep a nigger from the polls is to visit him the night before," the senator assured his colleagues that he meant only a peaceful, persuasive visit. At the close of his remarks, which lasted nearly two hours, Bilbo fielded questions from committee members, but there were no spirited exchanges. As Bernstein observed, the committee appeared "in a hurry to get the thing over with."[17]

Back in Washington the committee divided along partisan lines: the Democratic majority exonerated Bilbo; the Republican minority condemned him. Yet sentiment was building in Washington to deny Bilbo his seat when the Senate reorganized in January. Republicans had taken control of the Senate for the first time in nearly two decades, and, led by Senator Robert A. Taft, they saw in the Bilbo case an excellent opportunity to score points with black voters while embarrassing Democratic liberals.[18] Bilbo, however, was determined to keep his job. As the Republicans attempted to organize the Senate, minus Bilbo, southern Democrats led by Ellender began a filibuster to prevent the full Senate from taking action against their Mississippi colleague. A protracted debate was avoided when Bilbo agreed to step aside temporarily. He needed another operation, and under the terms of the Senate compromise, his credentials would lie on the table until he recovered his health. Bilbo left the capitol on January 5, never to return. After two more operations, Bilbo deteriorated rapidly. He died in New Orleans on August 21, 1947, succumbing (ironically, as numerous observers pointed out) to cancer of the mouth.[19]

Bilbo's death did not herald a new day in race relations for Mississippi. His successor, Judge John Stennis, though no race-baiter, was also dedicated to preserving white supremacy in the Magnolia State. Still, the 1946 primary election and the subsequent challenge to Bilbo is a significant event in the history of the black struggle for freedom. For four days that December, sixty-eight courageous black men and women publicly served notice that they would no longer accept the denial of their basic human rights. World War II veterans had led the way, along with older activists such as the Reverend William A. Bender. Few would predict in the winter of 1946 that victory was in sight, but in that crowded federal courtroom in Jackson the shock troops of the modern civil rights movement had fired their opening salvo.

• • •

In his classic *Southern Politics in State and Nation,* written in the late 1940s, V. O. Key observed that northerners and southerners alike agreed that Mississippi was in a class by itself, "the last vestige of a dead and despairing civilization." The image of Mississippi as America's dungeon not only persisted but intensified over the next three decades. Nonetheless, the traveler in 1945 entering the state for the first time and anticipating a 400-mile stretch of Tobacco Road was surprised to find instead a land of geographical diversity and considerable beauty. The Gulf Coast, with its sandy beaches and salt marshes, evoked images of Florida. In their efforts to attract tourists—by providing open gambling dens, saloons, and houses of prostitution—the citizens of coastal towns like Biloxi and Gulfport belied the stereotype of Bible-toting Baptists. Moving inland through the eastern half of the state, the traveler first encountered the "real" Mississippi, the Piney Woods, which cover roughly the state's southeast quadrant. The soil there was infertile, and the cut-over timberlands were testimony to the rapacious conduct of Yankee lumber barons in the late nineteenth century.

From east-central Mississippi northward to the Tennessee line lie the north-central hills, the state's largest section and its "geographical and cultural heart." Here, rich bottomlands along creeks and rivers give way to less fertile soil on the hillsides. At the northern edge of this section sits the University of Mississippi in Oxford, surrounded by Faulkner country. The Tennessee hills dominate the state's northeastern corner. Few blacks lived here, in Mississippi's Appalachia, and the white settlers who farmed this rugged land exhibited a stubborn independence both politically and culturally.[20]

The western half of the state is dominated by its border, the Mississippi River. Forty miles from the river, near the center of the state, lies the capital, Jackson, Mississippi's only real city. In the early nineteenth century, when Jackson was little more than an isolated frontier settlement, the river towns of Vicksburg and Natchez were thriving communities, and the Old Natchez District in the southwest comprised the heart of the antebellum slave empire. A Natchez aristocracy arose during the early 1800s and on the backs of their slaves built up huge fortunes and constructed great mansions. In the decades following the Civil War the Natchez aristocracy gave way to plantation barons to the north, who settled an area officially called the Yazoo Basin. Mississippians know that region, the state's most distinctive, simply as "the Delta."

The Delta was Mississippi's last frontier. This football-shaped expanse, which lies "flat as a tabletop" over the northwestern quadrant of the state, extends 200 miles from Memphis to Vicksburg and contains some of the richest soil in the nation. Blacks were a majority of this region's population. Prior to the Civil War most of the Delta was swampland and thick forests. There were no towns except for a few river settlements, and the regular flooding of the Mississippi made cotton cultivation an unacceptable risk. Between Reconstruction and World War I, settlers had the lands drained, levees built, and the forests cleared. A relatively small number of whites owned the land; tens of thousands of poor black families worked it. A "Delta aristocracy" soon emerged that dominated the state politically and economically for nearly a half century, maintaining its hegemony by exploiting the racial phobias of the poor whites from the hill counties to the east.[21]

The Delta is both a clearly defined geographical area and a state of mind. It is the birthplace of the blues, which was created by resilient black sharecroppers who labored on the plantations under

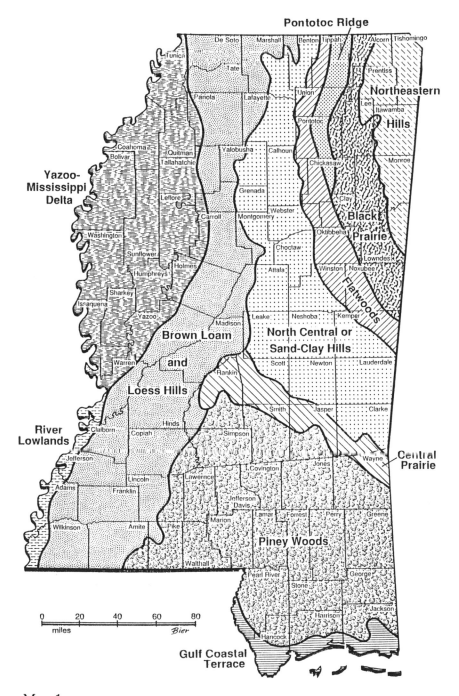

Pontotoc Ridge

Northeastern

Hills

Yazoo-
Mississippi
Delta

De Soto Marshall Benton Tippah Alcorn Tishomingo
Tunica
Tate Prentiss
Panola Lafayette Union Lee Itawamba
Pontotoc
Coahoma Yalobusha Calhoun
Bolivar Quitman Chickasaw Monroe
Tallahatchie
Leflore Grenada Clay
Webster
Carroll Montgomery Oktibbeha Black
Washington Choctaw Prairie
Sunflower Winston Noxubee Lowndes
Humphreys Holmes Attala
Sharkey
Issaquena Yazoo Leake Neshoba Kemper
Madison

Brown Loam

and

Loess Hills

Scott Newton Lauderdale

North Central or
Sand-Clay Hills

Flatwoods

River
Lowlands

Warren
Rankin
Smith Jasper Clarke
Hinds
Claiborn Copiah Simpson
Jefferson Wayne
Lincoln Lawrence Covington Jones
Adams Franklin Jefferson
Davis
Wilkinson Amite Pike Marion Lamar Forrest Perry Greene
Walthall
Pearl River George
Stone
Hancock Harrison Jackson

Central
Prairie

Piney Woods

Gulf Coastal
Terrace

0   20   40   60   80
miles   *Bier*

Map 1

conditions reminiscent of the old regime. The region is also home to the Percy family, who were representative of the small group of wealthy planters who regarded the Delta as their fiefdom and who pictured themselves as the embodiment of southern civility and gentility, Mississippi's natural aristocracy of wealth and talent surrounded by ignorant blacks and venal rednecks.[22] The Delta carries special meaning for the black freedom struggle. From Dr. T. R. M. Howard and Amzie Moore in the early 1950s to Fannie Lou Hamer, Aaron Henry, and Charles McLaurin in the 1960s, the Delta supplied much of the movement's leadership. Here key battles were fought, with names like "Greenwood" and "Ruleville" evoking the same bitter-proud-sacred memories in the new abolitionists as did "Shiloh" and "Gettysburg" for their forebears.

Mississippi blacks had fought for their freedom during the Civil War. Confederate troops put down slave revolts in two parts of the state, and when the Union army marched into Mississippi, blacks proved their worth as spies, guides, and combat troops. With the coming of freedom the state's 437,000 former slaves looked forward to full citizenship rights, including the economic opportunity provided by "forty acres and a mule." There followed instead a turbulent decade of Reconstruction that set the course of Mississippi history for the next century.

The stereotype of Reconstruction has died hard in Mississippi. Most whites today view that period as a tragic era of chaos, corruption, and—above all—Negro rule, an interpretation drilled into the minds of generations of schoolchildren. Reconstruction was in fact far more complex. Although blacks never controlled any branch of state government, many served with distinction in elective offices ranging from constable to United States senator. Corruption did exist (although it paled in comparison with that of the "Redeemer" regime that followed it), and some officials were unprepared to meet their responsibilities. Nevertheless, in a land devastated by war, the Reconstruction government rebuilt railroads and bridges, constructed hospitals and other health facilities, expanded the range of government services to the people, established Mississippi's first public school system, and wrote the most progressive constitution the state has had. When white conservatives brought an end to Reconstruction in 1875 through a campaign of intimidation and violence euphemistically called the "Mississippi Plan," it was not because black political participation had been a failure. Indeed, the progress of the Radical Reconstructionists in rebuilding Mississippi and in fostering a climate of democracy convinced privileged whites that they had to act quickly—and brutally—if they were to regain political control.[23]

Events in the late nineteenth century set the pattern for the twentieth. Racial segregation, which had not been rigidly observed even in the aftermath of Reconstruction, became a Mississippi "folkway" with passage of a series of Jim Crow statutes, beginning with an 1888 law segregating railroad passengers. Although for a time blacks continued to vote and hold minor offices, it was usually in alliance with conservative Democrats, who used the black vote to put down attempts by white insurgents to break the stranglehold that wealthy planters had on state government. Such "coalition" politics was risky—it could cut both ways—so in 1890 conservatives decided to eliminate forever the "threat" of Negro voting, enacting a new constitution with black disfranchisement as its centerpiece. By the turn of the century almost all white Mississippians agreed that the Negro was now in his proper place and must be kept there, whatever the cost.[24]

Over the next four decades blacks struggled against the forces of white supremacy with limited success. In his definitive *Dark Journey: Black Missisippians in the Age of Jim Crow,* Neil R. McMillen shows that by 1940 many of the gains made by blacks in the post–Civil War years had been swept away. Most major black businesses—particularly banks, insurance companies, and newspapers, which emerged in the post–Civil War era—had collapsed by World War I. Blacks owned less farmland in 1940 than they had in 1920, and during this period the value of their total farm holdings declined by more than 50 percent. Sharecropping and the crop-lien system, together with a racist judicial system, fostered on the vast majority of blacks a new slavery almost as pernicious and effective as the old. For blacks, racial violence was a daily reality. Between 1880 and 1940 nearly 600 Mississippi blacks were lynched, and no jury would convict a white man for killing a Negro. On the eve of World War II, then, it appeared that the caste system, in place for more than half a century, would continue to dominate the lives of Mississippians, black and white, well into the future.[25]

World War II brought change to Mississippi. Training camps and defense contracts poured money into the state. Thousands of Mississippians left the farm to work in defense industries or at military bases. Biloxi and Hattiesburg became boom towns, facing for the first time modern urban problems created by uncontrolled growth. Not since Reconstruction had outside forces intruded so dramatically. World War II was "a watershed for Mississippi," observed historian John Ray Skates, "before which there was basic historical continuity for a century, but after which nothing again was quite the same."[26]

Black Mississippians made marginal economic gains. Wartime labor shortages forced plantation owners to pay more attention to their tenants, and wages and working conditions improved to a degree both in the countryside and in the cities. At the same time, however, the demand for labor accelerated the mechanization of cotton farming. Chemical weed killers and cotton-picking machines were no longer a curiosity, particularly in the Delta. Farm population declined during the war years, while total acreage actually showed a slight increase. Few blacks were able to find jobs in the new industries. As a result of these developments, thousands of blacks left the state during the war years. Net outmigration among blacks during the 1940s totaled nearly 300,000. Most headed due north to Chicago or other midwestern cities, drawn by the expectation that the doors of industrial opportunity would open for them there. Moreover, the war had not improved the state's racial climate, for though they were enjoying the benefits of Yankee capital and technology, white Mississippians still clung to a caste system that seemed to have served them well for nearly a century. Jim Crow would not be a casualty of World War II; in fact, the major short-term impact of wartime upheaval in Mississippi was an increased level of racial tension.[27]

At first whites feared that the war would foster black militancy at home. Although blacks were not yet organized to demand their rights, rumors spread across the state that they were stockpiling weapons—guns, ammunition, even ice picks—for use in a race war now that so many white men were away in uniform. The wartime economy offered new opportunities to black women, but white housewives saw instead a conspiracy: Mrs. Franklin D. Roosevelt was sponsoring "Eleanor Clubs" among cooks and maids, designed to "put a white woman in every kitchen."[28] In this atmosphere of fear and uncertainty the historical pattern of white violence against blacks continued unabated.

Lynching had always been the ultimate form of social control, and neither youth, old age, nor social class offered protection to Negroes who did not stay in their place. In 1942 Charlie Lang and Ernest Green were both fourteen and lived in Shubuta, a small town near the Alabama border. The two black youths were playmates with a young white girl, and on an early October day of that year a passing motorist saw the two boys run out from under a bridge, chasing the girl. A short time later Lang and Green found themselves in the Quitman jail on charges of attempted assault. A mob stormed the jail and took the boys. Their bodies were found hanging from a river bridge. Less than a week later, a few miles away in Jones County, a mob lynched Howard Wash, forty-five, of Laurel. A jury had convicted Wash of killing his dairyman employer but had not recommended the death penalty. The U.S. attorney general ordered the FBI to investigate the lynchings, promising that if the investigation developed a case, "relentless prosecution will follow." No one was convicted.[29]

Six white men abducted the Reverend Isaac Simmons in Amite County in early 1944 and killed him with three shots into the back. When relatives found his body, they saw that Simmons's tongue had been cut out. He had not been charged with murder or with the "unmentionable crime." The sixty-six-year-old minister was lynched because he was a successful black man intent on keeping his property. Simmons owned 220 acres of debt-free land. When word got out that oil might be on the property, a local white man named Noble Ryder tried to take possession. Simmons then hired a white attorney from Jackson to protect his land. On the morning of March 26 Simmons and his son Eldridge were forced into a car and beaten. Eldridge Simmons later recalled that "they kept telling me that my father and I were 'smart niggers' for going to see a lawyer." The son witnessed the execution of his father. Before releasing him, one of the killers told the younger Simmons that "if this comes up again you had better not know anything about it" and gave him ten days to "get off the place." Simmons did leave, but he also brought charges against Noble Ryder, Ryder's brother, and four other men. The case did go to trial, and the prosecuting attorney urged the jury to disregard "all appeals to prejudice." None of the accused was found guilty. These events transpired in and around a Mississippi town called Liberty.[30]

White leaders were also concerned over the consequences of stationing thousands of black troops in segregated units in military camps across the state. To be a black soldier in Mississippi was to face daily abuse and humiliation. Strict segregation was the rule on all bases, and white officers went to ridiculous lengths to enforce it. Second Lieutenant Lowry Wright was one of the few black officers at Camp Shelby, which was located outside Hattiesburg. Wright reported that he and another black lieutenant were assigned their own latrine, consisting of four urinals, seven sinks, ten showers, and sixteen commodes, enough to bathe and flush an entire company. Black officers at Shelby had few responsibilities. Both white enlisted men and officers refused to recognize their rank. The army provided blacks with few recreational facilities on base and limited their access to Hattiesburg out of deference to local sentiment. Black soldiers were beaten by whites in the camp, and two black GIs were wounded in an altercation with the Mississippi Highway Patrol.[31]

The most serious racial trouble occurred at Camp Van Dorn, located near the small town of Centreville in an isolated section of southwest Mississippi. Clyde Blue, a Detroit native, was drafted in 1941 and assigned to the black 518th Quartermaster (Truck) Battalion at Camp Van Dorn. Blue recalled that when the 518th arrived, the camp was still under construction, "and the grounds would qualify for a massive mud puddle." Blue quickly learned that there was a black PX and a white PX, the latter out of bounds for black troops. Camp shows were also off limits: "Entertainers came and entertainers went; I guess they didn't know we were there since we never saw them." Although the men of the 518th resented these restrictions, they did not strongly protest against them. On the whole, the camp ran "smoothly"—until that day in May 1943 when the black 364th Infantry Regiment marched and rode through the gates of Van Dorn.[32]

Insofar as the United States Army was concerned, the 364th was a regiment of troublemakers. While stationed in Phoenix, Arizona, the unit became involved in two serious disturbances. As punishment—or so the men believed—the 364th was shipped to Mississippi. For Clyde Blue, the sudden appearance of the infantry regiment was like the cavalry coming to the rescue: "They had mounted guns, artillery, the works. . . . The real thrill for us was when we saw our first black officers; they were mostly lieutenants, but they were officers. With the coming of the 364th a whole new ballgame began." The men of the 364th had barely disembarked when they attacked Jim Crow head on, desegregating a whites-only USO show and invading the off-limits PX. On their first Saturday night in Mississippi about seventy-five men checked out Centreville and confronted its chief of police and nervous white townspeople, who were armed with shotguns. A military police officer intervened to prevent further trouble. The following night a private from the regiment became involved in a dispute with an MP just outside the base grounds. On hand to assist the MP was the county sheriff, who shot and killed the private. When word of the killing reached the barracks a race riot broke out. "That night I saw black hatred," recalled Private Blue. "I saw two or three black soldiers jump one white and give him a brutal beating." Whites retaliated in kind, and at one point the rumor surfaced that they were going to attack the black barracks with tanks. Sergeant Jeffries Bassett Jones was at the scene: "One of the officers from the 364th went into the white area and warned them that if this were true not to do it because the men of the 364th anti-tank company had sworn they would blow to hell any tank they saw coming near this area. All kinds of rumors were flying, along with fists, feet, cudgels, everything. It was a small war."[33]

Tensions remained high in the aftermath of the riot. Whites in the Centreville area armed themselves and demanded the regiment's immediate transfer. The War Department kept word of the riot out of the papers and eventually shipped the 364th to the Aleutian Islands to perform garrison duty for the rest of the war. Looking back on his basic training in Mississippi, Sergeant Jones remembers Camp Van Dorn as "the backside of hell," where "I saw and participated in more fighting than I experienced in all my days overseas."[34]

More than 85,000 Mississippi blacks served in the armed forces during World War II, and each felt the sting of racial discrimination. Whether they trained at Van Dorn, Shelby, or in camps in the North, they were always second-class citizens. Nonetheless, black Mississippians served their country well, whether on the battlefield or as support troops. Black GIs were not as naive in 1945 as their doughboy counterparts had been in 1918, when they had hoped that the war to make the world safe for democracy might make Mississippi a decent home for all its citizens. Still, blacks in Mississippi and across the land experienced shock mixed with outrage when James Eastland, a Delta planter and the state's junior senator, rose before his colleagues on June 29, 1945, and delivered an incredible speech on the performance of black troops in the war against Hitler's Germany.

Eastland began his harangue by posing a rhetorical question: "What is the history of the Negro soldier in the American army?" His answer: "The Negro was an utter and dismal failure in combat in Europe." Black troops were lazy, irresponsible, and "of very low intelligence." At crucial times they deserted their posts and refused to fight. Eastland dwelt at length on another familiar stereotype, charging that black soldiers raped white women in areas that the Allies occupied in Europe. His final judgment was that "Negro soldiers disgraced the flag of their country." Included in the senator's remarks was a personal plea for white supremacy. "I assert that the Negro race is an inferior race," the Mississippi statesman began. "I say quite frankly that I am proud of the white race. I am proud that the purest of white blood flows through my veins. I know that the white race is a superior race. It has ruled the world. It has given us civilization. It is responsible for all the progress on earth." Two weeks later, on the floor of the Senate, Robert Wagner of New York set the record straight. Where the Mississippi senator claimed that his information on the performance of black troops came from American generals in the field, Wagner quoted their denials, reading into the record numerous examples of individual and collective acts of black heroism in the European theater. But Senator Eastland had made his point—for the folks back home whose votes were counted.[35]

When World War II ended a month later, all Mississippians joined in celebrating the Allied victory over Japan. Beneath the surface, however, there lay a profound uneasiness over the uncertain period ahead. The war *had* brought change to Mississippi, yet it remained to be seen whether, in the critical area of race relations, the state would move forward with the times or continue to cling to the vestiges of the Jim Crow society that had for so long retarded the advancement of the majority of its citizens, black and white.

2

Rising Expectations, 1946–54

The decade following World War II was one of intensifying black activism in Mississippi, beginning with modest voter registration efforts and culminating in an attack on the color line in the state's public schools. Although local people did obtain some assistance from the National Association for the Advancement of Colored People and the NAACP Legal Defense Fund, the drive for political and educational equality was indigenous, receiving no support or encouragement from the federal government or from the labor movement, an ally of black activists in other southern states. The World War II veterans and traditional black leaders were facing a seemingly impossible task in Mississippi, for despite the wartime upheavals, whites were determined to maintain their supremacy by denying blacks political, educational, and economic opportunity and by maintaining racial segregation in all walks of life.

In postwar Mississippi most blacks were still working at jobs associated with slavery. Nearly two-thirds of the black male labor force engaged in some form of agriculture-related activity; more than 80 percent of these men were sharecroppers or day laborers on white-owned plantations. Few blacks held jobs in factories, and most of these were in the lowest-paying janitorial positions. For black women the designated place was still the white woman's kitchen. Of the 58,000 black women employed in nonagricultural jobs in 1950, two-thirds worked as domestics.[1]

Median annual family income for blacks in 1949 was $601; it was $1,614 for whites. More than a third of black families reported incomes under $500. The black professional class was small and concentrated in the larger towns and cities. In 1950 only five black attorneys, thirty dentists, and sixty-four physicians were practicing in the state. There were nearly 1,000 preachers and some 5,500 teachers, the largest professional group. Given their limited economic opportunity, blacks continued to leave the state in large numbers. Between 1940 and 1950 Mississippi's black population declined by nearly 300,000. Blacks now constituted 45.3 percent of the state's population, down from 54 percent in 1940. Contributing to the continuing black migration was the caste system, which had proscribed black freedom for generations.[2]

From drinking fountains and movie houses to schools and churches, Jim Crow dictated the pace of Mississippi life, and "keeping the Negro in his place" was the duty of every white citizen. That place might vary, depending on circumstance. When delivering the mail, letter-carrier Carsie Hall walked through the front door of the Heidelberg, Jackson's leading hotel, and rode the main elevator while making his rounds. Yet attorney Carsie Hall, at the Heidelberg to take the state bar exam, had to use the rear entrance and take the freight elevator to the floor where the test was given. Whites maintained their racial integrity on the playing fields, too, as when Mississippi State canceled its 1946 football game with the University of Nevada because of Nevada's "use of Negro players." A year later city officials in Jackson and Hattiesburg barred the Freedom Train, a government-sponsored "rolling showcase of democracy," rather than permit nonsegregated viewing of such documents as the Declaration of Independence.[3]

Mississippi's courts were the arbiters of the color line, and any number of judicial decisions illustrate the nature of justice, Jim Crow style. Consider the case of Davis Knight, who believed he was a white man, enlisted in the navy as a white man, and married a white woman. The state of Mississippi later charged Knight with violating the 1890 miscegenation law. At issue here was the ancestry of Knight's great-grandmother, a woman known as Rachel. The state contended that she was a Negro; Knight argued that she was a Cherokee Indian. The judge ruled that Rachel was black, and Knight drew a five-year sentence at Parchman penitentiary. Equally bizarre was the Mississippi State Supreme Court decision upholding an Adams County jury award of $5,000 to Mary Dunningham. It seems that the *Natchez Times* had incorrectly identified Mrs. Dunningham as "a negro," and that, in the eyes of the court, was "libel, *per se*."[4]

The courts were especially cruel in cases involving sex crimes allegedly committed by black men against white women. On the morning of November 3, 1945, a Laurel housewife named Wilmetta Hawkins reported to the police that she had been raped by a Negro. Thirty-two-year-old Willie McGee, married and the father of four children, was arrested and charged with the crime. His trial lasted less than a day. The Laurel jury deliberated only a few minutes before finding him guilty; the judge sentenced McGee to die in the electric chair. This was to be the first of three trials. The Mississippi Supreme Court threw out the first verdict by ruling that McGee should have had a change of venue, overturned the second on grounds that blacks had been systematically excluded from the juries, and then upheld the third conviction. The case dragged on for over five years. After the first trial McGee turned his defense over to the Civil Rights Congress (CRC); his chief counsel was a young New York attorney named Bella Abzug. The Communist party took an interest in the McGee case and transformed it into a *cause célèbre*. Rallies and protests took place around the world. Governor Fielding Wright received thousands of letters, including petitions signed by such notables as Josephine Baker, Jean-Paul Sartre, and Albert Einstein.[5]

McGee's lawyers had originally argued that the penalty was unfair because no white man had ever received a death sentence for rape, but in their final appeal the CRC attorneys exploded a bombshell: McGee and his wife Rosalee presented sworn statements that the alleged victim had been having an affair with McGee for a number of years before she claimed to have been raped. Although this new evidence smacked of desperation, the revelation did not come as a shock to a number of Laurel citizens who had long suspected such a relationship. The Mississippi Supreme Court rejected the new evidence as a "revolting insinuation and plainly not supported." The U.S. Supreme Court refused to review the case. Both Governor Wright and President Harry S. Truman denied appeals for clemency. Late in the evening of May 7, 1951, a crowd of some 700 whites gathered outside the Laurel courtroom, where the state's portable electric chair was now in place. At 12:07 A.M. they let out a loud, piercing rebel yell when word came that Willie McGee was dead.[6]

In addition to facing a discriminatory judiciary, blacks attempting to bring change to Mississippi had to deal with political institutions that were corrupt as well as racist. When the political scientist Alexander Heard toured the state in 1947, interviewing scores of elected and appointed officials, he uncovered a sordid picture of wheeling and dealing at all levels of government. Money changed hands at the polls during every election. The going rate per vote ranged from $1.00 to $2.50, depending on the closeness of the contest. The Delta was an exception. There, according to longtime political operative Wilbur Buckley, "the big planters merely call in their people and tell them who they are going to vote for."[7]

A major reason for such pervasive political corruption was the absence of ideological conflict within the white electorate. "In Mississippi," observed editor Hodding Carter II, "everybody more or less agrees on everything anyway." When asked to explain why poor whites did not rally around pocketbook issues that would ally them against planter and business interests, Carter pointed to the "common anti-black attitude" as a barrier to class politics, particularly "the campaign uses to which the Negro could be put by the 'rich' elements." The Delta still exercised disproportionate power in the affairs of state. George McLean, editor of the *Tupelo Daily Journal,* observed privately that "part and parcel of this control is the fact that the Delta returns the same old evil men again and again to the legislature and therefore gets seniority and influence out of proportion to the rest of the state."[8] Delta lawmakers were strongly influenced by the Delta Council, a conservative organization established in 1935 to promote the interests of the planter class. Poor whites had no significant voice in government. With the death of Bilbo they had lost their champion, but even "The Man" had posed no real threat to corporate interests, no matter how much he railed against them on the stump.

White voters gave overwhelming support to Franklin D. Roosevelt in each of his four election campaigns. Angered by federal programs assisting southern blacks, however, Mississippi Democrats had turned against the New Deal by the 1940s. Using the race issue to keep the white lower classes in their place, the men who ran Mississippi unabashedly proclaimed an economic conservatism that would preserve and widen the gap between rich and poor. Nowhere is there a better example of the privileged class at work protecting its privileges than in the campaign against the Congress of Industrial Organizations (CIO) in the years surrounding World War II.

Mississippi seemed overdue for a labor organization drive. By World War II only the Magnolia State had no worker's compensation law and no department of labor. One-third of the state's 71,400 factory workers were making less than thirty cents an hour, the lowest rate in the South. As late as 1947, a ten-hour day and a sixty-hour week was the norm for women workers, again the worst record in the region. Given such conditions, the CIO moved into Mississippi in 1946 as part of its "Operation Dixie" campaign to organize workers across the South.[9]

Resistance developed quickly. Although it was not an industrial state, Mississippi was attempting to attract factories from the North, and an abundant labor supply and an absence of unions were the state's best selling points. The American Federation of Labor (AFL) had established craft unions in the state, but these skilled white workers posed little threat to the status quo. The Congress of Industrial Organizations was another matter. The Mississippi establishment was paranoid about the CIO, linking it with racial integration and the international communist conspiracy. Jackson editor Fred Sullens labeled CIO organizers "strife breeders . . . more dangerous than rattlesnakes." In an open letter opposing the CIO, a group of citizens asked, "Do you want to be ruled from Russia by the Communists?"[10] White opinion makers went to such extremes in attacking the CIO because they believed the stakes were high. A unionized work force in Mississippi, so the argument ran, would be unattractive to northern capital. Moreover, the CIO policy of organizing across racial lines would, if successful, present Mississippi with a class movement threatening conservative rule. Thus, Delta planters joined with small-town editors in meeting the CIO challenge. The battle was primarily for the mind of the white worker, and while the union offered a vision of higher wages and better working conditions, CIO opponents dusted off the tried-and-true race-baiting arguments that had historically kept poor whites in line (and also poor).

Experience had taught the CIO to step gingerly around the race question. During the war years integrated teams of organizers had worked in the state. When Frank Davis, black, and Claude Welch, white, attempted to organize woodworkers in Vicksburg, the chief of police locked them up without charges for twenty-four hours and then turned the two men over to a mob, which handcuffed them to a tree and whipped them. In the postwar campaign most of the organizers in Mississippi were white, and they tried to finesse the race issue.[11]

The CIO enjoyed some success in Mississippi, winning fifty-seven union elections between 1946 and 1949 involving approximately 11,000 workers. The union did best in predominantly white counties in the southern half of the state, faring poorly in the north and in the Delta. The CIO base in the state was in Jones County, where the union won several elections, including a big victory against the AFL in the large Masonite plant in Laurel. Yet the Laurel success also demonstrated that Jim Crow held sway even in a union town.[12]

State CIO director Robert W. Starnes, a native white who had graduated from Mississippi College, told Alexander Heard in 1947 that union gatherings in Laurel were "segregated according to color" because whites refused to participate in integrated events. The Laurel CIO Political Action Committee worked to register white workers and see that they paid their poll taxes, but "they . . . made no effort among the Negroes." Heard expressed surprise that CIO leader Starnes was "not acquainted with Negro political activities in Mississippi."[13]

The CIO called off its Mississippi organizing drive in 1949, concluding that the campaign was too expensive for the results achieved. CIO (and AFL) locals survived into the 1950s, but the union movement was not a force for social change. Many union members supported the racist Citizens' Council and in the 1960s joined the Ku Klux Klan. Their leaders denounced the NAACP as a "communist-infiltrated organization." State CIO vice president J. W. Webb spoke for the rank and file when, in 1956, he vowed that "we'll support no movement that's opposed to segregation. We're very much a part of the national union, but we'll have nothing to do with integration."[14] As black activists began to put together a program in the postwar years, they had no more friends in the House of Labor than in other elements of white society.

That program centered on voter registration, the focus of the civil rights struggle in Mississippi for the next two decades. Desegregation of public facilities, including schools, was not as compelling an issue in Mississippi as in other southern states. White repression made direct action projects more dangerous, and endemic black poverty meant that the right to spend the night at the Heidelberg Hotel was not a high priority for most black citizens. Although the desegregation movement later took hold in the larger cities, the appeal of the ballot was statewide. Robert Moses, who directed the voter registration drive of the early 1960s, observed later that obtaining the franchise was a program behind which everyone in the community could unite: "There was almost universal agreement. Almost everyone you went to, whether they would go to register or not, believed that registration would help."[15]

Until the New Deal years, what black vote there was in Mississippi had gone to the party of Lincoln. The so-called Black and Tan Republican party was the political plaything of Perry W. Howard, a black Washington, D.C., lawyer and longtime Republican national committeeman from Mississippi. Howard, who made only occasional trips back to his home state to look after party interests, did not impress the younger blacks now becoming involved in the suffrage campaign. R. L. T. Smith, who would run for Congress in 1962, recalls that in the 1930s and 1940s the Republicans "had a rotten setup here. They had a group of blacks who were part of the apparatus to keep us down." Howard had a reputation as a wheeler-dealer and denied local blacks political participation and patronage. Nathaniel Lewis, the McComb resident who testified at the Bilbo hearings, said that the handful of "Negroes that ran the Republican Party in Mississippi . . . never said anything about getting more Negroes to vote. They didn't help one bit." Howard and his associates appeared content to dispense (or sell, as many claimed) patronage when the Republicans were in power and to handpick the Mississippi delegation to the national convention every four years. Neither Howard nor the Republican party played a role in the civil rights movement, and what influence Howard enjoyed in national Republican circles had ended by 1960.[16]

The organizational base for the postwar voter registration drive was the newly organized Mississippi Progressive Voters' League, which claimed approximately 5,000 members by 1947. With its headquarters in Jackson and with major branches in Clarksdale and Hattiesburg, the league mounted a nonpartisan effort to educate and motivate potential black voters. League president T. B. Wilson stressed the nonthreatening, cooperative character of the movement.

By adopting a moderate position, Wilson told Alexander Heard, the league had an easier time attracting church and lodge support and recruiting members than did local NAACP branches, which drew bitter opposition from whites.[17]

Dr. T. W. Hill, chairman of the league's Clarksdale branch, epitomized the organization's middle-class orientation. A successful dentist in his fifties, Hill impressed Alexander Heard as "a very canny man with the ability to understand and get along with people." Hill described the Clarksdale league's function as primarily that of voter registration. He urged members to register, to pay their poll taxes, and to "work individually to get other blacks to do the same." Yet Hill opposed any systematic block-by-block, door-to-door canvassing "for any purpose." Although other members urged Hill to send people into adjoining counties to stimulate interest in voting, he refused, explaining that "the Negroes who live in these nearby counties know their white people best and know best how to handle them." Hill also resisted efforts to organize an NAACP branch in Clarksdale, for though he supported the NAACP program, white opposition "was simply too strong. . . . Clarksdale cannot handle it yet." (The Clarksdale branch of the NAACP was organized in 1953 with Aaron Henry as president.)[18]

Despite efforts by people like Hill and Wilson to portray black political participation in positive, nonthreatening terms, whites took home a different message. "White Supremacy Is in Peril," screamed a *Jackson Daily News* headline early in 1947. Fred Sullens informed his readers that "Negroes in large numbers are paying their poll taxes down at the courthouse" and asked whether "you want a white man's government, or will you take the risk of being governed by Negroes?" White officials took a series of steps to ensure that such a calamity did not occur. First, in the spring of 1947, several months before the gubernatorial primary, the legislature passed a law stating that persons could vote in party primaries only if they were "in accord with" principles set forth by the party. Next, the state Democratic executive committee enumerated those "principles," including opposition to federal antilynching laws, anti–poll tax legislation, and the Fair Employment Practices Committee (FEPC). Blacks challenged at the polls in the primary, then, had to disavow their own beliefs in order to vote. In a move that surprised some observers, T. B. Wilson advised members of the voters' league to agree to the party principles because "we believe, as the party believes, in states' rights." Privately, Wilson said that blacks should go along because the Democratic primary was the only game in town.[19]

Reports of large numbers of blacks registering and voting had been exaggerated. Despite front-page stories and display ads in the Negro weekly newspapers urging blacks to register and vote, the rallies in major cities, and the unanimous endorsement of the most important black social, religious, and political organizations, turnout was disappointingly low for the 1947 primary. The *New York Times* reported that "only a comparative handful of Negroes" showed up to vote, and thus it was not necessary for white Democrats to challenge the "loyalty" of black voters. Only in the Delta's Washington County were a number of blacks denied the ballot because they refused to adhere to party principles. Other tactics of fraud and intimidation were reported in Jackson, where the few blacks registered had previously voted without incident.[20]

Having turned back this latest effort by blacks to play a political role, Mississippi whites soon faced another challenge, this time from the nation's capital. In 1946 President Harry S. Truman, under pressure from blacks and white Democratic liberals, had appointed a commission to study the race problem in America. Its report, *To Secure These Rights,* issued in October 1947, called for an ambitious federal effort to bring about "the elimination of segregation, based on race, color, creed, or national origin, from American life." Truman then sent a civil rights package to Congress that included a bill to strengthen voting rights. This was too much for Mississippi's governor, Fielding Wright, who early in 1948 set in motion the "Dixiecrat" movement. First, Wright called a meeting in Jackson, where 5,000 Mississippi Democrats attacked the president and his civil rights program and called for a convention of "true white Jeffersonian Democrats." Ten days later Democrats from Mississippi and nine other southern states convened in Jackson and unanimously agreed that unless the national convention adopted a states' rights plank, the southern delegates would walk out and nominate their own ticket. When the national Democratic party instead passed a strong civil rights plank at its convention, the Mississippi delegates and half of the Alabama delegation did walk out, while other southerners remained to wage a futile battle against the nomination of Truman. After the convention the Dixiecrats met to nominate South Carolina governor Strom Thurmond for president and Fielding Wright for vice president, a ticket that swept Mississippi in November, with Truman getting only 10 percent of the vote.[21] Nationally, of course, Harry Truman pulled off the biggest upset in American political history.

The estimated 7,000 black voters in Mississippi split three ways in this election. A few blacks joined with a handful of whites to support the Progressive party crusade of former vice president Henry Wallace, whose platform called for improved relations with the Soviet Union and for full equality for Negro Americans. Wallace had taken his campaign to Mississippi, speaking at Southern Christian Institute, a black college, and delivering a statewide radio speech in which he castigated Governor Wright for his racial views. The Black and Tan Republicans delivered some 2,500 votes for the Republican nominee, Governor Thomas E. Dewey of New York. President Truman had the support of most black Mississippians, whether they could vote or not. Percy Greene, the editor of the black *Jackson Advocate*, took charge of the Truman campaign in the black community, and from this effort emerged the Mississippi State Democratic Association, with Greene as its president. This organization, along with the Progressive Voters' League and local NAACP branches, led the effort to register blacks over the next few years. By 1952 the number of black voters had increased to 20,000, no small achievement, but this figure represented less than 6 percent of the eligible black electorate, and activists remained aware of the immense task that lay ahead.[22]

A number of factors accounted for the failure to register large numbers of black voters. As noted, tactics of intimidation did not die with Bilbo. Most blacks were afraid to try to register and vote, and with reason. Moreover, with all state and local candidates for office pledged to maintain white supremacy, there was simply no one to vote for. (At least Bilbo had been someone to vote *against*.) No candidate dared seek the black vote, and blacks realized that their numbers were too small to make a difference, even if they voted as a bloc. Finally, the registration campaigns of the late 1940s and early 1950s centered on the small black middle class. Not until the civil rights movement of the 1960s would activists attempt to register and organize the hundreds of thousands of black sharecroppers and unskilled urban workers.

With the voter registration drive making but limited progress, younger activists searched for other avenues to advance the cause and sensed that outside support would be necessary if meaningful change were to come to Mississippi. It was natural, then, that they would turn to the National Association for the Advancement of Colored People for help.

For three decades civil rights activity in Mississippi had been closely identified with the NAACP. Vicksburg blacks had organized the first branch in 1918. Mound Bayou followed in 1919, and Jackson, Meridian, and Natchez started branches in the 1920s. These branches all subsequently folded, only to be reorganized later. Several other cities received charters in the 1930s and early 1940s, but the NAACP did not become a viable presence in Mississippi until after World War II. Primarily a legalistic organization, the national NAACP had filed suits against the discriminatory laws and practices that violated the constitutional rights of blacks and lobbied Congress to enact federal antilynching legislation, abolish the poll tax, and establish a permanent FEPC. Although black Mississippians endorsed these goals, the world of Washington was far removed from that of Washington County. The New York national NAACP office, in return, gave low priority to work in Mississippi, believing that change must first come to the border states before the Deep South could be breached. National officials visited the state during the Depression years, but aside from legal advice and assistance in several court cases, the organization's work in Mississippi consisted mainly of limited solicitation of memberships.[23]

Simply belonging to the NAACP in Mississippi was risky business. Most whites accepted without question the false accusation that the NAACP was a communist organization, and thus any card-carrying member was by definition a traitor. The problem was most severe in the smaller towns. The Reverend R. G. Gilchrist of Aberdeen told the national office, "We have got to figure out some safe and effective way to get members. It is a dangerous risk for anyone to try to set up a branch of the NAACP in small towns or counties." Until the end of World War II, then, the NAACP maintained a holding operation in Mississippi. NAACP director of branches Ella Baker reported "with regret" that in 1944 there were only 129 members in the state's six branches.[24]

Jackson had the only branch to operate with any degree of regularity during this period. Living in the state's capital and largest city afforded black activists a degree of protection, but here too they took precautions, seldom meeting in the same place twice in succession.[25] Examination of the Jackson branch's leadership is instructive, for these people were representative of the small group of Mississippi blacks who placed themselves at risk during the darkest days of Jim Crow.

A trait that all Jackson NAACP leaders shared was their relative economic independence from whites. A. W. Wells, who "kept alive" the Jackson branch in the 1930s, was a federal railway postal clerk, as was A. J. Noel. Other postal employees active in the NAACP were John Dixon, R. L. T. Smith, Percy Greene, Carsie Hall, and Jack Young. Greene became editor of the *Jackson Advocate,* a black weekly, while Hall and Young later distinguished themselves as the state's first civil rights lawyers. A. H. McCoy was a dentist and businessman, M. C. Collins owned a funeral home, and William A. Bender was the chaplain at Tougaloo. All these men were "protected" from direct economic retaliation by whites, either through federal civil service laws or by providing services directly to the black community. As political activity expanded in the 1940s and 1950s, leaders throughout the state came from the thin ranks of small business owners, doctors, dentists, lawyers, government workers, and land-owning farmers.

An even more apparent characteristic was that the leadership was overwhelmingly male. In this the black community reflected the mores dominant in American society, as well as the tradition of the black church, which next to the family was the most important institution in the black community. Women did hold important positions in the NAACP hierarchy: Ella Baker was director of branches during the war years, and Ruby Hurley later provided distinctive leadership as southeast regional secretary. Within Mississippi several women were influential in the larger black community, most notably Mrs. Ruby Stutts Lyells. An educator, forceful orator, and president of the Negro State Federation of Women's Clubs, Lyells was a well-known Republican. A strong advocate of black rights, she was an independent force for social change for more than four decades.[26]

Nonetheless, leadership in the NAACP and in the black community as a whole remained a male prerogative through the decade of the 1950s. Among the officers of the Mississippi State Conference of the NAACP in 1953, for example, Mary E. Holmes, the assistant secretary, was the only woman. Only two of the twenty-seven members of the board of directors were women. As late as 1959 no women headed local branches, though thirteen branches had elected women to the traditional post of secretary. That emphasis began to shift over the years, and the daughters and wives of the NAACP's "founding fathers," women like Gladys Noel Bates, Clarie Collins Harvey, and Aurelia Young, later emerged as leaders in their own right.[27]

Inspired by the militancy of the war veterans and influenced by the civil rights agenda of the Truman administration, blacks in the late 1940s intensified their efforts to expand the NAACP presence in the state. Ten new branches in Mississippi were established between 1945 and 1947, and thirteen had the minimum fifty members needed to send delegates to the 1947 national NAACP convention. NAACP members had been active in the fight to unseat Bilbo, and the Jackson branch initiated a suit to equalize teachers' salaries in the public schools. Voter registration was a priority for Mississippi branches, which worked with the existing suffrage organizations.[28]

Because of the growth in membership activities, in 1946 the Mississippi State Conference of Branches was organized to coordinate efforts of local branches and to act as liaison with the national office. There was no paid fieldworker, a shortcoming that hampered efforts to expand the organization's influence in the black community. The national office's failure to provide adequate resources for work in Mississippi disturbed NAACP attorney Thurgood Marshall, who in August 1950 wrote director of branches Gloster Current, "We have never done a good job in Mississippi. . . . The only way to do a good job in Mississippi is to have someone there who knows Mississippi and who knows the people." Marshall recommended that the Reverend William A. Bender be "placed on the field staff and assigned to work there as our local representative," praising Bender as "the one contact we can rely upon in Mississippi."[29]

Current opposed the appointment, questioning Bender's leadership as president of the State Conference of Branches and citing the need to find "young men who can . . . develop into good field workers and fundraisers." Part of the problem was that Current disapproved of the Tougaloo chaplain's personality and style. Current was a bureaucrat very much at home in the NAACP's hierarchical structure. He demanded loyalty and obedience from his people in the field and regarded Bender as something of a loose cannon. Bender was his own man and possessed an explosive temper. When several members of the Yazoo City branch wrote the national office criticizing the manner in which Bender was mediating a local factional dispute, the chaplain fired back that "I felt like taking my .38 and walking to Yazoo City to do what ought to be done to the one or two scoundrels that got up that letter." This combativeness served Bender well as an organizer in a state where most blacks were afraid to get near the NAACP. Despite Current's objections, however, NAACP executive secretary Walter White agreed with Marshall that Bender was the best candidate, and the Tougaloo chaplain got the job. He was to be the first Mississippi NAACP official to organize branches across the state.[30]

Just as the NAACP was becoming more directly involved in Mississippi, there arose a new organization for racial advancement. The Regional Council of Negro Leadership (RCNL) was founded in Cleveland, Mississippi, in late 1951 by Dr. T. R. M. Howard, a prosperous Mound Bayou physician and businessman. The guiding force in the RCNL for the next six years, Howard became the state's most charismatic advocate of black rights. Howard was a native of Kentucky who moved to Mound Bayou in the early 1940s as chief surgeon at the Knights and Daughters of Tabor hospital. Within a short time he had set up his own medical clinic, bought a large plantation, and organized the Magnolia Mutual Life Insurance Company.[31]

At first glance the Delta physician did not appear to fit the image of a dedicated activist. A tall, powerful man in his early forties, Howard enjoyed life in the fast lane. His home on the outskirts of town was a showplace, replete with a staff of servants and chauffeurs, where he entertained in the finest tradition of a Delta planter. He raised pheasant, quail, and hunting dogs for sport; played the horses; and loved flashy cars. Myrlie Evers, whose husband, Medgar, began his career in Mound Bayou as a Magnolia Mutual agent, recalls seeing "Doc" Howard "sailing down the highway in a red Buick convertible on the way to visit a patient." She also remembers his "friendly smile, and a hearty handshake. . . . One look told you he was a leader: kind, affluent, and intelligent, that rare Negro in Mississippi who had somehow beaten the system."[32]

The national office of the NAACP was not so taken by this flamboyant upstart and believed that Howard had put together the RCNL for reasons of "self-aggrandizement." Always protective of its turf, the NAACP regarded Mississippi as its bailiwick and saw Howard as a potential rival. The RCNL, on the other hand, was more ecumenical, welcoming state and local NAACP people into its leadership. Aaron Henry has described the council as a "home-grown NAACP"; the young Clarksdale pharmacist served on the RCNL board at the same time that he was president of his local NAACP branch. Concerned by Howard's success in attracting much of the NAACP leadership into his organization, Ruby Hurley told Walter White that "the Council is a threat which I have recognized and tried to combat on my several visits to the state." Although its actual membership was never large—one source reported it had 500 members in twenty-nine counties—the RCNL knew how to attract a crowd. In May 1952 more than 7,000 blacks gathered in the comfortable surroundings of Mound Bayou to eat Doc Howard's barbecue and listen to a speech by Chicago Democratic congressman William Dawson, with additional entertainment provided by gospel singer Mahalia Jackson. Two years later 10,000 people showed up to hear Thurgood Marshall. T. R. M. Howard, Hurley realized, was a force to be reckoned with.[33]

The program of the RCNL was similar to that of the NAACP. The council was active in voter registration and stood for "first class citizenship for Negroes in Mississippi." Howard campaigned against police brutality, arranging an unprecedented meeting with state police commissioner Colonel T. B. Birdsong to air grievances against the Mississippi Highway Patrol.[34] As a local group the RCNL avoided the stigma attached to the national NAACP and thus had more freedom to operate.

National NAACP leaders saw more substantive differences. Current characterized the RCNL's program as "midway between that of the NAACP and the Urban League," and Hurley claimed that the RCNL accepted the doctrine of "separate but equal." There was some truth to the latter charge, at least in the council's early days. One of its first actions was a boycott against filling station owners who did not provide rest rooms for black patrons. The "Don't Buy Gas Where You Can't Use the Rest Room" campaign did not challenge segregation and would have accepted "separate but equal" facilities.[35] Still, the differences between the national NAACP and the RCNL were more territorial than ideological. Howard's organization was not accommodationist, as future events would prove. Both Howard and the NAACP members who supported the RCNL knew they were all facing a common enemy and could not afford the luxury of destructive interorganizational warfare.

Although the early 1950s was certainly no golden age of race relations in Mississippi—Jim Crow and everything it stood for remained firmly in place—there were signs of gradual improvement in the racial climate. The NAACP was experiencing slow but steady growth, with local branches becoming bolder in communicating their message to the general public. In urban areas several thousand blacks had added their names to the registration books, a development white politicians for the most part ignored. Younger men taking seats in the Mississippi legislature appeared to be more forward-looking than their hidebound predecessors. A racial moderate, Frank Smith, was now representing the Delta in the U.S. House of Representatives. After the black Natchez Business and Civic League urged its members to register and vote, an unprecedented 400 blacks did so in a special 1954 election, with "the calm acceptance of the white community." For the first time since Reconstruction, blacks served on a Natchez grand jury, and two blacks were jurors in a Greenville case. Indianola and Biloxi each quietly employed a Negro policeman to patrol black areas of town.[36]

Whites had not been aroused by these developments because they had become convinced that the racial status quo was no longer threatened. The dire predictions of masses of blacks registering and voting had proven false. At the current rate of registration, blacks would pose no political threat until well into the twenty-first century. Congress had failed to take action on Truman's civil rights measures. Now Ike was in the White House, the Korean War was over, and many white Mississippians were sharing in the returning prosperity. And yet, unobserved by most Mississippians, a number of school desegregation cases had been slowly working their way up through the courts. With *Brown* v. *Board of Education* the tranquility of the Eisenhower years would vanish overnight, plunging Mississippi into a period of violent interracial conflict unmatched since the bloody years of the 1870s.

Even the most ardent segregationist would admit that under the principle of "separate but equal," black children in Mississippi had been denied educational opportunity. As late as 1950, 70 percent of blacks twenty-five years of age and older had less than a seventh-grade education. Only 10,250, or 2.3 percent, had completed high school. During that year the state spent $122.93 per pupil for the education of whites and $32.55 for blacks. No less a champion of white supremacy than Fred Sullens had written in a 1949 *Jack-*

son Daily News editorial that "in the matter of education we have for many years been treating Negroes most outrageously. The type of education we have been providing for them is nothing short of a disgrace. It might well be called a public scandal." Sullens advised his readers to "go into any rural school building for Negroes and see for yourself . . . Negro schools are poorly equipped, shabby, delapidated, and unsightly. . . . Almost without exception they are one-room structures, rickety stoves are propped up on brickbats, blackboards are absent or worn to the point of uselessness, sanitation is sadly lacking." Conditions in city schools were often no better. Where city and county governments refused to appropriate funds, blacks had to provide their own school buildings while paying taxes to support white schools.[37]

The needs of white students always took priority. Their school year was nearly two months longer, their buildings were better, they had libraries—most black schools did not—and they received free bus transportation. The scholar J. Lewis Henderson, a white Mississippian, observed that "few southerners seem to resent it when the son of a millionaire cotton planter in Coahoma County rides to school in a free bus, while the Negro sharecropper's son must pay three dollars a month." Also blatant was the discrepancy in teachers' salaries. In 1948 the average yearly salary for white teachers was $1,861; for blacks, $711.[38]

In the spring of 1948 Gladys Noel Bates, a black science teacher at the Smith Robinson School in Jackson, filed suit in U.S. District Court charging that the local school board had denied her and all other black teachers and administrators salaries equal to those paid to white teachers with similar education and experience. A graduate of Tougaloo College, Bates had also done graduate work at the University of West Virginia. Her father, A. J. Noel, was a Jackson NAACP leader, and NAACP Legal Defense Fund attorneys Constance Baker Motley and Robert Carter represented her. The case dragged on for nearly three years. The Jackson school board had immediately fired Bates and her husband, also a teacher, and then argued in court that the case was moot since the plaintiff was no longer employed in the system. At that point R. Jess Brown, a teacher at Lanier High School, entered the case as an intervening plaintiff. (Brown, too, lost his job and went on to a career as an attorney.) Bates and Brown lost the case on a technicality. Taking his cue from a similar case in Georgia, Judge Sidney Mize ruled that the plaintiffs had not exhausted their administrative remedies before filing suit. In a significant footnote, Mize wrote that had he been forced to hand down a decision, he would have sided with the plaintiffs, as the weight of evidence was on their side.[39]

White political leaders had seen the handwriting on the wall. They came to believe that the only way to maintain their dual school system was to make separate-but-equal more of a reality, even though the economic costs would be substantial. A short time after the Bates decision, Governor Fielding Wright persuaded the legislature to allocate funds to begin equalizing teacher salaries. However, many local and county school boards, which were responsible for distributing the money equally, either refused to do so or engaged in subterfuges such as raising the monthly salaries of black teachers and then shortening the school year. Wright's successor, Hugh L. White, pursued equalization more vigorously. Starting from the premise that all Mississippi schools were underfinanced, White proposed an ambitious program of school consolidation and reorganization that would also allocate funds to build black schools, provide bus transportation for black students, and equalize the salaries of black and white teachers. The legislators were ambivalent; many members rejected the argument that they must take remedial action under threat of federal action. At a special session of the legislature called in November 1953 to deal with the educational budget, the Mississippi House passed a constitutional amendment permitting the abolition of the public school system if the U.S. Supreme Court required desegregation. The Senate voted down the amendment—this time.[40]

Both the special session and the regular January 1954 meeting of the legislature convened under the shadow of *Brown.* The U.S. Supreme Court was now hearing the cases, with a decision expected in late spring. Taking the easy way out, the legislature adopted a wait-and-see attitude. If the Court upheld the separate-but-equal principle, then Mississippi would spend millions of dollars to upgrade black education. If the decision called for desegregating the schools, more drastic measures would be in order.[41]

Black Mississippians were not of one mind about the school court cases. The state NAACP had consistently opposed segregation. At its sixth annual convention delegates passed a resolution calling on branches "to take any and all necessary legal steps to end segregation in public education." In January 1954 the NAACP assisted

Medgar Evers in his unsuccessful bid to enroll at Ole Miss law school.[42] Black principals and teachers, on the other hand, were understandably ambivalent about the prospect of school desegregation. With no tenure, and under the direct control of white school boards, they could be fired for taking any position opposed by the white establishment.

A number of black educators, especially administrators, had an economic interest in maintaining the status quo. The segregated environment had provided them both with a livelihood and with status in the community. They feared—in many cases appropriately, as it turned out—that they would not fare well in an integrated system. Moreover, after they had worked for years at low wages in dilapidated buildings with meager facilities, now white officials seemed prepared to raise their salaries and build new schools in the black community. Privately, and later publicly, leading black educators sided with the segregationists to preserve Mississippi's dual school system.

On May 17, 1954, Chief Justice Earl Warren spoke for a unanimous U.S. Supreme Court when he said, "Separate educational facilities are inherently unequal. . . . Segregation is a denial of equal protection of the laws." White Mississippi at first did not respond to the *Brown* decision with a single voice. Predictably, Senator Eastland breathed defiance: "The South will not abide by nor obey this legislative decision of a political court. . . . We will take whatever steps are necessary to retain segregation in education. . . . We are about to embark on a great crusade to restore Americanism." Other voices were at first more cautious. Senator John Stennis observed that "there is plenty of time, and I believe there are even years to seek a solution." Hodding Carter of the *Delta Democrat-Times* pleaded for moderation: "Let's keep our shirts on. The decision has been made. It is a momentous one. . . . And in the South it gives us the challenge to replace trickery and subterfuge with the honest realization that every child has the right to an equal education." And in the Delta town of Cleveland, a young Episcopal priest named Duncan Gray called on Mississippians to comply with the Court's decision—and kept his job.[43]

Most white Mississippians opposed *Brown,* but it was by no means immediately apparent that the state would defy the decision if the Eisenhower administration demonstrated a commitment to enforce it. (In the immediate aftermath of the decision, Duncan Gray talked with the Cleveland superintendent of schools and the president of the local school board, and both men said that they believed that Cleveland schools would be desegregated within a relatively short time.) At the state level, most discussion centered on strategies to avoid compliance without provoking a direct confrontation with the federal government. Attorney General James P. Coleman, whose apparent moderation made him the state's most effective segregationist, asked every white lawyer to sign up as a "Special Assistant Attorney General" to represent local school districts should blacks file desegregation suits, as they were threatening to do. Walter Sillers, the powerful Speaker of the House—and an opponent of Governor White's equalization plan—said he would reintroduce the constitutional amendment giving the legislature the authority to abolish the public schools rather than desegregate them. The unstated assumption here was that Mississippi would fund a private school system for white children. As for Governor White, who appeared to be genuinely committed to upgrading black schools, his plan was the most interesting of all: he would persuade the leaders of the Mississippi black community to endorse what he called "voluntary segregation."[44]

On July 1 the governor met with seven black men whom he believed to be key leaders in their community. Among those present were J. D. Boyd, the president of Alcorn College; J. H. White, president of Mississippi Vocational College; the Reverend H. H. Humes, a Delta minister, editor, and president of the 400,000-member General Missionary Baptist Convention; and Percy Greene of the *Jackson Advocate*. (Greene had by this time discarded the militancy of his earlier years and was currying favor with important whites.) Most of these men had previously gone on record against school desegregation, with Reverend Humes the most outspoken in his advocacy of all-black schools. They responded enthusiastically to the governor's pledge that if blacks supported voluntary segregation, then the legislature would begin allocating millions of dollars to improve black education.[45]

The group urged the governor to invite nearly 100 black leaders from across the state to meet with him in Jackson to discuss his plan, assuring him that 95 percent of those in attendance would endorse continued school segregation, provided that funds were immediately made available for equalization. The seven men were so confident of their position that they persuaded White to include representatives from the NAACP and the Regional Council of Negro Leadership on his guest list, arguing that if these spokespersons were excluded, any ensuing agreement would lack credibility in the black community.

White sent out approximately ninety letters on July 13, inviting the representatives to meet with him and his newly appointed Legal Educational Advisory Committee on July 30. Among those on the list was Emmett J. Stringer, a young dentist from Columbus and the new state president of the NAACP. Stringer accepted and used the NAACP network to learn the names of the other guests, calling them to a meeting at Farish Street Baptist Church in Jackson the night before they were to see the governor.

The "meeting the night before," as it would later be known, was a stormy one. Boyd, J. H. White, and the other members of the conservative faction soon realized they had miscalculated: they would not be able to persuade this group to go along with the governor. At one point during the meeting, Stringer recalled, the argument became so heated that Humes and T. R. M. Howard almost came to blows. After hours of debate, the group agreed to present a united front. They voted to select speakers to convey the message that black Mississippians expected the governor to enforce the *Brown* decision.

When the black delegation and Governor White and his entourage assembled at the State Office Building at 10:00 A.M., the atmosphere was tense. After a few opening remarks about the long history of good race relations in the Magnolia State, the governor turned the meeting over to House Speaker Walter Sillers to chair. The first black to get the floor was E. W. "Charlie" Banks of Jackson, who read a statement endorsed by the black delegation calling for "strict observance of the Supreme Court's integration order [through] consolidation and integration of the present schools on all levels." Subsequent speakers reiterated the theme. Howard minced no words. Although the governor had not yet introduced his plan, the Delta activist warned him that "the Negroes who have come here today have not come to help work out any trick plan to circumvent the decision of the Supreme Court outlawing segregation in the public schools. We believe that the decision is a just and humane decision."

Finally, in a desperate effort to salvage the situation, Speaker Sillers looked around for a friendly face and said, "I am going to call on Reverend Humes now." Humes strolled lazily to the floor and told the white leaders that "the real trouble is that for too long you have given us schools in which we could study the earth through the floor and the stars through the roof." At that, the governor hurriedly adjourned the meeting. Afterward, a visibly shaken Hugh White told reporters, "I am stunned." It was evident, he contended, that those blacks he had counted on for support had bowed "under pressure from members of their own race." "I have believed that a certain element representing a vast majority of the Negroes would go along," he said. "Now I am definitely of the conclusion that you can't put any faith in any one of them on this proposition."

Aaron Henry left the meeting with a different feeling. As the black delegation prepared to leave, "we shook hands, congratulating each other on what appeared to be a major triumph." It was an occasion, he recalled, "when I was really proud to be a Negro in Mississippi."

3

The Magnolia Jungle

The impact of *Brown* v. *Board of Education* extended far beyond the question of the future of the public schools. For Mississippi whites the U.S. Supreme Court decision had been a wake-up call, and preserving the southern way of life soon assumed all the trappings of a holy crusade. Black leaders, believing that the federal government had at long last come down firmly on the side of racial justice, prepared for the ordeal of desegregation hopeful that the Eisenhower administration would enforce the Court's mandate. *Brown* also energized the suffrage movement, with voter registration campaigns launched in areas of the state hitherto untouched by civil rights activity. The NAACP came into its own in Mississippi in the weeks and months following the meeting with Governor White. Aware that resistance in the Magnolia State would be strong, the NAACP sent in southeast regional secretary Ruby Hurley and director of branches Gloster Current to help organize new branches and to meet with local leaders to plan school desegregation strategy. From Oxford in the north to Pass Christian on the Gulf Coast, local blacks found new courage and signed up with the NAACP.[1]

In the Delta, Aaron Henry overcame opposition from conservative blacks and helped to establish the Clarksdale branch the year before *Brown*, and in 1955 postal worker and businessman Amzie Moore organized and became president of the branch in Cleveland, just down the road from Clarksdale. Further south a young physician, Dr. Clinton C. Battle, headed the Indianola branch. Both

Cleveland and Indianola were in Sunflower County, the fiefdom of James Eastland. In the state capital the "old guard" remained active, with attorney Carsie Hall now president of the Jackson branch. In southwest Mississippi the Natchez branch was led by Dr. A. Maurice Mackel, a dentist who had founded the branch in 1940. In Pike County a McComb railway clerk, Curtis Conway "C. C." Bryant, was elected president of the local branch, and E. W. Steptoe, a forty-three-year-old farmer whose courage and combativeness became legendary in the movement, organized the Amite County branch in 1954. To the east, Laurel dentist B. E. Murph headed the NAACP in Jones County, and Charles R. Darden, who would later serve a term as state NAACP president, led the Meridian branch.[2]

Emmett J. Stringer, state president of the NAACP in 1954, was representative of the new breed of NAACP activists. Stringer's mother had named him after Emmett J. Scott, Booker T. Washington's right-hand man at Tuskegee, and she taught young Emmett that as a gifted child he had a responsibility to work for the advancement of the race. (Mrs. Stringer took out NAACP memberships for Emmett and his sister "before we were teenagers.") The Stringers lived in Mound Bayou, and Emmett Stringer was strongly influenced by the nurturing environment of that all-black community. "Having seen black mayors and bankers and policemen and superintendents of schools, I knew what was possible, probable, and desirable," Stringer recalled. "People who had not been exposed to that could not see the possibilities." He also drew inspiration from the parade of prominent African Americans who came to speak at Mound Bayou. On graduating from Alcorn College in 1941, Stringer went directly into the army, where he served for nearly five years. After the war he enrolled at Meharry Medical College in Nashville, Tennessee. In 1950, Meharry degree in hand, the thirty-one-year-old dentist opened a practice in Columbus, Mississippi, where his wife, Flora, took a teaching job in the public schools. Stringer became active in the Columbus black community, serving as chairman of the board of directors of the 10th Avenue Branch YMCA in 1951 and as commander of American Legion Post 229 during 1951 and 1952. Early in 1953 Stringer organized the Columbus branch of the NAACP.[3]

Starting from a small middle-class base, the Columbus NAACP expanded to include members from all walks of life. At the organi-

zational meeting at the black Queen City Hotel, Stringer persuaded the group to go public and issue a press release. He recalled that
"we lost some of the people after that, especially some of the middle class leaders. They didn't come back. Working class people were
our main support."[4] As in most other branches, obtaining the franchise was the Columbus NAACP's priority. Stringer was relentless
in his efforts to convince people to register and vote. At one point
he personally collected the poll tax from forty American Legion
members, took the money to the courthouse, and returned with their
tax receipts. The branch grew rapidly under Stringer's leadership.
In little more than a year, more than 400 blacks had joined the
Columbus NAACP, making it the largest branch in the state. Practically unknown when he returned to Mississippi in 1950, Stringer
was elected president of the NAACP State Conference of Branches
in November 1953.[5] His year as state president was to be an event-
ful one.

Throughout the spring and summer of 1954 the implementation
of the school desegregation decision was at the top of the national
NAACP's agenda. Five days after *Brown* Stringer and Charles R.
Dardin attended an NAACP regional meeting in Atlanta. The resulting "Atlanta Declaration," mostly written by Thurgood Marshall, set forth the organization's position: "We here rededicate ourselves to the removal of all racial segregation in public education
and reiterate our determination to achieve that goal without compromise of principle." A week later Stringer convened an emergency meeting of local branch presidents and state NAACP officers,
who unanimously endorsed the Atlanta Declaration and outlined
the NAACP strategy to obtain compliance. First, local citizens
would petition their school boards to "take immediate steps to reorganize the public schools . . . in accordance with the constitutional
principles enunciated by the Supreme Court on May 17" and request a hearing to discuss the petition. Should school officials prove
recalcitrant, the NAACP was "prepared to carry to the courts any
infractions of this decision."[6]

This was an exhilarating time for NAACP activists. After years
of frustrating, mostly unsuccessful efforts to register voters (or even
sign up NAACP members), here was an opportunity to confront
the state on a Constitutional issue where the U.S. Supreme Court
had spoken directly. Long-standing fears over the consequences of
political involvement were diminishing, and the militant response

to Governor White's plea for "voluntary segregation" further emboldened black leaders. After a year of Stringer's leadership, the number of state NAACP branches had increased from twenty-one to thirty-four. Stringer also took steps to improve relations between the national office and the Regional Council of Negro Leadership, persuading T. R. M. Howard to take out an NAACP life membership in the name of the RCNL.[7]

The unity and euphoria surrounding *Brown* were to be short-lived, however, as conflict developed over questions of policy and strategy. One problem was that a group of the black educators who had gone along with the integrationist majority at the meeting with Governor White soon reverted back to their earlier position opposing school desegregation. White's strategy was to avoid compliance with *Brown* by acting as though the principle of "separate but equal" still applied in Mississippi. He now supported a constitutional amendment permitting the legislature to abolish the public schools rather than desegregate them, but he promised blacks that if the amendment passed, he would call a special session of the legislature and proceed with his school equalization plan. Black educators like Presidents White of Mississippi Vocational and Boyd at Alcorn saw that despite the earlier confrontation with the governor it was still possible to secure badly needed funds for their institutions, providing they once again toed the line. And they did.[8]

President White of Mississippi Vocational College led the counterattack. Labeled "our enemy #1" by the NAACP's A. M. Mackel, White was the governor's liaison with black educators. Furious over the rejection of the governor's voluntary segregation plan, J. H. White wrote Stringer that "the meeting we had at Jackson retarded the progress of the Negro" because "the white people of Mississippi are not ready. . . . we cannot change over night discrimination and irregularities." White concluded that Stringer was "wrong in attempting to push little Negro children in places where they are not wanted and where they are unhappy, and where they are not inspired."[9] Other black educators went public with their support of the governor's position. The white press praised these accommodationists; the black community labeled them "Uncle Toms." The NAACP desegregation strategy, however, did not depend on teacher support. At its annual meeting in Jackson in November 1954, the state NAACP reaffirmed its earlier plan of action: members were to file desegregation petitions with their local school boards, and if the boards rejected these petitions, then the NAACP would file suit to force compliance with *Brown*.[10]

A few black activists opposed this strategy. Although he had strongly endorsed *Brown*, T. R. M. Howard believed the decision to petition local boards was premature. When the Mound Bayou physician persuaded the RCNL board to support his opposition to the NAACP desegregation plan, the chairman of the RCNL executive board, Emmett Stringer, resigned. Stringer wrote Thurgood Marshall that "I should not and could not hold major offices in two similar organizations that differ so widely on such an important policy." Howard's objection to the petition drive's timing was twofold. First, he believed it a tactical error to "get ahead of the Supreme Court," which had not yet set down its desegregation guidelines. Second, assessing the current racial climate in the state, Howard warned that "to petition school boards in Mississippi at the present time is like going to hunt a bear with a cap pistol," an analogy that proved devastatingly accurate.[11]

On July 11, 1954, less than two months after *Brown*, Robert "Tut" Patterson, a thirty-two-year-old Delta plantation manager, called together fourteen Indianola men to discuss the problems created by the court decision. A former captain of the Mississippi State football team, the red-headed former paratrooper was drawn into politics because the thought of black and white children attending the same schools sickened him. "I became obsessed with the thing," he said, and "started agitating around town." Patterson drew together Indianola's civic and business establishment. Present at the July 11 meeting were a Harvard-educated attorney, a local banker, and the town's mayor and its city attorney. The group agreed that segregation in the schools could be maintained without resorting to violence. These upper-middle-class leaders were not interested in starting up a Klan klavern. At the close of the meeting the men decided to hold a public rally at the town hall. Approximately seventy-five Indianola whites joined Patterson and his cadre at that meeting, where they organized the first Citizens' Council.[12]

With Patterson as the primary organizer, Citizens' Councils sprung up first across the Delta and then throughout the state, with their best representation in black majority counties. By mid-October the council claimed 25,000 dues-paying members in Mississippi, and soon thereafter the movement spread into neighboring states. Among early supporters were Senator Eastland, scores of state legislators and local elected officials, and the powerful Hederman press, which controlled the state's two largest dailies, the *Jackson Daily News* and the Jackson *Clarion-Ledger*. Segregation could be preserved, council leaders always publicly stressed, through legal means. Indeed, as the historian Neil McMillen has noted, "In an atmosphere of unremitting hostility to social change in any form, where law was the servant of white supremacy, white supremacists had little need for lawlessness." Nevertheless, through its unrelenting attack on human rights in Mississippi, the Citizens' Council fostered and legitimized violent actions by individuals not overly concerned with questions of legality and image.[13]

Blacks got a taste of what was in store for them in August 1954 when a delegation from the Walthall County NAACP branch went to a county school board meeting to file the first desegregation petitions. After being harassed by the board chairman—"Nigger, don't you want to take your name off this petition that says you want to go to school with white children?"—the petitioners left the meeting, only to find themselves facing grand jury subpoenas on trumped-up charges. The district attorney quashed the subpoenas, but the tactic had succeeded. The Walthall County branch did not press the matter further, and the NAACP filed no new petitions in Mississippi until after the U.S. Supreme Court handed down its implementation decision in 1955.[14]

With a lull on the school desegregation front, the Citizens' Council directed a campaign of economic intimidation against the leaders of the two major black protest organizations, the NAACP and the RCNL. As president of the Mississippi State Conference of Branches, Emmett Stringer was an obvious target. In December 1954 Stringer reported that "since the advent of the Citizens' Councils we have experienced an increased amount and variety of pressures." Earlier in the fall the Columbus dentist found that the local banks, once eager to extend him credit, now refused to loan him money. His automobile liability insurance was canceled. The Internal Revenue Service took a sudden interest in Stringer, who had reason to believe the audits were initiated locally. Stringer's wife, Flora, who had a master's degree from Columbia University, lost her teaching job in the Columbus public schools. His dental practice began to suffer. Former patients stopped him on the street to explain that their white employers were now insisting that they patronize another dentist. A Columbus teacher who paid Stringer for her dental work by check was accused by a school official of making a donation to the NAACP and threatened with the loss of her job.[15]

Finally, there were the anonymous threatening letters and telephone calls. Stringer told NAACP official Clarence Mitchell that he and his wife were sleeping in the middle bedroom of their home as a defense against a bombing. He took other precautions: "I had weapons in my house," he explained later. "And not only in my house, I had weapons on me when I went to my office, because I knew people were out to get me. I would take my revolver with me and put it in the drawer, right where I worked."[16]

All this came down on Stringer and his family in the few months after Tut Patterson gathered the pillars of Indianola society to form a patriotic society dedicated to the preservation of white supremacy by legal means only. Less than a year earlier the young dentist had been the dynamic catalyst in the Columbus black community, with a promising professional career ahead of him. Now he walked the streets with a pistol in his pocket and faced financial ruin, if not assassination. The economic pressures eventually became too great, and he had to lower his visibility. In late 1954 Stringer announced that he would not be a candidate for a second term as state NAACP president. He did, however, remain as head of the local NAACP branch.[17]

T. R. M. Howard was the other primary target. Although a wealthy man by Mississippi standards, the Mound Bayou physician was vulnerable to economic pressures. In late 1954 Howard was in the process of buying several plots of land when the negotiable papers passed into the hands of a Citizens' Council member, who demanded immediate payment. The charismatic leader who had stood up to Governor White with all Mississippi watching was now being squeezed. Howard ultimately lost thousands of dollars of his property assets. He also suffered harassment, as when his local draft board attempted to reclassify him 1-A (Howard was forty-seven when he received his notice). Threats on his life were common; the word was out that there was a $1,000 price on his head. Howard took precautions, traveling with armed bodyguards and placing his home under twenty-four-hour protection. A rumor that whites had beaten Howard's wife brought fifteen carloads of blacks with guns ready to lend assistance.[18]

Registered black voters, school desegregation proponents, and

NAACP leaders across the state fell victim to Citizens' Council tactics. In September Gus Courts, a Belzoni grocer and president of the area's NAACP branch, learned from the local bank president that unless he resigned as NAACP head he would forfeit his credit rating with the bank. Courts did step down but continued to agitate for voter registration. Economic pressure continued, and he received the first of many death threats. In Cleveland Amzie Moore's banker called in Moore's $6,000 mortgage on his home and service station. And the sharecroppers who constituted a significant portion of Dr. Clinton Battle's clientele in Indianola received orders from plantation owners to find a new doctor. In Natchez A. M. Mackel reported that his telephone had been tapped, and other blacks had reason to believe their mail was being opened. Rank-and-file NAACP members also felt the heat. Indianola branch member Lovie F. Walker wrote the national office that "it is imperative that I no longer receive mail from the NAACP. Please, please discontinue sending me mail from there and take my name from your mailing list."[19]

The New York office of the NAACP attempted to counter the Citizens' Council's tactics. First, it called on the federal government to take action. In late December Channing Tobias, chairman of the NAACP's board of directors, sent a telegram to President Dwight D. Eisenhower. "Negro leadership in Mississippi is being subjected to undisguised economic intimidation," Tobias warned the president, and the Citizens' Council was responsible. He asked for a conference with the president to discuss "this threat to the well-being of our country." Ike answered with silence.[20]

In response to the actions of Mississippi banks in denying black activists credit, refusing to renew mortgages, and calling in existing loans, the NAACP acted on Howard's suggestion to create an independent loan fund to aid victims of economic retaliation. Early in 1955 the NAACP deposited $280,000 in the black-owned Tri-State Bank in Memphis and worked out a plan for financial assistance, stipulating that all applicants "will have to satisfy the usual requirements of the bank" and that "no money is to be ladled out on the mere assertion of prosecution." The Tri-State program was helpful in a number of cases, but the $12,000 monthly allocation for loans was insufficient to meet the need. In Mississippi, the NAACP was proving no match for the Citizens' Council.[21]

The NAACP's most important move in 1954 was hiring Medgar

Evers to be its first full-time field secretary in Mississippi. Evers was the ideal person for the job. Born and raised in Decatur, Medgar and his brother, Charles, grew up in a strong family environment. Their father, James, was a quiet, stern, hard-working man who refused to buckle under to the caste system. James Evers was the role model for his son, a father who "stood up and was a man." During World War II Medgar was stationed in France, and shortly after his return to Mississippi in 1946 he underwent his traumatic encounter with whites at the polls during the Bilbo election. Evers then enrolled at Alcorn College on the G.I. Bill and there met Myrlie Beasley. They were married during Medgar's senior year. On graduation Evers took a job with T. R. M. Howard's Magnolia Mutual Insurance Company, and the young couple moved to Mound Bayou.[22]

Evers's job selling insurance door to door in the Delta was in a sense his apprenticeship for his life's work. Distressed by the abject poverty of Delta blacks, he began to feel guilty about selling policies to people who could barely put food on their tables. Soon he was using his job as a cover for political work, talking up the NAACP and urging Delta sharecroppers to attend Doc Howard's mass meetings in Mound Bayou. At one of these meetings in 1953, Emmett Stringer asked for a volunteer to attempt to desegregate Ole Miss. When Evers stepped forward and subsequently applied to the University of Mississippi law school, his life took a fateful turn. From that point on national officers of the NAACP had their eyes on Evers, and in December 1954 they offered him the job as field secretary.[23]

Tall, low-keyed, intelligent, and dignified in appearance, Evers was from the outset loyal to his organization and to his superiors. But the new field secretary was also an angry young man. While living in Mound Bayou he became an interested observer of the freedom struggle then raging in Kenya and greatly admired the guerilla leader Jomo Kenyatta. (When the Everses' first child was born, a son, Medgar had the name picked out: Kenyatta. Somewhat distraught, Myrlie quietly inserted the name "Darrell" before "Kenyatta" on the birth certificate.) Myrlie Evers has written that before he went to work for the NAACP, her husband "flirted intellectually with the idea of fighting back, envisioning a form of guerilla warfare in the Delta." The NAACP's Ruby Hurley, who worked closely with Evers until his death, remembered her first impressions of the new field secretary: "Talk about nonviolent, he was anything but non-violent; anything but! And he always wanted to go at it in Mau Mau fashion."[24] Evers realized, of course, that armed resistance would be suicidal, and he channeled his rage into feverish activity on behalf of the NAACP, which he saw as the best hope for black Mississippians. Still, he remained a guerrilla fighter at heart.

The early months of 1955 were relatively quiet, as Mississippians awaited the Supreme Court's implementation decision. After an early burst of organizing activity, the Citizens' Council saw its membership leveling off, for most whites refused to believe that their way of life was in peril. NAACP branches in the state, shaken by the council's initial offensive, regrouped their forces to prepare for the next big push. On May 31, 1955, the Supreme Court declared that the initial responsibility for implementing *Brown* lay with federal district judges, "because of their proximity to local conditions," and that school desegregation should proceed "with all deliberate speed." Although the Court called for "a prompt and reasonable start toward compliance," Mississippi whites were relieved. Attorney Tom J. Tubb voiced a common sentiment when he welcomed the decision as "a very definite victory for the South. We couldn't ask for anything better than to have our local, native Mississippi federal district judges consider suits in good faith and act accordingly in the 'as soon as feasible' element." Tubb predicted "it may be 100 years before it's feasible."[25]

While disappointed that the decision had not been more forceful, on June 5 the state board of the Mississippi NAACP instructed local branches to take "immediate steps" to end segregation. Within weeks black parents filed desegregation petitions with school boards in Jackson, Clarksdale, Vicksburg, Natchez, and Yazoo City, cities with active NAACP branches.[26]

Across the state the Citizens' Council was preparing to meet the challenge. The council followed a similar strategy in each city, combining publicity and economic retaliation to intimidate the petitioners. In Yazoo City, the local council took out a full-page newspaper advertisement listing the names and addresses of the fifty-three black parents who signed petitions. Their names also appeared on large placards posted in every store in town and even in surrounding cotton fields. Almost immediately those petitioners working for white people lost their jobs. Independent black businessmen were also not spared. James H. Wright, a licensed master plumber whose clientele was "99 percent white," found himself the victim of a boycott so successful that he had to leave the state. Grocer Nathan Stewarts, whose patrons were black, could no longer obtain goods from distributors after he had signed the petition. The World War II veteran with six children relocated with his family in Illinois. Within a short time all but two of the fifty-three signers removed their names from the list, and both remaining signatories soon left the city. Removal of a name did not, however, mean restoration of a job. Eventually more than a dozen petitioners and their families had to leave the area to find work.[27]

This economic war of attrition stunned local black leaders. The Yazoo City NAACP had organized in 1948, but the school petition drive had been its first controversial action. "We got that petition straight from Roy Wilkins," said Jasper Mims. "We expected pressure, but not this much." Membership in the Yazoo City branch plummeted, while the local Citizens' Council grew from its base of sixteen founders to more than 1,500 members.[28]

Similar results occurred in the other cities targeted for desegregation. In Vicksburg, where 140 black parents had filed the first petition on July 18, publication of their names in the newspaper had been enough to end the drive. The Jackson NAACP was the state's strongest, and there forty-two parents petitioned the local board. Jackson Citizens' Council president Ellis Wright, who was also president of the local chamber of commerce, met with the mayor and school board officials and emerged to inform the press that the ultimate goal of school desegregationists was intermarriage. "If the NAACP thinks we have the slightest idea of surrendering our Southland to a mulatto race," Wright warned, "the NAACP had better think again." That, and strong editorial support for the council's stand in the Hederman press, was enough to sink the Jackson petition movement. Membership in the Jackson Citizens' Council rose dramatically. The petition drives in Clarksdale and Natchez also met early deaths and provided the opportunity for the council to organize affiliates in both cities.[29]

In retrospect, it is apparent that the NAACP petition drive in Mississippi was doomed from the outset. Ironically, this bold strategy proceeded logically from the NAACP's traditional conservative approach to the race problem: work through the courts and make sure the law is on your side before taking action. But here the national office made several miscalculations, underestimating the ferocity of white resistance and overestimating the federal government's commitment to law enforcement.

The Eisenhower administration stood by while Mississippi whites made a mockery of *Brown,* responding indifferently to repeated pleas for help by local and national NAACP officials. Privately, the president had opposed the *Brown* decision. His public comments offered little solace to black citizens: "It is difficult through law and through force to change a man's heart. . . . We must all . . . help to bring about a change in spirit so that extremists on both sides do not defeat what we know is a reasonable, logical conclusion to this whole affair, which is recognition of equality of men." In Mississippi, those "extremists" were presumably the Citizens' Council and the NAACP, those who would defy the law and those who were asking the president to enforce it.[30] The Supreme Court must also bear responsibility for the failure to secure compliance in the Deep South. Its implementation decree had in fact placed the burden of desegregation on the shoulders of black parents, with disastrous results. Given the powerful segregationist opposition, the federal government's inaction and the lack of a deep base of support in the black community, the school petitioners in Mississippi were sitting ducks, to be picked off one by one by the sharpshooters of the Citizens' Council.

The national NAACP office responded to this defeat by dropping Mississippi like a hot potato. Eight years passed before the NAACP filed its first desegregation suit against the Mississippi public schools, and it did so only after repeated, increasingly insistent requests by state field secretary Medgar Evers.[31] Having dealt the school desegregation movement a body blow in 1955, the Citizens' Council now moved to counter a renewed effort by blacks to obtain the franchise.

Black voter registration activities in the early 1950s had proceeded without fanfare and with limited success. By 1954 some 22,000 blacks were registered, about 4 percent of those eligible. Six counties with black majorities were among the fourteen that had no blacks registered. In exactly half of the state's eighty-two counties, fewer than 1 percent of eligible blacks were registered.[32] Confident that they had little to fear from the black electorate, white Mississippi voters had defeated a constitutional amendment in 1952 tightening registration requirements. Two years later, in the aftermath of *Brown,* the legislature passed a similar amendment requiring applicants to write a "reasonable" interpretation of a section of the state constitution given them by the registrar, who would judge the "reasonableness" of their answer. This amendment closed the loophole in the 1890 constitution that required only that an applicant be able to *read* a section of the constitution. (As previously noted, in the past registrars often conveniently forgot this provision when evaluating black applicants.) This time the amendment passed in a referendum by nearly five to one.[33]

Encouraged by the *Brown* decision, in late 1954 and 1955 blacks mounted registration campaigns in communities across the state. Whites responded as they had to the school challenge, with intimidation and force, dusting off tactics they had employed during the early postwar years. In Sunflower County, where only 114 of 18,949 eligible blacks were on the books, the registrar simply turned away black applicants. The sheriff's office in Tallahatchie County, two-thirds black and with no Negro voters, refused to accept poll tax payments from blacks. A black principal in Tallahatchie who attempted to register lost his job, and a Forrest County minister with two degrees from Columbia University failed the test twice. When pressed for an explanation, the registrar stated that the minister's membership in the NAACP had made him unfit to vote.[34]

In the spring of 1955 T. R. M. Howard held a mass voter registration rally in Mound Bayou that drew 10,000 blacks to hear Detroit congressman Charles Diggs and other speakers, including the Reverend George W. Lee. A vice president of the Regional Council of Negro Leadership and an NAACP activist, the fifty-two-year-old clergyman also operated a printing shop in the Delta town of Belzoni. Simeon Booker attended the Mound Bayou rally and remembered Lee as the "tan-skinned, stumpy spell-binder" who urged his audience to register and vote, predicting that if they did so someday the Delta would send a Negro to Congress.[35]

The Citizens' Council had already forced Lee's good friend Gus Courts to give up the presidency of the NAACP branch in Belzoni. When both men continued to urge blacks to vote, they began to receive death threats. On the night of May 7, two weeks after the Mound Bayou rally, Reverend Lee was driving along a Belzoni street when a convertible roared up from behind and pulled alongside his car. Shots rang out; Lee's car swerved and crashed into a shack. The lower side of his face and jawbone had been torn away by the gun blasts, yet he managed to pull himself out of the wreckage. Two black taxi drivers who heard the shots rushed over to assist the minister, but to no avail; George Lee died on the way to the hospital. The next day the *Clarion-Ledger* ran the story under the headline "Negro Leader Dies in Odd Accident."[36]

Immediately after the murder, Lee's wife contacted Dr. Howard, who telephoned Charles Diggs. The congressman demanded that the FBI investigate, and it did—in a perfunctory fashion. Dr. A. H. McCoy (who had succeeded Stringer as state NAACP president), Medgar Evers, and other blacks called on Governor White to send investigators to Belzoni. White refused, stating that he never responded to NAACP requests. No one was ever charged with the murder. It had been less than a month since a determined George Lee had stood before the mass of black faces in Mound Bayou and said, "Pray not for your Mom and Pop. They've gone to heaven. Pray you can make it through this hell."[37]

That the FBI had merely gone through the motions in investigating Lee's death was not lost on local whites. A week after the killing the NAACP learned that activist Gus Courts was "next on the list to go." Continued economic harassment had not shaken Courts's resolve, and he had spoken with a lawyer about bringing a damage suit against the Belzoni Citizens' Council. Shortly after the November elections, Courts was gunned down in his store. County sheriff Ike Shelton told the press that probably "some damn nigger just drove there and shot him." Again the FBI investigated, and again no arrests were made. The sixty-five-year-old Courts eventually recovered from his wounds, but he left the state. The NAACP helped him get back into the grocery business in Chicago.[38]

The most blatant political execution in that bloody year occurred in broad daylight on a busy Saturday afternoon on the crowded courthouse lawn in the southwest Mississippi town of Brookhaven. The victim was Lamar Smith, a sixty-three-year-old farmer and World War II veteran who had been urging blacks to vote in the Democratic primary. Although the sheriff saw a white man leaving the scene "with blood all over him," no one admitted to having witnessed the shooting. Again the killer went free.[39] Mississippi's reign of terror had received some coverage in the nation's press, but two weeks after Smith's murder news of yet another racial killing went out over the wires, and this case captured the attention of the world.

It was all so hauntingly familiar, a page from a Richard Wright story. On a late summer day in August several black teenagers gathered outside a country store in a Delta hamlet called Money. Several of the youths were playing checkers while others amused themselves by cutting up and telling tall stories. Conspicuous among the idlers was a stocky fourteen-year-old boy from Chicago, Emmett "Bobo" Till, who was down for a two-week visit with his granduncle, Moses Wright, a sharecropper. Streetwise and cocky, Till had learned to compensate for a speech impediment resulting from an early attack of polio.

That afternoon Till was boasting about having a white girlfriend in Chicago when several of the youths called his bluff, daring him to go inside the store and ask the white woman behind the counter for a date. He accepted the challenge. Inside he saw Carolyn Bryant, twenty-one, who was taking care of the family business while her husband Roy, a part-time truck driver, was out of the state on a delivery. What transpired next remains a matter of conjecture. Carolyn Bryant later testified that a Negro man, whom she did not identify, entered the store and asked for two cents' worth of bubble gum. As she handed him the gum he squeezed her hand and, speaking clearly but "with a northern brogue," asked her for a date. Then, as he left the store, he wolf-whistled at her.[40]

Till's defenders later claimed Carolyn Bryant fabricated the conversation. His mother, Mamie Bradley, said that to stop his stutter, her son would often "blow it out," causing the "whistle." His cousin, Curtis Jones, who was outside playing checkers, recalled no whistle but asserted that as Till left the store he said, "Bye, baby." Whatever the provocation, Bobo's friends immediately sensed that in some way he had violated the South's most sacred taboo, and they hustled him away from the Bryants' store, back to Moses Wright's house three miles from town.[41]

When Roy Bryant returned to the Delta two days later he learned of the incident while at work in the store—his wife had not mentioned it to him. He then talked with his half-brother, J. W. Milam, about taking revenge. "Big" Milam was just that: a hulking six-feet-two and 235 pounds, the balding World War II combat infantryman had been likened to "slavery's plantation owner." His friends claimed that he could "handle Negroes better than anyone in the county." Shortly after midnight on Sunday, August 28, more than three days after the incident at the store, Milam and Bryant awoke Moses Wright and demanded that he turn over his nephew to them for questioning. Wright's protest that "the boy ain't got good sense" and his plea that they "just take him out in the yard and whip him" were of no avail; the two men forced the youth into Milam's pickup and drove off. Three days later a white youth fishing in the Tallahatchie River discovered a partly submerged body tied to a cotton gin fan. It was dragged ashore and later identified as that of Emmett Till. The circumstantial evidence against Milam and Bryant was so overwhelming that local authorities arrested them and charged the two men with Till's murder.[42]

Three weeks later their trial took place in Sumner, a small Delta town in Tallahatchie County, where Till's body had been found. White men killing black men was nothing new in Mississippi, but this "wolf-whistle murder" of a fourteen-year-old boy captured international attention. Nearly 100 reporters from major newspapers, as well as network television camera crews, descended on the Magnolia State. At first Mississippi whites did not know what to make of all the media attention, but they soon grew to resent it, believing that their state was being maligned by outsiders determined to destroy the southern way of life. Mississippi newspapers focused their wrath on the NAACP, which had publicized the case, produced witnesses, and demanded that the killers be convicted. The defense would capitalize on local hostility toward the outsiders, shifting the focus of the jury away from the defendants to the NAACP.[43]

The early dramatic moment of the trial was the testimony of Moses Wright. Although friends advised him to go into hiding, Wright insisted on telling his story. When asked if he could identify the men who abducted his nephew, the tall, gaunt sharecropper rose in the courtroom and said, "Thar he," pointing first at Milam and then to Bryant. The defense conceded that the two men had taken Till from his uncle's home but claimed that they became convinced that Till was not the "guilty" party and released him unharmed at about 3:00 A.M. (Carolyn Bryant's refusal to identify Till as her antagonist was consistent with this scenario.) The prosecution produced a witness, a nineteen-year-old black man named Willie Reed, who testified that he saw Till in the company of Milam and five other men between 6:00 and 7:00 Sunday morning, that he heard cries coming from the barn of Milam's brother, and that he saw Milam, wearing a pistol, emerge from the barn.

The heart of the defense's case was that the bloated body dragged from the Tallahatchie was not that of Emmett Till—despite identi-

fication by Till's mother and the fact that Till's ring was recovered
on the body. Earlier, Sheriff H. C. Strider, in charge of the investigation, had claimed to be examining evidence that "the killing might
have been planned and plotted by the NAACP." There was no such
evidence, but in his summation defense counsel John C. Whitten, a
cousin of Mississippi congressman Jamie Whitten, warned the jury
that "there are people in the United States who want to destroy
the customs of southern people. . . . They would not be above putting a rotting, stinking body in the river in the hope he would be
identified as Emmett Till." In calling for acquittal Whitten expressed
confidence that "every last Anglo-Saxon one of you has the courage to do it." The judge in the case, Curtis Swango, had conducted the trial fairly, and the prosecutors argued vigorously for conviction. After being out for sixty-eight minutes, the jury returned
with a "not guilty" verdict. Milam and Bryant kissed their wives,
lit up cigars, grinned for the photographers, and accepted the con-
gratulations of the hundreds of well-wishers surrounding them.[44]

The verdict was generally well received in Mississippi, but there
were dissenting voices. Hodding Carter criticized the outcome.
Norma Bradley of the *Jackson State Times* wrote, "We showed the
world all right, that Mississippi does not bow to the dictates of the
National Association for the Advancement of Colored People, but
the NAACP is not the real loser. Justice is the real loser and when
that is true, Mississippi suffers." And William Faulkner asked
whether "the purpose of this sorry and tragic error committed in
my native Mississippi by two white adults on an afflicted colored
child is to prove to us whether or not we deserve to survive."
Faulkner concluded that "if we in America have reached that point
in our desperate culture when we must murder children, no matter
for what reason or what color, we don't deserve to survive, and
probably won't." More typical was the view expressed by the *Jackson Daily News* that "it is best for all concerned that the Bryant-
Milam case be forgotten as quickly as possible." But the story would
not go away. Thousands protested the verdict in rallies held around
the world, and anger intensified in early 1956 when Milam and
Bryant, in return for cash, admitted to *Look* reporter William Bradford Huic that yes, they had murdered Emmett Till.[45]

In the long run the Till lynching had an impact unforeseen by observers at the trial. Black teenagers like Sam Block in the Delta and
Joyce and Dorie Ladner of Palmers Crossing, Mississippi, identified

personally with "this boy our age, who could have been one of our brothers." Viewing the picture of his bloated body in *Jet* magazine, recalled Joyce Ladner, "we asked each other, 'How could they do that to him? He's only a boy.'" For fourteen-year-old Anne Moody, the Till case was the beginning of her political education. The young women and men who became the vanguard of SNCC and CORE in the 1960s were in a real sense members of "the Emmett Till generation." Amzie Moore later identified the Till lynching as the beginning of the modern civil rights movement in Mississippi.[46]

But in 1955 such thoughts were far from the minds of white Mississippians, some of whom took home a different message from the Till case. In early December Elmer Kimball, a white cotton gin manager, shot and killed Clinton Melton, a black service station attendant, after an altercation over the amount of gas Kimball ordered. (Kimball was driving the car of his good friend, J. W. Milam.) There was limited coverage of Kimball's trial, also held in Sumner; the NAACP did not get involved. Melton's white employer saw Kimball shoot down Melton in cold blood and said so under oath. Although the circumstances surrounding the murder of Clinton Melton were very different from those in the Till case, the results were the same: the jury set the killer free. When asked what all this meant, one local white man replied: "There's open season on the Negroes now. They've got no protection, and any peckerwood who wants can go out and shoot himself one, and we'll free him. Our situation will get worse and worse."[47]

• • •

In the wake of *Brown* white Mississippians had developed a siege mentality so pervasive it encompassed virtually every citizen and institution. "Keeping the Negro in his place" was no longer sufficient, for the real enemy lay outside the state's borders—in the New York offices of the NAACP, in the chambers of the Supreme Court, inside the Kremlin walls. As the Red Scare of the fifties was abating in the rest of the country, a homegrown McCarthyism took hold in the Magnolia State. Books were banned, speakers censored, and network television programs cut off in midsentence. To be certain that subversives did not operate underground, the legislature created the State Sovereignty Commission, a secret police force that owed its primary allegiance to the Citizens' Council.

Ole Miss historian James W. Silver lived through these times and later wrote of his adoptive state as "The Closed Society." Other Deep South states were harshly repressive, but Mississippi appeared to many observers to be in a class by itself. The historian David Donald, Silver's friend and a native white Mississippian, attempted to explain this distinction:

> The Mississipppian has always lived in a self-contained world. When he traveled, he went to Memphis (where he met other Mississippians in the lobby of the Gayso Hotel) or to his own Gulf Coast. When he traded, it was with other Mississippians. When he read, it was his own local newspapers, edited by Mississippians. When he got an education, it was at Mississippi colleges, where Mississippians taught. . . . These people had no idea that there was a world beyond themselves.[48]

Spokesmen for the Citizens' Council, and the politicians who followed them, exploited this provincialism, revealing to white Mississippians a "world beyond themselves" fraught with peril.

From 1954 to the early 1960s the Mississippi State Legislature enacted a series of statutes aimed at the enemies of white supremacy, a category so broad it encompassed literally every attempt to modify the status quo in race relations. As noted, in late 1954 and 1955 Mississippians had ratified constitutional amendments stiffening voter registration requirements and permitting the legislature to abolish the public schools rather than desegregate them. In 1956 the new governor, J. P. Coleman, signed a bill repealing the state's compulsory attendance laws, a measure designed to facilitate closing schools under desegregation orders (but whose major impact would be to reduce school attendance by poor black and white children). The legislature also tightened enforcement of segregation in bus and railroad facilities and authorized investigation of any organization deemed subversive, an act aimed at the NAACP. The law that proved most useful to segregationists was a sweeping "breach of the peace" statute making it a crime to advocate, urge, or encourage "disobedience to any law of the State of Mississippi, and nonconformance with the established traditions, customs, and usages of the State of Mississippi." Violators could be fined $1,000 and jailed for six months.[49] The spirit of defiance running rampant through the state capitol reached its peak in 1956 with the resolution of interposition, declaring the *Brown* decision to be "invalid, unconstitutional, and of not lawful effect." After voting 136 to 0 for the resolution, House members cheered as a quartet of legislators broke into a chorus of "Dixie."[50]

While the interposition resolution was an act of bravado signifying nothing, creation of the State Sovereignty Commission in 1956 had implications far beyond the hysteria of the moment. Officially established "to prevent encroachment upon the rights of this and other states by the Federal Government," the State Sovereignty Commission was, in the words of journalist Wilson F. Minor, "something akin to NKVD among the cotton patches." Commission agents engaged in wiretapping, bugging, and other acts of espionage against Mississippi citizens. According to former commission director Erle Johnston, Jr., by 1967 Sovereignty Commission files contained dossiers on "approximately 250 organizations" and listed "about 10,000 individual names," many of whom were alleged to "work for or represent subversive, militant, or revolutionary groups." Dozens of people were spies for the commission, gathering information and infiltrating civil rights organizations. At the commission's request, the *Jackson Daily News* and the *Clarion-Ledger* regularly killed news stories or published propaganda articles. Although it also carried on a campaign to "tell the truth" about Mississippi to the rest of the world, the Sovereignty Commission's major impact was to further narrow the boundaries of acceptable behavior in matters regarding race.[51]

Fearful that Yankee propaganda on the race question might corrupt the minds of Mississippi youth, white supremacists took a sudden interest in the curriculum of the public schools and the contents of their libraries. In south Mississippi a Jones County grand jury called for statewide screening of school and library books to eliminate those critical of the southern way of life. The Mississippi chapter of the Daughters of the American Revolution declared forty-four state public school texts "unsatisfactory," charging that the books promoted desegregation, labor organizations, and the United Nations. In 1956 the Mississippi House passed a bill requiring the State Library Commission to buy books promoting white supremacy. Among the volumes purchased were copies of Judge Tom Brady's *Black Monday,* a polemical attack on the *Brown* decision and a diatribe against the Negro race. A sample of Brady's rhetoric: "You can dress a chimpanzee, housebreak him, and teach him to use a knife and fork, but it will take countless generations of evolutionary development, if ever, before you can convince him that a caterpillar or a cockroach is not a delicacy. Likewise the social, economic, and religious preferences of the Negro remain close to the caterpillar and the cockroach." Segregationists embraced this unabashedly racist manifesto as scientific truth. Brady was elevated to the Mississippi Supreme Court in 1963.[52]

During the mid-1950s the Citizens' Council became the watchdog of the state's public schools, colleges, and universities. Under council pressure, the state superintendent's office withdrew the film *The High Wall*, donated by the Anti-Defamation League and shown in Mississippi schools for more than six years. The film did not even deal with black-white relations but instead dramatized prejudice against a Polish group living in a predominantly Anglo-Saxon community in the United States. When Ole Miss chaplain Will Campbell invited the Reverend Alvin Kershaw to speak at a Religious Emphasis Week program during the spring of 1956, the council objected. It seems that Kershaw, a minor celebrity after winning big on "The $64,000 Question" television show, announced he would donate part of his $32,000 prize to the NAACP. Over the protests of the Ole Miss school newspaper and a significant number of students, the university administration capitulated and withdrew Kershaw's invitation. In the aftermath of the Kershaw incident, the state college Board of Trustees issued an edict requiring the screening of all speakers brought to college campuses.[53]

Although the "speaker ban" did not apply to private colleges, church-related institutions such as Belhaven College and Mississippi College were philosophically committed to white supremacy and did not invite controversial speakers to their campuses. Millsaps College was for a time an exception. Located in Jackson and founded by the United Methodist church, Millsaps had enjoyed the reputation as the best white school in Mississippi—and the most liberal. Several Millsaps faculty members had established close relations with their counterparts at Tougaloo, the private black college six miles up the road, and some Millsaps and Tougaloo students held informal gatherings to discuss race-related issues. The driving force behind this interinstitutional cooperation was Tougaloo sociologist Ernst Borinski, who had emigrated to the United States after escaping the Nazis in the late 1930s. Borinski invited local whites to his social science forums and promoted closer relations between the two colleges. The short, portly professor was a familiar figure on the Millsaps campus, speaking in sociology classes, sitting in on comprehensive exams, and even conducting an informal, racially integrated course in conversational German.[54] Not surprisingly, the Citizens' Council regarded the situation at Millsaps as intolerable and moved to bring that errant institution back into the Mississippi mainstream.

The opportunity came in the spring of 1958, when the Millsaps Christian Council sponsored a forum on race relations and invited Glenn Smiley, an activist who was field secretary for the Fellowship of Reconciliation, to be the featured speaker. When the Citizens' Council objected to Smiley's appearance, the Millsaps administration reluctantly withdrew his invitation. The matter might have died there had announcement of the cancellation not come two days after Borinski had told a Millsaps audience that "racial segregation violates Christian premises." At that, Citizens' Council leaders launched a full-scale attack on the Millsaps administration, demanding to know whether the institution "supports racial segregation or racial integration." Millsaps president Ellis Finger, a racial moderate, eventually caved in to the pressure, announcing that it was "extremely regrettable" that Borinski and Smiley had been invited to speak at Millsaps. A short time later the Millsaps Board of Trustees issued a statement that "segregation always has been, and is now, the policy of Millsaps College. There is no thought, purpose, or intention . . . to change this policy."[55] Ernst Borinski continued to teach at Tougaloo and for the next quarter century remained an outspoken opponent of segregation. But with the capitulation of Millsaps, the Citizens' Council had eliminated the last hope in the white academic community for a rational dialogue on the race problem.

The Methodist ministers who sat on the Millsaps board were among the most liberal in the state, but their reaffirmation of the school's policy of racial exclusion was representative of the white churches' stand on the race question. With a few noteworthy exceptions, white clergy in Mississippi supported the status quo in race relations. When less than a month after *Brown* the Southern Baptist Convention adopted resolutions by overwhelming majorities urging support of the decision, Mississippi Baptists were quick to dissent. Representatives of the state's largest denomination pointed out that the convention resolutions were not binding on the autonomous Mississippi congregations. Dr. Douglas Hudgins, the pastor of Jackson's First Baptist Church and a resolution opponent, told reporters he did not expect Negroes to try to join First Baptist. Hudgins's reply to a specific question about *Brown* was that the Supreme Court decision was "a school question or a political question, and not a religious question." Other First Baptist leaders were less evasive. Alex McKeigney, a church deacon, pointed out that "the facts of history make it plain that the development of civilization and of Christianity itself has rested in the hands of the white race" and that support of school desegregation "is a direct contribution to the efforts of those groups advocating intermarriage between the races." Baptist lay leader Owen Cooper, who in the late 1960s worked to improve black-white relations, recalled that during the 1950s he avoided moral questions that would trouble him later: "To be quite honest I did not ask myself what Jesus Christ would have done had He been on earth at the time. I didn't ask because I already knew the answer."[56]

White ministers who had preached the social gospel became vulnerable to Citizens' Council pressure. Will Campbell was an early casualty. The director of religious life at Ole Miss, Campbell had survived the Kershaw affair only to clash again with the administration. The chaplain had violated southern customs by inviting as his house guest Carl Rowan, then a young black journalist gathering material for a book on race relations. To make matters worse, Campbell had been caught red-handed playing table tennis with a black minister in the YMCA building on campus. The irrepressible Campbell later assured his dean that the game "was really quite within the Southern pattern. We had used separate but equal paddles, the ball was white, and there was a net tightly drawn between us." The dean was not amused. Shortly thereafter Campbell took a job with the National Council of Churches as a civil rights troubleshooter and moved with his family to Nashville.[57]

A few other white clergy had taken a stand. The Reverend Brent Shaeffer, a Lutheran minister in Jackson, was chairman of the small Mississippi branch of the Southern Regional Council, an organization formed in the 1940s to promote racial understanding. When Shaeffer left the state in the mid-1950s, however, the SRC chapter went into decline. Rabbi Charles Mantiband of Hattiesburg was also active in SRC activities, and in 1958 the local Citizens' Council advised his congregation to get rid of the "mischief-making Rabbi." He survived that challenge, but five years later a dispirited Rabbi Mantiband moved away from Mississippi.[58]

The Reverend Duncan Gray was one of the few outspoken ministers to survive all attempts to drive him from the state. As the son of the diocese's Episcopal bishop, Gray was afforded some protection against recrimination, but he was also "a good pastor," and many of his parishioners who were segregationists supported him despite his racial views. While serving at Calvary Episcopal Church in Cleveland, Gray took to the pulpit to denounce segregation as "un-Christian" and wrote a pamphlet urging compliance with *Brown*. In early 1956 Mississippi State College officials forced Gray to cancel an appearance at a Religious Emphasis Week program because he would not retract his statement that "segregation is incompatible with the Christian faith." That same year Gray joined the board of the fledgling Mississippi Humans Relations Council, an integrated group whose effectiveness was limited by opposition from the Citizens' Council. He moved to Oxford in the late 1950s to become minister of the local Episcopal church and a chaplain at the University of Mississippi. Gray was in the middle of the Ole Miss riot the night of James Meredith's admission, pleading with the students to return to their dorms. Duncan Gray continued to champion the cause of racial justice and was later himself named bishop of the Mississippi Episcopal Diocese.[59]

Most white Mississippi clergy, however, either supported segregation, made their peace with white supremacists in their congregations and kept quiet, or left the state. With few exceptions the white churches opposed black demands for equality and offered virtually no leadership during the critical years of the 1960s. One of the most vivid images of that time would be the sight of deacons on the church steps denying entrance to the black men and women who had come to join them for Sunday worship.

Control over the media is essential to any repressive government. Mississippi did not resort to the heavy-handed tactics employed in totalitarian societies: censorship laws, troops storming newspaper offices, jailing or killing editors who did not follow the party line. It did not have to. With a handful of exceptions, the state's newspaper editors and radio and television station managers were white supremacists who held a visceral contempt for anything "Yankee." Mississippi had no moderating editorial voice with the influence of a Harry Ashmore of the *Arkansas Gazette* or a Ralph McGill of the *Atlanta Constitution*. Instead, Mississippi had the Hedermans.

The Hederman brothers, Thomas and Robert, bought the *Clarion-Ledger* in 1920 and three decades later purchased the *Jackson*

Daily News from Fred Sullens. With a combined circulation of about 90,000, these papers were the only dailies available statewide. Most Mississippians saw the world through the eyes of the Hedermans and their columnists, including such race-baiters as Tom Ethridge and Jimmy Ward. "To read the Hederman press day after day," wrote Jim Silver, "is to understand what the people of the state believe and are prepared to defend." From the lynching of Emmett Till to the summer of 1964 and its aftermath, the Hedermans poured out a steady stream of invective against black activists and their white allies. The Hedermans were unquestioning supporters of the likes of Eastland and Ross Barnett and had nothing but praise for the Citizens' Council, which honored the papers in 1955 for their "fair stories about the Councils." (Not until the late 1970s, when a younger, more progressive member of the family, Rea Hederman, took over as editor, did the *Clarion-Ledger* abandon its racist stance.)[60]

The Hederman brothers were extremely influential in other sectors. Serving as presidents of the chamber of commerce and local service organizations, they were also highly placed on the boards of colleges and insurance and banking concerns. Both were pillars of the Baptist church. Their wealth and respectability, together with their influence over the media, made the Hedermans segregation's most potent voice in Mississippi.[61]

On the morning of September 12, 1955, civil rights attorney Thurgood Marshall was appearing on the "Today" show, outlining his position on school desegregation. In the middle of his remarks viewers of the Jackson NBC affiliate, WLBT, saw their screens go blank, followed by a "Cable Difficulty" logo. WLBT rejoined the network once the problem had been solved—after the conclusion of the Marshall interview. Editor Hodding Carter reported the next day that NBC had no word of transmission problems from WLBT. At a meeting of the Jackson Citizens' Council a short time later a member of the audience, Fred Beard, rose to make a fiery speech about how the networks had become mouthpieces for "Negro propaganda." For those in the room who did not recognize him, Beard identified himself as the WLBT station manager and drew thunderous applause when he told the council faithful that he had in fact pulled the plug on Thurgood Marshall.[62]

Fred Beard's solution proved popular, and over the next decade "Sorry, Cable Trouble" became a familiar message on TV screens.

In Jackson, the major television market, the two network affiliates refused to carry programs or specials focusing on the race problem. Locally, station managers denied black spokespersons access to the media and gave black cultural activities little or no coverage. This crude combination of exclusion and self-censorship achieved its purpose. Most Mississippians could not see programs that discussed the social revolution underway in the South, and network newscasts could be dismissed as nothing more than Yankee propaganda.[63] With all television stations toeing the line, and the Hedermans and like-minded publishers fanning the flames of intolerance and blind resistance, it remained for that handful of moderate Mississippi editors to get at the truth of what was happening inside the closed society.

Mississippi editors with the courage to challenge the official orthodoxy included Hodding Carter of the *Delta Democrat-Times,* George McLean at the *Tupelo Journal,* Oliver Emmerich of the McComb *Enterprise-Journal,* Ira Harkey of the *Pascagoula Chronicle,* Hazel Brannon Smith of the *Lexington Advertiser,* and P. D. East, the irascible owner and editor of *The Petal Paper.* To this short list must be added the name of political correspondent Wilson F. Minor, whose "Eyes on Mississippi" column ran in the New Orleans *Times-Picayune* for more than two decades. Bill Minor's reporting on the civil rights movement as it unfolded in Mississippi was perceptive and accurate.[64]

For northern observers Hodding Carter II was the most reliable source of information on race relations in Mississippi. As a crusading young editor in Louisiana, Carter had taken on the Huey Long machine (and lost), and he continued to speak his mind after moving to Greenville in 1936. Then a town of about 30,000, equally divided between black and white, Greenville sits on the banks of the Mississippi in the heart of the Delta. Its leading citizens took pride in the community's reputation for civility and were quick to point out the bevy of nationally recognized writers and artists who called Greenville home. The city's patriarch was William Alexander Percy, whose book *Lanterns on the Levee* is the classic apology for racial paternalism. Percy and his friend, author David Cohn, joined with several businessmen to invite Hodding Carter and his wife, Betty, to start a newspaper. Within a short time the Carters had bought out their competition, and the result of the merger was the

Delta Democrat-Times. In the 1940s Carter took on Theodore Bilbo and won a Pulitzer Prize in 1946 for "distinguished editorial writing against racial and religious intolerance." He was one of the first journalists to warn the nation of the threat posed by the Citizens' Council.[65]

Although he was uncompromising in his opposition to the Citizens' Council and its followers, Hodding Carter was no ally of the state's black-led movement, as he assured his readers on many occasions. In the 1940s, while denouncing the crime of lynching, he opposed a federal antilynching bill, and although he spoke out against economic discrimination against blacks, he attacked Truman's FEPC proposals. In 1949 he wrote that "you can't legislate or deride segregation in the South out of existence" and claimed that "the southern Negro, by and large, does not want an end to segregation in itself any more than does the southern white man."[66] Carter also publicly opposed the desegregation of Mississippi schools. Although his editorial response to the *Brown* decision was temperate, he later wrote that "I also said then and have continually repeated that I am opposed to putting into practice public school desegregation in the Deep South." His condescending advice to black leaders: "concentrate upon improving the mass Negro level of morality rather than obtaining admission of a few Negro children to presently white schools." Carter repeatedly denounced the NAACP for its "angry racism . . . alienating white and black and setting a chasm of suspicion down the middle of the community."[67]

Although his positions on the race question appear contradictory, Carter was in fact consistent in his thinking. Like other Mississippi moderates, Carter was, in the words of the historian Anthony Newberry, a "fair play segregationist." Abhorring acts of racial violence, he courageously attacked the perpetrators of these crimes, but Carter was convinced that "separate but *equal*" was the best that Mississippi could hope for, at least in his lifetime, and he never identified with the civil rights movement. Betty Carter has said that her husband "was always a conservative" and that he saw his role as "interpreting the North to the South and the South to the North."[68] His many articles and books, written with the assistance of his wife, did provide nonsoutherners with a window into the closed society, an achievement not to be slighted. Still, Carter never grew beyond his paternalistic view of the Negro, and he could not conceive of a Mississippi where blacks shared all the freedoms that white people took for granted.

In February 1956 Mississippi's Nobel laureate, William Faulkner, sat down with a reporter from the London *Sunday Times* to talk about the race problem in the American South. During the course of the interview Faulkner said, "If I have to choose between the United States government and Mississippi, then I'll choose Mississippi. . . . As long as there's a middle road I'll be on it. But if it came to fighting I'd fight for Mississippi against the United States even if it meant going out into the streets and shooting Negroes." There appears to be no doubt that Faulkner was quoted accurately, although he later claimed that "they are statements which no sober man would make nor, it seems to me, any sane man believe." Faulkner had been drinking heavily during the interview, during the course of which he also affirmed that the *Brown* decision "had to be promulgated and it just repeated what was said in January, 1863." He also told the reporter that the NAACP was a "necessary organization" and even suggested that it might try to desegregate Ole Miss. Faulkner stated emphatically that "the Negro has a right to equality. . . . The Negroes are right—make sure you've got that—they're right." But it was his "Robert E. Lee Statement," as it came to be called, that made the headlines.[69]

That famous Faulkner interview exemplifies the dilemma and the limitations of the southern white moderate in the 1950s. Many southern whites, Mississippians among them, believed segregation to be immoral, and a few, like Faulkner, said so. Yet they could not bring themselves to enlist in the black struggle, partly because they were emotionally incapable of accepting black leadership, but also because as privileged members of the dominant caste they were fully aware of the price to be paid for their heresy. And many feared that if blacks pressed too hard they would bring on a bloodbath. "The South is armed for revolt," Faulkner warned. "These white people will accept another Civil War knowing they're going to lose."[70] Sensing that events were overtaking them, white moderates sought time to sort things out, hoping that a society would gradually evolve where the ugliest manifestations of racism would disappear while existing class relationships remained intact. (That, in fact, is an accurate description of the Mississippi of the 1990s.) Thus, Faulkner spoke for most southern moderates when he urged black activists to "go slow now. Stop for a time. You have the power now; you can withhold for a moment the use of it as a force."[71] The moderates' call for a gradual dismantling of the racially oppressive caste system evokes the memory of their ideological forebears over a century earlier who believed that slavery could be ended in phases, without outside interference. In both instances blacks were asked to endure their suffering a while longer, as their white counselors went on with their comfortable lives.

What it all comes down to is that in the mid-1950s white supremacists in Mississippi had a specific program: to maintain the status quo in race relations, whatever the cost. Moderates, on the other hand, could offer only cautionary admonitions—to blacks, to go slow, and to northern whites, to stop meddling. The result was a bankruptcy of both moral and political leadership at the most critical point in Mississippi's history since Reconstruction. What was happening was in many respects a replay of the year 1875: the Citizens' Council was busy implementing its own "Mississippi Plan"; the government in Washington was refusing to get involved; the new scalawags were being stunned into silence; and blacks were forced to run for cover. And from all sides of the white political spectrum the message to the nation was clear: leave us alone and we will solve our problems. It never did get to the point where the moderates had to decide whether to go into the streets and fire away at Negroes; instead, driven into submission, they watched from the sidelines as other whites did the shooting.

4

Toward a New Beginning

By the end of 1955 the black freedom movement in Mississippi was in disarray. With the school desegregation drive stopped in its tracks and voter registration campaigns crumbling in the face of intimidation and violence, activists were left without a viable program. Leaders who had rallied their communities around the banner of *Brown* were now exhausted, disillusioned, and frightened. Key people left the state. Gus Courts had been the first to go, and others soon followed. Dr. Clinton Battle, the young physician who had built the NAACP branch in Indianola, found he could not survive in the birthplace of the Citizens' Council. In Natchez Dr. Maurice Mackel, who founded the NAACP branch in 1940 and directed the school petition drive, was also hounded out of the state. And T. R. M. Howard, for years a symbol of black achievement, pride, and political activism, reluctantly concluded that he too had better cut his losses before it was too late. "I feel I can do more alive in the battle for Negro rights in the North than dead in a weed-grown grave in Dixie," Howard observed after reestablishing his medical practice on Chicago's South Side. These leaders were joined in exile by scores of others who had taken a stand for human rights, only to run afoul of the Citizens' Council.[1]

Although it is impossible to quantify repression, it is instructive to examine the decline of the movement's major program, voter registration. At the end of 1954, before passage of the new registration laws, some 22,000 blacks had registered to vote. A year later, only 12,000 could be found on the rolls. The gains made over the previous decade had been all but wiped out. Several factors account for this retreat. First, the constitutional registration amendment and subsequent enabling legislation discouraged all but the most dedicated from attempting to qualify. The new application form consisted of twenty questions, of which the final three were the most crucial:

> 18. Write and copy in the space below Section _____ of the Constitution of Mississippi: (Instruction to Registrar: you will designate the section of the Constitution and point out same to applicant.)
> 19. Write in the space below a reasonable interpretation (the meaning) of the section of the Constitution of Mississippi which you have just copied.
> 20. Write in the space below a statement setting forth your understanding of the duties and obligations of citizenship under a constitutional form of government.

A state legislator expressed a common feeling when he conceded that "if I wasn't already registered, I don't believe I could qualify to vote myself."[2]

The 1955 legislature raised yet another barrier to black registration by eliminating the nearly century-old practice of satellite registration. Instead of attempting to register in local election precincts, blacks now had to go to the county courthouse, historically the symbol of white power and oppression. Residents of the northern part of Sunflower County, for example, had to travel fifty miles to the county seat at Indianola. There they might have to wait in line for hours, or they might find the circuit clerk's office closed. The registration process itself was often humiliating and usually came to nothing. A requirement for dual registration with both the circuit clerk *and* the city clerk (to vote in municipal elections) meant that the applicant had to undergo the ordeal twice.[3]

Encouraged by the new voting laws, officials in several counties conducted "reregistration" campaigns. Originally designed to purge from the rolls the names of people no longer qualified, such as voters who had died or moved away, reregistration often meant reexamination of black voters under the 1955 laws. According to the New Orleans *Times-Picayune*, the Jefferson Davis County reregistration reduced the number of black voters in the county from 1,221 "to a reported 70." The discretionary authority of the registrar made such purges of black voters possible. When the U.S. Justice Department in 1956 announced plans to send investigators to the South to look into registration irregularities, state attorney general Joe Patterson assured circuit clerks that they need not cooperate with federal agents. Governor J. P. Coleman had called the Justice Department announcement a "cheap political shot" and "mass slander."[4]

Blacks responded to this new wave of intimidation by seeking redress in the federal courts. In 1957 Congress passed its first civil rights legislation since Reconstruction, and although it was inadequate, the law did provide black litigants easier access to the federal courts in cases involving voter discrimination. Nevertheless, building cases was extremely difficult. Circuit clerks were entitled to a jury of their peers, and the Eisenhower Justice Department was reluctant to prosecute. Voter registration, however, continued to be the major program of the state's racial advancement organizations. Those NAACP branches still active conducted classes so that blacks could "learn more about the state Constitution and thereby qualify themselves to vote." Aaron Henry announced a 1957 registration drive to add 100,000 Delta blacks to the rolls.[5] But with the new batch of repressive laws now in place and a state government hostile to Justice Department investigations, Henry and other black leaders in the late 1950s knew that their task was even more difficult than it had been a decade before.

Although Citizens' Council–inspired violence declined after 1955, the memory of that terrible year haunted Mississippi blacks. This was particularly true for the people who had an interest in maintaining the segregated economy. Teachers, preachers, and the handful of newspaper editors, along with some small business entrepreneurs, had lived relatively comfortable lives. Aware of the punishment inflicted on those blacks who had stuck their necks out in the early 1950s, they now retreated behind the Jim Crow wall. Lack of support from the black middle class frustrated and angered activists. Amzie Moore expressed his bitterness in a letter to Roy Wilkins in late 1955:

> The Negroes with money are in a world of their own here in the state of Mississippi. They live to themselves and they don't want things to change, they are happy, as you know they don't support our organization, they are not interested in the freedom of the common Negro of Mississippi, they have enough

money in the white banks to help all the Negroes of Mississippi, but they buy their fine cars, furs, homes, and stay very much to themselves. That's funny, isn't it. But that's how it is down here.[6]

C. C. Bryant experienced similar problems in southwest Mississippi. Although he was elected president of the Pike County NAACP branch in 1954, Bryant "wasn't the first choice for president. I wasn't a member of the elite. We have a class system [in McComb]." During the most difficult times in the mid-1950s Bryant felt like a pariah in his own community: "Many a time I walked down the streets of McComb and the black leadership—ministers, whatever—would move to the other side. They were afraid to do anything." Black journalist Simeon Booker, on assignment in Mississippi, concluded that "most professionals would have nothing to do with the crusade." A "very prominent family" in one city refused lodging to Booker and a photographer, stating that they "couldn't get involved in civil rights fights." When asked to elaborate, one family member, a physician, replied, "You can't win. Too many whites. Go along with them."[7]

No one was more dejected than Medgar Evers over this lack of support from black professionals. In a 1957 *Ebony* article the NAACP state field secretary declared that "as much good as the NAACP has done to make opportunities greater for teachers who once made $20 a month and are making up to $5,000 a year now, we don't get their cooperation." Myrlie Evers recalled that when they decided to build a house in a new Jackson subdivision that "attracted mainly Negro teachers," she and Medgar began hearing rumors "of a petition to keep us out. . . . There was talk that the wrong house might be burned down by mistake, that to have us in their midst would be dangerous for the whole community." There probably was no formal petition, but the teachers' uneasiness over having the state's best-known civil rights activist as a neighbor was genuine. Medgar also had harsh words for other professionals, observing that "only in isolated cases do they go all out to help us." He concluded that "our biggest support is with the rank and file of people."[8]

The reluctance of successful blacks to join the battle for human rights in the late 1950s reflects on the institutions they represented. By far the most accommodationist was the black press. Accord-

ing to the historian Julius Thompson, by 1954 only five black papers were published in the state, and four of these were "conservative (pro-segregation, white-dominated) sheets that continued to
make a niggardly response to the adverse human condition." The
one exception was Arrington High's *Eagle Eye,* a short mimeographed newsletter unequivocal in its advocacy of black rights.[9]

The best-known and most controversial editor was Percy Greene,
whose weekly *Jackson Advocate* had a circulation of about 5,000.
A champion of black voting rights in the mid-1940s, Greene grew
increasingly reactionary as the black agenda expanded to include
desegregation of schools and public accommodations. By the late
1950s he was on the payroll of the State Sovereignty Commission,
denouncing the *Brown* decision, the Montgomery bus boycott, and
President Eisenhower's decision to send troops into Little Rock to
enforce a court desegregation order. Greene carried on a running
feud with the NAACP. In a 1957 commentary widely reprinted in
the white press, Greene claimed that "the masses of Negroes in the
South are being led over the precipice by the siren calls of the new
Negro leadership." He defended those blacks (such as himself) who
urged moderation on the segregation issue and sought to maintain
"a friendly and respectful attitude" toward white leaders. "The
greatest need in Jackson, in Mississippi, and in the rest of the
South," Greene proclaimed, "is more and more 'Uncle Toms.'"
When Emmett Stringer took him to task for accepting favors from
segregationists, the *Advocate*'s editor replied, "Doc, I'm a practical politician. My policy is, 'whoever has the most to offer Percy.'"
By the end of the 1950s Greene had lost all credibility in the black
community, and the bitterness against him remained strong down
through the years. Two decades later R. L. T. Smith reflected on
his relationship with Percy Greene: "I worked with the man. He
was a mail carrier when they hired me." Then, after a long pause,
"I wish I knew something good about the man."[10]

Although few black educators endorsed the sycophancy of the
Jackson Advocate, black principals and state college presidents, who
were dependent on state funds for survival, tried to prevent discussion of civil rights issues or the NAACP in the classroom. The state
NAACP conference reported that "we have been reliably informed
that numerous qualified . . . teachers are told not to teach any citizenship rights, nor can they admit that the May 17, 1954 Supreme
Court decision is the law of the land." Some teachers disregarded

these directives. Many of the young Mississippi activists of the 1960s credit an inspirational teacher for opening their eyes to the systematic oppression of blacks. Alphonso Clark and Zola Jackson were role models for Dorie and Joyce Ladner of Palmer's Crossing. For Joe Martin and his classmates at Burgland High School in Mc-Comb, their history teacher, Mrs. Wade, revealed the international dimensions of the race problem. And Anne Moody's homeroom teacher, Mrs. Rice, supplied "a whole new pool of knowledge" about the nature of southern white racism. These teachers risked their jobs to raise the consciousness of the state's black youth.[11]

Yet for every Zola Jackson or Alphonso Clark there were scores of teachers and administrators who, through fear or indifference, refused to discuss racial problems in their classes and schools and avoided association with civil rights organizations. Arrington High attacked them for their timidity: "How can you Negroes teach young Negroes how to become self respecting when you yourselves are in the ditch through fear?" High urged teachers to set an example by joining the NAACP. Should the school board threaten them, they should "tell this Board here in Jackson or anywhere else that Yes, I am a card-carrying member of the NAACP, and if they don't like it they can go to Hell."[12] As a group, black teachers in the 1950s refused to take a stand, and the movement of the early sixties passed them by. Only after 1965, when the battle for the ballot had been won and the right to organize secured, did black educators finally step forward—to claim positions of political leadership in their communities.

Perhaps the most inspiring image of the Mississippi movement of the 1960s is the packed Delta church, with hundreds of blacks singing freedom songs and impassioned speakers urging them to join the march to the courthouse the next morning. Yet in Mississippi the institutional church did not stand in the forefront of civil rights activity, and black ministers were conspicuously absent from the front ranks of movement leadership. At the fourth annual RCNL meeting in 1955, only one of the twenty-one Mississippi speakers on the program was a minister, and when NAACP regional secretary Ruby Hurley called an important strategy meeting late in 1954, not one of the ten key people invited made his living as a minister. Medgar Evers was frustrated over the clergy's lack of support, complaining that "some ministers are . . . in that class of people who won't be hurt by belonging to the [NAACP], but who won't give us 50 cents for fear of losing face with the white man." Cora Britton, secretary of the Columbus NAACP branch, echoed Evers's disappointment. In a letter to the national office she observed that while "our people look to the Ministers of the Gospel for guidance and leadership," local preachers were afraid even to "mention the NAACP from the pulpit."[13]

Part of the explanation for the churches' reluctance to take a stand is historical and involves the relationship between influential black preachers and the white power structure. In Mississippi towns and cities whites selected "reliable" Negro ministers to be designated leaders of their communities, bestowing status on them, making financial contributions to their churches, and allowing them religious freedom in the pulpit. In return, as Benjamin Mays and Joseph W. Nicholson pointed out in *The Negro's Church,* "In any tense situation these Negro preachers could be relied upon to convey to their congregations the advice of the leading whites of the community. Examples of this kind could be multiplied indefinitely." In *Caste and Class in a Southern Town,* his community study of Indianola in the 1930s, John Dollard pointed out that planters welcomed the building of a church on the plantation, for the church "helped to keep the *status quo* by offering an illusory consolation to the Negroes." Whites believed that "religion centers the attention of the Negro on a future life while negating . . . the importance of effort here and now designed to better conditions."[14]

Employing religion as a means of social control and using black preachers to patrol the color line were tactics not peculiar to Mississippi, but the practice lingered there after it had begun to break down in other areas. As the most rural southern state, Mississippi had few urban centers capable of sustaining a strong, socially responsible ministerial alliance. The Southern Christian Leadership Conference (SCLC) never did establish a base in Mississippi, in part because of NAACP opposition; nor did Jackson, the only real city, produce a Fred Shuttlesworth or a Ralph Abernathy. The state's best-known black minister in the 1950s was Baptist leader H. H. Humes, the outspoken conservative who vied with Percy Greene for the white man's favor. Ministers most likely to assume leadership positions pastored churches with a predominantly middle-class membership. The most influential members of these congregations— the schoolteachers and relatively affluent businesspeople—had the most to lose from the brand of economic warfare that was the stock-in-trade of the Citizens' Council. Thus, any minister inclined toward political activism might meet stiff opposition from his own parishioners. Although a few ministers did preach the social gospel and participate in voter registration campaigns, most black preachers—conservative, frightened, or both—kept their distance from civil rights activity.

If the institutional church was not a positive force in the fifties, faith in God certainly was. Many black leaders, such as R. L. T. Smith and Emmett Stringer, were devout Christians. Prayer, the singing of hymns and spirituals, and the lessons of biblical teachings were a staple of mass meetings, and the belief that God was on their side sustained Mississippi blacks during the worst of the white reign of terror. Although the Mississippi movement's leadership was secular, and remained so throughout the struggle, no mass movement could succeed without the endorsement of the black community's most influential institution. One of the major goals of the grassroots organizers in the 1960s, then, would be to bring local ministers into the movement and open the doors of their churches to civil rights activities. It was no small task.

National NAACP officials had no program to deal with the range of problems facing Mississippi blacks. Executive secretary Roy Wilkins had discussed the situation in a September 1955 memorandum to his staff, setting down a number of options for consideration. While mentioning voter registration, Wilkins saw an immediate opportunity to capitalize on Mississippi's negative national image. The NAACP leader tried to "rally anti-murder sentiment against Mississippi" by distributing pamphlets, such as "M Is for Mississippi and Murder," and taking out ads in northern newspapers. A primary goal of this campaign was to bring contributions to the NAACP and increase national membership. Movement activists believed the NAACP was pursuing an "encircling strategy" rather than committing major resources to the state. Wilkins later claimed that "we never gave up on Mississippi" but conceded that "we didn't put as much energy into it as you put into places where you get a better response."[15]

Although its major resources were directed elsewhere, the New York office nonetheless wanted Mississippi to remain exclusive NAACP territory. NAACP activists in Mississippi, on the other hand, were more open to cooperation with other groups, particularly the Regional Council of Negro Leadership. After the murder of the Reverend George Lee in the summer of 1955, Medgar Evers and his former boss, T. R. M. Howard, talked of merging the state's two leading advancement organizations. At Lee's funeral Evers approached Ruby Hurley about the proposal. Hurley's views of Howard and the RCNL had not changed over the years, however, and she opposed the idea. Howard then suggested to Hurley that a statewide meeting take place within thirty days to discuss a merger. She again turned thumbs down. Hurley then reported to her superiors that "Evers seems to have too much of the Howard influence."[16]

A more serious threat to NAACP hegemony in Mississippi was that of Martin Luther King and the Southern Christian Leadership Conference. The rivalry between the NAACP and SCLC began almost as soon as SCLC was organized in 1957. Wilkins feared (justifiably, as it turned out) that the charismatic young preacher and his allies might undermine NAACP strength in the South. The national office was unhappy when Medgar Evers and Aaron Henry attended the SCLC organizational meeting in New Orleans and won election to the SCLC board. When Evers volunteered to serve as the SCLC's assistant secretary, Wilkins instructed him to "quietly ease out" of the new organization, and he reluctantly did so. Henry was more independent—he was not on the NAACP payroll—and continued to be an enthusiastic supporter of SCLC, inviting King to address the annual RCNL meeting in Clarksdale in 1958.[17]

Privately, Evers was disturbed by Wilkins's hostility toward other civil rights groups. "Our goals are identical," he once complained to attorney William Kunstler. "Why can't we join hands to get there?" Yet Evers was loyal to his organization. When in early 1958 SCLC explored the possibility of establishing a base in Mississippi, Evers "discouraged, 'tactfully,' any such movement here in Jackson." He informed Hurley that "it will be our design through the NAACP . . . to control the present state of affairs. . . . I shall await comments from you. In the meantime we are going to hold fast." SCLC backed off and did not become seriously involved in Mississippi until the mid-1960s.[18]

The late 1950s were years of frustration for Evers. With the Montgomery bus boycott in December 1955, black communities had begun to move, but as Myrlie Evers observed, "it was all happening somewhere else. Mississippi stood still." The NAACP field secretary was constantly on the road delivering "Pep Talks" at local branch meetings, attempting by his example to help blacks break through the cycle of fear. Returning from a regional NAACP meeting in North Carolina in the spring of 1958, he changed buses in Meridian, on the Mississippi border, took a front seat, and refused an order to move to the rear. Police arrived and brought Evers to the station for questioning but did not arrest him. Back on the bus, he took the same seat. Three blocks from the terminal a taxi driver flagged down the bus, got on, and slugged Evers in the face. Medgar kept his seat and did not fight back. The driver ordered Evers's assailant to leave, and the rest of the trip was uneventful. Three years later other "freedom riders" would travel that same road from Meridian to Jackson.[19]

Evers spent much of his time investigating racially motivated homicides. Between 1956 and 1959 at least ten black men were killed by whites, none of whom was convicted. Myrlie Evers recalls that Medgar "investigated, filed complaints, issued angry denunciations, literally dragged reporters to the scenes of crimes, fought back with press releases, seeking always to spread word beyond the state, involve the federal government, bring help from the outside." One such case occurred in Philadelphia in October 1959. Hattie Thomas and Luther Jackson, a friend from out of town, were sitting in a parked car when a patrol car drove up and a policeman ordered the two to get out. According to Thomas, the officer then pushed Jackson around the car, out of sight, and shot him twice. By the time Hattie Thomas reached him, Luther Jackson lay dead in a ditch. The Philadelphia police officer's name was Lawrence Rainey.[20]

Four days later, after a coroner's jury had rendered a verdict of justifiable homicide, Evers wrote U.S. Attorney General William P. Rogers demanding an investigation. Rogers promised that "this matter will receive our careful consideration, and should it develop that a violation of federal law is involved, appropriate action will be taken." A month later the Justice Department concluded that Rainey had not violated a federal statute and thus there was "no basis for action by this department."[21] The Philadelphia murder was typical of the crimes Evers investigated for the NAACP, but none affected him as deeply as the injustice committed against a young man whose only offense was a desire to attend a college near his home. The case of Clyde Kennard was, in many respects, the most tragic of the decade.

The basic facts are these: Kennard, a Forrest County native, had enlisted in the army in 1945 and served with distinction for seven years as a paratrooper, leaving the service with the rank of sergeant. He then enrolled at the University of Chicago and was in his senior year when his stepfather's poor health forced Kennard to return to Mississippi to run the family farm near Eatonville. Intent on completing his education, he made several unsuccessful attempts to enroll at the all-white Mississippi Southern College (now the University of Southern Mississippi) in Hattiesburg. In September 1959 the thirty-year-old farmer met with Mississippi Southern president William D. McCain to discuss his most recent application. After a brief exchange with McCain and State Sovereignty Commission agent Zack Van Landingham, Kennard was arrested on campus for reckless driving and possession of five bottles of liquor. Assisted by Evers and the NAACP, Kennard successfully fought the charge, vowing to continue his efforts to enroll at Mississippi Southern. A year later an illiterate nineteen-year-old black youth was arrested for stealing five bags of chicken feed, worth twenty-five dollars, from the warehouse where he worked and depositing the feed at Kennard's farm. The youth claimed that Kennard had planned the theft. Kennard was brought to trial; the jury deliberated ten minutes before finding him guilty. Judge Stanton Hall sentenced him to seven years in prison, the maximum penalty.[22]

But there is more to the story. The State Sovereignty Commission, always shrouded in secrecy, later deposited part of its Clyde Kennard file at the Mississippi Department of Archives and History. The commission's records provide an insider's account of the operation of Mississippi's secret police, the use of black "leaders" to do the commission's dirty work, and the "moderate" racial politics of the J. P. Coleman administration. State Sovereignty Commission agent Van Landingham, who had formerly worked for the FBI, had been assigned the Kennard case in 1958, and when it became apparent that the young farmer was serious about attending Mississippi Southern, Van Landingham prepared an extensive profile of Kennard and recruited reliable black ministers and educators to dissuade Kennard from applying. Van Landingham's report makes it clear that all who knew Kennard thought highly of him: "Persons who know Kennard describe him as intelligent, well-educated, quiet, courteous, with a desire to better the negro race in Mississippi." President McCain and Governor Coleman decided to appeal to Kennard's inherent decency. They befriended him and won his trust, never revealing that they had no intention of admitting him to Mississippi Southern.[23]

In pursuing this strategy Van Landingham contacted black professionals in the Hattiesburg area to persuade them to work with the Sovereignty Commission to bring Kennard to his senses. Van Landingham first spoke with the Reverend R. W. Woullard, who was recommended by the Forrest County sheriff and the Hattiesburg chief of police as a man who "had cooperated with them in the past and . . . had prevented a NAACP chapter from being organized in his church at Eatonville." Woullard, who also owned an insurance company and a funeral home, provided the Sovereignty Commission agent with names of black activists in the Hattiesburg area who would be supportive of Kennard, including NAACP leader Vernon Dahmer. Woullard agreed to "head up a committee of negroes" to talk with Kennard. The agent then contacted the black principal at Palmer's Crossing school, one of the English teachers at the school, and two black principals in the Hattiesburg school system. All agreed to serve on the visitation committee. Whether these citizens cooperated from fear of the Sovereignty Commission, genuine concern over Kennard's fate, or potential rewards for their assistance is difficult to determine. (Van Landingham reported there was "every indication that the negro educators on this committee want to bargain their efforts for a [new] Negro Junior College at Hattiesburg.") Perhaps all three factors came into play.[24]

Months passed, and as the fall term at Mississippi Southern approached, Van Landingham stepped up his efforts by enlisting the assistance of President J. H. White of Mississippi Vocational College. White was a willing accomplice. He agreed to go to Hattiesburg to talk with black leaders and suggested that McCain meet with Kennard personally, for "Kennard has a great admiration and respect for Dr. McCain." McCain stalled a few days before sending an application, hoping Kennard could not complete it before registration day. All these efforts came to naught. The black delegation visited Kennard, as did two Hattiesburg whites whom Kennard trusted. They could not shake his resolve. On September 14 Van Landingham met with Governor Coleman to determine the grounds for rejecting Kennard's application. The next day Kennard came to the campus for his meeting with McCain and Van Landingham and was subsequently arrested.[25]

The arrest was not part of the official game plan. Van Landingham was surprised when he learned that Kennard was in jail and reported to the governor that "it appeared to be a frame-up with the planting of the evidence [the liquor] in Kennard's car," a judgment with which both the local sheriff and the district attorney concurred. Apparently, two zealous constables at Mississippi Southern had acted on their own. A *Jackson Daily News* source reported that Coleman and other state leaders were "upset" about Kennard's arrest because, as Van Landingham put it, "no one would believe that the arrest was not connected in some way with Kennard's attempt to register at Mississippi Southern College."[26] Clyde Kennard's problems, however, were only beginning. Ross Barnett had just become governor, and the "civility" of the Coleman administration soon gave way to the police-state tactics of Barnett and his Citizens' Council henchmen.

Kennard's conviction on charges of stealing chicken feed is yet another example of racial justice in the closed society. His alleged accomplice, Johnny Lee Roberts, was so confused on the witness stand that he could not even get his original story straight. The frustrated district attorney ended up by leading Roberts through his testimony, supplying him with the information as to when and how Kennard allegedly set up the theft. While Kennard received the maximum penalty of seven years at Parchman penitentiary, Roberts got off with a suspended sentence. The employer whose feed Roberts had stolen promptly hired the thief back. When he heard the verdict, a furious Medgar Evers told a reporter that this was "a mockery of justice." For this Evers was arrested, charged with contempt of court, and sentenced to thirty days in jail, a conviction later overturned by the Mississippi Supreme Court.[27]

At Parchman, Kennard was put to work from sunup to sundown on the penitentiary's cotton plantation. On Sundays he wrote letters for illiterate inmates and set up classes to teach reading and writing. NAACP lawyers were working to obtain a reversal in Kennard's case, with Thurgood Marshall arguing before the U.S. Supreme Court. On October 8, 1961, the nation's highest court left standing the decision by the Mississippi Supreme Court, affirming the original conviction. Early in 1962 Kennard began complaining of abdominal pains and was taken to the University of Mississippi Hospital in Jackson. The diagnosis was cancer. University doctors operated, and a hospital staff report recommended parole "because of the extremely poor prognosis in this rather young patient." Instead, Kennard was returned to Parchman and literally dragged out to work in the fields each day. Prison authorities even canceled his appointment for a medical checkup.[28]

The realization that a political prisoner in critical condition was being denied medical attention and treated brutally shocked the black community. At Tougaloo College Joyce Ladner, who had been a member of Clyde Kennard's NAACP youth council chapter in Hattiesburg, mobilized students in an effort to free her friend and teacher. *Jet* magazine picked up the story, and national figures including Dick Gregory and Martin Luther King demanded that Kennard be set free. Finally, in the spring of 1963, Governor Barnett, aware that unfavorable publicity would accompany news that Kennard had died in Parchman, ordered his release. Kennard immediately went to Chicago, where he again underwent surgery for his malignancy.[29]

It was too late. When Kennard's friend, the author John Howard Griffin, visited him at the Chicago hospital, he was shocked to see that Kennard had wasted away: "He had become a tiny little dwarf. He lay with a sheet pulled up over his face so no one could see the grimace of pain on his face." Kennard told Griffin he was not bitter over what had happened to him and that it all would have been worthwhile "if only it would show this country where racism finally leads." He then sadly concluded, "But the people aren't going to know it, are they?" Months earlier, while Kennard was still in Parchman, Medgar Evers had spoken at a Freedom Fund banquet in Jackson about his friend Clyde Kennard and the agony that the state of Mississippi was putting him through. Normally a person of controlled emotions, this time Evers broke down and could not continue. Myrlie Evers recalled that "finally tears streamed down his face as he spoke, and he just gave way. He stood there in front of hundreds of people and cried as though his heart would break. Hundreds of us cried with him." Clyde Kennard died in Chicago at age thirty-six, on the Fourth of July, 1963.[30]

In April 1959, thirty miles down the road from Hattiesburg, a white mob in Poplarville abducted Mack Parker from his jail cell, beat him, drove him to the Louisiana border, shot him twice in the chest, and dumped his body into the Pearl River. Parker had been awaiting trial on the charge of raping a white woman, Mrs. June Walters. Two months earlier the Walterses' car had broken down late at night on a lonely country road; the alleged assault occurred after Jimmy Walters had locked his wife and young daughter in the car while he went for help. Coerced confessions from three of Parker's drinking companions that night formed the basis of the prosecution's case. Parker steadfastly proclaimed his innocence, repeated lie detector tests proved negative or inconclusive, and the victim never positively identified Parker as her assailant. Howard Smead, who has researched the case more thoroughly than any other scholar, is convinced that June Walters was raped that night but that "no conclusive proof will ever be forthcoming" as to Parker's guilt or innocence.[31]

The murder of Mack Parker shocked black Mississippians, even in the violence-plagued 1950s. Not since World War II had the state been subjected to a "traditional" lynching, where a mob abducted its victim from the custody of law enforcement officials. The FBI came to Mississippi in force, conducting an investigation that turned up substantial evidence. Director J. Edgar Hoover later told a House subcommittee, "We were able to establish the identity of a number of members of the mob who participated in the abduction of Parker and obtained admissions from some of the participants." Nevertheless, a local grand jury not only refused to return any indictments, it did not even ask to see the FBI report. Nor did Judge Sebe Dale, who had a copy, suggest that the jurors might want to take a look at it. A defiant white supremacist who belonged to the Citizens' Council, Dale instructed the grand jurors that "we should have the backbone to stand against any tyranny . . . [including] the Board of Sociology setting [*sic*] in Washington, garbed in Judicial Robes, and 'dishing out' the 'legal precedents' of Gunnar Myrdal." Subsequently, a federal grand jury in Biloxi also failed to return indictments. Three years later, while traveling in the North as a speaker for the Sovereignty Commission, Judge Dale was asked whether he thought Mack Parker's lynchers would ever be identified and brought to justice. Dale said he did not think so, then added, "Besides, two of them are already dead."[32]

For Medgar Evers the lynching of Mack Parker was almost the last straw. Upset at the failure of government at any level to curb white violence, disappointed in the national NAACP's refusal to pursue a more aggressive program in Mississippi, and frustrated over the "inertia" in the black community, Evers had written Gloster Current that he wanted to attend law school part-time in addition to carrying on his NAACP duties. Current wrote back rejecting this request. Three weeks later, after hearing the news about Mack Parker, Evers told his wife that "I'd like to get a gun and just start shooting."[33]

But the years that Evers had spent on the road meeting small groups of blacks across the state were about to pay off. Although largely unsuccessful in persuading middle-class blacks of his generation to enlist under the NAACP banner, Evers had reached young people who, inspired by his example and by the black awakening in other parts of the South, were ready to move. Joe Martin, a student at McComb's Burgland High School in the fall of 1958, heard Medgar give "such an inspirational speech" that he and his football buddies decided to form an NAACP youth group. "We were anxious to do something," Martin recalls. Joyce Ladner had the feeling that "things were going to change." She and her sister Dorie were active in the Hattiesburg youth council and attended NAACP meetings in Jackson. There they first met Evers, who became their friend and confidant when they later enrolled at Jackson State.[34]

NAACP youth council chapters had existed in Mississippi since World War II, but not until the late 1950s did young blacks begin to assert themselves as a group. Under the general direction of Mrs. Vera Pigee of Clarksdale, the youth councils were designed to provide citizenship training for black teenagers, preparing them to register and vote when they came of age. At the same time, however, local youth council leaders also exposed younger blacks to the world outside Mississippi, encouraging them to read the *Crisis* and other black publications and to attend rallies addressed by national figures.

The sit-in movement, which was initiated by black college students in Greensboro, North Carolina, in February 1960, inspired blacks across the nation. As the sit-ins spread throughout the upper South, some Mississippi youth council members were eager to stage demonstrations of their own, a strategy discouraged by their elders. NAACP leaders who had felt the brunt of the Citizens' Council recriminations in the mid-1950s feared that renewed protests would bring on another wave of terror. When Joe Martin and his friends told Pike County branch president C. C. Bryant that they wanted to sit in at Woolworth's in downtown McComb, Bryant put them off by telling them they needed Roy Wilkins's permission before doing so. Particularly outspoken in opposition to direct action was NAACP state president C. R. Darden of Meridian. At a state executive meeting in March 1960, Darden contended that "if members of our Youth Council were involved in protest movements of any sorts, hatred of the organization would be more pronounced than ever before." Moreover, there were "things far more important that the state conference should engage itself in, specifically registration and voting." Although some members of the board took issue with Darden, his position prevailed, at least for a while.[35]

Evers alerted the national office that the southern sit-ins had created divisions in the NAACP leadership, with branches in the Delta and on the Gulf Coast charging that "the state conference is being too cautious." He diplomatically suggested to Gloster Current that although "sit down strikes" in Mississippi were not at present "advisable," the NAACP needed to instigate "some form of brief protests." It would look bad to the nation if Mississippi blacks remained silent "while everyone else is protesting Jim Crow." Less than a month later Evers enlisted 200 students from black colleges in the Jackson area to distribute handbills announcing an Easter boycott of Capitol Street stores to protest poor treatment of Negro customers, failure of sales personnel to use courtesy titles, and refusal of store owners to hire blacks as clerks. Although moderately successful, the Jackson boycott was soon overshadowed by a direct action protest on the Gulf Coast.[36]

The Biloxi "wade-in" began inauspiciously on the morning of April 14 when Dr. Gilbert Mason and a few friends decided to go for a swim in the Gulf of Mexico. A city policeman spotted the group on the beach and ordered them off. Blacks were not permitted anywhere along the twenty-six-mile stretch of sandy beaches that constituted the heart of the Mississippi tourist industry.[37] Ten days later Mason led another group of black men, women, and children onto the beach at Biloxi. This time a mob of forty white men assaulted the swimmers with iron pipes, chains, and baseball bats. County police officers on the scene stood by and watched. When one bather went back onto the beach to assist a friend who had been beaten unconscious, a policeman stopped him, shouting, "Nigger, I told you to get your goddamn black ass off this beach before I blow your brains out." Another group of demonstrators met the same fate on a stretch of beach about a mile away. Violence later erupted in the town of Biloxi, with eight blacks and two whites wounded by gunfire.[38]

The wade-ins, which had been organized by adult NAACP members, presented a challenge to Darden and his fellow conservatives on the state board. In the fall of 1960 Darden stepped down and was replaced as state president by Aaron Henry, who favored a more militant course of action. The national NAACP office had also begun to rethink its strategy, for other civil rights organizations had gained considerable publicity from their direct action campaigns. Mississippi NAACP leaders met with Roy Wilkins and his office staff in New York on April 7, 1961, and launched "Operation Mississippi," a program that endorsed action by black students to attempt to desegregate facilities.[39]

Wilkins had been moved to action by pressure from below, for two weeks earlier nine members of the Tougaloo College NAACP youth council had made the headlines when they quietly sat in at the Jackson Public Library. Located on State Street in the heart of the city, the library catered to an exclusively white clientele. Blacks were shunted off to Carver Library, a small, inadequate "colored branch" in the black section of town. The main library presented an ideal target for the Tougaloo College chapter members. Because it was a public facility, it was supported by the tax dollars of black citizens. There could be no question here of a private business's "right" to choose its customers. Also, in the Deep South, a library was a safer area in which to stage a protest than, say, a lunch counter, which would quickly attract white antagonists to the scene. The students planned carefully, holding training sessions on the tactics of nonviolent resistance and alerting the press to the time, place, and purpose of their action.

On the morning of March 27 the nine students began their day by stopping at the Carver branch to ask for books they knew were not available there. They then moved to the main branch on State Street. One of the demonstrators, James "Sam" Bradford, later recalled that "when we got out of the cars the media was there. They popped out of the bushes or wherever they had been hiding, and the cameras started to roll." Accompanied by reporters and photographers, the students moved inside; one undergraduate perused the card catalog while the others took books off the shelves, sat at tables, and began to read. When library workers asked why they were there, the students replied that they were gathering research material for their college courses. The police arrived quickly and told them to go to the "colored library." When the students refused to leave, the police arrested them on charges of breach of the peace. Both the protests and the arrests were disciplined and orderly. Had officials at city hall simply booked the demonstrators and released them, Jackson might have been spared a good deal of unfavorable publicity. But the "Tougaloo Nine" remained in custody for thirty-two hours while the sheriff delayed attorney Jack Young in his efforts to post bond for the defendants. As word spread that the students were being held in jail, support developed quickly both at Tougaloo and at Jackson State.[40]

Working with Medgar Evers, Dorie and Joyce Ladner mobilized fellow Jackson State students to attend a sympathy prayer meeting in front of the college library at 7:00 P.M. The students were circumspect in rallying behind their jailed colleagues, for as a state-supported school, Jackson State was under the thumb of white supremacists. Its president, Jacob L. Reddix, had accommodated to this reality and had previously made it clear to students that he would not tolerate civil rights activity on his campus.

Nearly 700 people turned out for the meeting. Emmett Burns (later to become NAACP state field secretary) was in the middle of a prayer when President Reddix walked up, accompanied by members of the Jackson police force. Reddix angrily demanded that the students go to their rooms, but only after he threatened to expel them did the meeting break up. The president told the press that this was "more trouble than we have had here in the past twenty years." The next day Jackson State students boycotted classes and staged an illegal rally on campus, after which a group of fifty began a march to the city jail, where the Tougaloo students, still in custody, were meeting with their college president, Daniel Beittel, who came to demonstrate his support. About ten blocks from the jail the marchers came across a line of city police, who ordered them to disperse. When they refused, police charged into the group with clubs, tear gas, and police dogs. The next day the *New York Times* ran its first story on the sit-in and its violent aftermath. (Had the students made it downtown they would have come across the "biggest parade in the state's history," with 3,000 men wearing Confederate uniforms proudly passing in review before Governor Ross Barnett in front of the governor's mansion—a short block from the public library. The occasion? White Mississippi was celebrating the 100th anniversary of its secession from the Union.)[41]

The trial of the Tougaloo Nine took place the following day. The

"Negro side" of the courtroom filled early, and outside twenty-five Jackson police officers and two German shepherd dogs stopped other blacks who had come to watch. A tense calm prevailed until the Tougaloo defendants arrived and started walking up the courthouse steps; then the large crowd of blacks lining the street broke into spontaneous applause, an act that unleashed the police and their dogs. Medgar Evers, who was hit during this police riot, later reported that the scene "was indescribable. Men and women were beaten with clubs and pistols. The Negroes had done nothing to provoke the attack. They were not demonstrating . . . and were standing peacefully on the street." Inside the courtoom the Tougaloo students were quickly convicted, fined $100 each, and given thirty-day suspended jail sentences. The case was later thrown out on appeal.[42]

Myrlie Evers has written that "the change of tide in Mississippi" began with the Jackson library sit-in. Here for the first time student activism had created a dynamic that recurred during the 1960s in black communities across the state. Young people on their own initiative confronted the forces of white supremacy publicly and dramatically. Whites responded violently, and this in turn angered and mobilized older blacks who had hitherto steered clear of civil rights activity. The night after the library sit-in more than 1,500 blacks turned out to demonstrate their solidarity with the students. John Mangrum, Tougaloo chaplain and advisor to the campus youth council, later observed that the older people there were making a statement: "It was their way of saying, 'All my life I have resented the kind of treatment I have received. Now that someone has been brave enough to step out, I will identify with them.'"[43]

The library sit-in initiated a burst of activity by black youth in Mississippi. In Jackson students attempted to desegregate the public zoo. They were arrested, and the mayor promptly removed all benches from the zoo grounds. Other Jackson protests were aimed at segregated public parks and swimming pools. NAACP youth council members in Greenville picketed three chain stores; their counterparts in Clarksdale were arrested when they tried to buy train tickets at the "white" window; and in Vicksburg two students were jailed after picketing a segregated movie theater.[44] These and other direct action protests were unprecedented in Mississippi. But they went all but unnoticed, because by then the freedom riders had come to town.

5

Outside Agitators

They say in Hinds County, No neutrals they have met,
You're either for the Freedom Ride
Or you Tom for Ross Barnett

—Freedom song[1]

Welcome to the Magnolia State

—Mississippi state border sign

Early on the morning of May 24, 1961, a red, silver, and white double-decker Trailways bus pulled out of the Montgomery terminal bound for Jackson, Mississippi. On board were a half-dozen members of the Alabama National Guard, nearly a score of newsmen, and twelve civil rights activists. Sixteen highway patrol cruisers formed an escort, while three L-19 reconnaissance planes and two helicopters flew overhead. As the convoy moved through Selma at 10:30 A.M. a hostile crowd of whites shouted curses and threats. Inside the bus the Reverend James Lawson, one of the chief strategists of the Nashville sit-ins, conducted a workshop on nonviolent action. "If we get knocked down too often, let's kneel together where we are," he advised the group. Near the Mississippi border the bus stopped briefly while the Alabama troops got off, to be replaced by eight Mississippi guardsmen carrying bayonet-tipped rifles. As Mississippi Highway Patrol cars took over as escorts, one of the passengers remarked, "I'm going out of America into a foreign country."

At a densely wooded area near Meridian, helmeted guardsmen fanned out through the forest, while a helicopter circled overhead, alerted by a report that the bus would be dynamited shortly after it entered the state. Observing the activity from inside the bus, a reporter said that "it was like a scene from a bad war movie." Police had cleared traffic through the towns along U.S. Highway 80, and the caravan zipped through stoplights at high speed. Frank Holloway later recalled that "behind all these escorts I felt like the President of the United States touring Russia." Shortly before two o'clock the bus reached the outskirts of Jackson, where local police led the convoy to its destination. At the Trailways station the guardsmen stepped off the bus, followed by the twelve passengers, who walked through a sea of Jackson police officers, past the "Negro" waiting room, and into the area reserved for whites. Several of the activists headed for the rest rooms. Jackson police detective M. B. Pierce twice told the group to "move on," but they ignored his commands. Pierce then placed the passengers—eleven blacks and one white—under arrest, charging them with breach of the peace; officers took them to a paddy wagon parked outside the station. By then a second bus was making a fast trip from Montgomery to Jackson. One of its passengers was James Farmer.[2]

The forty-year-old Farmer was the national director of the Congress of Racial Equality (CORE), a civil rights organization that fourteen years earlier, when Farmer was a young CORE member, had sent a group of riders across the upper South to test a Supreme Court decision outlawing segregated seating on interstate carriers. Farmer remembered that tactic in 1960, when the Supreme Court, ruling in *Boynton* v. *Virginia,* also banned separate terminal facilities serving interstate passengers. CORE decided to test this decision by staging another ride, this time through the Deep South.

The original group of thirteen CORE freedom riders had left Washington, D.C., on May 4 in two buses, with New Orleans as their final destination. They met little resistance in Virginia, but as the riders entered the Deep South they began to encounter hostile white crowds. Violence erupted in Alabama. Outside Anniston a mob stopped one of the buses, hurled an incendiary device inside, and beat up the fleeing riders as the bus burst into flames. The other bus made it into Birmingham, where white men wielding baseball bats and chains worked out on the freedom riders for a full fifteen minutes before Public Safety Commissioner Bull Conner's police arrived. Several of the riders were seriously injured in the attack.

"Alabama," observed Jim Farmer, "had chewed up the original thirteen interracial CORE Freedom Riders," and the group reluctantly decided to complete the trip to New Orleans by plane.[3]

Mississippi might have escaped the freedom rides altogether had it not been for Diane Nash and a group of students in Nashville, Tennessee, who belonged to the fledgling Student Nonviolent Coordinating Committee (SNCC). Formed in the aftermath of the sit-ins, SNCC initially acted as a clearinghouse for student protest groups on southern campuses. Young veterans of the 1960 direct action campaigns, SNCC activists were eager to sustain the momentum created by the sit-ins. When Nash learned that CORE had decided to halt the rides, she recruited students from Nashville to continue the journey through Alabama and Mississippi. After a series of harrowing experiences, including another mob attack in Montgomery, the Nashville group, joined by a delegation of young CORE activists from New Orleans, boarded the Trailways bus for the ride into Mississippi. They were able to do so because the Kennedy administration had finally acted to guarantee their access to public transportation.[4]

The new administration's response to the freedom rides set the pattern for the Kennedy civil rights policy in Mississippi and throughout the South. Before embarking on the rides, James Farmer had written both President John Kennedy and Attorney General Robert Kennedy, providing information on the purpose, tactics, and itinerary of the freedom rides. He received no reply. Foreign policy, not civil rights, was the priority of the president, who in early May 1961 was preparing for his summit meeting with Soviet leader Nikita Khrushchev in Vienna. When he first realized what Farmer and CORE were up to, John Kennedy placed an angry phone call to Harris Wofford, his White House assistant: "Tell them to call if off!" the president demanded. "Stop them!"[5] The Kennedys adopted a wait-and-see attitude until the bus burning outside Anniston, but then Robert Kennedy ordered FBI investigators into Alabama and conferred with state officials to obtain assurances that they would preserve public order.

Avoiding violence would be the Kennedy administration's major goal during the freedom rides. After the mob attacked the riders in Montgomery, Robert Kennedy sent in federal marshals, who were on hand on the night of May 21 when a hostile crowd of some 500 whites surrounded the First Baptist Church and virtually imprisoned

Martin Luther King and the 1,500 blacks who had come to hear him. Late that night the attorney general persuaded a reluctant Governor John Patterson to lift the siege by sending in the Alabama National Guard.[6]

Robert Kennedy had been working frantically behind the scenes to make certain that the Alabama experience would not be repeated in Mississippi should the riders persist in their determination to go to Jackson. His task was made more difficult because Mississippi's governor was a rabid segregationist who had no use for the Kennedys. Ross Barnett and his Citizens' Council brain trust had apparently decided to declare martial law once the riders crossed into the state and call out the troops to intercept the buses, thereby provoking a confrontation with the federal government. Another idea was to haul the freedom riders off to the state mental hospital in Whitfield rather than bring them to trial. Given Barnett's volatility, Justice Department officials consulted with those Mississippi politicians who at least professed loyalty to the national Democratic party. Assistant Attorney General Burke Marshall spoke with former governor J. P. Coleman, a Kennedy supporter, who warned that Barnett could not be trusted and that the riders would be ambushed and killed before they reached Jackson. Robert Kennedy went to Senator James Eastland for advice, later recalling that "I talked to him probably seven or eight or twelve times each day about what was going to happen when they got to Mississippi and what needed to be done." Using Eastland, Coleman, and Jackson mayor Allen Thompson as intermediaries, the Kennedys made a deal with Barnett: if the state promised to protect the riders, the White House would not interfere while local police arrested them as they entered the "white" waiting room at the Jackson bus terminal. The assumption held by both sides was that there would be only one bus and that the riders would post bond after their arrest. Then things would return to normal.[7]

The Kennedys could have provided federal protection for the freedom riders in Mississippi. Segregated waiting rooms had been outlawed by the U.S. Supreme Court. Legally, they no longer existed. "To enforce segregation in a place that was prohibited by federal law from being segregated," observed Burke Marshall, was "unconstitutional in my opinion without any question." Robert Kennedy later told interviewer Anthony Lewis that the president was "very concerned about what could be done" for the freedom riders in Mississippi but that everyone in the Justice Department agreed that "our authority was limited," adding that "it's better not to impose things from above because people resent it." The president and his brother were convinced that strong federal support for civil rights activists would bring on another civil war in Mississippi, with dire consequences for the South and the nation.

Burke Marshall later attempted to justify this policy on constitutional grounds, invoking the doctrine of Federalism, which had as its basic premise that "the responsibility for the preservation of law and order, and the protection of citizens against unlawful conduct on the part of others is the responsibility of the local authorities." Only when local officials totally lost control of a situation—as when the mob took over in Alabama—would the federal government respond with outside force. Although scores of attorneys and law school deans cited a number of legal precedents for government protection of civil rights workers, the administration stood its ground. "We didn't have the power," Marshall later told an interviewer. "And," he added candidly, "we didn't want it."[8]

The Kennedys' objective in the freedom rides, to prevent violence, became the keystone of their Mississippi policy. They preferred to remain in the background and to avoid crises. When conditions demanded White House action, they were more comfortable working behind the scenes with Mississippi segregationists than with movement activists, a preference that, according to Martin Luther King, "made Negroes feel like pawns in a white man's political game." Leslie Dunbar, then head of the Southern Regional Council, has perceptively observed that in the Kennedy administration there was "a great reluctance . . . to accept the fact that you had to be on somebody's side in the South."[9]

When Farmer and fifteen other riders arrived in Jackson on the second bus, a Greyhound, they too were arrested peacefully and taken to the city jail. Mississippi officials had learned the lessons of Birmingham and Montgomery. They kept white mobs away from the terminals, treated the arriving passengers with civility, and even courted visiting representatives of the media. They hoped—along with the Kennedys—that the riders would post bond and go quietly into the night. With no dramatic story to cover, the reporters would soon follow. On the morning of May 24, as the first bus was roaring through Alabama, Robert Kennedy released a low-key statement that basically called for law and order. When the attorney general learned that the second bus of freedom riders had left Montgomery for Jackson, however, he publicly attacked the "curiosity seekers, publicity seekers and others who are seeking to serve their own causes." He praised Alabama and Mississippi law enforcement officials for "meeting the test" and called on civil rights activists to observe a "cooling-off period" and halt the freedom rides, a position he had been urging privately from the beginning. Farmer responded that Negro Americans "had been cooling off for a hundred years" and would be "in a deep freeze" if they cooled any further. Through Jackson NAACP attorney Jack Young, Farmer sent word to the national CORE office to "keep Freedom Riders coming into Jackson as fast as possible on every bus, every train."[10]

Two days later, when the first group of riders came to trial, Judge James L. Spencer quickly found all defendants guilty of breach of the peace, fined them $200, and gave them sixty-day suspended sentences. The defendants refused to admit their guilt by paying the fine. Nor did they post bail. Farmer and most of the other riders chose to remain in jail for thirty-nine days, the maximum time they could serve and still appeal their convictions. Moreover, with more riders on the road to Jackson, the strategy was shifting from one of "seeking token arrests to spur legal and administrative action" to that of filling the jails of Mississippi in the hope of "making segregationist practices so expensive and inconvenient as to become unfeasible." On May 28 seventeen new riders arrived in Jackson. Realizing that he had not resolved the crisis through his short-term *modus vivendi* with Governor Barnett, Attorney General Kennedy now acted on a suggestion from Martin Luther King and petitioned the Interstate Commerce Commission to issue a ruling to prohibit bus and railroad companies from using segregated terminals. While the ICC deliberated, more riders poured into Mississippi, and by the end of the summer, 328 of them had been arrested in Jackson. Of these riders, two-thirds were college students, three-fourths were men, and more than half were black. What had begun as a modest effort to secure enforcement of the *Boynton* decision had become, in Farmer's words, "a different and far grander thing than we had intended."[11]

Life behind prison bars was dehumanizing, but by and large, the glare of national publicity spared the riders jailed in Jackson from acts of violence. In early June they were moved to the county prison farm, where the Reverend C. T. Vivian received a blackjack beating from police interrogators because he refused to preface an answer with "sir." When a rider posted bond and demanded an FBI investigation of police brutality at the prison farm, the prisoners were immediately transferred back to the county jail in Jackson. With the city and county jails overflowing, and the county prison farm no longer an option, Governor Barnett decided to send the freedom riders up to Parchman penitentiary.[12]

Parchman in the summer of 1961 remains vivid in the memory of all movement veterans who did time there. When the first forty-five male prisoners arrived at the prison compound at dawn on June 15, they felt they had been transported back into another century.[13] From the observation tower inside the barbed-wire gate, guards looked out on miles of flat Delta land green with cotton plants tended by convicts (all but a handful of whom were black) in striped prison garb, with shotgun-toting overseers following behind—in the footsteps of their ancestors. The freedom riders did not work in these fields, although they had asked to do so. Instead, they served out the remainder of their sentences locked inside the prison's maximum security wing.

Aware of the horror stories surrounding the history of one of the South's most infamous prisons, the freedom riders at first expected the worst. But Barnett arrived at the penitentiary on the first day of their incarceration, no doubt to pass the word to Parchman officials that he wanted no recurrence of the C. T. Vivian assault at the Hinds County prison farm. The state's method of handling the prisoners had thus far succeeded in burying the continuing story of the freedom rides in the back pages of the *New York Times,* and Barnett and his advisors wanted to keep it there. Guards did use physical force, responding to acts of civil disobedience with cattle prods and wrist breakers, but there were no bloody beatings. Ironically, the activists were safer in Parchman than they were to be later as free citizens on the streets of McComb and Greenwood.

As the riders began to realize that their lives were not in immediate danger, boredom replaced fear. Inmates attempted to pass the time through daily rituals of calisthenics, religious and philosophical discussions, and song. The freedom songs boosted morale—and provided the most frequent confrontations between the prisoners and their jailers. When the riders ignored commands to stop singing, guards took their mattresses. One tall, young rider from Howard University refused, and the guard had to drag the mattress—and a determined Stokely Carmichael—out of the cell together. When that tactic did not stop the singing, guards brought in fire hoses and turned them on the prisoners. Huge exhaust fans chilled the prisoners at night, while cell-block windows were closed during the day to make the heat stifling. The jailers' tactics took their toll. Disputes broke out among the riders over the daily religious devotionals, the degree to which they should cooperate with their captors, and the advisability of hunger strikes.

Overall, however, a remarkable degree of solidarity had developed. Those men and women who walked through the prison gates after serving their thirty-nine days had forged a bond of shared experience. They had challenged the forces of white supremacy in the most repressive state in the union. Veterans of the freedom rides were among the shock troops of the Mississippi movement of the 1960s, fanning out across the state, organizing the dispossessed. The movement would undergo changes and adopt new strategies, but whenever SNCC and CORE organizers arrived at a new community, the word quickly spread through black neighborhoods: "Here come the Freedom Riders!"

At first, black Jacksonians did not know quite what to make of the freedom rides. Direct action protests were not new to the city— the Tougaloo students had sat in at the Jackson library less than a month before—but in the late spring of 1961 the black community was not yet prepared for the politics of confrontation. Aurelia Young, whose husband, Jack, was one of the riders' attorneys, recalls that initially "the blacks were complacent; we didn't get involved at first. It was as if we were onlookers." CORE and SNCC did not yet have staff people in Mississippi, and because of the frenzied pace of events, no one had come to Jackson to organize local support for the riders. The NAACP was still the only national civil rights organization operating in the state, and the freedom rides were not an NAACP operation. Whites lost no time in attempting to isolate the riders from the black community. Senator Eastland branded the rides as "a part of the Communist movement in the U.S.," warning that they had brought Mississippians "face to face with this world conspiracy." Mayor Thompson confidently predicted that "when you get rid of the outside agitators, our colored people will go right back to the old way." There was no going back, however, and although taken by surprise, blacks in Jackson did move to assist the riders.[14]

The most important support group was Womanpower Unlimited, established by Clarie Collins Harvey. Mrs. Harvey belonged to Jackson's black elite. Her father had been a successful mortician and one of the founders of the Jackson NAACP. Clarie Collins studied at Spelman College, where she received her B.A.; at Columbia, where she received her M.A.; and at New York University and Union Theological Seminary. As a young woman she became involved in the church and in 1939 was a delegate to the World Christian Conference in Amsterdam, where she met her future husband. That same year her father died and she returned to Jackson, took over management of the Collins Funeral Home, and for the next twenty years was active in church and civic work in black Jackson. When the first group of freedom riders came to trial, Harvey was in the courtroom: "It was a very cool day in May and I noticed that some of the girls were shivering—of course a lot of it was nerves, you know. I inquired if they needed sweaters or something." That night she and Aurelia Young sent some warmer clothing and sleepwear down to the Jackson jail. The following Sunday Mrs. Harvey made appeals in three churches in her neighborhood for offerings to support the riders. From these modest beginnings Womanpower Unlimited "just sort of evolved." Making use of her contacts outside the state, Harvey established an interracial network of some 300 women who "sent us all kinds of resources: food, sheets, clothes, magazines and books, blankets and everything to help minister to the needs of the Freedom Riders." Womanpower Unlimited also provided information to parents and families of the jailed riders, as well as food and lodging for the activists after their release from Parchman.[15]

As the summer progressed, these women worked to develop support for the movement in the black community, cosponsoring with SNCC rallies featuring James Farmer and Martin Luther King. Later, Womanpower Unlimited was active in voter registration campaigns and in the boycott of white Jackson businesses. The local response to these efforts was not always encouraging. Members of Harvey's own staff grumbled that she should spend more time at the funeral home comforting the families of the deceased, and "there were many blacks so brainwashed that they didn't understand, wouldn't have any part of the civil rights struggle, and wouldn't have any part of you because you were associated with it."[16] Still, defying stereotypes of gender, social class, and race, Harvey, Jesse Mosley, Aurelia Young, and the other women in the organization effectively mustered support for the freedom riders at a time when it was unpopular, if not dangerous, to do so. Independent of any male-dominated civil rights group, they acted quickly, free from bureaucratic inefficiency and territorial infighting. Brought into existence by the freedom rides, Womanpower Unlimited was symbolic of the changes beginning to occur in the leadership and direction of the black struggle.

The freedom rides also had an impact on the NAACP in Mississippi. When James Farmer first told Roy Wilkins of CORE's plans to test the *Boynton* decision, Wilkins tried to discourage him, adding that Medgar Evers "thought the Freedom Ride a bad idea and hoped we wouldn't come to Mississippi." With the freedom rides, the NAACP's domination of civil rights activity in Mississippi was nearing its end. In the summer CORE sent a field secretary, Tom Gaither, to Jackson to coordinate the freedom rides. Five SNCC veterans of the rides and the Nashville Student Movement, including Diane Nash, James Bevel, and Bernard Lafayette, also set up an office in Jackson after their release from Parchman.[17] Interorganizational tensions had been building in Jackson during the summer of the freedom rides. They came to the surface in September, seventy-five miles down the road in McComb.

· · ·

[Bob Moses' move into southwest Mississippi] was probably the most creative and heroic single act anyone in the New Left has attempted. Certainly much of the subsequent history of the New Left has flowed from that existential act of [Moses] disappearing alone into the most violent and desolate section of Mississippi.

—Jack Newfield, 1966

Last night there was a statement made that I initiated or started the movement, but anyone who thinks must know that I couldn't have done that cause I wasn't from McComb. And as far as I know things don't get started by somebody who is not from someplace just going in cold turkey and figuring that they are going to start something. And C. C. Bryant was the person who actually started this thing.

—Robert Moses, 1983

The "Camellia City of America," McComb was founded in 1872 by a Yankee capitalist as a repair station for his Illinois Central Railroad. Lacking the urban "sophistication" of Jackson or the paternalistic plantation aristocracy of Greenville, McComb grew up with a history of labor strife and a reputation as a rough blue-collar town. The railroad remained a major source of employment for the area's white and black workers well into the 1960s. The Illinois Central had demographic significance as well, for its tracks neatly separated McComb's 9,000 whites from its 4,000 black residents. As a relatively young city, McComb had missed out on slavery and most of Reconstruction, but that collective memory was deeply imbedded in the consciousness of local whites, and Jim Crow had been the arbiter of race relations in this isolated industrial community for nearly a century.[18]

The Illinois Central was important to black McComb, for it had supplied jobs—albeit often the most difficult and dangerous ones—and a degree of economic security. Black railroad workers were union men, belonging to segregated locals like the Railway Clerks and the firemen's union, which meant higher wages than the going rate for black labor. The union also afforded a degree of protection from local whites, who had historically applied economic sanctions against blacks who engaged in political activity. These railroad workers, along with a handful of independent business owners, provided the economic base for the McComb black community during the first half of the twentieth century.

For more than three decades Nathaniel Lewis had been one of the most important people in black McComb. Lewis, who was the grandson of slaves, and his father organized the McComb Independent Lodge of the Benevolent Order of Elks in 1928 with the hope that "we would be able to get some of our people in Pike County registered to vote. This didn't turn out too well." As a porter on the Illinois Central, Lewis enjoyed high status in the black community, and beginning in the 1930s he handled grievances for his fellow members of the Brotherhood of Sleeping Car Porters. Upon his return from service in the Pacific during World War II, Lewis and his brother Napoleon testified at the Bilbo hearings in Jackson, and that same year they founded the Pike County Voters' League. The Lewises and a small number of other blacks eventually succeeded in registering, and the voters' league conducted regular classes to encourage others to take the test. It was a low-key operation, limiting its political work to voter registration.[19]

As Mississippi heated up in the 1950s, the NAACP became the center of black involvement. The McComb NAACP had been founded in 1944 and limped along for the next decade, facing many of the same problems that plagued other Mississippi branches. When the leadership changed hands in the aftermath of *Brown,* the branch took on new life. Early in 1955 a campaign led by Webb Owens and recently elected president C. C. Bryant boosted membership by over 50 percent, surpassing the goal of 100 dues-paying members. Both Bryant and Owens worked for the Illinois Central and enrolled other railroad workers, as well as small-business owners like Ernest Nobles, a World War II veteran who operated a successful dry-cleaning establishment, and Aylene Quin, who had opened a restaurant after she moved to McComb in 1953.[20]

The reign of terror in Mississippi in 1955 drove the McComb NAACP underground. Aylene Quin recalled that "if you were a member of the NAACP you kept it kind of a secret. If you had any kind of a job or anything you couldn't let it be known." This repressive atmosphere kept the NAACP from going public with a program, much less confronting the white power structure on the other side of the tracks. McComb's city fathers had always dealt with the black community—when they had to—through "leaders," usually ministers, who accepted the status quo in return for recognition and small favors. This traditional arrangement was the only link between the black and white communities. Bryant recalls that although a few ministers "played on the black team," those with the most influence would go downtown and tell the whites "what they wanted to hear. Those preachers had no knowledge of civil rights. . . . they didn't speak for the people." (When black McComb began to stir in 1961, white officials were caught off guard. City attorney Joe Pigott did not recall ever having met C. C. Bryant before then: "At that time I thought the black leaders were all ministers. That was who we perceived as being the leaders in the community.")[21]

As the fifties ended, Bryant, Owens, and the other NAACP stalwarts were carrying on a holding operation in McComb. Most of the older blacks were afraid to act, aware that the retribution of the Citizens' Council and its poor white allies would be swift and brutal. Thus, in the spring of 1961, when Bryant read in *Jet* magazine that a young SNCC worker named Bob Moses was about to

launch a voter registration project in the Mississippi Delta, he expressed interest in initiating a similar drive in McComb. As it turned
out, Bryant got a good deal more than he had bargained for.

Robert Parris Moses' journey from the streets of Harlem to the
dirt roads of southwest Mississippi is part of the folklore of the
black freedom struggle. Born in 1935, Moses had spent his formative years in a Harlem housing project. His obvious intellectual talents enabled him to attend one of New York's best high schools,
and after graduating from Hamilton College, he went on to take
his master's degree in philosophy at Harvard. He was teaching
mathematics at Horace Mann High School in Westchester County
when the sit-ins began. Although he had been politically active
throughout his school years, Moses found the sit-ins to be a transforming experience. Viewing the photographs of the demonstrators
sitting at the lunch counters, he said, "I could feel myself in the
faces of the people that they had there on the front pages. I could
feel how they felt, just by looking at those pictures." Moses decided he needed a firsthand look, and during spring break he went to
Virginia to visit his uncle, William Moses, a prize-winning architect who for more than twenty years had taught at Hampton Institute.[22] Bob Moses joined a picket line at Newport News and met
Wyatt T. Walker, his first contact with the Southern Christian Leadership Conference. That summer the young teacher went to work
in the SCLC office in Atlanta, where he met Ella Baker, the veteran
activist and organizer who would have a profound impact on Moses
and SNCC in the early 1960s. Also working in the Atlanta office
was Jane Stembridge, a white southern student coordinating SNCC
activities. Part of Stembridge's responsibility was to plan a SNCC
conference for the fall. Having little information about black leadership potential in the Deep South, she asked Moses to make an
exploratory trip to Mississippi to recruit people for the conference.
He agreed and boarded a bus bound for the Mississippi Delta.[23]

Moses first stopped in Clarksdale, where he was warmly greeted
by Aaron Henry and a group of students. Next he made the short
trip down to Cleveland, where he began his long friendship with
Amzie Moore. The Delta businessman, post office employee, and
veteran activist was Moses' entrée into black Mississippi. Moore
was active in the state NAACP and had worked with T. R .M.
Howard in the Regional Council of Negro Leadership. During the
1950s he had developed close ties with, and received financial help

from, the Southern Conference Education Fund (SCEF), an inter
racial, southern-based human rights organization whose radical
politics were anathema to the NAACP. But Moore had grown impatient with the NAACP bureaucracy and questioned the New York
office's commitment to Mississippi. Moses realized that "Amzie saw
the students as a way out; I mean he really felt that these students
. . . were going to accomplish something . . . [they were] a force that
he and other people should try to tap." Moore had strong opin-
ions about what needed to be done in Mississippi. He was not interested in organizing direct action campaigns to desegregate public accommodations, for most Mississippi blacks were too poor to
derive any tangible benefits from such actions. Instead, Moore was
convinced that political power was the key to cracking open the
closed society and persuaded his young friend to return to Cleveland the following summer and launch an intensive voter registration campaign in the Delta.[24]

Having completed the final year on his teaching contract, Moses
came back to Cleveland in the summer of 1961, only to discover
that his mentor "just wasn't ready to start." Moore offered explanations—the meeting places and equipment needed by SNCC workers were not yet available—but Moses sensed that a lack of commitment from local blacks had made Moore reluctant to proceed.
Thus, when the president of the McComb NAACP branch let it be
known that he would welcome SNCC workers to work on voter
registration in Pike County, Moore told Moses, "We better send you
down to C. C. Bryant."[25]

Moses arrived in McComb in mid-July, moved in with the Bryants, and for the next two weeks did nothing but talk with local
people about the proposed voter registration project. Each morning Webb Owens, now retired from his job with the Illinois Central in Memphis, yet still active as membership chairman of the
NAACP, picked up Moses and began making the rounds. With them
was Jerry Gibson, also a retired railroad fireman and an NAACP
officer. "We went to every single black person of any kind of substance in the community," recalls Moses. The three men spoke with
Nathaniel Lewis, with local ministers, and with businesspeople like
Ernest Nobles and Aylene Quin. At each stop Moses talked about
SNCC and its plans for a month-long project to encourage McComb
blacks to attempt to register to vote. He promised that two other
SNCC workers would join him, provided that the black communi-

ty raised enough money to support the three workers. Then Owens asked for contributions, five or ten dollars from each person, stating that he was to be treasurer of the project. In this way the community demonstrated its endorsement of the program, which was financed before it got underway. Webb Owens was the key to the success of the fund-raising effort. He was one of the most respected members of the community, and people trusted him with their money.[26]

In this, his initial foray into community organizing, Moses established the pattern that SNCC followed for the next four years, involving local people in all phases of the movement and depending on them for support and, when needed, protection. He sensed then that the entrance into the community was through the black middle class, and in Mississippi this meant leaders of local NAACP branches. Once accepted, SNCC organizers made their own contacts and cultivated a different base for leadership, but initially, at least, SNCC needed the support of those men and women whose word meant something in the community. In McComb, Owens and Bryant were the key people. "The importance, the quality of the person, the local person, that you go to work with," Moses had learned, "is everything in terms of whether the project can get off the ground."[27]

Moses was able to establish his credibility not only because of his contacts but also because of his program. Voter registration had been the staple of black political activism in Mississippi for nearly a half century. Everyone agreed that registering and voting was important. It was a program around which the political extremes in the black community, from Nathaniel Lewis to the eager black teenagers, could all unite. Had Moses gone into the community with a direct action plan to desegregate downtown lunch counters and restaurants he would have gained virtually no adult backing, but McComb blacks rallied around the idea of a revitalized registration effort, spearheaded by enthusiastic full-time organizers from the outside. The Masons opened the doors of their meeting hall for voter education classes, Society Hill Baptist Church made available its mimeograph machine to run off copies of the complicated Mississippi registration form, and local churches even invited Moses to speak about the project from their pulpits. The black community of McComb was ready to move. Looking back at that moment from the vantage point of more than two decades, C. C. Bryant smiled as he recalled, "We had a zeal then!"[28]

During the first week of August, SNCC workers Reginald Robinson and John Hardy joined Moses in McComb. The three men began working door to door, attempting to persuade blacks to travel to the county seat in Magnolia to take the voting test. The SNCC workers were breaking new ground here. In the past, NAACP registration drives were directed primarily at the small black middle class. SNCC wanted to expand that base to include the entire community. The canvassers brought sample registration forms with them and asked, "Have you ever tried to fill out this form? Would you like to sit down now and try to fill it out?" This was the first step in breaking down the psychological barriers that had prevented local blacks from undergoing the ordeal of the registration procedure. The SNCC organizers also pointed out that the applicants had a chance to succeed: about 250 McComb blacks had previously made it onto the voter rolls.[29]

The first voter registration class met at the Masonic Temple on August 7. Moses went over the twenty-one-question form and familiarized the potential voters with sections of the Mississippi Constitution likely to appear on the test. That same day four people contacted during the canvassing went down to Magnolia to take the test, and three of them passed. Two days later two of three applicants registered. About twenty-five people were attending the classes, and word of the drive and its early success had spread to neighboring Amite and Walthall counties. Rural, poor, and violent, these areas made McComb appear by comparison a model of civility. In July the Justice Department had filed a suit against Walthall County officials, charging discrimination against black voting applicants. In Amite, a majority black county, there was reportedly only one registered Negro voter. The SNCC workers knew they were asking for trouble if they went into Amite. Moses' position was simply that "farmers came over and were very anxious to try and register and you couldn't very well turn them down. . . . you can't be in the position of turning down the tough areas because the people, then, I think would lose confidence in you." In mid-August John Hardy, accompanied by three students recently arrived from Jackson—MacArthur Cotton, Jimmie Travis, and George Lowe—left McComb to set up a registration school in Walthall. Their local contact was Robert Bryant, C. C. Bryant's uncle. Moses went into Amite to work with E. W. Steptoe.[30]

The fifty-three-year-old Steptoe was an Amite County native who owned a dairy and cotton farm on the Louisiana border. He had organized the Amite County branch of the NAACP in 1954 and was thereafter the subject of police harassment and threats from white neighbors. A man of courage and stubborn determination, the small, wiry farmer was legendary for his arsenal. One SNCC organizer who stayed with Steptoe remembers that "as you went to bed he would open up the night table and there would be a large .45 automatic sitting next to you. Just guns all over the house, under pillows, under chairs. It was just marvelous."[31] Bob Moses was committed to nonviolence and uncomfortable around all this weaponry, but he said nothing to his host.

Although they were caught off guard at first, whites soon took steps to neutralize this outsider who had come to town to stir up trouble. On August 15 Moses was arrested while accompanying three people to the registrar's office in Liberty, the Amite county seat. A week later Billy Jack Caston, a cousin of the local sheriff, attacked Moses with the butt end of a knife, resulting in three head lacerations that required eight stitches. Moses knew white violence was the most potent weapon against black protest in Mississippi, and he decided to press charges against Caston to demonstrate that this method of intimidation would no longer go unchallenged. Drawn by a mixture of curiosity and anger, 100 whites packed the courtroom on the day of Caston's trial. After Moses and other SNCC witnesses testified, the sheriff escorted them out of the courtroom, stating that he could not guarantee their safety once the trial had ended. Caston's defense was simple: Moses had picked a fight with him. Six white witnesses perjured themselves in court, and Caston walked out a free man. Inspired by Moses' courage and the receptiveness of local blacks, however, other SNCC workers joined the project. By the end of August a dozen SNCC organizers were in southwest Mississippi, including Ruby Doris Smith, Chuck McDew, Travis Britt, Charles Sherrod, and Marion Barry. These activists would have particular impact on the area's black youth.[32]

Hollis Watkins and Curtis Hayes, who grew up in Summit, a community just north of McComb, were the first young people recruited by Moses. Shortly after noon on a sultry Saturday in late August, the youths strolled into Woolworth's drugstore on Main

Street in McComb and sat down at the counter. Police on the scene asked them to move on and, when they refused, arrested Watkins and Hayes on charges of breach of the peace. Three days later a capacity crowd of more than 200 blacks attended a community meeting and heard James Bevel, who was now working in Jackson, speak about the power of nonviolent direct action. The following afternoon three blacks were arrested after attempting to integrate the white section of the Greyhound bus terminal. Two of the three protestors, Bobbie Talbert and Ike Lewis, were twenty. The third member of the group, Brenda Travis, was only fifteen, a fact that would have significant consequences for the McComb movement. All five demonstrators were held in jail for over a month until released on bond.[33]

The McComb sit-ins bore the stamp of the newly formed Pike County Nonviolent Movement, a group of McComb-area students led by Marion Barry, a veteran of the Nashville sit-ins and a strong proponent of direct action. Barry had recently returned from a stormy SNCC meeting at the Highlander Folk School in Tennessee where the young organization almost fell apart over the question of direct action versus voter registration. The Nashville faction, which included Diane Nash and James Bevel, had drawn up a plan they called "Move on Mississippi," which envisioned a massive effort to "move against all the institutions in Mississippi and desegregate them." The voter registration group supported Moses' program of focusing on registration in key areas of the state. Ella Baker finally resolved the dispute by suggesting that SNCC create two wings, one for direct action and the other for voter registration. The Nashville group returned to their project in Jackson, while Marion Barry headed for McComb.[34]

Moses had mixed emotions about the direct action protests. He believed that "it was important in terms of building unity with SNCC to give free access to Marion [Barry]." It was also advantageous "for young people like Hollis and Curtis, who had been working on voting, and who had gotten frustrated, to do something themselves.... I was glad for them to get involved in something they were enthusiastic about." On the other hand, Moses "was not personally enthusiastic" about the McComb sit-ins. "My problem was that I didn't think it was a program. And I was right on that. It was a one-event thing, and not something the movement could sustain." The direct action campaign also undercut Moses' credibility with middle-class blacks. Not once during his July conversations with black leaders had he suggested that SNCC would attempt to desegregate public facilities in McComb. C. C. Bryant and more conservative leaders had signed on to voter registration, nothing more. Although the initial response of the community had been to rally around the young people now sitting in jail, Bryant began to feel uneasy, and other blacks questioned the wisdom of the decision to welcome these young outsiders into their community.[35]

During September white intimidation and violence took a heavy toll. With the five sit-in students held in jail under a $5,000 bond, the Pike County Nonviolent Movement planned no further protests. Although the arrest and beating of Bob Moses had slowed the voter registration drive, a few people were still eager to take the test. On September 5 Travis Britt was beaten "into a semi-conscious state" while trying to assist blacks attempting to register in Liberty. Two days later John Hardy accompanied two applicants to the Walthall county seat in Tylertown, where the registrar struck the SNCC worker on the head with a pistol, shouting, "Stay out of here, you dumb son of a bitch." When the dazed Hardy staggered outside, Sheriff John Q. Wood arrested him on a charge of disorderly conduct. At this point the federal government intervened, and that for a time raised the flagging hopes of local activists.[36]

At first the Kennedy administration appeared more favorably inclined toward offering protection in voter registration activities than in desegregation protests. In mid-July, after SNCC had informed the Justice Department of its forthcoming project in McComb, Burke Marshall wrote Deputy Attorney General Byron White that "economic and other types of reprisals" might be employed against Pike County blacks attempting to register. If so, "we will have to move immediately to prevent the reprisals through court orders which may have to be enforced by federal marshals." Hardy's beating and arrest brought Justice Department troubleshooter John Doar to McComb to investigate. Doar immediately filed a suit that was ultimately successful in blocking the state's prosecution of Hardy. This move, following the federal government's inaction regarding the trials of the freedom riders, illustrates the Justice Department's belief that it was on firmer legal ground intervening in voting cases. Such action was also consistent with the Kennedys' ongoing efforts to divert the movement away from direct action and into voter registration. The Justice Department, however, soon retreated from its advanced position.[37]

At 9:00 A.M. on Monday, September 25, E. H. Hurst, a member of the Mississippi state legislature, shot and killed Herbert Lee, a black farmer and father of nine children, at a cotton gin near Liberty. Hurst later claimed that a dispute over money prompted Lee to attack him with a tire tool and that Hurst's gun had gone off in the skirmish, inflicting the fatal wound. The previous evening, shortly before returning to Washington, John Doar had talked with Moses and Steptoe about the dangers facing Amite County blacks active in the registration campaign. Steptoe had singled out Representative Hurst as a threat and mentioned Herbert Lee as a potential target. Although less visible than Steptoe, Lee was a charter member of the Amite County NAACP branch and had volunteered to drive Moses around the county to contact potential voters. The day after the killing a coroner's jury cleared Hurst.

Among those corroborating Hurst's account was a black eyewitness, Louis Allen. Allen later told Moses that his testimony had been coerced: Lee did not have a tire tool, and Hurst had shot him in cold blood. When an Amite County grand jury convened to examine the findings of the coroner's jury, Allen told Moses he would now tell the truth, but he needed protection. Moses immediately called the Justice Department: "They told us that there was no way possible to provide protection for a witness at such a hearing and that probably, in any case, it didn't matter what he testified and that Hurst would be found innocent." With no federal protection, Allen stuck to his original story, fearing for his life. Unfortunately, he had told FBI agents the truth about Lee's murder, and from that day on Lewis Allen was a marked man in Amite County.[38]

The murder of Herbert Lee brought the voter registration drive to a halt. The message was clear: standing up for your rights in southwest Mississippi could get you killed. Lee's murder also had a sobering effect on SNCC staff. As Chuck McDew put it, "It's okay to put our own lives in jeopardy, but when you can cause somebody else to get killed, then that's a different question. . . . we did have thoughts that if we had never come here, this would never have happened." McDew, Moses, and the other organizers "finally came to a decision that nothing would happen in Mississippi, and in the South, unless somebody was willing to die. We had made the commitment that we were willing to die; other people would have to make it on an individual basis, whether they were willing or unwilling to do so."[39] The SNCC workers did not have much time for reflection on these matters, for in McComb black high school students were up in arms about the punishment handed out to two of their classmates.

The week after Herbert Lee's murder, the five students jailed for thirty-four days as a result of the sit-ins were released on bond supplied by the NAACP and SCLC. Two of them, Ike Lewis and Brenda Travis, attended Burgland High, the town's black junior and senior high school with an enrollment of about 700. When Lewis and Travis attempted to go back to school, the principal, Commodore Dewey Higgins, refused to admit them. Anticipating this development, students walked out on October 4, marching first to SNCC headquarters at the Masonic Temple to pick up the signs they had made. SNCC staff divided on the question of whether the students should continue the march. Direct action advocates Marion Barry and Cordell Reagon urged them to go ahead. Chuck McDew and Bob Moses had reservations, correctly anticipating that black adults would not approve of the demonstration. "We did not want to have the parents alienated," recalls McDew. "We didn't want the parents to feel that we were using their kids." But the overriding factor was that the students wanted to march, so Moses and McDew supported the decision and accompanied them.[40]

McComb had never seen anything quite like it: more than 100 young people marching through the middle of one of the toughest towns in the country, carrying their handwritten banners and singing "We Shall Overcome." They stopped at city hall, where one by one they climbed the steps to pray. Police began making arrests. By this time, an angry mob of several hundred whites had surrounded the demonstrators and attacked a newly arrived SNCC worker, Bob Zellner, the only white person in the march. The son of a Methodist minister from Alabama, Zellner had come to SNCC on a SCEF subsidy and was assigned to work on white southern campuses. He had been reluctant to participate in the march, for he realized that his visibility might undermine his ability to organize white students, and he feared his presence in the demonstration "would cause more violence." Swept up in the emotion of the moment, however, he joined the students and fellow SNCC workers. Zellner took a savage beating while police stood idly by and FBI agents on the scene took notes. The SNCC organizers were arrested, as were 116 students. Police later released the 97 students who were under eighteen years old but charged the remaining 19 "adults" and SNCC workers Moses, McDew, and Zellner with breach of the peace and contributing to the delinquency of minors.[41]

Fifteen-year-old Brenda Travis received the cruelest sentence of all. An enthusiastic worker, she had canvassed neighborhoods each afternoon for weeks. She volunteered for the sit-ins, and when Marion Barry said that minors could not participate, she told him she was eighteen. After she was arrested the second time on the city hall steps, Brenda Travis was given an indeterminate sentence at the reformatory "for Negro delinquents" at Oakley.[42]

As Moses and McDew had feared, the student march eroded support in the black community. Commodore Higgins expelled the students who walked out, requiring that they promise not to participate in further demonstrations as the price for readmission. Most refused to sign the pledge. At first McComb blacks rallied behind their children. Aylene Quin, whose daughter helped organize the walkout, demanded that the students be readmitted without signing the pledge; Ernest Nobles attempted unsuccessfully to persuade the parents to stage a protest march; and C. C. Bryant was arrested and detained briefly after addressing a mass meeting, charged with contributing to the delinquency of minors. But many parents were furious over the walkout (some even whipped their children on the city hall steps after obtaining their release from jail), and they blamed SNCC for turning their sons and daughters into troublemakers. Nathaniel Lewis, who had supported Moses' initial voting project, was out of town during the march: "I came home and found out exactly what happened, they had deceived me, using the children was not my thing at all. I cut loose from Robert Moses."[43]

So did C. C. Bryant. For some time now Bryant had been the man in the middle. He had invited Moses into McComb and enthusiastically supported the early voter registration campaign, but he did not believe McComb was ready for demonstrations, and like many black adults, he was appalled that SNCC would permit a fifteen-year-old girl to participate in a sit-in. Thus, while black conservatives blamed Bryant for bringing on all the trouble, black youths began to see him as a person out of step with the times.

Although he held a deep respect and affection for Moses, Bryant decided that it was time for SNCC to pack up and leave, and he turned to the state NAACP for help.[44]

The NAACP's attitude toward the SNCC project in southwest Mississippi had been ambivalent. State field secretary Medgar Evers was miffed that SNCC had moved into McComb "without my knowledge" and accused the outsiders of refusing to acknowledge the McComb NAACP's role in getting the project underway. When SNCC went to the NAACP for legal assistance and bond money after the sit-in arrests, Roy Wilkins icily replied, "If we are expected to pay the bills, we must be in on the planning and launching, otherwise the bills will have to be paid by those who plan and launch." In the end, however, the NAACP Legal Defense Fund did supply bond money and assigned Jackson attorney Jack Young to represent the defendants. Evers made several trips to McComb and at a rally at the Masonic Temple on October 10 pledged the NAACP's support for the expelled students. Yet when fifty-four of the students refused to sign the pledge and staged another walkout, support in the black community diminished. Moses recalls that at the state NAACP executive committee meeting at the end of October, Bryant asked the board to "condemn the SNCC operation and have it moved out." SNCC had strong defenders at that meeting, however, including Owens, Steptoe, and Amzie Moore, and the organization took no position on the McComb project.[45]

Out on bond and awaiting trial for their participation in the student march, the SNCC organizers spent the last three weeks of October as teachers at "Nonviolent High," a makeshift school they had set up for the students still boycotting Burgland High. McDew taught history; Moses, math; and SNCC worker Dion Diamond took charge of chemistry and physics. McDew was appalled at "how systematic the school system is in messing up the minds of children." He recalled his bewilderment when a student asked whether they were going to study "the war for Southern Independence." Further questioning led McDew to understand that the student was referring to the Civil War.

For the students, this first "freedom school" was an unforgettable experience. Joe Martin, one of the organizers of the walkout, was impressed that social and class factors were unimportant to their teachers: "It wasn't like in the public schools that this was

Mr. so and so's daughter. If you had a good idea it was accepted regardless of what your social status was." Here, SNCC intuitively grasped a vital part of its future mission in Mississippi: developing a sense of worth and leadership among people who had never been held in high regard in their communities. Brenda Travis, for example, had come from a broken home. She was not "a well-known person at school," yet through SNCC she came alive and emerged as the symbol of the student movement in McComb. She had mobilized the Burgland High students, inspiring them to stand up for their principles. "It was really a sight to see," remembered Ernest Nobles, "all those kids leaving here and following Brenda Travis." Nonviolent High closed its doors shortly before its faculty went on trial at county court. Many of the students, still refusing to sign the pledge, enrolled at Campbell College in Jackson, an A.M.E. school that offered classes on the high school level. One of them, sixteen-year-old Emma Bell, later worked full time with SNCC.[46]

On October 31 McDew, Moses, Zellner, and the older McComb students were convicted of disturbing the peace and given prison terms of from four to six months. In announcing the sentences, Judge Robert Brumfield said that "some of you are local residents, some of you are outsiders. Those of you who are local residents are like sheep being led to the slaughter." (Nearly a quarter century later Brumfield admitted that "we found 'em all guilty, whether they were or not.") The county jail in Magnolia was home to the activists for more than a month while they attempted to raise bail. They passed the time there by playing chess, reading, singing, and writing letters that they smuggled out of the cells. Visitors came from McComb, and Aylene Quin brought food that she and other community people had prepared (Bobbie Talbert claimed to have gained twenty-five pounds during his period of incarceration!). Bob Moses captured the hopeful spirit of those early days of the movement in this note written in "the drunk tank of the county jail in Magnolia":

Twelve of us are here, sprawled out along the concrete bunker; Curtis Hayes, Hollis Watkins, Ike Lewis and Robert Talbert, four veterans of the bunker, are sitting up here talking—mostly about girls; Charles McDew ("Tell the story") is curled into the concrete and the wall. . . . I'm sitting with smuggled pen and paper, thinking a little, writing a little; Myrtis Bennett and Janie Campbell are across the way wedded to a different icy cubicle.

This is Mississippi, the middle of the iceberg. Hollis is leading off with his tenor, "Michael row the boat ashore, Alleluia; Christian brothers don't be slow, Alleluia; Mississippi's next to go, Alleluia." This is a tremor in the middle of the iceberg, from a stone that the builders rejected.[47]

While they were in jail, the group learned that there had been an outburst of violence at the McComb bus station when a group of six CORE activists attempted to test the ICC ruling forbidding segregation in bus terminals, which had gone into effect November 1. As the group entered the terminal, white men cursed and beat them. Although the police station was less than a block from the terminal, police officers did not show up until five minutes after the mob had done its work.[48]

Moses and the McComb students left the Magnolia jail on December 5. SCEF president James Dombrowski had supplied the $13,000 needed for bail. On their release, the students who were high school seniors went up to Campbell College in Jackson. Hollis Watkins and Curtis Hayes soon initiated a SNCC project in Hattiesburg. Moses moved on to work in Jackson, in part because he felt a responsibility to look after the McComb students now at Campbell. Brenda Travis remained at the Oakley reformatory until May 1962, when a German émigré teaching at Talledega College in Alabama persuaded the judge to release her into his custody.[49]

SNCC had, in Moses' words, "gotten its feet wet" in McComb. In terms of wins and losses, the score was not impressive. The registration drive had netted only a half-dozen new voters from the nearly forty attempts to register. Despite the sit-in protests, McComb remained the same Jim Crow town it had always been. Ernest Nobles had lost his white trade at the dry cleaners; C. C. Bryant was fighting to maintain his leadership in the NAACP; and Herbert Lee's widow and nine children were grieving their loss, confused as to why he had to pay the ultimate price. Yet the movement in southwest Mississippi would revive in 1964, with battle-tested veterans like E. W. Steptoe, Aylene Quin, Joe Martin, Ernest Nobles, and yes, C. C. Bryant continuing the struggle.

For the young men and women of SNCC, McComb was an invaluable testing ground. They found that they could stand up to intense white pressure and survive. They discovered their natural constituency among the young, and they saw that the activism of high school students brought adults into the movement. On the other hand, much of the black middle class was under severe economic constraints and could not be counted on to support the assault against segregated institutions. SNCC workers learned that although officials of the Justice Department listened to their grievances, the activists could not rely on the Kennedy administration to enforce the First and Fifteenth amendments in Mississippi.

SNCC also learned from its mistakes in McComb. It now understood that direct action protests conducted against an intransigent and lawless white establishment could be counterproductive and internally divisive when not endorsed by local black leaders. Moreover, in the Deep South the apparent dichotomy between direct action and voter registration had proven a distinction without a difference. Simply attempting to register could bring on the wrath of the mob. SNCC applied these lessons as it fanned out across the state, particularly into the Mississippi Delta.

6

Into the Delta

Throughout the summer and fall of 1961, as SNCC was developing its first voter registration project in southwest Mississippi, activists in Jackson were encouraging black high school and college students to carry out direct action protests against segregated public facilities. This small SNCC contingent, which included Diane Nash, James Bevel, Lester McKinnie, and Bernard Lafayette, all veterans of the Nashville sit-ins, formed the Jackson Nonviolent Movement and established the first "freedom house" in a black neighborhood on Rose Street. Capitalizing on the enthusiasm generated by the freedom rides, the young organizers found allies at the black colleges. When Jackson State president Jacob Reddix dissolved the student government association, more than 400 students boycotted classes to protest this attempt to put them back in their place. Tougaloo students worked closely with SNCC, forming the Non-Violent Action Group on campus. Among those active in the organization were future SNCC organizers Dorie and Joyce Ladner (who had transferred to Tougaloo from Jackson State), MacArthur Cotton, and Jimmy Travis, as well as Joan Trumpauer, a white freedom rider from Virginia who was now a full-time Tougaloo student.[1]

City officials moved quickly to destroy SNCC's beachhead in Jackson. When Bevel and Lafayette recruited a group of local youths—seven of whom were under eighteen—to go to the bus station, purchase interstate tickets, and then move into the white waiting room, police arrested the SNCC workers and charged them with contributing to the delinquency of minors. On July 19 Bevel and Lafayette were found guilty and received harsh sentences: four consecutive six-month jail terms. The prosecutor offered to suspend the sentences if the two left town, but they turned down the deal and appealed their convictions. Nash had been arrested on the same charge, but her trial was put off until November. Undeterred by the police, SNCC continued to work with the students, organizing a boycott of the segregated Mississippi State Fair. As a squad of pickets marched through the fairgrounds carrying signs reading "No Jim Crow Fair for Us," more than 100 blacks outside the gates staged a demonstration. Jackson police, led by six German shepherd dogs on leash, charged into the demonstrators and arrested seven protestors, four of them Tougaloo students, for "obstructing public sidewalks and streets." As a result of the protest, black attendance at the fair dropped markedly.[2]

Although a number of black adults were supportive, many viewed the new student militancy with concern. As the fair boycott was in full swing, Medgar Evers wrote a "Special Report" to the national NAACP office on "the operation of other civil rights organizations in Mississippi." Evers complained that the Jackson Nonviolent Movement had sponsored "hastily gotten together workshops . . . for the purpose of involving Jackson citizens into the freedom ride movement, which had not been advocated by the NAACP." Gloster Current shared Evers's report with the New York NAACP staff, noting that "this is going to be a continuing problem."[3]

Organizing the black community in Jackson proved as frustrating to SNCC workers as it had been for Evers. The relatively large black middle class, composed mainly of teachers, ministers, and a small but influential group of entrepreneurs, felt threatened by the Jackson Nonviolent Movement and wanted no part of the politics of confrontation. The young activists contributed to the tensions. They soon learned that Jackson was not Nashville. They were now outsiders, and they could not simply move into a community and ignore the existing black leadership. When Dave Dennis, a young black freedom rider from New Orleans, took over as CORE's Mississippi field secretary in the summer of 1962, he reported that "many of the students who came in to organize the Jackson Nonviolent Movement said and did some very harsh things to some of the citizens here who could serve a major part in our work at present but refuse because of this." Some of these slights—such as announcing that the Reverend R. L .T. Smith would speak at a rally without first securing Smith's commitment to do so—could be chalked up to youthful inexperience, but beneath the surface fundamental issues divided the two groups. The conflict was generational, organizational, and ideological. Both sides were attempting to win the hearts and minds of Jackson's black youth, who were ready to move.[4]

Evers admired the SNCC workers' courage and identified with their goals. For years he had worked almost alone to develop strong NAACP youth councils, but now he watched as black teenagers began to gravitate toward the young, hip, more aggressive men and women of SNCC and CORE. These organizers were impatient with the conservative NAACP bureaucracy and said so to anyone who would listen. A few, such as CORE's Tom Gaither, sympathized with Evers's position and regarded the national NAACP office as the source of the problem. Newer recruits criticized Evers personally, exacerbating an already tense situation. In Jackson, as in McComb, SNCC's direct action wing had alienated much of the black middle class. A certain amount of disagreement was inevitable, but the level and intensity of distrust and animosity threatened to destroy the fledgling Mississippi movement from within.[5]

Bob Moses first recognized the need for a united front while in McComb, where local blacks "felt threatened to the point where they really felt the need for unity among themselves to confront the opposition." After moving up to Jackson in December 1961, Moses came to believe that "if you had in this state this real strong feeling for a need for unity, then that becomes a very strong vehicle for building something, because it makes it possible to think of a common program." He talked with key people in the other civil rights organizations and found that they agreed that cooperation was essential to the movement's survival. Out of these discussions COFO was born.[6]

The Council of Federated Organizations was originally put together before the freedom rides in May 1961 by Aaron Henry and other black Mississippians as an ad hoc group that met once with Governor Ross Barnett. In February 1962 SNCC's Bob Moses, Tom Gaither of CORE, and Aaron Henry and Medgar Evers of the NAACP met in Jackson to revamp COFO into an organization incorporating all national, state, and local protest groups operating in the state. Historically, COFO has been viewed primarily as an umbrella agency set up to facilitate the transfer of funds from outside agencies to groups working in the state. COFO directors Moses and Dennis have taken sharp issue with that characterization, pointing out that black Mississippians "wanted to have the feeling that all of their organizations were working together," and thus they developed strong ties to COFO. National civil rights groups were fearful that this new organization might undercut their own fundraising activities. "But always," concluded Dennis, "we come back to the inescapable conclusion that the Negro people in Mississippi needed some organization which could belong to them (as opposed to their belonging to it) which could serve as a unifying force among the isolated Negro communities."[7]

Aaron Henry was COFO's president, but most influential in the COFO operation were Moses as program director and Dennis as assistant director. Although the Southern Christian Leadership Conference also participated, its presence in Mississippi was mostly limited to a voter education "citizenship" program, and it did not play a major role in COFO. The state conference of the NAACP was part of COFO, but the national NAACP, traditionally opposed to such alliances, was not. Local community groups like the Holmes County Voters League also allied with COFO. Thus, "through COFO the drive immediately became local and closer to the people," observed Dennis, who wrote in late 1962 that COFO "has been a very good idea and it has worked extraordinarily well." COFO staff retained their organizational affiliations. With the largest number of field workers in the state, SNCC became the dominant partner. CORE's national office insisted on its own territory, so COFO awarded CORE the fourth congressional district in central Misssissippi, which stretched from Canton east to Meridian. Dennis and Moses worked together closely, and the distinction between CORE and SNCC inside Mississippi was largely "whether one wore a red T-shirt or a blue T-shirt."[8]*

COFO projects were to be funded in part by grants from the Voter Education Project (VEP), administered by the Southern Regional Council. VEP was organized in the aftermath of the freedom

*Throughout the text *COFO* will be used to describe organized movement activity in Mississippi in the early 1960s. The SNCC, CORE, and NAACP projects, however, will continue to be identified by organizational affiliate. It should be understood that all these projects were operating under the COFO umbrella.

rides in the summer of 1961 after a series of meetings involving movement activists, Justice Department officials (including Burke Marshall), and representatives of the Taconic and Field foundations. The civil rights workers attending these sessions were suspicious, believing (correctly) that the Kennedy administration was attempting to influence the movement's direction by providing financial support for voter registration but not for direct action campaigns. Because the activists had already decided to organize around the franchise in Mississippi, they agreed to participate in the VEP program, provided that the federal government pledged to protect voter registration workers. They came away from these meetings convinced that both FBI and Justice Department investigators would be on the scene when trouble arose and would make arrests when federal laws were violated. Justice Department officials later denied they gave any such assurances. Other participants in the discussions, including Leslie Dunbar, head of the Southern Regional Council, insist that they did.[9]

The young activists in Mississippi needed money if they were to survive, so they accepted VEP funds while grumbling about bureaucratic regulations such as having to submit weekly reports from the field. Even with VEP help, the organizers led a spartan existence. The original VEP grant to COFO of $14,000 did not meet basic expenses. SNCC field secretaries, for example, scraped by on weekly stipends of ten dollars, and even these small checks came irregularly. As movement workers in Mississippi expanded their operations, the lack of adequate funding and the absence of federal protection hindered their efforts to unite black communities under the COFO banner.[10]

The most successful example of movement cooperation through COFO occurred in the Delta town of Clarksdale under the leadership of Aaron Henry. A native of Coahoma County, Henry had served for three years in the Pacific during World War II, after which he took a degree in pharmacy at Xavier University in New Orleans. Returning home to Clarksdale in 1950, he managed a drugstore, which he soon bought, and married Noelle Michael. In the 1950s Henry had been one of the "young Turks" challenging both Mississippi segregationists and NAACP leaders who advocated a cautious approach to racial advancement. In his first speech after being elected state NAACP president in 1960, the Clarksdale pharmacist called for a new militancy: "Our actions will probably result in many of us being guests in the jails of the state. We will make these jails Temples of Freedom." Until the summer of 1964, Henry was the most ecumenical of the Mississippi activists, working with and requesting help from all national civil rights groups. Such an independent stance did not endear him to Roy Wilkins and Gloster Current.[11]

The Clarksdale movement began over a racial snub. Every year "since God knows when," two black marching bands from the local high school and Coahoma Junior College had participated in the annual Clarksdale Christmas parade. But in November 1961 the new mayor, a segregationist hard-liner, persuaded the local chamber of commerce, which sponsored the parade, to cancel its invitations to the two bands. Angry students were set to march on city hall. No doubt with the recent student march in McComb fresh in his mind, Henry persuaded the students not to demonstrate. "There were too many students and too much bond money involved to go into this without it being well-planned in advance," Henry informed Current. Instead, he suggested a boycott of downtown merchants, since the chamber of commerce was ultimately responsible for withdrawing the invitation. The NAACP-led campaign adopted the following slogan: "If we can't PARADE downtown should we TRADE downtown?"[12]

Withholding trade from local white merchants would become a popular strategy in Mississippi, first in Clarksdale, then in Jackson, and later in communities throughout the state. Unlike signing school petitions, attempting to register to vote, or marching in picket lines, the boycott guaranteed a large degree of anonymity to the participants: the whole idea of the boycott was *not* to do something. Moreover, by refusing to buy groceries, clothes, and appliances from whites, blacks hit the merchants where it hurt most—in the cash register. More than half of Clarksdale's 21,000 residents were black, and Coahoma County was nearly 70 percent black. A successful boycott would either win the desired concessions or drive merchants out of business. Carrying on a boycott, however, required both unity and staying power. Whites would enlist their traditional black allies to discredit the boycott and eventually threaten boycotters with loss of jobs. The local press could be counted on to minimize the impact of the boycott, if the newspapers mentioned it at all.

By the end of November, Henry reported the boycott was "about 40 percent" successful, conceding that "we have a lot of work to do to make it truly effective." As in McComb, black youth led the way. "The best assist that we have had," Henry informed Current, "is that the school children have won the support of their parents in not going downtown." The goal of the boycott soon moved beyond the right to march in a town parade. By early 1962 the Clarksdale movement was demanding that merchants employ blacks "above the menial level" and use courtesy titles when addressing black customers. Later the agenda expanded to encompass voting rights, school desegregation, integration of public facilities, and formation of an interracial committee. Local whites were determined not to budge on any of these issues.[13]

During the first week of December, with the boycott still in its first month, police arrested Henry and four other Coahoma County NAACP officers, including youth council advisor Vera Pigee, charging them with conducting an illegal boycott. The group drew six-month jail sentences and $600 fines. NAACP lawyers posted bonds and filed an appeal. The arrests united the community behind the boycott, but harassment continued. Early in March, Henry was convicted on a trumped-up charge of molesting a white hitchhiker. When the NAACP leader accused the county attorney and the police chief of framing him, they countered with a libel suit and won $40,000 in damages. Shortly thereafter, Noelle Henry was fired from her teaching job.[14]

To counter these measures, Henry called in support from national civil rights organizations. Martin Luther King was among the first to respond. Addressing an audience of 1,000 Clarksdale blacks in early April 1962, the SCLC leader praised Henry and urged local people to "stand in, sit in, and walk in by the thousands." CORE sent in Tom Gaither to assist in the boycott. Gaither even edited the NAACP newsletter once when Henry was out of town. SNCC workers were in and out of the county to encourage voter registration and to help where needed in Clarksdale. Henry also enlisted the support of virtually every local black advancement group in the county, from the local chapter of the Mississippi Progressive Voters' League to the Coahoma County Ministerial Council. A respected and successful businessman with a down-home manner, Henry had won the endorsement of the black middle class to pursue a militant program, a considerable political achievement. Although the national NAACP had pledged support, Wilkins and Current were growing increasingly apprehensive over Henry's inviting

CORE, SNCC, and the SCLC to participate in what had begun as an NAACP operation. Still, the Clarksdale movement was unique in that it combined widespread support from the black middle class and a high degree of cooperation among competing civil rights organizations. Nevertheless, despite the remarkable degree of unity and the boycott's impact on the local economy, white officials refused even to meet with Henry and other black leaders. There matters stood in the summer of 1962.[15]

Down in Jackson, movement activity had continued throughout the spring and early summer of 1962, with mixed results. The NAACP kept up its voter registration efforts, as did CORE's Dave Dennis. Although he was living in Jackson, Bob Moses spent much time on the road, holding workshops on civil liberties and the philosophy of nonviolence in connection with the Mississippi Adult Education Program. The Jackson Nonviolent Movement promoted direct action, calling for a boycott of city buses to protest segregated seating, which had continued despite the Supreme Court's decision that such practices were unconstitutional. The boycott, along with a suit filed by the NAACP, resulted in the removal of signs designating segregated seating in the buses, but buses throughout Mississippi remained segregated, and challenges to that practice could produce tragic results. On April 16 army corporal Roman Duckworth, who was in Taylorsville to visit his ailing wife, refused to move to the back of a Trailways bus. In an altercation that followed, a city policeman shot and killed the unarmed serviceman. No charges were filed, and the murder of Corporal Duckworth received little media attention.[16]

In late April Diane Nash, now married to James Bevel, decided to abandon the appeal of her conviction the previous year on the charge of contributing to the delinquency of minors and to serve her two-year jail sentence. Expecting her first child in November, Nash concluded that "I can no longer cooperate with the evil and unjust court system of this state." When asked about the effect of her decision on her child, she replied, "This will be a black child born in Mississippi and thus wherever he is born he will be in prison. I believe that if I go to jail now it may help hasten the day when my child and all children will be free—not only on the day of their birth but for all of their lives." Judge Russell Moore delayed his decision on her request to serve her sentence but jailed her for ten days for refusing to sit in the "colored" section of the courtroom.

Three weeks later Moore ruled that Nash could not give up her appeal. SNCC workers Jesse Harris and Luvaughn Brown also refused to sit in the segregated section at the hearing, and Moore sentenced them to forty days at hard labor at the Hinds County prison farm, where they were repeatedly beaten by guards. On June 2 four members of the Jackson Nonviolent Movement who were protesting the arrests of Harris and Brown were arrested on the steps of the Federal Building.[17]

Although the daily newspapers reported these actions, and the new movement-oriented weekly, the *Mississippi Free Press,* provided detailed accounts, Jackson's 50,000 black residents did not rally to the defense of the SNCC workers. Without community support, the young activists were fair game for the local authorities, who jailed them every time they attempted a protest. By midsummer the Jackson Nonviolent Movement was in disarray. Dennis believed that local blacks were afraid to associate with the SNCC workers because "many people fear radical organizations." He also noted the lack of participation by "the ministers and other leading citizens." Without much support or money to pay their bills, the SNCC organizers concluded that Jackson was not yet ready for a campaign centered on militant protest. Several staff people, including Nash and Bevel, moved up to Cleveland, staying with Amzie Moore while they planned their next move.[18]

Direct action campaigns to desegregate public facilities had never held much interest for Moore, who two years earlier had persuaded Bob Moses that voter registration was the only viable program for Mississippi. Moore and Moses now envisioned a cadre of dedicated, full-time organizers fanning out across the Delta, enlisting the vast black majorities in county after county to attack the forces of white supremacy where they were most vulnerable—at the ballot box.[19]

Given the reality of life in the Delta, SNCC's mission appeared foolhardy, if not suicidal. This was the place where the Reverend George Lee had been gunned down for encouraging blacks to vote and Emmett Till had been lynched for allegedly whistling at a white woman. The fundamental problems facing blacks in Mississippi—racism, poverty, lack of educational opportunity—were writ large in the Delta. The big cotton plantation remained the dominant economic and cultural fact of life in the region, with blacks working as sharecroppers and increasingly as day laborers on land owned by whites. By the early 1960s, however, chemical weed killers and mechanical cotton pickers had displaced enough farm workers to create a surplus of black labor. The usual wage of three dollars a day for seasonal fieldwork led to widespread poverty and malnutrition. In 1960 three-fourths of all Delta families had incomes below the $3,000 poverty line; the median annual income for black families ranged from a high of $1,600 in Washington County to a low of $819 in Quitman County.[20]

Education, still segregated, offered no escape. Delta schools were the worst in the state. One classroom teacher in Ruleville "taught" seventy-seven students. Outdated textbooks, nonexistent libraries, and poorly prepared and underpaid teachers were the norm. White superintendents and school boards demanded that black teachers toe the Jim Crow line and avoid all civil rights activity. Some teachers even acted as labor agents for the plantation owners, forcing students to pick cotton each fall "to raise money for the school."[21]

Given the repressive atmosphere and lack of economic opportunity due to the mechanization of the cotton economy, many young blacks migrated to southern cities or to the North as soon as they came of age, in search of jobs and a better life. SNCC organizer Michael Thelwell worked in the Delta and observed the phenomenon: "This gap between generations lies like a blight on every Negro community, and especially in the Delta. You see it in any kind of meeting, in the churches—any gathering of Negroes in Mississippi consists of teenagers and older people."[22] These two groups formed the SNCC constituency in the Delta.

Where the voter registration campaigns of the 1940s and 1950s had been based in the cities and dominated by the NAACP, SNCC organizers in the Delta found the rural poor to be their natural constituency. Not since Reconstruction had anyone seriously proposed that illiterate sharecroppers had the same right to the franchise as did teachers, lawyers, and doctors. Donning overalls and work shirts, SNCC workers sneaked onto the vast plantations to talk with people who had never thought about voting in an election. Mrs. Fannie Lou Hamer described the impact of SNCC's work there:

Nobody never come out into the country and talked to real farmers . . . because this is the next thing this country has done: it divided us into classes, and if you hadn't arrived at a certain level, you wasn't treated no better by blacks than you was by the whites. And it was these kids what broke a lot of this down. They treated us like we were special and we loved 'em. . . . We didn't feel uneasy about our language might not be right or something. We just felt like we could talk to 'em. We trusted 'em.[23]

To gain the trust of Delta blacks, SNCC relied on older people for access into the community. Amzie Moore was the key figure, a mentor. Besides providing food and lodging for SNCC workers, Moore introduced them to respected local people who then spread the word that these young activists were there to help. Wherever movement organizers went in Mississippi, adults in their fifties, sixties, and seventies provided entrée into the black community. Although these men and women often had NAACP connections, they were not part of the local black elite. By and large, the professionals and ministers initially held back from supporting the movement. It was the small, independent farmers, along with a few struggling entrepreneurs, who risked their livelihoods and lives to legitimize the movement in their communities. Once the organizers had established a beachhead, local youth, mostly junior high and high school students, provided the energy and enthusiasm to carry the movement to its next stage.

The majority of the SNCC (and CORE) field secretaries in Mississippi were black men. They were the shock troops of the movement, the intitial contingent of organizers to move into McComb, Hattiesburg, Holly Springs, Canton, and the cities and small towns of the Delta. Having established a presence in the community, they became the focus of white hostility, as well as a source of inspiration for the local blacks who took them in and joined the struggle. There was, then, some continuity between the male-led NAACP campaigns of the 1950s and the movement of the 1960s.

Moreover, the cadre of young male organizers had assimilated much of the notion of "woman's proper place" then dominant in the larger American society. For example, men often assigned to themselves the most dangerous work, such as canvassing on white-owned plantations. Male chauvinism also manifested itself in other forms, and numerous examples of discrimination against women in the movement can be (and have been) recited. Still, SNCC activists never lost sight of their primary goal of black empowerment, and the organization's antibureaucratic, antihierarchical structure encouraged the contribution of people whose talents had hitherto been ignored. Local black women, as movement scholar Charles Payne has pointed out, "represented an enormous pool of untapped leadership potential . . . [and SNCC] was structurally open to female participation in a way that many older organizations would not have been."[24]

Beginning with the Delta campaign, women entered the movement in large numbers, participating in all phases of activity. They constituted a majority at the mass meetings, did voter registration work, led marches to the courthouse, served time in prison, and later ran for Congress. In his study of the movement in Greenwood, Payne found that a number of mothers came into the movement because of their children's involvement and that the strong religious beliefs of many black women gave them both the courage to participate and the conviction that the movement would succeed. Devotion to their churches was easily transferable to the movement, even when their ministers declined to participate.[25]

Although the movement of the 1960s did not eliminate gender discrimination within its ranks, it came closer to the ideal of an egalitarian community than had any major social movement in this nation's history. Wherever one looked in Mississippi in the 1960s, women were in the forefront of the movement. Fannie Lou Hamer is but the most widely acclaimed of a generation of women who influenced first the course of the black struggle and later the women's liberation movement. In 1964 she would be joined by Victoria Gray and Annie Devine in challenging the white men then representing their districts in Congress. The Mississippi movement, in short, was a liberating experience for thousands of black women.

A final point of contrast between the movement of the 1960s and its predecessor was ideological. The older NAACP leaders had come of age during the New Deal. They believed change had to come gradually, under the watchful eye of a strong and active federal government. Few were political radicals. Their goal was "simply" to abolish all forms of racial discrimination in the state, so that blacks might obtain their fair share of the American Dream. Many younger activists came into the movement committed to these same principles. And though they wanted "more than a hamburger," they had not developed an economic program that addressed the inequalities inherent in American capitalism. Experiences in the field, however, radicalized movement organizers. Working in the most poverty-stricken sections of America, they came to see that eliminating segregation, even obtaining the vote, would not fundamentally change the lives of the black poor.

As the struggle in Mississipppi intensified, the young activists began to lose faith in liberal institutions, particularly the federal government. What angered organizers most was not the behavior of white racists—for this was expected—but rather the federal government's failure to enforce the United States Constitution in Mississippi. Still, movement workers could not afford to turn their backs on Washington in the early 1960s, for along with the growing determination of blacks to defend themselves, the possibility of federal intervention had prevented white Mississippi from taking even more drastic action against the movement. An increased federal presence, some activists believed, would help break down the fear and isolation that kept many blacks from joining the struggle.

Organizers in Mississippi thus had to operate on two levels. Their major task was grass-roots organizing, first in the Delta and later in other areas of the state, working quietly and patiently to develop local leadership. At the same time, the movement needed to attract publicity to create public demand for federal protection. These two thrusts—low-key, long-term organizing and dramatic exposure of white lawlessness in areas where the movement was operating—were in a sense contradictory, creating internal tensions that later surfaced during the debate over bringing in hundreds of northern volunteers during the summer of 1964.[26]

• • •

When Sam Block began walking the streets of Greenwood he set in motion a movement that would involve thousands of Delta blacks in a militant campaign to overthrow a system that had oppressed them since the days of slavery. Block had grown up in Cleveland, Mississippi, where he came under the influence of Amzie Moore. Along with Bevel and Moses, Moore had convinced Block to work full-time in the movement, and on June 18, 1962, Moses took the twenty-three-year-old Block to Greenwood to begin organizing the black community. "I had no car, no money, no clothes, no food," recalls Block, "just me."[27]

Located in the eastern section of the Delta, eighty miles due north of Jackson, Greenwood is the Leflore county seat. In the early sixties nearly two-thirds of the county's 50,000 residents were black, but only 250 were registered to vote. Whites owned 90 percent of the land and had a median income three times that of blacks. The self-styled "Long-Staple Cotton Capital of the World," Greenwood was the center of the Mississippi cotton trade, processing more than 800,000 bales each year. The long row of elegant mansions on Royal Boulevard testified to the affluence of the cotton elite, who controlled the county and opposed any changes in the racial status quo. All public facilities were segregated. The state headquarters of the Citizens' Council was in Greenwood, along with a chapter of the ultraright John Birch Society. All in all, Greenwood seemed an unlikely spot for SNCC's first major Delta campaign.[28]

Sam Block was no stranger to Greenwood. He had attended Mississippi Vocational College in nearby Itta Bena, and with the help of several of his Greenwood classmates he found housing in the city with Mrs. E. H. McNease, the principal of the black elementary school, who "really didn't know then why I was there." Each morning the tall, gaunt young visitor from Cleveland went into the community, hanging out in the laundromats, grocery stores, pool halls, and juke joints—wherever local people congregated—listening to people's problems and subtly introducing the topic of voter registration. Block soon learned that the "people who were most receptive to me were the older people.... The movement in Greenwood was built with older people who were angry, who were looking for somebody who could give form and expression to ideas and thoughts that they had had in mind for years, that they wanted to do and just couldn't bring together."[29]

Block's initial contact was Cleveland Jordan, a World War II veteran who had first attempted to register in 1951 and had been encouraging blacks to go down to the courthouse ever since. Jordan introduced Block to others who had been active in the past, including members of the Leflore County Voters' League. Jordan also used his influence to make the Elks Hall available for meetings. Block proceeded cautiously, asking local leaders for their help but never pressuring them to make a total commitment. (As one SNCC activist later observed, in Greenwood "certain people were afraid to do one thing but would do another.")[30]

By late June, Block had gathered fifteen or twenty people for the first organizational meeting at the Elks Hall. After the second meeting, when he started teaching people freedom songs, the Elks closed their doors to Block, afraid that whites would now identify their

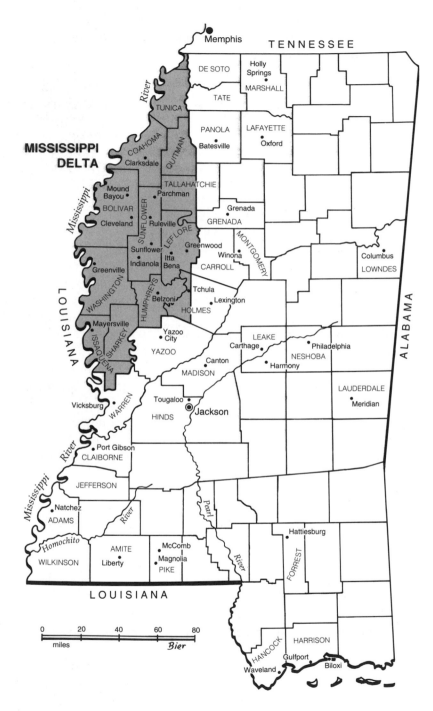

Map 2. Centers of Civil Rights Activity

lodge as a center for civil rights activity. The Citizens' Council was now onto Block, and Mrs. McNease had to evict her unpopular boarder. For the next week Block slept in a car in a junkyard until he found more suitable accommodations. But the SNCC organizer's patient approach paid off when the Reverend Aaron Johnson agreed to host a meeting at his First Christian Church.[31]

The "mass meeting" was perhaps the movement's most effective organizing tool, the culmination of weeks of one-on-one conversations concerning the problems that individuals faced in the community. Michael Thelwell described a typical Delta meeting:

> The meeting is called for eight, but will not really get started much before nine, as the women must feed their white folks their suppers before going home to feed their own families. But folks start gathering from seven. They use the time to "testify": to talk about whatever troubles their minds—mostly the absence of food, money, work, and the oppressiveness of the police. They talk about loss of credit, eviction, and voting, three things which form an inseparable unity in the Delta. . . . In the meetings everything—uncertainty, fear, even desperation—finds expression, and there is comfort and sustenance in "talkin' 'bout hit."[32]

For Bob Moses, the meeting was "an energy machine."[33] The combination of spontaneous testimony, old-fashioned preaching, wickedly hilarious observations about the character of the white opposition, and inspiring oratory from the young organizers transformed powerless individuals. Local people were especially moved to action by the freedom songs.

The day after the first gathering at Reverend Johnson's church, Sam Block recalled, "as I walked the streets I met a lot of people, and the thing that they remembered most about that meeting was the songs we were singing. And they asked me when we were going to have another meeting and sing those songs." In the Mississippi Delta the blues had sustained a generation of sharecroppers through lives bleak and without hope, and in the churches spirituals and gospel music held forth the promise of a rich life in the hereafter. The freedom songs sprang from this cultural tradition. Movement songwriters added political lyrics to traditional melodies, even adapting movement themes to current rhythm-and-blues hits. In addition, there were original compositions such as Bertha Gober's "We'll Never Turn

Back," the haunting anthem of the Mississippi movement, written in memory of the martyred Herbert Lee. Initially surprised at the response to the songs he led at that first meeting, Block soon "began to see the music itself as an important organizing tool to really bring people together—not only to bring them together but also as the organizational glue to hold them together."[34]

Throughout July 1962 Block worked alone and without pay. "I cannot send a budget for this week," he informed SNCC headquarters on July 26, "because I did not have any money to spend anyway." But the young organizer was making progress. He had secured both lodging and office space from a local black photographer, Robert Burns, and the backing of Jerry Chestnut, an insurance agent. A young pool hall owner donated ten dollars and promised to contribute more. Block began to recruit a cadre of local people to assist with canvassing and voter registration classes. Dewey Greene, Jr., a navy veteran now attending Mississippi Vocational College, became Block's most valuable co-worker.[35]

In early August, Block accompanied four local residents, a man and three women, to the courthouse. After some intimidation, the deputy registrar allowed the applicants to take the test, and they left without incident. When Block arrived home he received a call from a man identifying himself as speaking for the Citizens' Council, who warned the SNCC organizer that "if you take anybody else up to register you'll never leave Greenwood alive." Undeterred, Block took two other applicants to the courthouse. The registrar, Martha Lamb, summoned the police, who followed the registrants home and took down their addresses. On August 13 three white men jumped Block on a Greenwood street, dragged him into a vacant lot, and beat him.[36]

If SNCC were to continue to function in Greenwood, then Block could no longer operate alone. Three days after the attack on Block SNCC field secretaries Lawrence Guyot, a Tougaloo student from the Gulf Coast, and eighteen-year-old Luvaughn Brown joined Block at the SNCC office at 616 Avenue I. The new recruits found that the Citizens' Council pressures were taking their toll. Only three of the ten people who had agreed to register showed up. Brown tried to persuade the others of "the need to stand up and demand their rights and vote—but to no avail." When the three registrants arrived at the courthouse, the police chief cursed and threatened them, and they turned back.

Much later that night, as Block, Guyot, and Brown were trying "to find a way to get some of the fear out of people we were working with," they looked out the window of their second-floor office and saw a police car. Five minutes later the car moved on, but a second car had driven up filled with men carrying what looked like shotguns. Block tried to call Moses at Amzie Moore's home in Cleveland but could not get through. Then he placed a collect call to John Doar of the Justice Department, who conceded that their lives were in danger but offered no help except to suggest that they get out of the building. As eight men armed with guns, ropes, bricks, and chains piled out of the car and climbed the stairs, the three SNCC organizers scrambled out the bathroom window onto a neighboring roof. Crawling to the front of the building, they saw another car pull up carrying men similarly armed. The SNCC workers jumped to another roof, slid down a television antenna, and disappeared into black Greenwood. Stopping at the home of a man who had befriended the movement, they called Moses in Cleveland to report the incident. Early the next morning the SNCC workers returned to their office to find the door kicked in, files strewn across the floor, and Bob Moses and Willie Peacock asleep on the couch.[37]

A Delta native and graduate of Rust College in Holly Springs, Peacock was making plans to go north to earn money for graduate school when Moses and Moore persuaded him to stay in the Delta and work in a new SNCC project in Sunflower County. Peacock was at Moore's home when the emergency call came from Block, and he and Moses immediately headed for Greenwood, less than an hour's drive away. They arrived at the SNCC office around 2:00 A.M. to find it trashed and abandoned. It was Peacock's baptism into the movement:

We just walked in and Bob Moses went ahead of me into the office . . . turned the light on, let the couch out and put the covers on, turned on the fan, which makes a lot of noise and went to bed. I was very—I was scared. I just didn't understand what kind of guy this Bob Moses is, that could walk into a place where a lynch mob had just left and make up a bed and prepare to go to sleep, as if the situation was normal. So I guess I was learning, and I said, well, if Bob can go to sleep, I can go to sleep, so I guess about five minutes after I got in the bed I was asleep.[38]

The following day the SNCC organizers discussed the future of the Leflore County project. Since this was the opening wedge in a voter registration drive that would encompass six Delta counties, it was essential that SNCC remain in Greenwood. But the situation was critical. Fear was now endemic in the black community. Reverend Johnson remained the only minister supporting the movement, and no teachers had dared to take a stand. Block had just learned that the Citizens' Council had pressured Robert Burns to evict SNCC from his building. Block clearly needed support from the outside, but no one was eager to work full-time in Greenwood. Finally Peacock, who was scheduled to organize in Ruleville, volunteered to stay: "I got patriotic, since I had waited an hour I guess for somebody to get patriotic, I said, 'well, I'll stay,' and no one challenged me. Well, so there I was."[39]

For the next six months Block and Peacock maintained a holding operation in Greenwood: "From August to the first of next year all we were able to do was to walk the community," recalled Peacock. For a time they were ostracized by local blacks. "People would just get afraid of me," Block reported. "Women told their daughters, don't have anything to do with me . . . because I was a Freedom Rider. I was there to stir up trouble, that's all." The two field secretaries did not eat regularly; Peacock had to beg for a pair of shoes; without a car, they canvassed the countryside on a mule. Still, their spirits remained high. "We ain't complaining," Peacock wrote. "We just go on and raise hell all the time. We don't have to ride, we can walk, we don't care."[40]

The SNCC activists had two immediate goals in Greenwood: to show they were not there simply to stir up trouble and then leave, and to help local blacks overcome the paralyzing fear that had stopped the registration drive. Thus, when the county sheriff confronted Block in a crowd of blacks and told him, "I don't want to see you in town anymore. The best thing you better do is pack your clothes and get out and don't ever come back no more," Block shot back defiantly, "Well, sheriff, if you don't want to see me here, I think the best thing for you to do is pack *your* clothes and leave, get out of town, cause I'm here to stay."[41] Such bravado was calculated. Block knew nobody talked to the sheriff that way and that word of this confrontation would quickly circulate through the black community.

That Block was able to back down a sheriff and survive may

appear incredible, but SNCC's experience in Greenwood was part of a pattern repeated in other projects. When organizers first moved into a community, whites responded violently, yet after a time, as movement historian Howard Zinn has observed, "the SNCC people become part of the community." What initially appeared strange and threatening—door-to-door canvassing, meetings in local churches—"actually becomes a part of the pattern of the community. And while the violence certainly does not stop, it doesn't take on the same consistent, frenzied character that it had at the beginning, when there is a first appearance of this phenomenon in the town." Of course, once the movement adopted new tactics, such as mass marches, the level of violence would once again intensify. One by one, blacks overcame their fears. Students like June Johnson and Lenora Brewer, defying their high school counselors, began to hang out at the SNCC office and then joined in the door-to-door canvassing. Beautician Hattie Smith offered to house the field secretaries, and businessmen raised funds for a SNCC office.[42]

In Greenwood entire families became active in the movement. The children of Dewey Greene, Sr., president of the local NAACP in the 1950s, were among the first to join with the SNCC organizers. Mrs. Laura McGhee, the younger sister of Belzoni activist Gus Courts, used her small farm outside Greenwood for meetings and to secure bail bonds for arrested workers. Her sons, Silas, Jake, and Clarence, became legendary for their dedication and courage. June Johnson's family had had no previous history of civil rights involvement, and her early interest in SNCC drew reprimands from her mother. Eventually, the teenager won her over, and Mrs. Belle Johnson became one of the movement's stalwarts.[43]

The Greenwood voter registration drive was only one of a half-dozen SNCC-led COFO projects underway in Mississippi during the late summer of 1962. By then Hollis Watkins and Curtis Hayes were working down in Hattiesburg, and Frank Smith was organizing in Marshall County in the north-central part of the state. There had also been a short-lived project in Vicksburg. The Jackson operation shut down in September, as activists there moved on to the new projects. In addition to organizing in Greenwood, SNCC workers fanned out into other areas of the Delta, walking the streets of Ruleville, Greenville, and Clarksdale, encouraging people to register to vote. The programs were coordinated from Cleveland, where Moses had set up shop with Amzie Moore.[44]

Aside from Greenwood, SNCC's major initiative in the Delta was Sunflower County, site of Parchman penitentiary, birthplace of the Citizens' Council, and home of Senator James Eastland, who operated a 2,000-acre plantation near Doddsville. Blacks constituted a two-to-one majority in Sunflower, but whites owned 90 percent of the land, and the average black income was between $400 and $600 a year. Of the more than 13,000 blacks eligible to vote, fewer than 200 were on the books. Although Indianola was the largest town and the county seat, SNCC opened its first drive in Ruleville, twenty-three miles to the north. SNCC staff members had made several short visits to Ruleville, and local people were soon making the half-hour drive to Indianola to try to register. In contrast to blacks in Greenwood, where Block at first felt like a pariah, Ruleville blacks welcomed the SNCC workers, particularly Charles McLaurin, who had volunteered to head the project.[45]

Although only twenty-one, McLaurin was a movement veteran. The Jackson native first became active during the freedom rides. He was jailed during the protests at the state fair in 1961 and arrested twice more before coming to the Delta, serving seventeen days in prison. Arriving in Ruleville in early August, McLaurin was taken in by Joe and Rebecca McDonald, who would be mainstays of the Ruleville movement. "We were able to keep a place to stay because of Mr. Joe and his wife," McLaurin recalled. "Many times the mayor told Mr. Joe to get us out of his house or he would have real trouble, but Mr. Joe stood his ground." Although he soon lost his job, McDonald continued to support the movement. As Fannie Lou Hamer put it, "Brother Joe McDonald stood there until he died."[46]

Later in the month McLaurin made his first trip to the courthouse, accompanying three elderly women. As they approached the courthouse, McLaurin was overcome with fear, "realizing what danger could lie ahead for us, especially me." Then he suddenly realized that he "was no longer in command, the three ladies were leading me, I was following them." With pride and amazement, he looked on as the women got out of the car and "went up the walk to the courthouse as if this was the long walk that led to the Golden Gate of Heaven, their heads held high." As it turned out, they were not permitted to register that day; the door to the clerk's office was locked. For McLaurin, however, this was "the day that I became a man." He had recruited these three women, explained the registration procedures, and "when that day came I followed them.

The people are the true leaders. We need only to move them, to show them. Then watch and learn."[47]

The following week Fannie Lou Hamer was part of a group of eighteen people who tried to register. The youngest of twenty children in a family of sharecroppers, Mrs. Hamer had lived all but two of her forty-four years in Sunflower County. For eighteen years she and her husband "Pap" had worked on the B. D. Marlowe plantation, where they had sharecropped and she was timekeeper. At the courthouse only Mrs. Hamer and one other Ruleville resident were permitted to take the registration test. That night Marlowe came down to the Hamers' house and demanded that she withdraw her application. When Mrs. Hamer responded that "I didn't go down there to register for you, I went down there to register for myself," Marlowe threw her off his plantation. She spent that night with the Tuckers, friends in Ruleville.[48]

Marlowe's response was typical, for in Ruleville all the now-familiar Citizens' Council techniques immediately came into play. The local newspaper published the names of blacks who tried to register. Mayor Charles M. Durrough, who was *the* law in Ruleville, began harassing SNCC organizers from the moment they set foot in his town. Durrough used local ordinances and state laws to punish local blacks for stepping out of line. On the first Sunday in September, the mayor closed all black businesses, enforcing the state's blue laws for the first time within memory. He canceled the tax-exempt status of the Williams Chapel Missionary Baptist Church, which had welcomed the SNCC field secretaries, because they were "using the building for purposes other than worship services." Durrough dismissed a sanitation worker whose wife had attended SNCC's registration classes. Two black dry-cleaning establishments, including that of the father of SNCC recruit Lafayette Surney, were closed down for minor violations of city ordinances. White employers fired black workers with any connection to the registration campaign. Fred Hicks, who drove cotton workers to the plantations, lost the use of the bus he had been renting because his mother had attempted to register. The owner warned him, "We gonna see how tight we can make it—gonna make it just as tight as we can. Gonna be rougher and rougher than you think it is."[49]

When "legal" methods failed to stop the registration drive, night riders went into action. Ten days after Mrs. Hamer's eviction from the Marlowe plantation, a car drove by the Tuckers' house and pumped sixteen bullets into the bedroom where she had been staying. By this time Mrs. Hamer had moved in with her niece and no one was hit. Marylene Burks and Vivian Hillet were not so fortunate. The two girls were visiting in the home of Vivian's grandparents, Herman and Hattie Sisson, active movement supporters, when gunshots ripped into the house. Burks was shot in the head; Hillet was wounded in the arms and legs. Shortly before, occupants of a speeding car had fired into the home of the McDonalds. When SNCC worker Charlie Cobb, a Howard student organizing in Greenville, went to the hospital to visit the young women, Mayor Durrough arrested him, charging that Cobb shot into the home as a publicity stunt to raise money for SNCC.[50]

The shooting of the two young girls halted the Ruleville registration campaign. "After that," recalled Charlie Cobb, "you just couldn't get anybody to register." Although no one would now dare come to the voter education classes, SNCC workers remained on the scene, chopping wood, picking cotton, assisting the local people however they could. As with Peacock and Block in Greenwood, McLaurin and the other organizers working in Ruleville knew they had to remain. "It's very important that the Negroes in the community feel that you're . . . going to ride through whatever trouble arrives," explained Moses. "And in general, the deeper the fear, the deeper the problems in the community, the longer you have to stay to convince them."[51] There matters stood in the early fall of 1962. By then, grass-roots organizing in the Delta was being overshadowed by a sideshow in Oxford.

• • •

James Meredith's admission to the University of Mississippi is of signal importance in the battle against Jim Crow in the Magnolia State. Meredith became a powerful symbol for local blacks, who identified with him and closely followed the events unfolding in Oxford. Meredith's decision to desegregate the university was personal, however, not part of any COFO strategy. Always a loner, he only reluctantly accepted counsel from the NAACP Legal Defense Fund and did not attempt to enlist support from the black community. Despite its significance, then, desegregation of the University of Mississippi was not a "movement" campaign or priority. In fact, its immediate impact was to intensify white resistance to COFO activity in the Delta and throughout the state.

A native of Kosciusko, Meredith was born poor in a family of ten children. To escape the cycle of poverty, "J.M." enlisted in the air force in 1951. After eight years in the service Meredith decided to attend college, enrolling at Jackson State in 1960. While there he informed Medgar Evers that he was going to apply to Ole Miss and asked whether the NAACP would provide legal help if the university turned him down. Evers promised support.[52]

Meredith formally applied for admission to the University of Mississippi early in 1962. The NAACP defense team, headed by Constance Baker Motley and Derrick Bell, successfully countered efforts by Mississippi officials to deny him admission. Throughout the spring and summer, as the courts rejected appeal after appeal, Mississippi governor Ross Barnett began to call for resistance. On September 13, when the Fifth Circuit Court of Appeals demanded Meredith's immediate enrollment, the governor went on state television to invoke the long-discredited doctrine of interposition, pledging that "no school will be integrated in Mississippi while I am your governor" and demanding the resignation of any state official "who is not prepared to suffer imprisonment for this righteous cause. . . . We will not drink from the cup of genocide."[53]

Barnett's inflammatory rhetoric met with almost unanimous approval from the state's elected officials. With the exception of Congressman Frank Smith, the Delta moderate recently defeated for reelection, all of Mississippi's congressional delegation, including both senators, praised Barnett's defiance. State representative Karl Wiesenburg, who with Joe Wroten stood alone in the legislature against the governor, later wrote that "the leaders of nearly every community, bankers, lawyers, businessmen and workers went on an orgy of rebellion against constituted authority and the federal government."[54]

As the time for Meredith's enrollment drew near, a condition bordering on hysteria swept the state. Radio stations blared "Dixie" as announcers began the countdown to the final confrontation. When a rumor surfaced that Barnett was about to be arrested, thousands of loyal citizens surrounded the governor's mansion to protect him. On Saturday, September 29, the night before Meredith moved onto the Ole Miss campus, the school's football team was playing against Kentucky at Memorial Stadium in Jackson. At halftime the crowd demanded that Barnett speak to them. The governor rose, waving his arm in defiance, and shouted into the microphones, "I love Mississippi! I love her people! I love our customs!" These three short sentences sent the crowd into a frenzy. Gerald Blessey, an Ole Miss student at the time (and later mayor of Biloxi), was at the game: "I looked back at the crowd and I saw anger in the faces of the people right next to me, and it sort of flashed through my mind that those Rebel flags looked like swastikas. . . . [These] were just ordinary school kids who were being whipped into a fever-pitch of emotion by their own leaders. . . . it was just like the Nazis had done."[55]

The 46,000 spectators would have been horrified to learn that for the past two weeks Barnett had been in secret negotiations with Robert and John Kennedy over the logistics of Meredith's admission to the university. The Kennedys were unenthusiastic about Meredith's application, yet in the face of a constitutional crisis they had no choice but to insist that he be enrolled. Relying on Barnett's promise to keep order on the campus, the Justice Department sent only a small contingent of federal marshals to accompany Meredith into Oxford, keeping the army on call in Memphis. Trusting Ross Barnett to keep his word was the biggest of several mistakes the Kennedys made during the crisis.[56]

The Ole Miss riot of Sunday, September 30, 1962, became page-one news throughout the world. Before the nightmare had ended two men lay dead, a French reporter and an Oxford bystander. One hundred and sixty marshals were injured, twenty-eight of them by gunfire. While Meredith was under heavy guard in a dormitory (marshals with him had orders to "shoot anybody that puts a hand on him"), the bulk of the federal force had gathered in front of the lyceum in the middle of campus. There they suffered verbal and then physical abuse from a crowd of students and outsiders, which swelled to 3,000 before the night ended.[57]

By 7:30 P.M. the crowd was throwing bricks, bottles, and Molotov cocktails at the marshals and setting fire to vehicles thought to be federal property. At this point state senator George Yarborough, Governor Barnett's personal representative on the scene, ordered the Mississippi State Highway Patrol to withdraw. This force was the key to preserving order, and Barnett had promised that it would remain on campus. An enraged Robert Kennedy demanded their return. Some state troopers did come back, only to be caught in the first barrage of tear gas from the besieged marshals. (By that time eight marshals had been injured by flying objects.) Infuriated, the state police withdrew again, giving the crowd   now a mob   free rein. At this point the president had gone on national television to make a conciliatory speech and appeal for calm, unaware that all hell was breaking loose at Ole Miss.[58]

Within an hour after Kennedy's speech the first gunshots rang out, and the startled marshals saw one of their colleagues bleeding profusely from the neck. Another was hit in the leg. As the casualties mounted, the marshals requested permission to fire back, but Washington refused. Efforts by Ole Miss professors Jim Silver and Evans Harrington, along with the Reverend Duncan Gray, to talk sense to the students had been of no avail, but the gunfire frightened many of them back to their dormitories. The violence intensified as heavily armed outsiders took over the campus, incited by retired army general Edwin Walker, who for days had been urging patriotic Americans to join him at Oxford.[59]

By ten o'clock it was apparent in Washington that the army was needed to put down the riot, and Robert Kennedy sent word to Memphis to have the troops moved out. Because of an incredible series of snafus, however, it took over four hours for the soldiers to cover the sixty-five miles from Memphis to Oxford. At 2:15 A.M., with the marshals' supply of tear gas now exhausted, the first troops, the 503rd MPs, arrived on campus. "It was like a western movie," journalist Walter Lord concluded, "where the cavalry arrives in the nick of time." By dawn an overwhelming military presence of 23,000 soldiers had restored order to the Ole Miss campus and to the town of Oxford, where the rioting had spread. That same morning James Meredith walked through the rubble under heavy military guard, registered, and attended his first class—in American history.[60]

In the aftermath of the riot the Ole Miss campus had the appearance of a war zone. For the New Frontiersmen of the Kennedy administration, it should have been apparent that the doctrine of Federalism had not played well in Oxford. Relying on state officials to uphold the law and maintain order meant trusting Ross Barnett to keep promises made under extreme duress. As Victor Navasky has observed, the Kennedys had assumed that "white southern law enforcers, like themselves, were decent human beings, men who didn't break their word, who didn't lie." While the riot was at its peak, Robert Kennedy paused to reflect: "What are we going to say about all this? . . . We're going to have a helluva problem about why we didn't, uh, handle the situation better. . . . you see, we're going to be blamed for, uh, not doing enough."[61]

Mississippi officials realized that they too had an image problem. Their solution was to blame the riot on the U.S. marshals and on the Kennedy brothers who sent them to Oxford. From the governor on down, the party line was the same. Congressman John Bell Williams's response was typical: "The bestiality, cruelty, and savagery of Justice Department employees under the direction of Robert Kennedy . . . were acts beyond the comprehension of normal minds." Williams even drew a parallel with "the dastardly acts of Adolph Hitler and his infamous Gestapo." Although white supremacists had suffered a defeat at Oxford, the spirit of "Never!" was still alive and well in the Magnolia State.[62]

Ole Miss became a major casualty of Barnett's defiant stand. Faculty morale hit bottom, and at least thirty-seven professors resigned in protest at the end of the year, including most of the chemistry faculty and the entire philosophy department. One critic of Barnett who remained, James W. Silver, gained distinction as "the most hated white man in Mississippi" after his *Mississippi: The Closed Society* became a bestseller in 1964. Student enrollment also dropped. For those undergraduates remaining on campus, the integration crisis did not appear to have raised their level of racial tolerance. The few students who befriended Meredith were targets of crude reprisals. A fire was set in the room of one, and others came back to find their rooms smeared with excrement.[63]

Black Mississippians rejoiced at Meredith's victory over the combined weight of the Mississippi establishment, yet they saw it for what it was worth, nothing more. Fraternity row at Ole Miss was far removed from the lives of black people in Greenwood and Ruleville, who would bear the brunt of white rage over the defeat suffered at the hands of the federal government. As for James Meredith, he graduated in the summer of 1963. After having held up under intense pressures for over a year, he left his native state and all but disappeared from view. When he returned three years later to lead his "March Against Fear," he found a black community much more angry and radicalized than the one he had, for a brief moment, inspired through his quiet and courageous example.

Witnesses wait to testify at the Bilbo hearings in Jackson, December 5, 1946. (The Bettmann Archive)

Dr. T. R. M. Howard addresses a state NAACP meeting in 1954. Seated in the front row are Aaron Henry (first seat) and Dr. Emmett J. Stringer (to Henry's right). (Emmett J. Stringer)

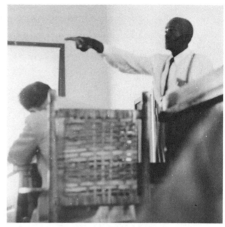

Moses Wright identifies Bryant and Milam as the abductors of Emmett Till. (The Bettmann Archive)

Emmett Till. (The Bettmann Archive)

Hodding Carter II, editor of the *Delta Democrat-Times*. (Hodding and Betty Werlein Carter Collection, Mitchell Library, Mississippi State University)

Tougaloo students are arrested after their sit-in at the Jackson Public Library, March 27, 1961. In the foreground (left to right) are Janice Jackson, Evelyn Pierce, and Ethel Sawyer. (AP/Wide World Photos)

The "Tougaloo Nine" (left to right): Joseph Jackson, Jr.; Geraldine Edwards; James "Sam" Bradford; Evelyn Pierce; Albert Lassiter; Ethel Sawyer; Meredith Anding; Janice Jackson; Alfred Cook. (Coleman Library, Tougaloo College)

SNCC activists and local organizers in southwest Mississippi, 1962 (left to right): Bob Moses, Julian Bond, Curtis Hayes, Willie Peacock, Hollis Watkins, Amzie Moore, and E. W. Steptoe. (Mrs. Mary Lee Moore and Blackside, Inc.)

James Forman, SNCC's executive secretary, in 1962. (Braden Collection, WHi [X3] 45655, State Historical Society of Wisconsin)

Dick Gregory unloads food cartons in Clarksdale, 1962. (Ernest Withers)

The Woolworth's sit-in in Jackson, May 23, 1963. Seated (left to right) are John Salter, Joan Trumpauer, and Anne Moody. (AP/Wide World Photos)

In the aftermath of the sit-in, the Reverend Ed King assists the demonstrators. Dr. Daniel Beittel, president of Tougaloo College, is seated at the far right. (John Salter, Jr., Collection, WHi [X3] 43068, State Historical Society of Wisconsin)

Roy Wilkins (left) and Medgar Evers are arrested as they attempt to picket Woolworth's, June 1, 1963. (The Bettmann Archive)

Mrs. Myrlie Evers comforts her son, Darrell Kenyatta, at Medgar Evers's funeral. Charles Evers is seated to her right. (Ernest Withers)

COFO Freedom House in the Delta. (Tamio Wakayama)

An advertisement for the Klan, found on a utility pole in Kosciusko. (Mitchell Library, Mississippi State University)

COFO activists at a workshop at Tougaloo College (right to left): Lawrence Guyot, Bob Moses, Dave Dennis, and Victoria Gray. (Highlander Folk School Collection, WHi [X3] 44678, State Historical Society of Wisconsin)

Summer volunteers at an Oxford, Ohio, orientation session. (Tamio Wakayama)

7

Greenwood and Jackson

As you can see, I do not plan to leave. I am anchoring
myself here for better or for worse (I hope better), but if
worse comes I'll be in the middle of it.
> —Medgar Evers, May 4, 1956

The aftermath of the Meredith crisis was similar to that of
the *Brown* decision nearly a decade earlier. Furious over what they
perceived to be the federal government's flagrant disregard for states'
rights, many Mississippi whites took out their frustrations on black
people, particularly those active in the struggle. But tactics of intimidation, violence, and murder, so effective in 1955, had less impact now, for this time blacks were building their movement on a
solid grass-roots foundation. Throughout the early fall of 1962,
while the state and nation focused on the drama unfolding in Oxford, SNCC workers in the Delta hung on in Greenwood, Ruleville,
and Cleveland. The Citizens' Council strategy of economic reprisal, coupled with night-riding attacks on the homes of local activists, had stalled the voter registration drives. Then the white leadership overplayed its hand, providing SNCC with an opportunity
it quickly exploited. The issue, quite simply, was food.

Since 1957 Greenwood and Leflore County had participated in
the federal surplus commodities program, providing welfare recipients with basic foods such as meal, rice, flour, and dried milk on a
twelve-month basis. In addition, during the winter months of January, February, and March, the county had extended the program
to other needy persons, particularly sharecroppers and farm workers who had no income during the off-season. Planters had previ-

ously supported this voluntary program because it sustained their work force, at federal expense (the county paid only the administrative costs), during the downtime between cotton picking and planting. In 1961–62 surplus commodities had gone to the 5,000 people on welfare—far fewer than the number eligible—and to an additional 22,000 people during the winter months. More than 90 percent of these recipients were black. In July 1962 the Leflore County Board of Supervisors voted to discontinue the winter program for people not on welfare, citing excessive adminstrative costs as the reason, although for the previous year the entire program had cost Leflore County only $12,500.[1]

The county's action was now feasible because the sharecroppers and farm workers were no longer important to plantation operations: between 1950 and 1960 mechanization had reduced the number of farm workers by more than one-half. Local blacks immediately concluded that the supervisors' decision was an act of retribution against SNCC's voter registration project.[2]

"If you want to know how to take care of *them,* come over and see how we do it. We're going before the Board tomorrow and we're going to cut off their water," a wealthy Greenwood man announced at the conclusion of a political meeting in nearby Lexington in early November 1962. On the following night the Leflore County Board of Supervisors held a unique forum to gain public support for its July decision to omit from its 1962–63 budget the winter distribution of federal commodities to needy people. After the all-white audience voted forty to twenty-nine to discontinue the winter program, the board reaffirmed its initial action. Neighboring Sunflower County also restricted eligibility for commodities. Previously, all it took to receive surplus food was to go to the city hall in Ruleville and sign up. In late 1962 Sunflower supervisors required that applicants fill out a registration form, to be countersigned by a "responsible" person. When Mrs. Gertrude Rogers completed the form and received a card, she overheard Mayor C. M. Durrough say, "Most of them with cards, ain't going to get any food," adding that he was "going to mess up all of them." The United States Commission on Civil Rights sent investigators into the Delta, who "urgently recommended that the President direct the Secretary of Agriculture to take immediate steps to provide for direct Federal distribution of surplus food commodities to needy persons in Mississippi." The federal bureaucracy moved slowly, and as winter set in, thousands of black parents in the Delta did not know how they were going to feed their children.[3]

SNCC workers in Greenwood and Ruleville saw the face of hunger all around them. Sam Block and Willie Peacock visited the Meeks family of eleven children and found seven youngsters staying home from schoool "because they have no money, no food, no clothes, and no wood to keep warm by." The two organizers walked up "little nasty alleys" and found families living without food or heat: "some of them will make you cry to see the way they have been trying to live." Shocked and angered by the supervisors' decision—and believing that their voter registration drive had precipitated this action—SNCC workers in the Delta sent out a national appeal for food and supplies.[4]

Among the first to respond were Ivanhoe Donaldson and Ben Taylor, black students at Michigan State University, who drove a truckload of food, clothing, and medicine down to the Delta during Christmas week. The two students were arrested in Clarksdale and charged with possession of narcotics; their cargo was confiscated. The "narcotics" were aspirin and vitamins. While Donaldson and Taylor were spending eleven days in the Clarksdale jail, the SNCC office in Atlanta was using the arrests to call attention to the desperate plight of Delta blacks. Friends of SNCC in northern cities responded. A Carnegie Hall fund-raiser headlined by Harry Belafonte provided much-needed support, and comedian Dick Gregory made the first of several trips to the Delta, chartering a plane loaded with seven tons of food. SNCC activists now made relief to the hungry their priority. Supervising the distribution of food also meant that SNCC could reach thousands of angry blacks who had hit bottom and were now ready to enlist in the struggle.[5]

SNCC "set up our own welfare system" using the commodities cutoff as an organizing tool. Word spread quickly as the first shipments of food and clothing reached SNCC headquarters, and blacks who had previously had no contact with the movement came by the office. SNCC linked food to the franchise. Applicants filled out a personal data sheet to determine their need. Each person then was handed a registration form and asked to try to complete it, with project workers offering instruction on the complicated registration process. Attempting to register was a requirement for receiving food and clothing, although it was not strictly enforced. But many of the destitute applicants found the organizers' argument persuasive: "The

Board of Supervisors could do this to you because you couldn't vote. Register and it won't happen again."[6]

Efforts to involve leaders of the Greenwood black community in the distribution effort received little initial support. Early in January James Bevel tried to persuade local ministers to file protests with the supervisors, but "most of them [were] afraid," refusing even to permit the use of their churches as distribution centers. At first only Father Nathaniel at the Catholic Center made his facilities available; later the Wesley Chapel agreed to participate. Food and clothing distribution centers soon opened in neighboring counties. Amzie Moore offered his home as the center in Cleveland. A group of local blacks in Ruleville took over the operation there, and in Coahoma County the NAACP's Aaron Henry and Vera Pigee operated a distribution center in Clarksdale.[7]

Organizers were delighted that hundreds of blacks were now associating with the movement, providing a steady stream of applicants to take the registration test, but the distribution of food and clothing was at times frustrating. To begin with, need far exceeded supply. In late February Bob Moses reported that in Leflore County, "We have been giving food and clothing to 1,000 out of an estimated 22,000 needy." To make matters worse, some of those in line for food were not among the needy. SNCC worker Frank Smith observed that "people lied to you about their incomes and family sizes and various other things. You find yourself becoming more and more inhuman and strict each day." Eventually, organizers had to take on the role of social workers, visiting homes to determine need.[8]

Despite these disillusioning experiences and long work days, SNCC workers were exhilarated by the sudden turn of events. Local people who pitched in to help with the distribution effort stayed on to become involved in the voter registration campaign. Poor blacks enraged at county officials defiantly went to the courthouse, although many could not read the registration forms placed before them. All this was not lost on the city fathers. As in the past, when economic intimidation failed to destroy a local movement, terror was certain to follow.

On February 19 a truck from Chicago loaded with 9,000 pounds of food and clothing arrived in Greenwood. Early the following morning a SNCC volunteer received an anonymous phone call "gloating that no food would be distributed the following day." At that moment a block in the black business district was ablaze, the fires consuming four buildings, including a dry-cleaning establishment located next to the SNCC office. Later that day 600 people received food from the Chicago shipment. Sam Block called the wire services to state the obvious: the SNCC office had been the target of a bungled attempt "to burn us out." When Block's remarks were reported in the local press, police jailed him for "public utterances designed to incite breach of the peace." It was Block's seventh arrest in the eight months he had been in Greenwood. When he came to trial on February 24, more than 100 local people, many of them from the plantations, flooded the courthouse. They were in an angry mood, even defiantly drinking from the "white" water fountains inside the building. This unprecedented display of support may have intimidated the judge, who offered the hated Block a suspended sentence if he left town. Block refused and appealed his $500 fine and six-month term at the county prison farm.[9]

The arson and Block's arrest accelerated the voter registration drive. The night after Block's trial the Reverend Aaron Johnson, the first local minister to support the movement, addressed a packed mass meeting at his church. Over the next two days more than 150 blacks went to the courthouse, the largest single registration effort in Mississippi since Reconstruction. The SNCC office in Atlanta couldn't believe the news, and the Voter Education Project sent staff member Randolph Blackwell to investigate the phenomenon.[10]

On the evening of February 28, as Blackwell was receiving a briefing from SNCC organizers in Greenwood, Jimmy Travis, a young worker from Jackson, interrupted with news that three white men were parked outside in a Buick with no license plates. Moses suggested that the group break up and return to their home counties. It was late, and Peacock, who knew the territory best, "tried to stop them from leaving town that night." But Moses, Blackwell, and Travis headed west on Highway 82 for Greenville. Seven miles outside Greenwood the Buick reappeared and pulled alongside. Its occupants sprayed gunfire into the SNCC car. Blackwell pushed Moses down, but Travis, the driver, was shot twice, once in the shoulder and once in the back of the neck. Two days later in Jackson doctors removed the bullet from Jimmy Travis's spinal cord and reported that he would have died instantly had the slug penetrated with greater force.[11]

After hearing the news of the ambush, an enraged Wiley Branton, the black civil rights attorney who headed VEP, wired Attorney General Kennedy demanding "immediate action by the federal government" in Greenwood. Branton next sent out a call to all registration workers in Mississippi to come to Leflore County immediately: "Leflore County has elected itself the testing ground for democracy and we are accordingly meeting the challenge there." (Later at a mass meeting Branton had the satisfaction of answering whites' charges that he was an outside agitator by informing them that his great-grandfather was Greenwood Leflore, a person of some historical importance to the area!) COFO leaders agreed to pull workers from other projects and send them to Greenwood. By the end of the first week in March two dozen SNCC organizers, along with a handful of CORE people, including Dave Dennis, were working in Leflore County. The NAACP also committed six people and employed Amzie Moore to work full-time during the campaign. The SCLC sent in Annelle Ponder and Bernice Robinson to set up citizenship classes that not only focused on politics but also helped illiterate local residents learn to read and write. The VEP office hired about twenty local blacks at ten dollars a week to work in a door-to-door canvass.[12]

Transferring all Mississippi personnel to Greenwood was a difficult decision for SNCC, for it ran counter to the principle that organizers should move into a community and stay there to build up trust among local people. On March 4 Moses informed Branton that "SNCC workers are reluctant to give up their projects in the other counties of Mississippi, as they feel that they are just beginning to crack the ice and to suspend the projects for 30 days or more would be detrimental." Outside the Delta, SNCC's major projects were in Hattiesburg and Holly Springs. Since the Hattiesburg program was now under the direction of Mrs. Victoria Gray, a local resident, that project could continue without interruption. Frank Smith, SNCC's principal organizer in Holly Springs, agreed to work in Greenwood, provided that he could commute back to Marshall County periodically to keep that program alive. The influx of so many "outsiders" into black Greenwood also created problems. Peacock was ambivalent about the decision. For over eight months he and Block had been working patiently to develop local leadership in Greenwood, and these efforts could be undermined by the arrival of the new workers, many of whom did not know the territory.[13]

Still, the benefits of bringing nearly forty people into Greenwood outweighed all risks. The food distribution drive was now in high gear, and workers were badly needed to keep up with the shipments, paperwork, and allotment. For the first time in Mississippi hundreds of local blacks were eager to register. The presence of the young organizers bolstered their resolve and put pressure on the black clergy and professional class to get off the fence. Moreover, the history of black protest in Mississippi since World War II had shown that white terrorism had always succeeded in destroying local movements. Branton voiced the sentiments of most activists when he said, "The time has come for us to pick up the gauntlet." Finally, the bold response to the Travis shooting put Greenwood on the media map. By March 5 Claude Sitton of the *New York Times* and Joseph Cumming of *Newsweek* were both filing stories from the Delta community. It was not coincidental that the Justice Department's John Doar began to make frequent trips to Greenwood. Wherever the press went, the federal government was sure to be close behind.[14]

When Randolph Blackwell visited the Greenwood project in late March, he found the office "buzzing like a gigantic telephone switchboard, or more like an army headquarters in the middle of a battlefield." Twenty people were at work in the three-room office, coordinating the major thrusts of the program: canvassing and registration; clothing and food distribution; youth work; mass meetings and Sunday speaking; and the citizenship schools. SNCC staff met at eight o'clock each morning to plan the day's activities and again at night to report. The voter registration effort remained the central project, requiring scores of people to carry out a systematic house-by-house, plantation-by-plantation canvass of the city and county. Canvassers kept notebooks recording information and impressions of potential registrants and followed up on those most likely to go to the courthouse to take the test. Some of the high school students involved in the youth program also canvassed. Others performed the more mundane but essential tasks of cleaning up the office and delivering handbills and church announcements. About thirty young blacks were actively involved in the project, with many more swelling attendance at the mass meetings.[15]

At one point a "mass" meeting had consisted of a dozen people, including the organizers, but by the early spring of 1963 large crowds were turning out for the weekly gatherings, featuring officials of the COFO affiliates such as SNCC executive secretary James

Forman, Aaron Henry and Medgar Evers of the NAACP, CORE's James Farmer, and James Bevel, now with the SCLC. Organizers were hoping that the meetings would generate enthusiasm for the movement among both the rank and file and the "leadership segment" of black Greenwood. Although throughout the campaign SNCC had received support from several prominent local people, Greenwood's black middle class as a whole was still unwilling to endorse the expanded program. In early March only one church, the Reverend Aaron Johnson's, was open for meetings, and no teachers were supporting the registration drive. (In an act of movement mischief, high school students placed bumper stickers on their teachers' cars that read, "Be a First Class Citizen. Register and Vote.")[16]

Late on the evening of March 6 Peacock and Block, along with two women workers, Essie Broom and Peggy Marye, pulled into a parking spot in front of SNCC headquarters on McLaurin Avenue. The four had been working late at the Wesley Chapel Methodist Church, sorting a large shipment of food and clothes that had just arrived from Chicago. As they stopped in front of the SNCC office, a car drove up and two shots—deer slugs from a double-barreled shotgun—knocked out the windows of both front doors of the car. Miraculously, the four workers escaped with only minor cuts from flying glass. When the police arrived they lectured Essie Broom: "Don't you know that you didn't have any business being in the car with that nigger Sam Block? That nigger is the most dangerous nigger in Mississippi." Greenwood mayor Charles Sampson later suggested that SNCC shot at its own workers to generate publicity.[17]

Police harassment and arrests continued throughout March. To counter the increased COFO presence, officials formed the Greenwood Auxiliary Police Force, a posse empowered to make arrests. "With the assistance of the Auxiliary Police," boasted Chief Curtis Lary, "we are able to double the size of the city police department in a matter of minutes." Preventing acts of violence against blacks did not seem to be a priority of this beefed-up police force. On March 24 the SNCC office was nearly destroyed by fire—this time the arsonists got the right address—with records burned and equipment destroyed. Two nights later buckshot tore through Dewey Greene's front door and a window in the bedroom where six of his children were sleeping. The Greenes had been identified with the movement more closely than any other family in Greenwood. Dewey Greene was a painter who early on had volunteered to work in the registration campaign. Dewey, Jr., Sam Block's first local recruit, was attempting to enroll at Ole Miss, the first black to apply since Meredith. Three other children, George and his sisters Freddie and Alma, were active in the youth movement. For many local blacks, the shots fired at the Greene home was the last straw: "They felt now that they had nothing to lose. They were really ready to move."[18]

The following morning, Wednesday, March 27, a crowd of 150 people gathered outside Wesley Chapel to hear Forman call for a protest march on city hall. Moses expressed reservations, no doubt remembering that the students' march to McComb city hall had sharply divided the black community there. To date, there had been no direct action in Greenwood, and although large numbers of people were now assembling at the courthouse each day to register, marching on city hall would almost certainly bring on police repression. Moses and Forman reached a compromise of sorts: the group would walk by the city hall, then go on to the courthouse to attempt to register. As they approached city hall, the marchers were met by Mayor Sampson, a dozen police officers, and a German shepherd on a leash. The mayor, a proud member of the Greenwood Citizens' Council, warned the demonstrators, "I'll give you two minutes to get out. . . . If you don't, we are going to turn the dog loose." As the blacks stood fast, police waded into the crowd. The dog bit marcher Matthew Hughes and tore up Moses' pants leg. After that, the marchers frantically retreated back to Wesley Chapel.[19]

Forman's direct action strategy paid off. The police violence brought the national media scurrying back to Leflore County and also set in motion a chain of events that persuaded the federal government to initiate unprecedented action against the city of Greenwood. Mayor Sampson had used the march as a pretext to arrest and jail ten key leaders of the Greenwood movement, including Peacock, Moses, Forman, McLaurin, Smith, and Lawrence Guyot. (Sam Block was out of town raising funds for the project.) By the weekend eight of the activists had been convicted of breach of the peace, receiving sentences of four months in jail and $200 fines. Guyot drew an extra charge of contempt of court. In an act of defiance that shocked black and white spectators alike, the flamboyant Guyot repeatedly interrupted Police Chief Lary during the latter's testimony. To force the federal government's hand, the group decided to remain in jail rather than accept bail.[20]

As it had two years earlier in McComb, direct action in Greenwood transformed what had been a voter registration and community organization campaign into a full-blown confrontation with city officials. Tactics of intimidation and violence, hitherto successful, now seemed to inspire greater unity and resolve in black Greenwood. The day after the march to city hall, 100 blacks went to the courthouse to take the registration test. The following morning more applicants stood in line. Later, they were led back to Wesley Chapel by the Reverend David L. Tucker, the charismatic young A.M.E. minister who had recently become active in the movement. As Tucker and forty-two prospective voters returned to the chapel, nearly 100 law officers and auxiliary police confronted them. With representatives of the national media looking on, one of the dogs charged into Reverend Tucker, biting him on the leg and drawing blood. While several blacks carried Tucker away, the others retreated to the chapel. The assault on the popular minister further enraged the black community. The police had attacked a group of people who were simply walking home after attempting to register. This was no direct action protest, but the police had responded as though a mob were about to tear the city apart.[21]

With Greenwood in the headlines and civil rights leaders, including Martin Luther King, pledging their support, important segments of Greenwood's black middle class now publicly embraced the movement. Over the weekend thirty-one ministers signed a manifesto: "We the undersigned Pastors and Ministers of the city of Greenwood and Leflore County do hereby endorse the Freedom Movement one-hundred percent and urge our members and friends of Leflore County and the state of Mississippi to register and become first-class citizens."[22] Hundreds of area blacks packed the mass meetings to hear their leaders urge them to sustain the struggle. Dick Gregory returned to the city on Monday to speak to a throng of more than 1,000 people. The following day he led forty blacks back from the courthouse. Gregory taunted the police (who had orders not to arrest him—Greenwood did not want the publicity), referring to them as "a bunch of illiterate whites who couldn't even pass the test themselves."[23]

The escalating tensions in Greenwood had not gone unnoticed

in Washington. The Kennedy administration sent in a team headed by John Doar that included at least six FBI agents. With the notable exception of its involvement in the Meredith case, the Justice Department had kept a low profile in Mississippi since the eruption in McComb, limiting its work to investigating reports of civil rights violations and filing lawsuits against recalcitrant registrars. A suit filed in Leflore County the previous August had become tied up in the lower courts, and the county registrar, Martha Lamb, continued to discriminate against black applicants. From August 8, 1961, when the Justice Department filed suit, through June 10, 1963, more than 80 percent of white Leflore applicants passed the test; of the 1,013 blacks who applied, only 23, or 2.3 percent, made it onto the books, despite the fact that the Justice Department was photographing all application forms.[24]

SNCC had forced the Kennedys to do what they did not want to do, to "be on somebody's side" in a direct confrontation between the movement and white Mississippi. Moreover, pressures were also increasing inside Washington. Liberal congressional representatives, including some members of the Republican opposition, were upset that President Kennedy had thus far refused to propose new civil rights legislation, and members of the U.S. Commission on Civil Rights, an agency nominally free from presidential control, were furious that the president kept postponing hearings that they had scheduled in Mississippi.[25] This combination of pressures, the fear that Greenwood might explode at any moment, and the realization that they were dealing with an irresponsible city government led the Kennedys on March 30 to file a sweeping lawsuit against the city of Greenwood.

Pending a full hearing in federal court, Justice Department attorneys asked for a temporary restraining order against city officials, directing them to release the eight black organizers remaining in prison. More than that, the order would force the city to "refrain from further interference with a registration campaign and those taking part in it" *and* to "permit Negroes to exercise their constitutional right to assemble for peaceful protest demonstrations and protect them from whites who might object." A Justice Department official termed the suit "highly significant," pointing out that this was the first time the department had interceded to protect the right of blacks to demonstrate.[26]

Greenwood blacks were jubilant. Chuck McDew reported to the

Atlanta SNCC office that local people "seem to see some concrete proof, for a change, that the government is on their side." Wiley Branton told a mass meeting that "it's the greatest thing the President of the United States can do to let the world know we believe in democracy." The Justice Department action had special significance for the SNCC workers in the Greenwood jail. Earlier in the year three of them—Moses, McLaurin, and Lafayette Surney—were part of a suit filed against Attorney General Kennedy and FBI director Hoover to "compel" the federal government to protect civil rights workers in the exercise of their constitutional rights. Now it appeared that the federal government had decided to do just that. Greenwood officials were stunned by the Justice Department's move. McDew observed that the threat of the injunction "has had a remarkable effect" on local law enforcement officials, who "are being half-way decent for a change."[27]

The euphoria was short-lived, for white Mississippi rolled out its big guns to shoot down the Justice Department initiative. On Monday, April 2, John Stennis rose on the Senate floor to inform his colleagues that in Greenwood "professional troublemakers have organized one of the most bitter hate campaigns ever devised in this country . . . purposely inflam[ing] the public mind, through their meetings, their organized mob marches on the courthouse, and their wild charges and speeches." Their sole purpose, continued Stennis, was "to create strife and discord and to overturn the peaceful and harmonious cooperation among the people of the two races built up over generations." Stennis was joined on his trip through fantasyland by his colleague Jim Eastland. Both denounced the Justice Department suit in the strongest terms and demanded that it be dropped. Back in Greenwood, city prosecutor Gray Evans threatened that "if the police power of the city, the county and the state is suspended, then we cannot be responsible for anything that happens." The Kennedy administration took notice.[28]

On Wednesday, April 3, the day before the federal court hearing on the injunction request, police again confronted a group of forty local blacks who were marching two-by-two on the sidewalk on their way to the courthouse to register. Chief Lary, with his auxiliary police out in force, demanded that the group disperse. "We will not," asserted Ida Mae Holland, a young Greenwood woman at the head of the march. Police then began making arrests, roughly herding nineteen of the marchers into a school bus, en route to the county jail. (In an act not countenanced in the book of passive resistance, Mrs. Laura McGhee grabbed a policeman's nightstick, yanked it from him, and had to be pulled away by Dick Gregory.) Sixteen of those arrested were local people not on the SNCC staff. This was the first time that Greenwood blacks had volunteered to go to jail in numbers. Abusing their prisoners in full view of FBI agents and the media, the police showed little concern over the threat of the injunction. Tensions in Greenwood had never been higher.[29]

Early the next morning VEP director Branton received an urgent telephone call from Justice Department attorney Doar. When the two met at 6:30 A.M., Doar told Branton that the federal court hearing scheduled for 10:00 A.M. that day in Greenville had been canceled. The previous day he had cut a deal with Greenwood officials, who promised to release the eight jailed SNCC workers and stay execution of their sentences pending a full hearing in late October. This, Doar said, had prompted the Justice Department to withdraw its application for a preliminary injunction. Branton calmly asked whether the arrangement included the release of the nineteen people jailed the previous day, dealt with the issue of police harassment and brutality, or said anything about the right of people to walk down the street in large groups. Doar replied that the agreement included only the release of the eight SNCC organizers.[30]

The Justice Department retreat shocked and saddened black Greenwood. Reverend Tucker concluded that "we're right back where we started—we have no protection." Dave Dennis accused the Kennedy administration of "taking the Negro people and playing politics with their freedom." Bob Moses simply withdrew. He had cooperated fully with the Justice Department for two years now, establishing a personal relationship with John Doar. Doar made it a point to seek out Moses to try to explain his actions, but he recalled that when he saw the look of total despair on Moses' face, he did not even bring up the subject. White Greenwood rejoiced over the sudden turn of events. The *Greenwood Commonwealth* adopted a restrained tone in its front-page editorial, headlined "Reasonable Accord." Referring to the agreement as "reasonable and timely," the editorial went on to "congratulate the Justice Department officials for their attitude." But for the average white person in the street, one reporter observed, "the attitude is 'we've licked them hands down.'"[31]

City officials made it clear that they had not backed down, that "no large organized groups will be allowed on the public streets of the city." Aside from a promise to permit blacks to take the registration test and an offer to transport registrants to the courthouse in a bus, the city conceded virtually nothing. When Branton met with the city commissioners to try to get assurances that the city would end harassment of blacks trying to register, he came away empty-handed. The county supervisors had also bested the bureaucrats in Washington. The board resumed the distribution of surplus food to the needy—but only after the U.S. Department of Agriculture had agreed to pay the county's costs in administering the program.[32]

The larger question remains: why did the Kennedy administration, after giving wide publicity to its proposed remedy in Greenwood (the president had referred to it proudly in a news conference), back down so quickly? No doubt the strong opposition from Stennis and Eastland was a factor. The Kennedy brothers did not want to alienate Mississippi's two powerful senators completely. Doar told Branton that the Justice Department was afraid it would lose its case in district court; but the department usually lost in the lower courts, only to have those decisions reversed in the Fifth Circuit Court of Appeals, as had been the case with James Meredith. A more plausible explanation is that the Kennedys feared a race war in Greenwood and that the injunction, if approved, would put the U.S. Army in the city's streets. It would be Ole Miss all over again, with local police withdrawing and a federal occupationary force responsible for maintaining law and order. A conciliatory gesture—withdrawing the injunction request—would keep Mayor Sampson and the Citizens' Council in control of Greenwood and keep the even more reactionary Klan-types on the sidelines.[33]

Finally, the request for the injunction was at odds with the Kennedy Justice Department's philosophy of Federalism, that Washington should intervene only when local or state authorities proved incapable of maintaining order. By jailing blacks as they peacefully walked down the streets, Sampson showed he was still in charge. Quite probably, the Kennedys were never really serious about following through with the injunction. While appearing to protect the rights of black citizens, they used the threat of an injunction to obtain token concessions from Greenwood officials and thereby defused a tense situation. If this was the administration's plan, it worked, but there was a price. Journalists Pat Watters and Reece Cleghorn have observed that in Greenwood, fear of white violence had "route[d] the federal government in a showdown on the most basic right of American citizenship. This point . . . seemed largely lost on the nation, but not on the white and Negro principals in the showdown."[34]

The Greenwood movement survived both the violent repression of local officials and the timidity of the Kennedys. The visiting SNCC workers returned to their projects, Forman went back to Atlanta, and Gregory was soon doing stand-up comedy again in northern nightclubs. Peacock and the other Leflore County SNCC staff members, however, continued to walk the city streets and country roads, knocking on doors, asking people whether they would like to sit down and look over the registration form. Each day one or two dozen local people showed up at the courthouse to take the test. Few of them passed, but SNCC had indeed secured a beachhead in the Delta and had proved that it could survive both white intransigence and federal indifference.

• • •

At the same time that the battle of Greenwood was raging, NAACP activists in Jackson were mobilizing for a campaign against segregated facilities and discriminatory employment practices. The Jackson movement began inauspiciously in late 1962 when the north Jackson NAACP youth council announced a boycott against downtown merchants, charging them with a broad pattern of discrimination against black workers and consumers. Movement demands included the use of courtesy titles, equality in hiring and promotion, and an end to Jim Crow practices.[35] In many respects, the program in Jackson was similar to the boycott underway in Clarksdale. Jackson merchants at first did not take this latest effort seriously, but local blacks were aware of the ongoing protests in Greenwood and in Albany, Georgia, and James Meredith's success in desegregating Ole Miss was proof that the white establishment was not invincible. The eager and dedicated young people who announced the boycott were determined to follow up with direct, door-to-door contact in the black community, for only grass-roots support could sustain a boycott in a city the size of Jackson.

The chief strategist for the boycott and the direct action campaign that emerged from it was John Salter, a Tougaloo sociology professor in his mid-twenties. A former labor organizer in northern Arizona, Salter and his wife, Eldri, had been inspired by the freedom rides and came to Mississippi in the summer of 1961. Shortly thereafter Colia Liddell, a Tougaloo student from Jackson, asked Salter to be an adult advisor to the north Jackson NAACP youth council, the only such group still active in the Jackson area and composed mainly of black high school students.[36] Although his father was a Micmac/Penobscot Indian, Salter was defined as white in Mississippi's color-conscious society. As an outsider and a "white man," Salter incurred the wrath of white Jackson and never gained the trust of the black community's conservative leadership. Nonetheless, the high school students in the youth council and undergraduates at Tougaloo recognized that Salter's background as an organizer—a commodity in short supply in NAACP circles—could provide the experience they lacked. A courageous and quietly charismatic person who preferred to work behind the scenes, Salter won the respect of the small youth council group, and together they planned to crack open Jackson's segregated society.

The boycott was planned for early December, to coincide with the Christmas season buying rush, and youth council leaders decided on early picketing in the downtown area to call attention to the campaign. Since Jackson police would probably arrest all picketers, securing adequate bail bond was important. Medgar Evers told Salter that the national office of the NAACP should have no trouble supplying bond money, and the youth council made plans to picket on December 3. The NAACP did not come through with any funds, however, and the picketing was postponed. A series of hurried telephone calls resulted in bail money for six pickets, the funds supplied by SCEF, the Gandhi Society, and New York attorney Victor Rabinowitz. On December 12, after alerting the media, the Salters and four students, including youth council president Bette Anne Poole, stopped in front of Woolworth's on Capitol Street, took out their signs, and formed a picket line. As expected, police immediately arrested the group, which was soon out on bail. Local media gave wide coverage to the small demonstration, and Jackson mayor Allen Thompson went on television to denounce the boycott and the picketers. With cooperation from their adversaries, the youth council had publicized the boycott to the entire Jackson community.[37]

Awareness of the boycott did not necessarily translate into observance, so the teenagers hit the streets, distributing thousands of leaflets in black neighborhoods, speaking in churches, and telephoning people who could not be otherwise reached, all to persuade black adults not to shop on Capitol Street. After Evers located two property bonds, Tougaloo students Dorie Ladner and Charles Bracey picketed downtown four days before Christmas and were arrested. Early in January Evers reported to the national NAACP office that the boycott was "60–65 percent effective." But Jackson's white leaders acted just as Clarksdale's had: they refused to negotiate with movement representatives.[38]

Initially, other activists working in Jackson responded ambivalently to the work of Salter and the young boycott organizers. CORE's Dave Dennis, who later played an important role in the Jackson movement, was at first skeptical, believing it a mistake to call for a boycott *before* "organiz[ing] the community for such a program." Dennis also had reservations about John Salter. In a letter to CORE official James McCain on December 6, Dennis wrote that "the leader of the group is rather headstrong and he is also white. . . . He has a reputation of being a Marxist which might or might not be true."[39] (Salter was not a Marxist.) SNCC workers in the Jackson area were by now absorbed in the Greenwood project. Tougaloo student Joyce Ladner, one of a number of SNCC activists commuting to the Delta, later recalled that the idea of a boycott did not strike her as particularly bold or adventurous: "For me it was like middle-class people in Jackson can run a boycott if they want to run a boycott." Bob Moses was also lukewarm toward the Jackson campaign, and Salter believed that Moses "did everything he could do to pull our student activists into his projects in the spring of '63."[40]

Since the boycott was an NAACP program, support from adult NAACP leaders was essential. Salter had developed a close friendship with Evers, who endorsed the boycott and assisted when and where he could. Evers was not, however, engaged in the day-to-day planning, nor was he initially optimistic about the chances for success. Frustrated over the timidity of the city's black leadership, Evers was now spending even more time on the road, assisting Aaron Henry in Clarksdale, lending support in Greenwood, and bolstering NAACP branches across the state. Even so, he soon became caught in a crossfire between the increasingly militant leadership of the Jackson movement and the cautious responses of his NAACP superiors in New York.[41]

Its failure to provide bail bonds for the first group of picketers indicated the national NAACP's attitude toward the boycott. In late January, director of branches Gloster Current recommended that "the NAACP should take some action backing up our North Jackson Youth Council and give this matter nationwide publicity, if at all possible," but the New York office took no action.[42] A frustrated Salter complained to New York attorney William Kunstler that "the NAACP has given us no tangible aid of any kind. Medgar is certainly with us but, for several reasons, is unable to give us the help that we need or get it for us. . . . The whole thing is pretty damned disheartening." Nor had the situation changed a month later, when Roy Wilkins, who was to address a boycott rally in Clarksdale, informed Evers that his schedule did not permit him to speak in Jackson.[43]

In the middle of May the national office changed course abruptly and made Jackson a priority, cranking out public relations releases, supplying bond money for picketers, and eventually flooding the city with top NAACP officials, including Ruby Hurley, Current, and Wilkins. The reason for this sudden shift in policy was, in a word, Birmingham. SCLC demonstrations there were capturing international attention in a direct action campaign where the demands were similar to those being pushed in Jackson. In a revealing memorandum to regional and field secretaries on May 13, Current called attention to the "apparent success of the Birmingham protest," speculating that "Jackson, Mississippi will be the next scene of attack by the King forces." Such a move would "make it much harder for the NAACP to carry on its work effectively." Current asked the field secretaries to suggest "possible focal points where action programs may be directed within the next thirty days. . . . As soon as the Birmingham crisis is past, we ought to hit hard two or three focal centers in each of the states where we presently operate in the South." Two days later the national office of the NAACP pledged its support to the "current selective-buying campaign of our North Jackson Youth Council and the general drive toward the objective of putting an end to all forms of racial discrimination and segregation in Jackson."[44]

With this welcome (albeit overdue) commitment from the national NAACP, the Jackson movement now gained new local recruits, as conservative black leaders publicly came on board. In mid-May black businessmen and ministers met to form the Citizens Committee for Human Rights in Jackson. The group, which included NAACP stalwarts I. S. Sanders, Sam Bailey, and the Reverend R. L. T. Smith, began to meet regularly with the Jackson movement strategy committee. They were joined by Dean Charles Jones, the chaplain at Campbell College, and Edwin King, a native white Mississippian in his twenties who had become the chaplain at Tougaloo College. Dave Dennis, having overcome his earlier misgivings, was now participating in planning sessions. The expanded strategy committee was of two minds as to how to proceed. The original boycott group, led by Salter, believed that the time was right for massive demonstrations. Birmingham was on their minds, too. The older, more conservative clergy and business faction favored new efforts to bring Jackson officials to the negotiating table. The strategy committee agreed on a compromise: Mayor Thompson would get one more opportunity to negotiate; if this effort failed, demonstrations would immediately begin.[45]

The 600 black Jacksonians attending a mass meeting on May 21 called for Mayor Thompson to meet with fourteen representatives of the Jackson movement to discuss a specific list of grievances. The group now added the hiring of black police and school crossing guards and the establishment of a biracial committee to their original demands for desegregated facilities and fair employment practices. If the city again refused to negotiate, Evers made clear in a telegram to the mayor, blacks would demonstrate. Aware of the broad support in the black community, Mayor Thompson resorted to tactics of divide and conquer. He agreed for the first time to meet with a black delegation but eliminated ten of the movement's representatives and replaced them with such reactionaries as Percy Greene and Jackson State president Jacob Reddix, men whom he could count on for support. Initially rejecting the mayor's obvious ploy, the Jackson movement strategy committee decided to meet with Thompson after he promised to include more members of the original group in the black delegation. On Monday, May 27, sixteen blacks arrived at city hall to see the mayor, hoping he had undergone a change of heart. They were to be disappointed, for Thompson once again rejected all demands. The next day, May 28, the Jackson movement took to the streets.[46]

At 11:15 on a hot and muggy Mississippi morning, Tougaloo students Pearlena Lewis, Memphis Norman, and Anne Moody sat down at the fifty-two-seat lunch counter at the Woolworth's drugstore on Capitol Street. Representatives of the media, alerted by

Evers, were on hand, but the lunch-hour crowd had not yet arrived, and business at the counter was slow. A gray-haired white woman came over and chatted amiably with the students, remarking that she would "like to stay here with you but my husband is waiting for me." At noon white students from nearby Jackson Central High School began pouring into the store, joined by downtown workers on their lunch breaks. At first the crowd was content to heckle the demonstrators, chanting racist slogans. Then former police officer Bennie Oliver came up to the counter, which had now been roped off, slugged Memphis Norman, dragged him off his stool, and kicked him repeatedly in the face. A police detective finally stepped in and arrested Oliver for assault—and Memphis Norman for disturbing the peace. As Pearlena Lewis and Anne Moody were joined at the lunch counter by Joan Trumpauer and white Tougaloo professor Lois Chafee, the crowd pressed in, taunting the demonstrators and dousing them with mustard and catsup.

When Salter joined the group at the counter the crowd had swelled to a mob of over 200. "I know you're a communist," one man yelled at the Tougaloo professor. "Worse than that, he's a nigger lover!" shouted another. At that, a member of the mob started beating Salter in the face. Others came up and poured salt and pepper on his bleeding cuts.

For two hours whites splattered, beat, and kicked the demonstrators, who had now been joined at the lunch counter by another Tougaloo student, Walter Williams, and George Raymond, a young CORE activist and freedom rider. Tougaloo president Daniel Beittel had been outside the store, frantically trying to get the police to stop the rioting. Officers told him that they could not act because the store manager had not requested their assistance. The sixty-three-year-old Beittel then went inside and sat down at the lunch counter. Only after the mob started emptying the shelves, hurling ashtrays, glass figurines—whatever they could get their hands on—did the Woolworth's manager turn off the lights and shut down the store. The demonstrators then left under police guard.[47]

The Woolworth's sit-in, a direct action protest, transformed the boycott into a mass movement. Scenes of white thugs attacking peaceful protestors flashed across television screens throughout the country, and that night nearly 1,000 enthusiastic blacks at Pearl Street A.M.E. Church sang freedom songs and greeted the sit-in demonstrators with a standing ovation. There they learned that Mayor Thompson had met late in the afternoon with the black delegation and had agreed to most of the movement demands. When later that night the mayor denied having made any concessions, movement strategists decided to launch massive demonstrations to bring the city to its knees.

For the next few days events moved at a frantic pace. On Wednesday twenty pickets were arrested at three different locations. Picketing continued the following day, and when hundreds of black students at Lanier High School met on the lawn during the noon hour to sing freedom songs, police with dogs charged, clubbing several and driving the rest of the group back into the school building. After school on Friday, May 31, hundreds of black youths, ranging in age from seven to eighteen, assembled at the Farish Street Baptist Church to begin the first mass march of the Jackson movement. Waving American flags and chanting, "We want freedom!" the demonstrators waded into a wall of Jackson police, backed by sixty shotgun-toting state troopers, who arrested 450 of the marchers and carried them in garbage trucks to a makeshift prison at the state fairgrounds.[48]

At first Medgar Evers had expressed reservations about mass demonstrations in Jackson, noting that similar mobilization campaigns by SCLC had had negative long-term impact on local movements. Now he became excited at the prospects for success. The enthusiasm of the young activists was contagious and no doubt rekindled his own youthful militance. Myrlie Evers recalled that her husband "moved through each day with an energy denied by a single glance at his face. . . . At night he was on the platform of whatever church hosted the meeting, reporting the events of that day and the plans for the next. . . . for the first time, the entire Negro community was behind him; for the first time, volunteers were everywhere." And also for the first time, national officers of the NAACP appeared to be enthusiastic. Roy Wilkins and much of the New York NAACP staff had arrived in town on the day of the first mass march. Wilkins gave a fiery speech to an audience of 1,500 that night. The following day, in a symbolic gesture of support, Wilkins joined Evers on a small picket line on Capitol Street, and both men were arrested. Unknown to Evers, Salter, and the young militants of the Jackson movement, however, Wilkins had not come to Jackson to stand in the front ranks of hundreds of marchers demanding their freedom. Roy Wilkins had no desire to become the NAACP's Martin Luther King.[49]

Although Wilkins and his New York staff ostensibly came to town to offer assistance, they quickly took over planning and strategy. Myrlie Evers later ruefully observed that "with his immediate superiors on the scene, Medgar was relieved of both the necessity and the opportunity of making policy decisions." On Sunday, June 2, the day after Wilkins's arrest, Salter learned that a meeting of the strategy committee—of which he was cochair—was about to begin. When the confused Salter arrived at the meeting, he heard Gloster Current introduce a proposal to add more conservative Jackson blacks to the committee and rotate the committee chairmanship, thereby stripping the Tougaloo professor of his influential position. To avoid sounding self-serving, Salter said nothing, and the motion passed. While Salter and the younger activists pushed hard for the resumption of mass demonstrations, Wilkins and Current applied the brakes. Several small demonstrations took place on Tuesday, with twenty-eight people arrested, but national NAACP officials, backed by local conservatives, declared that there would be no more mass marches in the foreseeable future. As a result, the Jackson movement lost momentum. Attendance at nightly mass meetings declined drastically, and the number of people attending Dennis's classes in nonviolent tactics dropped sharply. On Thursday the city of Jackson obtained an injunction forbidding further demonstrations. Twenty-six young people picketing downtown in defiance of the injunction were arrested the following day. The news spread, however, that the active phase of the Jackson movement was ending.[50]

There were no demonstrations on Saturday, June 8. Thelton Henderson, who was the only black Justice Department investigator in Mississippi and who had gained the respect of movement activists, reported that night that CORE workers Dennis and Jerome Smith had left Jackson "very disgusted and bitter." Dick Gregory, in town to lend his presence to the protests, also departed, informing Henderson that "it would be a long time before anyone tricks him into coming into a town again. He said that there appeared to be a kind of gulf between the NAACP and him."[51] Members of the north Jackson NAACP youth council, who started it all, felt betrayed as well.

Why the national NAACP officers decided to reverse the direction of the Jackson movement just when it was gaining widespread community support is not altogether clear. One reason put forward at the time was that the demonstrations were too costly. The NAACP had kicked in $64,000 to bail out the 640 protestors already arrested, and continued demonstrations, arrests, and appeals would have doubled or tripled that amount within a short time.[52] Wilkins and Current were also determined to undermine John Salter's position in the Jackson movement. Salter's commitment to direct action, his independence, and his connections with activists like leftist attorneys Kunstler and Rabinowitz did not sit well with the NAACP hierarchy, particularly given the Tougaloo professor's strong following among the young people who had been the movement's driving force. Finally, despite its eagerness to counteract the publicity that King and the SCLC were getting in Birmingham, the NAACP was never comfortable with the idea of massive civil disobedience. The black ministers and businessmen, now represented in larger numbers on the strategy committee, had opposed mass marches and had become increasingly fearful of white violence. Despite pleas from younger activists, the ministers had refused to stage a march of their own. The coalition of national NAACP officials and the traditional middle-class leadership of black Jackson agreed, then, that although the boycott should continue, there would be no further mass demonstrations and that the movement should initiate another voter registration drive in the Jackson area.[53]

Throughout this final phase of the movement Medgar Evers was once again the man in the middle. Despite his earlier misgivings about their strategy, he had given strong support to the young activists until the arrival of the New York staff. Now, torn between his friendship and loyalty to people like Current, Wilkins, Clarence Mitchell, and Ruby Hurley—his comrades in the earlier, lonelier struggles—and the demands of the militant young faction of the movement, Evers chose to withdraw, taking little part in the bitter infighting over tactics. Fatigue had also set in, and threats against his life were increasing. After someone threw a Molotov cocktail onto his carport the night after the Woolworth's sit-in, Evers began to adopt more elaborate security precautions, and he talked with Myrlie about the likelihood that his days were numbered.[54]

On the evening of Tuesday, June 11, President John F. Kennedy made a historic televison address, endorsing for the first time federal civil rights legislation. "We are confronted primarily with a moral issue," the president solemnly declared. "The heart of the question is whether all Americans are to be afforded equal rights and equal opportunities, whether we are going to treat our fellow Americans as we want to be treated." That night Evers was attending a rally in Jackson at New Jerusalem Baptist Church. It was a long and disappointing meeting. The small church was not full, and much time was spent discussing the new NAACP thrust in voter registration. Instead of singing inspiring freedom songs and listening to fiery oratory, the audience heard staff members promote the sale of NAACP T-shirts. Evers looked tired and said little. At 12:20 A.M. he pulled into his driveway and got out of his car carrying a bundle of the T-shirts. As Myrlie and the children jumped up to meet him, a sniper crouching 150 feet away in a honeysuckle thicket fired one shot from a high-powered rifle, dropped the gun into a patch of weeds, and fled. The slug hit Evers's back just below the shoulder blade. He staggered to his feet, groped toward the kitchen door, and collapsed in a pool of blood. Neighbors rushed him to the hospital, but he died en route from loss of blood and internal injuries. Later police recovered the rifle and identified fingerprints belonging to a Citizens' Council member from Greenwood named Byron De La Beckwith, who was soon arrested and charged with Evers's murder.[55]

For a time it appeared that Evers's assassination would revitalize the direct action campaign. The day after his death, hundreds of angry blacks poured out into the streets. For the first time, black ministers were marching, along with scores of poor blacks who hitherto had not been involved. Thelton Henderson reported to the Justice Department that he had heard conversations among the leading black ministers that they should stop preaching nonviolence. "The situation is terribly tense," he warned, "and Negroes are about to shoot." Police resorted to violence to stop this demonstration and another mass march later in the week. Veteran journalists Claude Sitton and Carl Flemming reported that "these were some of the worst incidents they had seen." On Saturday morning more than 4,000 black men, women, and children packed the Masonic Temple for Evers's funeral. There they heard tributes from Wilkins and from the veteran leader T. R. M. Howard, who had welcomed Medgar and Myrlie to Mound Bayou less than a decade before.[56]

After the service had ended, some 5,000 black mourners joined the funeral cortege for the long march from the Masonic Temple to the Collins Funeral Home, from which Evers's body would be sent by train for burial in Arlington National Cemetery. Aware that blacks were determined to march, with or without official sanction, Mayor Thompson had authorized it but stipulated that there be no singing or shouting of slogans. When the solemn procession reached its destination, several hundred young people began singing freedom songs and surged southward toward the white business district on Capitol Street. Caught unprepared, police responded with clubs and dogs to disperse the demonstrators. And then, for the first time, the angry blacks fought back, showering the police with bricks, bottles, and other available missiles. A full-scale riot was avoided only after Dennis, Current, several black ministers, and Justice Department lawyer John Doar pleaded with the crowd to disperse. The young activists who spearheaded the Jackson movement were hopeful that the police brutality following Evers's funeral would revive the direct action campaign, but the conservatives, now fully in control (Current had even tried to have John Salter removed from the steering committee), declared that there would be no further demonstrations.[57] At this point the federal government began to arrange a peaceful settlement in Jackson.

Although it had been preoccupied with the Birmingham protests, the Kennedy administration became directly involved in Jackson after the Woolworth's sit-in, when Assistant Attorney General Burke Marshall called city officials to express his concern. Marshall urged the mayor to appoint blacks to the police force, but the Kennedy administration also made it clear to the older black leaders that it wanted an end to demonstrations and supported the idea of a voter registration drive.[58] The Kennedys had employed a similar strategy in Alabama, but unlike Birmingham, where moderate white business leaders were open to discussion, Jackson was still under the thumb of the Citizens' Council, which had made it clear that there were to be no negotiations. The Kennedys' Jackson strategy, then, was to persuade the mayor to make token concessions and then to sell this package to the black community as a victory.

Two days after Evers's funeral, President Kennedy was on the phone to Mayor Thompson. As he had months earlier when he first held conversations with Governor Barnett, the president adopted a conciliatory tone with Thompson, ingratiating himself with attempts at good-old-boy camaraderie: "I understand Reverend Smith, is he, is he the stud duck down there?" Thompson responded with the same wily tactics employed by Barnett, at first sounding obsequious ("Yes sir—everything will be fine") and then later taking a hard line: "I've got a problem. I've got to handle it *my* way."[59]

Kennedy's intervention produced immediate results. On Tuesday, June 18, only three days after Evers's funeral, the strategy committee of the Jackson movement—now completely dominated by conservatives—called a mass meeting to discuss an agreement worked out that afternoon with the mayor. (At noon that day, John Salter and Ed King, who were among the most outspoken critics of the conservative coalition, were involved in a serious automobile wreck that left them both in the hospital.) That night the Reverend G. R. Haughton rose to present the mayor's offer to a large gathering at his Pearl Street A.M.E. Church. Many in the audience groaned in disbelief when they learned that the mayor had agreed only to hire six black policemen to patrol Negro areas and black crossing guards for Negro schools. That, and a handful of black promotions in the sanitation department, constituted his package, along with a vague promise to "continue to hear Negro grievances." Thompson had offered essentially the same concessions before, only to have them rejected by black leaders. The major movement demands—desegregation of public facilities, formation of a biracial committee, and an end to discrimination in hiring—were ignored. Jackson remained a Jim Crow city. Angry activists in the audience pointed out that the mayor had not budged from his previous positions, and a furious debate ensued. Nevertheless, by invoking the memory of their slain leader and citing the approval of the Kennedys, the leadership prevailed. The majority in attendance accepted the mayor's proposal and agreed to end marches and demonstrations.[60]

Later that summer Burke Marshall wrote briefly of the events in Jackson, noting in his report to Attorney General Kennedy that "upon urging from the Administration, the demonstrations in Jackson were discontinued and replaced by a voter registration campaign." Then he added, "As a consequence [of] the demonstrations having been discontinued, the Registration Office [in Jackson] was closed entirely"—a fitting obituary for the Jackson movement.[61]

In Jackson, the unbending resistance of local whites had for a time united blacks across lines of class and age, but as the level of violence intensified, the more conservative black ministers and businessmen became willing to settle on terms that stopped far short of the movement's original goals. These men kept their leadership positions in the years following Evers's death, but they were not a dynamic force for social change. John Salter left Mississippi in the summer of 1963 to become an organizer for SCEF. Several young people active in the direct action campaign remained in Mississippi to work in projects in other areas; others, disillusioned by their experience, dropped out of the movement. Jackson continued as a central headquarters for civil rights organizations, but the black community there never again sustained a movement of its own.

In death Medgar Evers became a heroic symbol of the black struggle, cut down at the very moment when he was leading a courageous battle against the forces of white supremacy. In his final days he had to contend not only with the unrelenting hostility of white Mississippi but also with a black community increasingly divided over questions of tactics and strategy. When Wilkins, Current, and other NAACP leaders came to Jackson in late May 1963, they did so with the assumption that they would take charge. Behind this assumption lay a certainty bordering on arrogance that they knew what was best for black Mississippians, a feeling shared by the Kennedy administration. In Jackson, as in Albany and Birmingham, the Kennedys' primary objective was to bring an end to violence, which meant getting black people off the streets. In arranging the so-called compromise in Jackson, the Kennedys demonstrated once again that in the short run, at least, they preferred order to justice.[62]

Evers had to contend with all these forces, with no blueprint to follow. In the lonely days of the 1950s he and a handful of black men and women had kept the spirit of protest alive in Mississippi. If at the end he displayed a certain ambivalence, a hesitancy to act, it was because the stakes were so high and the path ahead not clear. Had national leaders encouraged Evers to follow his basic combative instincts, the Jackson movement might have taken a different turn. One can only speculate as to the outcome of a sustained confrontation with the local power structure, which was unbending in its determination to preserve the racial status quo. But we do know this: both the inner turmoil of Evers's final days and the tragedy of his martyrdom are eloquent testimony to the courage and dedication of a leader who deserved—in his lifetime—the respect and the support of the powerful people who later publicly identified themselves so closely with this man and his cause.

8

Organizing Mississippi

They are making their last stand, Jim, and if we survive it
we'll be seeing a new day soon. . . . New leadership is
arising and it is not from the white collar man but from
the "down to earth" people. They are people in the rural
areas and areas where there is great pressure from the
whites. The people are tired, Jim, and they are beginning
to stand up for what they want. It's what I have been
dreaming of.
—Dave Dennis to James McCain, summer of 1963

For teenager June Johnson, the trip to Charleston, South
Carolina, had been an exciting adventure. After being among the
first young people to become involved in the Greenwood movement,
June had been chosen by Annelle Ponder as one of seven black Mississippians to attend the SCLC citizenship school, which was held
early in the summer of 1963 and directed by long-time South Carolina activist Septima Clark. At the end of the week-long training
session the group boarded a bus bound for home. Riding all night,
they arrived in Columbus, Mississippi, early Sunday morning and
made an unsuccessful attempt to desegregate the bus station. On
reboarding they received rough treatment from the Trailways driver, who shoved them into seats at the back of the bus.

At Winona, a rest stop only thirty miles from Greenwood, three
of the group remained on the bus while Johnson, Ponder, Euvester
Simpson, Rosemary Freeman, and James West went inside the station restaurant and lunch counter and asked to be served. At that

point the Winona police chief and a member of the Mississippi Highway Patrol emerged from the rear of the station (they may have been tipped off by the bus driver, who had stopped along the way to make a phone call) and evicted them. When Ponder wrote down the patrol car's license number, the police chief rushed out of the station and arrested the five activists. Fannie Lou Hamer, a member of the delegation who had remained on the bus, saw her friends being herded toward the patrol car and came out to ask what the others should do. Ponder told her to stay on the bus, but an officer grabbed Mrs. Hamer and placed her under arrest. The two remaining members of the group rode on to Greenwood.[1]

June Johnson recalled that at the jail the county sheriff greeted them with, "I been hearing about you black sons of bitches over in Greenwood, raising all that hell—you come over here to Winona, you'll get the hell whipped out of you." He then ordered everybody to get inside the cell block. June started in with the rest of them, but the sheriff pulled her aside: "Not you, you black-assed nigger!" The Greenwood teenager recalled what happened next:

He asked me, "Are you a member of the NAACP?" I said yes. Then he hit me on the cheek and chin. I raised my arm to protect my face and he hit me in the stomach. He asked, "Who runs that thing?" I answered, "The people." . . . Then the four of them—the Sheriff, the Chief of Police, the State Trooper, and the white man that had brought Mrs. Hamer in—threw me on the floor and beat me. After they finished stomping me, they said, "Get up, nigger." I raised my head and the white man hit me in the back of the head with a club wrapped in black leather. Then they made me get up. My dress was torn off and my slip was coming off. Blood was streaming down the back of my head and my dress was all bloody. They put me in a cell with Rosemary Freeman, and called Annelle Ponder.[2]

A graduate of Clark College who had been working with the SCLC in Greenwood since April, Ponder was next to receive Mississippi justice. Her refusal to answer questions with "sir" led to a beating with "blackjacks, and a belt, fists, and open palms. . . . That went on, I guess, off and on, for about ten minutes. . . . They really wanted to make me say yes, sir . . . and that is the one thing I wouldn't say." She emerged with her head bloody and swollen, a tooth chipped, and her clothes torn. James West was the next member of the group to be assaulted, both by a highway patrolman and by black prisoners forced to administer the beating.[3]

Fannie Lou Hamer received the worst beating. Again, black inmates had to do the dirty work.

> I said, "You mean you would do this to your own race?" So then I had to get over there on the bed flat on my stomach and that man beat me, that man beat me till he give out. And by my screamin'—it made one of the other ones, the plainclothesman—he got so hot and worked up off of it he just run there and started hittin' me on the back of my head. Well my clothes come up and I tried to pull 'em down. You know, it was just pitiful. And then one of the other white fellas just take my clothes and snatched 'em up. And this Negro when he had just beat me till I know he was give out. Well, this state patrolman told the other Negro to take me so he take over from there and they just beat till . . . and anywhere you could see me you could see I'm not lyin' because I just can't sit down. I been sleepin' on my face because I was just as hard as a bone. It was just hard . . . when they turned me loose, I was hard as a bone.[4]

Later, the six prisoners were booked on charges of disorderly conduct and resisting arrest.

That Sunday morning Willie Peacock had been looking forward to a holiday. He and his girlfriend had "dressed to the nines," gone to church, and were strolling through black Greenwood when they learned from the two returning members of the group that the others were being held in the Winona jail. For the next three days, Peacock recalls, he was constantly on the phone, calling the Justice Department and influential friends in the North—he even got through to Governor Ross Barnett. SNCC immediately sent a delegation headed by Lawrence Guyot to Winona to try to arrange bail. Guyot was immediately arrested, and he too was savagely beaten. Fearful that Guyot would be killed, Peacock organized a steady barrage of phone calls from all over the country to the sheriff's office, with the callers asking to speak to Lawrence Guyot. SNCC workers knew that, in situations such as this, the best protection they could provide for those in custody was to be certain that the jailers knew they were being watched.[5]

On Monday night the civil rights workers were brought to trial and convicted. Not until late Wednesday afternoon did Andrew Young and other members of the SCLC staff arrive with bail money. In their first moment of freedom in nearly four days, the activists learned that late the previous night Medgar Evers had been gunned down in his carport. The Justice Department filed suit against Montgomery County sheriff Earl Patridge, Winona police chief Thomas J. Herod, Jr., state highway patrolman John L. Basinger, and two other men, charging them with seven counts of conspiracy to deprive those arrested of their civil rights. At the trial held in federal court in Oxford that December, the FBI introduced photographs of the injuries, and an agent testified that he had examined the bloodstained clothes worn by June Johnson while she was under arrest. The federal jury of local white men found the accused not guilty on all counts.[6]

The year 1963 witnessed an explosion of civil rights activity and brutal white repression across the South. Direct action protests rocked Birmingham, Greensboro, Atlanta, Danville, and more than 100 other cities in eleven southern states, with over 20,000 people arrested.[7] In Mississippi the Winona beatings, followed by Evers's murder, were the opening salvos in a summer campaign of white lawlessness unmatched since 1955. Yet the spirit of the movement remained strong, and COFO activists deepened and expanded their base. The young organizers took everything the state of Mississippi threw at them and came back for more. Local people who had suffered quietly for generations gathered new strength and resolve, inspired by and inspiring the grass-roots leaders emerging in their midst.

On the evening of June 18, local blacks gathered at Hopewell Church in Itta Bena, a small town not far from Greenwood, for a voter registration rally. SNCC worker MacArthur Cotton introduced June Johnson, who described her beating in Winona only nine days before and told her listeners that if they registered, they could vote out people "who beat you up for nothing." As the group was singing "Ain't Gonna Let Nobody Turn Me 'Round," someone hurled a smoke bomb into the church, creating a panic that caused several members of the congregation to be hospitalized. The audience regrouped outside the church and decided to march to the sheriff's house and demand protection. Gun-toting whites stopped them along the way, and a deputy sheriff arrested them for breach of the peace. The next day forty-five local blacks were sentenced to six-month jail terms and carted off to Parchman penitentiary, where they stayed for two months until finally bailed out. One of those convicted was Mother Perkins, who was permitted to serve out her two months at the county prison farm. She was seventy-five.[8]

A week after the Itta Bena arrests MacArthur Cotton led 200 Greenwood blacks to the courthouse to register. At noon police demanded that the group disperse, and when the people refused, thirteen of the leaders were arrested. At 1:30 that afternoon there was a "five minute trial" in which all were convicted of disturbing the peace and given four-month sentences. Among those who served time, first at the county prison farm and later at Parchman, were local activists Mary Lane, George Greene, and Mary Booth, along with SNCC staff members Cotton, Hollis Watkins, and Guyot, back in custody again two weeks after his beating in Winona. The Justice Department investigated the Greenwood and Itta Bena incidents as fifty-eight people sweated it out in Parchman for nearly two months before being released on bond.[9]

Now, however, intensified white violence seemed to anger Delta blacks more than it frightened them. Greenwood was a case in point. Over the past year movement workers there had endured beatings, bombings, jailings, assassination attempts, the cutoff of food commodities and other economic reprisals, along with the disappointment that accompanied the Justice Department's withdrawal of its injunction request. In the summer of 1963 the local people's commitment remained strong, while SNCC staff received reinforcements, this time from the North. Stokely Carmichael and Jean Wheeler came down from Howard and Martha Prescod came from Michigan. For the first time, SNCC permitted white students to work in the Delta. Mike Miller and Dick Frey were in Greenwood, and Hunter Morey was in Greenville. Jane Stembridge, one of the original members of SNCC, later joined the Greenwood project. And although the national media were no longer drawn to Greenwood, entertainers like Lena Horne came to town, and Dick Gregory paid a return visit. On July 8, on a farm outside Greenwood, an unusual folk festival took place. Among the visiting musicians performing were Theodore Bikel, Pete Seeger, and a fervent young guitarist and songwriter named Bob Dylan. The entertainment was a welcome distraction and boosted morale, but the Greenwood story remained that of voter education and the daily trips by local residents to the courthouse to take the registration test. With the local ministers now committed—on paper, at least—to the registration drive, black Greenwood had a unity and sense of purpose that Sam Block and Willie Peacock could only have dreamed of a year earlier.[10]

Across the Delta in Greenville, Charlie Cobb reported intensified activity in Washington County, with his small staff augmented by a half-dozen black college students on summer vacation. Cobb had set up the Greenville Student Movement, young people recruited "for the most part . . . off the block, in the pool halls, and out of the cafes and juke joints, and they are probably the wildest crew of working freedom fighters in the state. . . . But they work, every day, the dull drudgery of canvassing in hot streets. As long as we work, they work." They also initiated direct action protests. Five local blacks and Hunter Morey were arrested after a sit-in attempt at the local Walgreen's drugstore on July 1. Later that month, after several black youngsters had been arrested for playing baseball in a "white" public park, SNCC fieldworker Charles McLaurin urged a crowd of blacks assembled in front of the courthouse to register and vote so they could deal with such injustices. For this, McLaurin was arrested for disturbing the peace and resisting arrest and drew a 180-day jail sentence, which he appealed all the way to the U.S. Supreme Court.[11]

McLaurin continued to organize in neighboring Sunflower County, assisted by SNCC's newest—and oldest—field secretary, Fannie Lou Hamer. Activity also continued in Indianola and Cleveland in Bolivar County, Amzie Moore's home base. There, Diane and James Bevel attempted to reach the larger community in a letter sent to 300 prominent Cleveland whites. The informative and polite statement ended with a warning that in "any community where people have been oppressed for hundreds of years," there exists "a dangerous potential." Included with each letter was a pamphlet entitled "How to Practice Nonviolence." After responding to Wiley Branton's call to come to Greenwood after the Travis shooting, Frank Smith returned in May to Holly Springs, where he worked with students at Rust College, forming a "Speaker's Bureau" led by Leslie McLemore, John Morris, and Johnnie Harris. These students canvassed the community, spoke at churches, and took part in a boycott against downtown white merchants. A threatened demonstration drew "some concessions" from the city, Smith reported, and for a time a larger percentage of applicants passed the registration test.[12]

There was no progress in Clarksdale, where blacks had been boycotting white businesses since December 1961. In the months following the Meredith crisis, boycott leader Aaron Henry had been forced to deal with escalating violence, police repression, and an intransigent white business community, as well as opposition from the national office of the NAACP over his ecumenical "COFO approach" in organizing black Clarksdale. By the spring of 1963, with the boycott holding firm, whites employed terrorist tactics to break the movement. In early March someone broke out the front windows in Henry's pharmacy, and on Good Friday two white men firebombed the Henrys' home. Their house guest, Detroit congressman Charles Diggs, helped to extinguish the flames. Later that month an explosion ripped a hole through the roof of Henry's drugstore. Vera Pigee was beaten by a white service station attendant for attempting to use the rest room and then arrested for disturbing the peace.[13]

Faced with mounting white violence apparently sanctioned by public officials, Henry sent out a call for help. The NAACP national office responded in early May by sending in its top leaders for a brief visit, including Wilkins, national board chair Bishop Stephen Gill Spottswood, and Arthur B. Spingarn. Later that month, after a similar appeal to the CORE national office, Henry received a "bawling out" over the telephone from Wilkins, who made clear the NAACP's displeasure over other movement agencies getting publicity from the Clarksdale campaign. Henry tried to explain the need for outside help during this critical phase, yet he conceded that "I do see how this does cause a problem in the areas where money is raised to support the program." Still, Henry continued to work under the COFO umbrella. Assisting him in Clarksdale were the SCLC's James Bevel, SNCC's Lafayette Surney, and CORE's Tom Gaither. Early in the summer Gaither reported that "unity is still eminent in the workings of all the civil rights groups here."[14]

On June 12, just hours before Medgar Evers's assassination, the Clarksdale mayor and commissioners rejected the movement's most recent request for an interracial committee. There followed a series of demonstrations and sit-ins that jolted the city throughout the summer. Local blacks set up picket lines at city hall, the public library, the circuit clerk's office, and at the Southern Bell telephone office to protest unfair hiring practices. Demonstrators defied a court injunction prohibiting picketing, with many choosing to stay in jail rather than post bail. The national NAACP, perhaps smarting from the criticism over having cut off bail money in Jackson, supplied over $20,000 to secure the release of demonstrators who could not remain in prison. By the middle of August nearly 100 protestors had been arrested. The prisoners sang freedom songs in overcrowded cells with windows shut even in 103-degree heat. Withholding food did not deter them. Work details included cutting grass with "swing blades" for women and an assignment to a garbage truck for Henry, an attempt at humiliation that only increased his prestige in the black community. The boycott continued, with transportation provided for shopping in neighboring towns.[15]

Despite the remarkable degree of unity and perseverance that Clarksdale blacks showed in sustaining the campaign for more than two years, white officials and businesspeople still refused to discuss any of the movement's demands. Even if the merchants had been willing to compromise, they probably would not have been able to persuade the politicians to go along, so strong was the feeling against civil rights "agitators." Backed by the law enforcement agencies and confident that federal intervention was unlikely, segregationists believed they could break the boycott without making concessions. Blacks still held no jobs above the menial level in government or in white-owned businesses, and the mayor refused to agree to an interracial committee.[16]

Down in Jackson the boycott continued during the summer and fall of 1963, but without the unity and intensity displayed by Clarksdale's black community. The death of Evers and the disillusionment over the Kennedy-supported agreement with Mayor Thompson demoralized the young people who had originated and sustained the boycott. The movement was thrown into further confusion when Charles Evers, Medgar's brother, appointed himself the new Mississippi NAACP field secretary.

Although Charles and Medgar had maintained a close relationship over the years, the brothers were distinct opposites in personality and profession. After graduating from Alcorn College, in 1951 Charles moved to Philadelphia, Mississippi, where for the next five years he held down a series of jobs as a teacher, mortician, cab driver, and disc jockey. His advocacy of black voting rights angered

Philadelphia whites, who bankrupted him and forced him to leave the state. For the next seven years Charles lived in Chicago, where by his own admission he was a bootlegger, numbers runner, and petty thief, as well as a teacher and tavern owner. Returning to Jackson for Medgar's funeral, Charles startled Wilkins by announcing that he was taking over as Mississippi field secretary. Rather than risk a public confrontation with the slain martyr's brother, Wilkins went along, a decision the NAACP chief regretted many times over the next several years.[17]

Mississippi blacks knew little about Charles Evers, but local people almost immediately began making unfavorable comparisons between him and Medgar. Myrlie Evers privately expressed reservations about her brother-in-law's appointment. Aware of Charles's checkered career in Chicago, she feared he would "mar the record made by her husband." Charles Evers made it clear from the start that he was his own man. Shortly after taking over the Mississippi operation, he told an audience of a 1,000 civil rights advocates in Detroit that northern Negroes did not give adequate support to the southern movement and should "stop blaming the white man for [their] troubles." Evers also hit out at southern blacks who moved north "to get on welfare or ADC," for the welfare system "makes the Negro lazy." This speech drew a sharp rebuke from Gloster Current, who instructed his new field secretary that "before making any other speeches outside of Jackson, I want to see the written text of all such speeches a week in advance." The speech, and Evers's flamboyant and domineering personality, did not go down well in black Jackson, and early in September Current reported to Wilkins that "Negro leaders in the community" were upset with Evers's conduct. Nevertheless, Current recommended that they give Evers a chance to prove himself and "try to give him some guidance."[18]

The emergence of Charles Evers was a setback for the Mississippi movement. Although Medgar had initially been wary of the young organizers in SNCC and CORE, and they of him, by late 1962 there had developed a mutual respect. Medgar had been comfortable working within the COFO framework, where Charles ignored COFO leaders and tried to undermine their programs. From the summer of 1963 on he began to chart his own course for the state NAACP, which frustrated and infuriated grass-roots activists and national NAACP officials alike.

With the notable exception of Hattiesburg, COFO had sustained no major projects in the southern half of the state before 1963. SNCC workers made occasional trips back to their initial base in McComb, but they found the black community there still divided and white resistance to voter registration as strong as it had been in the fall of 1961. There had been some NAACP voter registration activity in Natchez, but COFO did not initiate a project in that old river town until 1964. The Gulf Coast was also unexplored territory. Under the leadership of Dr. Felix Dunn and Dr. Gilbert Mason, the NAACP had undertaken registration efforts in Biloxi and Gulfport, yet there had been no significant movement activity since the Biloxi wade-in in the spring of 1960. SNCC had sent Nashville activist Lester McKinnie into Laurel after the freedom rides. McKinnie met strong opposition both from local whites and from Dr. B. F. Murph, the Laurel dentist who ran the NAACP.[19] The smaller rural counties were virtually untouched by civil rights activity of any kind, and race relations in these communities remained unchanged. Aware of the need to expand the movement to southern Mississippi, SNCC organizers worked to develop a strong project in Hattiesburg and, with that base secured, extend outward into other areas.

Hattiesburg is located in the middle of the state's southeast quadrant and contrasts sharply with the Delta towns of Greenwood and Greenville. Trees, not cotton, dominate this Piney Woods section of Mississippi, and small farms instead of plantations dot the countryside. Blacks constituted only one-third of Hattiesburg's 35,000 residents. Although far from affluent, Hattiesburg blacks were not so poor as those in the Delta, and white resistance to black advancement was more subtle. The presence of Mississippi Southern College and William Carey College no doubt had an ameliorating impact on race relations. No whites openly endorsed the movement, but several individuals in the white community were quietly supportive. The local daily newspaper, while staunchly segregationist, was not a hate sheet. Still, Hattiesburg was a segregated city, and blacks suffered from lack of economic opportunity, poor schools, and inadequate city services. Above all, in denying blacks the right to vote, Forrest County circuit clerk Theron Lynd put his Delta counterparts to shame.[20]

The 330-pound former football player and Citizens' Council member was elected circuit clerk in 1959. The following year U.S. Attorney General William P. Rogers requested that Lynd allow the

Justice Department to examine his registration files. When he refused, the federal government filed suit in January 1961. The Justice Department investigation had shown that although a substantial majority of the county's 22,431 white voting-age residents were registered, only about 25 of the 7,495 eligible blacks were on the books. During his first two years in office, Lynd had permitted no blacks even to attempt to register. He did allow some to apply after the suit was filed, but none passed the test. Among those Lynd ruled unqualified were David E. Roberson, a biology teacher at the local black high school who had recently been awarded a National Science Foundation scholarship for a year's graduate study at Cornell, and David Lewis, a chemistry and physics teacher with a master's degree.[21]

In the summer of 1961 the Kennedy Justice Department filed another suit against Lynd, and a year later, in *United States* v. *Lynd,* the government initiated its most sweeping action to date, asking the federal courts to prohibit Lynd from discriminating against black voters. Lynd refused to comply at each stage of the judicial process, assisted in his resistance by federal district judge Harold E. Cox, who consistently ruled against the Justice Department. (President Kennedy had appointed him at the urging of Senator Eastland, who had roomed with Cox in college. Judge Cox soon developed a reputation as the most openly racist of the federal jurists.) In a landmark decision, the Fifth Circuit Court of Appeals overruled Cox and issued an injunction against Lynd, prohibiting him from continuing discriminatory practices and subjecting him to contempt proceedings if he failed to comply. Despite all the evidence and the court rulings against him, Lynd still refused to register black voters.[22]

The Justice Department's interest in Forrest County was a factor in SNCC's decision to open a voter registration drive in and around Hattiesburg. In March 1962, not long after the collapse of the McComb project, SNCC sent in two of its new Pike County recruits, Hollis Watkins and Curtis Hayes. They came at the invitation of Vernon Dahmer, an NAACP leader who had grown impatient with the local branch's lack of an agenda. A successful farmer and businessman, Dahmer was "quite a militant person" who had for years worked on behalf of his community. Dahmer had a light complexion, and "unless he told you he was black you'd never know it." At the time he contacted the SNCC workers, Dahmer was leading the campaign to have his close friend Clyde Kennard released from Parchman. Dahmer told Watkins and Hayes that he "had a business and didn't have the time to organize" but was "willing to support somebody who had the time to do it." Local and state NAACP officials responded less than enthusiastically to Dahmer's plan to bring SNCC workers into Hattiesburg, and as a result the Hattiesburg project was slow getting started.[23]

Watkins remembers Dahmer as "a real down to earth father" who used his influence in the black community to overcome NAACP opposition. Since SNCC had supplied Watkins and Hayes with only fifty dollars for a six-month campaign, the young organizers had to rely on local blacks for food and shelter. Of inestimable assistance was Mrs. L. E. Woods, an older member of Hattiesburg's black elite who provided space on the first floor of her hotel for the COFO office, resisting repeated white demands that she evict her new tenants. For a time Hayes and Watkins worked half-time at a black-owned sawmill for room and board, spending their afternoons and evenings canvassing the community to persuade people that it was important that they go down to the courthouse and face Theron Lynd.

The first major breakthrough occurred in the spring of 1962 in Palmer's Crossing, the small settlement just outside Hattiesburg, when the Reverend L. P. Ponder opened St. John's Methodist Church to the movement. "That's really where the Hattiesburg movement started," one parishioner proudly recalled. "It started for all practical purposes in St. John's Church in Palmer's Crossing." There, at an early meeting, about a half-dozen people agreed to go to the courthouse in Hattiesburg to take the registration test. In addition to Reverend Ponder, three members of that original delegation played significant roles in the development of the Hattiesburg movement. Mrs. Virgie Robinson, age seventy, became involved "in every way, from walking a picket line to fixing a meal. She kept people in her home, and went to jail." The Reverend J. W. Brown, who made his living as a school bus driver, remained active in the struggle until the end: Brown "hung in with the movement until he closed his eyes." The third person to commit to the movement that night was a woman in her early thirties, a mother of three children who operated a successful business. Her name was Victoria Gray.[24]

Born in Palmer's Crossing and educated in the local schools, "Vickie" attended Wilberforce College in Ohio for a year before returning to Mississippi to marry Anthony Gray, a career military man, and begin raising a family. When Anthony was stationed in Germany during the Korean War years his family accompanied him, returning to the Hattiesburg area in 1955. She then opened a branch of a cosmetics firm and for the next six years concentrated on building up her business. Although she always possessed "a very high social consciousness" and was "looking for opportunities to make necessary changes," Gray did not join the Hattiesburg branch of the NAACP, which she regarded as "a closed social group." The male-dominated organization, under the leadership of J. C. Fairlie, did not even approach her about taking out a membership, although she was head of her local PTA and a leader in her church. When Watkins and Hayes arrived in Hattiesburg in early 1962, Victoria Gray was more than ready to work with them.[25]

That first small group to arrive at the courthouse to take the test found Lynd waiting for them behind a forty-foot counter that ran practically the length of the room. Mrs. Gray remembers her first encounter with the circuit clerk: "totally uncooperative; totally hostile; very rude; and just doing everything possible to discourage you aside from saying 'get out of here.'" Lynd refused to answer questions about the registration form. No one passed the test. Three of the people in the group were school bus drivers, and within twenty-four hours all had been fired. As was the case with other COFO registration projects, in Hattiesburg whites resorted to intimidation and economic reprisal to crush the local movement early on. They had help from a few key black allies, including the Reverend R. W. Woullard. Woullard, it will be recalled, had worked closely with the sheriff and police chief in discouraging black protest in the 1950s and cooperated with the Sovereignty Commission in its unsuccessful effort to dissuade Clyde Kennard from applying to Mississippi Southern. The pastor of the largest Baptist church in Hattiesburg and a wealthy businessman, Woullard used his considerable influence to thwart the COFO project and never endorsed the movement, even after many other ministers had come around.[26]

During the summer of 1962 Hayes and Watkins worked to build a broad-based movement, helping to establish the Forrest County Voters League. By September 100 blacks had attempted to register, and Lynd, increasingly under pressure from the Justice Department, had found four of them eligible to vote. As had the movement in the Delta, the Hattiesburg movement drew its greatest support from older people and youngsters. Victoria Gray, who was in her mid-thirties, was a notable exception. Among the adults, black business and professional people were more likely to support the movement clandestinely with cash donations, as would the small number of black men holding down factory jobs. Most teachers and ministers shunned the movement in its early stages. As it had in other projects, interorganizational rivalry developed in Hattiesburg, with the local NAACP at first resentful of the SNCC presence. Over time NAACP officials softened their opposition to the project, and by the middle of 1963 they had come on board.[27]

When Watkins and Hayes left Hattiesburg in September 1962 to join SNCC's major project in the Delta, Gray took over as project director. She paid less attention to her business as her involvement in civil rights activity deepened, and by November she was working full-time in the movement, at a salary of twenty-five dollars a week. After attending an SCLC workshop, she began holding citizenship-training classes in the Hattiesburg area, first in her church and later in private homes. She taught her students, most of whom were older adults, basic skills such as writing their names, addresses, and social security numbers. She taught them to read and used the Constitution and the Mississippi registration form as advanced texts. The citizenship classes were also an important recruiting tool. Gray remembers that the program gave the movement an important entrée into Hattiesburg churches: "Many times I was able to use the literacy thing where I couldn't use anything else. I would go to the churches and simply ask the question: 'Would you like to read and write? I am involved in a literacy program.' This is the way I would recruit people." Gray saw the graduates of the citizenship schools as the unsung heroes of the Hattiesburg movement. The pride and confidence they gained through learning to read and write was an empowering experience: "These were the people who were willing to walk those lines; to say 'Yes, we are going to jail,'and 'No, we don't want any bail.' . . . These people grew and were ready to do whatever they had to do, once things were made clear to them."[28]

Teaching people to read and write and canvassing black neighborhoods door to door was time-consuming, painstaking work, and the movement in Hattiesburg grew slowly. In the spring of 1963, when Greenwood was at fever pitch and the Jackson boycott was gaining momentum, Hattiesburg activists could point to fewer than 150 people who had attempted to register, and there had been no large mass meetings or marches to the courthouse.

In the summer, however, SNCC sent John O'Neal, Lawrence Guyot, and Carl Arnold to work full-time in Hattiesburg, for Forrest County had again become an important movement battleground. On July 15 a three-judge panel of the Fifth Circuit Court of Appeals upheld an earlier judgment against Lynd requiring him to register blacks on the same basis as he certified white applicants. The court also found Lynd in civil contempt and gave him ten days to purge himself by registering forty-three named black applicants whom he had previously rejected. To avoid being jailed, Lynd was also to cease giving blacks more difficult sections of the Mississippi Constitution to interpret than he gave whites; stop rejecting black applications for minor errors or omissions; and permit federal agents to check his voter records. Lynd once again appealed the decision, this time to the U.S. Supreme Court. SNCC leaders realized that Hattiesburg was now the major testing ground in the battle for the suffrage. Early in August Bob Moses wrote an urgent memo to national civil rights leaders noting that the Fifth Circuit Court decision was "the first such order handed down in Mississippi" and that it was "crucial for the civil rights organizations to launch a concerted drive in [Forrest] county to register Negroes before the 1964 elections."[29]

Throughout the fall of 1963 the movement's local base was broadening. One field report was signed jointly by Victoria Gray, now president of the Forrest County Voters League; J. C. Fairlie, president of the local NAACP branch; and SNCC field secretary John O'Neal. A weekly newsletter, the *Voice of the Movement*, circulated widely in the black community, and the NAACP was supporting two local full-time workers, Betty Davis and Geraldine Deas. In late September O'Neal reported that "we have reached a kind of plateau here. A congenial atmosphere has been established and I think that things are ready to move into another phase of development." Although not satisfied with the results of the registration effort to date, O'Neal was convinced that "if we've accomplished no more than to create the atmosphere in which this kind of realization (of self) is more likely, we have done something important."[30]

• • •

While SNCC had been expanding its efforts outside the Delta and local NAACP branches were taking on new life in areas where COFO was operating, CORE, the third major partner in the coalition, had been keeping a low profile in Mississippi. Except for Tom Gaither, who was working full-time with Aaron Henry in Clarksdale, Dave Dennis was the only CORE organizer in the state. Since his arrival in Jackson in the summer of 1962, the twenty-one-year-old Dennis had assisted with the ongoing programs of SNCC and the NAACP while trying to establish a CORE presence. Active in the Delta project and in the Jackson boycott, Dennis had begun a Home Industry Cooperative in Ruleville, working with eighteen local women who made rugs, quilts, and aprons in their homes for sale to movement supporters in the North. He also spent time working in Hattiesburg—and courting a local activist named Mattie Bivins, whom he married.

During his first year in Mississippi Dennis had become frustrated over CORE's lack of support: "I am very disappointed at the response which has been given to the local project here in Mississippi by the national office," he wrote Jim McCain, CORE's director of organization. Specifically, Dennis believed that CORE had not committed adequate financial resources and legal assistance and that it was not providing him with any sense of direction. "During the past six months I have been attempting to establish some type of an over-all program for CORE in Mississippi," he wrote McCain in the summer of 1963. "It has been difficult because of my inability to determine what positions CORE really wanted to take. Every time I would ask the national office about helping to set up such a program I would get the word to do what I thought was best. When I do that I'm confronted with what the national office can do or won't do, which is then too late because I would have committed myself as CORE on 'what I thought was best.'"[31]

CORE officials also had complaints about the operating style of their man in Mississippi. Dennis's primary loyalty lay with COFO rather than CORE. He worked effectively with Moses and the other SNCC organizers and was unconcerned about which organization got credit for movement successes. Dennis shared SNCC's distaste for bureaucracy and made no effort to establish CORE chapters in the state. CORE leaders believed that following the freedom rides their contributions in Mississippi had gone largely unrecorded, while SNCC garnered most of the credit. Since CORE depended on contributions from liberal whites to support its programs, this lack of visibility posed a serious problem.[32] On the other hand, they realized that Dennis was a person of extraordinary ability who combined passionate dedication to the cause with superior organizational skills and a vision that extended beyond the ongoing programs of voter registration.

From the beginning Dennis had been interested in dealing with the staggering problems of poverty facing black Mississippians, and he initiated the project to get food and clothing to destitute families in the Delta. His Ruleville cooperative was an unsuccessful attempt to help local blacks become economically independent. He also envisioned the creation of "educational centers" that would be "a central place for people from all over the country to come and acquire information." At the heart of these community centers would be libraries where "the people can come and learn more about their government, how to establish better living conditions, how to better their farm conditions. We want to be able to show films on agricultural development, health, history, government . . . and, of course, educate them in the importance of the movement." For Dennis, "the big problem in Mississippi is to get the people to understand exactly what we are attempting to do. If we can awaken the minds of the masses in Mississippi," he confidently predicted, "we can have the greatest movement ever."[33]

Dennis's request for more support from CORE and the national office's insistence on more visibility in Mississippi were reconciled with the establishment of CORE's first project in the state. National CORE's position that the organization must have its own territory in Mississippi had resulted in COFO's awarding CORE the fourth congressional district, but it was nearly a year before the financially strapped national office was able to give the go-ahead to launch a voter registration drive in Madison County. In March 1963 Dennis had proposed to McCain that CORE send more organizers to Mississippi and assign them all to work in and around Canton, the county seat. For Dennis, Madison County was the ideal location for a CORE project. Blacks there made up more than 70 percent of the county's 33,000 inhabitants and constituted over 60 percent of Canton's 10,000 residents. Blacks owned 40 percent of the land, providing an apparent economic independence. Moreover, this was virgin territory for the movement. SNCC had sent no workers there, and the local NAACP chapter was inactive.[34]

In making his case for Madison County, Dennis noted that Canton's proximity to Tougaloo College, which was located on the southern edge of the county, made it possible to involve college students in the project. Less than a half-hour from Jackson, Canton was easily accessible to national news media. National CORE did not need much persuasion. Key members of the New York staff, unhappy over not having been able to do more in Mississippi and desperate for visibility, saw the value of the proposed project. Dennis became director of the fourth district CORE project, which eventually expanded to Leake County and to Meridian on the Alabama border.[35]

The chief strategist and organizer in Madison County was George Raymond, one of the unsung heroes of the Mississippi movement. Born in New Orleans in 1943, Raymond first came to Mississippi as a teenager to participate in the freedom rides. In late 1962 he worked in Sunflower County with Fannie Lou Hamer. When CORE opened its Madison County project in June 1963, the twenty-year-old Raymond was its only staff person. A short, very strong man, Raymond was quiet and intense, yet fearless. Willie Peacock, an authority on the subject, put it simply: "George Raymond had guts." Although he was not a charismatic speaker, Raymond won the respect of the black community because, as much as any "outsider," he identified with the local people. Whenever and wherever there was trouble, Raymond, always clad in bib overalls, was on hand to investigate.[36]

When Raymond first moved into Canton he found a town and a county totally controlled by a handful of powerful whites. The second-largest cattle county in the state, Madison had the appearance and mentalilty of the western frontier. Racial violence and brutality had been widespread throughout the county. Several months before CORE came into Canton the body of a twenty-four-year-old black man was found castrated and mutilated near the home of a white family. Although judged "a probable lynching," this act of bestiality surprised few Madison County residents, black or white. Even though blacks did own 40 percent of the land, that statistic is misleading and did not translate into economic or political independence. Cotton was the major crop, and federal agricultural officials discriminated against black farmers when setting domestic production allotments. The farms were small, and many black landowners had to pledge their crop in advance in order to plant. This continual indebtedness relegated most of them, in effect, to the condition of sharecroppers. Almost half of all black families in Madison County had annual incomes of less than $1,000. Of a potential black electorate of nearly 10,000, only 121 were registered, and few of these people dared show up at the polls to vote.[37]

As in the other movement counties, a handful of local blacks supported Raymond and legitimized his presence in Canton. His major ally in Madison County was C. O. Chinn. Born and raised in Madison County, Chinn received little formal education, but his family had held on to 154 acres of land, and he also owned and operated a restaurant. Along with people like E. W. Steptoe and Hartman Turnbow, Chinn had a deserved reputation for courage and stubbornness. "He was the last of the frontiersmen," recalled CORE organizer Matt "Flukey" Suarez. "Every white man in that town knew that you didn't fuck with C. O. Chinn." "Most of the whites feared him," agreed co-worker Anne Moody. "He was the type of person that didn't take shit from anyone." The forty-one-year-old Chinn took an instant liking to young George Raymond, and during the hot summer days of 1963 the two men were always seen together making the rounds, talking to people in the city and county who could be useful in implementing the planned voter registration project. "When George had to go somewhere, Chinn took him," observed Suarez. "When he needed protection, Chinn protected him. When he and the other workers needed somewhere to sleep, Chinn found beds."[38]

The movement in Madison County got off to a promising start. In Raymond's first three weeks in Canton seventy-five blacks took the registration test, and twenty-five passed. Caught off guard by this initiative, white supremacists in Canton struck back. Foote Campbell, the circuit clerk, developed a reputation for unfairness in registering black applicants that rivaled that of Martha Lamb and Theron Lynd. The Citizens' Council was strong in Madison County, including in its ranks leading attorneys, bankers, elected officials, and businesspeople. Sheriff Billy Nobles was a member, as was his brother Gus, who ran an insurance agency and Canton politics. Almost immediately, blacks attempting to register met economic reprisals, and police set up road blocks to prevent people from attending mass meetings. But here again young people served as the shock troops of the movement. Anne Moody, a Tougaloo student who had been active in the Jackson movement, went to work in Canton early in the summer and reported that from forty to fifty young blacks were canvassing, despite all the threats and harassment. Then, on the evening of July 24, a white gas station attendant named Price Lewis leveled a shotgun blast at a group of five black teenagers active in the movement. Lewis was fined $500 on a charge of "unlawful discharge of a firearm within the city limits" and set free. Although none of the young people received serious injuries from the buckshot blast, Moody recalled that "the shooting really messed up our relationship with the teenagers," whose frightened parents ordered them to stay away from the Freedom House.[39]

August was the month of the Democratic primary elections for governor. All candidates were segregationists. The most moderate of them, former governor J. P. Coleman, lost to Lt. Governor Paul Johnson, Jr., who had "stood tall" in the schoolhouse door when James Meredith first attempted to enroll at Ole Miss. During the gubernatorial campaign blacks discovered an old state law that permitted citizens to vote by affidavit if they believed they had been illegally prevented from casting their ballots. Thirty Madison County blacks filed affidavits locally, and others sent their sworn statements to Washington. Three weeks later, in the runoff primary, Madison County blacks staged a preview of things to come when more than 2,000 voted in a mock election. By then CORE had a staff of five working in Madison County, including Moody and two other black college students who would be returning to their studies in the fall. CORE was now committed to Madison County, with veterans of New Orleans CORE like Suarez and Jerome Smith moving up to Mississippi to join their hometown colleagues Raymond and Dennis.[40]

Voter registration activities stalled during the early fall, as white resistance remained solid. After Chinn rented an office to CORE, police forced him to shut down his cafe and jailed him on a weapons charge, although Chinn had his pistol openly displayed on the front seat of his car in accordance with Mississippi law. But black adults were now taking an interest in the new movement, which gained an invaluable recruit in Annie Devine.[41]

Mrs. Devine played much the same role in Canton as did Victoria Gray in Hattiesburg. A mother of four children, in her mid-forties, and active in her church, she had taught elementary school in the early 1950s before becoming an agent for Security Life Insurance Company. Movement activist and historian Tom Dent has observed that Devine "represented the respectable center of the black community," complementing the leadership of Chinn, "a bar owner, opinionated, and regarded as something of an outlaw." Dent concluded that "the Chinn/Devine alliance in support of CORE and the movement symbolized the unification of the black community and provided the Canton movement with an important and unusual legitimacy in the history of the civil rights struggle."[42] Annie Devine was also an invaluable resource for the New Orleans CORE workers. Matt Suarez worked closely with her:

> We were young and full of energy. We were trying to bust down brick walls by running our heads through them. We understood very little about Mississippi and how whites and Blacks related to each other. [Mrs. Devine] knew her community and understood it. . . . She directed us to blacks who were trustworthy, to ministers and churches that would open, and [told us] how to approach these people. . . . She knew what we could get away with and what we could not. . . . She was a stabilizing force . . . the backbone of what we were doing.[43]

Within six months George Raymond had established a beachhead for CORE in Madison County. Devine and Chinn provided adult leadership. Young people were now once again becoming involved in the day-to-day canvassing, supplying the energy for the weekly mass meetings taking place in several churches. The local NAACP chapter had reorganized and joined the Madison County movement, the COFO affiliate that included all the civil rights groups working in the county. Madison County blacks appeared ready to move.[44]

Located immediately to the northwest, the part Delta/part hills county of Holmes at first glance appeared in many ways to mirror Madison. There too blacks constituted 72 percent of the county population of 27,000, and in 1963 only a handful were registered to vote. In addition, some 800 black farmers owned their land. Politically, however, Holmes developed differently from Madison. In fact, as activist Susan Lorenzi Sojourner has written, "Probably no other of Mississippi's 82 counties . . . developed a comparable political organization, sophistication, and level of accomplishment."[45]

A number of factors account for the success of the Holmes County movement, but foremost are the history and character of its people. Born in 1916, Ralthus Hayes was a lifelong resident of Holmes County. His father had sharecropped in both the Delta and hills sections, and when he came of age, Ralthus also worked on white-owned plantations. He married a Holmes County woman in 1938, and they began to raise a family. In 1940, in the last hurrah of the New Deal, the Farm Security Administration purchased 9,350 acres of rich Delta land in the county and divided it into 106 farms. This modest project made it possible for Hayes and other black sharecroppers and plantation workers to buy their own farms. "Always since I was a man," Hayes recalled, "I thought of buying land but there was no ways I could have done it. There was no ways to make enough on shares to ever get land." In 1941 Hayes got a long-term federal loan to purchase fifty-four acres and received low-interest federal loans to buy materials for a house, mules, and farming equipment. Because the land was fertile, he could make a go of it, and ten years later he bought sixty-four more acres in another federal project. The FSA program brought more than economic security to Hayes and the other beneficiaries; they developed an independence of mind and spirit rare among rural blacks. (Hayes had made his first attempt to register and vote in 1951.) These independent yeomen resisted efforts by whites to buy them out—Delta land had been, after all, white man's territory—and with shotguns at their sides, they made it clear that they would not be driven off their farms. In 1963 this small group of farmers and their families, located in the Mileston-Tchula section of the Delta, launched the Holmes County movement.[46]

The Delta region of Holmes borders on Leflore County, and in the early months of 1963 several blacks from the Mileston area drove to Greenwood to attend the mass meetings. Key people here were Alma Mitchell Carnegie, a sixty-six-year-old warrior who had for decades been traveling the state to NAACP and union gatherings, and her younger brother, Ozell Mitchell. The two "brought the movement to their home community." Soon Sam Block was holding meetings in Mileston, and another young SNCC worker, John Ball, conducted citizenship classes twice a week. Ralthus Hayes was involved from the beginning (he later attended an SCLC workship and returned to lead the citizenship program), as was another local farmer named Hartman Turnbow. Turnbow's grandfather had been a slave, the child of his master, who after emancipation sold his son a piece of Delta land. Turner's grandmother left him the farm, and he had been working it for most of his fifty-nine years. A short, solidly built man, Turnbow was known for his malapropisms (he once referred to SNCC as "the Student Violent Non-coordinated Committee"!) and for his fierce independence, which was backed by an impressive arsenal of weapons. Turnbow, Hayes, Carnegie, and Mitchell were part of a group of fourteen Holmes County blacks—the "First 14," as they would proudly become known in local movement lore—who quietly made their way to the county courthouse in Lexington on the morning of April 9, 1963, and announced that they had come to register to vote.[47]

All the prospective voters were over forty; at seventy-eight, Charlie Carnegie was the oldest. Most were independent farmers. The Reverend Nelson Trent, who had recently moved to Lexington, was the only person not from the Delta area. Three in the group were women. They were met outside the courthouse by Deputy Sheriff Andrew Smith, county and city officers, and nearly thirty members of the local auxiliary police force. Not eager for the kind of publicity that neighboring Greenwood had been attracting, the local authorities did not provoke a confrontation, but it was an intimidating show of force. When Smith bellowed, "All right now, who will be first? Who will be first?" the black delegation "commenced to lookin' at one another. . . . I stepped out the line. I said, 'Me, Hartman Turnbow, will be first.'" Only Turnbow and John D. Wesley, another farmer, were permitted to take the test, but the remaining twelve completed the complicated process the following day. Although none of the fourteen passed, they went home feeling proud that they had taken a stand—and relieved that they had not been physically assaulted and jailed.[48]

One month to the day after Turnbow attempted to register, night riders threw three Molotov cocktails into his living room and kitchen while he and his family slept. "My wife and daughter jumped up and run out, and the first thing they met was two white fellas in the backyard," Turnbow recalled. "And I didn't go out till I got my rifle, and when I got my rifle, I pushed the safety off, I got it into the shootin' position, and then I run out. The first thing I met was those two white fellas. They start to shootin' at me, and I start to shootin' at them. So they run off, and then we come back and put the fire out." The following morning Bob Moses was at the scene taking pictures of the damage when the deputy sheriff arrived and arrested him for "impeding an official investigation of the fire." Later, Turnbow, Moses, and three other SNCC workers were formally charged with arson and bound over to a Holmes County grand jury. John Doar then intervened on behalf of the defendants, filing a federal civil rights suit in Jackson. Six months later the charges were dropped for lack of evidence.[49]

The early stages of the Holmes County movement are indicative of the opportunities and problems confronting black organizers in Mississippi in the spring and summer of 1963. News of the movement was spreading, and local people, like the "First 14," increasingly overcame fear and took a stand. But there was still no movement activity in the majority of Mississippi counties, where life for blacks had changed little since the turn of the century. Moreover, the firebombing of the Turnbow home and the local authorities' response to that crime provided yet another reminder that segregationists would apparently stop at nothing to maintain white supremacy. The collusion between the police and vigilantes was still the major problem facing civil rights workers, who after two years of intense activity had not yet won the right to organize black communities. By the summer of 1963 a number of COFO activists had concluded that if the Mississippi movement were to survive, the Kennedy administration would have to be pressured to intervene directly to end the white reign of terror. To achieve that goal, new movement strategies were essential.

9

Conflicting Strategies

Mississippi has presented COFO with a major policy
decision. Either the civil rights struggle has to continue, as
it has for the past few years, with small progress in
selected communities with no real progress on any fronts,
or [it must establish a] task force of such a size as to force
either the state and municipal governments to change their
social and legal structures, or the federal government to
intervene on behalf of the constitutional rights of its
citizens.

—COFO, "Prospectus for the Mississippi
Freedom Summer," n.d.

National publicity, if correctly used and focused, is a
powerful weapon in any move for change in Mississippi.

—Bob Moses, Feb. 24, 1963

The Kennedy administration's reluctance to take a stand in
Mississippi was most apparent in its ongoing effort to prevent the
U.S. Commission on Civil Rights from holding hearings in the state.
Established under the Civil Rights Act of 1957, the commission (pop-
ularly known as the Civil Rights Commission, or CRC) is a presi-
dential advisory body charged with investigating human rights abuses.
Under the leadership of two college presidents, John Hannah of
Michigan State and Father Theodore Hesburgh of Notre Dame, the
commission established itself as an independent agency, goading the
Eisenhower and Kennedy administrations to expand the federal government's role in guaranteeing the rights of African-American citizens. Under the terms of the 1957 act, each state was to have its own

advisory committee to "hear complaints, make studies, and report its findings to the federal commission in Washington."[1]

More than two years had passed before the Mississippi advisory committee was organized, and the original board of four whites and two blacks immediately drew fire from segregationists. Congressman John Bell Williams charged that the participation of whites on the committee was "tantamount to collaboration with the enemy"; the Citizens' Council's W. J. Simmons warned that committee members faced the "contempt and ostracism that people feel for a traitor." Members received hate mail and telephone threats, a cross was burned on the lawn of white committee member Jane Schutt, and a week after James Meredith desegregated Ole Miss, the home of a black member, Dr. James L. Allen, was bombed. Undaunted, the Mississippi committee held meetings throughout the state to gather evidence on mistreatment of blacks and urged the CRC to hold hearings in Mississippi.[2]

The commission first scheduled a hearing for October 3, 1962, but postponed it when the Justice Department argued that the immediate aftermath of the Ole Miss crisis was no time for a public forum. Rescheduling the hearings for December prompted Attorney General Kennedy to ask for another delay, and the commission reset the hearings for January. On December 15, Robert Kennedy once more asked the commission to put off the Mississippi hearings. The Justice Department had filed criminal contempt charges against Governor Barnett and Lt. Governor Paul Johnson over their refusal to obey a court order admitting Meredith, and Kennedy argued that if there should be a jury trial (by no means a certainty), then "the claim will be made that the Civil Rights Commission is working with the Department of Justice publicly to prejudice the State of Mississippi and its officials in the minds of the jury." Kennedy suggested that "a report could be prepared, without any need for public hearings in the state." A disappointed commission chair John Hannah again acquiesced in the delay, but he told the attorney general that "this decision is difficult for us" because the situation in Mississippi "urgently demands the fact-finding activities the Commission is uniquely able to provide." By then, however, it was clear that the Kennedys did not want the commission to hold any hearings in Mississippi.[3]

Frustrated over the lack of support in Washington, the Mississippi advisory committee, now chaired by Jane Schutt, issued a stinging report in January 1963 on the current state of affairs in Mississippi. The committee declared that "terror hangs over the Negro in Mississippi. . . . The attitude of the State Government, rather than being one of protection, has been one of obstruction of the realization of the rights of our citizens." The report described the Justice Department's role as "unduly and unwisely narrow and limited" and once again called for the Civil Rights Commission to hold "a formal civil rights hearing . . . [which] is more urgently needed in Mississippi than in practically any other State in the Union."[4]

This urgent plea was lost on the Justice Department. Although President Kennedy stated at a March 21 press conference that the Mississippi hearings should not be delayed any longer, five days later his brother told John Hannah that he still opposed the hearings, again citing the Barnett contempt case as his reason. By now the members of the CRC were thoroughly disillusioned with the administration's refusal to cooperate. On March 29 Burke Marshall warned Robert Kennedy that "we may at some point have to face resignations" from four members of the commission, including Hannah and Hesburgh. The attorney general scrawled back the following cryptic note: "Can't we find something that would be worthwhile for the Civil Rts Commission to do? There must be something useful. I don't want them to resign."[5]

Instead of resigning, the following day the members of the CRC drafted a resolution on Mississippi, which they made public two weeks later over administration protests. It stated that "since October, open and flagrant violation of the Constitution has reached the point of crisis. . . . Citizens of the United States have been shot, set upon by vicious dogs, beaten and otherwise terrorized because they sought to vote." After rehearsing the history of the scheduled hearings' postponements, the commissioners appealed to the president to do the following:

1. Formally request and direct all persons in the State of Mississippi engaged in willful violation of the laws of the United States to cease and desist therefrom;

2. Do what he can to suppress the existing lawlessness and provide Federal protection to citizens in the exercise of their basic constitutional rights;

3. Give serious consideration to the withholding of Federal funds from the State of Mississippi, until [it] demonstrates its

compliance with the Constitution and laws of the United States.[6]

President Kennedy responded defensively. He praised the work of the Justice Department in Mississippi, adding the following incredible claim: "With regard to the incidents [of white violence] referred to in the Commission's report, I am advised that every case, but one, has been successfully resolved." Kennedy ignored the recommendation that he provide protection for civil rights workers but attacked the suggestion, originally put forward by the national NAACP, that federal funds might be cut off. Correctly sensing that this section of the resolution would not attract widespread support, Kennedy argued that black Mississippians would be among the victims hardest hit by such a move. It is, however, ironic that for months the Kennedy administration had been gathering specific data on federal money spent in the state, classifying the material under the heading "Stick It to Mississippi."[7]

Part of the Kennedys' opposition to the Misssissippi hearings stemmed from their displeasure with the Civil Rights Commission itself, a feeling shared by other administrations. With investigative but not enforcement powers, the CRC served as a gadfly to spur the administration to greater effort. The president ridiculed the commission in private, while his brother drew an unflattering comparison with the House Un-American Activities Committee. More important, in requesting that human rights abuses in Mississippi be publicized nationally and declaring that the administration had the obligation to protect civil rights workers, the commission was challenging the Kennedys' fundamental southern strategy.[8]

Until his death John Kennedy tried to maintain good relations with Mississippi's segregationist congressional delegation. The president went out of his way to avoid conflict, observing the amenities of senatorial courtesy in federal appointments even though it meant undercutting the handful of loyal white Democrats in the state. When Karl Wiesenburg, the moderate Mississippi legislator who publicly condemned Ross Barnett for his handling of the Meredith crisis, was asked to chair the Mississippi advisory committee, he sent back this acerbic reply:

It would appear to me that if the national administration is going to try to act through the so-called Mississippi Democratic Party, and through Senator Eastland, that it would be logical for you to ask Senator Eastland which of his various pigeons he would like to serve as Chairman of the Mississippi Commission on Civil Rights. This would be consistent with other actions taken by the administration in the past. In Mississippi the administration has consistently followed the policy of punishing their friends and rewarding their enemies.

After sarcastically observing that "the offer of the present appointment is one of the few offers that has been made to a loyal Democrat in this administration, and this offer is, of course, an invitation to commit social, political, and economic suicide," Wiesenburg concluded that "I am constrained to say 'a plague on both your houses.'"[9]

In its final days the Kennedy administration did more visibly identify with the black struggle in the South. After initially opposing the March on Washington, fearing it would alienate support for the administration's civil rights bill, John Kennedy eventually embraced it, enhancing the movement's status in the eyes of many skeptical northern whites. And the civil rights bill itself, largely aimed at discrimination in public accommodations and school segregation, was an indication of the administration's committment to the cause of freedom. Still, until the end, the Kennedy administration adopted a cautious approach to civil rights, opposing the stronger civil rights bill submitted by congressional liberals that would have expanded the coverage of the public accommodations and voter registration sections. Further, nine days before the president's assassination, Attorney General Kennedy recommended that John Hannah be relieved of his duties as chair of the Civil Rights Commission.[10]

Civil rights activists in Mississippi were unaware of the behind-the-scenes manuevering in Washington, but they clearly understood that the Kennedy administration had no intention of declaring a war against racist oppression in Senator Eastland's backyard. This policy of nonintervention had undercut the Mississippi movement for two years and was now threatening its existence.

In the late summer of 1963 Bob Moses wrote an analysis of the Mississippi Project for the SNCC executive committee. After summarizing the history of SNCC's work in the state, Moses assessed the movement's prospects. He noted that the organizers had established "beachheads" in a number of towns and counties; recruited and involved local blacks, particularly young people, while gaining the confidence of "many local Negro leaders"; and provided considerable evidence for the Justice Department's voter registration suits. The tone of Moses' report was pessimistic, however, and at times almost despondent. Among the lessons painfully learned was that "it is not possible for us to register Negroes in Mississippi." Moses believed that Mississippi authorities "will force a showdown over the right to vote in large numbers similar to the Federal-State showdowns over integration of schools." SNCC's first Mississippi organizer was equally blunt in his evaluation of the impact of nonviolent protests in Mississippi: "All direct action campaigns for integration have had their backs broken by sentencing prisoners to long jail terms and requiring excessive bail. It has not proved possible to get large enough numbers of people committed to staying in jail, or long enough money to overcome these two obstacles."[11]

Noting that the "Mississippi monolith" had survived the freedom rides, the desegregation of Ole Miss, and the assassination of Medgar Evers, Moses believed that the recent victory of Paul Johnson in the Democratic gubernatorial primary "reinforces all that is bad in the state." The core of the problem, then, was that "the full resources of the state will continue to be at the disposal of local authorities to fight civil rights gains." "The entire white population," Moses glumly concluded, "will continue to be the Klan."[12]

Not all Mississippi activists shared Moses' pessimism, for in some projects the movement was holding its own despite white terror and intimidation. Nevertheless, it was clear that by the late summer of 1963 COFO was facing a dilemma: as long as white hoodlums and police could attack black organizers with impunity, it would be extremely difficult for the movement to make further substantive gains. Although the patient, grass-roots organizing pioneered by SNCC in McComb and in the Delta had politicized many local people, the combination of fear and inertia had left the vast majority of black Mississippians on the sidelines; these men and women were unlikely to enlist in the struggle without some degree of protection from retaliation. All previous efforts to persuade the Kennedy administration to safeguard human rights in Mississippi had failed. Needing security to continue to organize, key movement strategists grudgingly conceded they must reach out to the largely indifferent national public and shock it into demanding federal intervention. To do so meant attracting the media to Mississippi and providing television cameras with action footage. The Mississippi movement was about to enter a new phase.

Allard K. Lowenstein first arrived in Mississippi early in July 1963. Perhaps the youngest of the post–World War II generation of cold war liberals, the thirty-three-year-old Lowenstein graduated from Yale Law School and was a dean at Stanford before moving on to teach at North Carolina State University. Confident, charismatic, and well connected (he had been a confidant of Eleanor Roosevelt), Lowenstein sought out Bob Moses to discuss the range of problems confronting COFO's voter registration campaign. From these conversations, and from COFO strategy sessions, emerged a plan for a series of protest votes, culminating in a "Freedom Ballot for Governor" in November.[13]

In the August 6 Democratic primary, 733 black Mississippians, including 400 from Greenwood alone, had taken advantage of an obscure state law to present affidavits at the polls, claiming they had been illegally denied the right to register. Hundreds more were turned away. In the gubernatorial primary runoff three weeks later, more than 27,000 unregistered blacks of voting age had cast protest ballots in special polling places set up in black churches and businesses.[14]

In September COFO activists began work on a massive "freedom vote" campaign, a mock election that "would demonstrate to Mississippi, Washington and the rest of the nation that the Negro people of Mississippi would vote if they were allowed to register free from intimidation and discrimination." This statewide canvass, culminating in the November election, would also be an ideal vehicle to expand the movement into new territory. Concentrated in the Delta and in central Mississippi, COFO still had no viable projects south of Jackson except Hattiesburg. SNCC organizers were eager to get back into McComb and to begin organizing in Natchez and on the Gulf Coast, but SNCC lacked the resources to send full-time organizers into any of these areas. The freedom vote could provide access to new territory and lay the groundwork for future community organization.

COFO strategists were also excited about the educational value of the mock election. Not only would it allow blacks to "walk through the process" of voting; it might awaken them to the shortcomings of both national parties and encourage local people to develop their own political institutions designed to address problems they identified. The concepts of independence and empowerment were foreign to most Mississippi blacks, who were brought up under segregation and the shadow of slavery. The freedom vote offered the opportunity to establish a structure for a statewide political organization independent of both major parties. (This prospect later became a source of considerable concern for Lowenstein, whose assumption was that once southern blacks got the vote, they would throw in with the liberal wing of the Democratic party.) Finally, COFO organizers hoped that by directing the nation's attention to Mississippi, the freedom vote might force the Kennedys to provide federal protection for civil rights workers.[15]

Bringing the spotlight back on Mississippi would prove difficult. Since the assassination of Medgar Evers, events there had been overshadowed by the debate over the civil rights bill in Congress and by the March on Washington. While national political leaders were basking in the reflected glow of Martin Luther King's "I Have a Dream" speech, a white mob in Meridian attacked a busload of Mississippi marchers returning from Washington, an event overlooked by the national media.[16] Americans could still be shocked by racial atrocities—the church bombing in Birmingham that killed four black girls is a grim example—but in the aftermath of the bloody summer of 1963 there appeared to be a lull in movement activity, with attention shifting to Capitol Hill and the debate over the civil rights bill. Mississippi had been all but forgotten.

The "Freedom Ballot Campaign" officially began with a statewide COFO convention held at the Masonic Temple in Jackson on Sunday, October 6, and open to all movement supporters. The convention adopted a platform calling for racial justice, school desegregation, and the right to vote. In demanding an end to the literacy section of the state's voting laws, COFO directly challenged the common assumption—held by some blacks as well as the majority of whites—that a person should be able to read and write in order to vote. Moses argued that a state that had denied blacks educational opportunity had no right to impose a literacy requirement. The platform also offered an economic program for farmers and factory workers. It called on the state to establish a farm loan program, encourage cooperative farming, and institute a progressive property tax on tracts of over 500 acres. Congress should raise the federal minimum wage from $1.00 to $1.25 an hour, and the rights of labor unions to organize workers should be protected. The most obvious omission from the platform was any reference to welfare rights. One delegate later reflected that "perhaps we all somehow assumed that all the ideas for jobs and education and economic security in the rest of the platform negated the need for a discussion of welfare."[17]

The delegates then chose Aaron Henry as their candidate for governor. The long-time NAACP activist was Mississippi's most recognized black leader, and he had won the respect of NAACP moderates and many SNCC and CORE activists. Henry's campaign for racial justice in Clarksdale was the longest ongoing COFO project in the state, and he had survived numerous jailings and bombings with both courage and humor. On the stump, his down-home oratory went over well with his audiences.[18]

The convention did not select a candidate for lieutenant governor, but a week later Bob Moses asked Tougaloo chaplain Ed King to be Henry's running mate. It was an agonizing decision for King. The white native Mississippian from a prominent Vicksburg family had graduated from Millsaps College in 1958, where he had been active in the interracial meetings at Tougaloo led by Ernst Borinski. After receiving two advanced theological degrees from Boston University, King and his wife, Jeannette, also a native Mississippian, moved to Tougaloo in early 1963. King worked with John Salter and Medgar Evers in the Jackson movement and was arrested twice during demonstrations. When Moses approached him about joining the freedom vote ticket, King was still recovering from the early June automobile accident in which he and Salter had been seriously injured. King's reservations about running included concerns about his health and the danger to himself and his family. The major reason for his hesitation, however, as he later candidly admitted, "was a small thing which suddenly seemed very large. I realized that I really did care what people thought about me—and that included the opinion of my old white friends and of other white ministers in the state." King's dilemma was that of every white Mississippian who opposed segregation. By now, all but a handful had either moved out or decided to keep quiet. King, however, overcame his misgivings and agreed to run with Henry. He became the most visible white activist in the Mississippi movement, and he paid a heavy price for honoring his convictions. King was ostracized by his family, scorned by his colleagues in the clergy, and later shunned by the "New South" white moderates who entered the political arena only after it was safe to do so.[19]

With the candidates and platform in place and the stated goal of nearly 200,000 black ballots, COFO now had to deliver. With less than a month before the election, the organizers had to build a campaign organization, arrange rallies for the candidates, line up polling places, and most important, reach the people. SNCC and CORE were confident they could handle these problems in the counties where there were ongoing projects, but since a major thrust of the freedom vote was to move into new areas, additional campaign workers were needed. Lowenstein suggested that he use his contacts at Stanford and Yale to bring down a number of students to assist in the canvass. COFO staff members had some reservations, for they understood that the students would be white. Although a few white SNCC staff members had been operating in Mississippi, the influx of 50 to 100 white students with little organizing experience and knowledge about Mississippi was problematical. Still, conducting the freedom vote with existing staff, even augmented by SNCC workers from other states, would limit the campaign primarily to existing COFO enclaves, with the strong possibility that the vote would fall far short of the stated goal. COFO accepted Lowenstein's offer. Eventually, more than seventy students, most of them from Yale and Stanford, spent a week in Mississippi getting out the vote.[20]

Although white politicians either ignored or scoffed at the freedom vote, police harassed and jailed campaign workers throughout the state. On October 22, one day after the first group of volunteers arrived from Yale, fourteen movement organizers were arrested in Indianola on charges of distributing leaflets without a license. Two days later, in Clarksdale, Lowenstein and two Yale students were jailed for violating the city curfew. Later that week Yale divinity student John Else found himself in custody on a traffic violation charge, and SNCC veteran Jane Stembridge spent time in the Greenwood jail for allegedly running a stop sign. More than 200 such incidents were reported during the three weeks of the campaign. More ominous were the life-threatening confrontations involving both volunteers and SNCC staff.[21]

A week before the election George Greene, the twenty-year-old SNCC field secretary recruited by Sam Block in Greenwood, was organizing in Adams County. Accompanying him were SNCC advisor Ella Baker, who had come to Mississippi to work in the campaign, and a twenty-one-year-old white Yale graduate student named Bruce Payne. At a filling station in Port Gibson four white men jumped Greene's car and assaulted Payne. Undaunted, the two young men went to work in Natchez the following day, only to find the same group of white hoodlums on their tail. Greene—whose driving prowess became legendary—led his pursuers on a wild 105-mile-per-hour chase, but eventually the whites forced the COFO "votemobile" off the road against a bridge. When one man drew his pistol, walked up to Greene, and demanded that the two get out of the car, the intrepid SNCC activist slammed his car into low gear, swerved past the startled locals, and shot back onto the highway. His would-be assailant fired four times, hitting the left tire. Greene lost his attackers by charging through three red lights, crossing double lines, and driving in oncoming traffic lanes. Back in Jackson, a shaken Bruce Payne asked Ed King, "Do you think those fellows really intended to kill us? Those bullets really hit the car sorta low." To which King sagaciously replied, "In Mississippi it is an error to confuse good intentions with poor aim."[22]

Despite white intimidation, the various groups constituting the COFO coalition stayed together to turn out the vote. The SNCC leadership of COFO had gone out of its way to include state and local branches of the NAACP in the campaign. Although Moses was campaign manager and Dennis chaired the policy committee, the NAACP's Henry headed the ticket, Charles Evers (no friend of SNCC) was given the role of chairman of the speaker's bureau, and R. L. T. Smith was finance chairman. Lowenstein, whose entrée into Mississippi had been through Henry and the NAACP, assumed the position of chairman of the advisory committee. The public meetings on behalf of the ticket reflected the ecumenical spirit. Although some SNCC staff grumbled that the NAACP did not pull its weight, Henry campaigned vigorously, and the "NAACP counties" would deliver a sizable percentage of the total vote.[23]

On the stump King emphasized the symbolic significance of the ticket, the first time that blacks and whites had run in tandem since Reconstruction. Henry stressed the major themes of voting, education, and racial justice, sprinkling his speeches with engaging humor. He always got a roar of approval when he observed, "Now white people will tell us that they have to have segregation because they don't want us fooling with their white women. [pause] I just wish the white men were as satisfied with their women as we are with ours!"[24]

As the election drew near, harassment increased. Hostile whites forced Henry to cancel speeches in Yazoo City and Belzoni, and in Hattiesburg a fire truck blared its siren throughout his address in a black church. Still, the candidates were able to speak in most cities. Nearly 1,000 blacks jammed the Elks Rest in Greenwood to hear Henry, and in Greenville he addressed a crowd of 500 on the courthouse steps with police protection. Perhaps what was most remarkable was that neither Henry nor King was assaulted or arrested throughout the campaign, a unique experience for both men. No doubt most state and local officials preferred peaceful public rallies to the unfavorable publicity that would accompany any outbreak of violence in their communities. The ballots were collected between November 2 and 4, the three days before the official election. Most blacks cast their votes at Sunday church services; boxes were also available for the full three days in such black businesses as beauty parlors, cafes, groceries, and pool halls. Since intimidation was heavy in some areas, campaign headquarters distributed about 25,000 ballots through the mail, to be completed and submitted anonymously.[25]

The results of the freedom vote were gratifying. More than 83,000 blacks, and a few whites, cast their ballots for Henry and King. While this total fell short of the goal of 200,000 (or about 40 percent of the eligible black electorate), given the brief campaign and the harassment by whites it was a victory worth celebrating. SNCC organizer Ivanhoe Donaldson spoke for many others when he wrote, "The Freedom Vote Campaign was definitely a step forward for the movement. . . . For the first time, the entire project was mobile and able to get to the people. . . . We laid the foundation to establish a really state-wide voter registration campaign. . . . It showed the Negro population that politics is not just a 'white folks' business. . . . There was less fear in the Negro community in taking part in civil rights activity." CORE's Dennis agreed that the freedom vote "did much more for the movement, toward uniting Mississippi, than anything else we have done."[26]

Dennis was particularly pleased that CORE's Madison County staff had delivered over 3,500 votes, despite many attempts by whites to disrupt the election. SNCC's Hattiesburg project accounted for an equal number of ballots, doing so in the face of numerous arrests and acts of intimidation. And though the question of participation by white volunteers soon became a major source of contention inside COFO, the initial verdict was more favorable. Donaldson concluded that "the mock election also pointed out that whites can work in Mississippi (at least white males). A lot of leg work which we didn't have the manpower to accomplish was done by the Yale and Stanford students, including canvassing in some of the hard core areas: Sunflower and Leflore Counties."[27]

Nevertheless, a closer look at the vote tally would have revealed the difficult problems that lay ahead. Two-thirds of the total vote came from eight counties, and twenty-five of the state's eighty-two counties reported fewer than 100 votes each. It was no surprise that a disproportionate percentage of the vote came from the Delta. But while Coahoma—Henry's home base—and adjoining Quitman and Panola counties combined for more than 30,000 votes, or 40 percent of the statewide count, Leflore County, SNCC's major project, contributed fewer than 2,000 ballots, despite the fact that COFO ran a slate of fourteen candidates for Leflore county offices, including veteran organizer Willie Peacock for district attorney. Sunflower, Fannie Lou Hamer's home county, turned in fewer than 300 votes for the ticket. The area surrounding Jackson, the state capital, contributed the largest single bloc, over 13,000 votes. Statistics can of course be misleading, and COFO staff emphasized the positive, rejoicing over all votes coming from areas that had not yet been organized. Still, the vote in all the counties where SNCC and CORE had ongoing projects was under 16,000, less than one-fifth of the total. That these were areas where white hostility toward the movement was greatest only underscored the problems remaining in organizing Mississippi. Bob Moses, speaking at the victory rally in Jackson, faced the issue squarely: "This election also makes it clear that the Negroes of Mississippi will not get the vote until the equivalent of an army is sent here," a pointed reference to the fact that throughout the campaign, the Kennedy administration had ignored repeated pleas to protect Mississippi blacks against white violence and intimidation.[28]

The other major disappointment, one directly related to the concern over federal inaction, was the paucity of national media coverage of the campaign. The Associated Press called the freedom vote "an election sidelight." Most news stories centered on the Yale and Stanford volunteers rather than on the local people and veteran organizers. Even journalists sympathetic to the movement fell into the trap. When Ronnie Dugger of the *Texas Observer,* in his positive article on the freedom vote, wrote of the violence in Adams County, his lead paragraph began "Bruce Payne is a white, blond-haired 21-year-old graduate student in political science at Yale." The media's fixation on the white students remained constant until the end of the campaign. Lowenstein recalled that at the election night celebration "the TV cameras were all there [and] they focused again on . . . the white students. And the bitterness of the SNCC workers was very understandable and intense." Without the presence of the white students, however, the media would have paid even less attention to Mississippi in the fall of 1963.[29]

COFO staff capitalized on the momentum generated by the freedom vote, sending SNCC organizers to work in "new" counties like Issaquena. CORE workers expanded into Leake County and Meridian. Now operating in all five congressional districts, COFO began holding monthly conventions to bring together local people from all parts of the state. The immediate question concerning COFO strategists was whether to continue with the decentralized grass-roots community organizing that had characterized the movement before the freedom vote or to put together another statewide project to bring more outsiders into Mississippi, thus generating national publicity and badly needed financial support. During the week following the freedom vote COFO staff met in Greenville for a workshop sponsored by the Highlander Folk School. They began a debate there that ran on into the spring over the character, composition, and direction of the Mississippi movement.[30]

• • •

The Greenville workshop agenda ranged from COFO's relationship to the NAACP to the advisability of forming a political party, but the overriding issue was the proposal for a Mississippi summer project and the role, if any, that white college students would play in it. Until the winter of 1963–64 the question of whites in the Mississippi movement had not been contentious. Although whites like Bob Zellner, Jane Stembridge, Dorothy Miller, Mary King, and Casey Hayden had long been active in SNCC, with the exception of Zellner's foray into McComb in 1961, no white staff members had worked in any SNCC or other COFO projects until the summer of 1963. COFO staff considered the presence of whites

too dangerous, both for them and for local blacks. Whites working in black communities brought the wrong kind of visibility, and
the sight of blacks and whites organizing together—particularly
white women and black men—was a red flag for segregationists.
In mid-1963, however, SNCC assigned two whites, Dick Frey and
Mike Miller, to work in the Greenwood office; another, Hunter
Morey, was in Greenville; and in Jackson Mendy Samstein, a white
northern graduate student, arrived to work in the COFO central
office. The freedom vote campaign had demonstrated that whites
could operate in the field as well as in the office. The question facing the COFO staff assembled in Greenville, then, was not whether it was possible for white activists to work in Mississippi but
whether more should be invited to come to the state in the summer of 1964.

The idea for a summer program incorporating large numbers of
students was not new. Many Yale and Stanford students active in
the freedom vote campaign and influenced by Allard Lowenstein
assumed they would return to Mississippi in June. A week before
the freedom vote the *Stanford Daily* had run a notice that Lowenstein "will come to campus in December to organize summer programs for students interested in working in Mississippi under more
organized conditions." Bob Moses seemed to share this assumption.
In a memorandum to the Mississippi staff written before the Greenville meeting, Moses posed the following question: "How large a
force of volunteer summer workers should we recruit? 100? 1,000?
2,000?"[31] When he arrived in Greenville for the second day of the
staff workshop, however, Moses learned that many of the veteran
organizers favored, at best, a limited future role for white students.

At the initial meeting the consensus of the seven whites and approximately thirty-five blacks in attendance was that in any summer program no white person should serve as a project director or
WATS line operator. Moreover, project directors would select the
white volunteers to work in their areas, and the major function of
whites would be to work in the white community on a new
project.[32] The evident hostility toward white volunteers was largely a backlash against the freedom vote participation of the Yale and
Stanford students. In addition to the obvious fact that the visitors
had gotten most of the media coverage, field organizers charged that
whites had "taken over the Jackson office" during the Henry cam-

paign, from operating the WATS line to making policy decisions. "I came into SNCC and saw Negroes running the movement and I felt good," remarked Ivanhoe Donaldson, "and then the whites take over leadership. We're losing the one thing where the Negro can stand first." Lowenstein, the person responsbile for recruiting the volunteers for the fall campaign, received harsh criticism: "I remember a situation where a kid couldn't take orders from whom he was working under—he wouldn't take orders from you," Dona Richards later reminded Bob Moses. "He said his orders came from Al Lowenstein." Class differences intensified racial feelings. "It was hard to establish a tone appropriate to the task," one black staff member complained, "with a bunch of Yalies running around in their Triumphs."[33]

On learning of the previous day's discussions, the normally reserved Moses uncharacteristically took a leading role in the debate. Dismissing the charge that whites tried to take over the Jackson office ("We had a lot of work to do in Jackson. It was simple as that"), Moses addressed the larger question, charging that the debate over limiting the role of whites was really a move to exclude them altogether, an accusation staff members vigorously denied. Moses then stated his own position: "Whiteness is no argument. That's an irrational, racist statement. That's what we're fighting. [If] no white person can be head of any project, [then] I don't want to be part of an operation like that."[34]

Among the Mississippi staff at the Greenville meeting, only Guyot and Fannie Lou Hamer strongly supported Moses' position. "If we're trying to break down this barrier of segregation," Mrs. Hamer observed, "we can't segregate ourselves."[35] Those opposing an expanded role for whites included northern SNCC organizers Cobb and Donaldson, along with native Mississippians recruited by Moses like Peacock, Watkins, and Curtis Hayes. They were concerned that the proposed summer project, with its heavy emphasis on untrained volunteers, would divert resources away from SNCC's primary mission: organizing local communities and developing indigenous black leadership. Peacock conceded that white volunteers might be effective in the short run—but for the wrong reasons. He later expanded on this argument: "I know that if you bring white people to Mississippi and say 'Negro, go and vote,' [they will respond] 'Yassah, we'll go and try to register and vote.' I know that's not permanent. . . . When the one who looks like the oppressor comes and tells them to do something, it's not commitment. It's done out of that same slavery mentality."[36]

Personal feelings also came into play. With the confidence born of money and education, white students from elitist universities could intimidate and embarrass local people. (During the 1964 summer, Forman later recalled, "One of our project directors . . . began to feel ashamed of the fact that he had completed only the sixth grade in school and told people he had graduated from college.") Finally, for more than two years the young men and women in SNCC had dedicated their lives to the movement, forming a strong emotional bond. Expanding the circle to include large numbers of people of a different race, class, and culture, they feared, would fundamentally change the nature of their organization.[37]

Arguments favoring extensive white participation in the summer project were pragmatic. Movement activists knew from experience that as long as it was black people who were being brutalized in Mississippi, white Americans paid little attention. But they would respond "to the death of a white college student," Dennis has observed. "That's cold, but . . . we were trying to get a message over to the country, so we spoke their language." Perhaps white volunteers could bring a degree of protection and prevent such a tragedy. They definitely would bring visibility and publicity. In any event, if COFO were to continue to expand its operations throughout the state, many more workers were needed.[38]

The staff at the Greenville meeting took no action on the question of white volunteers. Although intense and at times painful, this first lengthy discussion of the role of whites in the Mississippi movement did not break down the feeling of camaraderie between black and white staff members, who played touch football between meetings and visited black Greenville clubs together at night. The sessions themselves had their lighter moments, too, as when, in response to a comment that the purpose of the volunteers was to create confrontation with Mississippi racists, Donaldson suggested that "we bring down 5,000 whites and put 'em all in Belzoni!" There was general agreement that although voter registration would continue as its major program, COFO needed to establish community centers to provide local people with a wide variety of services, a project Dennis had been pushing for some time. As discussions continued throughout the winter, Charlie

Cobb's proposal that the movement establish "freedom schools" during the summer months drew enthusiastic response. Slowly, a consensus began to emerge around the program that later became known as Freedom Summer.[39]

Less than a week after the Greenville conference President John F. Kennedy lay dead in Dallas. In schools across Mississippi white children cheered when they heard the news, reflecting the prejudices of their parents, but many Mississippians were shocked by the tragedy. More than 1,200 people attended a memorial service at Ole Miss, and in Jackson 2,000 packed the Episcopal cathedral for "one of the most integrated gatherings that Mississippi has seen in modern times."[40] Black Mississippians were stunned and saddened. Five months earlier Medgar Evers had been gunned down by an assassin, and now the national leader who, more so than any previous president, had identified with the civil rights cause had also been shot. Sam Bailey of the Jackson NAACP branch stated that "we have lost one of the greatest men of our time. . . . He looked on the Negro as a man, and upheld an attitude indispensable to the Movement." Among SNCC and CORE activists the response was respectful but not eulogistic. SNCC opened its fourth leadership conference in Washington with a moment of silence for the slain president. Author James Baldwin no doubt voiced the sentiments of many in the audience when he said, "Let us not be so pious as now to say that President Kennedy was a great civil-rights fighter."[41]

Once the initial shock of John Kennedy's death had worn off, Mississippi activists began to assess the potential impact of Lyndon Baines Johnson's accession to the presidency. Although the new president's pledge to carry out the Kennedy program—including passage of the civil rights bill then being debated in Congress—was encouraging, many blacks in the movement were uncomfortable with Johnson. An editorial in the November 25 issue of COFO's *Mississippi Newsletter* warned that the movement must face the "probablility of a major setback" now that LBJ was in office: "We face the prospect of a Southern President controlling the country [who] is fundamentally a conservative." SNCC's Forman was less pessimistic. Reflecting the frustration shared by a majority of movement activists over the gap between rhetoric and action during the Kennedy years, Forman predicted that although "Kennedy could get by on words, Johnson has to deliver." Whatever their feelings about the transition in the White House, black organizers agreed that the events in Dallas should not deter them from intensifying the pressure on Mississippi.[42]

That task had become more difficult because, less than two weeks before Kennedy's death, the Voter Education Project announced that it was cutting off funding to all registration projects in Mississippi. VEP head Wiley Branton explained to Aaron Henry and Bob Moses that the $50,000 allocated to COFO in 1962 had added only 3,228 new voters to the rolls. In short, the Mississippi project was not cost effective. COFO workers suspected a hidden agenda. Although they respected Branton, Mississippi activists knew that VEP depended on foundations for support, and these organizations made it clear that money was not to be spent for "partisan political activity." COFO had ignored that restriction, accepting the funds and filing reports but placing a much broader interpretation on the term "voter registration." That the VEP announcement came a week after the freedom vote may have been coincidental, but it was nonetheless symbolic. One SNCC worker later stated that VEP "stopped the grants because we just wouldn't do some of the things they wanted us to do . . . particularly around the political organizing, like the Freedom Vote." Given the Mississippi movement's meager financial resources, elimination of the modest VEP support created problems in projects throughout the state.[43]

The VEP cutoff contributed to a general malaise that had settled over COFO projects in the aftermath of the freedom vote. Part of the problem was the natural letdown accompanying the end of three weeks of frenzied activity, but the difficulties facing the Mississippi movement, outlined by Moses earlier in the fall, remained unchanged. White Mississippi was as intransigent as ever, and the new Johnson administration gave no indication that it would abandon the Kennedy policy of Federalism in the Deep South. SNCC and CORE were reaching out into new areas, but with inadequate resources, and it was too early to tell whether the interest generated by the freedom vote could be sustained in these communities. The ongoing CORE project in Canton was facing increasing white resistance, with local leaders jailed on false charges. In Hattiesburg project director Lawrence Guyot had complained of lack of personnel, and SNCC worker Mendy Samstein reported that in the weeks following the freedom vote the Hattiesburg black community "has shown very little life." Dissatisfaction and unrest were also running high in the Delta, particularly in SNCC's flagship project, Greenwood.[44]

Years later, Bob Moses recalled that one of the reasons he had pushed so hard for a summer project that included hundreds of white volunteers was that by the end of 1963 the COFO staff "was exhausted. . . . they were butting up against a stone wall, no break-throughs for them." Veteran organizers "were already burnt out. They had now been out there for a couple of years and that's a long time in that situation: where you're in a given area, and you're strug-gling against the same thing every day, and you don't see any progress." Nowhere was movement burnout more evident than in Greenwood. Against overwhelming odds, SNCC had established its Delta beachhead there, organizing the black community into an ef-fective political force. But white intimidation and violence had in-tensified during the spring and summer of 1963, and only a hand-ful of blacks had managed to pass the registration test. Although the Henry-King campaign had provided an alternative, the freedom vote turnout in Leflore County was disappointing and left the Greenwood staff frustrated and demoralized.[45]

In late November Jane Stembridge wrote her friend Mary King about conditions in the Greenwood project. "The report from the field is one of sadness," she began. "With all of the forces of hu-man fear and hatred arrayed against us, we must somehow draw together around the fire, around the table. But, instead, we are de-stroying each other." There was work to be done—reorganizing the library, planning for a community center, and distributing a ship-ment of clothes sent down from the North—but little enthusiasm for the tasks at hand. This was particularly true for Sam Block, whose courage, patience, and organizing skill had brought the Greenwood movement into being. Eighteen months of beatings and jailings, along with disagreements with other staff members, had taken their toll on Block. Stembridge wrote that although Block was still on the scene, "walking upon his territory," he was now dispir-ited, "telling how much he doesn't care about the movement." Oth-er project veterans shared this feeling of alienation. "To get to the point, finally, about the field," Stembridge sadly concluded, "no one is in it."[46]

As the year ended, movement activists were beset by conflicting emotions. There had been progress: throughout the state more black men and women were taking a stand. Despite the decline of morale in Greenwood and in other projects, local people and COFO organizers were determined to carry on the struggle. Nevertheless, there were few solid victories to point to, and it was clear that white Mississippi would remain hostile and intransigent until forced to change its ways. As if to underscore that point, the new year saw the revival of the Ku Klux Klan in the Magnolia State.

10

Freedom Days

On the evening of January 31, 1964, Louis Allen was gunned down outside his home in Amite County. Married and the father of four children, the forty-five-year-old independent logger was hit in the face with two loads of buckshot, dying almost instantly. Three years earlier he had seen state legislator E. H. Hurst shoot Herbert Lee in cold blood; after word got around that Allen had talked with Justice Department officials about the case, his life became a nightmare. Over the next two years Allen suffered economic harassment, was jailed on false charges, and had his jaw broken by a deputy sheriff. When, early in 1964, he learned that whites were planning to kill him, the terrified victim made plans to join his brother in Milwaukee. Allen was to leave Mississippi on February 1—one day too late. Both the sheriff and the FBI investigated the murder, but no one was ever charged.[1]

The killing of Lewis Allen coincided with the rebirth of the Ku Klux Klan in Mississippi. Throughout the winter and spring of 1964 night riders roamed unchecked across the state. Cross burnings announced the Klan presence in an area—on one night in May crosses burned in sixty-four counties—followed by bullets and bombs. Black churches, businesses, and homes were the targets, and local people began to stand guard at night with their own shotguns and rifles. The terror was greatest in southwest Mississippi. In addition to operating in Amite, the Klan was active next door in Pike County. Early in January whites fired into six black businesses and two homes, wounding a fourteen-year-old boy. McComb Police Chief

George Guy downplayed the shooting, commenting that the youth was not badly hurt, that the shots only "blistered his tail a little bit." Klan activity continued through the spring and included the bombing of longtime NAACP activist C. C. Bryant's barber shop.[2]

The violence was intense in Adams County, where the Klan revival began. Natchez, the county seat, was a city of some 25,000, 42 percent of whom were black. This historic river town had been home to the state's antebellum slave-owning aristocracy. Now it boasted an industrial base, and white factory workers were prime recruits for Klan organizers from Louisiana. Mississippi klansmen broke away from the Louisiana group in December 1963 to form the White Knights of the Ku Klux Klan of Mississippi, which emerged as the dominant and most violent Klan faction in the state. Its leader in Adams County was twenty-nine-year-old Edward Lenox McDaniel, a Natchez native with a tenth-grade education who had worked at the Red Ball Express Company. (Four years earlier McDaniel had been fired from his job at Johns-Manville for stealing coins from a milk-vending machine.) Under E. L. McDaniel's leadership, the Klan struck quickly in Natchez, terrorizing the black community as the local police looked the other way.[3]

On the evening of February 15, the mortician Archie Curtis received a call from a man requesting an ambulance for his wife, who had supposedly suffered a heart attack. Arriving at the scene, Curtis and his assistant were jumped by four men wearing hoods and carrying guns. The klansmen drove the two blacks to a deserted field, stripped them, and whipped them repeatedly. Although Curtis later identified the make of the car and provided physical descriptions of his assailants, police made no arrests. Archie Curtis was the longtime chairman of the Natchez Business and Civic League's voter registration drive. The night before the attack on Curtis, whites had abducted and whipped Alfred Whitley, a janitor at the Armstrong Rubber Company. The Klan bombed the home of Leonard Russell, who was active in the Negro Pulp and Sulfite Workers local. Another victim was Clinton Walker, who had worked at the International Paper Company since 1950. Married with children, Walker was considered "a good employee who was regular in his attendance." On February 28 Walker finished his regular shift at 11:00 P.M. He never returned home. At noon the next day he was found dead in his car, shot in the back with buckshot and rifle slugs. Again, there were no arrests.[4]

Two hundred klansmen gathered at Brookhaven on February 15, 1964, to establish the White Knights as a statewide organization. They adopted a forty-page constitution and agreed on a plan of attack that escalated through four stages, or "projects." Project 4 bore a simple but ominous label: "extermination."[5] The leader of the White Knights, its Imperial Wizard, was Sam Bowers, a forty-year-old Laurel resident who ran a coin machine business, the Sambo Amusement Company. A World War II veteran who had attended the University of California School of Engineering for two years before returning to Mississippi, Bowers made it clear that the White Knights' mission was the destruction of the Mississippi civil rights movement. In his first executive order, the Imperial Wizard decreed that "weapons and ammunition must be accumulated and stored; squads must drill . . . counterattack maps, plans and information must be studied and learned; radios and communications must be established." Mindful that his was a holy crusade, Bowers piously concluded that "a Solemn, determined Spirit of Christian Reverence must be stimulated in all members."[6]

White violence directed against blacks was, obviously, not new in Mississippi, but the Ku Klux Klan as an institution had not been active since the 1930s. The Klan's revival in late 1963 resulted from frustration, a gut feeling that the battle for white supremacy was being lost. For nearly a decade the Citizens' Council had led the forces of resistance, assuring the white masses that the state's business and professional class would take care of any agitation on the race question. Although the Citizens' Council had prevented the movement from making any major breakthrough, it had not driven the COFO organizers out, and in the aftermath of the freedom vote more volunteers appeared to be headed for Mississippi. Moreover, the positive national impact of the March on Washington, growing support for passage of a strong federal civil rights bill, and the expectation that the courts would soon force Mississippi elementary and secondary schools to desegregate convinced many whites that the tide of history was running against them. Thus, although the Citizens' Council could claim that it had brought the civil rights movement in Mississippi to a standstill, less affluent whites were now both impatient and angry, consumed by anxiety over the future. By the summer of 1964, nearly 5,000 of these latter-day "fireaters" had joined the Ku Klux Klan.[7]

Mississippi's state and federal elected officials were disturbed by the Klan renaissance, for it was certain to generate bad publicity, create a negative climate for outside investment in new industry, and increase the likelihood that Congress would enact civil rights legislation. Thus, in November 1963, Attorney General Joe Patterson, the state's chief legal officer and a member of the Citizens' Council, declared that there was no place for the Klan in Mississippi. "I think the people of Mississippi are fully capable of taking care of themselves . . . without resorting to the known tactics of the Ku Klux Klan," he said. Senator John Stennis, while not mentioning the Klan by name, condemned the rash of cross burnings, warning that such actions "can only hurt us in our efforts to defeat the [civil rights] bill because it gives our opponents an additional weapon to use against us." Even Ross Barnett denounced as "wholly untrue" a report that he had sent a letter of support to the new Yazoo County Klan klavern. The Yazoo City chapter of the Citizens' Council went on record opposing the Klan, adding that "your Citizens' Council was formed to preserve separation of the races, and believes that it can best serve the county where it is the only organization operating in this field."[8]

White opposition to the Klan, however, was largely rhetorical. In smaller communities police and elected officials were ignoring Klan-inspired violence and in some cases supporting it. Klan infiltration into law enforcement agencies was widespread, with police officers and members of the Mississippi State Highway Patrol on the Klan's secret membership rolls. Thus, while Mississippi's political leaders were nervous about the Klan and wished it would go away, they were afraid to confront it directly. They wasted no sympathy on the Klan's victims, nor did they attempt to apprehend the perpetrators of its crimes.[9]

For some COFO organizers, the Klan revival added weight to the argument that the proposed summer project needed hundreds of white volunteers to focus national attention on the area. At the SNCC executive committee meeting held in Atlanta in late December, Marion Barry won unanimous approval for a resolution that read, "During the Presidential election year of 1964, SNCC intends to obtain the right for all citizens of Mississippi to vote, using as many people as necessary to obtain that end." Barry's motion finessed the controversial question of white volunteers. At the next COFO staff meeting held in Hattiesburg in mid-January, three-fourths of those present voted for a summer project that included an unspecified number of volunteers from outside the state. Opposition to white student participation, however, had run strongest among organizers in COFO's two largest projects—Greenwood and Canton—and they were not represented at the meeting. Thus, although COFO had given an endorsement of sorts, and an official announcement of the summer project would soon be forthcoming, the question of the volunteers remained very much up in the air.[10]

For Bob Moses, the murder of Louis Allen had resolved any doubts about the need for outside help: "There was no real reason to kill Louis, and they gunned him down on his front lawn. We were just defenseless; there was no way of bringing national attention. And it seemed to me like we were just sitting ducks . . . people were just going to be wiped out." Moses had gone to Amite County to conduct his own investigation of the murder, and from that point on he used his considerable influence to persuade reluctant staff members to invite white students to join them in Mississippi. Activists like Willie Peacock and Hollis Watkins, on the other hand, rejected Moses' conclusions. They maintained that far from being "defenseless," local blacks were armed and prepared to fight back; they would later argue persuasively that at no point was massive white participation essential to the survival of the Mississippi movement. But in the spring of 1964 Moses' arguments would carry the day, in part because of the important support he received from older local people, who almost unanimously favored the project. Charlie Cobb, one of the strongest opponents of the plan, later recalled that Mississippi blacks were "very pragmatic. They wanted things to change, and if it took bringing in a bunch of white kids, OK. Local people were not into all these ideological kinds of things."[11]

The immediate problem in early 1964 was to counter the threat posed by the intensified campaign of white violence. Realizing that their only security lay in numbers, COFO borrowed a tactic first used by SNCC in Selma, Alabama, the previous October. On January 22, Hattiesburg became the sight of Mississippi's first "Freedom Day." Freedom Day was a logical extension of the voter registration campaigns already in place. Instead of applicants going to the courthouse one or two at a time, on the designated day large numbers of local blacks marched to the courthouse and lined up to take the test, while supporters set up a picket line to protest unfair practices by the circuit clerk. Such a show of strength would "give heart to other blacks" who were afraid to make the registration attempt alone. Hattiesburg was the ideal setting for such a demonstration, for on January 6 the U.S. Supreme Court upheld the lower court decisions requiring that Forrest County registrar Theron Lynd desist from discriminatory practices. When he once again resisted the court order, COFO decided to throw a national spotlight on Lynd and force a showdown. "We can't ask people to go down and take a test which is going to be reviewed by a man who has no regard for federal court orders," stated Hattiesburg project director Lawrence Guyot. "The only recourse is federal intervention or community action."[12]

Taking a page from the freedom vote campaign, COFO sought national media coverage by inviting outsiders to Hattiesburg, this time a delegation of white clergy representing the National Council of Churches. To ensure that sufficient staff was on hand, organizers from other COFO projects came down to help, including Fannie Lou Hamer and Amzie Moore, who drove down from the Delta. Jim Forman and SNCC chairman John Lewis from SNCC's Atlanta office were also there, as was Ella Baker. At a mass rally the night before, a large gathering heard speeches by representatives from all the national organizations in COFO, including Lewis, Aaron Henry, Dave Dennis, and Annelle Ponder. It began to rain as the marchers gathered on the following morning, and although the day-long downpour may have discouraged some from participating, by 10:30 nearly 200 people were at the Forrest County courthouse, including fifty clergymen from out of state. Hattiesburg officials were uncertain about how to respond to this new tactic. Earlier, the police chief had contacted a Negro businessman in an unsuccessful effort to prevent the demonstration from taking place. Now that it was a reality, downtown businesses closed for the day. Police on the scene attempted to disperse the picketers, but when the marchers refused to move, the lawmen took no action. The historian Howard Zinn, an observer-participant at the courthouse, wrote that "something unprecedented was taking place in . . . Mississippi: a black and white line of demonstrators was picketing a public building, allowed to do so by the police."[13]

Obviously, the presence of network televison cameras affected police behavior, as did the large delegation of visiting clergy. Inside the courthouse a smiling Theron Lynd assured reporters that this was just another day at the office: "Yes, indeed. I will treat all applicants alike, just as I have always done." By noon, however, only twelve people had been permitted to take the test, and Lynd did not release the results. At 5:00 P.M. some seventy-five demonstrators still stood in the rain at the courthouse. Police were now harassing black men in the group by demanding that they produce their draft cards. Nevertheless, Freedom Day organizers were surprised that only one person, Bob Moses, was arrested at the courthouse. Later they learned that Yale law graduate Oscar Chase had been jailed on a traffic charge and beaten by a white cellmate.[14]

The success of Freedom Day in Hattiesburg revitalized the local movement. By the end of the week approximately 150 people had taken the test, and in the days that followed a steady flow of applicants converged on the courthouse, where picketing continued, even after the city obtained a court injunction to prohibit it. Nor was the ministers' visit a one-shot guest appearance. Each week a new delegation of clergy arrived in Hattiesburg to assist in the canvassing and to show up at the courthouse. Nine ministers were arrested on January 29 on charges of breach of the peace for violating the injunction on picketing. The police did crack down once the media had departed, arresting Guyot, Sandy Leigh, and other project organizers, but a new spirit had arisen in the black community. Encouraged by the results in Hattiesburg, COFO now planned additional Freedom Days, beginning with Canton.[15]

In early 1964 CORE's Madison County project was the most active in the state. Led by George Raymond, the CORE task force there now consisted of seven organizers, five of whom were local people. C. O. Chinn had agreed to provide a building for the proposed community center in Canton; the twice-weekly mass meetings were well attended; and each day potential voters arrived at the courthouse, hoping that circuit clerk Foote Campbell would see fit to administer the registration test. After six months of concerted effort, however, only about 120 of some 10,000 adult blacks in the county had qualified to vote, while more than 97 percent of the 5,600 eligible whites were on Foote Campbell's books. White hostility to the movement was intensifying, with police conduct in Canton worse than in any other COFO project area. The major problem facing Madison County blacks remained that of poverty: average annual income for black families was only $1,100, one-fourth that of whites. To dramatize the lack of economic opportunity, police brutality, segregated businesses and schools, and denial of voting rights, Madison County blacks in January announced a boycott of twenty-one stores in downtown Canton. By the end of the month CORE claimed that the boycott was 75 percent effective.[16]

For white Canton, the selective buying campaign posed a more immediate threat than did voter registration. On January 21 the Canton City Council passed an ordinance prohibiting the distribution of literature without a permit (news of the boycott had been announced through leafleting in the black community) and added two constables and a patrol car to the police force. Two days later police raided the CORE office, seized the names of people who had signed a petition outlining movement demands, and arrested Clarence Chinn, C. O.'s brother, for violating the city's building code (Chinn had been making repairs on the office). When CORE worker Theodis "Pete" Hewitt protested, he was booked for intimidating an officer. Later that day police arrested nine registration workers for "distributing leaflets without a permit." Now nearly all of the staff was in jail. On January 25 police began stopping all cars entering town. Two nights later lawmen were out in force at a mass meeting in a black church, taking down license tags, photographing the crowd, stopping all cars after the meeting, and following some of the cars home. In spite of this harassment, more than 150 local people showed up to hear Raymond, Dennis, and NAACP leaders Current, Charles Evers, and R. L. T. Smith.[17]

The success of the Hattiesburg Freedom Day encouraged Madison County blacks, who scheduled their own event for February 28. CORE sent down six field secretaries and two other workers to help organize what the white *Madison County Herald* called Canton's "first 'racial demonstration' since carpetbagger days." SNCC and NAACP representatives were out in force, ministers from out of state were in town to observe, and all three major television networks were in attendance, as were the local police. The *New York Times*'s Claude Sitton described the scene:

> Police auxiliaries in blue helmets and makeshift uniforms mounted a shotgun guard along the route. Sheriffs and deputies from Madison and surrounding counties wearing 10-gallon hats and driving white cars . . . patrolled the streets. City policemen armed with nightsticks, revolvers and a variety of shotguns and rifles snapped orders at the Negroes as they shepherded them through a crosswalk to the courthouse grounds.

. . . The State Highway Patrol manned a police-radio network set up in a command post in the courthouse.

Undaunted, approximately 350 Madison County blacks gathered to form long lines outside the courthouse, waiting to take the test. Only 5 of them made it into Foote Campbell's inner sanctum, where they were greeted by a poster of the confederate flag with the message: "Support Your Citizens' Council." But there were no arrests and no violence. Dave Dennis, noting the presence of FBI and Justice Department officials, stated that "direct Federal intervention appears to be necessary, perhaps Federal registrars," and he called on the government to file suit against circuit clerk Campbell.[18]

Less than a week later the Justice Department did just that, arguing before Judge Harold Cox that Campbell should be directed to speed up the processing of black voter applicants. Cox's comments at the hearing illustrate the depth of racism in Mississippi. Throughout the hearing the Kennedy appointee and former college roommate of Senator Eastland referred to those Canton blacks who attempted to register as "a bunch of niggers." To Cox it "appeared that these people went to a church and were pepped up by a leather-lung preacher, and they gathered in the streets like a massive dark cloud and descended on the clerk." Then he asked, "Who is telling these people they can get in line and push people around, acting like a bunch of chimpanzees?" Still, less than a month later Cox directed Foote Campbell to process at least fifty applicants each day.[19]

Freedom Day lifted the spirits of Canton blacks. Early in March nearly 2,700 black students staged a boycott of their schools, protesting overcrowded classes, insufficient library resources, and other inadequacies typical of the state's Jim Crow school system. A second Freedom Day took place on March 13, the boycott remained in effect, and blacks continued to attempt to register. In the absence of federal protection, however, white violence and police intimidation took their toll. Aware of the declining support for the boycott and increasing fear in the community, CORE director James Farmer came down to speak at a third Freedom Day on May 29. With the national media largely absent, police barred a march to the courthouse and arrested fifty-five demonstrators, yet Dennis and other CORE staff remained defiant, if not optimistic. Addressing a mass meeting shortly before the final Freedom Day, Dennis stated that "we're demanding this time . . . to be first-class citizens. . . . We've got to sweat, we've got to bleed, a lot of us are going to have to die for it." Earlier, in a telegram to President Johnson and Attorney General Kennedy, the angry young activist had warned, "You have proven to us by your refusal to act that we have no other recourse than to defend ourselves with whatever means we have at our disposal."[20]

Buoyed by the earlier successes in Hattiesburg and in Canton, Greenwood organizers made plans for their first Freedom Day, which was set for March 25. At a mass meeting at the Elks Hall the evening before the rally, between 400 and 500 people learned that the police had arrested Willie Peacock and three other workers earlier in the day for distributing leaflets. Later that night the Klan burned crosses in front of SNCC headquarters and on the courthouse lawn. Still, 200 Leflore County blacks lined up to register on Freedom Day, supported by nearly 100 people (including several white ministers) who formed a picket line around the courthouse. Unlike previous demonstrations, this saw the police make no arrests. Only about thirty-five blacks were permitted to take the test, and although white ministers were conspicuous on the picket line, national figures declined to attend the rally. The media may have decided that yet another Freedom Day in Mississippi was no longer news. The *New York Times* did not send a reporter and buried a brief Associated Press dispatch on the story in the middle of the paper. Of the televison networks, only NBC showed up—with one correspondent.[21]

The Mississippi state legislature responded to the Freedom Day protests with a law passed on April 8 to prohibit picketing of state buildings. The following morning, on Greenwood's second Freedom Day, police arrested forty-six picketers, all charged with violating the new statute. Shortly thereafter, eight of the people who attempted to register were thrown off the plantations where they had worked, and night riders fired shots into the homes of three movement supporters. Although the Freedom Day tactic had given the movement a temporary boost—Freedom Days were held in a number of smaller communities, including the Klan town of Liberty—the results were always the same. Bob Moses' observation in the summer of 1963 still held true: "It is impossible to register Negroes in Mississippi."[22]

• • •

Although desegregation of public facilities was not a COFO priority, the spirit behind the freedom rides remained alive in Mississippi. In communities across the state blacks attempted to obtain service at lunch counters or to use the "white" waiting rooms in bus terminals. Many of the direct action protests occurred in Jackson and were led by students and faculty from Tougaloo College.

For Mississippi activists, Tougaloo had been a safe haven, an "oasis in the desert." The school's president, Daniel Beittel, had welcomed SNCC and CORE workers, who could meet on campus in a secure setting. In 1963 Bob Moses had worked with Tougaloo officials and the Field Foundation to initiate the Work-Study Project, a program that enabled young Mississippi blacks to participate in the movement and at the same time earn credit toward a college degree. Moses also used Tougaloo as the base for the Literacy Project, which employed innovative techniques to teach blacks lacking formal schooling to read and write. A number of SNCC field secretaries, including Hollis Watkins, Lafayette Surney, MacArthur Cotton, Euvester Simpson, and Dorie and Joyce Ladner, were also Tougaloo students working toward degrees.[23]

Tougaloo stood apart from Mississippi's other black colleges in its commitment to the freedom movement. Rust College, a private school in Holly Springs supported by the Presbyterian church, permitted its students to engage in some political activity, and a few, like Leslie McLemore, worked with SNCC organizer Frank Smith in Marshall County. The state's public four-year black colleges— Jackson State, Alcorn, and Mississippi Valley State College—were all controlled by the segregationist state legislature. When protests did erupt on these campuses, the presidents had to crack down on the dissent or lose their jobs. Dorie Ladner, who with her sister Joyce enrolled at Jackson State in the fall of 1960, recalled that while there she was "politically repressed. . . . I was forced to go to chapel. . . . I could not read the textbooks I wanted." After President Jacob Reddix put down the student protests following the Tougaloo library sit-in in the spring of 1961, the Ladners transferred to Tougaloo, where they found "free speech, freedom of religion, political freedom . . . and a caring faculty."[24]

Still, Tougaloo's reputation as a hotbed of movement activity has been exaggerated. A majority of the faculty and administration were uncomfortable with the school's civil rights image, and only a relatively small group of students actively participated in the struggle. Most Tougaloo students were no different from their peers on other campuses, black and white: their goal was obtaining a college degree to improve their socioeconomic status. While students at Tougaloo were concerned about the state's racial problems and could be mobilized for brief periods around dramatic issues, few were willing to make a major commitment to the movement. The small contingent of Tougaloo activists, however, did have an impact far beyond its numbers.[25]

During the summer of 1963 Tougaloo students and faculty began a series of "pray-ins" in which integrated groups attempted to attend the Sunday services of white protestant churches in Jackson. There they were usually met by stone-faced deacons who denied them entrance. Church doors were locked to prevent late arrivals, with police cars cruising by to preserve law and order. That fall, when the pray-ins intensified after the beginning of the school term, police began arresting the Tougaloo churchgoers.[26]

Although worshiping with Mississippi whites was never high on the movement agenda, the pray-ins, perhaps more than any other tactic, revealed the moral bankruptcy of racial segregation. Several white ministers resigned in protest over their congregations' refusal to admit blacks to Sunday services, but the prevailing view of the white clergy was expressed by Dr. Marvin Franklin, the Methodist bishop for Mississippi, who declared that "integration is not [to be] forced on any part of our church" and concluded that it was the respsonsibility of white Methodists to "move on to do the work of the Church, loving mercy, doing justly, and walking humbly with our Lord."[27]

The Tougaloo-initiated project that created the most controversy—and was the most fun—involved a letter-writing campaign to nationally known artists and celebrities, asking them to refuse to perform at whites-only or racially segregated public events in Jackson. It all began in early November 1963, on the eve of the freedom vote, when Tougaloo music major Robert Honeysucker and Nicolas Bosanquet, a white Cambridge graduate studying in this country, were arrested in Jackson when they presented their tickets for admission to a concert given by the Royal Philharmonic Orchestra of London. Police dropped the charges after a representative of the British Consulate in New Orleans showed up at their trial. Two weeks later the Original Hootenanny USA troupe from the network television show was to perform at the Jackson auditorium. When three Tougaloo students tried unsuccessfully to buy tickets, members of the newly formed "Tougaloo Cultural and Artistic Committee" contacted the performers and explained that blacks were to be excluded from the event. The Hootenanny group canceled its concert at the last minute and instead performed for free before a large, appreciative audience at Tougaloo, which contributed seventy dollars to the performers. The musicians returned the money, asking that it be added to the bond fund for those arrested in Jackson churches on Sunday mornings.[28]

Early in January Dan Blocker, Lorne Greene, and Michael Landon were to appear at the Mississippi Industrial Exposition in the Jackson coliseum. The three were the stars of "Bonanza," the most popular television program in the country. After receiving a letter from student Austin Moore, the chair of the Tougaloo committee, explaining that seating would be segregated, Dan "Hoss" Blocker replied, "I will not be there. I have long since been in sympathy with the Negro struggle for total citizenship, therefore I would find an appearance of any sort before a segregated house completely incompatible with my moral concepts." When Greene and Landon also canceled, Jackson mayor Allen Thompson was beside himself. In a long, rambling radio address to his constituents, the mayor struck back: "I've enjoyed 'Bonanza.' I thought it was a wonderful program. I could hardly wait to get settled, so I could enjoy 'Bonanza.' But let me tell you one thing . . . *'Bonanza' will never come through the air into my home again*—I'll never listen to it and it will never come into my home again!" The most dramatic cancellation was that of trumpeter Al Hirt, who met with Austin Moore shortly before he was to perform at a segregated March of Dimes benefit. The large crowd had already assembled in the Jackson auditorium when it learned that Hirt had honored the students' request. Late that evening night riders fired into the Tougaloo campus.[29]

Other cancellations followed, including scheduled appearances by Birgit Nilssen, Sammy Kaye, Stan Musial, and NASA director James Webb. The one notable exception was the Holiday on Ice revue, which did appear before segregated audiences. At one Holiday on Ice performance Tougaloo students Marion Gillian, black, and Eli Hochstedler, white, were arrested when they tried to sit together. Later that night Hochstedler was badly beaten by a white inmate at the Jackson jail, a reminder that no protest activity in Mississippi was without risk. Tougaloo students expanded their "visits" to include other cultural activities in the Jackson area. They were thrown out of a Little Theatre production of *The Miracle Worker*, a Shakespeare festival at Belhaven College, and a choir concert at Mississippi College. Integrated groups attended events at Millsaps College without incident, but the administration there assured the public that the college had no intention of desegregating its student body. Blacks gained admission to a white movie theater located near Millsaps, and faculty members unsuccessfully attempted to integrate several Jackson restaurants.[30]

Perhaps the most encouraging sign that spring came when folksinger Joan Baez gave a concert at the Tougaloo chapel. White students from across the state were a majority of the audience (Mississippi College students had been called in the day before and threatened with expulsion, but they came anyway) and joined hands with blacks when Baez closed her performance with "We Shall Overcome." Tougaloo student Joan Trumpauer was hopeful that this would be "the beginning of real contact with liberal white kids."[31]

Such interracial contact among young people frightened Mississippi's hard-core segregationists, and they were enraged when in March 1964 U.S. District Court judge Sidney Mize reluctantly decreed that the school boards in Jackson, Biloxi, and Leake County must submit school desegregation plans to be implemented in the fall. A year earlier several black parents, including Medgar and Myrlie Evers, had filed suit on behalf of their children. As expected, the Citizens' Council breathed defiance. Believing that "no education is better than integrated education," the council demanded that schools close rather than admit blacks. This time, however, the council's position was publicly challenged by a group called Mississippians for Public Education, which was led by Mary Ann Henderson, a native Mississippian with children in the schools. Although many of the members, including Henderson, were integrationists, for political reasons this organization of white women took no official position on the desirability of school desegregation. Still, their campaign to keep the public schools open in the fall took courage. The Citizens' Council viciously attacked Mississippians for Public Education and kept up the pressure on the state legislature to enact laws designed to counter the new tactics employed by the civil rights coalition.[32]

The 1964 spring legislative session was dominated by the specter of the summer project. In addition to enacting the antipicketing statute preventing courthouse demonstrations during Freedom Days, Mississippi lawmakers expanded coverage of the breach of peace statutes and increased maximum penalties for violation of municipal ordinances; permitted local governments to enforce curfews; and facilitated transfer of prisoners to Parchman penitentiary. Referring to the latter act, one senator said that "this bill applies to those visitors who might be coming into our state this summer." Since a large number of the people participating in demonstrations were under twenty-one, legislators removed minors charged with breach of peace from the jurisdiction of the Youth Court. The spirit dominating this legislative session is exemplified in the introduction of House Bill 180. As originally passed by the House, the bill would have penalized the birth of a second illegitimate child by a prison term of one to three years for the parents or, as an alternative, voluntary sterilization of the mother. By the time the bill reached the Senate it had been picked up by newspapers across the country. SNCC issued a pamphlet detailing the debate under the heading "Genocide in Mississippi." Embarrassed, the Senate eliminated the sterilization section and softened the penalties, but the amended version became law. One observer believed that with this act the legislature "was expanding its program." Instead of maintaining the oppression of blacks through "the harassment of civil rights workers, it was showing its hatred of civil rights workers by harassing [local] Negroes."[33]

Enactment of this latest package of antiblack legislation intensified the pressure on the handful of lawyers handling civil rights cases in Mississippi. Since 1961, black attorneys Jack Young, Jess Brown, and Carsie Hall had been receiving some aid from the NAACP Legal Defense Fund, as well as assistance from individual lawyers like white Mississippian Bill Higgs and New Yorker William Kunstler. But the prospect of 1,000 volunteers flooding the state in the summer and the likelihood that many of them would be arrested convinced Mississippi activists of the need for more legal help. Among those groups volunteering were the Lawyers' Committee for Civil Rights under Law, which was formed in the aftermath of the Birmingham demonstrations with the blessings of the Kennedys, and the Lawyers' Constitutional Defense Committee (LCDC), which was organized during the winter of 1963–64 by Melvin Wolf of the

American Civil Liberties Union with the backing of Protestant, Catholic, and Jewish leaders. Both LCDC and the Lawyers' Committee were mainstream organizations, and they and their backers were horrified when COFO announced that it was also accepting legal assistance from the National Lawyers' Guild, a leftist organization founded in the 1930s. The guild had achieved a reputation as a "communist" organization, largely because it did not exclude communists and because its lawyers defended American communists during the witch-hunts of the post–World War II era. Two attorneys associated with the guild, Len Holt and Ben Smith, had been active in Mississippi since 1961 and had pioneered the innovative legal maneuver of using a Reconstruction statute to remove civil rights cases from local to federal jurisdiction, thereby improving the chances for favorable verdicts.[34]

COFO's announcement that the Lawyers' Guild would participate in the summer project drew immediate criticism from white liberals active in civil rights causes. Jack Greenberg, director of the Legal Defense Fund, warned Moses that if the guild were in Mississippi during the summer, the "Inc. Fund" would stay out. After the SNCC executive committee refused to withdraw its support of the guild's offer, Greenberg backed down some but informed Moses that "the Legal Defense Fund will not support or participate in any litigation in which the guild is involved or enter into any agreement with it." Nor would the Inc. Fund represent SNCC workers. The Lawyers' Committee also stated that its attorneys would not cooperate with the guild. LCDC lawyers decided that they would represent SNCC clients, despite misgivings about the Lawyers' Guild. Robert W. Spike, executive director of the National Council of Churches' (NCC) Commission on Religion and Race, reminded Moses that the NCC was making a major commitment to COFO's summer project and warned that SNCC's decision to welcome the guild "jeopardizes not only the possibility of extensive legal help this summer but also many other joint projects in which we have common interests. We believe this deliberate link with the National Lawyers' Guild is a great mistake for SNCC."[35]

For the embattled Mississippi activists the flap over the Lawyers' Guild was not their first encounter with outsiders' concerns over alleged communist influence in the movement. Liberals had attacked SNCC's early and continuing association with the Southern Conference Education Fund, which the House Un-American Activities

Committee had labeled a communist front. SNCC's relationship with SCEF, as previously noted, began back in McComb in the fall of 1961, when SCEF director James Dombrowski supplied $13,000 to bail out the young organizers languishing in the Pike County jail. Thereafter, SCEF made annual donations of $5,000 to SNCC to support the work of a white organizer (first Bob Zellner and later Sam Shirah and Ed Hamlett). Anne and Carl Braden, SCEF's field-workers in the South, had won the respect and trust of SNCC activists. They supported SNCC's growing militancy while not attempting to influence its direction.[36]

In the summer of 1962 Bob Moses had invited Anne Braden to come to Mississippi to help with a series of workshops on civil liberties and nonviolence. She could not make the trip, but Carl did. The *Jackson Daily News* learned of his visit through a leaked SCEF internal memo, and it trumpeted the event in a front-page headline: "Red Crusader Active in Jackson Mix Drive." Black leaders in the Delta received copies of the *Daily News* stories, and the linking of SNCC with "communism" undercut the movement there for a time. Moses later recalled that "we were tied up in Mississippi after the Braden incident."[37]

The mainstream civil rights leadership had tried to keep SCEF at arm's length, but following the furor over Carl Braden's Mississippi trip, VEP's Wiley Branton suggested that the Bradens and SCEF totally withdraw from civil rights activity in the South. At that, an angry Anne Braden wrote Branton that "I find it completely shocking that you would make such a proposal. . . . Do you really mean this? Do you really want to be party to putting this sort of power in the hands of the opposition—to say to them that if they yell 'red' loud enough and long enough they can knock their opponents out of the struggle?" Branton, however, was not alone in his fear that SCEF was hurting the movement. Several months later, when James and Diane Nash Bevel worked with Anne Braden to propose an educational center for the Delta, the SCLC's Andy Young advised the Bevels against involvement with SCEF. Although Young did not "believe there is anything wrong with SCEF," he said, "We have to stay relatively free of the Communist *charge* even. I don't think that we can ignore this and go on." The Bradens continued to work in the South, and SNCC refused to alter its "open-door" policy. At its December 1963 executive committee meeting, Charles Sherrod spoke of meeting Anne Braden for the first time and being impressed with her, only later learning that she was with SCEF. "What should I do?" asked Sherrod. "I took the position that I'm going head on into this stuff—I don't care who the heck it is—if he's willing to come down on the front lines and bring his body along with me to die—then he's welcome."[38]

SNCC's insistence on independence of association and action would be severely tested in the coming months. By late January COFO and SNCC staff had agreed to enlist approximately 1,000 volunteers for the summer project and began contacting Friends of SNCC groups in northern cities to handle recruitment. The Northern Student Movement, a national campus-based organization led by black activist William Strickland, was of major assistance. Also involved was Allard Lowenstein, who since December had been drumming up enthusiasm for the summer project among college students.

For a time COFO officials welcomed Lowenstein's efforts. His connections were valuable, and at first he kept in close contact with the Jackson office. COFO planners invited him to talk about the summer project at their state convention, held in early February. Problems soon arose, however, over Lowenstein's assumption that he had the authority both to recruit students and to *accept or reject* them as summer volunteers.[39]

In late February, Dorothy Miller Zellner, the white SNCC veteran now working with Boston Friends of SNCC, informed the Jackson office that Lowenstein had set up his own Boston recruiting office headed by Harvard graduate student (and later Massachusetts congressman) Barney Frank. Lowenstein "was up here and left several times without having contacted a single person I knew or me," reported Zellner. She finally reached Lowenstein by phone in Raleigh and explained that prospective volunteers should "apply directly to Jackson and then receive instructions from Jackson about being interviewed in their areas." This information "did not go over with a big bang with Lowenstein," who insisted that local groups should do their own selecting. He later told Zellner that "Yale, Stanford, and some other colleges were all upset about this." Mississippi staff were enraged that Lowenstein had assumed he would do the screening, and COFO made it clear to him that all decisions on volunteers would be made in Jackson.[40]

The larger issue here was the overall direction of the summer project. Lowenstein believed that leadership should come from the outside. He told student supporters that William Sloane Coffin, the chaplain at Yale, was the ideal person to head up the project and was dismayed when COFO did not approach Coffin. For black activists working in Mississippi, the idea that their summer project would be headed by a white outsider was preposterous, and they were correct in assuming that Lowenstein had another agenda. As a cold war liberal, Lowenstein was disturbed at the rumors surfacing that SNCC had been infiltrated by communists. Although no one had produced any evidence of communist involvement, Lowenstein was unhappy over SNCC's connections with SCEF, the Highlander Folk School, and the leftist *National Guardian*. But it was the decision to accept the services of the National Lawyers' Guild that pushed the young white activist into an open break with SNCC.[41]

At first Lowenstein enlisted his student disciples at Stanford to try to force his program on SNCC. The former Stanford dean reiterated his position that an outside group, "with representatives of the volunteers and of each of the constituent organizations of COFO," should make basic decisions concerning the summer project. Later Lowenstein persuaded the Stanford students, who were naive about the politics involved, to invite Bob Moses to the campus and insist that he agree to exclude the Lawyers' Guild. Moses did come to Stanford during the last week of April. "I had to make a special trip out to the West Coast to talk to the Stanford group," Moses later recalled. "They were considering whether they . . . should pull out, and not go down [to Mississippi]." He listened patiently long into the night while the students repeated their mentor's warnings about the dangers of associating with communists. Moses then explained "our viewpoint about being open and not having that whole atmosphere of the fifties injected into the movement."[42]

For Moses, the possible defection of Lowenstein and the students who were loyal to him presented a troubling dilemma. Moses had made it clear that there would be no compromise on the question of the leadership of the summer project or of COFO's decision to accept the support of the Lawyers' Guild. On the other hand, as late as February 1964 he believed that Lowenstein's continued support was important to the success of the summer project and wrote the white activist imploring him to stay on board: "If you pull out it won't reduce any tensions absolutely, it will merely be an exchange of one set for another. . . . You not only have to stay—*you must* . . . come to the March . . . meeting. . . . We are just beginning to open up the pandora of inter–civil rights organization tensions. You have got to help us iron them out. If we lose dialogue, then we will be lost." In a postcript to that February letter Moses even raised the possibility that Lowenstein might come to Mississippi to "handle the program to unseat the Mississippi Democratic Party," a reference to the proposed challenge at the national Democratic convention in August.[43]

In late April, however, after Moses had made it clear to the Stanford students that the question of the participation of the Lawyers' Guild was not negotiable, Lowenstein urged student organizers at Stanford, Yale, Harvard, and the University of Oregon to hold a press conference and dramatically announce their own withdrawal as volunteers. So enraged was Lowenstein that at one point he told the Stanford students that Bob Moses was "being run by Peking." By now the white college activists realized that their primary allegiance lay not with their friend and mentor but with the embattled movement veterans in Mississippi. Lowenstein himself refrained from publicly denouncing the summer project, but throughout the late spring he continued to attack SNCC in the inner circles of the liberal political community. Moses, who had gone the extra mile to placate Lowenstein, now distanced himself from his one-time ally, refusing to return Lowenstein's calls.[44]

At the same time that Moses and COFO were fighting to protect the Mississippi movement from a hostile takeover by some of its northern "friends," the white president of Tougaloo College, Daniel Beittel, was encountering similar pressures in his efforts to maintain Tougaloo as a institution open to and supportive of civil rights activities. From the outset of his presidency in 1959 Beittel had refused to discourage student political activity. He had visited the jailed "Tougaloo Nine" after the library sit-in in 1961 and risked personal injury by joining the students at the Woolworth's lunch counter during the 1963 sit-in. Although no wild-eyed radical— Beittel ran a tight ship on the Tougaloo campus—he was greatly admired by activists for his courage and commitment. For white Mississippians, President Beittel was the symbol of "communist" influence at "cancer college." The state legislature had even threatened to revoke the school's charter to bring the institution into line.

Dan Beittel had resisted these pressures, and his tenure at Tougaloo seemed secure. On taking the job at age fifty-nine, Beittel had received assurances from the Tougaloo board of trustees that he could serve until his seventieth birthday. In January 1964, however, the board informed him that he would be "retiring" as president that year, on reaching the age of sixty-five.[45] Although it was not a major movement story, the events and intrigue surrounding Beittel's forced retirement are illustrative of the efforts by well-placed outsiders to influence the course of events in the Mississippi black community during the civil rights years.

The previous year Tougaloo had begun a cooperative relationship with Brown University. Brown's president, Barnaby Keeney, had taken an immediate interest in the southern black school, meeting with Tougaloo board members and contacting northern foundations on Tougaloo's behalf. Keeney had his own agenda, however, one that did not include Tougaloo's active involvement in the black struggle.[46] When Beittel received word from the board in late March that its decision was irrevocable and that he would need to clean out his desk before the summer session—and the onset of the Mississippi summer project—even though his successor would not yet be in place, Beittel made inquiries at the New York office of the United Church of Christ, Tougaloo's founding body, as to why the board had so abruptly terminated his contract in violation of their earlier agreement. Beittel then wrote to Keeney, reporting that "I was told that I was to be replaced at the urgent request of Brown University. It was indicated that Brown University would not continue our promising cooperative relationship unless I am replaced, that without Brown University the Ford Foundation will provide no support, and without foundation support the future of Tougaloo College is very uncertain."[47] President Keeney and Tougaloo board members were quick to deny any complicity. Keeney wrote Tougaloo board president Robert Wilder that "it would be disastrous if the word got around that Brown was interfering in the internal affairs of Tougaloo." Keeney's private correspondence, however, substantiates Beittel's accusations.[48]

The Brown relationship did prove financially and academically rewarding for Tougaloo; for example, shortly after Beittel's exit the Ford Foundation came through with a large grant to improve the school's educational program. But the college would never again be at the center of civil rights activity. Keeney used his influence to terminate Tougaloo's association with Moses' promising literacy project in the Delta and a year later to reverse the college's tentative commitment to serve as administrative agency for the Child Development Group of Mississippi, a movement-related Head Start program. Throughout the period of his involvement with Tougaloo College, Barnaby Keeney was on the payroll of the Central Intelligence Agency (an association that, when later made public, he cheerfully acknowledged), and though there is no evidence available to prove a link between his Tougaloo activities and his CIA work, Keeney personifies the interrelated network of government agencies, private foundations, and the intellectual community that needs to be explored more fully, particularly in relation to the southern black struggle of the 1960s.[49]

Although they were disappointed at Beittel's dismissal, COFO staff members had little time to speculate on the circumstances and timing of his ouster, for there were more pressing matters at hand. In preparation for the summer project, they needed to make arrangements for the freedom schools, plan community centers, and find housing for hundreds of volunteers. Activists also pushed ahead with their political agenda, a program now complicated by changes taking place in the structure of the Mississippi movement.

For nearly two years COFO had served as a loose confederation of organizations operating in Mississippi. Now, as the movement expanded statewide after the freedom vote, COFO adopted a constitution and began holding monthly meetings attended by blacks from all parts of Mississippi. The result was the gradual evolution of "a staff thing into a community thing," recalled Mendy Samstein. "We began to dig in at the idea of making COFO into a people's organization." Such a development was consistent with SNCC's philosophy of community organization. Still, a number of SNCC staff members outside Mississippi had reservations about the "new" COFO, fearing that "through this summer project COFO could swallow SNCC up," particularly in the critical area of fund-raising. SNCC executive secretary Jim Forman has written that in the summer of 1964 he "saw the continued existence of COFO as detrimental to SNCC's growth" and expressed his distaste at "being in a coalition with Toms and especially with the NAACP," one that could "make decisions in conflict with important principles of ours." At a SNCC executive committee meeting on the eve of the summer project, Guyot assured the skeptics that "in Mississippi SNCC *is* COFO," and when questioned about his commitment, Moses affirmed that his primary allegiance lay with SNCC. But doubts remained, and the debate over the relationship between SNCC and COFO would intensify in the months ahead.[50]

A logical outgrowth of COFO's new thrust was the formation of an independent, movement-led political party. At its monthly state convention held in Jackson on March 15, which was open to all movement supporters, COFO officially decided to challenge the state Democratic party's delegation at the national convention in Atlantic City in August and announced a "freedom registration" campaign for the summer. The delegates also voted to nominate candidates to run in the Democratic congressional primary on June 2. At its April convention COFO made it official, as the delegates assembled voted to establish the Mississippi Freedom Democratic party.[51]

Black political activity in the late spring of 1964 was carried on in an atmosphere of escalating white violence. While the Citizens' Council was busy issuing proclamations denouncing the civil rights bill and urging defiance of school desegregation orders, the Klan and local police were continuing to terrorize Mississippi blacks. On May 30, the night after Canton's third Freedom Day, police stopped Otha Williams, a businessman and farmer, on a deserted back country road and beat him severely. Williams finally escaped into the woods, where George Raymond found him and brought him safely back to town. Four days later two cars loaded with armed white men pulled up in front of the COFO office in Jackson. The occupants jumped out and fired away gangland style, shatttering the plate-glass front and injuring several workers inside. That same week three blacks, two men and a woman, were found dead in a car near Woodville. The sheriff blamed carbon monoxide poisoning for the deaths, but the black mortician who prepared the bodies for burial "said it was buckshot." Earlier, on May 19, Charles Evers had written his friend Attorney General Kennedy that black citizens in Neshoba County, particularly the Philadelphia township, were being "threatened and beaten by local police officers."[52]

Aware of the escalating Klan violence in Mississippi, federal officials feared that the invasion of hundreds of volunteers would make a bad situation worse. Lee White, a holdover from the Kennedy administration, advised President Johnson to urge civil rights leaders to avoid demonstrations and "channel their energies into registration drives" instead. In late May a worried Robert Kennedy reported to the president that "there has been an increase in white extremist activity in Mississippi. . . . Some forty instances of Klan type activity or police brutality have come to the Department's attention over the past four months. I have little doubt that this will increase." During the first week of June, Burke Marshall made a trip through the Klan stronghold of southwest Mississippi and reported his findings to the attorney general. Kennedy wrote the president on June 5, reminding him that "I told you . . . that I considered the situation in Mississippi to be very dangerous. Nothing in the reports I have received since then changes my view on that point."[53]

Marshall had gone to Mississippi to see things firsthand because the Justice Department possessed little information about Klan strength there. The FBI simply had not done its job. Marshall later recalled that prior to the summer project, "the Bureau just wouldn't put any resources into Mississippi, and they weren't any good, and they didn't have any informants." Lyndon Johnson had continued his predecessor's policy of handling J. Edgar Hoover with kid gloves. In his report drafted for the president, Marshall told Robert Kennedy that he had avoided "as much as possible any appearance of criticism of the Bureau's handling of specific investigations." Instead, he had attempted "to describe what is happening in such a way as to permit the Bureau to develop its own new procedures for the collection of intelligence." Nonetheless, Marshall made an end run around Hoover by sending the Justice Department's organized crime unit, led by Walter Sheridan, to Mississippi to investigate the Klan. Sheridan later observed that "we were sent because the Bureau wasn't doing anything. There were twenty FBI guys in the state, mostly Southerners, but they weren't doing anything unless they had to." Hoover was furious when he learned about Sheridan's group, but Marshall's move may have goaded the FBI director into becoming more active in Mississippi.[54]

Marshall had learned that both whites and blacks were arming, preparing for confrontation. Early in February, after a young black woman was hit by a car driven by whites on a street than ran through the Jackson State campus, more than 700 students went on a rampage, throwing rocks, bricks, and bottles at cars driven by whites. When the Jackson police arrived they were treated to the same reception and responded by firing into the crowd and wounding three students. Mississippi had become a powder keg.

The White House wanted to keep the lid on, while COFO leaders continued to demand that the Johnson administration offer protection for staff workers and volunteers throughout the summer.[55]

In early April Bob Moses wrote a memorandum to "Friends of Freedom in Mississippi," including the leaders of the major civil rights organizations, as well as celebrities like Harry Belafonte, James Baldwin, and Marlon Brando. The memorandum asked that they seek a meeting with Lyndon Johnson and make the case for direct federal intervention. "The President must be made to understand that this responsibility rests with him, and him alone," wrote Moses, "and that neither he nor the American people can afford to jeopardize the lives of the people who will be working in Mississippi this summer by failing to take the necessary precautions before the summer begins." At the same time COFO made plans for a public hearing to be held in Washington on June 8. There, before a panel of attorneys, educators, and authors, Mississippi blacks told their stories of violence and repression in the Magnolia State, again with the aim of increasing the pressure for federal action. Moses, Henry, and Dennis wrote the president in late May, requesting a meeting on June 18 or 19 to "discuss preparations for the summer."[56]

The White House response was to ignore the hearing and refuse all requests for a meeting. On June 17 presidential assistant Lee White called Henry to say that Johnson could not meet with the COFO delegation because "the President's schedule at this particular time is unusually heavy." When a group representing the parents of the volunteers also asked to meet with the president to urge him to offer protection for their children, White advised his boss against it, adding that "it is nearly incredible that those people who are voluntarily sticking their head into the lion's mouth would ask for somebody to come down and shoot the lion." On learning of these negative developments, the first group of summer volunteers, now meeting in Oxford, Ohio, on June 17 wrote an impassioned plea to the president, asking, "as we depart for that troubled state, to hear your voice in support of those principles to which Americans have dedicated and sacrificed themselves since our country's founding." Lyndon Johnson remained silent. (Nearly two months later the White House sent its reply in a form letter, stating that the federal government was doing all it could in Mississippi and had sent troops to search for the three missing civil rights workers. Among the signatories of the June 17 letter was volunteer Andrew Goodman.)[57]

Blacks in Mississippi looked ahead to the arrival of the summer volunteers with mixed emotions. Among local people anticipation and excitement ran high. Perhaps there is no better barometer of community support for the project than that so many blacks had agreed to open their homes to the northern students, for to do so meant risking retaliation and even death. Given the Klan's operations over the past five months, there was every reason to believe that homes housing volunteers would be bombed. Nonetheless, hundreds of black families prepared to welcome the civil rights workers, whatever the cost. The COFO staff in Jackson was too overwhelmed by the logistics of preparing for the summer activities to give much thought to the possible consequences of the decision to invite the students down. Out in the field, the publicity and excitement surrounding the summer project had little positive impact among the weary movement veterans who had opposed it from the outset.

On the evening of June 8 Sam Block, Willie Peacock, Charles McLaurin, James Jones, and James Black left Greenwood by car for a SNCC meeting in Atlanta. All were black Mississippians, veteran activists who had been organizing in communities for at least two years. Just outside Columbus, near the Alabama border, a state highway patrolman named Roy Elder pulled them over and then called the sheriff, who came out and took four of the men to the Lowndes County jail. Elder took Black in his patrol car. Twenty minutes after the first group arrived at the jail Elder showed up with his prisoner: "Black's head was dirty; one side of his face was swollen out of shape; one of his eyes was blackened and bloodshot, and blood was running from his swollen mouth. His clothes were also torn and disarranged," reported McLaurin. The five were placed in a cell and taken out individually for "interrogation." Sam Block was the first to go:

> Elder hit me on the cheek with his fist. I staggered and fell back to the window, and he grabbed me and hit me in the groin with his fist very hard. I fell down and he kicked me hard in the shin. . . . He asked me if any white person has mistreated me in Mississippi. I answered, "Yes, you are mistreat-

ing me now." He hit me again with his fist and knocked me back. When it was over, I could just barely make it back upstairs to the cell. I fell to the concrete floor and blacked out and just lay there for about 20 minutes.

Peacock, McLaurin, and Jones were then taken out for the same treatment. Badly beaten and in pain, the five men spent the night in jail, unable to make a phone call, uninformed of the charges against them. The next morning Black was found guilty of a traffic violation. The group was then released and drove on to the Atlanta meeting.[58]

A week later at the Oxford, Ohio, orientation sessions, white student volunteers, fresh from their final exams, were perplexed because a number of the black Mississippi SNCC workers there did not appear hospitable.

11

That Summer

We've been 'buked and we've been scorned.
We've been talked about sure's you're born.
But we never will turn back,
No, we'll never turn back
Until we've all been freed
And we have equality

We have walked through the shadows of death,
We've had to walk all by ourselves.
We have hung our head and cried
For those like Lee who died,
Died for you and died for me,
Died for the cause of equality.

—"We'll Never Turn Back," by Bertha Gober

As part of their orientation, the 250 young men and women gathered in Oxford, Ohio, were viewing a CBS documentary entitled "Mississippi and the Fifteenth Amendment." They watched attentively as a ludicrous image appeared on the screen: an obese, redneck registrar explaining in his heavy southern drawl why Mississippi Negroes really did not want to vote. He was a caricature, a political cartoonist's delight, and the volunteers laughed at the spectacle. They became quiet when the scene shifted to an elderly black man describing the shotgun blasts that had torn into his living room and wounded two young girls staying with his family. Then the camera focused on his wife, an old woman with a birdlike face and an absurd hat balanced atop her thin, gray hair, and some in the audience began to giggle, even as she unfolded the story of her nightmare.

The SNCC and CORE workers gathered in the room that night were watching a very different program. Instead of a ridiculous fat man, they saw Theron Lynd, the powerful symbol of white repression in Forrest County who had humiliated hundreds of black men and women attempting to register to vote: "This was no abstract injustice. This was the guy who said 'No' after you had worked your tail off for months getting frightened people to the point of walking up his county courthouse steps." And they knew the elderly black woman whose eccentricities the volunteers had found amusing as Mrs. Hattie Sisson, who with her husband, Herman, had been among the handful of local people to welcome the movement to Ruleville in the heart of the Delta. She too was a symbol—of courage and inspiration. Even the months and years spent organizing Mississippi had not prepared black activists for this display of insensitivity by the mostly white volunteers, who had come to Oxford for a crash course on the southern way of life. When the lights came on an angry black organizer leaped to the stage. "You should be ashamed!" he shouted. "You could laugh at that film! Six of the SNCC workers left this hall when you laughed. They couldn't believe their ears, and neither could I." Fighting back tears, he concluded, "I hope by the end of the summer you will never laugh at such a film again."[1]

The audience sat stunned. For three days they had listened to COFO staff and outside speakers discuss the summer project. Now, as one volunteer wrote, "We were afraid the whole movement was going to fall apart." Later that night the staff and volunteers "had the whole thing out" in an informal meeting. The northern students complained that the black organizers were aloof, unappreciative, and disdainful. SNCC workers tried to explain the reality the volunteers would soon face. "If you get mad at us walking out," one veteran observed, "just wait until they break your head in, and see if you don't have something to get mad about." Jimmy Travis, who had almost died in a Greenwood ambush, relieved the tension: "When the trouble comes I want to help you and I want you to help me. We may be angry tonight, but SNCC will not let you down." The long evening ended with volunteers and staff joining together to sing freedom songs, including the haunting "We'll Never

Turn Back," the anthem of the Mississippi movement. After this traumatic yet cathartic experience, one volunteer predicted hopefully that "the crisis is past, I think."[2]

It was, for a time, yet though the gulf separating the summer volunteers from the veteran COFO staff might narrow, it would never be bridged. Given the fear, the life-threatening situations, and the clash of cultures, interracial tensions lay uneasily near the surface throughout the Mississippi summer project.

The volunteers attending the first week-long orientation were assigned to voter registration work in ongoing and new projects throughout Mississippi. A week later another group would arrive for training as teachers in the freedom schools. The typical volunteer was white, affluent, politically liberal, and enrolled at a prestigious university. Just how many volunteers worked in Mississippi is subject to conjecture, for COFO never compiled a final tally. The most accurate information is in a list of volunteers released by the Jackson COFO office in mid-July, which stated that as of July 3 "approximately 450 volunteers are now in Mississippi." Not counted were volunteer lawyers and law students, members of the clergy, and physicians, many of whom were in the state for short periods of time. The oft-cited figure of "a thousand volunteers" appears credible if these latter categories are included. Probably no more than 650 students worked in Mississippi, and not all of these people worked all summer. Of the 382 people listed by name in the July 3 count, 155 were from New York and California, while only 26 came from southern states. Although women constituted 40 percent of this total, by the end of June COFO had stopped accepting white female volunteers, "as the areas to which they may be sent are very limited."[3]

No more than 10 percent of the volunteers were black. The difficulty in attracting black college students to work in Mississippi had concerned SNCC staff in their initial discussions of the project at the November meeting in Greenville. Although part of the justification for the summer project was to use white volunteers to focus national attention on Mississippi, no one wanted the volunteer contingent to be overwhelmingly white. Freedom school coordinator Staughton Lynd, a white historian then teaching at Yale, worried about the problems inherent in "an almost-all-Negro registration staff . . . working alongside an almost-all-white teaching staff." In the spring SNCC exempted black volunteers from the requirement that they bring with them to Mississippi $150 in cash, and organizers recruited on southern black campuses. The results were discouraging. In their public comments on the relatively low black volunteer turnout, staff members always cited the economic factor: most black students were not affluent and needed to work during the summer to make money for their college tuition. That, and the fact that blacks in 1960 constituted fewer than 3 percent of the nation's college undergraduates, accounted in part for the problem.[4]

Yet it is also true that the Mississippi summer project did not capture the imagination of black students as had the sit-ins three years earlier. The sit-ins and freedom rides had produced the SNCC and CORE cadre in Mississippi, but since 1962 few black students had made the decision to work full-time in the movement. Even at Tougaloo organizers were asking "why so many students are dropping from the movement." In a candid interview Dave Dennis concluded that "we didn't have that many Negroes to apply as volunteers because they just didn't happen to want to do it." The CORE activist speculated that northern black students were not interested in coming south because "that's what they want to escape from." Their parents, many of whom had faced southern racism firsthand, often strongly opposed the idea of their children leaving the relative safety of the North to go to Mississippi. Those black students who did volunteer played an important role in the summer project. Several were placed on the SNCC staff and remained to work in the state.[5]

At Oxford the preponderance of white volunteers was duly noted by the large press contingent in attendance, but the business at hand—orientation—absorbed both the students and COFO staff. Classes in voter registration, nonviolence, and Mississippi history were augmented by role playing, where the volunteers walked through interviews with black sharecroppers and confrontations with white mobs and police. They listened sullenly while the Justice Department's John Doar told them not to expect protection from the federal government: "The blunt truth is that federal protection for you . . . can be assured only by the creation and employment of a federal police force. . . . The creation of such a force, once taken, is not easily undone." The most enlightening presentation was that of the scholar and activist Vincent Harding, who anticipated and analyzed every major problem the white volunteers would face in Mississippi, from the deference of local blacks to the question of interracial sex and the hostility of a paranoid white citizenry. Finally, on Saturday, June 20, the first volunteer contingent boarded buses and cars for the long drive to Mississippi. It was, as one student wrote, "a strange [combination] of children headed for summer camp and soldiers going off to war." One of the volunteers, Andrew Goodman, rode down with CORE organizers James Chaney and Michael ("Mickey") Schwerner, bound for the relatively safe COFO project in Meridian.[6]

The twenty-one-year-old Chaney, who was born and raised in Meridian's black community, had become active in the movement in the fall of 1963 after he was recruited by CORE's Matt Suarez. In February 1964 Chaney joined Suarez and George Raymond in Canton, where he helped to organize the first Freedom Day, and he later worked briefly in Greenwood and Carthage before returning to Meridian. There he met Schwerner and his wife, Rita, a New York couple who had joined the CORE staff in Mississippi that January. The Schwerners' first task was to organize a community center, the first such facility in the state. By the end of March, Mickey reported that the center was providing reading instruction, classes to prepare people for government and clerical jobs, a Saturday story hour for children, a library, and a ping-pong table in constant use. The community responded enthusiastically to the sewing program Rita had established with equipment and materials supplied by northern supporters.[7]

Impressed by the young couple, CORE staff members appointed Mickey director of the eastern section of the fourth district project, covering six counties—including Neshoba. Although he was a Cornell graduate who had done graduate work at Columbia, Schwerner had a congenial and self-effacing manner that belied the Ivy League stereotype. He and Chaney worked together and became fast friends. ("Mickey and my boy were like brothers," Mrs. Chaney recalled.) Early in the spring they began to prepare for the summer project, planning freedom houses and freedom schools in Lauderdale, Clarke, and Neshoba counties. They were delighted when Cornelius Steel, a farmer who lived outside Philadelphia, offered to help organize a freedom school and community center there. In reporting this breakthrough to the New York CORE office, Schwerner added a cautionary note: "As promising as things look there, though, one must keep in mind that Neshoba is a very 'tough' county."[8]

A member of Mount Zion Methodist Church in the Longdale

community outside Philadelphia, Steel arranged for Chaney and Schwerner to speak to his congregation on Memorial Day about their summer plans. Parishioners readily agreed to let them use Mount Zion as a freedom school. On the evening of June 16, while Chaney and the Schwerners were meeting the first group of volunteers in Ohio, a delegation from the White Knights of the Ku Klux Klan appeared at Mount Zion just as the church board meeting was breaking up. Klan members threatened Steel and then assaulted three of the church leaders, including fifty-eight-year-old Bud Cole and two other church leaders as Cole's wife, Beatrice, looked on in horror. Later that night klansmen returned and burned Mount Zion to the ground.[9] As Chaney and Mickey Schwerner began the long drive from Oxford to Meridian after the first week's orientation, they knew their first order of business was to return to Longdale. They had won the trust of the local people, and the Klan had made them pay for it.

The two CORE staff members brought six volunteers to Mississippi, including Goodman, a twenty-year-old student at Queens College. Schwerner had recruited Andy Goodman for his project. The two young men shared similar backgrounds: both were Jewish, New Yorkers, and left-of-center in their politics. (On his application form Goodman had listed the radical *National Guardian* as one of his hometown papers.) Having driven much of the night, the group arrived in Meridian before dark on Saturday, June 20, and Chaney and Schwerner invited Goodman to accompany them to Neshoba County the next day as they tried to keep the fragile project there alive.[10]

The tragic journey of Chaney, Schwerner, and Goodman into the heart of Klan country on Sunday, June 21, is the most depressingly familiar story of the Mississippi movement: their arrest by Neshoba deputy sheriff Cecil Price on the outskirts of Philadelphia shortly after 3:00 P.M.; the incarceration in Sheriff Lawrence Rainey's jail; their release at about 10:30 that night, only to be stopped again ten miles south of town by Deputy Price, who turned the young men over to a mob; the gangland-style executions by klansmen; and their burial in a dam under construction in a remote area of the county. The Neshoba lynchings provoked international outrage and provided the Mississippi movement with the visibility it needed to force a reluctant federal government to take action against the Klan. The killings were decisive in persuading the state's white elite that continued violent resistance to federal law would lead to political anarchy and economic devastation. Within the movement, however, the tragedy left only feelings of grief and rage. Publicly, the anger focused on the federal government's failure to prevent the killings; privately, veteran activists also blamed themselves for the deaths of their three comrades.[11]

COFO's most serious charge was that the FBI did not arrive on the scene until nearly twenty hours after the three men's disappearance. Movement representatives also remembered that the Johnson administration had refused numerous requests to create the kind of visible presence in Mississippi that would have discouraged the Klan from carrying out such a crime. The chronology of events prepared by the COFO office documents Justice Department neglect, but it also indicates that the Meridian and Jackson COFO offices failed to follow the procedures established for such emergencies. When the three men did not return to the Meridian office at 4:00 P.M., the designated time, Louise Hermey, a volunteer who was spending her first day on the job in charge of the telephones, called the Jackson COFO office, where a more experienced staff person told her to wait until 5:00 before beginning to make inquiries. With still no word from the missing workers, at 5:30 COFO staff began calling the six jails in the immediate area. All law enforcement officers they spoke with denied that the young men were in their custody, including the receptionist at the Neshoba County jail in Philadelphia. Inexplicably, once the initial calls were made, COFO appeared immobilized for several hours. Mary King, who was in charge of SNCC communications, recalls that "there was a gap of six hours between the time that the Meridian office notified Jackson of the disappearances and the time that Atlanta [SNCC office] was notified."[12]

Dave Dennis was not in Mississippi on June 21. Because he was suffering from a severe case of bronchitis, the CORE activist had gone to his mother's home in Shreveport to recuperate while the other staff members were in Oxford. When the Meridian office called Dennis at about 9:00 P.M., he was horrified to learn that no one had contacted the FBI or sent people into Neshoba County to investigate. Dennis knew that Chaney and Schwerner "would not have stopped between Meridian and Philadelphia for anyone but cops. . . . If you didn't hear from people by 4:00, you call the FBI, the press, you sent a car in. . . . Instead they waited until 9:00."

Dennis blamed himself for the tragedy: "I feel very responsible for Chaney and them. . . . I don't know whether I would have been able to stop it. The one thing I do know, I feel we would have been on top of it much quicker if I had been there. The people who were there just didn't know what to do."[13]

The delay in responding was probably not decisive. Given that the FBI did not enter the case until nearly twenty-four hours after being contacted, there is no reason to believe that agents would have moved more quickly had they been called earlier. Sending people into Neshoba County could have given the Klan second thoughts, or it could have resulted in more deaths. COFO should have alerted the press earlier, but there were no leads, no evidence that the three men were in jail rather than in the hands of a mob, and it is doubtful that a call from a reporter to the Neshoba jail would have dissuaded the Klan from doing its work. Still, the murders extracted a heavy psychological toll on veteran organizers. Two decades later Dennis observed that "you never get over that. I guess I will live with it until the day I die." He believed that "a lot of people were hurt or killed because, indirectly, Bob Moses and I would say go do this and go do that. . . . So you don't get over that stuff. It happens. It is part of the ball game. But the thing that hurts more than anything else is the question that you can't answer: it is whether or not it was worth it for the gains that you got at the time." Above all, Neshoba convinced Dave Dennis that nonviolence as a tactic was "a waste of good lives. You have to put some injury on your enemy to get respect."[14]

At dawn on Tuesday, June 23, CORE workers George Raymond and Landy McNair left Meridian for Philadelphia to investigate the disappearance of their comrades. Dona Richards, Gwen Gillon, and Matt Suarez drove to Neshoba County from Jackson. Shortly after word reached Oxford, Ohio, where the second week of orientation was underway, four teams of SNCC organizers immediately left for Mississippi to join the search. On arriving in Neshoba County they were taken in by local people, who themselves had been combing the woods and swamps during the day, carrying shotguns and pretending to hunt. Cleveland Sellers, not yet twenty and new to Mississippi, recalled that he, Stokely Carmichael, Charlie Cobb, and other members of the search party slept in the homes of black sharecroppers during the day and went out after midnight to avoid klansmen in the area: "Piling from the truck at 1:30 or 2 A.M., we would fan out. Walking slowly, and almost never talking—we searched swamps, creeks, old houses, abandoned barns, orchards, tangled underbrush and unused wells. . . . Our search was complicated by the poisonous snakes and spiders that abound in rural Mississippi." It soon became apparent to Sellers and his friends that "the situation was utterly hopeless. The unknown killers had made certain that no one was going to stumble over the bodies accidentally."[15]

The disappearance of two young middle-class white men finally moved the White House to action. On Tuesday, June 23, FBI inspector Joseph Sullivan arrived in Meridian with five agents to take charge of the search. President Johnson had been on the phone to Senator Eastland and Governor Johnson and sent former CIA director Allen Dulles to Jackson to meet the governor and important businessmen. Dulles did not, however, have time for Rita Schwerner. When SNCC's Bob Zellner confronted Dulles outside a state office and said, "Mr. Dulles, this is Rita Schwerner. We'd like to talk with you about the search going on for the civil rights workers," Dulles replied, "I'm sorry, but I have to rush off to a very important meeting." Dulles made clear his opposition to federal protection for civil rights workers, but he did recommend that the president authorize an increased FBI presence in Mississippi. Dulles's trip set the stage for a visit by J. Edgar Hoover, who on July 10 opened a new field office in Jackson, the largest in the nation.[16]

The FBI director's trip to Jackson was a media event in which Hoover gave public assurance to Mississippi whites that the FBI was their friend. He explained that the bureau was coming to Jackson because the state's burgeoning economy would inevitably attract "criminal scum" from other areas and promised that "we most certainly do not and will not give protection to civil rights workers. . . . The FBI is not a police organization. It is purely an investigative organization." At the same time Hoover privately warned the governor, law enforcement officers, and business leaders that Klan violence must end and that they must comply with the new civil rights law. Although he had opposed equality of the races since the beginning of his career at the end of World War I, Hoover knew his reputation was on the line and that the bureau would have to deliver in Mississippi. Before the end of the summer 153 agents were working out of the Jackson office. Hoover reported to the president that Governor Johnson had deplored the violence and "emphasized that as long as he sat in the Governor's chair, ignorance, hatred and prejudice would not take over in his state."[17]

Earlier that spring, however, the governor's State Sovereignty Commission had circulated to local sheriffs and police chiefs a description of Michael Schwerner, the blue Ford station wagon he drove, and its license tag. Schwerner was not wanted for any crime. Sheriff Lawrence Rainey no doubt already had that information, but the implied message was clear: civil rights workers were the enemy, and the highest state officials supported their local police. Given this assurance, it is not surprising that Neshoba County lawmen and klansmen seemed unconcerned about the possibility that they might be prosecuted for their crime. But now Governor Johnson, like Director Hoover, was under pressure. Johnson feared a military occupation of his state and thus had to move against the Klan. At their meeting in Jackson, Hoover gave the governor a list of state highway patrol officers who were Klan members, and Johnson promptly fired them. Agents of the Justice Department also quietly moved into communities with COFO projects.[18]

The Klan and its supporters did not seem to get the message, for the summer of 1964 was the most violent since Reconstruction: thirty-five shooting incidents and sixty-five homes and other buildings burned or bombed, including thirty-five churches. One thousand movement people were arrested, and eighty activists suffered beatings. In addition to the Neshoba lynchings, there were at least three other murders.[19]

On July 12, the day after J. Edgar Hoover left Jackson, a fisherman near Tallulah, Louisiana, reported seeing the lower half of a man's body caught on a log in a bayou near the Mississippi River. The next day the lower half of a second body was discovered nearby. The victims were twenty-year-old Charles Moore, an Alcorn College student, and Henry Dee, twenty-one, neither of whom had been active in the civil rights movement. On May 2 klansmen had abducted the two young men and taken them deep into the Homochitto National Forest, where they bound them to a tree and beat them to death. Their bodies were then tied to an engine block and dumped into the river. Four months later the FBI arrested two white men, a truck driver and a paper mill worker, charging them with the murders of Dee and Moore. State authorities later refused to prosecute, claiming the evidence was insufficient. The body of a black teenager, never identified, was also found floating in the Big Black River. He was wearing a CORE T-shirt. Once it became clear that these three victims were not the missing COFO workers, the press and the public quickly lost interest.[20] As the search for Chaney, Schwerner, and Goodman dragged on in an atmosphere of constant terror and tension, COFO workers, local people, and the outside volunteers pushed on with the summer project.

• • •

Shocked by the disappearance of the three men in Neshoba County, organizers nonetheless moved ahead with their original program for the summer. From its state headquarters in Jackson, COFO secured locations for freedom schools, proceeded with plans for community centers, and mapped out areas to be covered in the voter registration canvas. Existing projects in all five congressional districts were to be staging areas for expansion into new territory. From its base in Canton CORE moved west up Mississippi Highway 16 to Carthage and Harmony, and from there later to Philadelphia, where a large "COFO" sign on a storefront defiantly proclaimed the movement's determination to confront the Klan at its doorstep. SNCC likewise sent organizers back into McComb, ignoring Justice Department warnings to avoid southwest Mississippi, where the police were the Klan. On the Gulf Coast COFO experimented with a "White Folks Project," originally designed to reach white moderates but ultimately focusing on economic issues aimed at the working class. A major goal of the summer project, then, was to create a truly statewide movement. Not surprisingly, the most intense activity occurred in the Mississippi Delta, where SNCC had been operating continuously since the summer of 1962.[21]

SNCC chose Greenwood, the symbol of its presence and commitment in Mississippi, as its national headquarters for the summer. Bob Zellner, having taken leave from his graduate studies at Brandeis University, headed the local COFO project, while Stokely Carmichael was in charge of operations for the entire second congressional district. Born in the West Indies, the twenty-two-year-old Carmichael was a graduate of Howard and already a veteran SNCC activist. Although he was flamboyant and charismatic, Carmichael was also a disciplined organizer who insisted that the student volunteers keep a low profile and respect the religious and cultural traditions of Delta blacks. In movement communities like Ruleville and

Clarksdale, the presence of the young whites and the promise of the freedom schools added a dimension to the ongoing voter registration activities. The influx of the volunteer workers also made it possible for the movement to expand to areas of the Delta as yet untouched by civil rights activity, such as Issaquena County.[22]

Situated at the southern end of the Delta just north of Vicksburg, Issaquena was sparsely populated and overwhelmingly black but had no registered black voters. Charlie Cobb, Ivanhoe Donaldson, and Stokely Carmichael had gone into Issaquena in the spring of 1964 to meet with Henry Sias, an eighty-three-year-old World War I veteran who owned and farmed 160 acres of rich Delta land. Sias introduced the SNCC workers to local blacks, including Unita Blackwell, who had recently moved to the county and was "pickin' and choppin' cotton at three dollars a day." During the summer more workers came into Issaquena, including black volunteer Muriel Tillinghast. At a church rally in the county seat of Mayersville they asked local people to volunteer to take the voter registration test. Blackwell, one of the five women and three men who went to the courthouse, later recalled that "I was just starting to learn about myself and history in a brand new way." Angered by the circuit clerk's refusal to register her, Blackwell became a SNCC organizer. Although unheralded at the time, SNCC's move into counties like Issaquena expanded the base of the Mississippi movement and brought new people into leadership positions.[23]

The summer project also stimulated movement activity in Holmes County, where a year earlier that handful of independent black farmers had first attempted to register to vote. COFO staff members under the leadership of Hollis Watkins set up operations in Mileston, and more than fifty volunteers moved into Holmes, operating freedom schools and canvassing nearly every black residence in the county. Local morale received a boost when Abe Osheroff, a fifty-year-old white activist from Los Angeles, raised $10,000 for a community center, moved in with Hartman Turnbow for the summer, and with a carpenter friend built the center and donated the building to the Holmes County movement.[24]

White residents of Holmes did not take kindly to this invasion by outsiders. Night riders burned a SNCC car, attempted to bomb the new center, and threatened local people active in the movement. The violence was not as severe in Holmes as in several other counties, in part because black residents set up nightly patrols, letting it be known that they had weapons and were prepared to use them. After one bombing scare Margaret Rose, a white freedom school teacher, reported that the family she was staying with "were up all last night, Mr. on the road patrolling with his new rifle and Mrs. walking from room to room in the house with a shot gun, peering out of every window." Later Rose looked into the bedroom where one of the children lay sleeping, and "on the bed next to her was a large shot gun, waiting." Although she was a pacifist, Rose expressed the sentiments of many other volunteers—and staff people— when she observed that "I cannot help feeling more secure knowing that they are armed."[25]

Although Delta organizers drew encouragement from the response of local people in Holmes and Issaquena, progress was slow in hard-core areas of resistance such as Sunflower County. Project director Charles McLaurin, along with Ruleville leaders Fannie Lou Hamer and Joe McDonald, worked to solidify and expand the movement in Sunflower; white officials, assisted by the Citizens' Council, resorted to familiar tactics to discourage black participation. Before the volunteers reached Ruleville, Mayor Charles Durrough visited several black families, warning that if they housed the northern workers their white guests would beat and kill them. When these scare tactics failed, local whites imposed economic penalties. By the end of the summer nearly all Ruleville blacks "known to support the civil rights movement" had lost their jobs. When in mid-July McLaurin and other COFO workers attempted to organize a registration drive in Drew, just north of Ruleville, police arrested seven workers for distributing literature without a permit. The following day, after a black church withdrew permission for a meeting, McLaurin led a group of young Drew blacks onto the sidewalk for an impromptu rally. Police were on the scene, while a group of black men looked on from across the street. McLaurin urged the men to join the gathering. When they failed to respond, the frustrated SNCC leader shouted, "Are you gonna let them see that you're afraid? That you won't join these kids and women?" No one moved—except the police, who arrested twenty-five of the activists for blocking the sidewalk.[26] This pattern of breakthroughs and setbacks, of defiant courage and sullen resignation, coexisted in COFO projects across the state.

Influenced by the disappearance of the three movement workers, the CORE national office increased its efforts in Mississippi's fourth congressional district. Delegates to the CORE convention in early July unanimously approved a plan to build a large community center in Meridian as a memorial to Chaney, Schwerner, and Goodman; vowed to send more staff, cars, and money for the existing projects in Canton and Meridian; and decided to expand into Leake and Neshoba counties. Throughout the district whites resisted these movement initiatives. Gus Noble, the president of the Canton Citizens' Council, warned that if local blacks received their rights, the results would be the same as in the former French and British African colonies: "Those natives were not prepared for self-government. They were unstable. They ate each other." By early June many of the fifty-five blacks arrested while picketing the courthouse during the May 29 Freedom Day were still in jail, including C. O. Chinn. There was a drive-by shooting at the freedom house, and on June 8 the headquarters was rocked by a bomb that bounced off the outside wall and exploded on the sidewalk.[27]

Despite Madison County's reputation as one of the toughest in the state, CORE staff members at the Oxford orientation recruited a strong contingent of summer volunteers for the area. Rudy Lombard, a black student from New Orleans, recalled his ambivalence about spending the summer in Mississippi, but when Mrs. Annie Devine "looked me in the eye and said, 'Rudy, I *know* you won't deny us the benefit of your talents in Canton this summer. I'm depending on you.' I knew I was trapped. No way I could turn that woman down." The volunteers joined CORE staff led by George Raymond to open ten freedom schools throughout the district, promote the ongoing "blackout" boycott of Canton's white merchants, and work in the local project's community center. Voter registration efforts continued throughout the county. CORE staffer Mike Piore organized a Farmers League, which was designed to educate the county's black farmers about the federal government's complex acreage allotment program and to organize them for the fall Agricultural Stabilization and Conservation Service (ASCS) elections. Predictably, Madison County whites responded violently. Over the summer nine black churches in the district were burned or bombed. Canton workers were shot at and arrested on false charges. Despite this intimidation, local blacks supported CORE's work, and Canton activist Annie Devine became a leader of the new Mississippi Freedom Democratic party.[28]

The CORE project in Leake County, next to Madison, received

less attention from the press, yet it was an important and in many ways unique example of local community spirit and organization. The movement here was centered in the all-black community of Harmony, which was located on a dirt road about fourteen miles from the county seat at Carthage. Rural and isolated, Harmony had about it a timeless, mythical quality, a black Brigadoon in the heart of Klan country. The *New York Times*'s John Herbers observed that "most of the several hundred families own their farms and they live in well-kept bungalows scattered over the rolling clay hills." Evoking the image of the old frontier cabin-raisings, Herbers noted that as volunteers were building a new community center, "women in the community serve lunch every day to the volunteer workers— fish deep-fried out-of-doors in large iron kettles and black-eyed peas." CORE worker Jerome Smith remembers Harmony as providing "a safe haven for movement people." It was "a together community" of "powerful people who would defend themselves." Harmony, concluded CORE's Tom Dent, "really lived up to its name."[29]

The movement had first come to Harmony in the late 1950s, when Medgar Evers spoke at a rally and helped to organize a local NAACP branch. Its president was Mrs. Winson Hudson, who along with her sister Dovie led a voter registration campaign and the drive to desegregate the schools. "Women," recalled Jerome Smith, "were the backbone of the community." The Hudson sisters, along with fifty other Leake County blacks, joined with NAACP plaintiffs in Jackson and on the Gulf Coast to file desegregation petitions in 1962. The Harmony community had become enraged that year when county officials, using consolidation as their rationale, closed the school in Harmony and began busing students to the black school in Carthage. The Harmony school had been a gift of the Rosenwald Fund, and local people had helped to build it. The school was a symbol of community pride and independence; Harmony residents believed that the whites had shut it down for that reason. If they could not have their own school, they would see to it that the white schools were integrated. Whites responded as they had to the suits filed across the state in 1955, attempting to intimidate plaintiffs to remove their names from the suit. But a dozen signatories held firm, including Dovie Hudson, whose daughter joined the children of Medgar and Myrlie Evers as participants in the court action. They won the case, and in the fall of 1964 Leake County joined Jackson and Biloxi as the first public school systems in the state to desegregate.[30]

The school suit, the influx of CORE workers beginning in the fall of 1963, the voter registration drive, and now the presence of a group of white volunteers working in the black community had turned Leake County into an armed camp. Shortly after the Harmony freedom school opened, the Klan burned a cross in front of the only store in town. That same night whites threw large-headed nails on the only road into town; the first casualty was a car driven by two FBI agents investigating the cross burning. Local activists had their deliveries of butane gas stopped, and Winson Hudson and other leaders had their credit cut off by Carthage merchants. Two volunteers, an Iowa minister and a Harvard student, were beaten by a mob inside a doctor's office in Carthage, where the student had gone to get medical attention. Police arrested the two white volunteers. With no local, state, or federal authorities to deter them, white terrorists began to make forays into Harmony. There they found the community armed and ready. When Dovie Hudson learned that whites were on the road placing bombs in mailboxes, she "called my boys and one got one gun and one got the other one. And just as they drove up and put the bomb in the mailbox, my boys started shooting. They just lined that car with bullets up and down."[31]

Harmony's response to the terror exemplified the determination of Mississippi blacks throughout the summer. "The more they did to us," Winson Hudson recalled, "the meaner we got." The freedom school prospered. The Citizens and Parents Committee for Equal Schools in Leake County sent a manifesto to the county superintendent demanding desegregation and "equality in all the public schools of Leake County immediately." Under the guiding hand of Winson Hudson, the Leake County Freedom Democratic party met at the Galilee Baptist Church on July 26 to elect a full slate of delegates to attend the district caucus in Meridian. One observer who had visited movement operations across the state reported that Harmony was "the happiest project I have seen in Mississippi."[32]

For the most part, the summer project expanded and extended existing COFO programs throughout the state. The freedom schools, however, were something new to the Mississippi movement and represented a creative contribution to the teaching of children—

and adults—who lacked basic skills and training. SNCC field secretary Charlie Cobb first came up with the idea for the freedom schools late in 1963. Working in the Delta, Cobb had seen the inequities inherent in Mississippi's two-tiered educational system. The state spent four times as much money on white schools as on black schools, and local funding, especially in the rural areas, was even more one-sided. The Holly Bluff school system, for example, spent $191.17 each year per white student and only $1.26 for each black student. In 1960 the average black adult had completed six years of school; the average white, eleven years. Equally disturbing was what transpired in the classroom. Black history and contemporary race relations were taboo subjects. "The only thing our kids knew about Negro history," observed freedom school teacher Ralph Featherstone, "was about Booker T. Washington and George Washington Carver and his peanuts." Moreover, teachers were often badly trained and autocratic in their pedagogy, stressing rote memorization and discouraging student inquiry. Since "students are forced to live in an environment that is geared to squash intellecutal curiosity," Cobb concluded, it was the responsibility of the movement "to fill an intellectual and creative vacuum in the lives of young Negro Mississippians, and to get them to articulate their own desires, demands, and questions."[33]

Throughout the spring of 1964 COFO worked with local community leaders to create interest in the freedom schools and to arrange for meeting places and housing for the teachers, most of whom would be white women volunteers. At the same time a group of educators and activists led by Staughton Lynd developed a program based on maximum student participation. Such an approach would turn the traditional role of the teacher "upside down." Educator Florence Howe, who taught in the Jackson freedom schools, drove that point home: "The teacher is not to be an omnipotent, aristocratic dictator, a substitute for the domineering parent or the paternalistic state. He is not to stand before rows of students, simply pouring predigested, pre-censored information into their brains. The Freedom School teacher is, in fact, to be present not simply to teach, but rather *to learn with* the students." The key to the freedom schools was the awareness that the students brought with them valuable knowledge and experiences: the culture of black Mississipians was important and must be preserved. The curriculum reflected this emphasis. In addition to offering more traditional classes in reading, writing, and mathematics, each school devoted part of the day to black history and its relationship to the civil rights movement.[34]

The freedom schools captured the imagination of Mississipi blacks. Where Cobb's original proposal envisioned "about twenty-five" schools serving approximately 1,000 tenth- and eleventh-grade students, by summer's end about 2,500 students ranging in age from preschool to adults were attending nearly fifty schools scattered across the state. Hattiesburg became the "Mecca of the Freedom School world." Under the leadership of Carolyn and Arthur Reese, a black couple from Detroit, Hattiesburg boasted the largest freedom school program in the state, with more than 600 students showing up on the first day of registration.[35] All this occurred in the face of white opposition. Local authorities warned black ministers not to make their churches available as schools and black families not to house the volunteer teachers. In Harmony, after local people renovated the abandoned Rosenwald school, the sheriff declared that the school was county property and denied permission to use it. Undaunted, Harmony blacks held classes under the trees while the new community center was under construction. The morning after a bomb leveled the church serving as the McComb freedom school, seventy-five students showed up for class on the lawn in front of the smoldering ruins. Whites feared that more was going on in the freedom schools than the teaching of the three Rs, that the schools were an extension of the movement.[36]

And in fact they were. Cobb made it clear in his original proposal that a primary goal of the freedom schools was to "form the basis for statewide student action . . . to be assured of having a working force that remains in the state high schools putting to use what it has learned." Moreover, along with the Freedom Democratic party, the freedom schools represented an early attempt to create "parallel institutions" in the black community: "If we are concerned about breaking the power structure, then we have to be concerned about building our own institutions to replace the old, unjust decadent ones which make up the existing power structure. Education in Mississippi is an institution which must be reconstructed from the ground up."[37]

Throughout the state students responded. Merely showing up for classes could be an act of protest, as in McComb, where the freedom school served "to loosen the hard knot of fear and to organize the Negro community." Freedom school newspapers reflected the growing political consciousness of the students. "Reporters" investigated working conditions in their communities, wrote essays critical of their segregated school systems, and urged support for the Freedom Democratic party. Students at the Palmer's Crossing freedom school wrote their own declaration of independence. After listing specific grievances, the document concluded with "We do hereby declare independence from the unjust laws of Mississippi which conflict with the United States Constitution." In early August delegates from freedom schools across the state assembled in Meridian for a convention, which adopted resolutions ranging from a call for enforcement of the Civil Rights Act of 1964 to economic sanctions against South Africa. Staughton Lynd observed that as the convention proceeded, "these teenagers were rejecting the advice of adults whether in workshops or plenary sessions, for they had discovered they could do it themselves." Among the adult observers was Bob Moses; Lynd recalls "it was the single time in my life that I have seen Bob happiest. He just ate it up. . . . He just thought this was what it was all about." Freedom school students formed the nucleus of the SNCC-sponsored Mississippi Student Union and in the fall continued to be active, organizing boycotts of the segregated schools in Shaw and in Issaquena County.[38]

The freedom school experiment was not an unqualified success. School coordinators in the Delta had to schedule their classes around the black public schools' summer session, which was held so that children would be free to pick cotton in the fall, thereby limiting student participation. In most projects, makeshift provisions were necessary to accommodate individuals considerably younger and older than the high school students for whom the schools had been planned. Teaching personnel changed frequently, upsetting students who had begun to develop friendships with favorite teachers. (Early in the summer Staughton Lynd had complained that some project directors were arbitrarily reassigning freedom school staff to voter registration work.) Not all students were eager participants. Teachers had to contend with the disruptive influence of "hangers on and drop-outs" who "wanted to hang around the center but were unwilling to join a class." And while the majority of volunteer teachers adapted well to their environment, a number were incapable of adjusting to the innovative teaching program or of relating to young black Mississippians as equals.[39]

Still, the freedom schools stand out as a major achievement of the summer project. Howard Zinn noted that although it was difficult to point to concrete results, "nine-year-old Negro children sounded out French words whose English equivalents they had not yet discovered. . . . They learned about Frederick Douglass, wrote letters to the local editor about segregation, and discussed the meaning of civil disobedience. Some wrote short stories about their lives, and others wrote poems." Freedom school students listened to Pete Seeger sing African, Indian, Chinese, and Polynesian songs; they sat attentively while A. Philip Randolph spoke of his life's work as an activist in the freedom struggle; and they attended performances of Martin Duberman's play *In White America,* put on by the Free Southern Theatre. Organized at Tougaloo College by John O'Neal, Doris Derby, and Gilbert Moses, this touring company remained active long after the end of the summer project, performing before black audiences in towns and hamlets throughout the Deep South.[40]

The freedom schools opened new worlds to several thousand black youngsters, enhancing their self-esteem and raising their expectations. One such student was Walter Saddler, who attended the freedom school in Gluckstadt, about a dozen miles from Canton in Madison County. Saddler wrote of his experiences that summer, of his interest in "Negro history, because it was something new to me and it really taught me a lot." He recalled the night that the freedom school in Gluckstadt was burned to the ground and how he continued to attend a freedom school in Canton that fall in the evening, after his regular schoolday had ended. Saddler said that he had "hopes of going on to college, and I know I could do a good job." Little more than a decade later, Walter Saddler was the anchor on the state's most widely watched television news program. Although Saddler's achievement was not typical, the volunteer teachers in the freedom schools proved that a creative, anti-authoritarian, student-centered approach to teaching and learning had and still has much to offer the tradition-bound educational establishment, both in Mississippi and throughout the nation.[41]

As for the performance of the volunteers as a whole, each project had its stories of compassion and courage, insensitivity and arrogance. To an extent, the reservations expressed by SNCC staff who opposed bringing in the white students proved accurate. Many volunteers were articulate, confident, and naive, a combination of qualities that drove some to attempt to assume leadership positions and to dictate policy. Some volunteers came to Mississippi to teach, not to learn. They believed in the American dream—it had, after all, worked for them—and stereotyped the enemy as a big redneck who drove a pickup with a gun rack. They were not prepared for the refusal of liberal northern politicians to act decisively in Mississippi or for the resentment and hostility they met from a number of veteran COFO staff. Examples of the "Ugly American" volunteer abound. None is more revealing than the recollections of one northern white student, the late Paul Cowan.

A graduate of Choate in 1958 and Harvard in 1963, Cowan epitomized the best and brightest of his generation. After he was assigned the job of communications officer in the relatively safe project in Vicksburg, Cowan quickly became impatient with what he perceived as the autocratic leadership of the SNCC worker heading the project, a twenty-two-year-old black man who had dropped out of college to work full-time in the movement. Cowan nicknamed the project director "Papa Doc," after Haiti's dictator. "It sounds like a barely disguised code," Cowan later reflected, "a liberal's way of saying Rastus or Burrhead." Along with several other volunteers who worked in the office, Cowan lectured the SNCC veteran on the strategies they needed to pursue. Cowan later saw that "it must have been torment for him to enter the Vicksburg office and listen to us discussing local problems as if they were issues that had arisen in a college seminar." When the project director responded by withdrawing, Cowan "moved to assume the leadership that Papa Doc seemed incapable of exercising."[42]

With funds solicited from the North, the volunteers founded a movement newspaper, the *Vicksburg Citizen's Appeal*. Late in the summer they invited Bob Moses to come to a meeting so that they could share with him the results of their work. The Vicksburg project director accompanied Moses and was visibly angry: "Local people didn't want our newspapers, he said in a quiet, bitter voice. . . . They wanted freedom. And that was the one thing we would never be able to give them." Cowan expected this criticism, but he was shocked when Moses supported the project director, informing Cowan that if his newspaper were to retain formal ties with the movement, it would have to be controlled by SNCC's communications people. Cowan replied that that would be censorship, and thus intolerable. An angry exchange followed, and Cowan left the meeting—and Mississippi—sad and chastened. Years later he would write that "we were so intent on transforming Mississippi in a summer that we were unable to relate to its people as human beings." He concluded that "there is a kind of Jesus Christ complex that many middle-class whites bring to their relations with people whom they consider oppressed."[43]

A concern in several of the projects was interracial sex, particularly relationships that developed between black men in the movement and white women volunteers. Frowned upon by many local blacks and resented by black women activists, these summer romances enraged local whites and thus were potentially dangerous. Ivanhoe Donaldson told his Holly Springs workers he did not intend to have any interracial courtships among staff members, for such activity would "provide local whites with the initiative they need to come in here and kill all of us. Even if the whites don't find out about them, the [local] people will, and we won't be able to do anything afterwards to convince them that our primary interest is political."[44]

No doubt the extent of sexual activity between blacks and whites during the summer of 1964 has been exaggerated, in part because white segregationists had made interracial sex a centerpiece of their attack on the summer project itself. More recently, historians of the women's movement have examined the issue. Sara Evans, for example, has written that "interracial sex became a widespread phenomenon in local communities in the summer of 1964" and called attention to the exploitation of white women by black men. Sally Belfrage, a white volunteer-journalist in Greenwood, has taken issue with these generalizations: "I must say it baffles me. I didn't see any white women being victimized by black men. . . . At the time it seemed we were just too busy and crowded. I can't even work out where they did it, where people *went* to be victimized. My greatest problem in Greenwood was the absolute impossibility of being alone." And Mary King, a veteran white SNCC worker, has stated that "there was no undercurrent of sex affecting my experiences in the civil rights movement."[45]

Still, whether for reasons of guilt or youthful physical and emotional attraction, some white women volunteers did have sexual relationships with black men, who at times came on aggressively. Mary King also observed that "lack of awareness coupled with sudden exposure to the sexual frankness of some of the black men meant that a few of the [white women] fluttered like butterflies from one tryst to another. Sexual dalliances were one way for a volunteer to prove that she was not racist and I'm certain any number of black men manipulated this anxiety."[46] Viewed strictly in political terms, such activity weakened the links between COFO and local communities while exacerbating racial tensions within the movement.

Nevertheless, the stereotypes of the women volunteers as naive and foolish and of the men as arrogant and uncooperative are misleading and unfair to the vast majority of volunteers. In community after community local people welcomed the northern white students into their homes, finding their Yankee eccentricities more amusing than threatening. And it is certain that summer volunteers did not throw their weight around in projects headed by SNCC activists like Ivanhoe Donaldson, Hollis Watkins, Curtis Hayes, and Stokely Carmichael. Differences of race and social class obviously created internal problems, as did the COFO veterans' growing disenchantment with white liberals. Facing a common enemy as they did, however, black and white workers generally worked together harmoniously, and in projects like McComb, where Klan activity was most severe, feelings of true camaraderie developed.[47]

In assessing the role played by the men and women who came to Mississippi in the summer of 1964, one must also note the work of nearly 150 lawyers and law students who took on civil rights cases; the 300 ministers representing the National Council of Churches; and some 100 physicians, nurses, and psychologists who came to offer their services to movement workers and laid the foundation for the Medical Committee for Human Rights, which took on the task of providing health care for thousands of impoverished Mississippi blacks. Although many of these individuals stayed for only a week or two and operated largely outside the glare of publicity, they possessed the skills and training to provide immediate assistance where needed. These older, short-term volunteers worked quietly but effectively in many projects across the state.[48]

It is difficult to generalize about the impact of the volunteers. They did not "save" the Mississippi movement. Despite the white reign of terror, local people in COFO projects across the state were dedicated to carrying on the struggle, and they would have continued to do so whether or not the white students had come down. Along with other developments in the summer and fall of 1964, however, the continuing presence of large numbers of white volunteers did push the movement in a new direction, one that increasingly relied on directing the national spotlight onto Mississippi through activities such as the Atlantic City and congressional challenges. Later, a number of black organizers would look back negatively on their experiences with white volunteers. Many local black families, on the other hand, maintained their friendships with the outsiders who had lived with them during the summer, and these locals greeted the young northerners enthusiastically when they returned to visit over the years. When all the stories of white insensitivity, paternalism, and exploitation are finally recorded, one simple fact stands clear: the white students came to Mississippi because they had been invited. The conclusion of civil rights scholar Doug McAdam—that "they were tried and not found wanting"—applies to the vast majority of the volunteers who came to Mississippi in the summer of 1964.[49]

• • •

The most symbolic achievement of the summer project was the movement's return to McComb, where three years earlier SNCC had initiated its first voter registration project. Southwest Mississippi was even more dangerous now, for the Klan there was organized and running wild. Justice Department officials pleaded with COFO organizers to stay away from the area. Although several movement workers had been in and out of McComb, particularly during the freedom vote campaign in the fall of 1963, SNCC had not committed full-time staff to the area despite the presence of a core of dedicated local people who were eager for outside help. SNCC veterans, then, felt a moral obligation to reestablish the McComb project during the summer of 1964. The disappearance of the three men in Philadelphia delayed deployment of staff to McComb for two weeks and led to stringent guidelines in selection of personnel. At first only seasoned SNCC activists like Jesse Harris and Curtis Hayes were to go, but soon, particularly at the urging of Jim Forman, inexperienced white volunteers took up residence in the McComb freedom house. No women were in the first contingent, so when the freedom school opened all the teachers were men.[50]

For nearly three years the movement had stagnated in McComb, in part because leadership in the black community remained divided among three major factions. On the right were the older members of the black establishment. This group included some, but not all, of the ministers and teachers, as well as men like Nathanael Lewis, whose support for voting rights went back to the 1940s but who in recent years had become known for his accommodating stance toward whites. Much more militant were the activists whom SNCC had cultivated in 1961, including a number of young people and adults like Webb Owens, Aylene Quin, Ernest Nobles, and Joe Martin, who had worked with SNCC and returned to his hometown in the spring of 1964. Sitting rather uncomfortably in the middle were C. C. Bryant and those NAACP members who followed his leadership. Project director Curtis Hayes, a native of the area who had played a key role in the student actions in 1961, worked to bring these factions together under the COFO umbrella.[51]

Middle-class whites in McComb viewed the oncoming summer project with alarm. Although *Enterprise-Journal* editor Oliver Emmerich had run a series of editorials in late May urging his readers to remain calm, the response of many whites bordered on hysteria. Some were convinced, for example, that black men wearing white bandages on their throats had been designated to rape white women. Sale of small arms, ammunition, dynamite, and Ku Klux Klan memberships boomed. The most preposterous example of white paranoia was Help, Inc., a self-defense group hastily organized in a middle-class white neighborhood. Members set up an alarm system to warn of any imminent COFO attack, and Help guidelines alerted citizens to "keep inside during darkness or during periods of threats. . . . Know where small children are at all times . . . [and] do not stand by and let your neighbor be assaulted."[52]

There was total hostility toward the summer project among the city fathers. Attorney Robert Brumfield, then president of the Chamber of Commerce, recalled that "at the time I detested 'em coming in here and disrupting things. The way of life we had lived through the years was crumbling around us, and I'm sure I didn't like it." More extreme were the elected officials. Mayor Gordon Burt, Jr., was county chairman of the Citizens' Council. Police Chief George Guy later admitted that for a time he had headed the local branch of the extremist Americans for the Preservation of the White Race (APWR). A month before the summer project began Pike County sheriff R. R. Warren told a meeting of the APWR that if the law proved insufficient to handle the COFO threat, he would "recruit some of you," adding, "They say we are going to have a long hot summer, and I sort of believe that."[53]

The Ku Klux Klan thrived in this atmosphere. Bankrolled by J. E. Thornhill, a local man who had struck it rich in oil, Klavern no. 700 of the Realm of Mississippi of the United Klans of America boasted well over 100 members and included such "respectable" citizens as businessman Sterling "Bubba" Gillis, the son of one of McComb's civic leaders. The Klan had been waging war on black McComb since the beginning of the year, with dynamite the weapon of choice. As an oilman, Thornhill had easy legal access to explosives. On the night of June 22—twenty-four hours after the Philadelphia lynchings—explosions shook three houses in black McComb, including that of C. C. Bryant, who grabbed his rifle and fired away at the car carrying the bombers. "A lot of people sat back and enjoyed what was going on," recalled Brumfield, comparing their reaction with the jubiliation in much of white McComb over the news of President Kennedy's assassination. Whites approved of police harassment of civil rights workers and did nothing to curtail Klan violence. In 1961 the combination of legal and extralegal forces had driven SNCC from southwest Mississippi. The summer project provided an opportunity to deal the movement a death blow.[54]

The initial all-male COFO contingent, six blacks and two whites, drove down from Jackson to open the McComb project on July 5. They moved into a Wall Street freedom house that was owned by a local supporter, Mrs. Willie Mae Cotton. The following day the group received a visit from congressional representative Don Edwards of California, whose son was a summer volunteer in Mississippi. Ed King, who drove Edwards to McComb, recalls that the congressman was determined to spend a night in the freedom house as a show of support. When Edwards called the Justice Department that evening, a horrified official "warned Edwards that there might be serious violence in McComb, that he was in a dangerous situation," and urged him to leave the freedom house. Edwards angrily replied that if Washington officials had reason to fear violence in McComb they should be providing protection for the civil rights workers. The Justice Department informed local police that they had a member of Congress in their midst, and there was no incident that night. Edwards left McComb the following morning. Two nights later night riders threw a bomb at the freedom house, blowing away the outside wall of one of the bedrooms. No one was killed, but project director Curtis Hayes was knocked unconscious, receiving glass cuts over his face, arms, and body, and white volunteer Dennis Sweeney suffered a minor concussion. The following day police and FBI agents investigated the crime and—as was the case throughout the summer—made no arrests.[55]

The Klan bombing of the freedom house sent a message to McComb blacks: associate with these "outside agitators" and you will receive the same treatment. In practice, however, white terrorists did not distinguish between local people active in the movement and those who were not. Over the next month the Klan burned three black churches in Pike and neighboring Amite counties; none of the church buildings had been used for civil rights activities, nor were any of the parishioners politically active. On July 19 whites assaulted SNCC field secretary Mendy Samstein on a McComb street, again with no arrests. A week later Ora "Dago" Bryant and her husband, Charlie (the brother of C. C. Bryant), were awakened by the sound of a car pulling into their driveway. Mrs. Bryant grabbed a shotgun and fired at the car just as someone threw a package at the house. The subsequent explosion blew out all the front windows, tore the asbestos siding off the house, and uprooted the shrubbery. Following the attack the Bryants, both of whom were active in the movement, took turns standing guard over their house every night, a pattern that became standard procedure in black McComb, which was now in effect under a state of siege.[56]

Faced with this reign of terror—McComb soon gained a reputation as "the bombing capital of the world"—except for FDP canvassing, the COFO project made little headway during July. Churches closed their doors to the movement, and few local residents would risk their jobs and physical safety by making the trip to the Magnolia courthouse to take the registration test. With most activities at a standstill and "mass" meetings poorly attended, it was once again the youth of McComb who kept the movement alive.[57]

The McComb freedom school, which opened in mid-July, at first conducted its classes in the backyard of the recently bombed freedom house, for no local black institution dared offer facilities for a school. Joyce Brown, a sixteen-year-old freedom school student, addressed the problem in a poem:

> I asked for your churches, and you turned me down,
> But I'll do my work if I have to do it on the ground.
> You will not speak for fear of being heard,
> So you crawl in your shell and say, "Do not disturb."

Moved—and shamed—by Joyce Brown's poem, local people soon made church facilities available for the freedom school. Over 100 youths enrolled, many of them younger brothers and sisters of the students who had walked out of Burgland High School three years earlier. The director of the freedom school was Ralph Featherstone, a quiet, kind, dedicated black activist and speech teacher from Washington, D.C. He and other COFO staff soon noticed that "the Freedom School is inspiring the people to lend a hand in the fight. The older people are looking to the young people, and their courage is rubbing off."[58]

The turning point came in early August, when ten black businessmen met secretly with COFO representatives at Aylene Quin's cafe. To avoid detection by whites—or betrayal by black collaborators—they took elaborate precautions, including the use of passwords at the door. Several of the men arrived in the back of a panel truck that Ernest Nobles used to make laundry deliveries and slipped into a side entrance. It was an emotional and inspirational gathering. Everyone was deeply affected when Joyce Brown's poem was read, and one of the men broke down, stating that he was "so *happy* to see such a meeting." He had been "thinking these things for so long, and thought he was alone." After the group formed a housing committee and a food committee to assist the COFO staff and volunteers, each man contributed fifty dollars toward the purchase of a lot on which to build a community center, which was to be the focal point for the Pike County movement. (The Martin Luther King Memorial Center in McComb today is the result of that initial meeting.)[59]

Through these and other more public actions, local leaders made it clear that they were an integral part of the movement and that they supported the summer project. Their example sent a message through the black community. Shortly after the meeting, St. Paul's Methodist Church agreed to permit movement gatherings there once again. Attendance at nightly meetings grew. Webb Owens made daily collections, providing money for COFO workers and the project. Community people donated food for freedom house residents. The Reverend Harry Bowie, a black Episcopal priest turned summer volunteer, recalls that "we never felt that stern rejection because of fear. What we felt instead was some real solid support for what we were doing."[60]

The high point of the summer activity was McComb's first Freedom Day, which was held in mid-August in the midst of a firestorm of repression. A week earlier the Klan had burned crosses in front of the homes of two white McComb residents. One, a physician, had made a contribution to rebuild the Negro churches that had been destroyed; the other, a local businessman, had resisted pressure to fire several of his black employees who had tried to register. On August 14 klansmen bombed the Burgland supermarket, which was owned by a black man named Pete Lewis, a sixty-five-year-old registered voter and movement supporter. Three years earlier Lewis had made the upper floor of the building available to SNCC for the state's first freedom school. This was the sixth bombing in a two-month period. Two days later twenty-four officers representing city, county, and state police forces staged a midnight raid on the two buildings serving as the freedom house. They had a warrant to search for illegal liquor. Finding none, they stayed to inspect the office files. Undeterred, project workers hit the streets the following morning, distributing 3,000 leaflets announcing the Freedom Day. That afternoon Police Chief Guy informed the organizers that they had violated a new city ordinance prohibiting the distribution of leaflets without a permit, and he threatened to sign out John Doe warrants and arrest everyone. Guy backed down after being contacted by John Doar from the Justice Department.[61]

Later that evening several hundred McComb blacks attended a rally called to drum up support for Freedom Day. The audience listened to songs by folksinger Len Chandler and SNCC freedom singer Cordell Reagon. They heard testimony from members of the audience and a talk by Hayes, who laid out the plans to take registrants to the Magnolia courthouse the following day. A COFO observer reported back to the Jackson office that "the meeting was a good success both in numbers and in spirit." The same could be said for Freedom Day itself. Although only twenty-three people were permitted to take the test, the event drew newsmen, photographers, FBI agents, and a surprisingly cooperative local police force. Freedom Day was not a turning point in McComb. The worst, in fact, was still to come, but this public display of solidarity served notice that the black community *was* the movement in McComb and would not be deterred by the stormtrooper tactics of the Klan and the police.[62]

The rebirth of the movement in McComb was a major achievement of the summer project. In the face of the most violent and sustained campaign of intimidation and terror in the state, SNCC workers returned to Pike County to take up where they had left off three years earlier. They were assisted by a talented group of white volunteers, several of whom became full-time organizers after leaving Mississippi. McComb demonstrated the possibility that "black and white together" could be more than a movement slogan.[63] Yet more important than the SNCC organizers and their volunteer assistants were the local people themselves, who demonstrated that they could overcome their political differences as well as their fears to pursue a common goal. The conservative Sunday school teacher and NAACP president C. C. Bryant, firing at the klansmen who had just thrown a bomb at his home; the dapper "Cool Daddy" Webb Owens, now an old man, still the most trusted person in the community, making his daily rounds raising money for the movement; and the fearless, inspirational Mama Quin, leading as well as feeding the troops, fully aware that at some point she and her family would have to pay the price—these McComb leaders had their counterparts in other black communities as the summer project moved them from their fields and shops to the gates of power at the Atlantic City Democratic Convention.

Years later, recalling his first weeks in McComb, volunteer Harry Bowie eloquently captured both the meaning and the spirit of the summer project: "You saw people with relatively low levels of education, very little money, beginning to stretch themselves, beginning to see themselves as worthwhile, to overcome the years of deprivation. To see people grow out of that deprivation, to begin to believe in themselves, and to believe in the possibility of their future, was one of the most rewarding experiences of my life, and I will always treasure it." Then, after a long pause, he added: "I won't look for it to be *that* way again."[64]

12

The Mississippi Freedom Democratic Party and the Atlantic City Challenge

On July 19 Bob Moses sent out an "Emergency Memorandum" to all COFO field staff stating that *"everyone* who is not working in Freedom Schools or community centers *must* devote all their time to organizing for the convention challenge." Admitting that the summer project directors "did not properly stress the importance" of preparing for the Democratic National Convention in Atlantic City, Moses observed that "the various political programs which comprise the Freedom Democratic Party's Convention Challenge are in very bad shape all around the state" and warned that there was a "high degree of probability that we will not be prepared" for the national convention. The problem was that relatively few blacks had signed FDP registration forms. While more than 80,000 had voted in the November 1963 freedom vote, only 21,000 blacks and a handful of whites were on the FDP rolls in mid-July 1964. A low registration figure could undermine the challenge's credibility. Alluding to the ambitious goal of enrolling 200,000 members by convention time, only a month away, Moses concluded that "all of us must now pull together behind the program in order to make it at least a partial success."[1]*

*Throughout the Mississippi Freedom Democratic party's existence, its members referred to it both as "FDP" and "MFDP." Both abbreviations will be used here.

Thus, during midsummer COFO shifted its emphasis from voter registration to FDP recruitment. Moses called for a moratorium on the traditional Freedom Days at the county courthouse, replacing them with "Freedom Registration Days" at a location in the black community. COFO staff and volunteers should no longer take people down to the courthouse, "*unless* they *ask* to be taken down." Moses noted that "after August 20th or so we will have ample opportunity to try to convince people to register" but then added pessimistically, "*if* we feel that the psychological value of getting a few people 'to try' is worthwhile."[2]

To challenge successfully the legitimacy of the Democratic party in Mississippi, FDP needed to prove that blacks were systematically excluded from participating in the regular party's selection of delegates to the national convention. That process began at the precinct level, where assembled Democrats chose representatives to a county convention. There delegates were elected to the district meetings, which selected representatives to the state convention. This final assembly chose the thirty-four delegates and an equal number of alternates to attend the national party conclave. The FDP strategy was, first of all, to attempt to participate in the state party's pyramid structure of delegate selection. If, as expected, black delegates were not welcomed, then FDP would set up its own parallel pyramid structure, culminating in a state convention that elected a rival slate of delegates and alternates.[3]

On June 16—before the official start of the summer project— local blacks had attempted to participate in a number of the 1,884 precinct meetings held across the state. A few blacks were admitted in larger cities such as Greenville and Jackson, but these were rare exceptions. The vast majority of blacks who showed up for the meetings either were turned away at the door, found that the meeting site had been changed, or learned that no meeting was held in their precinct. A week later, blacks claiming to represent the precincts where meetings did not take place attempted to gain admittance to the county conventions. They were turned away. The district and state conventions, then, were all white, as was the official delegation sent to Atlantic City. At their statewide meeting the white Democrats passed a series of resolutions denouncing the Civil Rights Act of 1964, urging the United States to get out of the United Nations, demanding a purge of the U.S. Supreme Court, and calling for "separation of the races in all phases of our society." The *New*

York Times reported that "virtually every delegate" was supporting Senator Barry Goldwater, the Republican presidential nominee.[4]

FDP had only a month remaining to increase its membership,
organize and hold precinct meetings and county and state conventions, and select an Atlantic City delegation, all the while lobbying
northern delegates to support the challenge. Under the best of circumstances this would have been a formidable task, but the summer project staff had to contend with the ongoing wave of white
intimidation and terror and at the same time deal with a serious
division within the Mississippi movement, a split encouraged by the
national office of the NAACP.

NAACP executive secretary Roy Wilkins and director of branches
Gloster Current continued to view COFO with suspicion, if not
alarm. Particularly troubling was state NAACP president Aaron
Henry's continuing identification with COFO. At one point Current grumbled to Wilkins that "COFO has captured the imagination of our state president, who offers little to his own organization except lip service." He then added, without a trace of irony,
that Henry "believes that whosoever frees him and his people should
be used." During the middle of the summer of 1964, Current had
written Charles Evers that "every effort should be made to encourage Dr. Henry to wean himself away from [COFO]," promising that
"we shall review our relationship with that outfit at the end of the
summer."[5]

Evers shared Current's reservations about both COFO and its
summer project. He attempted to organize an independent NAACP
project, plagiarizing a COFO recruiting pamphlet and requesting
that applications—and funds—be sent to his office in Jackson. Late
in June he publicized a telegram he had sent to Wilkins asking the
national NAACP office to consider recruiting an additional 1,000
volunteers to work in Mississippi. For this, he drew an angry rebuke from Current: "This attempted pressuring of the NAACP for
a project of dubious value is irresponsibility at its worst. . . . We are
not following SNICK's leadership and we don't want you to either.
Keep in mind that we have a major project of our own to implement in Mississippi and it can best be done under our own strategy and not someone else's."[6]

Current expressed a major concern of a number of Mississippi
NAACP officials: despite the COFO "umbrella," the summer project
was essentially a SNCC-led operation and was perceived as such

by the media. State NAACP leaders felt shut out from the decision making. Moreover, the young radicals working in local communities were often impatient with and condescending toward the older established leaders and undermined their efforts to recruit local students into NAACP youth councils. Dr. B. E. Murph, a Laurel dentist and longtime president of the NAACP branch, spoke for other moderates that summer when he wrote Wilkins that "COFO is no friend of ours. The people are so confused. The job is more difficult than at anytime since I have been working for the organization."[7] By the middle of the summer it was clear that the COFO coalition was fragmenting, but both factions maintained a public facade of unity.

In a move "to keep our own public relations posture prominent," the national NAACP hit on the idea of sending a delegation to Mississippi to test the public accommodations section of the 1964 Civil Rights Act. This decision angered COFO, which had made it clear that it was not going to engage in desegregation protests during the summer. There was no need to further incite whites already upset about the summer "invasion" by dramatically staging sit-ins at restaurants and hotels.[8]

Mississippi's white leaders divided sharply over the question of compliance with the new civil rights law, which went into effect on July 1. The Citizens' Council called for defiance, recommending a boycott of white restaurants and hotels serving black customers. Supported by the state legislature, Governor Paul Johnson urged noncompliance until the courts ruled on the law's constitutionality. In a surprise move, however, the Jackson Chamber of Commerce, led by president-elect Robert Ezelle and bank presidents Nat Rogers and Robert Hearin, called on its members to obey the law: "We may not be in sympathy with all of the laws of the land," the statement read, "but we must maintain our standing which abides by the law." Jackson mayor Allen Thompson, a staunch segregationist, bowed to the wishes of the business community, telling reporters that although it made him "sick all over," he was urging local establishments to comply.[9]

With the white leadership split on the question of compliance, the integrated nine-member delegation of NAACP leaders headed by Gloster Current arrived at the Jackson airport on July 5 not knowing what to expect. City police escorted the group into town, where members checked into the three most expensive hotels and motels in Jackson. At the Heidelberg, the city's most prestigious hotel, black NAACP officials registered without incident (the hotel manager greeted them "with a smile"), had their bags carried to their rooms by a white bellhop, and returned to dine at the hotel restaurant, surrounded all the while by a sea of reporters and cameramen. The story made the front page of the *New York Times* and provided favorable publicity for the city of Jackson, as well as for the NAACP.[10]

The following day a three-car caravan, including Charles Evers and other local leaders, headed out to test facilities in other cities. They paid a courtesy call at the police station in Canton, deciding not to test facilities there because of Canton's "reputation of being extremely tough on racial issues." The testers met a hostile reception in Philadelphia, where a large crowd of whites forced an early departure. The rest of the tour, which ranged from the Gulf Coast to Clarksdale in the Delta, went largely without incident. The NAACP delegation tested public facilities only in the larger towns, where the likelihood of trouble was minimal. Back in New York Current wrote Evers that the "fact-finding tour" had been a success: "We were indeed fortunate that the break in public accommodations came. . . . Other citizens must be encouraged to take advantage of the facilities throughout the state at every opportunity."[11]

"Other citizens" attempting to test the law found Mississippi not so accommodating as it had been to those national NAACP officials touring the state in the protective glow of the national media. Nowhere was this double standard more apparent than in Greenwood. On July 5, the same day that the NAACP delegation made its much-heralded landing in Jackson, twenty-one-year-old Silas McGhee took it on himself to desegregate the Leflore Theater. McGhee "wasn't involved in the Greenwood Movement at that time. This was something I had planned on my own." His family, however, had long been active. His older brother Jake had worked with SNCC. Clarence Robinson, his half-brother, was a career army man, a Korean War veteran who spent his furlough time in Greenwood. Clarence was an imposing figure. Sally Belfrage remembers him as "a six-foot-six paratrooper [with] a thirty-six-inch reach and a 136 I.Q. . . . He walked down the street in his uniform like Wild Bill Hickok on the way to a duel, cool, tough, infinitely menacing." Their mother, Mrs. Laura McGhee, had been one of the first local people to open her doors to the movement, inviting SNCC workers to hold rallies on her fifty-eight-acre farm. Years earlier a member of the Mississippi legislature had coveted her land, and when she refused to sell, he arranged to have her committed to the state asylum at Whitfield for a year and persuaded the bank to institute foreclosure proceedings. But the McGhees had fought back, and in the summer of 1964 they found themselves at the center of a violent confrontation between Greenwood whites and the movement.[12]

The management of the Leflore Theater had decided to comply with the civil rights act, so Silas McGhee had no trouble at the ticket window. Shortly after he took his seat, however, whites began pelting him with paper and trash. McGhee went out to complain to the manager, who refused to intervene. Silas returned to his seat, only to be jumped and beaten by about fifteen white men. Fleeing the theater, he went directly to the police station. The only question on the officers' minds was "Who put you up to this?" McGhee told them, "I only wanted to see a movie."[13]

Silas and his brother Jake went back to the theater seven times that month, enduring harassment, physical assault, or both. Soon white men, including Byron De La Beckwith, began picketing the theater, protesting the manager's decision to obey the law. After Thatcher Walt, the editor of the *Greenwood Commonwealth,* crossed the picket line with his family, his home was shot at and he received threatening phone calls. Less than a week later he was fired from his job. Greenwood's elected officials, all segregationists, divided over how to handle the crisis brought on by the McGhee brothers' determination to go the movies. At one point Mayor Charles Sampson, who wanted to close the theater rather than integrate it, got into a fistfight at city hall with City Commissioner Buff Hammond, who favored compliance with federal law.[14]

Although desegregation of public facilities was not part of the summer project program, there was no question that COFO (and the national SNCC staff, headquartered in Greenwood for the summer) would provide the McGhee brothers with all possible support. Tensions had been building in Greenwood since the first northern volunteers arrived in town, and the continuing confrontation at the moviehouse cast a long shadow over Greenwood's fourth Freedom Day on July 16, held three days before Bob Moses' call for a moratorium on such activities. Greenwood police and deputies jailed 111 demonstrators, the largest mass arrest of the summer, charging them with violating the state's new antipicketing law. Silas

McGhee, in line to take the registration test, was abducted by three white men who forced him into a car at gunpoint, took him to a plumbing shop, and beat him with a wooden board and a pipe.[15]

On the night of July 25 night riders fired into the McGhee home. COFO worker Muriel Tillinghast remembers that Mrs. McGhee "called the sheriff and told him . . . she knew exactly who was out there and that the sheriff should come and tell these here boys to go home, because they were going to be picking up bodies the next time that she called." The following evening Silas was back at the Leflore Theater, with his brothers Jake and Clarence, who was home on a furlough. This time they were able to watch the movie in peace, but outside a mob of nearly 200 whites was waiting. A call brought two cars from the SNCC office to the theater. As the brothers climbed into a car, someone threw a bottle through the rear window, spraying them with glass and damaging one of Jake's eyes.[16]

Instead of returning to the relative safety of black Greenwood, they drove to the emergency room of the hospital, followed by angry whites. SNCC sent another car to the hospital, this one driven by Atlanta staff worker Judy Richardson. Two carloads of whites followed and fired at the workers. At the hospital they found armed whites outside, blocking all exits, and Clarence Robinson inside, armed and ready to shoot it out. Richardson immediately called SNCC headquarters, and Greenwood project director Bob Zellner notified the FBI, which was noncommital about intervening, and the Justice Department's John Doar, who told Zellner that "you have to make your own decisions in these matters." Eventually FBI officers, the police commissioner, and the sheriff arrived at the hospital, but all refused to offer the civil rights workers protection. Richardson then defiantly stated that they would not leave without an armed escort. The stalemate ended at 1:00 A.M. when the sheriff had a sudden change of heart and led the activists away from the mob. Perhaps the Justice Department had finally persuaded local officials to do their job.[17]

The police were not finished with the McGhees. Three weeks later an officer ticketed Silas for parking on the wrong side of the street and told him to move his car: "And I took my own time going back to the car. He told me to move the car right then . . . and I told him that I got the ticket and was fixing to move the car, you know. Well, he cursed me out . . . and he told me he would blow my damn brains out." A short while later McGhee was back at the COFO office, picking up a group of workers on their way to Lula's Cafe for a farewell party for the summer volunteers. McGhee did not join the party; it had begun to rain hard, so he remained in the car and dozed off. "For some reason, I don't know, for some reason I woke up. And just as I woke up . . . I looked out the window . . . and I saw this white car right there in the middle of the street. And I could see the man's arm pointing toward me. And before I could do anything, the shot went off."[18] The celebrating summer workers and COFO staff members poured out of the cafe, saw McGhee's bleeding face, and rushed him to the hospital. He had been hit just below the left temple, with the bullet lodged in his throat. He survived and was taken to University Hospital in Jackson for surgery. No one was arrested for the crime, but McGhee, and black Greenwood, were convinced that the police officer who had threatened him only a short time before was in fact the man who pulled the trigger.[19]

Later that night new faces showed up at the COFO office, black men in their late twenties and thirties who had not previously been involved in the movement. They were carrying guns and eager to use them. SNCC field secretary Jesse Harris led them to Friendship Baptist Church, where they were joined by several hundred other angry local people. Harris was able to talk them down, to channel their anger into peaceful protest, and thus avoid a bloodbath.[20]

Two days later police arrested Jake McGhee on a traffic violation. When his mother went to the station to pay his fine, two officers harassed her. When a third policeman hit her in the chest, Laura McGhee countered with a right to the jaw, staggering the officer, and then calmly walked out of the station. She was later arrested. On the eve of the Atlantic City convention, Mrs. McGhee and Jake were out on bail; Silas was lying in a Jackson hospital, also on bail. Clarence Robinson was in Greenwood jail, rearrested on an old charge. The army had also brought court-martial charges against him (later dropped) for being AWOL. Undaunted, the McGhee family persevered and remained strong within the movement. Silas joined the SNCC staff, and in February 1965 he was elected to the executive committee, its youngest member.[21]

In this atmosphere of extreme racial tension and increasing interorganizational rivalry, the Mississippi Freedom Democratic party moved ahead with its plan to unseat the regular Democrats at the national convention. Party registration efforts intensified, but staff workers across the state had to contend with more conservative black leaders who did not take the challenge seriously, as well as with the continuing fear among many poor blacks of signing *any* voter registration form. Canvassers in Greenwood reported that people were afraid to register as Freedom Democrats because they "still think that [whites] put their names in the newspaper, just like they do when you go to the courthouse."[22]

When the first FDP precinct meetings took place during late July, some people in rural areas were afraid to attend, and when they did come they were at times reluctant participants. At one Pike County precinct all ten people nominated to chair the meeting refused. Attempts to draft a secretary led to the same result. Not until Curtis Hayes took over the meeting and persuaded the group of the importance of the business at hand were officers chosen and a delegation elected. At a nearby meeting in Summitt only seven people of voting age showed up. Since their precinct was entitled to ten delegates to the county convention, they elected themselves and then appointed additional delegates and alternates. COFO had anticipated these problems. In his July 19 memo, Bob Moses had urged the staff not to "give up because you can't pull a big meeting off. Round up a few people for a meeting . . . even if means that all the people at the meeting come as delegates.[23] The process ran more smoothly in the larger towns and cities. For many local people, the precinct meetings were their first experience with electoral politics. One summer volunteer in Columbus was enthusiastic at how quickly the caucus took shape: "Within ten minutes they were completely at ease and had selected a chairman, secretary, and ten delegates. . . . The delegates were teachers, housewives, packinghouse workers, a toy factory worker, in short a genuine cross-section of the community. . . . It was tremendously interesting to watch and indicative, I think, of the innate political nature of all men."[24]

Momentum began to build at the county and district conventions. The sight of delegates arriving from such embattled outposts as Ruleville and Liberty inspired all who attended. In Madison County, where the meeting convened on a black farmer's property, convention chair Annie Devine grouped the 300 delegates by precinct under the trees. As in the other conventions, resolutions were passed calling for racial justice in Mississippi and pledging loyalty to the national Democratic party. The following day the Leflore County FDP had a similarly successful meeting in Greenwood, where Stokely Carmichael spoke. Of the sixteen delegates and alternates selected there to attend the second district convention, twelve were women.[25]

When the Mississippi Freedom Democratic party held its state convention in Jackson on August 6, nearly 2,500 people packed the Masonic Temple. Speaking at the convention was the activist Washington attorney Joseph Rauh, recruited by Ella Baker to be FDP's legal counsel. A leader of the Democratic party's liberal wing, Rauh told the cheering crowd that several northern delegations had already pledged to support FDP at the convention. He then explained the challenge process: FDP would first take its case to the credentials committee to argue that blacks had been excluded from the "regular" party and that FDP was the only party in the state loyal to the national ticket. Should that committee refuse to seat FDP, then with the votes of only eleven members of the 108-person credentials committee, the issue could be brought to the convention floor, where a roll-call vote would take place if eight state delegations requested it. Should the question come before the convention as a whole, Rauh assured his Jackson audience, chances for success were excellent.[26]

Ella Baker gave the keynote address. The veteran movement activist had in late April opened a SNCC office in Washington and was coordinating the effort to win northern support for the challenge. Baker's speech was not the usual convention peroration, replete with catchy phrases and alliteration. Instead, she gave her audience a lecture on the history of race relations in this country and called on blacks to prepare for the coming battle by educating themselves:

> Now, this is not the kind of a keynote speech, perhaps, that you like. But I'm not trying to make you feel good. We have to know what we are dealing with and we can't deal with things just because we feel we ought to have our rights. We have to deal with them on the basis of knowledge that we gain . . . through sending our children through certain kinds of courses, through sitting down and reading at night instead of spending our time at the television and radio just listening to what's on. But we must spend our time reading some of the things that help us to understand this South we live in.[27]

At one point in her address Baker issued a warning that went almost unnoticed among outsiders at the meeting: "We must be careful lest we elect to represent us people who, for the first time, feel their sense of importance and will represent themselves before they represent you." Baker was aware that during the past month traditional NAACP leaders in places like Jackson and Meridian had decided that it was time for them to join the challenge and gain places in the delegation. One dismayed volunteer reported on the Warren County convention held in Vicksburg:

> After those great precinct meetings which I told you about on the phone, the county convention was a disappointment. The Old Guard—the Warren County Improvement League—the comfortable middle-aged "We Don't Want Any Trouble" Uncle Toms—monopolized the meeting and the votes. Most of the Great New Blood which pulsed through the precinct meetings was slyly siphoned out. It was a sad night for all of us. We had forgotten that machinery is quickly formed even in something as new as the FDP and our defenses were down.[28]

The volunteer's characterization of the opposition as "Uncle Toms" was harsh. These men had been active in the earlier campaigns to secure the vote, and many had run risks to advance the race, but their gradualist approach to social change had made them distrust and resent the young activists in SNCC and CORE. Yet now that the train had arrived and was getting ready to pull out, these establishment leaders scrambled to get on board. Movement leaders worked behind the scenes to keep as many of them as possible standing at the station.

Moses later recalled that he and the other FDP organizers wanted to get "as radical a delegation as you could . . . people who would stand up when they got to Atlantic City." Three SNCC veterans— field secretaries Charles McLaurin, Jimmy Travis, and Lawrence Guyot—were elected to the FDP delegation. At the party's convention in Jackson, where most of the sixty-eight-person delegation was to be selected, COFO organizers took steps to make sure that the delegation was representative of the majority of the state's blacks, the rural poor. To do so it was necessary to engage in old-style politics, with staff members distributing a slate of delegates to be elected at large—a practice common at state conventions. Ironically, Al Lowenstein had earlier suggested this procedure, but his motive was to "slate" traditional leaders like the Reverend R. L. T. Smith, who was eventually defeated in his bid to become a delegate. The balloting divided roughly along rural and urban lines, with delegates from the countryside uniting to elect their people and to defeat "big city" businessmen and professionals. The traditional leaders were by no means excluded, but the FDP delegation that was selected in the caucuses and at the state convention was militant, including as it did such grass-roots activists as E. W. Steptoe, Winson Hudson, Hazel Palmer, and Fannie Lou Hamer, men and women who had little formal education or social status but who spoke—with authority and from experience—in the name of the dispossessed. Before adjourning, the convention delegates elected Guyot as FDP chair, Henry as chair of the delegation, and Fannie Lou Hamer as vice-chair. Victoria Gray and Ed King were representatives to the Democratic National Committee. (Guyot would not go to Atlantic City, instead spending convention week in the Hattiesburg jail after having been convicted on false charges.)[29]

On the evening following the FDP convention James Chaney was laid to rest on a sandy hill four miles south of Meridian. A week earlier a paid informant (whose identity was so secret that the FBI would not divulge it to Assistant Attorney General Burke Marshall) revealed that the bodies were buried under an earthen dam at a Neshoba County farm known locally as the "old Jolly Place." A bulldozer was hauled out to the dam on the morning of August 4, and by late afternoon the bodies of Chaney, Mickey Schwerner, and Andrew Goodman had been recovered. Autopsies revealed that Schwerner and Goodman had each been shot once; James Chaney, three times, twice in the head and once in the chest.[30]*

On the afternoon of Chaney's funeral Meridian blacks assembled in different churches and staged a silent walk to the First Union Baptist Church, where they were joined by movement people from all over the state, as well as by representatives of the media. Mrs. Fannie Chaney sat in the front row, her twelve-year-old son, Ben,

---

*Dr. David Spain, a New York pathologist, conducted an independent autopsy on James Chaney's body and found multiple fractures. Spain's conclusion, that "in my extensive experience of twenty-five years as a pathologist . . . I have never witnessed bones so severely shattered, except in tremendously high-speed accidents such as airplane crashes," was shocking. However, two klansmen at the scene of the crime who gave separate, independent confessions did not mention any severe beatings of the victims. FBI and Justice Department officials concluded that Chaney's body was crushed by the bulldozer initially used to bury the corpses.

huddled next to her. TV crews kept the glare of their lights on the family, and photographers hovered with their flash cameras to capture each sign of emotion. For almost an hour local ministers conducted a low-key service, careful not to inflame the emotions of the congregation. The Reverend Ed King, also on the program, recalled that "the tone of the service was so cautious a stranger might have thought the victim had been killed in an auto accident." King could see that Dave Dennis, who was waiting to deliver the eulogy, "became more and more angry the longer the preachers went on."[31]

When Dennis's turn finally came, he delivered one of the most powerful addresses in the movement's short history:

> I feel that he has got his freedom and we are still fighting for it. But what I want to talk about right now is the living dead that we have right in our midst, not only here in the state of Mississippi, but throughout the nation. Those are the people who don't care. . . . That includes the president on down to the governor of the state of Mississippi. . . . I blame the people in Washington, D.C., and on down in the state of Mississippi for what happened just as much as I blame those who pulled the trigger.
>
> I don't grieve for James Chaney. He lived a fuller life than most of us will ever live. He's got his freedom, and we're still fighting for ours. I'm sick and tired of going to the funerals of black men who have been murdered by white men. I've got vengeance in my heart tonight, and I ask you to feel angry with me.

Overcome with emotion, Dennis directed his final remarks to the local people in his audience: "Don't just look at me and go back and tell folks you've been to a nice service. Your work is just beginning. If you go back home and take what these white men in Mississippi are doing to us . . . if you take it and don't do something about it . . . then God Damn your souls!"[32]

Memorial services for Mickey Schwerner and Andrew Goodman took place in New York City. The Schwerner family had wanted their son buried next to James Chaney in Mississippi, but integration there was prohibited even in cemeteries. One week later SNCC field secretary Ralph Featherstone led an interracial group of twelve workers to open a COFO office in Philadelphia and announced that the first freedom school in Neshoba county would open on September 1.[33]

• • •

The Democratic National Convention of 1964, held in late August in Atlantic City, was to be a coronation of sorts for President Lyndon B. Johnson. No other names would be placed in nomination; there would be no major platform fights. A week before the convention the only item of suspense was Johnson's choice of a running mate. But the sixty-four blacks and four whites who constituted the Mississippi Freedom Democratic party delegation threw a monkey wrench into the president's plans for an orchestrated convention. For four days the FDP challenge of the Mississippi regulars was the major event in Atlantic City.

The FDP delegates arrived in Atlantic City by bus on Friday, August 21, the day before the all-important hearing with the credentials committee. Housed in the small, run-down Gem Hotel, about a mile from the convention hall, these Mississipians stood out among the rank-and-file party faithful. Sharecroppers and small landowners, maids and mechanics, schoolteachers and businessmen, the Freedom Democratic party delegation accurately reflected the socioeconomic composition of the state's black population. SNCC worker Mary King recalls that the delegates were at first "dazzled and bewildered" by the scene and by the media attention they immediately attracted. But they quickly got down to business, fanning out over the convention grounds, button-holing delegates, and bringing them the word on life in Mississippi and the righteousness of the challenge.

The lobbyists quickly adapted to their new surroundings. On arriving at the delegation's hotel, Jim Forman observed that "everywhere in the lobby there were Mississippi farmers, all dressed up in their Sunday-go-to-meeting best." He spied Ivanhoe Donaldson and Charlie Cobb, "the blue jeans twins of Mississippi . . . all dressed up now in Ivy League outfits . . . suits, button down collars, striped ties, the works." The Mississippi contingent did not, however, let down its guard. Joyce Ladner remembers seeing Mrs. "Sweets" Turnbow, whose husband Hartman was a Holmes County delegate, lobbying members of the Oregon delegation. "A very gentle woman," Mrs. Turnbow calmly presented the FDP case as she stood before the Oregon Democrats carrying a brown paper bag. Inside the bag was a gun. "Sweets never went anyplace without her brown paper bag and gun," observed Ladner.[34]

Although the FDP delegates were objects of interest and curiosity at a convention that otherwise promised to be dull, few political observers had taken their challenge seriously. A week earlier Mississippi governor Paul Johnson had told the press that he had the president's assurance that the Freedom Democrats would not be seated. Now that the Republicans had nominated Senator Barry Goldwater, the Arizona conservative who had voted against the civil rights bill, Lyndon Johnson believed that his base among black voters was secure, but he feared a white backlash in the South if FDP gained recognition. More immediately, Johnson was concerned that Deep South delegations would walk out of the convention if FDP won its challenge. In its Saturday edition the *New York Times* reported that "the general belief here is that there is little chance of any of the Freedom Democrats being seated." Instead, the word on the floor was that FDP would be given "special status at the convention without the right to vote."[35]

The Mississippi challengers nonetheless had some cause for optimism. Throughout the summer, Democrats meeting in convention in several states, including Oregon, Michigan, and New York, passed resolutions calling for the seating of FDP. The Americans for Democratic Action, the most potent liberal influence on the party, had done the same. The civil rights establishment also backed the challenge. Martin Luther King had toured Mississippi in July to encourage blacks to sign up with FDP and on August 19 sent a telegram to the president urging that FDP be seated "as the only democratically constituted delegation from Mississippi." Two days later twenty-five congressional Democrats signed a statement that "elementary justice" demanded that FDP be certified as the official Mississippi delegation. Moreover, thanks to the summer project, every convention delegate was aware of the conditions facing blacks in the Magnolia State. To be sure that no one forgot, SNCC and CORE supporters at Atlantic City kept a constant vigil on the boardwalk outside Convention Hall, with large portraits of the three slain civil rights workers mounted on tall poles in the background.[36]

Mary King overstated the case when she recalled that "it never occurred to us that our delegation would be turned down." On the eve of the convention COFO leaders like Moses and Dennis, as well as Ella Baker, who had directed the lobbying effort from Washington, were not optimistic. In the days that followed, however, events unfolded so rapidly—and positively—that seasoned movement veterans became caught up in the enthusiasm of the moment, almost in spite of themselves. "Initially I thought we would go down in defeat," recalled Hollis Watkins. "But then based on the response that had come from other parts of the country and those in Congress, I felt we would be victorious."[37]

Whatever chances FDP had in Atlantic City depended on the outcome of the credentials committee hearings, which were scheduled for Saturday afternoon, August 22. Both FDP and the regulars would present their cases there before a jury of 108 Democrats. Since supporters of the president dominated this committee, no one expected it to act favorably. The strategy of the insurgents remained the same as outlined by attorney Rauh earlier in Jackson. If 10 percent of the committee—eleven members—filed a minority report supporting FDP, then that report would come to the convention floor. If eight states then requested a roll call, every delegation would have to go on record, avoiding the voice vote "rubber stamp" that convention chairs so often used to decide unpopular issues. Going into the credentials committee meeting, Rauh was confident that he had his "eleven and eight" with room to spare.[38]

When committee chair David Lawrence, a former governor of Pennsylvania and a Johnson loyalist, gaveled the meeting to order, network cameras were there to cover the proceedings live. In an effort to prevent such coverage, Lawrence had originally scheduled the meeting in a room barely large enough for the committee members, but Rauh and the networks forced a change to a larger meeting hall. Chief spokesperson for the regulars was Mississippi state senator E. K. Collins of Laurel, who argued that his delegation should be seated because of the overwhelming support that Mississippi had given party presidential nominees in the past. Collins also denied that blacks had difficulty in voting in Mississippi. Members of the credentials committee knew, however, that the regulars, who were highly critical of both President Johnson and the national party, had recessed their state convention rather than adjourn it in order to reconvene after the national meeting. Most observers believed that when the regulars met again they would endorse Barry Goldwater for the presidency (as they in fact did).[39]

The challengers argued that FDP should be seated because

blacks had been shut out of the Mississippi Democratic party. The Freedom party had observed all regulations in selecting its delegation and had pledged its loyalty to the national ticket. Legal arguments would count for little at this session. Rauh brought forth a number of witnesses, including delegation chair Aaron Henry, national committeeman Ed King, Rita Schwerner, and Martin Luther King, who warned that "if you value your party, if you value your nation, if you value the democratic process, then you must recognize the Freedom party delegation." Yet even the eloquent symbol of the civil rights movement was overshadowed that day by the testimony of the former sharecropper from Ruleville, Mrs. Fannie Lou Hamer.[40]

The several million Americans watching the proceedings on television had known little if anything about Mrs. Hamer, but as she graphically described her life, her eviction from the plantation when she registered to vote, and, most dramatically, her beating in the Winona jail, it soon became apparent that hers was an authentic voice describing simply yet powerfully the reality of life in the closed society. This was high drama, and it did not go unnoticed in the White House. President Johnson hurriedly called a press conference in the middle of her testimony, and the networks dutifully cut away to the president before she had completed her remarks. Aware that they had been manipulated, however, and sensing the importance of the story, the networks played back her testimony that night, where a prime-time audience heard Mrs. Hamer state that "if the Freedom Party is not seated now I question America." In a voice filled with emotion she concluded, "Is this America, the land of the free and the home of the brave, where we have to sleep with our telephones off the hooks because our lives be threatened daily, because we want to live as decent human beings, in America?"[41]

Credentials committee chair Lawrence, in a surprise move, postponed a decision on the Mississippi challenge until Sunday, hoping to work out a formula "to avoid a bruising floor battle in front of the television cameras." Telegrams of support began flooding the convention immediately after Mrs. Hamer's testimony, and they continued to pour in throughout the night. FDP had won the first round.[42]

When the credentials committee reconvened on Sunday afternoon, Joe Rauh was confident. He had seventeen committee members pledged to sign a minority report supporting FDP, six more votes than needed to bring the challenge before the entire convention. He also had ten states, including New York, Michigan, and California, pledged to ask for a roll call on the convention floor, two states more than needed. So when the president's representatives on the committee put forward the proposal that the Freedom Democrats be "honored guests" at the convention, FDP supporters contemptuously rejected it. Oregon congressman Al Ullman then made a motion that FDP be awarded two seats at the convention. At that, Rauh recalled, "my heart sunk, because he was on our side and here our side was reducing its demand to two before the fight had started." The Ullman proposal split the FDP forces on the committee, but after a quick count Rauh saw that he still had eleven members who would sign a report even if Ullman's measure should pass, so the committee was again stalemated. Without taking a vote on the Ullman amendment, Lawrence formed a subcommittee to make a recommendation to the full committee about the Mississippi question. Minnesota attorney general Walter Mondale, a protégé of Senator Hubert Humphrey, chaired this subcommittee, which included black congressional representative Charles Diggs. The full committee then adjourned until Monday.[43]

That evening a caucus of black delegates met at the Deauville Motel. Although not invited, many black FDP delegates attended and listened while "some of the most prominent Negro politicians in the country" concluded that blacks must support their president. At this implied rebuff of the FDP position, Annie Devine of Canton took the floor and responded angrily, with tears in her eyes: "We have been treated like beasts in Mississippi. They shot us down like animals. We risk our lives coming up here. . . . politics must be corrupt if it don't care none about people down here. . . . these politicians sit in positions and forget the people who put them there." At that, the meeting adjourned without taking any action. SNCC field secretary Charles Sherrod, who was at the caucus, later reflected that "at President Johnson's 'coronation' in Atlantic City there were no blacks with power to challenge the position of the administration. Moreover, there was opposition by blacks to any attempt to wield power against the administrative position."[44]

SNCC's Courtland Cox recalls that at an FDP strategy meeting held a short while earlier, a black congressman befriended Bob Moses and asked for the names of credentials committee members supporting FDP. This list, he said, would persuade committee chair

Lawrence of the FDP's ability to bring the challenge to the convention floor. Moses was reluctant to part with the list, but he did so at Cox's urging. What happened next, in Cox's words, "was something unbelievable. Every person on that list, every member of that credentials committee who was going to vote for the minority, got a call. They said, 'Your husband is up for a judgeship, and if you don't shape up, he won't get it.' 'You're up for a loan. If you don't shape up, you won't get it.' And you began to see how things worked in the real world."[45] Having failed to satisfy black Mississippians with minor concessions, Lyndon Johnson had now decided to play hardball.

In his memoirs Johnson did not even mention the Mississippi challenge, remembering Atlantic City as "a place of surging crowds and thundering cheers." In fact, the president had become obsessed by the FDP effort to unseat the regulars. Throughout the summer Johnson and his aides had lobbied important northern governors about potential problems with Mississippi and Alabama, where the state party had nominated a slate of unpledged electors. On July 20, New Jersey governor Richard Hughes talked with White House aide Jack Valenti about the FDP challenge and passed on the message that "we are ready to do anything the President wants us to do on this—we are waiting to be told the President's desires." A week later Governor Karl F. Rolvaag of Minnesota wrote presidential assistant Walter Jenkins to "assure you that the Minnesota delegation will abide by the wishes of the President."[46] The northern party faithful would go along with whatever recommendation the president made. Not so in the South. Stung by the success of Alabama governor George Wallace in the presidential primaries, and aware of the enormous popularity of Republican nominee Goldwater among white southerners, Texas's John Connally was not alone when he warned the president that "if you seat those black buggers, the whole South will walk out."[47]

The White House strategy, then, was to prevent important northern delegations from supporting FDP while keeping the "responsible" southern delegations—Mississippi and Alabama were written off as lost causes—from bolting. Placed in charge of this delicate operation was Senator Hubert Humphrey of Minnesota, an ideal choice for the assignment because he was a liberal whose civil rights record was impressive. In 1948 he had led the national convention fight for a strong civil rights platform plank, which resulted in the

Dixiecrat walkout. He also had close ties with members of the left wing of the Democratic party, like Rauh, who were supporting the Mississippi challenge. Humphrey had good reason to do the president's bidding, for he was the front-runner for the vice presidential nomination. Word quickly passed that the president would choose Humphrey as his running mate—if the senator kept FDP in line.

Rauh had felt pressure from the White House weeks before the convention opened, receiving a series of phone calls from Humphrey and Walter Reuther, head of the United Auto Workers, for which Rauh was legal counsel. Rauh recalls that "the most hysterical of all the phone calls" was from Reuther:

> Walter said, "I've been talking to the President and we have agreed that if you go through with this, we're going to lose the election." I said, "Are you serious? Goldwater has been nominated! How can you lose it!" He said, "We both think the backlash is so tremendous that either we're going to lose the Negro vote if you go through with this and don't win, or if you do win, the picture of your black delegation going on the floor to replace the white one is going to add to the backlash. We really think that Goldwater's going to be president."[48]

On Tuesday morning, August 18, four days before the credentials committee meeting, Johnson had called a strategy session in the Oval Office to discuss the Mississippi problem. In attendance were Humphrey, convention chair David Lawrence, and presidential advisors Abe Fortas, Clark Clifford, and Walter Jenkins, who was to direct the operation against FDP at the convention. The following day Johnson met with civil rights leaders in what was supposed to be an "off the record" meeting about Mississippi. Once word of the meeting became public, Johnson refused to say anything about the FDP challenge, and no one else raised the subject. James Farmer, Roy Wilkins, and A. Philip Randolph, all of whom supported the challenge, attended. Martin Luther King did not, but he sent a telegram calling for the seating of FDP. Neither King's absence nor the telegram came as a surprise to the White House, as the FBI had alerted the president of these developments. For in addition to his standard arm-twisting approach, Lyndon Johnson had turned to J. Edgar Hoover to provide his own "coverage" of the convention.[49]

The White House campaign of surveillance and espionage at the

1964 convention was a Watergate that worked. In 1976, in the aftermath of the Nixon scandals, the Senate Select Committee to Study Governmental Operations, the "Church Committee," summarized the Atlantic City operation with devastating clarity:

> Approximately 30 Special Agents, headed by Assistant [FBI] Director Cartha ["Deke"] DeLoach, "were able to keep the White House fully apprised of all major developments during the Convention's course" by means of "information coverage, by use of various confidential techniques, by infiltration of key groups through use of undercover agents, and through utilization of agents using appropriate cover as reporters." Among these "confidential techniques" were: a wiretap on the hotel room occupied by Dr. Martin Luther King, Jr., and microphone surveillance of a storefront serving as headquarters for the Student Nonviolent Coordinating Committee and another civil rights organization [CORE].[50]

FBI involvement had begun on July 22 with a White House inquiry as to whether the bureau had a file on the Freedom Democratic party. Receiving a negative reply, Walter Jenkins then asked Hoover for a "name-check" on all FDP delegates.[51] FBI intelligence gathered at the convention proved valuable. Agents posing as NBC correspondents (the network cooperated with the FBI) were able to gain off-the-record information through "interviews." The wiretaps provided important data on FDP strategy throughout the convention, and FBI agents planted an informant who attended all FDP meetings and caucuses. Correspondence in the Johnson Library reveals a constant stream of memoranda to the president's desk during convention week. DeLoach passed on the FBI reports to Johnson's operatives on the floor, Walter Jenkins and Bill Moyers, whose FBI code name for the week was "Bishop." They in turn passed on the information to Lee White at the White House or to Johnson directly. The president's diary ledger for convention week is filled with calls from Johnson to Jenkins and Moyers.[52] Two weeks after the convention Moyers wrote a congratulatory note to Deke DeLoach, who replied "that it was a pleasure and privilege to be able to be of assistance to the President, and all the boys that were with me felt honored in being selected for the assignment. . . . I'm certainly glad that we were able to come through with vital tidbits from time to time which were of assistance to you and Walter. You know you have only to call on us when a similar situation arises."[53]*

Despite the Freedom Democrats' distrust of Lyndon Johnson, not even the veteran SNCC and CORE activists at the convention suspected that the president had resorted to tactics normally employed against spies and gangsters. Instead, they went about the business of lining up delegates to support the challenge, while the delegation debated whether to accept a compromise on the question of seating. FDP met twice on Sunday, August 23, for that purpose and found acceptable a proposal put forward by Representative Edith Green of Oregon, an FDP supporter and member of the credentials committee. Under the Green initiative, the convention would seat all members of both Mississippi delegations pledging loyalty to the party and the presidential ticket, dividing seats proportionally according to the number who signed the oath. Since FDP leaders knew that no more than three or four members of the regular delegation would comply, in effect the "compromise" would exclude the regulars while seating the challengers. For this reason the Green proposal was unacceptable to Lyndon Johnson.[54]

Monday was a day of caucuses, lobbying, and closed-door meetings. The convention officially opened that night, with the credentials committee scheduled to make its report. Rauh still had his eleven and eight, FDP had rejected the Ullman two-seat suggestion in favor of the Green proposal, and the administration had not yet shown its hand. Humphrey was now frantically searching for some sort of solution and that afternoon called a meeting with dissident members of the credentials committee, FDP delegation leaders, Martin Luther King, and Bob Moses, whom the administration regarded as a major stumbling block to a settlement. Fan-

*Four years later Vice President Hubert Humphrey's executive assistant asked the FBI to send a "special team" to the Democratic National Convention in Chicago, where Humphrey was making his bid for the party's nomination. Lyndon Johnson allegedly told Humphrey that "the FBI had been of great service to him and he had been given considerable information on a timely basis throughout the entire convention." Democratic party treasurer John Criswell made a similar request, noting that former Johnson staff member Marvin Watson had spoken "of the great service provided by the FBI during the last Democratic Convention." Although not enthusiastic about supplying the candidate of the liberal establishment with political intelligence, Hoover did send his agents once again to the convention floor, assigning five of them to gather information on the new delegation of Mississippi challengers.

nie Lou Hamer, one of the FDP delegates in attendance, was flattered by the invitation, because with "all that we had been hearing about . . . Hubert Humphrey and his stand for civil rights, I was delighted to even have a chance to talk with the man." But Humphrey had nothing substantial to offer the delegates, and when the point was raised that a floor fight over the challenge might cost Humphrey the vice presidency, Mrs. Hamer turned to him and said, "Well, Mr. Humphrey, do you mean to tell me that your position is more important to you than four hundred thousand black people's lives?" She left the meeting in tears—and was not invited back to the final conference with the senator.[55]

Because Rauh still had enough support for a minority report and the Mondale subcommittee had not yet come up with a recommendation, Lawrence took the unusual step of postponing the full committee meeting scheduled for Monday afternoon for one day and its report to the convention until Tuesday night. Rauh welcomed the breathing space, for he had not yet prepared for a convention floor debate. The delay, however, ultimately benefited the Johnson forces, which were now pressuring FDP supporters on the credentials committee to desert the cause. Monitoring the situation closely from the White House, Johnson had also contacted Walter Reuther, then in the midst of important UAW negotiations with General Motors in Detroit. The convention opened without incident, with the entire FDP delegation seated in the gallery.[56]

Tuesday was the day of decision. Everyone knew that the Mississippi question could not be put off any longer. The only issue was whether there would be an acceptable compromise or a floor fight. Rauh did not get much sleep Monday night. As he had done at the end of each day, he stopped by Hubert Humphrey's hotel suite to discuss the challenge and did not leave the senator's rooms until five or six o'clock Tuesday morning.[57]

At about 1:00 P.M. on Tuesday Rauh arrived at the FDP caucus, which was already in session. By then he was aware that Reuther, at Lyndon Johnson's insistence, had left the GM negotiations and arrived at about 3:00 A.M. in Atlantic City, where he had met with Humphrey, Mondale, Lawrence—"all the big shots"—to formulate a compromise. Rauh later claimed he had been shut out of this discussion and had no idea of the compromise agreed on at that meeting, but when delegation chair Aaron Henry called on him to address the Tuesday afternoon caucus, Rauh made a rather curious speech. As he later put it,

> I decided to make a speech for tolerance. And it just came out. I said I think something's going to happen. We're going to have a meeting at 2 o'clock and I'm going to be made an offer and I haven't the vaguest idea what's in it. . . .
>
> I made a plea for tolerance for Hubert Humphrey who they felt wasn't supporting them, but who I felt was doing all he could. . . . I made a plea for people to understand each other and not have bitterness come out of this. Because there was going to be—I said, "We are within 12 hours [of] a settlement now." I don't know whether; I honestly don't know why I did that.[58]

Many of the civil rights activists at the convention thought they knew why. Looking back at what transpired on Monday night and Tuesday, they became convinced that their attorney had deceived them. SNCC's Mendy Samstein saw it this way:

> But here is the way most people interpret it. That a deal was made during the night, that Rauh knew all the time about the compromise, that when he came to the church [Tuesday afternoon] he was dishonest. Because he couldn't have very well told them about the compromise and then they say under no condition accept it. . . . So he makes a deal during the night, goes to the caucus, tells them nothing new has been added . . . but in fact the deal has been made . . . [and he then] goes to the [credentials] committee.[59]

The question "What did Joe Rauh know and when did he know it?" may never be resolved. Perhaps he did not know the exact form of the final compromise, but it seems likely that he knew enough about the offer to plead with the FDP delegation to show "tolerance for Hubert Humphrey" and not "to have bitterness come out of this." These remarks sound like those of a lawyer preparing his clients for an unfavorable verdict.

In fact, by then the Johnson administration's pressure on FDP supporters in the credentials committee had taken its toll. Governor Pat Brown of California told Verna Canson that her continued support of FDP would cost her husband a promised judgeship. Another friendly delegate from the Canal Zone was threatened with the loss of his job. When Abe Fortas (later elevated to the U.S. Supreme Court) heard a report that Puerto Rico had decided to support the Freedom party, he dashed over to bring that delegation back into line. By late Tuesday morning Walter Jenkins was optimistic that FDP support on the credentials committee had dropped below the magic number of eleven. Now Reuther was on the scene to exert pressure on Rauh, the union's attorney, and on Martin Luther King, whose SCLC had been the recipient of UAW money.[60]

According to Rauh's account, he first learned of the specifics of the White House–supported compromise shortly before the final session of the credentials committee on Tuesday afternoon. When he arrived for the 2:00 P.M. meeting, Congressman Charles Diggs instructed him to call Reuther immediately. Reuther told Rauh that "the decision had been made . . . and I want you to take it." When Rauh pressed for details, Reuther laid out the terms of the settlement the Mondale subcommittee was about to propose to the full committee: FDP representatives Aaron Henry and Ed King would be seated as at-large delegates, with the remaining FDP delegates "welcomed as honored guests of this convention"; only those members of the "regular" Mississippi delegation who signed a loyalty oath agreeing to support the party's nominees in the November election would be seated; finally, the national Democratic party pledged to eliminate racial discrimination in state delegations in all future conventions and would convene a committee before the 1968 convention to draw up guidelines for all states to follow.[61]

Rauh told Reuther that it was "a great proposal" but that he could not vote for it until he talked with Aaron Henry, the FDP delegation chair. If Henry gave his consent, then Rauh would return to the credentials committee session and propose that the compromise be endorsed unanimously. (Two decades later Rauh still believed that Henry's agreement alone would have legitimized Rauh's endorsing the compromise and abandoning the position voted on by the entire FDP delegation.) Rauh pushed for an adjournment until he could speak with Henry, but the Johnson forces on the credentials committee, including Mondale, wanted the vote before hearing from Henry or anyone else in the Freedom Democratic party. A strong negative response from an FDP caucus *before* the vote might encourage wavering supporters on the committee to overcome White House pressures and send a minority report to the floor.[62]

While Rauh unsuccessfully tried to win an adjournment of the committee, Henry, Ed King, and Moses were conferring with Humphrey, Reuther, Bayard Rustin, Martin Luther King, and several other representatives of the SCLC and the Johnson administration. According to Ed King (the only participant who has written extensively about this meeting), Rustin, who had set up the meeting, wanted to exclude Moses but relented when Ed King insisted that the SNCC leader be present. When King, Moses, and Henry arrived, "It was soon clear to us from MFDP that everyone else at this session was already 'in the know' about the details of the compromise" and that they were committed to support it. While Ed King and Henry were willing to discuss the terms of the offer, Moses was not and spoke instead of the wretched conditions in Mississippi and the failure of the federal government to do its job. Humphrey and Reuther were clearly frustrated, for their purpose was to present the final settlement, not to negotiate; they wanted Moses, Ed King, and Henry to agree to the compromise as it stood, then and there. When all three FDP representatives insisted that the entire delegation decide the question, Rustin interrupted to say that there would not be time for a lengthy debate before the convention that evening.[63]

Although it was now apparent that Humphrey and Reuther would not get what they wanted from this meeting, the discussion dragged on. Then one of the senator's aides burst in to say that there was important news on television. Everyone rushed into the next room to hear a bulletin that the credentials committee had unanimously approved the two-seat compromise and that this was a great victory for the civil rights forces. A furious Bob Moses, believing he had been sandbagged, shouted at Humphrey, "You tricked us!" The normally reserved SNCC activist then stormed past Humphrey, slamming the door on the next vice president of the United States. Moses grabbed a cab and hurried back to the FDP delegates to assure them that he had not agreed to the compromise. But the damage had been done. Unable to get a recess, Rauh and the handful of remaining FDP supporters on the credentials committee had in fact voted against the proposal, not wanting to commit themselves until they heard from the Mississippi delegation. The number of committee loyalists, however, was now down to eight. There would be no minority report submitted to the convention, and in the short time remaining the Freedom Democrats' choices had narrowed to accepting or rejecting a compromise that was certain to be passed by voice vote on the convention floor that evening.[64]

After the credentials committee vote, attention shifted to the Union Temple Baptist Church, where the Freedom Democrats were caucusing. Moses got back to the delegation first, followed by Ed King, Martin Luther King, and Henry. Then came Rauh and the seven other credentials committee delegates who had voted against the compromise, including Edith Green. Rauh spoke first, outlining the compromise and recommending that the delegation accept it, pointing out that they no longer had the "eleven and eight" needed to bring the FDP position to the convention floor. Then, Rauh recalled, "Edith Green got up and attacked the compromise and Hubert, and then . . . King was denied the right to speak and it got to be an awful shambles in there." That the delegates did not choose to hear from Martin Luther King Tuesday afternoon is indicative of their frustration and anger. This proposal had been sprung on them after the fact, and now the outsiders who had supported their challenge—Rauh, Rustin, and Dr. King—appeared to have sold them out. At the end of a chaotic session, the FDP delegation voted to reject the two-seat compromise. After meeting with the seven other credentials committee members, Rauh announced to the press that they would file a minority "statement" saying that "we think more should have been done."[65]*

Unwilling to sign any loyalty oath, the Mississippi regulars also rejected the compromise, defiantly contending that "the Mississippi Democratic delegation did not leave the national Democratic party; it left us." Most members of the all-white delegation packed up and left town. Four of the regulars did sign the pledge, and three

---

*One of the enduring myths surrounding the "two-seat compromise" is that had the Johnson people only permitted the FDP to select its own delegates, or even if Mrs. Hamer had been designated for one of the two seats, then the FDP delegation would have accepted the compromise. FDP members did react strongly to having their "leaders" chosen by the White House. For COFO militants, the choice of Henry and King, two middle-class men from urban areas who were not SNCC or CORE people, added insult to injury. Still, there is no evidence that the choice of the two delegates was the sticking point. Moses recalls that Rustin suggested that Mrs. Hamer could be given one of the seats, but Moses did not find that prospect appealing. An eleventh-hour suggestion that the delegation ask for control over the two seats also met with little enthusiasm from FDP delegates.

of them attended the Tuesday evening session, including Greenville attorney Douglas Wynn, a personal friend of Lyndon Johnson.[66]

Although they were to be denied official recognition at the convention, the Freedom Democrats and their supporters were not through yet, resorting to direct-action techniques to dramatize their disappointment and anger. As nearly 500 FDP supporters continued to picket on the boardwalk at the Tuesday night session, about fifty SNCC and CORE activists joined hands to form a circle around three of the FDP delegates and then attempted to push through the convention gates. State police stopped the charge, but friendly delegates from other states had been passing on credentials to members of the FDP delegation, twenty-one of whom gained access to the floor and moved into the seats abandoned by the Mississippi regulars. This "sit-in" immediately attracted the attention of convention officials, who tried unsuccessfully to evict FDP members from the Mississippi section. (When the sit-in began, the three Mississippi regulars quickly moved out, escorted by Walter Jenkins to the convention's VIP lounge, where Doug Wynn received a phone call from the president.) Representatives of the media raced to the scene. ABC's John Scali lectured one of the demonstrators: "Ma'am, now that you've made your point, don't you think it would be best to leave?" And when NBC's John Chancellor asked Bob Moses about the compromise, Moses angrily replied, "What is the compromise? We are here for the people and the people want to represent themselves. They don't want symbolic token votes. They want to vote themselves."[67]

The convention did proceed with its business Tuesday night. Temporary chair John Pastore read the compromise proposal to the assembled delegates and with a single bang of the gavel dismissed contending voices from the floor. Within thirty seconds, the compromise had passed. Later that evening President Johnson indirectly sent word to Senator Humphrey that he would be the vice presidential nominee. Humphrey had apparently passed his test.[68]

The sight of black Mississippians engaging in acts of civil disobedience against the party of Lyndon Johnson made liberal Democrats uncomfortable, and they made one final effort to persuade the Freedom party to accept the compromise. Aaron Henry, now openly supporting the Johnson proposal, called for a caucus on Wednesday morning, where the delegation would hear from the leaders of the civil rights establishment. Prior to that meeting members of the delegation who supported the compromise lobbied hard to convert those who had rejected it. Essentially, the delegation divided here along socioeconomic lines. Moses recalled that the delegates favoring the compromise were largely oriented toward the NAACP, the "more established people from the large cities." Mrs. Hamer described this group more graphically: "Everybody that would compromise in five minutes was the people with a real good education. I don't understand that—I really don't to save my life. Them folks will sell you—they will sell your mama, their mama, anybody else for a dollar." Unita Blackwell remembers a confrontation with a wealthy black Meridian businessman:

> He had on a silk suit and he called us off and told us we've got to get this thing together. . . . And, them people had not been even talking to us poor folks. They had a certain clique that they would talk to. The big niggers talked to the big niggers and the little folk, they couldn't talk to nobody except themselves, you know. . . . They had decided they was going to take that compromise, but the little folks told them no, they wasn't going to take it and they meant business.[69]

The array of speakers lined up on Wednesday morning to address the delegates and their supporters was impressive. Among those defending the compromise were Jack Pratt and Bob Spike of the National Council of Churches, which had contributed financially to the summer project; Senator Wayne Morse, a staunch FDP supporter, who had "sat in" with the dissidents the previous night in the Mississippi section; and Bayard Rustin, who lectured the FDP delegates on the difference between protest and politics: "The former is based on morality and the latter is based on reality and compromise. . . . You must accept the compromise. If you don't, then you are still protesting." Rauh told the delegates that he believed the two seats represented a victory and that "I am with you and I want you to know that we're going to make the resolution work." Martin Luther King did not employ his considerable oratorical skills to sway the delegation, but he did say that he had talked with Humphrey, who "promised me there would be a new day in Mississippi if you accept this proposal."[70]

Moses had earlier made clear his opposition to the compromise, but now he did not ask the delegation to reject it. Characteristically, Moses told the delegates that it was up to them to decide. Forman delivered the strongest attack against acceptance, asking, "What effect will a decision to accept the honored guest status and the two seats-at-large, with the delegates named for you—what effect will this have upon your friends and your relatives and your fellow workers in the state of Mississippi? It seems you have no other choice but to reject support of this resolution."[71]

At the conclusion of the speeches everyone except the delegates left the room. As their debate began, the issue was in doubt. A number of the delegates who had angrily rejected the compromise the day before now seemed to resign themselves to the inevitable, to follow the lead of the important people who claimed that the compromise was a victory for the struggle. Henry Sias, the elderly FDP stalwart from Issaquena County, was at first persuaded by these arguments: "Well, quite a few of us wanted to accept it. . . . I thought we was getting somewhere." All the arguments against the compromise were once again rehearsed: that the compromise recognized the legitimacy of the racist white delegation; that if King and Henry took the seats, they would be registered as at-large delegates and would not represent Mississippi; and that the Johnson forces had had the audacity to decide who the FDP delegates would be. As to the pledge that things would be different in 1968, since only a few thousand blacks were registered to vote in Mississippi, that seemed an empty promise.[72]

The most persuasive appeals to reject the compromise came from the three women who later challenged the state's congressional delegation. Victoria Gray recalls that "at the appropriate moment, personally, when I realized some decisions were going to be made soon, I took the floor, and I simply said to people in no uncertain terms why we were there, and reminded them of what the people back in Mississippi were expecting from us, and that I for one was not going back to Mississippi and tell those people a lie. Then Fannie Lou and Devine spoke." Henry Sias remembered that when he had taken the floor to recommend accepting the two seats, Fannie Lou Hamer and Annie Devine had hit the ceiling: "Mrs. Hamer just hollered out and cried when I said we'd accept those two votes. . . . Mrs. Hamer and Mrs. Devine . . . when they got through talking and hoopin' and hollerin' and tellin me what a shame it was for me to do that, I hushed right then. . . . I changed my mind right there. Those two women just shamed me right there."[73] In the end it was Fannie Lou Hamer, now the symbol of grass-roots activism in Mississippi, who stated the case simply yet powerfully: "I got up and I soon said what I had to say and I sat down. I said, we didn't come all the way up here to compromise for no more than we'd gotten here. . . . We didn't come all this way for no two seats." After hours of discussion and debate, the FDP delegation once again rejected the Atlantic City compromise.[74]

"For many people," observed SNCC's Joyce Ladner, "Atlantic City was the end of innocence." The 1964 Democratic convention was in fact a turning point in the black struggle. Bob Moses believed that "Atlantic City was a watershed in the movement because up until then the idea had been that you were working more or less within the Democratic party. We were working with them on voting, other things like that. With Atlantic City, a lot of movement people became disillusioned. . . . You turned around and your support was puddle-deep." SNCC's Cleveland Sellers expressed that disillusionment: "Never again were we lulled into believing that our task was exposing injustices so that the 'good' people of America could eliminate them. We left Atlantic City with the knowledge that the movement had turned into something else. After Atlantic City, our struggle was not for civil rights, but for liberation."[75]

13

Aftermath in McComb

On the evening of August 27, as Lyndon Johnson was accepting the nomination of his party in Atlantic City and promising a "Great Society" for all Americans, Willie Dillon was at home in McComb, repairing a car owned by COFO. Although Dillon had not been active in the movement, his wife, Matti, attempted to register during Freedom Day a week earlier and had participated in the meetings setting up the Mississippi Freedom Democratic party. Their two oldest children had attended the McComb freedom schools. Shortly after midnight the Dillons were jolted by an explosion twenty feet from their front door. There was no serious damage, but on the lawn lay an unexploded package of nine sticks of dynamite, wrapped in brown paper and bound with red tape. A crowd of neighbors soon gathered, followed by Police Chief Guy, Sheriff Warren, and agent Frank Ford, who headed the FBI's McComb task force. According to Matti Dillon, the officers lost interest in the immediate circumstances of the bombing once they discovered the COFO car, which they searched. The victims now became chief suspects. Both Warren and Ford asked the Dillons to take a lie detector test; when they refused, saying, "We haven't done anything," the FBI man shot back, "If you haven't done anything why are you afraid to take it?" Sheriff Warren warned that "if you don't cooperate with us more than the COFOs, more than that [the bombing] is going to happen to you."[1]

The FBI agent and the police officers then stepped aside and talked among themselves. When they returned Sheriff Warren arrested Willie

Dillon for operating a garage without a license and for stealing electricity by attaching a wire outside the meter. Dillon had done so to install a floodlight to guard against attacks by night riders. He did not operate a garage but occasionally fixed cars for friends after returning from his job at the McComb Scrap Iron Company.

Dillon's trial was set for the following day at 3:00 P.M. at the county courthouse in Magnolia. His lawyer, Jackson attorney R. Jess Brown, arrived to discover that the trial had been moved to 2:30 and switched to McComb. By the time that he and Mrs. Dillon got back to McComb, the verdict was already in. Pike County authorities had held Willie Dillon incommunicado, tried him without an attorney present, and persuaded him to plead guilty by arguing that "it'll save you a lot of money." The judge fined Dillon $600 and sentenced him to nine months in jail. Matti Dillon caught up with her husband as he was led back to jail and asked him why he had pleaded guilty. "I couldn't think of anything else to do," was his sad reply. Dillon's appeal bond was $1,200, and with COFO's help Mrs. Dillon raised it. When she went to post bail, however, Sheriff Warren hiked the bond to $2,000. Dillon remained in jail for a month until finally released on bail. He was also fired from his job. Two days after the trial Matti Dillon met again with FBI agent Ford, who "talked the same way, like *we* did it."[2]

The town of only 12,000 residents had seen more than a dozen bombings since June 22. Throughout the summer Frank Ford had fifteen agents working out of McComb, yet the FBI had come up with nothing. On "most of these investigations," Sheriff Warren later proudly told the Civil Rights Commission, "Mr. Frank Ford was working side by side with me." The bombers clearly believed that they had little to fear either from local police or from J. Edgar Hoover's men, and they were no doubt further emboldened when in late August the FBI reduced its McComb contingent to four agents.[3]

Like the FBI, McComb whites believed that life would return to normal after the summer project officially ended. Having reestablished its base in southwest Mississippi, however, SNCC let it be known that it had come back to stay. Although a number of the white volunteers left, some remained, along with a veteran SNCC staff including Jesse Harris as project director, Mendy Samstein, and Cephus Hughes. Local people also remained strong in the movement. Most visible was Mrs. Aylene Quin. "Mama Quin is kind and good to everyone," wrote Samstein, "but more than that, she is a towering figure of strength. She can't be intimidated. Three years ago she was one of the first to welcome Moses and lend him and the SNCC workers her support. Her cafe has always been open— despite the threats. And this summer, again she leads the community. She serves black and white, night after night. And the pressures increase."[4] On August 30 the police raided Mama Quin's cafe and arrested her after planting liquor on the premises. A short time later her white landlord threatened to evict her if she did not stop serving COFO people. She closed her cafe but made plans to open another in a building owned by a local black man.[5]

Throughout it all, McComb's white leadership remained silent. Even Oliver Emmerich, the town's moderate newspaper editor, had said nothing about the violence throughout the summer. "Nobody could have gotten through to the people of McComb," he later explained. "Almost everybody was hysterically afraid." The handful of whites who befriended COFO activists had paid for their support. Mrs. Libby Price, an elderly matriarch from Magnolia who welcomed movement people into her home and helped to furnish the freedom house, was subjected to constant threats and eventually moved to Jackson. Then there were the Heffners. Red and Malva Heffner were solid citizens. Red was a successful insurance agent; Malva's daughter by her first marriage was the reigning Miss Mississippi, a title carrying considerable status in the Magnolia State. The Heffners lived in a middle-class neighborhood and had never been active in civil rights activities. They had, however, made the mistake of inviting volunteer Dennis Sweeney and a visiting white minister to their home for dinner, after which their lives became a nightmare. Within two months Red's insurance business was a shambles, his wife and children were ostracized, and the family's pet dog was poisoned. Finally, on September 5, they moved away from McComb. Their crime, a COFO notice stated, was that "they had tried to arrange peaceful relations between the summer project and the community."[6]

Throughout September the Klan ran wild in McComb. On September 2 white volunteer Bob Stone was assaulted in the middle of town; police made no arrests. Five nights later the Klan bombed the homes of a black minister and a school principal; neither had been active in the movement. That same evening dynamite damaged a black-owned grocery; its owner had no civil rights connections. Nor did the Reverend James Baker, a minister and farmer whose home near Summit was bombed two nights later. Having failed to expel the COFO organizers, the Klan was now resorting to indiscriminate violence against McComb blacks in an effort to separate COFO from its local base of support. With the bombing escalating nightly, project director Jesse Harris wrote Burke Marshall, detailing the latest acts of terror. Harris ominously concluded, "We of the McComb project are convinced that our situation has become critical. We must again make it clear that unless responsible forces are brought to bear in McComb, what happened in Neshoba County will happen here. We plead with you to take action now before it is too late." But Mississippi was now out of the limelight. The press had given the situation in McComb little attention. The Justice Department took no further action.[7]

McComb was now an armed camp. Black residents posted guards at their homes, businesses, and churches. NAACP president C. C. Bryant bought a high-powered rifle and exchanged gunfire with the terrorists who had hurled dynamite at his brother's home. Blacks in isolated areas lit up their neighborhoods at night with makeshift streetlights draped on posts and trees in their yards. They knew they would receive no help from law officers, who ignored information from black victims, even when they provided accurate descriptions of cars fleeing the scene of a bombing. Local blacks were convinced that the police knew the identities of the dynamiters all along and that some officers were participating in the bombings. Ernest Nobles reported that on the night his laundromat was bombed, his brother standing guard saw a police car stop in front of the laundry and shine a light into the building moments before it started to burn. Reports such as this circulated through the community.[8]

Shortly before eleven o'clock on the night of September 20, Jimmy P. Wilson, the manager of the Edgewood Service Station, pulled his black 1961 Ford up in front of the home of Aylene Quin. Mrs. Quin was on her way home from an FDP meeting in Jackson at the time. She had left her two youngest children, Jacqueline, nine, and Anthony, four, in the care of a babysitter. Sitting next to Jimmy Wilson was Billy Earl Wilson (no relation) cradling a sixteen-gauge shotgun. In the back seat Paul D. Wilson, an Illinois Central employee, lit a long fuse attached to fourteen sticks of dynamite and handed the bundle to Ernest Zeeck, a clerk at the Western Auto Company store. Given the honor because it was his first bombing,

Zeeck heaved the dynamite onto the porch of the Quin home. The explosion shattered the eight-room house, collapsing the front wall and ceiling of the room where the children lay. Anthony was pinned to his bed by the fallen ceiling but was not injured. Jacqueline suffered a punctured eardrum from the explosion. A half-hour later a second blast destroyed the Society Hill Baptist Church, where C. C. Bryant had long served as a deacon.[9]

Almost immediately several hundred angry blacks stormed into the streets surrounding Mama Quin's home. Some were carrying guns, while others made Molotov cocktails by pouring gasoline into empty beer bottles. Aylene Quin described the scene as she returned home: "They came up here and they were throwing bricks and everything. They hit Chief Guy on the leg with a brick. The police found out that black people weren't afraid any more. They had gone far enough. There was gonna be a riot right here in McComb." When Pike County sheriff Warren arrived he saw "a riot, you might say, in progress. There was three or four hundred Negroes. A lot of them was drinking. They were cursing, they were calling us everything but white people. They even was threatening to kill us." A full-scale race war was avoided that night largely through the efforts of COFO workers to control the crowd. Local SNCC activist Joe Martin screamed at blacks, "They're gonna kill you if you keep throwing those bricks," and disarmed a man with a .22 rifle. "Some guys," Martin recalls, "were ready to take somebody out."[10]

Unable to control the situation, police called in the highway patrol. Once order was restored, officials fell back into the familiar pattern. Sheriff Warren accused Mrs. Quin of bombing her own home (and children!), and the next day he told the press that he believed both bombings had been "COFO plants." That day McComb was crawling with over 100 highway patrolman, who had sealed off the black neighborhood surrounding the Quin home. Police jailed scores of blacks over the next seventy-two hours, including COFO leaders. Twenty-four people were charged under the "criminal syndicalism" bill passed by the legislature in May but applied here for the first time. This was a catchall measure that in effect outlawed free speech and political organization among groups deemed subversive. Police charged Dennis Sweeney as an accessory to the "production of Molotov cocktails" but had to release him when their black "witness" refused to testify against Sweeney in court. Many of the blacks arrested were high school students. Jerry Lee Hill's experience with the police was typical. A tenth-grade student at Burgland High School, Hill was picked up near the scene of the disturbance after the Quin bombing. During interrogation, Hill denied participating in attacks on the police. Even though there was no evidence against him, Hill was locked up for twenty-nine days at the county jail, where he shared a cell with eight other prisoners.[11]

With the police busy jailing COFO workers and local teenagers, the Klan resumed its activities. Three nights after the Quin and church bombings, two more residences were dynamited. One was the home of twenty-seven-year-old Ardis Garner, who had been hired as one of two black police officers earlier in the summer. When Garner learned that his job was to plant an informant inside the COFO office and to start a petition to demand that COFO workers leave town, he resigned. Garner was in Jackson testifying before the Mississippi Advisory Committee to the Civil Rights Commission on the day the Klan bombed his home. From there he flew to Washington to meet with Burke Marshall. The McComb story was now again in the headlines, for earlier that week Aylene Quin, Matti Dillon, and Ora "Dago" Bryant had stopped by the White House to give President Johnson a firsthand report on life in the Camellia City.[12]

The day after the Quin bombing, COFO had sent the three women—all bombing victims—to Washington to meet with Justice Department officials. Lee White advised the president to avoid the women, noting that he had discussed the matter with Burke Marshall and black presidential aide Louis Martin "and both agree that there is no political benefit in meeting these people." On Wednesday Marshall assured the women that "the FBI is investigating the bombings as vigorously as possible. Everything that can be done is being done." Mrs. Quin responded that blacks in McComb had little faith in the FBI, who "work with the local police" and had not made a single arrest. Later at a news conference she ridiculed Sheriff Warren's charge that she was responsible for the destruction of her home: "Do you think I would work 11 years to keep a house and then plant a bomb under it while two of my children were in it?" The three women were getting their message across, and the following day President Johnson did meet them privately. Aylene Quin asked Johnson to send federal troops to McComb, and though he made no commitments, the president assured the women he would take action. The McComb delegation then met with several members of Congress, one of whom, William Fitts Ryan, promised to ask the Justice Department to convene a grand jury in McComb to investigate possible "collusion between local police and white terrorists."[13]

All this was not lost on McComb's business leadership. Network news programs now featured nightly reports on the latest acts of Klan terror, and Drew Pearson focused on McComb in his widely syndicated column. In an October 6 editorial, the *New York Times* told its readers that in McComb "a pattern has developed of open warfare against Negroes who assert themselves or seek to organize in any way," warning that "if the pattern of violence and intimidation in the state is to be broken, further federal action is needed." Such publicity did not bode well for the local economy. Hodding Carter II observed that in McComb, "Business was at its lowest ebb since before World War II. Too many housewives were nervous about going downtown on leisurely shopping expeditions and too many Negroes were either doing without or driving across the Louisiana line to make their purchases." Attorney Robert Brumfield remembered staring out the window of his second-floor office in downtown McComb the day after the Quin bombing: "You could look out across Main Street and three-fourths of the parking spaces in town were empty. People were actually afraid at that time to come on the streets." New industry would not consider locating in McComb, and several national insurance companies directed their local agents not to write any more coverage. The major McComb manufacturer was now shipping his products from a point across the line in Louisiana to avoid the "made in McComb" stigma.[14]

Editor Emmerich was the first white civic leader to break the conspiracy of silence. In a cautious September 25 editorial he wrote for the first time on the reign of terror's adverse effects ("bombings create tension") and warned of the consequences if the federal government imposed martial law in McComb ("business would dry up").[15] Two days later Emmerich and other white moderates met in McComb with John A. Griffin and Jerome K. Heilbron of the Community Relations Service (CRS). This Justice Department agency, headed by former Florida governor LeRoy Collins, was created under the Civil Rights Act of 1964 to assist troubled communities settle racial disputes peacefully. The two mediators met with people representing a broad range of interests. Griffin recommended that a statement calling for law and order be endorsed by as many leading citizens as possible and published in the local newspaper. Griffin and Heilbron reported back to Governor Collins that tensions remained high, that many prominent whites still identified or sympathized with extremist organizations, and that white businesspeople were "anxious about the possibility of federal intervention."[16]

On September 29, while the CRS representatives were still in McComb, Pike County district attorney Joseph Pigott got a telephone call from a man he knew in the Justice Department, who asked, "Did you know that they are going to alert a battalion of troops to declare martial law in McComb?" Within five minutes Pigott received another call, this time from Governor Paul Johnson, who said, "I want a meeting in your office this afternoon at five o'clock." Johnson had gotten a similar call from Washington.[17]

Late that afternoon Johnson and T. B. Birdsong, head of the Mississippi Highway Patrol, met with Pigott and all the major elected officials in McComb and Pike County. The governor informed the group that he was going to move a battalion of the state's National Guard into McComb. "In other words," concluded Pigott, "he was going to beat President Johnson to the draw." Obviously distressed, the Pike County officials asked the governor for a forty-eight-hour extension to give them one last chance to clean up the situation. He agreed. Twenty-four hours later the first Klan bombers were apprehended.[18]

Attorney Pigott argues emphatically that the arrests occurred when they did because an eleventh-hour tip revealed the residence of several of the bombers.[19] McComb blacks believed that the sheriff and the police chief had known the bombers' identity all along. Whatever the speculation, the fact remains that until the end of September the Klan had its way in McComb, and the bombers were arrested only after blacks engaged in retaliatory violence and after both the president and the governor had threatened to send troops to occupy McComb.*

---

*The evidence that the federal government did threaten to send troops is circumstantial but persuasive. Emmerich has written that "the report was not hearsay. Roughly one thousand soliders were readied to be sent to McComb." Burke Marshall has said that he "might have" made such threats and that Emmerich would no doubt have used them to move whites to take action to end the violence. Whether President Johnson would in fact have sent the army into McComb a month before the presidential election is another question. As it was, the threat was sufficient to produce the desired result.

Within a week eleven Klan members were in custody, along with enough weapons, ammunition, and explosives to start a small war. Six of the men worked for the Illinois Central Railroad; three others had jobs in McComb businesses, two as store managers; one Klan member was a painting contractor and a former Army demolitions expert. Another man arrested was Sterling "Bubba" Gillis, the proprietor of an upholstery shop, who was also charged with the $40,000 robbery of a bank in Lawrence County on March 2. At first all of those charged professed their innocence, but when nine of the defendants went to trial on October 23, they pleaded either guilty or *nolo contendere* to charges ranging from attempted arson to bombing. Under Mississippi law the maximum penalty was death, yet the presiding judge, W. H. Watkins, gave the defendants suspended sentences and immediately released them on probation. In justifying his leniency Judge Watkins stated that the men had been "unduly provoked" by civil rights workers, some of whom "are people of low morality and unhygienic." The bombers, on the other hand, were from "good families" and were "mostly young men starting out and . . . deserve a second chance." Five of the nine "young men" were over thirty-five years of age. That afternoon thirteen COFO staff members were jailed on charges of operating a food-handling establishment (the freedom house, where they lived) without a permit. On that same day federal judge Sidney Mize rejected Willie Dillon's appeal to have his trial removed to federal court. Judge Mize ruled as he did because "there is no hostility among the general public in Pike County to the Negro race."[20]

The McComb black community was shocked and angry that the bombers had gotten off with a lecture. In Washington, J. Edgar Hoover said that letting them go free was "a scandalous thing to do." Yet, as Charles Dunagin wrote in the McComb *Enterprise-Journal,* "It seems a logical assumption that the defendants would never have changed their 'not guilty' pleas if they were not reasonably sure that they would have received suspended sentences. . . . Had the cases gone to trial there would have been a good chance a jury would have found the defendants not guilty or mistrials would have resulted from hung juries." For local officials, then, the guilty pleas made it appear that they had solved the cases and thus the city could return to normal. It did not, for the city fathers were as determined to drive COFO out of McComb as they were to destroy the power of the Klan. Harassment arrests continued, and although there were no more bombings in the black community, several local whites designated as Klan enemies were fired at by night riders.[21]

Throughout October editor Emmerich had been writing strong editorials. On October 14 he admitted that "Negro churches have been burned. Negro homes have been bombed. A Negro store has been dynamited. And with a sense of irresponsibility we have blamed the Negroes for the burnings, the bombing, the dynamiting. This is the sordid story of McComb." A week later he asked, "Can community tranquility prevail and progress proceed if we, as advocates of constitutional government, turn our backs upon the Constitution of the United States?" One response to the editorials was gunfire directed at the newspaper's office. Plate-glass windows were smashed; someone tossed a stink bomb into the circulation department. The Klan burned a cross on Emmerich's lawn the night his mother died. (In an act of civility peculiar to the mind of the South, Emmerich later received a call from a man who said, apologetically, "We would not have burned that cross in front of your home had we known of your mother's death.")[22]

Emboldened by Emmerich's stand, other civic leaders led by insurance agent Newton James and attorney Robert Brumfield followed through on John Griffin's suggestion and began collecting the first of over 650 signatures for a "Statement of Principles," which appeared in a full-page advertisement in the *Enterprise-Journal* on November 18. It was, on the whole, an impressive document, specifically calling for an end to harassment arrests, economic threats, and sanctions and advocating "the widest possible use of our citizenship in the selection of juries." "There is only one responsible stance we can take," the statement concluded, "and that is for equal treatment under the law for all citizens regardless of race, creed, or position of wealth; for making our protests within the framework of the law; and for obeying the laws of the land regardless of our personal feelings." The statement carried a thinly veiled attack on COFO ("For too long we have let the extremists on both sides bring our community close to chaos"), but given the recent history of McComb, it represented a remarkable change in the public position of white people of social standing and political and economic influence.[23]

The statement was rushed into print on November 18 because that was the day the state NAACP had planned to test the public accommodations section of the Civil Rights Act of 1964. Ernest

Nobles remembers the occasion: "I tell you what, I have never seen that many people in McComb. Oh, I bet you it was 20,000 at least. . . . I mean, it was so crowded it was like a parade." Nobles and his wife were part of a twenty-person delegation headed by NAACP leader Charles Evers. Guarded by local police, forty state patrolmen, and twenty FBI agents, the group "desegregated" the Continental Motel and the Holiday Inn, the Palace Theater, the Woolworth's lunch counter where Hollis Watkins and Curtis Hayes had been arrested three years earlier, and the Trailways Bus Station, the scene of a white riot when CORE workers attempted to desegregate the terminal in 1961. C. C. Bryant was served a bowl of gumbo in the restaurant at the Continental Motel. The white waitress "smiled and said 'Thank you,'" reported the local NAACP head. "She even asked us to come back."[24]

Bryant did not return for more gumbo at the Continental. As with the earlier NAACP test in Jackson, this was a one-shot affair, with no follow-up planned. Once the media, highway patrol, and FBI pulled out, McComb returned to its segregated ways. Early in 1965 only the Holiday Inn, located just off the highway, was open to black patrons.[25]

This confluence of events—the brief desegregation of downtown businesses and the statement of principles—symbolized both the progress made in McComb and the problems that remained. Two months earlier, such developments would have been unthinkable. Even so, Newton James and most of the white men and women who signed the statement remained segregationists and paternalists. They would now deal with black McComb, but not with COFO. Mayor Burt put it bluntly as he surveyed the downtown scene on November 18: "See, we want to split off these people from the COFO bunch. . . . These local people on their own, they ain't about to do anything." Within the black community, the battle for these "local people" would now be waged between forces representing the grass-roots movement led by SNCC and the NAACP, symbolized in the person of Charles Evers. (Evers, who had never spent much time in McComb, had not even informed the COFO leadership of the desegregation test. SNCC people resented his intrusion almost as much as did the white business community.)[26]

The white leadership of McComb would continue to fight Aylene Quin, Ernest Nobles, Joe Martin, and the outside people who supported them. C. C. Bryant represented a moderate NAACP alternative, but he too would continually be frustrated by the instransigency of the white establishment. Still, the movement had won a major victory in southwest Mississippi. It had moved into the heart of Klan country and survived. Blacks and their white allies had won the right to organize in McComb, and the city would never be the same again.

Nor would the state of Mississippi. The COFO summer project and the attendant national publicity, grudging compliance with the new civil rights act, and the peaceful desegregation of a handful of elementary schools in the fall of 1964 marked the end of the policy of "massive resistance" in the Magnolia State. White Mississippi no longer spoke with a single voice. The Citizens' Council, for nearly a decade the dominant political force, was now discredited for its its failure to prevent the desegregation of schools and lunch counters. It would never again control state government, as it had during the Barnett administration. The voices of moderation in white Mississippi, silent for a decade, once more were being heard, albeit timidly.

The embattled veterans of the black freedom struggle, however, did not see much cause for celebration in the fall of 1964. Widespread poverty remained the dominant economic fact in black Mississippi. Despite its setback in McComb, the Ku Klux Klan remained a feared presence in the southern half of the state. Governor Paul Johnson was a strong segregationist who made concessions only grudgingly. And the Atlantic City convention had demonstrated that the federal government and northern liberals were unwilling to accept an independent, black-led third force in state and national politics.

Still, the movement had made impressive gains in the three years since Bob Moses and a handful of activists had moved into McComb to open a voter registration drive. By holding firm and refusing to back down in the face of intimidation and terror, the movement did win the right to organize black communities, driving a wedge into the closed society. Ironically, these victories also created serious problems for local people and their SNCC and CORE allies, as moderate whites and more conservative blacks soon joined forces to establish themselves as the authentic voice of the "new" Mississippi. To succeed they would have to do battle with those black women and men at the grass roots who had risked their lives to make such political activity possible. A new phase of the Mississippi movement was about to begin.

A volunteer leads a freedom school class during the summer of 1964. (Staughton Lynd Collection, WHi [X3] 37060, State Historical Society of Wisconsin)

Students sing freedom songs at the freedom school convention in Meridian. (Staughton Lynd Collection, WHi [X3] 45643, State Historical Society of Wisconsin)

Mississippi Freedom Democratic party protest outside the convention hall at Atlantic City, August 25, 1964. Aaron Henry is holding the microphone. Next to him are Fannie Lou Hamer, Ed King (in the background), and the parents of Michael Schwerner. (The Bettmann Archive)

Remains of Zion Hill Baptist Church, July 1964. (McComb *Enterprise-Journal*)

The home of Aylene Quin in McComb after the Klan bombing, September 1964. (McComb *Enterprise-Journal*)

Hearing of the U.S. Commission on Civil Rights, Jackson, January 1965. (McComb *Enterprise-Journal*)

COFO staff at a meeting in McComb in 1965 (left to right): Jean Wheeler Smith, Lorie Smith, unidentified worker, Dennis Sweeney, J. D. Smith, Marshall Ganz, Janet Jemmott, Phil Lapansky, Lorne Cress, and Dorie Ladner. (McComb *Enterprise-Journal*)

A Panola County resident listens to a COFO worker discuss the ASCS elections. (Tamio Wakayama)

Fannie Lou Hamer, Victoria Gray, and Annie Devine, on the steps of the Capitol, react to the news that the House of Representatives had rejected the congressional challenge, September 18, 1965. (AP/Wide World Photos)

Troops evict protestors from the Greenville Air Force Base, February 1, 1966. (Photograph by Maria Varela. Braden Collection, WHi [X3] 48685, State Historical Society of Wisconsin)

James Meredith, moments after being shot on the second day of his march through Mississippi. (AP/World Wide Photos)

El Fondren, triumphant after registering to vote at the Panola County courthouse. (The Bettmann Archive)

Martin Luther King, Jr., Stokely Carmichael, and an unidentified black youth on the Meredith March. (Ernest Withers)

A civil rights symposium in Jackson, Mississippi, April 21–23, 1989 (left to right): Curtis Hayes, Willie Peacock, June Johnson, Chuck McDew, and Winson Hudson. (Robert Townsend Jones)

A panel discussion at the Jackson symposium (left to right): Bob Moses, Dave Dennis, Hollis Watkins, Victoria Gray-Adams, and Lawrence Guyot. (Robert Townsend Jones)

Local people. (Photograph by Bruce Davidson, Magnum Photos)

14

Battle Fatigue

White liberals and black moderates wasted no time in moving to undermine the SNCC-led COFO coalition. On September 18, three weeks after the Atlantic City convention, the National Council of Churches assembled a group in New York "to discuss ways of cooperating in Mississippi in the future." The national civil rights organizations were represented: Gloster Current and John Morsell of the NAACP, James Farmer of CORE, and Andrew Young of the SCLC. SNCC sent Courtland Cox and Mendy Samstein to the meeting. (At the time, most of SNCC's leaders, including Bob Moses and Jim Forman, were touring Africa as the guests of Guinea president Sekou Touré.) Whites were in the majority at the session, including four NCC staff members, NAACP Legal Defense Fund attorney Jack Greenberg, Joseph Rauh, and Allard Lowenstein. Current set the tone with an opening salvo directed at COFO, SNCC, FDP, and Bob Moses. Young jumped in as conciliator, calling for development of a "structure of cooperation. . . . Now we must work to reestablish the coalition we had on Saturday and Sunday in Atlantic City. Our main concern must be to put this back together."[1]

Atlantic City and the Mississippi summer project were very much on the minds of SNCC's critics. Even CORE's Farmer echoed the NAACP charge that SNCC had failed to consult other COFO participant organizations when making decisions. The NCC's Jack Pratt accused SNCC of having "railroaded" FDP delegates into rejecting the convention compromise. Joe Rauh, fired as COFO counsel for his role at Atlantic City, attacked SNCC's friends on the left. "I

would like to drive out the Lawyers' Guild," Rauh bluntly asserted. "I think it is immoral to take help from communists." Everyone understood that while in the past Mississippi had been of relatively minor concern to the civil rights establishment, the summer
project and the Atlantic City challenge had transformed the Magnolia State into the movement's central battleground. The NCC's
Bob Spike observed that "Mississippi is no longer a local problem. . . . Mississippi has now become so large, it exerts leverage on
the national scene: this is the problem." After Lowenstein's asser-
tion that "we can't leave Mississippi, though we might talk about
the possibility," the NAACP's Morsell replied, "Precisely the point.
We're caught."

COFO's critics wanted to set up a committee to oversee civil rights
activity in Mississippi. Lowenstein proposed "the formation of a new
central body . . . responsible for handling money and making other
decisions." This group would have a written constitution and elect
officers. COFO, then, would be assisted in planning and implementing its program by representatives from organized labor, student volunteers, doctors and lawyers who had spent time in Mississippi, and
"other groups," presumably including those represented at this meeting. Such a structure was necessary, Lowenstein argued, because
COFO had excluded NAACP leaders like the Reverend R. L .T. Smith
and had made "authoritarian decisions [that] others have no way of
escaping." The new governing body would be "regularized and de-
mocratized and broadened in its base." COFO would "submit [its]
decisions to this body, [such as] the question of the Lawyers' Guild."
"We need structured democracy," Lowenstein concluded, "not amor-
phous democracy."

SNCC's Cox countered that no one had asked how COFO really operated, pointing out that the "people on the scene make the
decisions. It so happens that most of the people on the scene are
SNCC people so SNCC plays a major role in the decisions." Cox
denied that SNCC had manipulated FDP convention delegates, who
themselves had decided to reject the compromise. "I was willing to
sit and be quiet," he said, "but this whole meeting has been aimed
against SNCC." The NCC's Art Thomas, one of SNCC's few defenders, commented on the "air of unreality about this . . . for an
ad hoc group to meet in New York and determine what should go
on [in Mississippi]."

It soon became clear that although Lowenstein's proposal for a central committee to oversee COFO's activities had broad support, no decisions were possible without the participation of the SNCC leadership. Current proposed another high-level meeting, this time with Moses and Forman present. To Cox's suggestion that the next meeting be held in Mississippi, where local people could "speak to their needs," Current shot back, "The more I listen to Cox the more I know we need a top-level meeting. I have been listening to the crying of people from Mississippi for seventeen years. I don't want to listen to Steptoe. We need high-level meetings so we can cut away the underbrush." The gathering closed with Spike's promise "to get in touch with Bob and Jim and try to set up a meeting as soon as they get back into the country." Forman later wrote that "as might be guessed, the meeting with Bob and myself called for by that group never materialized."[2]

In the fall of 1964 Lowenstein was in residence at Yale, warning summer volunteers back on campus that SNCC had been infiltrated by communists and that the students should not return to Mississippi under SNCC's auspices in 1965. Through Lowenstein protégé Barney Frank, then a Harvard graduate student, SNCC's Dorothy Zellner learned of a series of follow-up meetings in New York "to change the decision-making base of COFO." Frank said that the people representing the NCC, NAACP, and other organizations "wanted to avoid a public split" with SNCC, but that if "we did not accept the idea of a governing board . . . there would probably be [a split]." When Zellner asked Frank for specifics, he replied that if there were to be another summer project, the northern-based group would recruit students for its own program.[3]

In November Curtis Gans, a staff member for the Americans for Democratic Action (ADA), reported on his recent fact-finding tour of the South. The quintessence of American liberalism, the ADA had on its board such important Atlantic City players as Hubert Humphrey, Walter Reuther, Wayne Morse, and Joe Rauh. Gans questioned "the political reliability of a number of people in and around SNCC," including Forman, Ella Baker, and SCEF's Anne Braden, and recommended that the ADA "use whatever influence it has to urge SNCC to abandon the Freedom Democratic orientation of its black belt party as being harmful to the freedom and representation the Negroes seek." The ADA should push hard for voting rights legislation, because "quick granting of voting rights will mean quick recruitment by the Democratic Party, which in turn will mean quick scuttling of the Freedom Democratic parties and SNCC control." At the same time, the ADA should use its considerable influence to "assist in a quiet freeze of funds on these projects which have a Freedom Democratic Party orientation."[4]

In the fall and winter of 1964, then, officials in the NAACP, the NCC, and the ADA were moving to isolate SNCC, COFO, and MFDP and to create a new leadership base in Mississippi. This development came as no surprise to the increasingly embittered Bob Moses: "The liberals getting upset at us was inevitable. We are raising fundamental questions about how the poor sharecropper can achieve the Good Life, questions that liberalism is incapable of answering."[5]

For the young organizers in SNCC, the fall of 1964 was a time of reassessment and uncertainty. At its September executive committee meeting in Atlanta, Jim Forman had unveiled a plan to expand the summer project in 1965 to encompass the entire southern Black Belt. Mississippi would serve as a model, but the emphasis now would be to recruit black volunteers. The "Black Belt Project" was a major item on the October staff meeting agenda, along with the question of the status of more than 100 summer volunteers who wanted to remain and work in Mississippi. By the time the meeting ended it was apparent that SNCC staff members divided sharply over the organization's direction and leadership.[6]

The broad support expressed for the Black Belt Project at the executive committee meeting by such activists as Stokely Carmichael, Ivanhoe Donaldson, and Mendy Samstein ran into a storm of criticism once the SNCC field secretaries began to examine it. Frank Smith, one of the original Mississippi organizers, asked who had made the decision; Lawrence Guyot joined in the attack and then angrily stomped out of the meeting. According to Forman, Guyot's real objection was not procedural but substantive: the MFDP chair was concerned that the Black Belt Project would drain SNCC resources from Mississippi to support programs in other Deep South states. Throughout the debate Moses, who in the September executive committee meeting had actively participated in planning the 1965 project, said nothing. Forman later attributed this silence to Moses' growing concern over Moses' own influence in SNCC. In a 1983 interview with historian Clayborne Carson, however, Moses denied he had once been enthusiastic about the Black Belt Project: "I felt at that time that it was useless to try and go into another student project like we had, because of the problems with the staff. I felt that we just couldn't handle that."[7]

As a result of the staff's rebellion against the leadership—epitomized in Forman—"the Black Belt Summer Project of 1965 was tabled—never again to hit the floor of SNCC for discussion." Forman later maintained that the failure to adopt the proposal was a "crucial defeat," for it left SNCC without a program: "SNCC had reached a high point of power and influence, which had been slowly and painfully built since 1960. The Black Belt Summer Project would have extended the acquisition of power for poor people. But it was tabled, and the clock turned back." Moses, on the other hand, believed SNCC needed some breathing space to recuperate: "I was waiting for SNCC to resolve the basic problems that had surfaced as a result of '64. And I felt that it was worth whatever amount of time it took to resolve them."[8]

What to do with the remaining summer volunteers, most of whom were white northern college students, was the other major question at the October staff meeting. In September the executive committee had recommended that the volunteers become part of a SNCC-supervised "freedom corps" in Mississippi, but now eighty-five of the summer workers had petitioned to become full members of the SNCC staff. Forman has written that he and Ruby Doris Robinson led the opposition to the proposed expansion. Such a move, Forman argued, would change the racial and class composition of SNCC and would endanger security by increasing the possibility that police and FBI infiltrators would be among those put on staff. Furthermore, these young people needed more education in the history and objectives of SNCC before being admitted to the inner circle. When a vote was taken, which was in itself a departure from SNCC's normal procedure of making decisions by consensus, the volunteers were put on staff.

Given the the general debate that would soon begin over the role of whites in the movement, the decision to add so many of them to SNCC staff in the fall of 1964 appears remarkable. Forman argues that class and geographical considerations played a major part in the decision. The staff additions strengthened the ideological position of the northern blacks who were now playing an increasingly articulate and highly visible role in SNCC's deliberations. Among those requesting staff appointments were the black volunteers who had remained to work in the South, most of whom were northern college students. SNCC, Forman concluded, was moving away from its working-class, southern black base. Antagonism toward Forman himself was also an issue: his opposition to adding staff could easily be interpreted as a move to protect his own position of power within the organization. Whatever the combination of factors, the decision to add these newcomers to the staff altered the composition and personality of SNCC, exacerbating the tensions that would plague the organization over the next two years.[9]

The disagreements among SNCC staff members over personnel and program had a direct impact on the movement in Mississippi. Given the uncertainty over SNCC's future commitment to grass-roots organizing in the rural Black Belt, the young Mississippi Freedom Democratic party now began to go its own way, asserting its independence from SNCC, the organization that had created it.

• • •

Three days after the close of the Atlantic City convention, Aaron Henry, who had chaired the FDP delegation, wrote President Lyndon Johnson that "this was the greatest experience in most of our lives. We rejoiced with you and Senator Humphrey in your greatest hour. We hope that we can make some small contribution to insure your success." After expressing regret that the convention had not seated the Mississippi challengers, Henry stated his conviction that "the problems we have here in Mississippi will come nearer being solved by the National Democratic Party than any other unit in America." Henry certainly understated the disappointment of the majority of the FDP delegation, but the executive committee of the Mississippi Freedom Democratic party soon decided to endorse and campaign for the Johnson-Humphrey ticket, arguing that "support for Johnson will help in its fight against the Regular Democratic Party because of the latter's opposition to the candidates and Platform of the national Party" and stating that it "believes, despite Atlantic City, in the ultimate ability of the Democratic Party to meet the challenge of the FDP and eliminate racism from its ranks."[10]

The decision to support the national ticket did not sit well with many SNCC field secretaries. For them, Atlantic City had proven that Democrats could not be trusted, and they were uncomfortable with FDP campaign posters reading "Freedom Means a Vote for Lyndon Baines Johnson–Hubert Humphrey."[11] Although they disagreed with the FDP's endorsement of Johnson, Moses and other staff members were reluctant to impose their will on the new party and its indigenous leadership, for "letting the people decide" had been the cornerstone of SNCC's philosophy. Moreover, support for Lyndon Johnson was but part of another "freedom vote" campaign that featured black candidates running for Congress. FDP's goal, then, was to demonstrate loyalty to the national party while at the same time developing increased political consciousness among black Mississippians.

Spearheading this effort was Lawrence Guyot, who on his release from the Hattiesburg jail had resumed his role as FDP chair. A strong, forceful person whose vocabulary matched his imposing physical stature, Guyot developed both a loyal following and bitter enemies within the movement. His credentials were impressive. The Tougaloo graduate had been in the first wave of SNCC activists to follow Sam Block and Willie Peacock into Greenwood. In 1963 he had been brutally beaten by Winona police, and the following year he had worked with Victoria Gray and other local blacks in organizing Hattiesburg. A person of unsurpassed physical courage, Guyot was also headstrong and combative, traits that better equipped him to confront sheriffs than to deal with the subtleties of movement politics. More so than any other FDP leader, Guyot staked out his (and his organization's) independence from SNCC's Atlanta-based leadership.

The 1964 presidential campaign was bizarre, even by Mississippi standards. Virtually the entire Mississippi Democratic establishment had lined up behind Republican Barry Goldwater. Although most of the state's congressional delegation—fearing for their seniority—stopped short of formally breaking with their party, Governor Paul Johnson openly endorsed the Arizona senator. Goldwater's following among Mississippi segregationists was fanatical. They saw his vote against the 1964 civil rights bill and advocacy of states' rights as evidence that, once elected, the Arizonan would allow white Mississippians to handle their race problems as they had in the past. Among the faithful there was little doubt that the senator would occupy the White House come January. Despite all national polls to the contrary, Bill Simmons released a Citizens' Council "survey" predicting a Goldwater "landslide of major proportions," with an electoral total as high as 405 votes.[12]

So strong was the Goldwater movement in Mississippi that it

took a petition campaign to secure a place on the ballot for the Johnson-Humphrey ticket. That task had fallen to Doug Wynn, chair of the president's state campaign. Studiously avoiding any contact with FDP, the Greenville attorney and a handful of white loyalists attempted to persuade Democrats to stick with their party's candidate. To neutralize the race issue—the only matter of importance in the Mississippi campaign—Wynn reprinted and distributed a pamphlet put together by the Goldwater Committee in the District of Columbia to attract black voters there. The broadside quoted Goldwater on civil rights—"I am unalterably opposed to discrimination on the basis or race color, creed, or any other basis"—and charged that "Lyndon B. Johnson has fought viciously against civil rights and voted against it—39 times out of 50." In the topsy-turvy world of Mississippi politics, white Democratic loyalists hoped that circulating this pamphlet would win votes for Johnson and Humphrey! No doubt sensing that Mississippi was a lost cause—Goldwater would win 87 percent of the Mississippi vote—the president did not campaign in the state. Ladybird Johnson did make a brief appearance on the Gulf Coast as part of a campaign train through the lower South. She was dutifully welcomed there by Senators Eastland and Stennis and by Governor Johnson, who was concerned for the first lady's safety. "The Ku Klux had gotten together and were going to blow up the train," the governor later told an interviewer.[13]

The Freedom Democrats in Mississippi received no recognition or support from the national Johnson-Humphrey headquarters, and though all their campaign literature stressed FDP's allegiance to the national ticket, the primary purpose of the 1964 freedom vote was to promote the congressional candidacies of Fannie Lou Hamer, Aaron Henry, Annie Devine, and Victoria Gray. The four had been denied places on the official state ballot, and the freedom vote was to lay the basis for an FDP challenge of the Mississippi delegation when Congress convened in January.[14]

As it had during the 1963 freedom vote, COFO again provided the organizational support for the election campaign, this time with a larger staff covering more areas in the state. In the fall of 1964 SNCC reported ninety-eight paid fieldworkers in more than thirty projects, augmented by 104 "freedom corps" volunteers, most of whom were white students remaining to work in the state after the summer project. Operating out of the fourth congressional district, the twelve full-time CORE workers were reinforced by twenty new staff members who were paid a subsistence wage by the national CORE office.[15] In late October nearly 100 short-term volunteers, most of whom were white college students, came to Mississippi to help get out the vote. Despite the increased number of workers, however, only about 60,000 ballots were cast in the 1964 freedom vote, down by more than 25 percent from the total amassed by the Henry-King ticket a year earlier. Part of the reason for this decline lay in the intensified white resistance to black political participation, even in an election with no official sanction.[16]

As there had been in 1963, there were the usual harassment arrests of workers canvassing for the freedom vote. Among the charges were distributing leaflets without a permit, reckless driving, trespassing, and criminal syndicalism. But the fall of 1964 was marked by an even greater level of violence. On Sunday, October 4, a dynamite explosion "largely destroyed" the residence housing the Vicksburg COFO office, library, and freedom school. Mrs. Bessie Brown and her family of seven children, who lived on the first floor, miraculously escaped serious injury. Movement workers had considered Vicksburg one of the safer projects. In Holmes County night riders fired into the home of FDP delegate Hartman Turnbow, and in Jackson they bombed the offices of Hazel Brannon Smith's *Northside Reporter* and the home of NAACP leader I. S. Sanders.[17] The most concentrated attacks occurred in Sunflower County.

Under the leadership of SNCC field secretary John Harris, COFO had expanded from its Ruleville base into Indianola and the town of Sunflower. During the summer of 1964 the Indianola Citizens League and the Sunflower County Citizens League had formed to carry on voter registration activities, and in a five-month period approximately 400 local blacks had attempted to register; only ten succeeded. Among those recruited by SNCC in the Indianola area was Mrs. Annie Mae King, age sixty, who lost her job as a cook at a white school after attempting to register in mid-September. She then became active in COFO and took movement workers into her home. "I fed the civil rights boys when they came in," she later recalled. "I slept them; gave them a place to stay." On October 28 a tear-gas bomb hurled through her window injured a fourteen-year-old boy working with COFO. The previous day the building housing the Indianola freedom school had burned, and on October 29 club-swinging police broke up a rally attended by some 230 people at the freedom school site. Despite these efforts to destroy the fledgling Indianola movement, local blacks refused to be intimidated and cast more freedom votes in November than the city total in the official balloting.[18]

While community organizing intensified in some areas, movement activity as a whole declined throughout the fall of 1964. The FDP's Guyot saw this period as one of missed opportunities: "That was a crucial time. We had jolted the country. The state of Mississippi was on the defensive." Instead of maintaining the pressure, what resulted was "utter chaos. . . . for three months there was nothing but anger [and] frustration." The organizers "were completely disillusioned, completely alienated," Guyot recalled. "They would have been better absent than in Mississippi."[19] While he may have overstated the problem, the summer project and Atlantic City had taken their toll in Mississippi. The COFO project in Holmes County exemplified the postsummer malaise. A September 13 report filed from Holmes noted that "illness, police harassment, staff migration . . . and the cotton harvest have disrupted the local project. . . . To compound our problems, local community leaders have been in disagreement over a number of issues, thus straining our relations with the local community." Nor had the situation changed much in Holmes by late November: "Meetings are poorly attended. There is a lack of purpose. . . . There has been little registration since summer. . . . The budget is insufficient. SNCC has not been paying much of the time."[20]

The difficulties related directly to changes in personnel. A number of organizers who had worked in Mississippi for nearly three years now decided to take time out to resume their formal studies. Hollis Watkins, MacArthur Cotton, Euvester Simpson, Emma Bell, Gwen Gillon, and George Greene enrolled at Tougaloo under SNCC's work-study program, while Sam Block spent the fall semester at Marlboro College in Vermont. Veteran Mississippi activists did remain full-time in the field, including Charles McLaurin and Fannie Lou Hamer in Sunflower County, Dorie Ladner and Jesse Harris in southwest Mississippi, Annie Devine in Canton, and Victoria Gray in Hattiesburg. Prominent among the project directors were former Howard University students Stokely Carmichael, Cleveland Sellers, Muriel Tillinghast, and Ed Brown. Given the reduced activities of the Mississippi activists who had returned to school, the increased visibility of the Howard group, and the addition of more than 100 white volunteers, many of them stationed in newer projects, strong movement leadership was essential. In the fall of 1964, however, the two most important figures in the COFO coalition, Bob Moses and Dave Dennis, began their withdrawal from Mississippi.[21]

Unlike the other civil rights organizations, SNCC had consciously avoided projecting anyone into the role of "leader," yet in Mississippi Bob Moses had become the first among equals, a role with which he grew increasingly uncomfortable. Although he had attempted to keep a low profile, Moses was the person others turned to in times of indecision or controversy. It was he who had overcome the opposition of the Mississippi SNCC staff and turned the tide in favor of the 1964 summer project. His quiet yet charismatic personality had attracted a devoted following, particularly among local blacks and northern white activists. The summer volunteers were awed by him. But the summer project had exhausted Moses, and the FDP defeat at Atlantic City had left him embittered and thoroughly disillusioned with the nation's liberal white leadership. For Moses and an increasing number of veteran activists, the goals of racial integration and mainstream political participation were now neither feasible nor desirable. In the months after Atlantic City he began to articulate a nationalistic program based on the concept of "parallel institutions."

The success of the freedom schools and the organization of the Mississippi Freedom Democratic party, together with the intransigence of the white South and the paternalism of northern liberals, led Moses to conclude that blacks needed to move independently to take charge of their destiny. He shared his thoughts at a SNCC-sponsored meeting in California in the fall of 1964. After rehearsing the events of the summer—the Neshoba lynchings, the failure of local and federal officials to curb the Ku Klux Klan, the "compromise" at Atlantic City—Moses went on to envision a society where blacks would develop alternative organizations and institutions responsible to their own communities: "We have to ask ourselves what is the government? Who sets it up? The people set it up. . . . Why can't we set up our own government? So that in 1967, if we get organized enough between now and then, we can set up our own government and declare the other one no good. And say the federal government should recognize us." Moses also suggested expansion of the concept and scope of the freedom schools:

"Now, why can't we set up our own schools? . . . Because when you come right down to it, why integrate their schools? What is it that you will learn in their schools? Many of the Negroes can learn it, but what can they do with it? What they really need to learn is how to be organized to work on the society to change it."[22]

While Moses was talking about the need for black people to organize outside the system, MFDP was out campaigning for the man who personified it, Lyndon B. Johnson, and laying the groundwork for the congressional challenge. Along with a number of SNCC veterans, Moses was uncomfortable with the course now being charted by FDP: "Basically they were following the national programs, programs geared at a national level—the Congressional Challenge. My feeling was that they needed, we needed to retrench and let the party [FDP] . . . do basic organizing in the state . . . begin at the local level in electing people, building the party like that." But he knew that "there was no way to take that disagreement to the people without clashing with Guyot at that point," and Moses would not bring on that confrontation: "I felt that the other principle was more important, the principle about leadership and of the people who are at the local level moving and assuming leadership roles. So there was no way to do that." In the fall of 1964 Moses began to spend more time outside the state and was no longer involved in the day-to-day operations of the movement he had helped build. In 1965 he changed his name to Parris (his mother's family name), left the South, and eventually moved with his family to Tanzania, where he taught for seven years before returning to the United States in 1976.[23]

For CORE's Dave Dennis, the deaths of Chaney, Schwerner, and Goodman, followed by the debacle at Atlantic City, had left him cynical and bitter, and he began to question both the tactics and the costs of the southern freedom movement. "The thing that hurts more than anything," he said in a 1983 interview, "is the question you can't answer: whether or not it was worth it for the gains that you got at the time."

> We had told a lot of people to put down their guns and not be violent in Mississippi, and I wasn't so sure that the nonviolent approach was the right approach anymore. And I had to do a lot of soul searching about that. I guess I made the decision prior to that that it was not, but I did not make any

decisions about what to do about it. And the next step was, what was my role to be in Mississippi? It looked to me as if there was a need for something else, but whether I was the person to try to develop that, I just didn't know. There was total confusion. . . . You get to a certain point and then people say "Where do we go from here?" I just didn't have answers. . . . I guess I never did get back on the track after that in terms of participating in the movement.[24]

Like Moses, Dennis drifted in and out of Mississippi in the fall of 1964. Early in 1965 he moved back to New Orleans to work with CORE there, but "none of the CORE stuff made any sense." Dennis ended up in law school and later opened an office in Lafayette, Louisiana.[25]

The disillusionment expressed in different ways by Dennis and Moses and shared by many movement veterans was part of a larger phenomenon that psychiatrist Robert Coles identified as "battle fatigue." Coles, who had worked in Mississippi during the 1964 summer, wrote that "in many ways these young civil rights workers are in a war and exposed to the stresses of warfare." Movement leaders were "generals worried about 'war neuroses' in their front-line troops."

Briefly the symptoms reveal fear, anxiety, and anger no longer "controlled" or "managed." Depressions occur, characterized by loss of hope for victory, loss of a sense of purpose, and acceptance of the power of the enemy where before such power was challenged with apparent fearlessness. The youth affected may take to heavy drinking or become silent, sulky, and uncooperative. Frequently one sees real gloom, loss of appetite, withdrawal from social contacts as well as from useful daily work in the movement.

Coles concluded that "in such cases the non-violent movement itself may be attacked instead of the segregated society formerly felt to be the enemy."[26]

Throughout the fall and winter of 1964 exhausted SNCC and CORE organizers had to contend with declining morale within their projects, problems exacerbated by the presence of the relatively inexperienced white volunteers. Full of enthusiasm and ideas, these young men and women at times became confident to the point of arrogance. In such an atmosphere black-white tensions, which had flared in some projects during the summer, now exploded. Volunteers who had submitted to organizational discipline now demanded to be treated as equals and often chafed at what they perceived to be authoritarian conduct by black project directors. At times the race question remained beneath the surface. At a fifth district meeting in Hattiesburg, the Reverend Harry Bowie concluded that "there is really a black-white problem here which you don't say but which is at the bottom of a lot of what you are saying. Why don't you deal with your black-white problems? Here you are in the middle of Mississippi and if as much bitterness could be directed at the white man out there as has been at each other . . . things would really be moving here."[27]

Across the state the debates over tactics, strategy, involvement of local people, and the chain of command all came down to a matter of black and white. The CORE project in Canton was a case in point. Led by project director George Raymond, CORE had worked effectively in the fourth district after Atlantic City. Freedom school classes still met; the Canton community center boasted "one of the best libraries in the state"; voter registration efforts continued; and FDP was "pushed a great deal" due to Annie Devine's campaign for Congress. Throughout the fall Raymond had put in long days working both in Canton and in neighboring Rankin County.[28] Inside the project, however, white staff members and volunteers had begun to criticize Raymond, charging that he made decisions arbitrarily and would not listen to advice.

The issue came to a head at a staff meeting in early December, when Raymond suggested that whites in the project should take a six-week leave of absence and go north to raise money. Denying that he meant "white boy go home," Raymond argued that the increased full-time staff had "turned this into our movement, not the people's" and that he wanted to "get local people to take over again." For the next month Raymond became the center of attack from white project workers, led by Tom Ramsay, a volunteer in charge of "Federal Programs." When during a heated exchange Ramsay said, "Nobody tells me what to do and I don't tell people what to do," Raymond replied, "I'm sorry, Tom, you'll have to leave the project." At this, Ramsay shot back, "You're a dictator, a little Caesar; you're everything I'm in the movement to be against. I'm in the movement to get guys like you out." Whites at the meeting supported Ramsay.[29]

Annie Devine defended the veteran black activist: "Nobody in here has had George Raymond's experience," she stated. "This kind of talk goes on and on. Somebody like George has to finally make decisions about how to get some work done. Otherwise all people do is sit around and cry about their personal problems. . . . My objection to Tom is that he tried to run the show." "You all soon will be gone," she predicted. "Unless you forget yourself and relate to the people, you'll go away without doing anything." Whites at the meeting then criticized Mrs. Devine, at times condescendingly: "If you're speaking to my point speak to it," one white staff member icily replied. "If you don't understand it ask me to repeat it."[30]

Ramsay left the project, along with several other whites, but in late January the fourth district's new project director, a dedicated and sensitive white activist named Richard Jewett, reported to CORE's New York office that the Madison County staff "is still beset with internal difficulties—the tendency has been strong to turn in on themselves rather than to involve themselves in the community and to absorb community problems. A start of a change is evident, but it will take time to see results."[31]

Race was also a factor in the breakdown of COFO's central headquarters in Jackson. Beginning with the summer project, the Jackson office had served as the nerve center of the Mississippi movement, allocating funds to the individual projects, alerting the FBI and the press when COFO workers were in jeopardy, handling the stream of applications from white northern students, and in general coordinating all COFO programs. But by the fall, the office was in disarray. Letters went unanswered, relations with the media deteriorated, and money needed by the projects was often not forthcoming. Holly Springs project director Cleveland Sellers threatened to shut down his operation in December unless Jackson responded with financial support. The manager of the Jackson office was Jesse Morris, a black activist from California who had moved to Mississippi in 1963. Morris had taken the job temporarily and reluctantly because nobody else wanted it. Many Jackson staff members were white women volunteers who handled correspondence and operated the WATS line. Although office workers were the movement's second-class citizens, the centralization of state operations had made their jobs more important. A breakdown in communications from Jackson could literally be a life-or-death matter. Thus, the problems in the COFO office in Jackson directly affected every project in the state.[32]

White SNCC worker Hunter Morey, who had coordinated COFO's legal assistance program during the summer, bluntly and somewhat hysterically laid out his assessment of the problem in a December 3 memorandum:

> The state headquarters in Jackson is almost completely disfunctionally [*sic*]. . . . Staff and volunteer discipline has broken down so far that the state headquarters has had several race riots, white workers are often subject to severe racial abuse and even violence from Negro workers . . . cash, checks, clothes, and supplies have been stolen totalling several thousands of dollars, Negro workers are frequently played-up-to and looked-down-on by white workers, juvenile delinquency sometimes appears to have taken over certain offices, Bob Moses has retained the position of Project Director while taking no part in key day to day decisions in areas such as personnel, distribution of resources, etc., and the staff has allowed all this to develop, contributing to the problem by the relatively high number of drunks and goof-offs all over the state.[33]

Although perhaps exaggerated, Morey's description of office conditions was not far off the mark. Jackson staff member Charlie Horwitz observed that "there's a small-scale siege in the office every day." Things got so bad that Jesse Morris shut down the COFO headquarters for a week.[34]

CORE's Matt Suarez, who was brought in as a troubleshooter, concluded that the difficulties centered on the tensions between the white female office staff and the local black teenage males who hung around the office seeking financial and sexual favors. He believed that the women, in trying to relate to the youths, to "be a big sister," sent out the wrong signals: "the young cats figured she's just somebody to hit on." When the women resisted these overtures, the youths responded with thefts and violence. Suarez advised the women to avoid their antagonists and if harassment continued to turn the matter over to the black man in charge. The problem was that no one in the office wanted this responsibility.[35] Thus, although they may not have handled the situation well, the fact remained that these women were subjected to intimidation and abuse that earlier in the year would not have been tolerated on any project. The situation improved only after Muriel Tillinghast, the no-nonsense former Howard student, agreed to leave her position as project director in Greenville to take over as state office manager. By the end of the year COFO headquarters in Jackson had returned to its normal state of controlled chaos. Still, although a number of the white summer volunteers, such as Marshall Ganz, now organizing with Steptoe in Amite County, continued to do important work, resentment against the presence of white northerners in Mississippi did not abate.[36]

SNCC discussed the black-white question, along with other controversial issues, at a week-long retreat held in early November 1964 at the Gulfside Methodist Church in Waveland, on the Mississippi coast. Its purpose was to discuss SNCC's goals, programs, and structure. Most Mississippi SNCC people were present, at least for part of the retreat, and SNCC's relationship to COFO and MFDP did receive some attention. Most of the workshops centered on broader questions, however, such as the relationship of SNCC staff to local people and the problems in communication that resulted when college-educated activists dominated community meetings. Much discussion focused on SNCC's organizational structure. One faction, identifying with the views of Moses, believed that SNCC should remain a small cadre of organizers working independently to create autonomous local movements. Forman and an increasing number of "hard-liners" argued that to survive SNCC would have to become a strong, centralized body that emphasized planning and staff discipline. There was no immediate resolution to this question, which preoccupied SNCC in the months ahead. And at Waveland SNCC veteran Mary King, with assistance from Casey Hayden, anonymously submitted a position paper on the role of women in SNCC.[37]

The King-Hayden statement directly confronted the issue of sex discrimination within the organization, claiming that "women who are competent, qualified, and experienced are automatically assigned to the 'female' kinds of jobs such as typing, desk work, telephone work, filing. . . . Women are the crucial factor that keeps the movement running on a day-to-day basis. Yet they are not given equal say-so when it comes to day to day decision-making."[38]

SNCC men at Waveland did not take the paper seriously, and

most black women there did not identify with it. In Mississippi black women like Cynthia Washington, Dorie Ladner, and Muriel Tillinghast were project directors, and three women were preparing to contest the congressional seats held by white men. Black women in SNCC were more influential than were white women or white men. King later claimed that authors like Sara Evans had oversimplified the meaning of the protest, reducing it to the argument that women were second-class citizens in SNCC. "Our status in the movement was never the issue," wrote King. "This distorted characterization represents an imposition of a later feminist construction on a period of ferment. . . . Casey and I were not inquiring about our roles but about whether there would be room in the civil rights movement for differing social and political concerns, as various groups and, in our case, women defined them."[39]

At Waveland the overriding issue was race, not gender. King and Hayden were well aware of the intensifying discussion of their position as *whites* in the movement, an issue that, when finally resolved two years later, resulted in the exclusion of all whites from SNCC. Male chauvinism was a reality in SNCC, and the two women raised this legitimate issue because the Waveland meeting was called to allow SNCC people to voice whatever concerns they might have. For most SNCC activists, however, exhausted, disillusioned, and uncertain about their future course, the "new" question of sexual discrimination did not seem terribly important.

Despite the problems concerning SNCC's identity and future, the turmoil in the state COFO office, and the constantly changing movement personnel, all Mississippi projects reported some civil rights activity during the fall of 1964. The freedom schools still met in many communities, although at a reduced level because the regular school term was now in session. Capitalizing on the political consciousness developed over the summer, COFO started chapters of a new organization of high school students, the Mississippi Student Union. These students were now eager to take on school administrators over issues ranging from curriculum to student freedom. In Philadelphia forty-five high school students were suspended for wearing "Freedom" buttons and refusing to remove them when ordered, and in Holmes County a Lexington principal expelled two students for singing freedom songs during lunch. Students continued earlier efforts to desegregate public facilities, as there was statewide noncompliance with the 1964 Civil Rights Act. Sunflower

County teenagers attempting to desegregate the Indianola Public Library were allowed to fill out library cards but were then turned away. Police arrested them for trespassing when they sought service in a local restaurant. In Ruleville whites shot at a group of young people who had been denied service at a local cafe. Young blacks in particular were eager to confront the establishment over the issue of compliance with the civil rights law.[40]

The vote remained a COFO priority. Although many SNCC and CORE workers had little enthusiasm for the freedom vote campaign, tied in as it was with support for the Johnson-Humphrey ticket, most projects still retained a commitment to voter registration. Several communities held Freedom Days. In Meridian Mrs. Fannie Lee Chaney, mother of James Chaney, led a procession of blacks to the county courthouse. Blacks still faced the usual registration difficulties: complicated forms administered by dishonest registrars, with harassment and economic retaliation awaiting those brave enough to attempt to get their names on the voting books. Seventeen people attempting to register in Philadelphia were met by a crowd of whites wielding clubs and pistols. Sheriff Rainey was on the scene, and though there was no violence, Rainey and his officers harassed the applicants as they stood waiting their turn to register.[41]

There was, however, one election in Mississippi that required no registration, literacy test, or poll tax. Each year the Agricultural Stabilization and Conservation Service (ASCS) of the U.S. Department of Agriculture held elections in farm areas to select county committees whose major function was to allot acreage for crops. In Mississippi this meant cotton. Designed to control production of basic commodities and thus stabilize prices, the program operated under a complicated formula wherein the Department of Agriculture set the basic allotment for each farmer, while the county ASCS committees could provide additional acreage to individual farmers. The ASCS program in Mississippi had always been run by whites, and black farmers received disproportionately smaller acreage allotments. In the 1964 ASCS county committee elections, set for December 3, COFO decided to run candidates in twelve heavily black rural counties.[42]

Movement activists faced many problems from the outset. Although any farm owner, renter, or sharecropper could vote, few black farmers were familiar with the complicated election procedure. A county was divided into "communities" of from 200 to 300 farmers. Each community elected a committee of five, with the top three vote-getters serving as delegates to the county convention, which in turn elected the county committee. Practically speaking, blacks would have to win a majority of community elections in order to have any representation on a county committee. Since few if any blacks had ever participated, COFO launched an intensive campaign in the weeks following the freedom vote to educate farmers about the election process and to convince them that it was worth the risks to go to the polls or, in some counties, to mail in the ballots. COFO worked frantically during November to turn out a large vote, for in most of the twelve selected counties black farmers, renters, and sharecroppers were in the majority.[43]

Yet the ASCS vote followed the same pattern as general elections. COFO poll watchers were thrown out of polling places, and officials harassed black farmers who came to cast their ballots. Whites with questionable farming credentials were permitted to vote. Among the Panola County voters were three nurses from the Batesville hospital who insisted that their mothers had left them some land. Election officials took their word. The situation was worst in Madison County, where police arrested four CORE staff members, including George Raymond, who along with organizer Eartiss Crawford was beaten. Two white men then attacked Marvin Rich outside a polling place and broke his nose. The national CORE official had come down from New York to observe democracy at work in Mississippi.[44]

When the ballots were counted, five blacks had led the tickets in their communities, but blacks failed to win a majority of the community elections in any county. Thus, there was no chance for black farmers to win election to any ASCS county committee. COFO reported election abuses to the Department of Agriculture, and Secretary Orville Freeman eventually ruled that new elections should be held in several communities; but even if blacks were to win these contests, the makeup of the county ASCS committees would not change. Black farmers decided to boycott these new elections, claiming that the abuses were countywide and thus the Department of Agriculture's action was meaningless. Otha Williams, president of the Madison County Farmers' League, which had worked closely with COFO in the December elections, now called on black farmers to tear up their ballots: "We are tired of tokenism and half-way

measures. So we are asking you to join us in boycotting the elections. When you get your ballot, throw it away! Don't vote!"[45]

Still, organizers who had worked on the ASCS elections believed
the experience worthwhile. The vote had been a means of reaching
new people with a program important to the farmers, who in many
areas turned out in unexpectedly large numbers. Despite fraud, intimidation at the polls, and disappointing results, both the farmers
and movement activists looked forward to the next election. Starting from scratch, they had waged an impressive campaign. At a time
when the Mississippi movement appeared to be losing touch with
its constituency, the ASCS elections proved that local people would
still respond, given a practical reason to do so.

• • •

The fall of 1964 had witnessed a change in the Mississippi movement, with veteran organizers moving on to other arenas and new
civil rights–related agencies coming into the state. After Atlantic City
COFO took steps to institutionalize the medical and legal services
made available during the summer project. The Medical Committee for Human Rights (MCHR), a group of New York physicians
organized in June 1964 to provide health care for the volunteers,
continued to be active after the summer and now planned to establish "an efficient public health program in Mississippi" that
would include immunization services, child care, and family planning for the state's black poor. Dr. Alvin Poussaint was one of the
MCHR's national organizers, and Dr. Robert Smith of Jackson
played a major role in establishing its presence in Mississippi. From
its inception MCHR worked closely with COFO and took on a
political role was well, as when it later endorsed the congressional
challenge of MFDP.[46]

As noted, during the summer project movement workers had received legal assistance from a bevy of lawyers representing a wide
spectrum of political interests, from the NAACP's Legal Defense
Fund (Inc. Fund) to the radical National Lawyers' Guild. To coordinate these independent efforts, COFO established a legal department with Hunter Morey as coordinator and Henry Aronson, a
northern white attorney, as full-time staff counsel. In the fall COFO
also set up a legal advisory committee with representatives from
the Lawyers' Constitutional Defense Committee (LCDC), the Inc.

Fund, and the Lawyers' Guild. The Lawyers' Committee for Civil Rights under Law opened an office in Jackson in 1965.[47]

COFO accepted legal assistance from "all who offer it under our policy," an arrangement unsatisfactory to the NAACP, which still strongly objected to COFO's reliance on guild lawyers Arthur Kinoy and Ben Smith. Inc. Fund attorney Marian Wright joined the advisory committee only after making it clear that she would not accept any directives from that committee. Early in 1965 staff counsel Aronson resigned after a dispute with guild attorneys on the committee, and COFO's financial and political problems made it impossible to replace him. Even with all of the political infighting, the movement legal force in Mississippi was impressive. By the middle of 1965 four national civil rights legal organizations had full-time staffs working out of Jackson, more than in any other southern state.[48]

The summer project gave birth to another organization, the Delta Ministry, which over the years would play an increasingly important role in the movement. The National Council of Churches had sponsored the Oxford training session for the volunteers, sent scores of clergymen into the state during the summer, and invited the Lawyers' Committee to provide legal defense when these ministers were arrested for civil rights activities. That fall the NCC's Commission on Religion and Race announced that a permanent office would open in Greenville for a long-term program of community development in the Delta. The Reverend Art Thomas, who had worked in Mississippi during the summer, was the first director. Although centered in the Delta region, the Delta Ministry immediately opened offices in Hattiesburg, headed by a white minister, Robert Beech, and in McComb, under the leadership of the Reverend Harry Bowie.

COFO leaders at first viewed the Delta Ministry with suspicion, if not hostility. The NCC, which was known for its middle-of-the-road position on the question of black activism, had called the New York meeting in September that attempted to limit SNCC's influence in Mississippi. Now, under white leadership and with a healthy bankroll, the NCC was hanging out its shingle in Greenville, determined to play a role in the civil rights struggle in Mississippi. In the months and years to come the Delta Ministry remained controversial, both in Mississippi and with its parent body, the NCC. Yet it also filled a void when other movement organizations pulled out of the state, providing community organizers, financial assistance, and logistical support to those waging the war on poverty in Mississippi and to the Freedom Democratic party.[49]

At the end of 1964 the Mississippi Freedom Democratic party was still struggling to establish an identity apart from that of COFO and SNCC. Within the Mississippi movement there was disagreement over whether FDP should become an independent political party advancing a black agenda or work to displace the white segregationist Democrats and win recognition from the national party. The congressional challenge would provide answers to some of these questions and establish the Freedom Democratic party as an independent force within the movement, the successor to both COFO and SNCC.

15

The Collapse of
the COFO Coalition

Although the "congressional challenge" had originated in COFO discussions in the spring of 1964, the idea itself was not new. Back in 1956, J. Francis Polhaus, an NAACP attorney, had proposed the same course of action in an eighteen-page document entitled "Memorandum on the Possibility of Unseating the Mississippi Congressional Delegation." In early December 1964 attorneys for the Mississippi Freedom Democratic party filed a notice of contest, asserting that the House should not seat the five white men who composed the Mississippi congressional delegation because blacks had been "systematically and deliberately excluded from the electoral process." The brief also contended that Annie Devine, Victoria Gray, and Fannie Lou Hamer, three FDP congressional candidates who ran in the freedom vote election after being denied a place on the official ballot, were entitled to the seats in their respective districts.[1]

For the next ten months most FDP resources were directed toward the challenge. The Freedom Democrats opened a Washington office, headed by SNCC's Michael Thelwell, who organized a nationwide lobbying effort. The three most militant movement organizations—SNCC, CORE, and SCLC—endorsed the challenge, including the seating of the three women. Both Martin Luther King, Jr., and James Farmer held press conferences in December to demonstrate their personal support.[2] As the opening day of Congress drew near, however, it became apparent that although the national civil rights coalition agreed that the House should vacate the Mississippi seats, it was divided over whether the three challengers were entitled to fill them.

The Americans for Democratic Action was the first group to express misgivings. In late December the ADA's national executive committee stated that "the contention that Mrs. Hamer, Devine, and Gray should be seated in Congress is without legal support and has dangerous implications. They were not elected in any regularly-constituted state election." The ADA, then, would "support the challenge to the Mississippi congressmen *unconnected* with the effort to seat the three ladies." The national office of the NAACP conceded that although "it would be a good thing to get rid of the Mississippi Congressmen . . . the NAACP does not endorse the method proposed by the MFDP." In a January 1 editorial the *New York Times* stated that the House "can and should refuse to seat the five Mississippi Representatives pending a full investigation by one of its own committees" but rejected the claim of the three FDP candidates as "a preposterous gesture." Faced with this criticism, FDP backed away from its position. Although it never formally withdrew the claim that the three women were entitled to the seats, in a later brief FDP conceded that "the most appropriate form of relief . . . would be the vacating of the [seats] and the ordering of new Congressional elections."[3]

The Freedom Democrats' decision not to press for the seating of its candidates made sense. As the ADA and NAACP had pointed out, that part of the challenge rested on shaky constitutional grounds, at best. More important were the political realities: had FDP stuck by its position that candidates Devine, Gray, and Hamer were entitled to represent their districts, there would have been little congressional support, and the challenge would never have gotten off the ground.

At noon on January 4, 1965, members of the U.S. House of Representatives assembled for the opening ceremony of the 1965 session. Also on hand at the Capitol were more than 600 black Mississippians, who were there to lobby against the seating of the Mississippi delegation. When Speaker of the House John McCormack gaveled the session to order, Congressman William Fitts Ryan of New York rose to object to the seating of the Mississippians. After a debate, the House passed a resolution to administer the oath of office to the delegation, but 149 representatives—more than one-third of the House membership—voted to bar their colleagues from the Magnolia State. Moreover, the resolution stated that the challengers had the right to pursue their case further "under the laws governing contested elections."[4]

The following evening President Lyndon B. Johnson delivered his State of the Union address outlining his plans for the "Great Society," setting in motion the most significant burst of domestic reform legislation since the New Deal. Johnson expected his program to encounter stiff opposition from southerners in Congress, particularly over those measures that addressed the needs of African Americans. The president did not, however, want a Dixie rebellion on Capitol Hill, a distinct possibility if the Mississippi congressmen were told to pack their bags and go home. Thus, from the outset of the challenge Johnson made it clear to House leaders that he opposed it. According to columnist Drew Pearson, shortly before Congressman Ryan introduced the motion to unseat the Mississippi delegation, House majority leader Carl Albert told Ryan that "the full weight of the Johnson Administration leadership would be thrown against him in favor of the [white] Mississippians." Johnson did not appear outwardly vindictive. He had invited ten members of the FDP Atlantic City delegation, including Devine, Gray, and Hamer, to his inauguration, and they attended. Nonetheless, the Freedom Democratic party had crossed him twice, first refusing his two-seat compromise at Atlantic City and now jeopardizing his Great Society agenda by challenging the Mississippi delegation. Lyndon Johnson was not one to take such insults lightly.[5]

The president's opposition came as no surprise to the Freedom Democrats, who now went back to Mississippi to prepare their case. The statute on contested elections authorized challengers to take depositions for forty days. Drawing on the network of the National Lawyers' Guild, FDP recruited more than 150 attorneys to come to Mississippi at their own expense. Throughout February and March they fanned out across the state, recording the now-familiar stories of the black women and men who had faced economic reprisal and violence in their unsuccessful efforts to register and vote. The lawyers also deposed white registrars and public officials, who testified that no barriers existed to black voting. Former governor Ross Barnett said that he did not know of a "single Negro who has been discriminated against," adding that some blacks received "better treatment than whites." (Deposing white officials had a positive impact on organizational efforts in small counties like Amite, where blacks were emboldened by the spectacle of powerful segregationists being forced to account for their behavior.)[6]

Upset by the invasion of the lawyers and the attendant negative publicity, Mississippi officials engaged in red-baiting to shift attention away from the charges of voter discrimination. Prentiss Walker, one of the five challenged congressmen, charged that "this deposition caravan . . . is staffed with either known communists or those affiliated with communist front organizations." Senator Eastland singled out guild attorney Morton Stavis for abuse, concluding that the congressional challenge was "a Communist-planned attempt to influence the Congress of the United States." Although harassed and threatened, the attorneys compiled 600 depositions—3,000 single-spaced pages of testimony—which they submitted to the House as evidence that the 1964 congressional elections were unconstitutional. FDP leaders hoped that the House would hold public hearings quickly and then bring the challenge to the floor for debate. They were to be disappointed, for procedural delays put off consideration of the challenge until September.[7] Still, the Freedom Democrats had once again brought Mississippi into the national spotlight, establishing their party as a force Washington had to reckon with.

Back home, however, serious internal problems threatened the future of the civil rights coalition. On January 6, two days after the first House vote on the challenge, NAACP head Roy Wilkins publicly charged that "Chinese communist elements" had infiltrated SNCC. The timing was not coincidental. The national office of the NAACP had been hostile to SNCC since its inception, resenting its predominant position in Mississippi and refusing to join the COFO coalition.[8] On November 5, 1964, Gloster Current had written a memorandum to Wilkins presenting a grim picture of the NAACP's relative decline in Mississippi. Current believed that the NAACP had "lost considerable ground" to COFO, which "has grown stronger. . . . We possibly have lost many of our younger persons to COFO." Current posed the question, "Can the NAACP [in Mississippi] survive by working within the COFO framework?" and answered, "I believe not." He recommended that the state NAACP withdraw from COFO and pursue its own program in Mississippi. Two days later Current repeated his concern at the meeting of the Mississippi state NAACP conference, whose executive board recommended that the national board of directors "take appropriate action to sever NAACP relationships with the COFO movement." Surprisingly, the national board delayed its formal approval of the state NAACP's request.[9]

Although there was opposition to the move within the state NAACP, the Wilkins-Current position on COFO had support among "old-guard" Mississippi leaders. Their most common criticism was that after they had welcomed COFO workers into their communities and homes, these activists began to undermine the NAACP, persuading younger blacks that the older leaders were "Uncle Toms" who could not be trusted. NAACP stalwarts C. C. Bryant, Vera Pigee, Felix Dunn, and B. E. Murph, representing NAACP branches in all parts of the state, wrote letters endorsing the break with COFO and recounting in detail how their overtures of friendship and cooperation toward COFO workers had met with betrayal. Although political considerations were doubtless a factor, the traditional leaders were echoing complaints that had surfaced in communities during the summer project and intensified throughout the fall.[10]

Local people who had worked closely with COFO were angry and hurt by the state NAACP's call for withdrawal. At a statewide COFO convention held in Jackson on March 7, they pressed Aaron Henry, who had remained as COFO president, for an explanation of the NAACP's action. Henry responded that the NAACP was excluded from the planning of COFO projects and contacted "only after people were in jail." He also mentioned reports that the COFO workers' casual dress and life-style had offended local leaders. Fannie Lou Hamer defended decision making on the local level and pointedly rejected the charge that the COFO workers were unkempt: "How much have the people with the suits done? If they, dressed up, had been there, then the kids in jeans wouldn't be here." Other activists attacked the NAACP, while NAACP loyalists reiterated the charges against COFO. The general mood of the meeting, however, was that COFO embodied the hopes of the Mississippi black community and must be saved. Hartman Turnbow spoke for the majority when he observed that "we have many parts, like a body, and it takes all of them to reach our goal. We shouldn't split up."[11]

NAACP leaders were determined to go their own way. The state NAACP board was scheduled to meet at 2:00 that afternoon in the same room, but because the COFO session had run over its allotted time the NAACP moved its meeting upstairs. Current later reported that "we commandeered the Universal Insurance office and had to bring chairs upstairs because I did not want eavesdroppers from COFO in our meeting; and we had strict screening of the NAACP representatives to determine if all of them were in fact representatives of our group." Henry excused himself from the COFO meeting to chair the NAACP gathering. There the assembled representatives discussed plans for a 1965 NAACP summer project in Mississippi totally separate from any activity sponsored by COFO or MFDP.[12] The state NAACP's decision to withdraw from the coalition was not fatal, but it accelerated COFO's decline, coming as it did at a time when movement leaders themselves were questioning COFO's relevance now that the Mississippi Freedom Democratic party was emerging as the major voice of the movement in the state.

At its executive committee meeting in Atlanta in early March, SNCC reassessed the role of COFO in the light of the NAACP defection and the emergence of FDP. Jim Forman, who had never been happy with COFO, said that "there is confusion in my mind about what COFO is." He suggested that COFO should be a convention organization, holding statewide meetings to discuss common concerns and leaving FDP to develop and implement political programs. A month later, when the executive committee met at Holly Springs, Forman called attention to "a very serious problem of leadership of [COFO] project directors, poor morale, and no programs." Muriel Tillinghast agreed, noting that "when Moses left, there was a vacuum. People used to be able to go to him about their problems; now they have no one." She later observed that "the staff of Mississippi is tired. They just don't have the energy to start over knocking on doors." From these discussions a consensus emerged that COFO had outlived its usefulness and that for the coming summer SNCC should devote its resources to assisting the Mississippi Freedom Democratic party. The recommendation to abolish COFO was ratified at a statewide meeting of Mississippi activists held at Tougaloo in late July. Local COFO projects were to turn over all resources and contacts to the FDP executive committee in each county, and those workers whose primary identification had been with COFO were invited to become part of the FDP organizational structure.[13]

Although it was perhaps inevitable, the decision to abolish COFO was shortsighted, for COFO had been the one civil rights group representing the interests of virtually all black Mississippians. Moreover, with COFO's demise, SNCC and CORE became less active in the state. Bob Moses believed that the move was a mistake, and later said that COFO could have been reconstituted around another program that the entire black community could support, such as adult literacy. In the summer of 1965, however, the Mississippi Freedom Democratic party was designated to fill the void left by COFO.[14]

While its lobbyists were busy in Washington drumming up support for the final vote on the congressional challenge, in Mississippi FDP was preparing for another summer of activity. The demonstrations in Selma, Alabama, that spring, culminating in the march to Montgomery led by Dr. Martin Luther King, had all but ensured passage of a voting rights law that included a provision to send federal registrars into counties with a history of discrimination against black voters. To assist in the FDP summer program, which again was to include freedom schools and community organizing as well as voter registration, volunteers were once more recruited from northern campuses. This time there was a conscious effort to limit the number of outsiders and to place the volunteers only in communities requesting them. Fewer than 200 volunteers would come to Mississippi in the summer of 1965.[15]

FDP plans to mount an intensive voter registration drive were sidetracked when in mid-June Governor Paul Johnson called the Mississippi legislature into special session to repeal the state's discriminatory voting laws. Johnson's surprise move caught both whites and blacks off guard. On the surface his recommendations were stunning. Johnson called for the repeal of laws requiring voter applicants to be of "good moral character" and to be able to read, write, and interpret any section of the state constitution. He wanted to eliminate the requirement that prospective voters have their names published for two consecutive weeks in the local newspaper and reduce the power of local registrars to determine the qualifications of applicants. The governor had experienced no eleventh-hour conversion, however, and he made it clear he was not promoting black suffrage. Johnson told legislators he wanted to bring voting and registration requirements into line with those of northern states to pave the way for a court test once the new voting rights bill became law. And, of course, repealing the discriminatory statutes might also undermine the congressional challenge.[16]

FDP strategists saw the special session as an opportunity to generate publicity and support for the challenge. Employing the argument previously used against the Mississippi congressional delegation, FDP claimed that since the overwhelming majority of blacks had been denied the vote, the state legislature was illegally constituted, and thus the special session was in violation of federal law. On the morning of June 14, FDP chair Lawrence Guyot led 500 demonstrators out of Morning Star Baptist Church to begin a mile-long silent protest to the state capitol. Nearly half of the marchers were in their teens. About seventy-five of the demonstrators were white summer volunteers who had been in the state less than a week. Halfway to the capitol, Jackson police halted the march and began arresting participants for parading without a permit. Police crammed demonstrators into paddy wagons and large caged trash trucks, delivering them to the state fairgrounds nearby, where they were deposited in two large buildings used for industrial and agricultural exhibits. The 482 people arrested were literally herded into cattle barns. The story of the demonstration and arrests made the front page of the *New York Times,* and more FDP supporters from across the state converged on Jackson, which had not seen such movement activity since the demonstrations following Medgar Evers's funeral two years earlier. Led by SNCC chairman John Lewis and the NAACP's Charles Evers, who had temporarily laid aside his antipathy toward FDP to participate, 204 more marchers were arrested on Friday and sent to the stockade.[17]

Police treated the demonstrators cruelly. Sunflower County activist Annie Mae King, well into her sixties, recalled that "they put us in those paddy wagons and they packed us in so tight until you couldn't get breath, you couldn't move. . . . It was so hot we was just about to suffocate." Mrs. King spent four days incarcerated at the fairgrounds stockade under deplorable conditions. Inmates were served grits and syrup for breakfast and string beans and hominy for other meals. At night they slept on bare mattresses with no covers. During the day police removed the mattresses, and prisoners had to sit on cement floors.[18]

Reports of police brutality inside the compound were numerous and well documented, yet local officials denied all charges of mistreatment. An investigating team from the National Council of Churches, however, described the stockade as a "concentration camp" designed to "break the spirit, the will, the health and even the body of each individual."[19]

Sensing that the Jackson demonstrations had the potential to become another Selma, MFDP issued a call to "concerned citizens across the country to come to Jackson to continue demonstrating against the state's denial of the right to vote." On Friday 103 more marchers were jailed, bringing the total number of arrests to 859.[20] Yet Jackson was not to be Selma. Although a few clergy answered the FDP call, there was no outpouring of outside support for the Mississippi campaign. Perhaps the novelty of coming south to participate in demonstrations was wearing thin. The marches continued, however, and 169 more people were arrested over the next two weeks, bringing the total to more than 1,000. Morale was now low at FDP headquarters. Bail bond money was hard to come by, and most of those arrested had not planned on a lengthy stay in prison. After the first week of demonstrations the national media lost interest; by June 24 Guyot reported that "press coverage is practically non-existent." Most disheartening was the lack of active support from black adults in Jackson, whose children constituted the largest local movement contingent. On June 30 a three-judge panel of the Fifth Circuit Court of Appeals enjoined the city of Jackson from making further arrests of demonstrators. Although several peaceful marches took place in early July, FDP planned no further protests and turned its attention once again to Washington and the congressional challenge. The legislature adjourned after passing Governor Johnson's repeal package. Few white officials now believed that a court challenge of the new voting rights act would succeed, but they did hope that the legislature's action would keep federal registrars out of Mississippi.[21]

• • •

In addition to dealing with the legislature, police, and the Klan, civil rights activists now had to face a political challenge brought by a coalition of former opponents and erstwhile allies. Early in July, as the Jackson demonstrations were winding down, Claude Ramsey, state president of the AFL-CIO, sent out a letter to more than 100 white and black moderates, inviting them to meet in Jackson to build "a Loyalist Mississippi Democratic group to restore relations with the national party." Labor organizers in Mississippi were about as popular as civil rights workers, and Ramsey had kept a low profile on the race question during the early 1960s, in part because the rank and file of the Mississippi labor movement was strongly segregationist. The passage of two civil rights laws and the decline of the Citizens' Council had encouraged people like Ramsey to step forward. Working with him in planning the Jackson conference were a group of white professionals, most of whom lived in the Delta, including attorneys Doug Wynn and Wes Watkins, planter Oscar Carr, and Hodding Carter III, editor of the *Delta Democrat-Times*. Sensing that the politics of the future in Mississippi would be interracial, these whites wanted to lead an integrated state Democratic party back into the mainstream. Since none of these men had impressive civil rights credentials, they needed black allies if they were to establish credibility as a progressive force for change. They found them in that group of NAACP leaders, most of whom were successful businessmen, who had become disenchanted with COFO.[22]

It was significant that Ramsey had restricted his guest list for the Jackson meeting to middle-class black men like Aaron Henry, Charles Evers, and Charles Young, the wealthy Meridian cosmetics manufacturer, for although this new alliance was built across racial lines, its membership consisted of people who had achieved at least a degree of economic security. No black sharecroppers, maids, or day laborers were invited to participate in the creation of the "Loyalist Mississippi Democratic group."

This "class thing," Bob Moses recalled, had "first come to a head at Atlantic City," where a new group of black leaders had emerged who were poor and without much formal education. Atlantic City had given political legitimacy to people like Fannie Lou Hamer, E. W. Steptoe, and Unita Blackwell, and the traditional leaders resented it. FDP leader Ed King observed that "suddenly a real class barrier developed the minute we got back from Atlantic City. The old Negro leadership class refused to work with the Freedom Party," and there developed "a kind of internal feuding within the Negro community from a displaced leadership class to restore itself and take the leadership over from this new class of leaders."[23]

For men like Henry and Young—both of whom had endorsed the Atlantic City compromise—joining together with a group of well-placed white moderates made good political sense. Believing that MFDP had little chance of recognition by the national party and eager to reassert their leadership, middle-class blacks cast their lot with their white counterparts and set out to build a new political force in Mississippi, positioned to the left of the regular Mississippi Democrats and to the right of MFDP.

On Sunday afternoon, July 18, about 125 people answered Ramsey's call and assembled at the Heidelberg Hotel in Jackson. There they formed the Mississippi Democratic Conference (MDC), which was pledged to the politics of interracialism and eager to accept the leadership of the national Democratic party. Nearly three-fourths of the delegates were white, and they elected as chairman a white attorney from Pascagoula, Robert Oswald. Charles Young was elected vice chairman, and R. L. T. Smith, treasurer. Despite the hopes of its founders, the MDC all but died aborning. The Johnson White House, which did not want unnecessarily to offend powerful segregationist Mississippians on Capitol Hill like Senators Eastland and Stennis, withheld support from the MDC. A number of white members had no use for the labor movement and were uncomfortable working with Ramsey. Oswald soon realized that the group he headed was too liberal for his tastes and resigned as chairman. Most important, the MDC had little support in the black community. Men and women associated with SNCC, CORE, and FDP were excluded from the meeting that organized the MDC, and movement activists were outraged at this apparent effort to undermine their credibility. After several meetings the Mississippi Democratic Conference quietly passed from the scene. By this time, however, the coalition forces had found an alternative political vehicle in the Mississippi Young Democrats.[24]

Although overshadowed by the Jackson demonstrations and the congressional challenge, the fight for the charter of the Young Democrats was of considerable political significance. The Mississippi Young Democrats had ceased to function even before the 1964 election campaign. Movement activists had attempted to gain the Young Democrats' charter at the Atlantic City convention but were rejected, ostensibly because of "technical failures in their application." Early in 1965 a small group of Delta whites led by Carter and Wynn began to reorganize dormant Young Democrats clubs on white college campuses. Allied with state NAACP leaders, they prepared to do battle with activists representing the Freedom Democratic party at a state Young Democrats convention, called in early August to adopt a new constitution and to elect officers. Representatives of the Carter and FDP factions met prior to the convention to lay out the ground rules. They selected Gordon Henderson, a political science professor at Millsaps College, as chair and agreed that no elections would take place before the afternoon. Students at Tougaloo and Millsaps had summer school classes in the morning, and a number of blacks from out of town would also be arriving late.[25]

Yet when the convention opened it was apparent that the NAACP-Carter faction, a majority at the morning session, had a separate agenda. Ignoring the earlier agreement, they elected their own convention chair, black NAACP youth leader Johnny Frazier, and proceeded to elect officers, choosing Hodding Carter and Cleveland Donald, one of a handful of black students enrolled at Ole Miss, as permanent Young Democrats cochairs and filling other offices with anti-FDP delegates. By the afternoon, however, FDP supporters commanded a strong majority at the convention and voted 175 to 114 to censure and remove Frazier as chair. At this point Hodding Carter called on all "true" Young Democrats to follow him downstairs to a room reserved earlier to convene a "true Young Democratic state convention." About a third of the delegates walked out with Carter. The two groups met separately for the rest of the afternoon, with the majority FDP faction choosing its own slate of officers. Eventually, the national Young Democrats, who shared the national Democratic party's reservations about MFDP, recognized the Carter-NAACP group as its legitimate Mississippi representative.[26]

All this might appear to be much ado about very little. Many SNCC activists, now alienated from mainstream politics, saw nothing to be gained from fighting over the charter. Nationally, the Young Democrats had no power within the party: the organization was mostly a training ground for ambitious politicians. For the new white-black coalition, however, recognition by the national Young Democrats was important, for it provided both visibility and an organizational base from which to operate now that the MDC had failed to take hold. Looking back at these developments Doug Wynn, who became the Mississippi Young Democrats' legal counsel, observed that obtaining the state Young Democrats charter was essential to the later success of the white moderate–NAACP coalition.[27]

The MFDP leadership, however, had little time to reflect on the Young Democrats confrontation in Jackson, for the party had just become the center of a firestorm of criticism over a statement concerning events thousands of miles from Mississippi. In late July 1965 a black man from McComb named John Shaw was killed while serving in Vietnam. Four years earlier, as a teenager, Shaw had been active in SNCC's first direct action campaign in Mississippi. Enraged that a man who could not find freedom at home had lost his life on a foreign battlefield, McComb activists Joe Martin and Clint Hopson circulated a leaflet through the community and sent a copy to Jackson, where it was published in the MFDP *Newsletter,* the party's official publication. The McComb statement listed "five reasons why Negroes should not be in any war fighting for America," bluntly asserting that "Negro boys should not honor the draft here in Mississippi. Mothers should encourage their sons not to go." Although the *Newsletter* printed the statement without endorsement—it had previously published, without comment, letters opposing the war—FDP opponents inside and outside the state seized the opportunity to portray the Freedom party as unpatriotic and extremist. Denunciations from the white Mississippi establishment were to be expected, but what damaged FDP most was criticism from blacks. Charles Evers said that "for Negro citizens to ignore the draft can only serve to destroy that which they have fought so hard to achieve." R. Jess Brown, the Jackson attorney and movement supporter, took issue with the McComb statement, declaring that blacks needed to "fight on a battlefield" as part of the struggle to win freedom at home. Michigan congressman Charles Diggs blasted the statement as "ridiculous and completely irresponsible."[28]

The FDP leadership attempted to control the damage. Guyot and executive committee member Ed King issued a statement that the leaflet did not represent FDP policy, and Guyot later told the *New York Times* that if drafted he would serve in the armed forces. Yet both men upheld "the right of our members to discuss and act upon all issues" and stated that "it is very easy to understand why Negro citizens of McComb, themselves the victims of Klan-inspired terrorism, and harassment arrests, should resent the death of a citizen of McComb while fighting in Viet Nam for 'freedom' not enjoyed by the Negro community of McComb."[29]

The McComb antiwar leaflet was one of the first broadsides calling on young men to refuse to fight, a position that gained widespread acceptance among antiwar activists as the conflict in Southeast Asia intensified. In the short run, however, the Freedom Democratic party lost credibility at the time it was fighting for its political life against the new coalition of moderates, who had pledged allegiance to Lyndon Johnson's Vietnam policy and who exploited the McComb statement to their advantage. In an August 8 *Delta Democrat-Times* editorial Hodding Carter III charged that the FDP statement was "close to treason" and accused Guyot and King of "deliberately collaborating in the Communist line." The AFL-CIO's Claude Ramsey went so far as to equate FDP with the Ku Klux Klan and expressed the conviction that the "great majority of Mississippi Negroes . . . will continue to follow the responsible Negro leadership of this state in lieu of the anarchists in their midst today."[30]

The Vietnam statement also worked to FDP's disadvantage in Washington as members of the House of Representatives finally, in mid-September, got around to examining the charges that the Mississippi congressional delegation was illegal, that the seats should be vacated, and that new elections should be held. In the months since the House had voted to seat the Mississippians pending an investigation, Congress had enacted much of the Great Society program, including the voting rights act, which President Johnson had signed into law on August 6. In addition to authorizing the attorney general to send federal examiners into counties where discrimination against blacks had been apparent, the new voting law suspended literacy tests in these areas, authorized the Justice Department to dispatch observers to monitor elections, and required Mississippi and the other affected states to submit any new voting requirements to the attorney general for prior approval. FDP lobbyists now had to contend with the argument that the voting rights act had made their challenge irrelevant.[31]

When the House Subcommittee on Elections met to consider the challenge on September 13, they did so in closed session, despite the protests of hundreds of Mississippi blacks who had come to Washington to attend the hearings. Moreover, subcommittee chairman Robert T. Ashmore of South Carolina limited debate to the issue of dismissing the challenge. Thus, the question of discrimination against black voters—evidence compiled in thousands of pages of depositions—could not even be discussed. Black Mississippians did testify before the subcommittee, but the result was a foregone conclusion. It voted to dismiss the challenge on September 14; the following day the parent House Administration Committee ratified the subcommittee recommendation 15 to 5; and on September 16 the full House membership concurred, 228 to 143.[32]

FDP supporters were disappointed with the House vote and angry that the Johnson administration had dealt with the challenge in such a cavalier fashion. Movement spokespersons tried to put the best face on the setback. In a story headlined "MFDP Wins Victory in Defeat," SCEF's *Southern Patriot* proclaimed that the Freedom Democrats "broke through a powerful alliance to force an open showdown. . . . It showed what little people can do when they organize." Challenger Victoria Gray optimistically stated that "the people are confident and ready to work; they feel we are just beginning." Guyot predicted that FDP "would make 1966 the year of free elections in Mississipi." In October FDP filed a federal suit calling for reapportionment of the Mississippi legislature, vacating all the seats and holding new elections. It also petitioned the National Democratic party for authorization to hold the party's primaries in Mississippi. On the surface, at least, FDP appeared to take the defeat of the congressional challenge in stride.[33]

In assessing the impact of the congressional challenge, its supporters claimed that the action had put the Mississippi Freedom Democratic party on the political map as a force to be reckoned with, both at home and in the nation's capitol. Moreover, although the SCLC campaign in Selma had been the immediate catalyst for the voting rights act of 1965, the congressional challenge had kept the issue of voter discrimination on the agenda, reinforcing the hand of congressional liberals who succeeded in enacting a strong bill. Still, the congressional challenge generated controversy within movement circles. FDP had spent thousands of dollars on the challenge and left Washington broke. It would never again have adequate funding to support its programs. Some activists who had worked for the challenge now believed that the movement needed to adopt new political strategies. For Michael Thelwell, who ran the FDP Washington office and spent months trying to enlist the support of white liberal organizations, the "lesson the movement learned is simply this: that we need power of our own. We cannot depend on our allies."[34]

Throughout the fall and winter of 1965 the Mississippi Freedom Democratic party struggled over questions of identity and mission. Should FDP continue its campaign to win recognition from the national party, or should it go its own way? With racial tensions increasing inside the movement, should whites continue to be active in FDP? What role should FDP play in relation to SNCC and to the emerging coalition of old-line NAACP leaders and white Mississippi moderates? These issues remained unresolved when trouble broke out in Natchez, where FDP took part in the last major organizing campaign of the Mississippi movement.

• • •

"The Old South Still Lives in Natchez," proclaimed an Adams County public relations brochure, a reference to the annual pilgrimage tour of elegant antebellum mansions that attracted thousands of visitors to this city built on bluffs above the Mississippi. Before World War II race relations in Natchez resembled the paternalism of the old regime, with organizations like the NAACP tolerated as long as blacks did not challenge the caste system. Now, however, Natchez had become a "New South" city boasting an industrial base anchored by Armstrong Tire and Rubber, the International Paper Company, and the Johns-Manville Corporation. When in the early 1960s black activists began to press for social change, whites responded as they had during the days of the first Reconstruction. With a substantial white working-class base, the Ku Klux Klan, under the leadership of E. L. McDaniel, was stronger in Natchez than in any other Mississippi community, even McComb.[35]

In the late summer of 1964, when SNCC organizers Dorie Ladner, Chuck McDew, and Charles Neblett inaugurated COFO's first project in Adams County, a bomb destroyed the building next to the house where the SNCC workers were staying. Chief of Police J. T. Robinson told Ladner that the "bomb was meant for you. I'm surprised you haven't been killed already." A year later Ladner was still in Natchez, heading an FDP staff of about fifteen people, about half of whom were northern volunteers. George Greene, the Greenwood native who had first come to Adams County with the freedom vote campaign in 1963, returned to Natchez, joined by SNCC workers Burt Watkins and Bill Ware. The Natchez contingent had experienced its share of internal problems: there was barely enough money for people to eat; several of the white male volunteers were unhappy working under the leadership of a black woman; and local people, intimidated by the Klan, were reluctant to come forward. The local NAACP branch had also conducted a voter registration project in Natchez during the 1965 summer. An uneasy truce had existed between the two civil rights organizations, as Ladner and

Greene had established good relations with several of the NAACP leaders, including George Metcalf, the president of the Natchez branch.[36]

A fifty-three-year-old worker in the Armstrong plant, Metcalf had assisted Greene in the fall of 1963, and when COFO began its Natchez project the following summer Metcalf housed the SNCC workers until they could arrange for their own lodging. Because of his open support of the movement, Metcalf became a marked man. In late January 1965 someone fired a shot through the window of his house. Throughout the summer he received numerous threatening phone calls and was harassed at work. Although nearly 400 blacks worked at Armstrong, most were employed in menial positions; the Klan had many members and supporters among the white workers at the plant. On August 27, as the early shift at Armstrong let out, Metcalf climbed into his car in the plant parking lot and turned on the ignition. The resulting explosion demolished Metcalf's car and damaged several vehicles nearby. Inside the plant some of the white workers who heard the blast "decided it was a holiday, just like November 22, 1963." Miraculously, Metcalf survived, but he was hospitalized for weeks, suffering from a fractured arm and leg, lacerations, and a serious eye injury.[37]

Just as the bombing of Aylene Quin's home had galvanized McComb's black community a year earlier, the attempted assassination of George Metcalf aroused and enraged black Natchez. Local people who had been afraid to attend movement meetings were now out in the streets demanding revenge. At a hastily called mass meeting on the day of the bombing, the NAACP's Charles Evers told a large crowd not to initiate acts of violence, but "if they do it any more, we're going to get those responsible. We're armed, every last one of us, and we are not going to take it." Younger blacks in the audience began a chant, "We're going to kill for freedom!" Following the meeting hundreds of blacks, many of them armed, roamed the streets of black Natchez. When a police car drove through the Negro section, someone in the crowd threw a rock that shattered the side window. One visiting journalist reported that "with the exception of military posts and hunting resorts, this city probably has been more heavily armed, man for man, than almost any other city."[38]

Alarmed at the prospect of race war breaking out in their community, moderate blacks associated with the NAACP tried to de-fuse the explosive situation by preparing "A Declaration of the Negro Citizens of Natchez," which included a list of twelve demands presented to the city government. The declaration called for the mayor and board of aldermen to denounce the Ku Klux Klan publicly; to secure equal employment opportunities for blacks, including positions on the police force; to desegregate all public accommodations, in compliance with the Civil Rights Act of 1964; to provide equal public services to residents in Negro sections of Natchez; and to desegregate Natchez schools and appoint blacks to the school board. Charles Evers let it be known that if the city refused to act on these demands, blacks would begin to march.[39]

Although he had not spent much time in Natchez, Evers was widely known in the black community, and with the attempted murder of the local NAACP president, the state field secretary moved in to take charge. The FDP workers who had been in Natchez for over a year resented his intrusion, because although Metcalf had been their ally, Evers had opposed FDP activities in Jackson and throughout the state. Evers had also alienated the national leadership of the NAACP. He rarely cleared his activities with the New York office and often ignored NAACP policy, as when he endorsed Robert Kennedy in the 1964 New York senate race. By the summer of 1965 Roy Wilkins was so angered by Evers's conduct that when he learned that Evers had been invited to the White House signing of the voting rights act, he called presidential aide Larry O'Brien and threatened to stay home. Two weeks before the Metcalf bombing, Gloster Current had prepared a four-page memorandum for Wilkins detailing the case for Evers's dismissal as Mississippi state field secretary. Evers knew he was about to be fired. For him, the trouble in Natchez was a godsend.[40]

The Natchez city council was to meet on Thursday, September 2, to consider the list of twelve demands. Blacks were holding nightly mass meetings and planning to demonstrate if the council did not take positive action. The city responded by prohibiting the sale of alcoholic beverages and imposing a 10:00 P.M. curfew, which was enforced only against blacks. Anticipating trouble, Governor Johnson dispatched 650 national guardsmen to patrol the city on the day of the council meeting. It was in this atmosphere of increasing tension and anticipation that, on Thursday morning, Natchez mayor John Nosser and the board of aldermen rejected the demands. More than 500 blacks had gathered to await the decision, ready for action, for at a mass meeting the night before Evers had told them to be prepared to march on the courthouse. Yet after announcing the disappointing news, Evers canceled the march, citing as his reasons the presence of the National Guard and the likelihood of violence. Instead Evers called on blacks to boycott all the downtown white businesses to protest the council's action. Many in the crowd were stunned and disappointed at Evers's caution. FDP activists were furious at Evers's move (characteristically, he had not consulted them beforehand), for they had mobilized the community to take action. SNCC worker Bill Ware urged the crowd to defy Evers and march anyway. When several in the audience cheered, Evers shot back, "Don't listen to these people. These outside agitators are gonna get you killed!" There was no march, and the NAACP branch, now following Evers's lead, proceeded with plans for the boycott.[41]

Although unsuccessful in gaining concessions from Natchez whites, Evers had won the first round against FDP, but he was still vulnerable locally and lacked support from the national NAACP office. Faced with these difficulties, Evers sent a telegram to Dr. Martin Luther King urging him to come to speak in Natchez; at the same time he sent out a call to the Delta Ministry for workers to assist in the boycott. The Delta Ministry responded immediately, and though King did not appear, he sent Andrew Young to speak in his place and soon dispatched a team of SCLC organizers. For the last time in the Mississippi movement, leading civil rights groups moved in to organize a black community.[42]

On the surface, the Natchez movement resembled the earlier campaigns in Clarksdale, Greenwood, Jackson, and McComb. Police repression and violence, coupled with the refusal of local government officials to negotiate with representatives of the black community, led to large nightly mass meetings, protest marches, arrests, and escalating racial tensions. Governor Johnson pulled the National Guard out of Natchez on Labor Day weekend, and while the curfew remained in effect, the first organized demonstration took place on September 9 when about 200 people staged a peaceful march on city hall. The boycott of white businesses was almost totally successful. Local NAACP observers called out the names of those blacks continuing to trade at white stores, and such public censure brought most of the violators into line. Behind the scenes, however, the Natchez movement was in turmoil. SCLC, NAACP, and FDP organizers were competing for the allegiance of the black community, with the Delta Ministry performing the increasingly difficult task of mediation. Charles Evers was at the center of the controversy, skillfully playing off one faction against the other, establishing himself as *the* leader of the Natchez movement.[43]

When Evers had originally contacted SCLC and the Delta Ministry, neither organization was aware that the other was being called in. He had also kept the national office of the NAACP in the dark. SCLC organizer Stoney Cooks reported that Evers had come to SCLC "in pseudo-desperation, explaining that difficulties with his parent organization, NAACP, had occurred and that Natchez needed a movement philosophy." Dr. King, believing that Natchez might be the proper setting for a campaign to secure legislation making violence against civil rights workers a federal crime, sent in a team of five organizers led by the Reverend Al Sampson. Sampson assigned each member the task of organizing segments of the community—ministers and entrepreneurs, young people, and "street corner" loiterers and bar patrons—following the organizational model of northern activist Saul Alinski. He tried to gain the cooperation of all the civil rights forces in Natchez, but Evers prevented him from garnering broad support, excluding representatives of the Delta Ministry and FDP from Sampson's first strategy sessions. Once SCLC, with its staff and financial resources, had assumed a high profile in Natchez, Evers took steps to isolate and then eliminate the SCLC presence.[44]

Things came to a head on the evening of Monday, September 27. A demonstration the previous Saturday had brought nearly 1,000 people into the streets, and organizers planned a mass march on Monday night to test the curfew. Stoney Cooks reported that "people were packed into the church, cars were lined up for three blocks. . . . There was a complete turnout, in excess of 1,500 people at the mass meeting. Old ladies in tennis shoes and old men in basketball shorts were ready to march." SCLC believed it had the white power structure in Natchez "in a bind," that the momentum of the movement was unstoppable.

Evers was out of town, but one of his representatives, a local black minister, got up at the meeting and told the throng that "the leader" had sent word that there should be no march and that "the people should do as the leader says do . . . and what the leader says is best." There would be no march. Three days later a local judge issued a sweeping injunction prohibiting marching and picketing, and the following day the city lifted the curfew. An embittered Sampson, believing that in calling off the march Evers had played into the hands of the whites, recommended that SCLC think about "pull[ing] out of Mississippi." For the majority of Natchez blacks, however, the behind-the-scenes struggles were of little consequence. They had found their leader in Charles Evers, and through October they continued to pack the nightly mass meetings and answer *his* call for demonstrations.[45]

On Saturday, October 2, more than 300 people defied the court injunction against marching; on Sunday another 150 blacks took to the streets. All were arrested on charges of parading without a permit, and those over twelve years of age were sent to Parchman penitentiary, over 200 miles away. City officials hoped that this action would crush the movement, for at Parchman male prisoners were stripped naked and for two nights suffered through temperatures in the forties with windows open and fans blowing. Men and women both were force-fed laxatives and given only "sparse supplies" of toilet paper. The intimidation did not succeed, however, for Natchez blacks posted property bonds and most prisoners were released within five days.

Back home, they once again took to the streets. More than 100 marchers were arrested on October 4, as E. L. McDaniel and about 150 of his klansmen stood by. Two days later, in a surprising move, Judge Harold Cox lifted the injunction against demonstrations, resulting in the largest march to date, with 1,200 people participating. Observing this march were members of the newly formed Natchez Deacons for Defense and Justice, a militant organization patterned after the group organized earlier in Louisiana to protect the black community from white attacks. Police made no arrests, and there was no violence. Shortly thereafter Mayor John Nosser sent out word that the city wanted to open negotiations with the committee of NAACP members and supporters.[46]

Mayor Nosser was the man in the middle. A native of Lebanon, Nosser had migrated to the United States when he was nineteen, later moving to Natchez. He had succeeded through hard work and now owned a number of businesses. Nosser had narrowly won reelection as mayor in 1964, his margin supplied by the small but decisive black vote. The Klan in Natchez believed that Nosser was too moderate on the race question and bombed his home in September 1964. Blacks soon became disappointed with Nosser's second administration. When the mayor refused to hire black clerks in his stores, blacks began to boycott the businesses even before the Metcalf bombing. Beset by the Klan on one side—two of his sons were active Klan members—and angry blacks on the other, Nosser vacillated. At the first negotiating session in mid-October the mayor and board of aldermen agreed to significant parts of the original twelve demands, yet two days later they renounced the agreement. Blacks took to the streets once again and throughout late October and November kept up the pressure, including the boycott of white stores, still nearly 100 percent effective.[47]

Evers was now firmly in control of the Natchez movement and had thus made himself indispensable to the national NAACP. He in turn began to cooperate with Current and Wilkins, accepting advice that the Natchez movement be more flexible in its demands "to get the operation in bounds." SCLC activists were now at loggerheads with Evers, and when in late October the Natchez NAACP chapter asked SCLC to leave, Sampson did so, but not before publicly denouncing the NAACP leadership as "unreliable, untrustworthy, and incapable." Although they too had misgivings about Evers and his operation, Delta Ministry workers remained in Natchez.[48]

With Evers's growing local popularity and his largely favorable image in the national media, the Mississippi Freedom Democratic party's fragile position in the community further deteriorated. Unlike in the earlier SNCC campaigns, from the outset middle-class adult males associated with the local NAACP branch were prominent in the Natchez demonstrations, and they were Evers's natural constituency. Looking back on her experiences in Natchez, Dorie Ladner acknowledged Evers's appeal: "He was an older man who looked good and dressed well. I can see now how people would readily identify with him, as opposed to some 17- or 18-year-old kids." Moreover, Evers had "turned the community against" FDP by denying the young militants any representation on the governing board of the Natchez movement, refusing to recognize FDP representatives at the mass meetings, telling local people not to feed or house "anyone who is working against us," and red-baiting Ladner and her young colleagues. Dorie Ladner recalled that immediately after Evers had canceled the September 2 march, he had attempted to discredit his critics by "calling us communists. I told him that if he said another God-damn word I was going to hit him with my God-damn fists. That's how angry I was."[49]

FDP organizers stepped up their criticism of Evers while trying to gain community support. They called attention to his dictatorial methods, his unaccountable handling of contributions to the Natchez campaign, his secretive relationship with the police chief and other white officials, and the apparent conflict of interest when he purchased a grocery store in Natchez while urging blacks to boycott white stores. But the FDP's animosity toward Evers served mainly to reenforce his image—in both the black and white communities—as a responsible moderate.[50]

By late November it was apparent that some sort of settlement was in the making. The boycott, picketing, and marches had taken their toll on downtown Natchez. Six businesses had already folded, and with the prospect of no Negro trade during the Christmas season, white merchants pressured their elected officials to do something to end the boycott. National NAACP officials, who had favored a compromise, asked Evers to lift the boycott "on those merchants who proceed in good faith." On November 29 Evers and the NAACP negotiating committee met with city officials and twenty-three merchants, reaching a tentative agreement. The city would hire six Negro policemen, desegregate "all City-operated public facilities," including the schools, and appoint a "qualified Negro" to the school board. The twenty-three merchants, who represented about one-fifth of the city's businesses, pledged to hire or promote blacks to the positions of sales clerks. Beyond that, concluded a Delta Ministry staff person, the agreement consisted "mostly of fine-sounding phrases and promises of limited action at some future time." The handful of jobs, agreement to obey the 1964 civil rights law, and token desegregation of the schools in 1966 (which the federal courts would have mandated anyway) were of little direct benefit to the thousands of black women and men who had made the Natchez movement.[51]

At a mass meeting on December 1, Evers announced the terms and called for an end to the boycott. There had been no advance notice that this critical subject would be on the agenda, and Evers permitted no discussion of the agreement before taking a vote. When an FDP worker tried to get the floor, "NAACP bouncers" seized him and prevented him from speaking. Evers had put his prestige on the line, and after a voice vote, the chair of the meeting declared the boycott over. Two days later Mayor Nosser formally announced the agreement, which was widely praised in the national media. In a memorandum to "Editorial Writers and Columnists," NAACP public relations director Henry Moon called the Natchez agreement "far more meaningful than any settlement ever achieved as the result of a direct action program by the Negro community in any other southern city."[52]

There was some truth in this claim. Under Evers's direction the Natchez movement had sustained its momentum and forced concessions from the city's business leaders and elected officials. The more militant blacks, however, believed that these concessions were inadequate, that Evers had compromised at a time when the movement could have demanded and gotten more, and that they "had been sold out, or at least tricked, once again."[53]

On the night after the vote to end the boycott, FDP workers in Natchez called a meeting and demanded its continuation: "Only by keeping up our boycott can we get what we want: a really DEMOCRATIC Natchez, where all the people have a say in making a better town for everyone." Only seventy local people showed up for the meeting, and blacks once again started patronizing white stores. Evers attempted to blunt FDP criticism of his role in the settlement by calling for a continued boycott of the stores that had not agreed to hire black clerks, and when white police assaulted a small group of black picketers on December 23, he decreed that the full boycott was again in effect, threatening a downtown demonstration to disrupt traffic on Christmas Eve. By now, however, the momentum of the last three months had dissipated. One outside participant captured the mood of black Natchez in late December: "The feeling of excitement, the feeling of membership in a community of good purposes, the experience of helping fashion a more just society, of being active and significant citizens for the first time, was gone. Their massive and prolonged struggle had produced minimal results in action and only a few vague assurances and limited promises that, even if kept, would not make a dent in the problems."[54]

Natchez was to be the last major mobilizing campaign of the Mississippi movement. Five months later the civil rights organizations participated in the Meredith March, but they never again worked together as they had under the COFO banner in the early 1960s. Charles Evers left Natchez with his own position strengthened statewide. Nationally, the charismatic brother of Medgar Evers had come to symbolize the civil rights movement in Mississippi. Now the media, the liberal wing of the Democratic party, MFDP, and the national office of the NAACP all had to take him seriously. The emerging coalition of black and white moderates—the Hodding Carter–Aaron Henry faction—never brought Evers into their inner circle, for they did not trust him, but they too had to deal with him, and usually on his terms.

For the Mississippi Freedom Democratic party, the defeat in Natchez, following on the heels of the failure of the congressional challenge, did little to enhance its stature. As a statewide political organization FDP lacked both the financial resources and the staff to implement its programs. The political ground was shifting in Mississippi, and the movement needed to develop new strategies now that the right to vote had been won. For in the summer of 1965 a battle had begun to take shape over Lyndon Johnson's "War on Poverty," a conflict that was to have major consequences for Mississippi and the movement.

16

CDGM and the Politics of Poverty

The domestic programs enacted by Congress between 1964 and 1966 were the most ambitious and far-reaching since the early years of the New Deal. President Lyndon Johnson secured passage of legislation providing for federal aid to education and health care for the elderly and poor, a reform agenda that had been stalled in Congress for decades. Programs like Medicaid, foodstamps, the Job Corps, and Operation Head Start were targeted specifically at the poorest Americans. To coordinate this "War on Poverty," Congress established the Office of Economic Opportunity (OEO), headed by Sargent Shriver. At the heart of the poverty program were the community action agencies under the Community Action Program (CAP). Designed to provide "a hand up, not a handout," CAP sought to develop neighborhood solutions to poverty-related problems and called for "maximum feasible participation" of poor people in both the planning and implementation of the programs that affected them.[1]

The War on Poverty would meet with but limited success in Mississippi. Moreover, antipoverty efforts in the Magnolia State were to be complicated by the interaction of impersonal economic forces, the unintended consequences of federal policies, and the determination of white Mississippians to block or control federal poverty programs. Well aware that the state's racial and economic problems were inseparable, civil rights activists themselves had made several attempts to address the problem of poverty among Mississippi blacks, beginning with a drive to organize farm and domestic workers in the Delta.

The Mississippi Freedom Labor Union (MFLU) was formed in the Bolivar County community of Shaw in early April 1965. Several white COFO workers met there with about fifty black cotton choppers and tractor drivers who had for years been struggling to support their families on abysmally low wages. The choppers, whose task was to weed the cotton rows in the summer, received three dollars for a ten-hour day. The tractor drivers, the "elite" of the black rural labor force, made only six dollars a day. News of the union, which was to be staffed and run by local blacks, quickly spread through the Delta, and within a month nearly 1,000 workers in six counties had signed on. The first labor action occurred at the end of May in Tribbett, a small community in Washington County near Greenville. Representatives of the dozen families living on the A. L. Andrews plantation asked for an hourly wage of $1.25. Andrews rejected their demands, and when the workers refused to go into the fields, he evicted all his tenants. In a display of planter solidarity, neighboring farmers supplied the labor to hoe his fields. The MFLU arranged for the displaced families to live in tents in a small community that became known as "Strike City" and sent out a call to northern unions for support. Farm workers struck in Shaw, Indianola, and Rosedale; in Cleveland ten women working as maids walked off their jobs when their demands for a $1.25 hourly wage were denied.[2]

The MFLU, however, was unable to sustain its campaign for higher wages. Planters remained united, and local police harassed and arrested strike leaders. The $15,000 strike fund the union had raised was quickly exhausted in supporting those families evicted from plantations. A strike planned for the fall cotton-picking season did not materialize.[3]

The MFLU failed to take hold in the Delta in part because of the traditional hostility of white Mississippians toward all labor unions but also because farm workers had no leverage to use against the planters. By the mid-1960s over 90 percent of the cotton crop was harvested by machines, and the use of chemical herbicides to eliminate weeds reduced the need for cotton choppers.[4] Although tractor drivers were essential to the operation of the modern plantation, few of them supported the MFLU, for they had the most to lose by going out on strike. Simply put, there were no longer *any* jobs for thousands of Delta blacks who had for generations worked in the fields, first as sharecroppers and more recently as seasonal laborers. The attempt to organize farm workers in the Mississippi Delta was the most ambitious effort since the Southern Tenant Farmers Union had organized in the state in the late 1930s and early 1940s. MFLU was a bold and romantic venture, but it was anachronistic, and activists began to explore other initiatives to deal with the changing agricultural economy.

One such program was the formation of cooperatives. In the summer of 1965 black farmers in Panola County, angry that the local white purchaser paid only four cents a pound for their okra crop, organized their own marketing cooperative, which under the leadership of Robert Miles soon expanded to include other vegetables and cotton. With a $113,000 grant from the Farmers Home Administration, the cooperative purchased land and equipment, thus providing food and work for some farm workers who had lost their plantation jobs. That same summer Delta Ministry staffer Owen Brooks, a black activist who had moved to Mississippi from Boston, began working with farmers to organize cooperatives in Bolivar County. Within three years the North Bolivar County Farm Cooperative became the largest in the state, with 900 families producing over 1 million pounds of vegetables for the market and for their own consumption. Blacks formed other cooperatives in the Delta later in the decade. In Sunflower County Fannie Lou Hamer organized the Freedom Farm Cooperative to obtain land for the unemployed plantation workers. Freedom Farm eventually grew to 680 acres and included a "pig bank" that provided cooperative members with free pigs to raise and slaughter for food.[5]

To address the scarcity of nonagricultural jobs for black unskilled workers, the Poor People's Corporation (PPC) was formed in the summer of 1965 under the leadership of SNCC activist Jesse Morris. Designed "to assist low-income groups to initiate and sustain self-help projects of a cooperative nature," the PPC was open to all poor people, charging nominal dues of twenty-five cents a year. With an initial fund of $5,000, the PPC loaned money, provided training, and set up a marketing network for small groups that worked together to produce a variety of craft items, including quilts, leather handbags, and children's clothing. Within a year there were sixteen "self-employment enterprises" underway in ten counties, and

"Liberty House" outlet stores opened in Jackson and in New York City.[6]

The cooperative movement, however, barely made a dent in the problems of black unemployment and poverty. From the outset the Poor People's Corporation had faced insurmountable difficulties in training workers, supplying materials and machinery to the cooperatives, and marketing the finished products. Factionalism developed in several of the centers, and morale suffered when checks were small and did not arrive on time. The major problem facing the PPC was inadequate capital. Lacking corporate or government support, and with local banks refusing to extend credit, the PPC barely scraped by during the late 1960s as a shoestring operation forced to rely on small contributions from civil rights supporters. Several of the farm cooperatives developed a more solid base, but the lack of financial resources to buy land and equipment meant that the number of displaced agricultural workers assisted remained quite small. By the early 1970s, cooperative farming was in decline.[7] Yet even in the early days of the cooperative movement, when enthusiasm was running high, movement activists realized that black poverty was so endemic that only the federal government had sufficient resources to combat the problem.

Early on the morning of January 31, 1966, a caravan of about a dozen cars moved through the streets of Greenville toward the U.S. Air Force base, a complex of 300 buildings, most of which had been empty since the military closed its pilot-training program there in 1960. At 6:30 A.M. the group of about forty poor blacks and ten civil rights workers swept past the startled guard at the gate, pulled up in front of a big gray wooden barracks, pried loose the padlock on the building's main door, and began unloading blankets and boxes of food. A half-hour later the base commander appeared, charged the interlopers with trespassing on government property, and demanded that they leave. The occupants refused, handing him a statement drafted the night before: "We are here because we are hungry and cold and we have no jobs or land. We don't want charity. We are willing to work for ourselves if given a chance." There followed a list of demands for food, land, job training, and jobs. The manifesto ended with a question for President Johnson: "Whose side are you on—the poor people's or the millionaires?"[8]

The decision to occupy the abandoned air base came out of a meeting held two days earlier that was attended by nearly 700 poor people and movement activists. The War on Poverty had had little impact on the impoverished farm workers in the Delta, whose suffering was intensified by an extremely cold Mississippi winter. Taking over the base, the group concluded, would send a strong message to Washington that "people were not only hungry in the Delta, but people needed homes and land."[9]

The audacious move took local and federal authorities by surprise. Fearing unfavorable publicity, city and county officials refused to evict the demonstrators. A Justice Department official showed up and unsuccessfully tried to convince the group to leave. At noon a second wave of about fifteen people moved in—no one had thought to lock the gates—bringing more food, blankets, and two small wood-burning stoves. Inside, the group began to organize for a long stay. The elected spokespersons were Isaac Foster, a young Delta labor organizer; Ida Mae Lawrence, an activist from Bolivar County; and Unita Blackwell, the Issaquena County leader who had been an FDP delegate at the Atlantic City convention. The group selected committees responsible for keeping the barracks clean, tending the stoves, and preparing meals. They agreed that the protest must remain nonviolent. Throughout the day other demonstrators arrived, climbing over the fences now that the gates had finally been locked. That evening the protestors, now numbering almost 100, ate a spaghetti dinner brought in by supporters from Greenville. Beginning around midnight, planes were heard circling around the base. "Thank the Lord," a plantation mother told her two children. "President Johnson is sending food for the folks in the Delta."[10]

The president was sending in troops, not food. The force included more than 150 air policemen, including two full colonels, three majors, and Major General R. W. Puryear. Early the following morning Puryear demanded that the demonstrators leave; when they refused the troops moved into the barracks, four at a time, escorting, carrying, and dragging the protestors out of the building and depositing them outside the base gates. There, Isaac Foster, speaking for the group, told reporters that "we had got our message across."[11]

They had indeed. Attorney General Nicholas Katzenbach warned President Johnson that "the situation demonstrated by the invasion of the Greenville Air Base . . . is potentially explosive." Katzenbach reported that in the Delta "many thousands of poor Negro workers are losing their jobs, and, in many instances, their homes as well." The situation was "even more acute because of the unwillingness of the white community to attempt to deal with the problem even at the welfare level," which had resulted in "great delays in getting federal programs carried out by state officials." The attorney general recommended that "we deal with this problem expeditiously and directly through surplus food distribution, crash employment programs, and as many poverty programs as we can fund. If we do not do this," Katzenbach concluded, "there is a real possibility that Mississippi will be the Selma, Alabama of 1966."[12]

The federal government did make available substantial quantities of food commodities, and officials promised to develop job-training programs in the Delta and provide housing for unemployed farm workers. Blacks, however, demanded that the air base be converted into housing for the displaced tenants. Greenville officials objected, for they did not want "a raft of unskilled Negroes" living near the community. Senator John Stennis then entered the debate, informing health, education, and welfare secretary Wilbur Cohen that unless the base was turned over to the city of Greenville (as agreed to earlier), "my only recourse will be through the HEW appropriations bill." Specifically, Stennis threatened funding for the president's new Teacher Corps. Although a compromise eventually resulted, the federal government backed away from its earlier commitments once the crisis surrounding the occupation of the base had passed.[13]

The Office of Economic Opportunity had not been totally insensitive to the problems facing blacks in the poorest and most racially torn state in the Union. In the summer of 1965, six months before the Greenville air force base occupation, OEO had made a major grant to provide preschool training for several thousand Mississippi children. The story of Operation Head Start in Mississippi is instructive, illustrating both the possibilities and limitations of federal programs designed to eliminate the causes and the condition of poverty.

• • •

The Child Development Group of Mississippi (CDGM) was one of the nation's pioneer Head Start programs. CDGM provided poor children with preschool training, medical care, and two hot meals a day; it also provided employment at decent wages for hundreds of local people who served as teachers and paraprofessionals at

Head Start centers. OEO cited it as a model program, one of "the best in the country," and praised CDGM for its parent involvement. Robert Coles testified that "in ten years of work in child psychiatry I have yet to see a program like this one. . . . against almost impossible odds children have been taught and also receive the benefits of medical care in a manner and with a thoroughness that is truly extraordinary."[14]

CDGM was the creation of Tom Levin, a forty-one-year-old psychoanalyst from New York who had worked in Mississippi during the summer of 1964 with the Medical Committee for Human Rights. In the spring of 1965 Levin met with other white activists involved in Mississippi, including Art Thomas of the Delta Ministry and Jeannine Herron, a freelance journalist. Together with Polly Greenberg, a program analyst with Head Start, they hammered out a proposal for a preschool program to run for seven weeks during the summer months. OEO officials were receptive, granting CDGM nearly 1.5 million dollars to serve 6,000 children through eighty-four centers in twenty-four counties. It was the largest Head Start program to be funded in the nation that summer. Mary Holmes Junior College, a private black school in northeast Mississippi, became CDGM's sponsoring agency, thereby avoiding the governor's veto of the program. A state board headed by Dr. Daniel Beittel, who had remained in Mississippi after being dismissed as president of Tougaloo College, was to oversee CDGM operations. Its central office was in Mount Beulah in central Mississippi on a twenty-three-acre campus, formerly the site of a black junior college and now the headquarters of the Delta Ministry and the Mississippi Freedom Democratic party.[15]

With only a few weeks to implement the program, Levin knew that the support of civil rights activists who had earned the trust of local people was essential if CDGM were to succeed. He discussed the program with Jim Forman, who invited him to a SNCC staff meeting at Waveland. Levin tried to persuade the veteran activists that CDGM "can be much more than simply early childhood education. It can act as a focus to organize a community around all their social aspirations." Now totally alienated from the federal government, SNCC saw the War on Poverty as a blatant move to co-opt the movement. And while CDGM was a natural extension of the freedom schools and based on egalitarian principles, it was a program conceived and developed by northern whites. Most of those present at the meeting opposed participation, and SNCC did not endorse CDGM. Levin did, however, convince veteran SNCC field secretary Frank Smith to sign on as director of community staff. Although not a "team player," more than any other member of the CDGM administration Smith knew black Mississippians and had their trust. Other movement people soon joined the staff, including SNCC's John Harris, Jim Monsonis, and Jim Dann and white Mississippi activist Jeannette King, the wife of the Reverend Ed King. Of the fifteen workers in the top administrative positions, thirteen had civil rights credentials. Eight were women and six were black.[16]

CDGM staff members contacted community people who had identified with COFO. They in turn formed hiring committees—the equivalent of school boards—employing some 1,100 workers to work in the eighty-four Head Start centers. Thus, CDGM took seriously OEO director Sargent Shriver's call for "maximum feasible participation of the poor in the solutions of their own problems." Although CDGM looked for teachers and teachers aides who could effectively work with preschool children, political considerations were also a factor. Privately, Levin admitted that "it is true that the poverty program has distinct 'pork barrel' aspects. The question to be asked will be, who will distribute the pork—the establishment or the poor?" Although several other Head Start programs were operating in Mississippi in the summer of 1965, CDGM was unique in that it was led by people who did not apologize for their civil rights involvement and who saw CDGM as an opportunity to provide education and services for poor children while at the same time advancing the movement agenda. CDGM centers were staffed by women, and a few men, who identified with the Mississippi Freedom Democratic party rather than with the NAACP. A frustrated Gloster Current reported that several NAACP branches were complaining that CDGM committees "are doing everything possible to deny to NAACP persons recommended to work on the 'Head Start' Project any opportunity to serve."[17]

As might be expected, Mississippi's white establishment vigorously opposed both CDGM and the entire War on Poverty. In 1964 all of Mississippi's congressional representatives had voted against funding the poverty program. The *Jackson Daily News* compared Head Start with programs in "Soviet Russia . . . Red China . . . [and] Hitler's Germany," concluding that "here is one of the most subtle mediums for instilling the acceptance of racial integration and ulti-mate mongrelization ever perpetuated in this country." Local school boards refused to rent their buildings and buses to Head Start. Rac-ists fired shots into several Head Start centers and harassed CDGM workers. In the Delta town of Anguilla plantation owners refused to permit sharecroppers' children to enroll in the program, and the Klan burned a cross at the center. Nevertheless, blacks in these com-munities, toughened by their experience in the movement, carried on, and all the centers opened on schedule.[18]

When the state's political leaders woke up to see an ongoing fed-erally financed institution operating independently and committed to racial equality, they moved quickly to destroy CDGM. Early in June Mississippi congressmen William Colmer and John Bell Williams charged that CDGM funds were being used to support civil rights activities. On June 29 Governor Paul Johnson wrote Shriver that CDGM was "an effort on the part of extremists and agitators to sub-vert lawful authority in Mississippi and create division and dissen-sion between the races." That same day the Senate Appropriations Committee, at the urging of committee member Stennis, sent staff members to Mississippi to inspect CDGM operations. Senate inves-tigators received assistance from the Mississippi State Sovereignty Commission, which had placed two informers in the CDGM central office. Commission director Erle Johnston shared this intelligence first with the Stennis committee and later with OEO itself. Most damag-ing was the revelation that early in June, CDGM had paid the fines of staff members jailed in the FDP demonstrations in Jackson. CDGM officials responded that they had only supplied "salary advances" to those arrested. Unfortunately, they recorded that entry in the finan-cial ledger as "bail fund." Stennis accused CDGM of mismanaging the grant as a whole and demanded that Shriver withhold remaining funds.[19]

The administrative structure of CDGM was, in fact, a mess. Staff member Joann Bowman wrote that "the difficulty lay in teaching our new administrators—both in the communities and on central staff—a financial system which by its very nature must be both in-tricate and unwieldy. It would have been comic had not the results been so disastrous in proportion and consequence." A basic prob-lem was meeting the payroll on time. Withholding forms submit-ted by the centers were misplaced, and when checks finally arrived to pay Head Start workers, they often lacked a signature or the recipient's name. School supplies often arrived late. Staff members in the field were careless about collecting and submitting receipts for expenses and left some funds unaccounted for. After Stennis publicized his charges, OEO auditors came down to Mississippi and instituted new procedures that corrected many of the problems. At no point had anyone made accusations of fraud or graft in connection with the CDGM grant, and according to Head Start associate director Jule Sugarman, the irregularities auditors uncovered "never exceeded more than 1 percent of the total cost of the program." In the end, less than $5,000 of the $1.5 million grant was disallowed.[20]

John Stennis was not appeased. As a ranking member of the powerful Senate Appropriations Committee, the Mississippi senator was critically important to the Johnson administration for funding not only the War on Poverty but also the war in Vietnam. OEO knew Stennis was most upset by CDGM's civil rights orientation and its association with the Delta Ministry and FDP. To pacify him, in late July OEO ordered the "immediate transfer" of the CDGM office from the movement center at Mount Beulah to Mary Holmes College, which was located in a remote area 150 miles from Jackson. They hoped this symbolic gesture would placate Stennis while preserving the program. CDGM staff did not see it that way. Frustrated by weeks of OEO scrutiny and angry at the CDGM board for agreeing to the relocation, the central staff threatened a mass resignation if the move to Mary Holmes were carried out. With only a month remaining in the Head Start program OEO officials finally admitted that "it was ludicrous to insist that the program move" and reversed themselves. But this controversy poisoned the atmosphere between OEO administrators in Washington and CDGM staff members.[21]

Surprisingly, the bitter battles waged by the politicians and bureaucrats had little impact on the operation of the Head Start centers themselves. Despite logistical problems involving materials and money, Head Start teachers and their aides, assisted by the local committees, reached more than 6,000 children that summer. In addition to receiving meals and medical care, the preschoolers were taught numbers, colors, and the alphabet—all parents wanted their children "to learn their ABCs." CDGM also included a "living arts" component, a traveling road show where actors, artists, and musicians would drop in on centers and engage the children in creative activities.[22]

Not all centers were exemplary. Polly Greenberg, now working for CDGM after quitting her job at OEO, observed most of the programs during the summer and concluded that nineteen of the eighty-four centers were "pretty terrible." There, strict discipline kept children "quiet and afraid." They did not see their parents "in new and dignified roles because parents played no part." Even in the worst centers, however, children were exposed to some new experiences, got enough to eat, and received some medical care. Greenberg found twenty-two centers to be "excellent," with the remainder "astonishingly adequate."[23]

The first CDGM program was a success. It did offer a "head start" to several thousand preschool children, all but a handful of them black. CDGM also provided meaningful jobs for 1,100 women and men in these communities. Where the going wage for plantation labor was three dollars a day, teacher's aides and trainees were paid from fifty to sixty dollars a week. Thus, despite the problems with OEO in Washington and the chaotic atmosphere surrounding the staff headquarters at Mount Beulah, CDGM was developing a dedicated following among blacks in the communities it served. Like COFO before it, CDGM was *their* organization. As Unita Blackwell put it, "When you say CDGM you are talking about the local people—we are talking about the people in the community."[24]

Impervious to the achievements of the program at the local level—which OEO readily acknowledged—politicians led by Senator Stennis continued to demand CDGM's scalp. By this time the War on Poverty was also under attack nationally, particularly from big-city mayors who, like the white Mississippi officials, resented their lack of political control over the new federal programs. On the defensive, OEO took immediate steps either to bring CDGM into line or to close it down.

The first casualty was CDGM's founder, Tom Levin. Freewheeling, at times arrogant, and a poor administrator, Levin alienated both OEO officials and important members of the CDGM board, including the Delta Ministry's Art Thomas and Marian Wright, the NAACP attorney now working full-time with the Inc. Fund in Jackson. He had also developed enemies on the CDGM staff, who resented his insistence that OEO procedures be followed. Levin, how-

ever, had set the tone for CDGM by staffing the program with movement workers and ensuring that local people would control their
own centers. His commitment to CDGM as not only a preschool
program but also an agency for social change was what had made
CDGM unique in Head Start. But pressured by OEO officials, the
CDGM board removed Levin as director even before the program
ended in late August. His replacement was a twenty-six-year-old
white man named John Mudd, the choice of board members Thomas and Wright. The Harvard-educated Mudd had run a summer
enrichment program for Tougaloo students in 1964 and was back
in the state working on a project to set up cooperatives. Although
he saw his new job as temporary, Mudd would preside over the
CDGM's fortunes for the next 2½ years.[25]

The replacement of Levin with Mudd was one of several major
changes affecting the structure, and mood, of CDGM. With most
of the federal grant expended, only a skeleton staff remained. Frank
Smith and other SNCC workers left, convinced (if they ever needed convincing) that grass-roots organization and federal funding
were incompatible. At OEO's insistence, CDGM shifted its operation from the movement community at Mount Beulah to the Mil-
ner Building in Jackson, which housed, among other mainstream
organizations, the Mississippi office of the FBI. With the encouragement of OEO, the CDGM board now began to exercise more
control over the day-to-day operations and to help write the new
grant.[26]

CDGM's second proposal, submitted in early November 1965,
met with foot dragging and petty criticisms from OEO. As the political infighting over CDGM became intense, Shriver backed away
from his Mississippi program. Jule Sugarman later recalled that he
would come to an agreement with CDGM only to have it overturned in Washington. "It really boiled down to the fact," Sugarman conceded, that Shriver had "added conditions after the agreement had been reached." Throughout the negotiations blacks in
more than fifty Mississippi communities continued to operate Head
Start programs without pay, providing their own transportation,
food, facilities, and classes for 3,000 preschool children.[27]

In early February 1966, the CDGM staff hit on the idea of taking their case directly to the U.S. Congress by sending two busloads
of preschool children to Washington. There, with their teachers and
teacher's aides, they would show what Head Start in Mississippi

was all about. With instant funding from wealthy northern supporters, the delegation took off for Washington. "A romper lobby from Mississippi petitioned Congress today for a redress of grievances" was the *New York Times*'s lead in its February 12 story on what others were calling "the children's crusade." Forty-eight black children and their teachers turned the hearing room of the House Education and Labor Committee into a kindergarten, complete with scissors and paste, crayons, and toys. They sang and clapped, drew pictures, and "dragged quacking Donald Ducks across the floor." Their teachers were less charming and more direct, telling the five congressional representatives present that CDGM wanted OEO funding "now, not maybe next week, next month, next year."[28]

Two weeks later OEO awarded CDGM a grant of 5.6 million dollars to operate for six months in 125 centers serving 9,135 children in twenty-eight counties. Stennis protested vigorously, joined by his colleague James Eastland, who charged that OEO money was funding "the extreme leftist civil rights and beatnik groups in our state, some of which have definite connections with Communist organizations."[29]

With the refunding of CDGM, Mississippi officials had to concede that the poverty program was there to stay, but they had found a way to control the flow of federal dollars into the state by creating Community Action Programs. As originally conceived by Congress, CAP was to be the core of the poverty program. The legislation provided for city, county, or multicounty boards composed of representatives from government, private civic agencies, and the poor to allocate all antipoverty funds in their area, including money for Head Start. OEO envisioned CAP as a cooperative effort by government, the private sector, and poor people to attack the problems of poverty at their most basic level. White Mississippians wanted no part of a program in which blacks participated as equals and for more than a year had refused OEO pleas to establish community action agencies. In the midst of the CDGM controversy, however, Governor Johnson and his allies came to see that by setting up CAP agencies in Mississippi communities, local whites could prevent the flow of federal dollars into programs like CDGM.[30]

Under continuing attack from segregationists, OEO was eager to recognize any CAP agency in Mississippi, regardless of its composition. In Greenwood the strongly segregationist county board of supervisors appointed all fourteen members of the CAP board.

SNCC activist Willie Peacock reported that the seven blacks on the board "have always been against the movement." When the Indianola police chief was appointed head of the local CAP, Sunflower County Progress, Inc., Congressmen Augustus Hawkins of Los Angeles and Joseph Resnick of New York were outraged, charging that under the chief's administration "Negro citizens of the town have endured a continuing experience of terrorism, beatings, harassment, bombings, and interference with their civil rights." The congressmen were successful in securing the chief's resignation, but the policy of the Sunflower CAP remained antiblack. Fannie Lou Hamer, for one, could not believe "that the landowners on the CAP board, who got us into poverty in the first place, are about to get us out."[31]

The strategy behind the sudden blossoming of community action programs in Mississippi first became apparent in Bolivar County, where the board of supervisors appointed eight whites and eight black "moderates" (whose "moderation," journalist Christopher Jencks reported, "was manifested by their invariable habit of agreeing with whatever their white counterparts said"). OEO approved the new agency. Immediately thereafter the Bolivar CAP voted to withhold money from the county's CDGM centers, with all eight blacks on the board supporting the decision. The local black community, however, remained loyal to CDGM, with unpaid volunteers staffing centers for 1,300 children.[32]

OEO was aware of the problem. One investigator concluded that "our present reliance on CAP boards in Mississippi seems unrealistic. . . . CAP boards were appointed by the local board of supervisors. Only hand-picked, rather wealthy Negroes are chosen. They are always either silent or compliant when faced with numerous and powerful whites. No CAP is responsive to the idea of elections in the poor community to allot to the poor representation." Yet Washington listened instead to white moderates like Doug Wynn, who in a letter to his friend Harry McPherson, Lyndon Johnson's special assistant, defended the Bolivar County CAP as "real progress, and I do not believe that such progress should be penalized, but rather, that it should be lauded, and encouraged to the fullest." Wynn dismissed opponents of the Bolivar CAP as "the same old Delta Ministry–CDGM–SNCC coalition which has been trying in every possible way to defeat the attempts of moderate right thinking people in Mississippi of both races to [develop] some sort of racial harmony rather than strife and disharmony."[33]

Although concerned over the threat posed by CAP boards controlled by white segregationists, CDGM pushed ahead with plans for expansion. Since the second Head Start grant was to expire at the end of the summer of 1966, in early July CDGM submitted an application for $41 million for a full-year program to cover 30,000 children. The proposed increase of some $35 million would triple the number of children served. OEO rejected this request as inconsistent with departmental guidelines; CDGM then scaled it down, asking for $21 million to serve 13,500 children.[34]

On August 5, Senate investigator Paul Cotter submitted a report highly critical of CDGM to Stennis and the Senate Committee on Appropriations. Cotter attacked CDGM's leadership, citing examples of adminstrative mismanagement. The Senate investigator found "a few [CDGM workers], both white and colored, who clearly fall into the category of extremists. They are not healthy for the program and should not be on the payroll." While conceding that Mississippi schoolteachers "attest that there is marked improvement in those children entering the first grade who have had Head Start training," Cotter could not help but "wonder whether these children are not being used as pawns to serve other purposes." After receiving the report, Stennis once again demanded that OEO cut off funding for CDGM. This time Shriver complied.[35]

While keeping CDGM in the dark about their plans, in August top OEO officials asked several Mississippi moderates to form a Head Start corporation, which OEO would then recognize as the successor to CDGM. Faced with mounting pressures from powerful segregationists on Capitol Hill, Shriver held an urgent meeting in Washington with Hodding Carter III and Aaron Henry. Carter candidly recalls that meeting: "I got the call and Aaron got the call and we came up here [to Washington]. We met with Sarge, and Sarge said: 'I need somebody to get my ass out of this sling. I gotta keep the Head Start program going and we're going to have to dump this one [CDGM], and I want you to put together a biracial board.' And so Aaron went back and got his brother-in-law, and I got Leroy Percy and Leroy got Owen Cooper and Oscar Carr . . . and we did this thing."[36]

On September 13, Cooper, a Yazoo City industrialist; Percy, a wealthy Delta planter; and Carter filed a charter for a new nonprofit corporation, Mississippi Action for Progress, Inc. (MAP). Governor Paul Johnson signed the charter the same day. Two weeks later the *Jackson Daily News* broke the story under the headline "12 MAN BOARD REPLACES CDGM." Owen Cooper was to be the MAP chairman, and he, Percy, and Carter appointed nine other people to the MAP governing board. No women or poor people were chosen, and a majority of its members were whites. On October 3 OEO formally announced its rejection of the new CDGM proposal. Counties with CAP boards were to take over existing CDGM programs. In the CDGM counties with no CAP boards, Head Start operations would be transferred to MAP. CDGM officials were stunned by the news. As more information became available, it became clear that the decision to replace CDGM with MAP had political implications beyond the question of who would run Head Start.[37]

MAP's original appointed governing board included Aaron Henry, R. L. T. Smith, and Charles Young. These three black men, along with Hodding Carter, were supporters of the ill-fated Mississippi Democratic Conference, set up the previous year to challenge MFDP. Carter was also cochair of the Mississippi Young Democrats. In short, the MAP board of directors was composed of the same men who had been working to undermine FDP and win recognition from the national Democratic party. This coalition of Delta whites and old-line NAACP leaders had not initiated the contact with OEO, and the MAP incorporators were genuinely concerned about keeping Head Start alive in Mississippi. Still, they must have been aware that control over millions of dollars of Head Start funds would give them political patronage and power, enhancing their position as a credible alternative to the Freedom Democratic party.[38]

Mississippi movement leaders—including those who had previously been lukewarm toward CDGM—denounced the OEO decision and demanded that CDGM be refunded. On October 8, some 3,500 blacks gathered in Jackson to protest the "political deal" and to hear Fannie Lou Hamer defiantly proclaim that "we aren't ready to be sold out by a few middle-class bourgeoisie and some of the Uncle Toms who couldn't care less." The audience endorsed the recommendations of the resolutions committee to boycott "the MAP board and all CAP boards not responsive to the poor" and to operate CDGM centers voluntarily until funds could be raised—from private sources, if necessary. That same day OEO released a telegram from John A. Morsell, the asssistant executive director of the NAACP, supporting the decision to fund MAP, and State Sovereignty Commission director Erle Johnston began cranking out telegrams to be signed by a dozen newspaper editors assuring Sargent Shriver that MAP "would restore confidence in Head Start. . . . people would support MAP but would not support CDGM."[39] Mississippi officials were so concerned about the CDGM "threat" that they endorsed an alternative Head Start program over which they had no direct control, a move unthinkable only a few months earlier.

OEO now moved rapidly to restructure Head Start in Mississippi. On October 3 CDGM had learned it would not be refunded. Four days later OEO announced Head Start grants of $700,000 to Southwest Mississippi Opportunities and $1.2 million to Rust College to operate in areas where CDGM had been active. A Rust official later conceded that the college had never submitted a "formal" proposal and that OEO had rejected its previous applications. On October 11 OEO awarded MAP $3 million for a year-long program covering thirteen counties, with Shriver pledging an additional $7 million to support MAP programs. The MAP application, OEO official Jule Sugarman later admitted, "was written in considerable degree by members of our own staff."[40]

If by pouring money into Mississippi Shriver had hoped to achieve a *fait accompli,* he miscalculated, for almost immediately a national coalition formed to demand that CDGM be refunded. Because of its educational focus and interracial composition, CDGM did not carry the stigma attached to black radicalism, and liberal organizations like the National Council of Churches and the Field and New World foundations rallied to its cause. The campaign to save CDGM was coordinated by the Citizens' Crusade Against Poverty (CCAP), an organization headed by former OEO official Richard Boone and bankrolled by elements of organized labor led by Walter Reuther. CCAP set up a "Citizen's Board of Inquiry," cochaired by A. Philip Randolph and National Council of Churches activist Robert Spike, to investigate the OEO decision to drop CDGM. The panel issued a stinging report defending CDGM against all charges of misconduct and accusing OEO of caving in to political pressure:

> We are unable to avoid the conclusion that the charges levied are a thin mask for a politically dictated decision . . . a yielding to those forces which have stood in historical opposition to progress for the poor and underprivileged in Mississippi. . . .

We cannot account for this decision on the basis of charges which are so insubstantial, so trivial, so unsupported in fact, so exaggerated and inflated and not supported by objective inquiry.[41]

CCAP also put together the ad hoc National Citizens' Committee for the Child Development Program in Mississippi, which on October 19 ran a full-page advertisement in the *New York Times* under the headline "Say it isn't so, Sargent Shriver," accusing OEO of abandoning the Head Start program "considered 'the best in the country.'" Shriver was stung by the ad, which he interpreted as a personal attack on his integrity, and OEO launched its own public relations effort. But the crusade to save CDGM had given the White House pause, and Vice President Hubert Humphrey, after meeting in early December with religious leaders at a Miami Beach conference, "promised his good offices."[42]

In mid-December, after a round of negotiations, OEO announced "an agreement in principle" with the CDGM board. MAP would still take over Head Start programs in nineteen counties formerly under CDGM control, but CDGM would also receive funds for a year to operate in nineteen of its original counties. The Washington press reported that CDGM had won "a hands-down victory." Two weeks later, however, OEO reversed itself, awarding five of the CDGM counties to MAP. These counties had been given to MAP in its October grant but "tentatively reassigned" to CDGM in December. Believing that OEO had double-crossed them, MAP leaders had insisted that OEO return the counties to them, rejecting an OEO compromise to permit both MAP and CDGM to work in the five disputed counties. (MAP officials knew that their program could not withstand CDGM competition in these counties.) Rather than jeopardize the grant renewal, CDGM officials accepted the reduced amount of nearly $5 million to run programs in their fourteen remaining counties. Several CDGM staff members, upset that the organization had accepted the grant without the five counties, helped to organize Friends of Children of Mississippi (FCM), which continued the Head Start program in these counties on a volunteer basis, assisted by grants from the Field Foundation.[43]

CDGM had won a Pyrrhic victory. OEO wrote into the new grant "a whole volume of conditions" that immobilized CDGM central staff. CDGM official Marvin Hoffman reported on the atmosphere at CDGM headquarters: "It's one thing to trade punches with Shriver out in the open, but the hidden bureaucrats are masterful guerilla fighters. . . . We have nothing to fight any of this with. We're tired and our supporters think the fight was won a long time ago. All of this would be too complicated to explain to them, and besides they've moved on to other things."[44]

Throughout 1967, the period of its third and final grant, CDGM was beset by internal problems. Black power advocates within CDGM deeply resented the continuing influence of white outsiders like Mudd and Hoffman. Charges of mismanagement surfaced in several centers, most notably in Madison County, now CDGM's largest program. Reverend James McRee, the state CDGM board chairman, formed an alliance there with veteran activist George Raymond, and the two men controlled CDGM hiring and policy in Canton, alienating many local blacks. The white leadership in the CDGM central office in Jackson was unable to resolve these problems, as McRee exploited the race issue to prevent close scrutiny of his operations, including allegations that he and Raymond demanded and received kickbacks from food suppliers and transportation contractors. In such an atmosphere many CDGM staff members became demoralized and disillusioned. There were recriminations and angry resignations.[45]

Relations between MAP and CDGM continued to be hostile, particularly in the disputed counties, where supporters of the Friends of Children of Mississippi were determined to maintain their programs free of local white control. In each of these areas deep resentment developed between black MAP and FCM workers as they fought over their children. Whatever its original intentions, the poverty program in Mississippi had divided the black community into warring factions, often pitting the poor men and women who had become politicized in the early 1960s against the old, traditional, middle-class leadership. Fannie Lou Hamer commented on this phenomenon in Sunflower County, where Head Start people associated with the movement were doing battle with the local CAP-sponsored program: "Now, the ministers, to get a little money, are selling their church to the white folks so the CAP program can run Headstart. . . . They're these middle-class Negroes, the ones that never had it as hard as the grass roots people in Mississippi. They'll sell their parents for a few dollars. Sometimes I get so disgusted I feel like getting my gun after some of these school teachers and chicken-eatin' preachers."[46]

The battle over Head Start in Mississippi ended in an uneasy accommodation. Helen Bass Williams, a black Tougaloo professor and former CDGM staff member, took over as director of MAP in mid-1967, and under her leadership MAP rewrote its bylaws to give Head Start parents more control over local programs. After CDGM's third grant ran out in December 1967, the organization dissolved as an administrative entity, with local CDGM programs now contracting directly with Mary Holmes Junior College, the original CDGM sponsor. In April 1968 OEO divided the disputed territory, giving four counties to the FCM and two to MAP. Early in 1968, however, OEO had also cut Head Start funding by 25 percent in Mississippi, a move dictated both by increasing demands for financing the war in Vietnam and by conservative backlash in Congress against the poverty program. Blacks united to protest these reductions, but to no avail.[47]

In drastically cutting funding for Head Start and the poverty program in general, the Johnson administration left a legacy of bitterness and distrust in the black community. In Mississippi, where fundamental economic changes underway for decades now literally threatened the survival of thousands of poor black families, the reduced commitment to fight the war against poverty would have serious consequences.

· · ·

In April 1967, in the midst of the battle between the FCM and MAP, attorney Marian Wright testified before the Senate Subcommittee on Employment, Manpower, and Poverty, which was holding hearings in Jackson. Charging that "the poverty program has done nothing to change the basic economic structure, which needs to be changed," Wright challenged committee members to accompany her up to the Delta and see firsthand the living conditions of America's poorest citizens. Taking her up on the offer, the senators made a highly publicized tour of several Delta counties. They were appalled at what they saw. Returning to Washington, committee member George Murphy, the conservative Republican senator from California, called on President Johnson to "declare an emergency situation exists in these areas, send in investigators and emergency aid." Senator Robert Kennedy of New York reported that the conditions he observed were "a condemnation of all of us . . . that this could exist in a prosperous nation like ours."[48]

The impressions gathered by the Senate subcommittee were reinforced by the findings of a team of distinguished physicians, which conducted a four-day inspection tour of Humphreys, Leflore, Clarke, Wayne, Neshoba, and Greene—the six FCM counties. Focusing on the impact of poverty on young people, the doctors examined children "whose nutritional and medical attention we can only describe as shocking—even to a group of physicians whose work involves daily confrontations with disease and suffering." Specifically, "in child after child" they saw "thin arms, sunken eyes, lethargic behavior, [and] swollen bellies," along with

> evidence of vitamin and mineral deficiencies; serious, untreated skin infections and ulcerations; eye and ear diseases . . . severe anemia. . . . We saw children with chronic diarrhea, chronic sores, chronic leg and arm (untreated) injuries and deformities. We saw homes without running water, without electricity, without screens, in which children drink contaminated water and live with germ-bearing mosquitoes and flies everywhere around. We saw homes with children who are lucky to eat one meal a day. . . . We saw children fed communally—that is, by neighbors who give scraps of food to children whose own parents have nothing to give them.

The physicians reported that "not only are these children receiving no food from the government, they are also getting no medical attention whatsoever. They are out of sight and ignored. They are living under such primitive conditions that we found it hard to believe we were examining American children in the twentieth century." The panel's conclusion was grim: "We do not want to quibble over words, but 'malnutrition' is not quite what we found. . . . They are suffering from hunger and disease and directly or indirectly they are dying from them—which is exactly what 'starvation' means."[49]

Thousands of Delta blacks had been living in poverty for generations, but the reports of starvation in America sent shock waves throughout the country, bringing journalists and television documentary crews to Mississippi to conduct their own investigations. Predictably, the white Mississippi establishment reacted defensively. In a television interview Governor Johnson countered that "nobody is starving in Mississippi," adding that "the nigra women I see are so fat they shine." But the evidence of widespread hunger was irrefutable, and the explanation—the collapse of the old plantation system—was no secret in Washington. Ironically, those federal policies designed to improve the quality of life in rural America had in fact made things worse for black Mississippians.[50]

Beginning with the Agricultural Adjustment Administration of the New Deal, the federal government had provided direct subsidies to farmers who took part of their land out of cultivation. The goal of this program was to reduce the supply of food and staples and thereby stabilize prices. Under the leadership of Delta congressman Jamie Whitten, the powerful chairman of the House Appropriations Subcommittee on Agriculture, the subsidy program expanded with the passage of the Food and Fiber Act of 1965, which provided cotton growers a payment of 10.5 cents per pound on projected yields for land taken out of cotton production. More than 70 percent of the Delta plantation owners in the program took advantage of the maximum reduction of 35 percent of their acreage, thereby reaping a financial bonanza. In 1966, 224 Mississippi farmers—nearly all of them Delta planters—took home payments of at least $50,000 each for not planting cotton. Thirty-six planters had subsidies in excess of $100,000, including Senator Eastland, who received $130,000 for his Sunflower County plantation. Altogether, Mississippi cotton farmers received more than $39 million in 1966, and this figure did not include government payments under the price-support program for crops harvested.[51]

For the following year the numbers would be even higher. The historian James C. Cobb has shown that in 1967, "22 percent of all payments in excess of fifty thousand dollars for the entire nation were made in the Delta, which also accounted for 17 percent of the national total for payments above one hundred thousand dollars." Although the planter elite profited immensely from this federal welfare program, the one-third reduction in cotton production devastated black farm workers. Demand for plantation seasonal labor fell by more than 75 percent between 1965 and 1967, and even the number of jobs for tractor drivers had declined by at least 25 percent.[52]

But it was Congress's extension of the federal $1.00 an hour minimum wage to agricultural workers in February 1967 that sounded the death knell for black farm workers. The Mississippi Freedom Labor Union had been one of a number of progressive organizations lobbying for the law, for theoretically the average Mississippi farm laborer would now earn $10 for a day's work, significantly more than the going rate of $3.50. Now legally obligated to pay higher wages, those farmers who had hired day labor to chop cotton immediately switched to herbicides. According to one estimate, after passage of the statute, chemical weed killers became approximately twelve times less expensive than human labor. Three months after the minimum wage law took effect White House official Lisle Carter "conservatively estimated that an additional 11,000 farm workers, representing families in excess of 50,000 members, have lost or will lose their jobs."[53]

For thousands of black families now without income the implementation of the highly touted federal food stamp program came as a cruel blow. Phased in gradually beginning in 1964, food stamps were to replace the commodities program, where staples like flour, powdered milk, and eggs were distributed monthly to impoverished residents. The family with stamps, supporters argued, would enjoy a greater variety of fresh, nutritious food and be spared the humiliation of lining up each month for a government handout. The commodities program in Mississippi was flawed, and as noted earlier, in the early 1960s counties cut off commodities to punish blacks engaged in civil rights work. Even so, the program was generally accessible to those who needed it, for planters were happy to have the federal government feed their work force during the winter months. Unfortunately, the food stamp program had been introduced at a time when there was no longer a demand for black labor, and the white Mississippi bureaucracy administered the new program "selectively, politically, and with racial considerations in mind."[54]

The most serious problem was that while the commodities program had been free, recipients of food stamps had to pay hard cash to get them. The minimum charge for stamps was two dollars per participant. A family of six would have to pay twelve dollars each month for stamps for seventy-two dollars' worth of groceries, even if the family had no income at all. Thus, counties that switched from commodities to food stamps saw a dramatic decline in the number of people receiving assistance. In Leflore County, 20,751 people had been receiving commodities in 1965. After two months under the food stamp program, only 8,331 were signed up. Since a county had to opt for one program or the other, this meant that 12,000 Leflore residents were no longer receiving any food. In 1967 the changeover in 50 percent of Mississippi counties from commodities to food stamps left an estimated 64,000 people who had received free food unable to buy food stamps. An NAACP investigator who toured the Delta in the spring of 1967 reported, "I am finding scores of people who are eating perhaps half of what they did under the commodity program. Many are living on leftover commodities, which are fast disappearing."[55]

The food stamp problem surfaced when the Senate subcommittee made its inspection trip to the Delta in April 1967. Among its recommendations to the president were that Secretary of Agriculture Freeman "should make food stamps available without cost to people who have no cash income" and that the purchase requirements for low-income families "should be lowered to reflect more realistic standards." The problem here once again was Jamie Whitten, who fought the proposal because "when you start giving people something for nothing, just giving them all they want for nothing, I wonder if you don't destroy character more than you might improve nutrition." The same Congressman Whitten who opposed giving hungry people in his district "something for nothing" was, of course, demanding and getting millions of dollars in federal subsidies for his Delta planter friends. In July the Department of Agriculture did lower the minimum price of stamps to fifty cents per person, with a maximum of three dollars per family, but even this amount was beyond the reach of many families.[56]

That unemployed people had *no* money to buy food stamps was an indictment of Mississippi's welfare system. State and local welfare offices were notoriously discriminatory in their treatment of blacks, with only a small percentage of those in need making it onto the welfare rolls. Mississippi's contribution to the AFDC (Aid to Families with Dependent Children) program was the lowest in the nation. Dependent children received payments amounting to about 25 percent of what the state of Mississippi estimated to be the minimum necessary for bare subsistence, and aid payments actually decreased from $13.30 per child per month in 1964 to $9.25 in 1966.[57]

As the physicians who inspected the state in 1967 learned to their horror, health conditions among poor blacks were appalling. Where in the heyday of the plantation system sharecroppers might have expected the planters to provide some minimal health care, now they were on their own. With only fifty-five black physicians in the state, most blacks had to rely on white doctors, and without money up front they might not even be treated. Dr. Raymond Wheeler, a white North Carolinian representing the Southern Regional Council on the physician's investigating team, estimated that "nine out of 10 children that we saw had never seen a doctor. I was told by some mothers of outright refusal of hospitals to care for their youngsters when they were sick because they were unable to pay." From the beginning of the Great Depression until the end of World War II, infant mortality among blacks had declined significantly in Mississippi, but over the next two decades there had been a steady *increase,* from 40.8 deaths per 1,000 live births in 1946 to 55.1 in 1965. "In no State other than Mississippi is the infant mortality of the Negro child steadily rising," Dr. Joseph Brenner informed the Senate subcommittee, "in no other State."[58]

Dr. Wheeler told the senators that in the Delta the doctors frequently "heard charges of an unwritten but generally accepted policy on the part of those who control the State to eliminate the Negro in Mississippi, either by driving him out of the State or starving him to death." Wheeler at first felt that "the charge seemed to . . . be beyond belief," but after "now reviewing what we saw and heard, it becomes more and more credible." On hearing Dr. Wheeler's remarks, Senator Eastland angrily took exception, adding, "I live around Negroes. If they were all to leave the State and move out of the State, I would move out with them, because I have always associated and been around them."[59]

Although circumstantial, the evidence to support this allegation—accepted without question by most Mississippi blacks—is persuasive. By 1967 the mechanization of cotton farming was almost total; the state's agricultural economy no longer needed black labor. In 1966 two Delta state senators had even introduced legislation designed to relocate Mississippi Negroes to other states. Whites realized that with the passage and enforcement of the voting rights act, African Americans had the potential to gain political power, particularly in those Delta counties where they were still a majority. Moreover, poverty programs such as CDGM had instilled the hope among blacks that they and their families could have a better life in Mississippi. Viewed in this context, the state political establishment's monolithic opposition to the poverty program, CDGM, job retraining, and adequate welfare for the needy carries with it a Machiavellian logic supporting New York congressman Joseph Resnick's conclusion that "the policy of the state of Mississippi is to drive the Negro out."[60]

Unable to keep the poverty program out of Mississippi, white leaders had moved to control it, establishing CAP programs run by local whites, waging war on CDGM, and finally accepting MAP as a less-threatening alternative. They also adopted policies whose impact was to accelerate the black migration—particularly in the heavily black Delta counties—that had been underway since the 1940s. Civil rights activists, who had for years pursued a program based on black enfranchisement and the end of legal segregation, had to deal with this new set of realities as the movement of the 1960s entered its final phase.

17

The Last March

At 1:45 P.M. on Sunday, June 4, 1966, James Meredith stood outside the Peabody Hotel in Memphis, surrounded by a handful of supporters and journalists. Wearing a yellow pith helmet and carrying an ebony African walking stick, Meredith stepped off toward U.S. Highway 51 to begin a 220-mile walk to Jackson, Mississippi. His purpose was "to challenge the all pervasive and overriding fear" still dominant among most black Mississippians and to convince them it was now safe to register and vote. The thirty-two-year-old Meredith had all but dropped out of sight since his graduation from Ole Miss three years earlier. He had toured Africa, moved to New York with his wife and son, and was now a student at the Columbia University law school. Always a loner, Meredith did not discuss his plans with any national civil rights leaders, nor had he been in touch with movement people in Mississippi. His first day on the road was uneventful: he walked twelve miles to within a few hundred yards of the Mississippi border and then returned by car to Memphis.[1]

The activists in the Mississippi Freedom Democratic party had not paid much attention to Meredith's venture, for they were in the final stages of their first statewide campaign, running candidates in the Democratic congressional primary. Although no one expected any victories, it was important that FDP make a respectable showing. The Delta Ministry had stepped in to provide support, but only a handful of outside SNCC and CORE workers remained in the state. At the same time, FDP's competitors were gaining strength.

Fresh from his "triumph" in Natchez, Charles Evers was adding to his base in the southwestern counties, registering voters, conducting boycotts in Fayette and Port Gibson, and expanding the NAACP membership rolls by more than 2,000 adults (with an additional 800 members in youth groups) in Claiborne, Jefferson, and Wilkinson counties. The NAACP–Young Democrats coalition was developing ties with the national Democratic leadership. In late November 1965 Doug Wynn and a group of "loyal Democrats" met secretly with Vice President Hubert Humphrey in New Orleans to discuss "the problems of the Democratic Party in Mississippi." Wynn advised Humphrey that "it would be extremely detrimental to our efforts should you maintain any contact or make any response to . . . Mr. Guyot or the so-called Mississippi Freedom Democratic Party."[2]

While no longer openly defying federal authority, the state's elected officials had not enforced the Civil Rights Act of 1964: Jim Crow was still the rule rather than the exception. Only a few restaurants and hotels in the larger cities served black patrons, and blacks attempting to desegregate public facilities were still being arrested for disturbing the peace. Although by the spring of 1966 more than half of Mississippi's school districts were technically in compliance with Title VI of the Civil Rights Act of 1964, which cut off federal funds to segregated schools, under Mississippi's "freedom of choice" plan only about 6,300, or slightly more than 2 percent, of the state's black children were attending previously all-white schools. Whites retaliated against many of the parents of these children by canceling credit, firing them from their jobs, evicting them from their homes, and in some cases resorting to violence. In school systems such as Issaquena's, children were driven to the white schools in separate buses, ate in segregated cafeterias, and sat together "in a completely segregated class." Local and state authorities refused to assist Justice Department investigations of these cases.[3]

State officials at first largely ignored the voting rights act. (They would soon pass legislation to subvert its intent.) Passed in the summer of 1965, the law prohibited circuit clerks from using the discriminatory practices that had kept blacks off the voting rolls. All that blacks now needed to register was proof of age and residency. The law also gave the attorney general power to dispatch federal registrars into areas where discrimination was blatant. Although thousands of new black voters were being added to the rolls in Mississippi, there were widespread reports of violations of the law in both letter and spirit. The federal government, however, was reluctant to move in. Steven Lawson, the leading historian of the voting rights act, has written that the administration sent federal registrars "only as a last resort," preferring to rely on voluntary compliance. Federalism remained the operating principle of the Johnson administration. Initially, the attorney general dispatched registrars to only eight Mississippi counties, and as late as March 1966 no registrars had been sent to thirty Mississippi counties where less than 25 percent of the adult black population was registered, including Senator Eastland's home base in Sunflower. Even in counties with federal registrars, blacks were reluctant to make the trip to the courthouse, still fearing white retaliation. They had good reason to be afraid, for the Ku Klux Klan's response to the voting rights act had been to step up its reign of terror.[4]

Spurred on by the new voting law, long-time Hattiesburg activist Vernon Dahmer had been urging Forrest County blacks to register and vote. Dahmer was a wealthy man by Mississippi standards, owning a 400-acre farm, a saw mill, and a grocery store. He lived with his wife and three of their seven children in an attractive ranch-style home. Late one night in January 1966 two carloads of klansmen pulled up outside Dahmer's home and store. One group torched the store while the others fired their shotguns into the house, shattering the big picture window. Two men hurled gasoline containers and a flaming, gas-soaked rag through the window. The explosion turned the front part of the house into an inferno. Dahmer, who had been sleeping with his family in the back room, grabbed his shotgun and threw open the door to the living room. The sudden draft sucked the flames through the doorway, enveloping Dahmer. He commanded his wife to get the children out while he fired into the darkness to hold off the attackers. Only after they were safe did he follow them outside. Vernon Dahmer died the next afternoon, his respiratory tract seared from inhaling so much fire and smoke.[5]

Two days later, as blacks grieved over the loss of yet another courageous leader, Lyndon Johnson in his State of the Union Address called on Congress to enact "legislation to strengthen authority of Federal courts to try those who murder, attack, or intimidate either civil rights workers or others exercising their constitutional rights" and to increase the penalties for civil rights crimes. As Congress debated the bill into the summer, down in Mississippi business went on as usual, as James Meredith was soon to learn.[6]

Again accompanied by a few friends and several reporters, Meredith crossed into Mississippi on the second day of his journey, covering some sixteen miles by late afternoon. Then, just south of Hernando, a white man named Aubrey James Norvell stood up in the roadside brush, twice shouted out the name "James Meredith," raised his shotgun, and fired three loads of buckshot. Some sixty to seventy pellets struck Meredith in the head, neck, and body while his horrified companions and the media representatives looked on. About fifteen law officers "in the vicinity" quickly apprehended Norvell, an unemployed hardware contractor from Memphis, and rushed Meredith to a Memphis hospital.[7]

The reaction of the politicians and the press was swift and predictable. President Johnson deplored the shooting as "an awful act of violence that every sensible American deplores"; the *New York Times* praised Meredith's courage and editorialized that "the nation cannot allow Mr. Meredith, as a symbol of the Southern Negro, to fail in his journey against fear." A Hernando grocer voiced a common sentiment among local whites: "It's terrible. Why did it have to happen in Mississippi? Why couldn't it have happened in Tennessee?" Governor Paul Johnson preferred to look on the positive side, stating, "I am particularly pleased that [Meredith's attacker] was not a Mississippian." As it turned out, Meredith's wounds were superficial—an AP story had gone out over the wires stating that he had died—but the attempted assassination transformed what had been a lonely walk through Mississippi into the last great march of the civil rights years.[8]

Almost immediately after the shooting, leaders of the national civil rights organizations rushed to Meredith's bedside and won his endorsement to continue the march while he recuperated from his wounds. Martin Luther King and Floyd McKissick, the new head of CORE, were the first to arrive, followed by SNCC's Cleveland Sellers, Stanley Wise, and Stokely Carmichael. The three had been visiting a SNCC project in Arkansas and drove to Memphis when they heard the news. A month earlier Carmichael had replaced John Lewis as SNCC's chairman in a hotly contested election. Carmichael's ascendancy had signified a new emphasis in SNCC, one that stressed black consciousness and the building of independent institutions in the community. He saw the Meredith March as an opportunity "to organize in communities along the march route," as well as to expose SNCC's new program to a national audience.[9]

The NAACP's Roy Wilkins and Whitney Young of the Urban League flew to Memphis for a late Tuesday night strategy session with the other leaders of "the big five" civil rights organizations. Carmichael arrived at the meeting with an agenda and an attitude. With Selma in mind, Wilkins, Young, and King wanted the march to marshal national support for the president's civil rights bill; but Carmichael, with support from CORE's McKissick, insisted instead that "the march serve as an indictment of President Johnson over the fact that existing laws were not being enforced." Reflecting the nationalist, militant SNCC mood, Carmichael called for the exclusion of whites from the march and asked that the Louisiana-based Deacons for Defense be invited to provide protection for the marchers. Carmichael later told journalist Milton Viorst that it was his intent to alienate the more conservative Wilkins and Young: "So I started acting crazy, cursing real bad. . . . We wanted to let them know it would be impossible to work with us. . . . Young and Wilkins fell completely into the trap and stormed out of there."[10]

Carmichael had been careful not to direct his anger at King, and the SCLC leader remained largely silent throughout Stokely's harangue. Carmichael eventually dropped his demand that whites be excluded, and King reluctantly agreed to let the Deacons participate.[11] King and Carmichael had arrived at an unspoken understanding. SCLC needed SNCC's cooperation, for the march's route bordered on the Mississippi Delta, "SNCC territory." SNCC wanted Dr. King as a drawing card to turn out large crowds along the way and to attract the national media. The press later exploited the two leaders' ideological differences, but without their cooperation and willingness to "agree to disagree," the march might never have made it to Jackson.

After Wilkins and Young had left the meeting, those remaining agreed to a march "manifesto." Calling on the president to "actively enforce existing federal laws to protect the rights of all Americans," to send federal registrars to all 600 Deep South counties, and to propose "an adequate budget" to deal with black rural and urban poverty, it went on to urge Johnson to strengthen the 1966 civil rights bill by accelerating the integration of southern juries and law enforcement agencies. Strident in tone, the manifesto was nonetheless a realistic assessment of the problems facing African Americans, calling attention to federal foot dragging in dealing with poverty, voting rights, and law enforcement. Now back in New York, Young and Wilkins refused to sign the document because it put "the blame for everything, personally, on the President." Representatives of the various civil rights organizations operating in Mississippi—the FDP, Delta Ministry, and state NAACP—endorsed both the march and the manifesto. However, a day later Charles Evers, perhaps influenced by Wilkins's position, charged that someone had forged his name to the document and that he actually opposed it "because it was too critical of President Johnson."[12]

On Tuesday—the day after Meredith was shot—Mississippi held its primary elections. The Freedom Democratic party was running a slate of candidates in all five congressional races and was also contesting the seat of Senator James Eastland. As a result of the voting rights act, nearly 140,000 blacks were now registered, one-third of the eligible black electorate and an increase of some 100,000 since 1964, a significant achievement in the face of the continued harassment of applicants in many counties. Yet only about one-fourth of registered blacks voted in the primary. FDP chair Lawrence Guyot won less than 5 percent of the vote in his fifth district congressional race; the party's best congressional showing was in the third district, which included Jackson, where Tougaloo chaplain Ed King, the only white FDP candidate, won 22 percent of the vote against incumbent John Bell Williams. The major "victory" occurred in Claiborne and Jefferson counties, where FDP senatorial candidate Clifton Whitley ran ahead of Eastland. These counties had been organized by Charles Evers, and for FDP leaders it was cold comfort that the strongest black turnout occurred in areas controlled by their bitter rival. The Justice Department received complaints throughout the state from blacks who had been barred from voting or harassed at the polls. The low black turnout strongly suggested that thousands of black voters had stayed home because, in the immediate aftermath of the Meredith shooting, they feared white intimidation and reprisals.[13]

Mississippi activists wanted the Meredith March "to deliver some concrete results for Mississippi black people" by registering new voters and providing political education through mass rallies. Once again, voter registration would be the program to unite all factions. March leaders agreed that instead of following Meredith's original route straight down Highway 51, the march would veer westward into the heart of the Delta. Teams of organizers split off from the main group, spread out into the surrounding counties, and used the march as a catalyst to encourage blacks to get their names on the voting rolls. An early emotional high point occurred in Batesville, when a 104-year-old farmer named El Fondren registered for the first time. As he emerged from the courthouse young black men hoisted him to their shoulders and carried him through a cheering crowd.[14]

The first week of the Meredith March had an informal, relaxed quality. There were a few white hecklers, but local officials were eager to avoid incidents and urged whites to stay away from the marchers. Seeking to avoid federal intervention, Governor Johnson had made good on his promise to protect the marchers, with twenty highway patrol cars on the scene during the day. At night, the Deacons for Defense took over, guarding the campsites "with pistols, rifles, and shotguns." The number of marchers varied from 30 to more than 250 each day. Many local blacks joined the march briefly as it passed through their towns. Freedom Democratic party and Delta Ministry representatives made local arrangements for food and lodging and directed voter registration efforts. The national leaders—King, Carmichael, and McKissick—left the march from time to time, but their organizations were always represented.[15]

The march achieved its greatest triumph in Grenada, a town of some 10,000 halfway between Memphis and Jackson. Believing that "the less trouble there was, the sooner the marchers would leave," local officials did not inhibit the activities of the marchers, with the result that for a day and a night Grenada became—for Mississippi—an open city. The festivities began when 200 marchers filing across the Yalabusha River Bridge "sang and danced their way into Grenada." Local blacks more than doubled the size of the march as they joined the procession to the courthouse square. The crowd cheered when SCLC's Bob Green climbed up the courthouse's Confederate monument and placed an American flag atop a statue of Jefferson Davis, a sacrilege that sullen white bystanders let go unchallenged. Blacks then moved into the courthouse, forming long lines into the "white only" restrooms. They also lined up to register. City authorities had agreed to hire six black teachers as deputy registrars and to permit nighttime and neighborhood registration. Before the march only 697 Grenada blacks were registered; that number literally doubled overnight. The 1,300 blacks added to the county's voting lists in two days was more than Governor Paul Johnson had bargained for. Using the excuse that the march had "turned into a voter registration campaign," Johnson cut the number of patrol cars accompanying the march from twenty to four and turned over responsibility for protecting the marchers to local authorities. That he did so just as the marchers headed west toward Greenwood, widely known for its oppression of civil rights activists, appeared more than coincidental.[16]

Greenwood marked both the halfway mark and the turning point of the Meredith March. For a week and a half political differences among march leaders had been kept largely beneath the surface, white community leaders along the way had gone out of their way to avoid confrontation, and the press, on the whole, was sympathetic. In the final ten days of the march, however, white authorities resorted to familiar tactics of repression in Greenwood, Philadelphia, and Canton; the march turned more militant, with the divisions among leaders becoming apparent; and the national media exploited these interorganizational tensions while adopting a more cynical attitude toward the march itself.

The trouble began in Greenwood when police arrested Carmichael and two other SNCC workers as they defied a city order by putting up tents to house the marchers on the grounds of a black public school. They were hauled off to jail in handcuffs. The city then relented and allowed the marchers to spend the night on the school grounds. Six hours later an angry Carmichael, just out on bail, told an agitated crowd of 600—most of them local people—that "this is the 27th time I have been arrested—I ain't going to jail no more. I ain't going to jail no more." Then Carmichael shouted five times, "We want black power!" The crowd cheered and with each repetition grew more enthusiastic. "Every courthouse in Mississippi ought to be burned tomorrow to get rid of the dirt," he proclaimed. "Now, from now on when they ask you what you want, you know what to tell 'em. What do you want?" Stokely asked rhetorically, and the crowd thundered back, time and again, "Black power!" The nation would quickly get the message.[17]

Carmichael's cry for black power was no spontaneous outburst. SNCC advance man Willie Ricks had tried out the slogan at rallies earlier in the week. The crowds had responded enthusiastically, and Ricks urged Carmichael to use it in Greenwood. Nor was the idea itself new. SNCC had been moving in a nationalist direction since the 1964 Atlantic City convention. Carmichael's Greenwood speech was a dramatic public revelation of a course that SNCC had decided on when Carmichael replaced John Lewis as chairman in May. Subject as it was to many interpretations, the slogan's ambiguity for a time enhanced its appeal.[18]

Most white Americans quickly came to see black power as a threat, as "racism in reverse" with violent implications. During his Greenwood speech, Carmichael had come close to a working definition (one largely ignored by the press) when he said that "we have to do what every group in this country did—we gotta take over the community where we outnumber people so we can have decent jobs." For black Mississippians this made sense—it was what they had been about since the first voter registration drive in McComb. Nonetheless, "black power" became the bogeyman for much of the media covering the march, and as such it created problems for the moderate civil rights leadership symbolized by Martin Luther King.[19]

For some time SNCC had been burning its bridges to the white liberal community—renouncing the philosophy of nonviolence, decreeing that integration was irrelevant, and deciding that its white members should not organize in black communities—yet King and the moderate civil rights forces had remained committed to a program based on nonviolent direct action and to the goal of an integrated society. The idea of black power represented a direct challenge to King's leadership as well as his to philosophy, and he was so upset by Carmichael's actions that for a time he considered pulling SCLC out of the march. Instead, he took the offensive, stating that "the term 'black power' is unfortunate because it tends to give the impression of black nationalism," adding that "black supremacy would be as evil as white supremacy." King's criticism was considerably more restrained than that of the NAACP's Roy Wilkins, who in a *Life* magazine article defined black power as "the reverse of Mississippi, a reverse Hitler, and a reverse Ku Klux Klan," an intemperate characterization he later retracted. Many white liberals shared Vice President Hubert Humphrey's view that "racism is racism—and there is no room in America for racism of any color."[20]

Despite these attacks, many blacks along the march route were drawn to the slogan and to Carmichael's fiery denunciations of a caste system that had oppressed them for generations. Yet they also revered Dr. King and continued to flock to the roadsides to catch a glimpse of their hero. Black Mississippians did not want to be forced to choose between the two men. The fervent desire by local people that their leaders work together had brought COFO into existence four years earlier; that same spirit made it possible for the Meredith March to continue, albeit in an atmosphere of increasing distrust and tension.

The main contingent of the march moved down the Delta to Belzoni, where George Lee and Gus Courts had been shot eleven years earlier, and through the hamlets of Midnight and Louise. About twenty marchers led by King then split off and drove across the state to Philadelphia to hold a service commemorating the second anniversary of the deaths of Chaney, Schwerner, and Goodman. (The previous day the Justice Department had announced that eighteen men, including Sheriff Lawrence Rainey and his deputy Cecil Price, would be tried in federal court for "violating the civil rights" of the three victims.) In Philadelphia 200 local people joined the Meredith marchers to walk from the Mount Nebo Baptist Church to the county courthouse. Prevented by the police from assembling on the courthouse lawn, the group moved a block away to the county jail. Several hundred whites surrounded the marchers, taunting them during a prayer led by the Rev. Ralph Abernathy. Deputy Price and other police officers stood behind Martin Luther King as he said, "I believe in my heart that the murderers are somewhere around me at this moment." When a white man shouted, "They're right behind you!" the courthouse crowd roared approval. King later said that at that moment he had "yielded to the real possibility of . . . death." The Delta Ministry's Owen Brooks recalled, "I was scared to death. We were just ringed with hostile people who had all types of armaments with them."[21]

As the marchers began to work their way back to the relative safety of Philadelphia's black section a group of twenty-five whites attacked the demonstrators with clubs while the police looked on, as did several Justice Department observers and FBI agents. Police intervened only when blacks started fighting back. Whites continued to hurl bottles and insults at the retreating marchers. "This is a terrible town, the worst I've seen," remarked King, who vowed to return to Philadelphia and called for federal protection for the next rally there. President Lyndon Johnson denied King's request, stating that "the Attorney General informs me that Governor Paul Johnson has assured him that law and order will be maintained . . .

throughout the march, and that all necessary protection can and will be provided."[22]

That night Governor Johnson's highway patrol was out in force in Canton, as the main contingent of the marchers had closed to within twenty miles of their destination in Jackson. Tensions had been building in Canton. The previous day police had arrested C. O. Chinn, the community's boldest black activist, on charges of "assault with a deadly weapon with intent to kill." Chinn and others had chased a carload of whites who had thrown a homemade firebomb at FDP headquarters and caught up with them at a service station. According to police, Chinn then shot and wounded one of the whites in the left arm, a charge he denied. Chinn was released on bail in time to join other Canton blacks in welcoming the 200 marchers, who arrived about 6:00 P.M. and proceeded directly to the courthouse, where more than 1,000 people had gathered for a rally. As in Greenwood, the marchers planned to pitch their tents on the campus of a black public school. Canton officials refused permission. A defiant Carmichael told the crowd that "they said we couldn't pitch tents on our own black school-ground. We're going to do it now," and he led a march from the courthouse to the school, which was about fifteen blocks away. When they arrived there, the crowd, now numbering about 3,500 people, saw sixty-one state troopers lined up in full battle gear and carrying nightsticks, carbines, automatic shotguns, and pistols. Faced with this show of force, about a third of the crowd melted away into the purple twilight, but nearly 2,500 remained to begin putting up the tents and to listen while a worried Martin Luther King, speaking from atop a flat-bed truck, told them, "I don't know what they plan for us, but we aren't going to fight any state troopers. But we are willing to fill up all the jails in Mississippi."[23]

At 8:40 P.M. a state trooper issued a warning: "You will not be allowed to erect the tents—if you do you will be removed." Two minutes later, having put on their masks, the troopers began firing tear gas across the field. The first volley scattered the crowd, but the troopers kept on firing and then waded in with their guns and nightsticks. Paul Good, a journalist on the scene, wrote that "they came stomping in behind the gas, gun-butting and kicking the men, women, and children. They were not arresting, they were punishing." Mrs. Odessa Warrick, a black woman in her late thirties, tried to get up after being stunned by the gas. A trooper kicked her down, shouting, "Nigger, you want your freedom, here it is!" Another local resident who worked for CDGM observed the scene from her home across from the field: "Suddenly, I saw this smoke rise, [and] heard somebody scream, 'Oh, God, they're going to kill us all.'" A young woman tackled her mother, who was walking around in shock: "She screamed, 'Mama, crawl, crawl, don't rub your eyes Mama, crawl.' She couldn't crawl. It had bursted into her eyes. She was overcome. She just lay in the field on her face. She thought she was dying. The skin on her face was all burned off. Here eyes were paining her terrible, and she was blinded, and her chest burned like fire for weeks." Fifteen minutes after the police fired the first tear gas canisters, the field had been cleared. The area resembled a war zone after a battle. Dr. Alvin Poussaint, who was on the march representing the Medical Committee for Human Rights, set up a makeshift clinic and called in his colleague Dr. Robert Smith in Jackson for emergency help. "We were up that whole night treating the victims," Poussaint recalled.[24]

The march leaders anticipated that the state troopers might use gas, but they were unprepared for the gestapo tactics that had followed. Stokely Carmichael, who became hysterical during the attack, was near collapse. A calmer, but equally bitter Martin Luther King tried to reassemble the demonstrators and told reporters, "This is the very state patrol that President Johnson said today would protect us. Anyone who will use gas bombs on women and children can't and won't protect anybody."[25]

The police riot in Canton equaled in ferocity the assault on the marchers at the Selma bridge a year earlier. After the Selma violence the president had federalized the National Guard to protect the demonstrators marching to Montgomery, but the Johnson administration's response to the events in Canton was strikingly different. The next day Attorney General Nicholas Katzenbach merely said that he "regretted" the use of tear gas against the marchers, for "it always makes the situation more difficult." Katzenbach refused to condemn the police action, commenting that the whole matter was under investigation. Deputy White House press secretary Robert Fleming told reporters that the president had "no specific reaction" to the gassing of the demonstrators. Later that day a delegation of ministers, unsatisfied with Katzenbach's response, requested an audience with Johnson, but they were turned away by White House aide Harry McPherson, who informed the president, "I told them that your schedule would simply not permit them to meet with you today." McPherson added, "I am certain that there is no legitimate way to satisfy these people, and unless you are prepared to send in Federal Marshals or troops today, a meeting with [this group] would only serve to exacerbate the situation." Back in Canton, Dr. King told Paul Good that he had "heard that terrible statement of Katzenbach's. . . . I've heard nothing from President Johnson. It's terribly frustrating and disappointing." The despondent civil rights leader confessed, "I don't know what I'm going to do. The Government has got to give me some victories if I'm gonna keep people nonviolent. I know *I'm* gonna stay nonviolent no mattter what happens. But a lot of people are getting hurt and bitter, and they can't see it that way any more."[26]

After Canton, the last leg of the march was anticlimactic. James Meredith now rejoined the marchers, and after several minor disputes with other leaders, he led a group to the campus of Tougaloo College, the staging area for the final day's march. That night 9,000 supporters, including Hollywood celebrities Sammy Davis, Jr., Burt Lancaster, and Marlon Brando, attended a mass rally on the football field. Across from the field, at the campus home of Tougaloo dean A. A. Branch, the march leaders held their final strategy session, an angry meeting that lasted far into the night. At issue was the question of who would be permitted to speak at the Jackson rally the next day.[27]

After some debate they agreed that Whitney Young, who had now signed the manifesto, and UAW president Walter Reuther could address the rally, but by a four-to-two vote they barred Charles Evers of the NAACP from the platform. SCLC and the Medical Committee for Human Rights favored Evers's participation, while SNCC, CORE, MFDP, and the Delta Ministry opposed it. The stated reason for excluding Evers was his continued refusal to sign the march manifesto. Although he initially had been critical of the march, Evers had joined it in Greenwood. Once it became apparent that local blacks were supporting the march and registering to vote along the way, Evers urged local NAACP branches to participate. Allowing him to speak would have promoted march unity, but Mississippi militants were in no mood to provide another forum for their political rival. The NAACP's Roy Wilkins was furious at the snub, but Evers shrugged it off with "It's all right. I'll be here when they're all gone."[28]

On Sunday, June 26, exactly three weeks after James Meredith set out alone on his march against fear, 2,000 people streamed through the Tougaloo campus gates and headed down Highway 51 for the final eight-mile trek to the state capitol. Several thousand black Jacksonians joined in along the way, and by the time the speeches began in the late afternoon some 15,000 people had assembled to hear Martin Luther King declare that the march and rally "will go down in history as the greatest demonstration for freedom ever held in the state of Mississippi." As had been the case since Greenwood, SNCC and SCLC supporters took up competing chants of "black power" and "freedom now," and Stokely Carmichael drew loud applause when he said that blacks "must build a power base in this country so strong that we will bring [whites] to their knees every time they mess with us." The overwhelmingly black audience cheered all the speakers, and outwardly the rally was a display of unity.[29]

From the standpoint of the Mississippi movement, the march appeared to have been successful. Nearly 4,000 blacks had registered to vote, and an estimated 10,000 local people had marched at least part of the way. National attention had focused on Mississippi for the first time since the summer of 1964, and the brutal attacks on the marchers by a white mob in Philadelphia and by the highway patrol in Canton were sobering evidence that, despite passage of two civil rights laws, white supremacy remained the central fact of life in the Deep South.[30] After Carmichael's Greenwood speech, however, reporters had become obsessed with the black power slogan, and from that point on conflict within the ranks of the march commanded their attention. Thus, media coverage shifted away from racial injustice in Mississippi to the ideological differences between Carmichael and King. Although important to the press—and to march leaders—the controversy was of minor importance to the thousands of black Mississippians who had cheered both King and Carmichael on the steps of the capitol.[31]

• • •

Following the Jackson rally the march leaders met one final time, and the tensions that had been building for three weeks now erupted. At issue was the question of who would pay the bills. SCLC's Andrew Young later charged that although SNCC and CORE had originally agreed to contribute, they now claimed to be short of funds, thus leaving SCLC with a tab of between $25,000 and $30,000. (SNCC's and CORE's insistence that Charles Evers be excluded from the speaker's platform had let the NAACP off the hook.) This, on top of the running dispute over black power, convinced SCLC to initiate "our own campaign in Mississippi, and let the others run theirs." Dr. King chose his militant lieutenant Hosea Williams to head the Mississippi project, a direct action campaign to begin immediately in Grenada.[32]

Grenada appeared to be a logical choice for SCLC's first—and only—Mississippi project. Almost equally divided between black and white, the town had not been a movement center, so SCLC would not be poaching on somebody else's turf. Grenada was fresh in the minds of SCLC staffers because it had been the scene of the Meredith March's greatest success, with more than 1,000 local blacks registered to vote and a city administration that had backed down before the marchers' challenge.

Hosea Williams and a staff of SCLC workers moved into Grenada in July. They did not appear interested in developing local leadership. From the outset Williams and his aides were calling the shots, mobilizing young blacks to test public facilities and presenting white officials with a list of fifty-one demands calling for "total integration." When Stokely Carmichael and other SNCC people came to Grenada in early July to present a black power alternative to SCLC's traditional integrationist approach, Williams refused to let Carmichael speak at a mass meeting and, according to a Sovereignty Commission informant, told him to get out of town because "SCLC was running the show." The SNCC chairman did leave, commenting that "when they get tired of marching, we'll be back with our program."[33]

Grenada in July was not the same town that had all but welcomed the marchers in June. When Williams kicked off the campaign with a series of demonstrations, police arrested sixty-six people the first week, with highway patrolmen using nightsticks and gun butts to scatter the protestors. A white civilian fired his submachine gun at two civil rights lawyers and a representative of the federal Community Relations Service who was in town to help bring the races together. The city refused to discuss any of SCLC's demands. "There will be no concessions of any type or degree made to anyone anywhere," officials proclaimed. Sheriff Suggs Ingram added a warning: "They had it so easy during the march they thought they could come back and take over. We are not going to put up with what we have in the past, even if it takes force." Throughout July and August black-white tensions intensified. Williams called for night marches—always dangerous—and wanted to initiate even bolder protests to provoke white violence and attract national media attenion. SCLC field staff, fearing reprisals against local people, disregarded his instructions. Williams settled for a boycott of white stores and service stations, which soon "severely crippled trade." SCLC also registered two-thirds of the town's eligible black voters and desegregated the public library. In addition, staff members got a positive response when they urged parents to enroll their children in the white elementary and high schools in September.[34]

School desegregation had never been a priority for SNCC and CORE, and now for black power advocates the idea of sending black children to be taught by southern whites in a hostile environment made no sense at all. Still, many black Mississippians valued school integration as an opportunity for their children to better themselves. Grenada's schools had remained totally segregated until the summer of 1966, when federal judge Claude F. Clayton, whose previous record in civil rights cases was almost as bad as that of Judge Harold Cox, reluctantly approved a "freedom of choice" plan covering all twelve grades at John Rundle High School and the adjacent Lizzie Horn Elementary School. Officials anticipated that fewer than 100 black students would ask to transfer to the white schools. After nearly 300 black children applied, the school opening was delayed for ten days.[35]

When the Grenada schools finally opened on Monday, September 12, about 150 black students entered unchallenged. An estimated 40 late arrivals were turned away by a crowd of whites that had begun to assemble outside the school grounds. Two young girls who tried to pass through the whites were pushed to the ground and fled to a nearby church. Classes met for only a half-day on Monday, and shortly after noon white students filed out, many accompanied by their parents.[36]

When the black students tried to leave, however, a mob of white men set on them with ax handles, pipes, and chains. Memphis reporter Charles Goodman arrived to find a black boy lying on the sidewalk, his ankle injured and his hands covering his bloody head. Further down the sidewalk "some husky young men were whipping a little Negro girl with pigtails. She was running. The men chased after her, whooping and leaping up and down like animals." ("How can they laugh when they beat them up?" asked a shocked white Grenada woman. "How can they laugh when they are doing it?") One twelve-year-old boy was caught in "a surging, cursing gauntlet." For a full block he walked through the mob, emerging with his clothes torn, limping, bleeding from the head. After a white woman tripped up thirteen-year-old Richard Sigh by ramming her umbrella between his legs, a mob beat him with clubs as he lay on the ground. Sigh's leg was broken, and later that day his father was fired from his job.[37]

Throughout all of this, local and county law enforcement officers made no move to help the children or arrest their attackers. FBI agents took pictures and communicated with each other through walkie-talkies. Sheriff Ingram himself watched five white men pull a ten-year-old black boy to the ground and pummel him. Ingram started toward them, hesitated, and then walked away. Whites in pickup trucks cruised the area and attacked black parents and children in their cars. Altogether, more than thirty black children were assaulted that day; several were hospitalized. Two Memphis reporters and a photographer were also beaten. Although probably no more than seventy-five whites were involved in the beatings, they were cheered on by nearly 400 bystanders, including cursing and screaming women.[38]

The violence in Grenada appeared to be a premeditated assault on black children approved by local law officials, not a spontaneous outburst by an uncontrolled mob. Later in the week Judge Clayton, in handing down an injunction ordering city officials to protect black students from further attacks, said that he was "astonished that such violence could happen once. But it is absolutely incredible that it could have happened as many times as it did with so little reaction on the part of public officials." On Monday night, after Governor Johnson sent state troopers into Grenada, 500 whites protested at city hall. "You get the Highway Patrol out of here and in 24 hours there won't be a nigger left," one man shouted to a city council member. The following day there were sporadic acts of violence as only about twenty black students showed up at the white schools. City manager J. E. Meachin resigned under fire—he had a local reputation as a racial moderate—and blamed the violence on the decision to desegregate all twelve grades at once.[39]

On Tuesday night Hosea Williams led 150 people in a protest march around the town square, where they were confronted by about 200 whites, some of whom used slingshots to shoot lead fishing sinkers at the demonstrators. After Judge Clayton issued his injunction on Friday, black students returned to the white schools, where classes were for the first time segregated by sex. Martin Luther King paid a one-day visit to town, leading marchers escorting black students to class. Black students reported constant acts of harassment by white students throughout the fall term and staged a two-week school boycott as a protest. On September 17 the FBI charged thirteen men with assaulting the students. Most of those arrested were shopkeepers and service station operators; one was a justice of the peace. In June 1967 eight of the men were brought to trial, and Judge Clayton instructed the jurors to reach a decision "based on the evidence without bias, without prejudice." The white jury found all the defendants not guilty.[40]

The violence directed against black students attempting to desegregate the Grenada schools was the worst in the twelve years since the Supreme Court had handed down the *Brown* decision, surpassing in ferocity the harassment of students in Little Rock in 1957 and in New Orleans in 1960, incidents that at the time led to public outrage. There were similar condemnations of the violence in Grenada—*The Christian Century* labeled the assaults "one of the vilest displays of hideous prejudice, hatred and sheer bestiality ever produced in this nation's history of racial strife"—but the nation's attention span was short. In 1968, two years after the Grenada riots, fewer than 8,000 black students were enrolled in previously white Mississippi schools, 3.9 percent of the total black school-age population, a statistic few Americans appeared to notice. Angered by the rioting in northern ghettoes and the militant black power rhetoric of activists like Carmichael, most northern whites now seemed unmoved by events in Mississippi.[41]

As for the SCLC project in Grenada, it limped along beset by problems of leadership and growing distrust in the black community. Its mobilization campaign, the last of its kind, had produced few positive results. A civil rights attorney close to the scene later concluded that "by and large SCLC has used the local people as conduits for implementing its decisions, without really involving them in the decision-making process, and without training them to take over."[42]

After the Meredith shooting the national civil rights leaders had come into the state with a flourish, marched from Memphis to Jackson, and then quickly departed, leaving local people once again to pick up the pieces. At the end of 1966 signs of progress were hard to come by in the Magnolia State. For all intents and purposes, Mississippi was still segregated, from its lunch counters to its classrooms. CDGM was fighting for its life, black poverty was getting worse, and community organizers were facing serious internal problems. Feeling abandoned by their friends, ignored by the federal government, and facing continuing harassment from the Klan and the police, local activists once again rallied around the ballot, the program that for decades had been synonymous with the black struggle.

18

A New Mississippi?

What could have been a beautiful revolution just
petered out.
                    —Mrs. Annie Devine, Sept. 29, 1968

For the Mississippi Freedom Democratic party 1966 had
been a frustrating year. The poor showing in the congressional primary election was a major disappointment, and FDP participation
in the Meredith March had gained the party little recognition. With
the SCLC move into Grenada, however, some FDP supporters held
out hope that other national civil rights organizations might again
come in to provide much-needed help. Buoyed by their reception
in the Delta during the march, SNCC activists considered moving
back into Mississippi in force. At the SNCC central committee meeting in Knoxville in late October several organizers maintained "that
Guyot and the FDP were open to SNCC becoming actively involved
again. People in Mississippi feel isolated." SNCC now had only seventeen people in Mississippi, more than a third of whom lived in
the Jackson area, where SNCC had no ongoing programs. Its most
active project was in Clay County in the eastern part of the state,
where John Buffington had begun work in 1964.[1]

Despite the talk, SNCC did not make a renewed commitment to
Mississippi, for it had become preoccupied with internal problems
centering on the definition and implications of black power. In December 1966 SNCC had voted, narrowly, to expel all whites from
the organization. Its most famous Mississippi member, Fannie Lou
Hamer, then resigned in protest. Although veteran Mississippi SNCC
organizers like Hollis Watkins and Charles McLaurin continued to

be active in the state, SNCC as an organization had little impact on the Mississippi movement after 1966. The same held true for CORE. Of the original contingent of CORE organizers in Mississippi, only George Raymond remained (in Canton), and he was no longer on the CORE payroll.[2]

In late October 1966 Mrs. Hamer sent out a call to fifty Mississippi activists—more than a quarter of whom were whites—to meet in Jackson a week later "to see if we have common purposes, goals and needs." Organizers who spoke at that meeting presented a grim picture of the state of the Mississippi movement. FDP executive committee members reported that the party "has lost personnel and has never reached the stage where it could keep up a WATS line and provide subsistence for an office staff." There had been little work done for the November general elections, where several FDP candidates were running as independents in U.S. House and Senate races. Jesse Morris of the Poor People's Corporation "made the point that black conservatism was taking over" in the state. Tougaloo College's Ed King agreed, noting that the NAACP "was building a machine that could deliver votes and bring federal programs." King concluded that local people "might not want to wait for the slow development of 'democratic leadership.'" The organizers set up committees dealing with economic development, fund-raising, and federal programs, and they all agreed that "political education in preparation for the 1967 local elections" should take priority over all other programs. Concerning the November election only a week away, the group seemed resigned to a negative outcome, agreeing only that "the decision to work on the election is a personal one—people may or may not do so."[3]

Following the defeat of FDP candidates in the Democratic congressional primary in early June, party leaders had decided to run three candidates as independents in November. Doc Drummond ran again in the first congressional district race, as did the Reverend Clifton Whitley for the Senate seat held by James Eastland. In the third district Emma Sanders, a black Jackson activist, replaced Ed King on the ticket. The Tougaloo chaplain had been the party's only white candidate in the primary election, and the decision to run a black person to oppose incumbent John Bell Williams in the fall, while not officially acknowledged as such, was an FDP nod in the direction of black power. White Democrats tried to prevent them from running as independents, but after a long court battle the three candiates were placed on the ballot. Although the delay cost FDP valuable time in launching the campaign, the result was foreordained: all three FDP candidates lost decisively. Most disturbing to FDP leaders were the results of the one statewide race, where Whitley's total vote dropped by 20 percent from June to November, despite the registration of several thousand new black voters over the summer. A major reason for this decline was Charles Evers, who had supported Whitley in the primary but endorsed Prentiss Walker, Eastland's unsuccessful Republican opponent, in the general election. The results in the southwestern counties were dramatic: where Whitley had polled 1,639 votes in the Claiborne County primary with Evers's support, he received only 120 votes in November; and in Jefferson County his 1,725 primary total fell to 69 in the fall. Evers had demonstrated that black voters in these counties were securely in his pocket.[4]

Shortly after the November election, in a confidential report to SNCC headquarters in Atlanta, John Buffington concluded that "the MFDP has failed in all of its efforts, beginning with the Convention Challenge and ending with the running of independent candidates in this year's election. In other words, the MFDP hasn't given the Black community a victory since it has been alive." Buffington's harsh assessment reflected the growing frustration of militant activists over the direction of the Mississippi movement. The local people at the grass roots who had been the backbone of the COFO coalition still identified with the Freedom Democratic party. Passage of the voting rights act, however, had brought new challenges from black and white moderates, and the departure of most of the SNCC and CORE field secretaries had left the movement without a strong contingent of full-time organizers. Although denying that their efforts had produced nothing of substance, FDP leaders agreed that the 1967 state and local elections could make or break their party.[5]

The 1967 elections took place in an atmosphere of continuing racial tensions. Ku Klux Klan terrorism showed no signs of abating, and the police power of the state continued to be directed against civil rights activists. The FBI became more involved in "racial matters," infiltrating and undermining both the Klan and the black protest movement with its Counter-Intelligence Program (COINTELPRO). Assisted by the presence of federal registrars in thirty-one counties, both the NAACP and FDP stepped up voter registration activity. The Mississippi legislature responded to the inevitability of an increased black electorate by enacting a series of laws designed to negate the effect of the voting rights act. Charles Evers directed NAACP-sponsored boycotts against white merchants in several cities, winning some concessions from white officials in small towns like Fayette and Woodville.

The ambiguity of the phrase "black power" and the subsequent lack of a clearly defined program enabled Mississippi activists to interpret the slogan broadly, enlisting it in behalf of boycotts, voter registration drives, and economic self-help endeavors such as the cooperatives. As far back as the fall of 1964 FDP leaders had been open to the ideas of Malcolm X, who had addressed an FDP rally in Harlem and introduced Fannie Lou Hamer at his Harlem mosque. (Malcolm had agreed to come to Mississippi to address an FDP meeting in February 1965 but canceled shortly before he was assassinated.) The strident black nationalism of Stokely Carmichael and SNCC, however, with its underlying theme that whites had no role to play in a black movement, did not attract a large following among local people. As Lawrence Guyot observed, "Once black power became anti-white, you couldn't sell it to Miss Jones, who's a Baptist lady, and believes the Bible, which states everybody should be treated equally. . . . You can't sell an anti-white thing in the churches."[6]

Resisting demands by nationalists, the Freedom Democratic party remained open to white participation and continued to work with the integrated staff of the Delta Ministry, which was now led by Owen Brooks, a black activist less concerned with ideology than with finding solutions to the economic problems facing local people. The Delta Ministry now had twenty-six full-time staff members in Mississippi, and organizers like Rims Barber, Harry Bowie, and Charles Horwitz worked closely with Guyot and the FDP leadership. At a time when northern cities were erupting in violence and black militants were calling for revolution, then, the Mississippi Freedom Democratic party continued to work within the political system. Becoming more militant in its rhetoric, and now running only black candidates on its tickets, FDP nonetheless continued to welcome support from all people who identified with its program of black empowerment.[7]

FDP's first 1967 election campaign, in Sunflower County, provided the party with a unique opportunity. The Fifth Circuit Court of Appeals had called for new elections in the town of Sunflower, ruling that blacks, who constituted 70 percent of the town's 800 residents, had been unlawfully excluded from political participation. The prospect that Mississippi blacks could take political control of an "integrated" town attracted financial and political support for FDP from the National Committee for Free Elections in Sunflower. Led by twenty-one-year-old Delta Ministry and FDP worker Joseph Harris, Sunflower blacks held mass meetings, conducted workshops in political education, registered voters, and appointed block captains to make sure that everyone turned out on May 2 to support an all-black slate in races for mayor and five aldermanic positions. MFDP historian Leslie McLemore has concluded that this "was perhaps the best organized political campaign conducted in the rural South." With registered black voters outnumbering whites by 185 to 154, and with most black ballots cast within two hours after the polls had opened, optimism ran high in the FDP camp. Yet when the votes were counted, with federal observers on the scene, blacks had lost every race by an average margin of nearly seventy votes.[8]

What had gone wrong? "Our people did not stick together," lamented Joe Harris. It was clear from the results that while virtually all whites voted for the white candidates, some blacks had split their tickets. For the first time white politicians had actively sought black votes. Before the election town officials laid gravel on dirt roads and put up street signs in the black community. Obtaining paved roads and street signs had been part of the platform of the black candidates.[9] But the determining factor in the election was white intimidation.

Letters sent out to black voters warned them to stay away from the polls, and a number of blacks were threatened with the loss of their jobs if the black candidates won. On election day menacing groups of whites stood around the one polling place, the town hall, taking photographs of blacks as they lined up to vote. Trucks parked nearby had shotguns plainly visible in their gunracks. Voting lines were segregated, and each black voter had to pass by the chief of police. City officials reneged on an earlier agreement to permit Joe Harris to assist illiterate voters in the booth, so on election day those needing help got it from a white candidate for sheriff in the fall election. His brother was a candidate for alderman. One observer commented that "it was not unlike having to vote in the middle of the town square with all the community watching." (Such tactics remained widespread in rural areas well into the 1970s.) Three days before the election Guyot had told Sunflower voters that they would be setting an inspirational precedent for blacks in other communities, where the sentiment would be "if they can do it in that little town we can do it here." At a Sunflower rally after the election an angry Guyot declared that in November FDP would be lining up "a complete black slate to run as independents throughout the Delta" and that FDP would "stay the hell out of the goddam Democratic Party."[10]

A week after the Sunflower elections city police came onto the Jackson State College campus to arrest a student for speeding, triggering a protest on May 10 that quickly escalated into a confrontation between about 1,000 students and hundreds of police and national guardsmen. On the following night police opened fire on a group of protestors, wounding several people and killing a bystander, Ben Brown. A movement activist since the freedom rides, Brown had participated in voter registration drives in 1964, demonstrated in Jackson the following summer, and worked with the Delta Ministry "Freedom Corps" until late 1966. He then married a movement worker, rented an apartment in Jackson, and took a job as a truck driver. On the night of the riot Brown had gone out to buy hamburgers for himself and his wife. City officials claimed he had been caught in a crossfire between police and demonstrators; local activists believed otherwise. Brown had been arrested in Jackson seven times in civil rights protests and was well known to local police. He died from bullet wounds in his back and in the back of his head.[11]

The police killing of Ben Brown set off a new wave of demonstrations in Jackson, with a number of students from Tougaloo College participating. Concerned that their classmates would be caught downtown and arrested after a 10:00 P.M. police curfew, Tougaloo student leaders commandeered the college's school bus and brought them back to the campus. When the Tougaloo business manager filed disciplinary charges against students Bennie Thompson and Constance Slaughter, president of the Tougaloo Student Association, for taking the bus off campus without authorization, the campus erupted in protest. Students boycotted classes, demonstrated on the lawn of the president's home, and closed the campus to outside traffic. The furor over the administration's handling of the bus incident regalvanized campus activists, who began to promote a black power agenda, demanding that the administration institute a black studies program and employ more black faculty.[12]

The more than 1,000 people attending Ben Brown's funeral heard speakers from the contending political factions unite in their outrage. "They have taken the hoods and sheets off the murderers and issued them uniforms and badges," charged Charles Evers. "We all know Ben was murdered," said Owen Brooks, who had worked closely with Brown in the Delta Ministry. "Let's do something, let's pull together. There is still no change in Mississippi." FDP's Guyot decreed, "We must organize Mississippi, or we will keep returning to this hall for more funerals. We must organize around one thing—survival."[13]

The death of Ben Brown served as a tragic reminder to black political leaders that, whatever their ideological differences, they still faced a common enemy, and political infighting was a luxury they could not afford. FDP and Delta Ministry officials made the first move toward unity, issuing a statement that endorsed all black candidates running for office in 1967, including those backed by the rival NAACP. "If 1967 is to be the year for political victory in Mississippi, open and abrasive disunity must be avoided," they declared, mentioning "an informal and unarticulated agreement among the differing political camps within the Black community to co-exist throughout the election year." They noted that both the NAACP and FDP factions had decided to avoid statewide races, concentrating on city and county races in areas with heavy black populations.[14]

The statement did touch on the differences between the two groups: the NAACP was running candidates in the primaries because "that camp believes that political power can be realized within the structure of the Mississippi Democratic party"; FDP supporters were convinced that "the only way Black people can acquire power is to develop an independent Black political force," and thus most of their candidates would skip the primaries and run as independents in the November election. In fact, the differences between MFDP and the NAACP were less ideological than political. The candidates of both groups ran on similar platforms attacking racial discrimination and demanding equal services in black communities. The tone of the FDP–Delta Ministry statement, while guarded, was conciliatory, a first step toward ending the bitter factional fighting that had plagued the black community since Atlantic City.[15]

The 1967 primary and general elections marked a turning point of sorts in Mississippi politics, for race-baiting all but disappeared as white candidates sought black votes. The reason for this sudden change in white political behavior was the impact of the voting rights act in Mississippi. The U.S. Commission on Civil Rights reported that while in early 1965 only 28,500 Mississippi blacks had registered, that number had climbed to 181,233 by the fall of 1967, over half the eligible black electorate. Although blacks constituted only 24 percent of the total number of registered voters, they held a majority in four counties, including Madison and Holmes.[16]

To counter this alarming trend, beginning in 1966 the Mississippi legislature enacted a series of laws that diluted the black vote, making it extremely difficult for blacks to win office. In his authoritative book *Black Votes Count: Political Empowerment in Mississippi after 1965,* Frank R. Parker has demonstrated the debilitating impact of laws that (a) gerrymandered congressional districts by dividing the predominantly black Delta among three other districts, thereby denying blacks a voting majority in any district; (b) created multimember legislative districts to require at-large voting that would "submerge black population concentrations that were large enough for separate legislative representation"; and (c) increased filing requirements for independent candidates. In addition, the legislature made it legal for counties to eliminate elections for certain offices, such as county school superintendent. Anticipating an increase in black registration, forty-six towns and cities adopted at-large city council elections to prevent blacks from gaining office, and twenty-two counties switched to at-large elections for county school boards. City annexations of white suburban areas and last-minute changes in polling places further minimized black voting strength. "Outright denial to black Mississippians of the right to vote, now prohibited by law, was replaced with these more subtle strategies to dilute and cancel the black vote," Parker concluded. "Not until these legal barriers were removed through court battles many years in duration would Mississippi's newly enfranchised black voters be able to exercise a meaningful vote."[17]

Overcoming these legal obstacles, the Mississippi Freedom Democratic party won its first—and greatest—victory in 1967 when a

Holmes County school teacher, Robert Clark, became the first African American to sit in the Mississippi legislature in this century. Clark's successful race for state representative was the culmination of years of organizing by local leaders, most of whom were landowning farmers, in a county 72 percent black. As a teacher, Clark was known throughout the county, and his credentials served him well with members of the small but important black middle class. FDP organizers, including Henri and Sue Lorenzi, a white couple who had been working in Holmes County for three years, had developed an impressive organization, with block captains in all parts of the heavily rural county ensuring a large election-day turnout. Differences between FDP and the NAACP were set aside. The newly formed Holmes County Independent Campaign Committee, though dominated by FDP supporters, included local NAACP leaders. Still, with the most sophisticated black political organization in the state behind him and a comfortable majority of black registered voters in a single-member district, Clark defeated his white opponent, twelve-year House veteran J. P. Love, by a slim margin of 116 votes: 3,510 to 3,394. Of the ten other black candidates running in Holmes County only one was elected, and that in a race for a minor constable's position.[18]

Both the NAACP and MFDP waged aggressive campaigns in the 1967 elections, registering new voters, holding mass meetings, conducting political education classes, and selecting and encouraging black candidates for office. Seventy-six blacks in twenty-two counties ran as Democrats in the August primary, and thirty-two sought election as independents in eight counties, all but one in the Delta. Despite the hard work and enthusiasm, election results were disappointing. Twenty-two blacks won office, an achievement of no small historical significance. (Most of those elected were from Evers's southwestern counties.) Still, although they represented one-fourth of the state electorate, blacks won only about 1 percent of the races. Fifteen of the victories were for the relatively minor positions of justice of the peace and constable. Four blacks were elected to the important post of county supervisor, yet only two, in addition to Clark, won countywide races (for chancery clerk and coroner). Whites won all contests for county sheriff.[19]

The 1966 election laws contributed heavily to the outcome of many races. Counties that changed to at-large voting elected no black supervisors, and all seven blacks running for the legislature in multimember districts also lost. Nineteen independent candidates, most affiliated with FDP, were denied places on the ballot for failing to meet the requirements of the new law. Fannie Lou Hamer was disqualified in her independent race for the state senate because she had voted in the August Democratic primary. Finally, the pattern of the Sunflower municipal elections was repeated, with threats and harassment reducing black voter turnout in many areas of the state.[20]

For Mississippi whites, the focus of the 1967 election was the hotly contested governor's race. Of the four candidates, State Treasurer William Winter, the most progressive, led the field and faced a runoff with congressional representative John Bell Williams, the only Mississippi congressman to endorse Barry Goldwater openly in 1964. Winter had sought black support behind the scenes—to do so openly in the 1967 governor's race meant certain defeat—and his had been a quiet voice of reason during the turbulent early 1960s. Yet Winter disappointed black supporters by his public endorsement of the racial status quo. Appearing at a Citizens' Council forum, the Mississippi moderate drew cheers with his boast that "as a fifth generation Mississippian whose grandfather rode with Forrest, I was born a segregationist and raised a segregationist. I have always defended this position. I defend it now." Even so, Winter was still too liberal for the white electorate. Williams won the primary runoff by 60,000 votes (most of the 100,000 black ballots cast in the runoff went to Winter) and in November defeated Rubel Phillips, a Republican who had openly campaigned for the black vote. John Bell Williams was a mean-spirited segregationist who evoked memories of Ross Barnett, but like his predecessor, Paul Johnson, Williams was a realist who knew that continued open defiance of federal authority was futile.[21]

The Mississippi Ku Klux Klan had not yet gotten that message. Klan terrorism in 1967 had begun with the car-bombing murder of Wharlest Jackson in Natchez in February. Jackson had just been promoted to a factory job formerly held only by whites. In the fall Klan violence centered on the state's capital city, targeting white moderates who had spoken out for civil rights. Within a two-month period beginning in mid-September, dynamite explosions hit the Jewish Temple Beth Israel, the campus home of the white Tougaloo academic dean, and the homes of a white Jackson businessman and the Beth Israel rabbi. On November 15 a bomb blasted the home of the Reverend Allen Johnson, a black NAACP activist in Laurel. The Klan then moved east to Meridian, where a series of bombings in the spring of 1968 culminated with a police shootout and the capture of Klan terrorist Thomas Albert Tarrants, who had driven to Meridian to bomb a Jewish merchant's home.[22]

After the Meridian bombings, however, the Klan quickly went into decline. White Mississippians increasingly came to see the Klan as a group of outlaws whose violent acts could no longer be tolerated. Late in 1967 an all-white jury had convicted seven men, including Neshoba County deputy sheriff Cecil Price and Klan leader Sam Bowers, of "violating the civil rights" of James Chaney, Michael Schwerner, and Andrew Goodman. The verdicts made it clear that klansmen engaging in acts of terrorism now risked punishment by a jury of their peers. Moreover, since the summer of 1964 the FBI had infiltrated the Mississippi Klan to the point where members could no longer trust one another. The capture of Tarrants, for example, had been an FBI sting operation assisted by one of the klansmen convicted in the Neshoba case. The Klan continued to exist in Mississippi, but its reign of terror had ended.[23]

· · ·

On September 17, 1967, Lawrence Guyot announced that the executive committee of the Mississippi Freedom Democratic party had decided that the party would challenge the white regular state delegation to the 1968 Democratic National Convention in Chicago. The news surprised the FDP rank and file, because less than five months earlier Guyot had responded to the defeat in the Sunflower municipal elections by pledging that FDP would "stay the hell out of" the Democratic party. When asked to reconcile the two statements, Guyot replied that had FDP controlled the election machinery in Sunflower, its candidates would have won, and that "unless and until we become the Democratic party in the state, elections will continue to be a farce." The executive committee decision drew sharp criticism from party members who believed that FDP should work independently to build strong organizations in the black community. One angry militant declared that the 1968 challenge would be "a pathetic new pilgrimage to Chicago to seek the blessings of the American fuhrer." From September until the following May, FDP leaders debated the question of the challenge, and though the party never changed its position, neither did it follow up with concrete plans to set the challenge in motion.[24]

At the end of September the Mississippi Young Democrats held their annual convention in Jackson, deciding to try to work within the state Democratic party to open it to participation by blacks. If that effort failed, then they would put together a coalition to challenge the regular delegation in Chicago. Since receiving their charter from the national party in 1966, the Young Democrats had kept a low profile inside Mississippi. They were nowhere to be seen—or heard—during the Meredith March, and although its membership overwhelmingly supported Winter for governor in 1967, the organization did not endorse him, for to have done so would have hurt Winter politically. At the September meeting the Young Democrats rejected resolutions by the Millsaps College delegation to "support all black candidates in the November 8 election" and to declare opposition to the Vietnam war. The Young Democrats had, however, worked hard to improve their image nationally and to cement their ties with northern liberal Democrats. In June, for example, Senator Edward Kennedy had held a fund-raiser in Boston for the Mississippi Young Democrats.[25]

National and international events in the early months of 1968 overshadowed all political activity in Mississippi: the Tet Offensive in Vietnam, which increased domestic opposition to the war and led to President Lyndon Johnson's decision not to seek a second term; the entrance of Robert Kennedy into the presidential race; Martin Luther King's Poor People's Campaign (PPC), which envisioned an army of the dispossessed descending on Washington to demand that Congress enact sweeping economic reforms; and finally, the assassinations of King and Kennedy. These events, unprecedented in recent American history, stunned the nation.

Ironically, these developments paved the way for improved relations among the contending civil rights factions in Mississippi. By early spring most leaders of the NAACP–Young Democrats group opposed the war, ending a long and bitter controversy with the Freedom Democrats, who since 1965 had spoken out against the role of the United States in Vietnam. Lyndon Johnson's decision not to seek reelection removed another barrier, for FDP members could not have entered any coalition that required loyalty to Johnson or his administration. Robert Kennedy's decision to enter the race drew wide support among FDP members and Young Democrats alike. In organizing the Poor People's Campaign, Martin Luther King and his SCLC aides spent several days in Mississippi to enlist the support of all black leaders. Both moderates and militants were initially unenthusiastic about the PPC. Owen Brooks remarked, "We've been going and going to Congress and we can't see what can be gained from going one more time." King's personal appeal won them over, however, and they cooperated to recruit local people and organize the mule trains that kicked off the march in Marks and Mount Beulah. King's tragic death in Memphis on April 4 shocked all black Mississippians, and their outpouring of grief in memorial services in communities across the state reinforced their solidarity.[26]

An important step toward political cooperation among the opposing black factions had occurred earlier, in January 1968, when Charles Evers announced his candidacy for Congress in a special election to fill the seat of newly elected governor John Bell Williams. In a marriage of political convenience, Evers chose Guyot as his campaign manager and FDP national committeeman Ed King as coordinator for speaking engagements. Evers led a field of six white candidates in the first election, winning more than 25 percent of the total vote, but lost in the runoff when the white vote went to his remaining opponent, Charles Griffin. FDP leaders had made it clear that the party was supporting Evers only in "his role as a candidate" and not in his capacity as state NAACP field director. Still, that he would receive the endorsement of his bitter rivals was a remarkable turn of events.[27]

It now appeared possible that the competing factions might agree to send a united delegation to challenge the white regulars at the Democratic National Convention in Chicago. The NAACP–Young Democrats coalition participated in the regular party's precinct meetings and county conventions, where the regulars did select three black men as Chicago delegates—Charles Evers, Dr. Matthew Page, and Dr. Gilbert Mason. At the regulars' state convention, however, the majority of delegates had opposed the NAACP–Young Democrats forces at every turn. It was apparent that Governor Williams, who led the regulars, was in no mood to open his party to meaningful black participation, and Evers and Page resigned from the delegation. (Dr. Mason remained, the only black member of the regular delegation in Chicago.) Late in June FDP leaders agreed to join with the Young Democrats and the state NAACP to form the Loyal Democrats of Mississippi. The black Missisippi Teachers Association and the Prince Hall Masons also became part of the coali tion, and later the Mississippi AFL-CIO came on board as well. The Loyalists, as they were now being called, announced that they would challenge the regulars in Chicago.[28]

The new Loyalist alliance was fragile. Guyot's demand that FDP representatives constitute 50 percent of the delegation was rejected by the other five groups, who wanted equal division of the twenty-two delegation votes. FDP had no desire to share the seats equally with the teachers and Masons, who had neither supported the 1964 challenge nor been active in the early days of the struggle. Eventually, FDP was given five votes (with each member given one-half vote, that translated into ten of the forty-four delegate seats). Many activists were unhappy with this compromise. John Buffington bluntly stated that FDP "had no business" in an alliance that included Charles Evers, Claude Ramsey of the AFL-CIO, and Hodding Carter. Fannie Lou Hamer observed that "these same folks in 1964 were willing to sell us down the drain and tried to do it." Guyot, however, forthrightly defended the decision: "This challenge is indigenous, issue oriented, and broad based. This is a mass challenge and the people support it."[29]

In the end, the Loyalist coalition held together out of necessity. The NAACP–Young Democrats forces realized that to legitimize their challenge they needed the endorsement of the FDP people who had captured the nation's attention four years earlier at Atlantic City. MFDP, on the other hand, was at a crossroads. Abandoned by SNCC activists who believed it was too conservative and by northern liberals who thought it too radical, the Freedom Democratic party lacked the resources to mount a serious challenge on its own. FDP's only alternative to joining the coalition was to stay at home and have no impact on the convention proceedings.

After holding precinct and county conventions that picked the majority of the delegates, the Loyalists held their state convention on August 11 at the Masonic Temple in Jackson, where FDP had met four years earlier. In contrast to those attending that earlier gathering, the 1968 audience "seemed more affluent and content." With Aaron Henry chairing the meeting, the moderates were in control, and selection of delegates was a cut-and-dried affair. An at-large slate of delegates had been agreed to in advance by representatives of the six groups in the coalition. (FDP delegates not privy to that meeting were dismayed when party leaders did not support nominations of FDP members from the floor.) To promote unity, the nominating committee had selected FDP's Robert Clark as the Loyalists' male representative to the Democratic National Committee, but here Evers engineered the convention's only surprise. Although he had finished second to Clark in the committee vote, Evers had himself nominated from the floor, whereupon a "spontaneous" demonstration broke out, complete with confetti tossed from the balcony and a rock-and-roll band playing near the stage. When Buffington rose to speak on the nomination, "one guy asked if I was for Charles Evers. I said no, and the mike was cut off. I tried to speak and was pulled from the stage and my jacket was ripped." Evers won the vote by a landslide. One convention observer commented, "That's as close to a machine as you can get."[30]

That the Loyalist delegation would be seated at the stormy Democratic National Convention in Chicago was a foregone conclusion. In contrast to 1964, all major contenders for the party's presidential nomination—Hubert Humphrey, Eugene McCarthy, and George McGovern—had endorsed the challenge well in advance of the convention. The Mississippi challenge was not the major story in Chicago, as it had been in Atlantic City; this time the controversy over the war in Vietnam and the battle between the police and demonstrators in the streets commanded the nation's attention. Although it was a minority in the delegation, the FDP contingent made its voice heard, pressing the Loyalists to take a strong stand in favor of the minority platform plank opposing the Vietnam war, which it did by a vote of 19½ to 2½. The convention as a whole defeated the minority plank, however, and a plurality of the Loyalist delegation voted for Humphrey, who supported the war. The FDP delegates lost their bitterest battle when they called for the delegation to walk out of the convention to protest the treatment of the demonstrators by the Chicago police. Guyot, who knew police brutality firsthand, nearly came to blows with Carter, who insisted that the Loyalists remain on the floor. In the end, the pragmatism of the Carter-Henry faction prevailed, and though they registered a protest against the police action, the Loyalist delegation did not walk out.[31]

Although they had fought for their principles, many MFDP delegates left Chicago disillusioned and demoralized. After the convention FDP continued to function in areas like Holmes County, where it had a strong indigenous base, but attempts at reorganizing the party on the state level failed. Some FDP activists chose to work with the Loyalists, while others continued to organize outside a formal party structure. A few, like FDP chair Lawrence Guyot, left the state to pursue other movement-related activities.

The demise of the Freedom Democratic party symbolically marked the end of the grass-roots movement of the 1960s in Mississippi. Assigning starting and termination points for the movement is, of course, arbitrary. Blacks had struggled for their freedom in Mississippi since the earliest days of slavery and continue to fight for their rights as citizens down to the present. Still, the period beginning with World War II and ending with the Chicago Democratic Convention in 1968 encompasses the most intensive and comprehensive period of grass-roots organization and protest in that state's history; as a result of that campaign, Mississippi experienced more sweeping changes in the area of race relations during those three decades than at any time since the end of the Civil War.

· · ·

> Men fight and lose the battle,
> and the thing that they fought for
> comes about in spite of their defeat,
> and when it comes
> it turns out not to be what they meant,
> and other men have to fight for
> what they mean under another name.
> —William Morris[32]

For generations, in the treatment of its African-American citizens, Mississippi had been, as Roy Wilkins bluntly put it, "the worst state." In no other southern state was the use of terror against the black population so systematic and pervasive. Both the Citizens' Council and the Ku Klux Klan had made a mockery of the law, employing economic sanctions, intimidation, and violence to maintain white supremacy. Elected officials and business leaders had either cooperated with these extremists or stood by hoping that somehow calm would return, with the racial status quo maintained. Mississippi had no racially enlightened white political leadership, no locally influential voices of moderation in the media, no white ministerial associations pleading for racial justice. Since the collapse of Reconstruction, segregation and economic proscription had defined the pattern of race relations; any challenge to the caste system had to be dealt with immediately and, if necessary, violently. Nowhere in America were the prospects for a black protest movement less encouraging.

Despite the intensity of this white opposition, the Mississippi movement became the strongest and most far-reaching in the South. Of course, parts of other states experienced similar patterns of community organization, voter registration campaigns, and direct action protests (the SNCC projects in southwest Georgia and in Selma, Alabama, come quickly to mind). Yet in no other southern state was mass protest as extensive and as enduring as in Mississippi, nor did competing civil rights organizations elsewhere work together as closely as they did under the COFO umbrella in Mississippi from 1962 to 1965. The movement, to be sure, was not all-encompassing. Some counties passed through the 1960s hardly touched by civil rights activity. Nonetheless, through COFO first, and later the Freedom Democratic party, blacks were organizing their communities in all sections of the state, with activity coordinated through a central headquarters.

Several explanations account for the character of the Mississippi movement. First, and foremost, were the local people themselves. Beginning with the World War II veterans who stood up against Theodore Bilbo in 1946; through the unsung activists like Emmett Stringer, Amzie Moore, and Medgar Evers in the 1950s; and culminating in the new indigenous leadership of the 1960s, exemplified by Fannie Lou Hamer, Annie Devine, and Victoria Gray, black Mississippians had fought for their rights. Without them there would have been no organization, no movement, no victories.

The young SNCC and CORE organizers were, however, the catalyst for the movement of the 1960s, bringing with them enthusiasm, energy, and commitment. An obvious point often overlooked is that these activists were full-time workers: their "job" was to organize, and they were independent of the local white-dominated economy. Their fierce independence and defiance of local law and custom first inspired and then empowered blacks in communities throughout the state, who began to believe they, too, could take control over their lives. Without the support and example of the outsiders, local people would have remained trapped in the cycle of intimidation and reprisal that had succeeded in stifling the movement in the mid-1950s.

The third reason for the distinctiveness of the Mississippi movement was the state itself. Mississippi attracted young activists from all parts of the country simply because of its reputation. The lynching of Emmett Till in 1955 had made an indelible impression on black teenagers everywhere, and less than a decade later some of the most dedicated had either come to or remained in the state to join the struggle against the forces of white supremacy. To serve in Mississippi, then, became a badge of courage for movement activists, and more of them worked in that state than in any other. Although the most symbolic movement triumphs came in Birmingham and Selma, Mississippi remained the standard by which this nation's commitment to social justice would be measured.

By the end of 1968 it was clear that the movement had won significant victories in Mississippi. More than 250,000 blacks were now registered to vote, 60 percent of those eligible.[33] Although such numbers did not immediately transfer into political power, the level of political discourse was now changing, and overt race-baiting was strikingly absent in campaign oratory. The War on Poverty was by then falling apart, but Head Start, reforms in food stamp allocation, and Medicare and Medicaid brought some improvement in the lives of the black poor. Activists continued—with some success—to press for welfare reform and to encourage local people to demand the benefits due them through AFDC and other government programs.

School desegregation had continued at a slow pace, but in 1969 a unanimous Supreme Court in *Alexander* v. *Holmes County* ruled that the time for all deliberate speed had ended. Mississippi's public schools were desegregated forthwith, accompanied by massive white flight to hastily organized private academies. Still, the leading symbol of segregation had fallen, and whites accepted a Court mandate that only a few years earlier would have led to massive resistance.

Segregation remained a fact of life throughout much of the state, but the Jim Crow signs had begun to come down, and it was no longer unusual in cities like Jackson and Greenville to see blacks eating in white-owned restaurants, staying at the local motels, or patronizing the previously segregated public libraries. As the years passed, even officials in the smaller towns no longer fought to preserve their "customs." A degree of civility had come to the Magnolia State.

The movement had enabled the black middle class to make significant gains. By the early 1970s Mississippi corporations were employing blacks in positions previously reserved for whites; opportunities became available in local, state, and federal government agencies; and the nation's leading graduate and professional schools recruited young blacks, many of whom returned to the state to practice law and medicine, to teach in the colleges and universities, and to administer federal programs.

The major victory of the movement, however, had been the substantial reduction in the use of terror to control the state's black population, a direct result of the black electorate's increasing political influence. Blacks had won the right to organize their communities and to take political action without fearing brutal reprisal. Racial violence remained a fact of life in Mississippi, but the systematic use of terror, which had been the mainstay of the hardline segregationists down through the mid-1960s, condoned and often directed by law enforcement officers, gradually abated.

In the 1970s and 1980s there emerged a new group of black political leaders, most of whom had not been active in the movement of the early 1960s, either by choice or because they had been too young then to participate. For example, in 1979 there were seventeen blacks serving in the Mississippi legislature, all of whom were college-educated males. All but five of these men were under the age of forty-five when they first took office, and seven were under thirty-five. Seven years later a young attorney named Mike Espy became the first African American elected to Congress from Mississippi since Reconstruction. A self-styled moderate, Espy won the respect of the white planters in his Delta district by supporting their interests as a member of the House Agriculture Committee. Espy won reelection easily, receiving an amazing 40 percent of the white vote, and in 1993 he was chosen by President Bill Clinton to be Secretary of Agriculture.[34]

By the end of 1992 there were over 825 black elected officials in Mississippi, more than in any other state. Included in this figure were two chancery court judges, four circuit court judges, and a justice of the state supreme court, attorney Fred Banks, who was elected in a predominantly white district. As a result of redistricting changes following the 1990 census, forty-two blacks sat in the Mississippi legislature in 1993, nearly one-fourth of the total and again more than in any other state. There were twenty-eight black mayors; the majority were elected in small Delta towns, but some held office in larger cities like Clarksdale. Six of these mayors were women, as were both chancery court judges. Ten black women served in the Mississippi legislature, and seventy-five were elected to city council positions. Although they were not represented in proportion to their numbers, overall nearly 200 black elected officials were women.[35]

Many of the most significant political gains occurred in areas where the movement had major projects in the 1960s. Of the eight black sheriffs, four were from strong movement counties: Claiborne, Coahoma, Holmes, and Marshall. Blacks held a majority of the important county supervisor positions in seven counties, including Hinds, Holmes, and Leflore. They were elected to city council positions and to the state legislature in all the movement counties, as well as to school boards and election commissions. And in a demonstration of "old" movement strength, Bennie Thompson, a young MFDP activist in the late 1960s, was elected to fill Mike Espy's congressional seat in a special election in 1993.[36]

Despite these substantial achievements, the Mississippi movement failed to bring about the social revolution envisioned by the militant activists. Whites continued to hold most of the positions of real political power and to dominate all aspects of economic life. In the early 1990s Mississippi still led the nation in poverty, infant mortality, and illiteracy. Gains made by the black middle class were offset by the economic problems facing the majority of blacks, who once again became Mississippi's forgotten people. According to Children's Defense Fund figures, more than half the state's black children, nearly 200,000, were living below the poverty line in 1990. Although black economic development agencies like Mississippi Action for Community Education (MACE) and the Delta Foundation worked to bring industry into black communities, black per capita income was less than half that of whites, and the state's per capita income remained the lowest in the nation. Black solidarity across class lines, evident in the early sixties under COFO, had begun to fragment in the middle years of the decade, and with the rise of the younger moderates, the agenda of the Mississippi Freedom Democratic party, which had called for economic as well as political democracy, seemed to fade into the background.[37]

The Mississippi movement, then, had gone through a cyclical pattern of development, one common to other major American social movements, such as the abolitionist crusade of the mid-nineteenth century and the labor movement in the 1930s. In these cases, grass-roots insurgency had led to substantial victories: the slaves were freed and workers won the right to organize. The larger goal, however, that of creating a society where all people could live productive lives free from exploitation, never materialized, as more conservative forces moved in to bring those movements into line with the philosophies of the major political parties. Thus, the radical abolitionist goal of "40 acres and a mule" found few supporters in the Republican party of Reconstruction, and the shop-floor militancy of workers in the 1930s culminated in the co-optation of much of organized labor by the Democratic party of Franklin D. Roosevelt.

Such was also the case in Mississippi. In the late 1940s and 1950s, middle-class leaders affililated with the NAACP, the Regional Council of Negro Leadership, and local progressive voters' leagues attempted to expand the black electorate and, later, to implement the *Brown* decision. After the white opposition led by the Citizens' Council crushed these early efforts, a new group of militant leaders arose in the early 1960s. This grass-roots insurgency focused its efforts around community organization, engaged in direct action protests to dramatize its program, and won major victories, culminating in the civil rights acts of 1964 and 1965. Ironically, passage of these important laws had a divisive impact on the black community. Once black political participation was both safe and acceptable, it became possible for the traditional leaders to reassert themselves and, after bitter battles with the Mississippi Freedom Democratic party, to bring black voters back into the Democratic mainstream.

The questions remain: Was this result inevitable? Could different strategies have produced more substantial and permanent gains for the majority of Mississippi blacks? Was the decision to focus on voter registration the correct one? Should fundamental economic questions have been raised earlier and more forcefully? Did MFDP crr in pursuing an independent course after the 1964 Atlantic City convention? Was the move to disband COFO a mistake? Looking back on the movement years, a number of black activists have singled out the decision to bring in large numbers of white students during the summer of 1964 as the point where their movement began to decline. Thereafter, they contend, the focus shifted from community organization to a goal of federal protection and political recognition by the national Democratic party, ultimately resulting in the co-opting of the movement by the federal government, exemplified in the poverty program and its divisive impact on the black community. Thus was a grass-roots insurgency transformed into a more moderate reform movement, one willing to sacrifice the needs of the poor to obtain rewards for the black middle class.

It is, of course, impossible to comment with assurance on roads not taken. It was, however, inevitable that events occurring outside the state would influence developments in Mississippi. Particularly after the passage of the civil rights laws of 1964 and 1965, the pace of social change in the South as a whole was moving so rapidly that it would have been extremely difficult, under any circumstances, to maintain the organizational structure and cohesiveness that had effectively united black communities in Mississippi in the early 1960s. The observations of two activist-scholars, Frances Fox Piven and Richard Cloward, appear relevant to the larger question here: "If there is a genius in organizing, it is the capacity to sense what is possible for people to do under given conditions, and to then help them do it. . . . Both the limitations and opportunities for mass protest are shaped by social conditions."[38]

In his evaluation of the contributions of Dr. Martin Luther King, Jr., Vincent Harding expressed that sentiment more succinctly when he wrote that King "made all the history he could make."[39] If black Mississippians and their allies did not achieve all their goals during the movement years, in those decades following World War II they did bring about extraordinary changes in a state that had been locked up in the caste system for nearly a century. They had transformed the closed society, opened up the political process to African Americans, and made it possible for a new generation to build on the solid foundation laid by that band of brothers and sisters who had "challenged America" in search of the Beloved Community. Bob Moses has observed that the movement "brought Mississippi, for better or worse, up to the level of the rest of the country."[40] That was no small achievement. It also reminds us of the distance still to be traveled.

Afterword

Over the years a number of movement reunions have been held in Mississippi, beginning with a 1979 event commemorating the fifteenth anniversary of "Freedom Summer" sponsored by Tougaloo and Millsaps colleges. Organizers who had long since left the state returned to renew friendships with the local people they had worked with during the early 1960s. Among the SNCC people making the trip to Mississippi were Sam Block, Dorie and Joyce Ladner, Lawrence Guyot, Michael Thelwell, Julian Bond, and Bob Zellner, who caught up on recent developments from veteran organizers still working for social change in Mississippi, people like Hollis Watkins, Annie Devine, Willie Peacock, MacArthur Cotton, Owen Brooks, June Johnson, and Henry Kirksey (who over the previous decade had played a key role in the redistricting court cases). Ella Baker, now in her seventies but still combative, gave an inspiring address. NAACP leaders also spoke, including Aaron Henry and Charles Evers, whose controversial career had led him into the Republican party of Richard Nixon and Ronald Reagan.

Bob Moses, who had returned to the country after years of living and teaching in Tanzania, did not attend, but three years later Moses made his first trip back to Mississippi since 1965 when he came to a movement reunion held in McComb. There he spoke once again with C. C. Bryant, the man who had invited Moses into his community in the summer of 1961, and listened while Aylene Quin, Ernest Nobles, Joe Martin, and Harry Bowie talked of the movement days and the problems facing blacks in McComb in the present. Other movement reunions followed, commemorating the congressional challenge of the Mississippi Freedom Democratic party and the Child Development Group of Mississippi. In the spring of 1989 Ronald Bailey, then head of the black studies program at Ole Miss, arranged a conference in Jackson to discuss *Mississippi Burning,* the Hollywood movie that stood history on its head by trivializing the work of movement activists and glorifying the FBI. A high point of that meeting was a panel discussion reuniting Bob Moses, Dave Dennis, Lawrence Guyot, Hollis Watkins, and Victoria Gray.

Moses and Dennis had not seen each other since 1965, when both men had left the state, it appeared, for good. The two veteran activists talked of the past and the directions their careers had taken, but Moses kept coming back to a project that he had begun in Cambridge, Massachusetts, in 1982 to teach algebra to sixth-graders in inner-city schools. Beginning with the assumptions made in the freedom schools—that students bring with them experiences that are essential to their future learning—Moses had developed a revolutionary technique whereby middle school students draw on their own environment to learn complex mathematical skills. Believing that "math literacy holds the key . . . to open the doors to citizenship," Moses took his program into urban schools across the country, with impressive results.[1]

Dennis became intrigued with the Algebra Project, and he and Moses talked of expanding the program into the predominantly black public schools in the Delta. "When I left Mississippi," Dennis said, "I felt there was a part of me missing. I didn't finish something." As a result of these discussions, the Delta Algebra Project of Mississippi was born, and by 1992 schools in the old movement counties of Leflore, Sunflower, and Washington were participating in this program. Dennis gave up his Louisiana law practice and moved with his family to Jackson, where he directed Algebra Project programs in Louisiana, Kentucky, and Arkansas, as well as Mississippi. "It's our version of Civil Rights 1992," Moses maintained. "But this time we're organizing around literacy—not just reading and writing, but mathematical literacy."[2]

At each of the movement reunions the participants paid tribute to those activists who had been martyred in Mississippi during the 1960s—Herbert Lee, Medgar Evers, James Chaney, Mickey Schwerner, Andrew Goodman, Vernon Dahmer, Ben Brown—as well as to

others who had died over the years. The person most fondly remembered was Mrs. Fannie Lou Hamer.

More than any other individual, Mrs. Hamer had come to symbolize the black struggle in Mississippi. Her name was honored by
virtually every black political leader in the state; both Bill Clinton
and Al Gore praised her in their acceptance speeches at the 1992
Democratic Convention. Over the years she had become a revered
figure in the women's movement as well. In her final years Mrs.
Hamer labored quietly at home in Ruleville, raising thousands of
dollars to feed displaced sharecroppers through her Freedom Farm
Cooperative and pig bank, securing funds for housing and the day
care center that bears her name. She remained active politically,
speaking out against the Vietnam war in the late 1960s and early
1970s and calling attention to abuses in the poverty and Medicaid
programs in Mississippi. After the triumph of the Loyalists in 1968,
however, she became a peripheral figure in state politics, shunted
aside by the new college-educated black leadership. During the last
months of her life Mrs. Hamer was in constant pain, fighting the
ravages of breast cancer, diabetes, and heart disease. During her last
days she felt abandoned by all but a few old friends, movement
colleagues like Owen Brooks, Charles McLaurin, June Johnson, and
L. C. Dorsey, a woman who shared Mrs. Hamer's background as a
sharecropper and who, inspired by Mrs. Hamer's example, became
active in the struggle in the mid-1960s. When Fannie Lou Hamer
died on April 14, 1977, in a Mound Bayou hospital, she did not
have a penny to her name. Owen Brooks made the arrangements
for her funeral and raised the money to pay for it.[3]

All the major newspapers reported Mrs. Hamer's passing, and
movement activists and prominent national political figures came
to Ruleville on the day of her funeral to join hundreds of local people in paying tribute. Among those eulogizing Mrs. Hamer were
SNCC colleagues Julian Bond, John Lewis, and Stokely Carmichael,
but former political opponents like Aaron Henry and Hodding Carter III also offered their testimony. The principal speaker was Andrew Young, the SCLC activist who had recently been appointed
ambassador to the United Nations by President Jimmy Carter. Addressing the more than three hundred people who had packed into
Williams Chapel, with hundreds more gathered outside, Young
praised Mrs. Hamer as "a woman who literally helped turn this
nation around. . . . Governors and heads of state know of this hum-

ble woman from Ruleville, Mississippi." In a reference to the other Carter administration officials in the room, Young observed that "none of us would be where we are now had she not been here then." He ended his oration by leading the mourners in one of Mrs. Hamer's favorite songs, "This Little Light of Mine." Two days later the Mississippi House of Representatives unanimously passed a resolution commending Mrs. Hamer for her contributions to the state of Mississippi.[4]

Like Martin Luther King and Malcolm X before her, in death Fannie Lou Hamer had become a person for all seasons, her name invoked by politicians and self-proclaimed leaders across the ideological spectrum. She is remembered for her deep religious faith, her ability to move an audience, and her refusal to hate those who oppressed her. Yet the Fannie Lou Hamer who speaks loudest and with the greatest sense of urgency today is the angry crusader for social justice who relentlessly attacked power and privilege and believed that progress depended on continual struggle. "Ain't nothing going to be handed to you on a silver platter, nothing," she said in a 1972 interview. "That's not just black people, that's people in general, the masses. See, I'm with the masses. So, you don't ever get nothing, just walk up and say, 'Here it is.' You've got to fight. Every step of the way, you've got to fight!" Her friend Charles McLaurin recalled that "when I talked with Mrs. Hamer for the last time shortly before her death, she said, 'Mac, we ain't free yet. The kids need to know their mission.'"[5]

Acknowledgements

In the dozen years I lived and worked in Mississippi I met many extraordinary people who contributed much to my understanding of that state's history and its cultural distinctiveness. I hope this book will honor the memory of Mississippi friends—moderates, liberals, and radicals—who shared a commitment to bring racial justice to the Magnolia State: Ed Akin, Ernst Borinski, Julia "Ma" Bender, Rose Branch, Lenora Brewer, Henry "Daddy" Briggs, Virgia Brocks-Shedd, Zenobia Coleman, Jim Silver, and Howard Spencer.

I owe an immense debt to Julian Bond, John Bracey, Joseph Herzenberg, Steven Lawson, Neil McMillen, August Meier, James T. Patterson, and Barbara Steinson, who read earlier drafts of a rather bulky manuscript. In addition to pointing out factual errors and suggesting new approaches, these scholars offered sound advice on the book's organization and style. Ken Bode, Marshall Ganz, Dorie Ladner, and John Salter critiqued parts of the manuscript. Charles Payne generously shared his insights on the history of the movement in the Mississippi Delta. All these readers have improved the book significantly. Its shortcomings are, of course, my own doing.

Other scholars, including William H. Chafe, Donald Cunnigen, David Chalmers, James Findlay, Raymond Gavins, David Garrow, Martha Prescod Norman, Frank R. Parker, Armstead Robinson, Joseph Sinsheimer, and Patricia Sullivan, have been helpful in many ways. Clayborne Carson made available his extensive collection of SNCC materials at a time when the SNCC papers were not open. Jim Brown, my long-time colleague at Tougaloo College, has for nearly a decade kept me posted on events in Mississippi through his personal clipping service. And David Dittmer assisted with the index.

Many librarians, archivists, and secretaries have assisted me in this project. They include Esme Bhan, Louise Cook, Sara Cooper, Odelle Dockins, Melinda Glidden, Clarence Hunter, Peg Lemley, Kathryn Millis, Karen Mota, Lynne Mueller, Elaine Owens, Mary Rose, Gail Shirley, Mattie Sink, Elinore Sinnette, and Ann Wells. Every scholar doing research on civil rights in Mississippi owes a huge debt to Jan Hillegas. A volunteer in 1964, Jan remained in Mississippi to work with the Freedom Information Service. For more than two decades she preserved, at considerable expense, thousands of valuable documents that otherwise would have been lost, adding to the collection as new materials became available.

Other friends, family, scholars, journalists, and activists have provided source materials, photographs, housing, encouragement, and companionship. Among the people I am particularly indebted to are Donna Barnes, Anne Braden, Sarah Brown, Charles Dunagin, Avery and Melba Dittmer, Charles and Brenda Eagles, Mary and Paul Gaston, Victoria Gray-Adams, Lawrence Guyot, Henry Hampton, Gordon and Mary Ann Henderson, June Johnson, John Jones, Ed King, Joyce Ladner, Bob Lavelle, Ken Lawrence, George A. Owens, Constance Slaughter-Harvey, Susan Lorenzi Sojourner, Emmett J. Stringer, Mabel and Raymond Tobey, and Robert Zellner.

My greatest obligation is to the movement activists, government officials, and other participants who, in interviews and informal conversations, shared their experiences with me. Their names are found in the text and throughout the notes. Without their assistance, their insights and analysis, this book could not have been written.

The Rockefeller Foundation, the American Council of Learned Societies, and the Fisher Foundation provided year-long fellowships that greatly facilitated my research. I owe special thanks to President Robert Bottoms of DePauw University, who has encouraged my work on this project for the past eight years. The Lyndon Baines Johnson Foundation supplied a travel grant for work at the Johnson Library in Austin, Texas. During the 1988–89 academic year I was a fellow at the Center for the Study of Civil Rights in Charlottesville, Virginia, and in that congenial atmosphere wrote the early chapters of the book. At the University of Illinois Press, Richard L. Wentworth, Theresa L. Sears, Stephanie Smith, and my copy editor, Bruce Bethell, have provided sound advice, encouragement, and understanding. John Bracey, coeditor of the series, offered important suggestions for improving the manuscript, and his continuing strong support for this project has meant a great deal to me.

Two scholars have served as mentors over a period spanning three decades. I first met Jim Patterson when I was a graduate student at Indiana University in the 1960s. Since then he has critiqued practically everything I have written, enabled me to experience new and challenging academic environments, and been as good a friend as anyone can hope to have.

My initial contact with August Meier came in 1971 when I submitted my doctoral dissertation to his Blacks in the New World series, which had just moved to the University of Illinois Press. I vividly recall his first telephone call, a forty-five-minute monologue in which he described in detail everything that was wrong with the thesis, concluding that if I took his advice he would do the book. It took me only six years to get him to sign off on that manuscript. My relationship with Meier is unique in that he was an early participant in the story I have tried to tell. When I began teaching at Tougaloo, Mrs. Julia Bender recalled for me her memories of "Gus" Meier—a young Tougaloo history professor in the early post–World War II years and a card-carrying member of the NAACP—striding purposefully across campus, carrying his briefcase (it must have been new then), agitating the cause of racial justice. Augie and his colleague, the late Elliott Rudwick, persuaded me that the world of historical scholarship could be accessible to teachers at small liberal arts colleges, and over the years they made certain that I subjected myself to the rigors of our profession. For more than a quarter of a century Augie's encouragement and friendship have sustained me in good times and bad. His contribution to this book has been immeasurable.

This book is dedicated to the people who are most important to me, my family. Julie and Dave spent their formative years in Mississippi, first on the Tougaloo campus and later in Jackson. There they, along with thousands of other youngsters, attended the public schools at a time when the crisis over desegregation was at its peak. They came through that ordeal with a strong set of values, as well as a keen understanding of the possibilities and problems facing Mississippi and the South today. Our shared Mississippi experience has kept us close over the years. That and our mutual passion for the Atlanta Braves.

My wife, Ellen, read each draft of this manuscript, taking time from her work to help me with mine. Her editorial advice, as well as her insights into the people and politics of Mississippi, have strengthened this book at every stage. Sixteen years ago, in another book, I wrote that Ellen was a demanding critic—and my best friend. That still holds true today.

Notes

Carson Collection	Collection of SNCC papers in possession of Professor Clayborne Carson, Stanford, Calif.
C-L	Jackson *Clarion-Ledger*
CORE Papers	Congress of Racial Equality Archives, 1941–67, on microfilm, Martin Luther King Center, Atlanta, Ga.
CORE Addendum	CORE Archives, 1944–68, on microfilm, State Historical Society of Wisconsin, Madison, Wisconsin
Cox Papers	Eugene A. Cox Papers, Mitchell Library, Mississippi State University, Starkville, Miss.
Dent Collection	Oral history interviews conducted by Tom Dent, not transcribed, Amistad Research Center, Tulane University. Copies of the tapes are also available at the L. Zenobia Coleman Library, Tougaloo College, Tougaloo, Miss.
Ed King Papers	Papers of Edwin King, Coleman Libary, Tougaloo College
Hillegas Collection	Freedom Information Service Archives, preserved and expanded by Jan Hillegas
Howard CRDP	Civil Rights Documentation Project, Moorland-Spingarn Research Center, Howard University, Washington, D.C.
JDN	*Jackson Daily News*
JFK	John F. Kennedy Presidential Library, Boston, Mass.

LBJ	Lyndon Baines Johnson Presidential Library, Austin, Tex.
Marshall Papers	Papers of Assistant Attorney General for Civil Rights Burke Marshall, Kennedy Library
Mississippi Archives	Mississippi Department of Archives and History, Jackson, Miss.
Mississippi OHP	Oral history collection at the University of Southern Mississippi Library, Hattiesburg, Miss.
MLK	Martin Luther King Center Archives, Atlanta, Ga.
MLK Papers	Papers of Dr. Martin Luther King, Jr., King Center Archives
NAACP Papers	National Association for the Advancement of Colored People Papers, Manuscript Division, Library of Congress
NYT	*New York Times*
Romaine Papers	Interviews conducted by Anne Romaine, State Historical Society of Wisconsin
SCLC Papers	Southern Christian Leadership Conference Papers, King Center
SHSW	State Historical Society of Wisconsin Library, Madison, Wis.
SNCC Papers	Papers of the Student Nonviolent Coordinating Committee, on microfilm, King Center
UCLA	Civil Rights Movement in the United States Collection, Special Collections, University Research Library, University of California, Los Angeles
VEP Papers	Papers of the Voter Education Project, on microfilm, Southern Regional Council, Atlanta, Ga.

Unless otherwise noted, oral history interviews are my own.

Chapter 1: We Return Fighting

1. Medgar Evers, "Why I Live in Mississippi," *Ebony,* Sept. 1963, 142–44; Jack Mendelsohn, *The Martyrs: Sixteen Who Gave Their Lives for Racial Justice* (New York: Harper & Row, 1966), 65–66. The men had registered to vote under a recent state law exempting all veterans from payment of poll taxes for the preceding two years; *NYT,* July 4, 1946.

2. Mendelsohn, *The Martyrs,* 66.

3. *JDN,* June 23, 1946; Hodding Carter, "The Man from Mississippi—

Bilbo," *New York Times Magazine,* June 30, 1946, 12; *JDN,* May 19, 1946.

4. United States Senate, 79th Congress, 2d Session, *Hearings Before the Special Committee to Investigate Senatorial Campaign Expenditures, 1946* (Washington: GPO, 1947), 19, 88–90 (hereinafter cited as *Bilbo Hearings*).

5. Steven F. Lawson, *Black Ballots: Voting Rights in the South, 1944–1969* (New York: Columbia University Press, 1976), 101; *NYT,* July 3, 4, 1946; *NAACP Bulletin,* Oct. 1946, 7, in the Papers of the National Association for the Advancement of Colored People, Library of Congress. (During the course of my ten years of research in the NAACP Papers, the staff at the Library of Congress recataloged some of the files and added new files from the Landover, Maryland, center. To avoid confusion and error, I will refer only to the general collection in my notes.) *New South* 3 (June-July 1948): 3; *Bilbo Hearings,* 3–6.

6. Lawson, *Black Ballots,* 107; *PM,* Dec. 5, 1946; "Investigators' Report," Oct. 31, 1946, *Bilbo Hearings,* 10; Charles Houston, "Report to NAACP on Bilbo Hearings," undated, 2, NAACP Papers (hereinafter cited as "Houston Report").

7. *NYT,* Dec. 2, 1946; "Houston Report," 2; Charles Houston, "Notes," Dec. 2, 1946, NAACP Papers; *Pittsburgh Courier,* Dec. 14, 1946.

8. *Bilbo Hearings,* 2; *NYT,* Dec. 10, 1946.

9. *PM,* Dec. 3, 1946; "Houston Report," 1, 2.

10. *Bilbo Hearings,* 196–203; "Affidavit of V. R. Collier," undated, NAACP Papers.

11. *Bilbo Hearings,* 13, 45–48.

12. Ibid., 245–55, 260–69.

13. Henry Lee Moon, *Balance of Power: THE NEGRO VOTE* (Garden City, N.Y.: Doubleday, 1948), 245–481. The $2.00 annual poll tax was cumulative and had to be paid for the two years preceding the election year; ibid., 247. *Bilbo Hearings,* 176. In 1954 the voting law was rewritten to conform to the common (illegal) practice.

14. *Bilbo Hearings,* 121, 137; "Houston Report," 5; *Bilbo Hearings,* 191, 205.

15. *Bilbo Hearings,* 12–15.

16. Ibid., 16.

17. *Pittsburgh Courier,* Dec. 14, 1946; *PM,* Dec. 8, 1946; *NYT,* Dec. 6, 1946; *Bilbo Hearings,* 333–61.

18. Committee to Investigate Senatorial Campaign Expenditures, 80th Congress, 1st Session, *Report on Senate Resolution 224* (Washington: GPO, 1947), 9, 22; *NYT,* Dec. 24, 1946. Although he had been Bilbo's Senate colleague for more than a decade, on becoming president Harry S. Truman distanced himself from the Mississippian and took no active role in the Senate deliberations. Theodore Bilbo to "Dear Harry," April 13, 1945; Harry S. Truman to "Dear Bilbo," Aug. 28, 1945; Bilbo to "Dear Mr. President," Aug. 7, 1945, president's personal files, 533, Harry S. Truman Library, Independence, Missouri.

19. Lawson, *Black Ballots,* 112–15.

20. V. O. Key, Jr., *Southern Politics in State and Nation* (New York: Knopf, 1949), 229; Claude Sitton, "Inquiry into the Mississippi Mind," *New York Times Magazine,* April 28, 1963, 13; John Ray Skates, *Mississippi: A Bicentennial History* (New York: Norton, 1979), 6.

21. Skates, *Mississippi,* 7; James W. Loewen and Charles Sallis, eds., *Mississippi: Conflict and Change* (New York: Pantheon, 1974), 17.

22. For the most comprehensive history of the Delta, see James C. Cobb, *The Most Southern Place on Earth: The Mississippi Delta and the Roots of Regional Identity* (New York: Oxford University Press, 1992).

23. Richard Aubrey McLemore, *Mississippi Through Four Centuries* (Chicago: Laidlaw, 1945), 231, 234, 247–48, 249; Vernon Lane Wharton, *The Negro in Mississippi, 1865–1890* (Chapel Hill: University of North Carolina Press, 1947), 180, 170; Lerone Bennett, *Black Power, U.S.A.: The Human Side of Reconstruction* (Chicago: University of Chicago Press, 1967), 232–33.

24. Loewen and Sallis, *Mississippi,* 186–88; Neil R. McMillen, *Dark Journey: Black Mississippians in the Age of Jim Crow* (Urbana: University of Illinois Press, 1989), 8. For a detailed analysis of the 1890 constitution and its disfranchisement provisions, see *Dark Journey,* 38–57.

25. Ibid., 306–7.

26. Skates, *Mississippi,* 153.

27. Dorothy Lee Black, secretary and manager of the Delta Council, interviewed by Alexander Heard, July 7, 1947, Somnerville, Mississippi, in Alexander Heard Papers, Special Collections, Joint University Libraries, Vanderbilt University; Skates, *Mississippi,* 151; Julius S. Scott, "Blacks and Wartime Industrial Expansion in Mississippi, 1940–1950," 29, unpublished essay in my possession.

28. Skates, *Mississippi,* 153.

29. Press release, Office of War Information, Oct. 20, 1942, copy in NAACP Papers; "Minutes of the Meeting of the Board of Directors," November 1942, NAACP Papers.

30. Affidavit, "Statement of Eldridge Simmons made to John E. Rousseau, Jr.," New Orleans, Aug. 1, 1944; "Minutes of the Meeting of the Board of Directors," Sept. [11], 1944; E. R. Dudley to Paul M. Katzenburg, Nov. 10, 1944, NAACP Papers; undated clipping, Office of War Information, box 28, Truman Library.

31. Alan M. Osur, *Blacks in the Army Air Forces During World War II* (Washington: Office of Air Force History, 1977), 32; Ulysses Lee, *The United States Army in World War II: The Employment of Negro Troops* (Washington: Office of the Chief of Military History, 1966), 213; Lowry G. Wright to T. K. Gibson, Jr., May 13, 1943, in Phillip McGuire, ed., *Taps for a Jim Crow Army: Letters from Black Soldiers in World War II* (Santa Barbara, Calif.: ABC-Clio, 1983), 37–38; William T. Schmidt, "The Impact of Camp Shelby in World War II on Hattiesburg, Mississippi," *Journal of Mississippi History* 39 (Fall 1977): 48; Norman Brittingham to Truman K. Gibson, Jr., July 17, 1943; Jerry M. Miller to Gibson, July 16,

1943, in McGuire, *Taps,* 18, 215. Judge William Hastie reported on the incident with the Highway Patrol; ibid., 187.

32. Clyde Blue, interview in Mary Penick Motley, ed., *The Invisible Soldier: The Experience of Black Soldiers in World War II* (Detroit: Wayne State University Press, 1975), 124–25.

33. Ibid., 126–27; Lee, *Employment of Negro Troops,* 368; Jeffries Bassett Jones, interview in Motley, *Invisible Soldier,* 118.

34. Motley, *Invisible Soldier,* 117; Lee, *Employment of Negro Troops,* 369–70.

35. *Bilbo Hearings,* 390–92; *Congressional Record,* 79th Congress, 1st Session, vol. 91, part 5 (Washington: GPO, 1945), 6994–96, 7000; ibid., part 6, 7420–22.

Chapter 2: Rising Expectations, 1946–54

1. Census of the Population, 1950, vol. 2, *Characteristics of the Population, Part 24, Mississippi* (Washington: GPO), 192; Morton King, Jr., and others, *Mississippi's People, 1950* (University, Mississippi, 1955), 55; U.S. Census, 1950, *Agriculture, Vol. 1, Part 22, Mississippi: Counties and State Economic Areas* (Washington: GPO, 1952), 5, 21.

2. 1950 Census, vol. 2, 21, 39, 177, 179, 180.

3. *C-L* (undated clipping in James Brown collection, Tougaloo, Miss.); *NYT,* Nov. 5, 1946; Nov. 20, 1947.

4. *NYT,* Dec. 19, 1948; *Delta Democrat-Times,* May 24, 1954.

5. Jessica Mitford, *A Fine Old Conflict* (New York: Knopf, 1977), 162; McGee Folder, NAACP Papers; *NYT,* Dec. 9, 1947.

6. Civil Rights Congress, undated press release, in Hodding and Betty Werlein Carter Papers, Special Collections, Mitchell Library, Mississippi State University; Mitford, *Fine Old Conflict,* 176; Carl Rowan, *South of Freedom* (New York: Knopf, 1952), 177–78; *Nation,* May 5, 1951, 5.

7. *NYT,* May 8, 9, 13, 1951; *Commonweal* 54 (May 25, 1951): 158; Rowan, *South of Freedom,* 187, 190; Wilbur Buckley, interviewed by Alexander Heard, June 24, 1947, Jackson; A. B. Friend, interviewed by Heard, Aug. 16, 1947, Sardis, Heard Papers. Heard was in Mississippi doing research for V. O. Key's *Southern Politics in State and Nation* (New York: Knopf, 1949).

8. Hodding Carter II, interviewed by Heard, Jan. 4, 1947, Greenville; George McLean, interviewed by Heard, July 10, 1947, Tupelo, Heard Papers.

9. Eugene Albert Roper, "The CIO Organizing Committee in Mississippi, June 1946–January 1949" (master's thesis, University of Mississippi, 1949), 5–6.

10. *JDN,* Jan. 20, 1937, quoted in John Ray Skates, Jr., "A Southern Editor Views the National Scene: Frederick Sullens and the Jackson, Mississippi *Daily News*" (Ph.D. diss., Mississippi State University, 1965), 227; Donald C. Mosely, "A History of Labor Unions in Mississippi" (Ph.D. diss., University of Alabama, 1965), 211.

11. *Workers Defense Bulletin,* Spring 1943, 1, copy in NAACP Papers; *Crisis* 50 (May 1943): 134.

12. Roper, "CIO," 10; R. W. Starnes, interviewed by Heard, June 21, 1947, Jackson, Heard Papers.

13. Starnes, interviewed by Heard.

14. *Jackson State Times,* March 13, 1956; undated *State Times* clipping, Eugene A. Cox Collection, Mitchell Library, Mississippi State University.

15. Robert Moses, remarks at the Mississippi Voices of the Civil Rights Movement conference, McComb, Mississippi, July 8–9, 1983, conference tape recording in my possession (hereinafter cited as "McComb Conference").

16. Interview with the Reverend R. L. T. Smith, Aug. 1, 1988, Jackson; Nathaniel H. Lewis, interviewed by Thomas Healy, Oct. 24, 1978, McComb, in the Mississippi Oral History Program, University of Southern Mississippi Archives (hereinafter cited as Mississippi OHP). For an illuminating account of Perry Howard's checkered political career, see Neil R. McMillen, "Perry W. Howard, Boss of Black-and-Tan Republicanism in Mississippi, 1924–1960," *Journal of Southern History* 68 (May 1982): 205–24.

17. T. B. Wilson, interviewed by Heard, May 31, 1947, Jackson; "One-Party-System," notes taken by Heard at Jackson meeting, June 23, 1947, Heard Papers; Andrew A. Workman, "Closing the Door: The *Brown* Decision and the Decline of Accommodationist Leadership in Mississippi," 4, paper delivered at annual meeting of the Organization of American Historians, Louisville, Ky., April 11, 1991.

18. Dr. T. W. Hill, interviewed by Heard, July 8, 1947, Clarksdale, Heard Papers.

19. *JDN,* Jan. 29, 1947; Mississippi Legislature, *Extraordinary Session, 1947,* House Bill no. 38, copy in NAACP Papers; *NYT,* March 14, 1947; Aug. 5, 1947; T. B. Wilson, interviewed by Heard, June 21, 1947, Jackson, Heard Papers.

20. *NYT,* Aug. 6, 1947; T. B. Wilson to Thurgood Marshall, Aug. 21, 1947, NAACP Papers; New Orleans *Times-Picayune,* Jan. 26, 1947.

21. William F. Winter, "New Directions in Politics, 1948–1956," in Richard Aubrey McLemore, ed., *A History of Mississippi, II* (Hattiesburg: University and College Press of Mississippi, 1973), 141–43. (For a thorough account of the Dixiecrat campaign, see Robert A. Garson, *The Democratic Party and the Politics of Sectionalism, 1941–1948* [Baton Rouge: Louisiana State University Press, 1974].) Frances Butler Simkins, *A History of the South* (New York: Knopf, 1963), 604; Frank Smith, interviewed by Orley B. Caudill, July 2, 1976, Mississippi OHP; F. Glenn Abney, *Mississippi Election Statistics, 1900–1967* (University, Mississippi: Bureau of Government Research, 1968), 2.

22. *NYT,* Sept. 3, 1948; Abney, *Mississippi Election,* 2; *Jackson Advocate,* May 21, 1949; *New South* 8 (Jan. 1953): 4.

23. A. W. Wells to William Pickens, March 7, 1940, NAACP Papers; Neil McMillen, *Dark Journey: Black Mississippians in the Age of Jim Crow* (Urbana: University of Illinois Press, 1989), 314–15.

24. Rev. R. G. Gilchrist to NAACP, April 3, 1945; Daniel E. Byrd to

Gloster Current, April 26, 1948; Ella Baker to Carsie Hall, April 28, 1944, NAACP Papers.

25. Clarice T. Campbell and Oscar Rogers, Jr., *Mississippi: The View from Tougaloo* (Jackson: University Press of Mississippi, 1979), 186; R. L. T. Smith interview.

26. See Ruby Stutts Lyells, "A Look Ahead: What the Negro Wants," *Vital Speeches* 15 (Aug. 15, 1949): 659–62.

27. "Officers of the Mississippi State Conference of the NAACP," Dec. 13, 1953, NAACP Papers; Gloster Current, "Women in the NAACP," *Crisis* 66 (April 1959): 205–10.

28. "Monthly Reports of the NAACP Board of Directors," 1945–47; "Annual Conference Proceedings," 1947, NAACP Papers.

29. Memorandum, Marshall to Current, Aug. 28, 1950; Marshall to White, July 13, 1950, NAACP Papers.

30. Memorandum, Current to White, Aug. 14, 1950; Bender to Current, March 15, 1951; Bender to Lucille Black, May 7, 1952, NAACP Papers.

31. Simeon Booker, *Black Man's America* (Englewood Cliffs, N.J.: Prentice-Hall, 1964), 166; Workman, "Closing the Door," 9.

32. Mrs. Medgar Evers with William Peters, *For Us, the Living* (New York: Doubleday, 1967; citations are from the 1970 Ace paperback edition), 82; Booker, *Black Man's America,* 166.

33. Memorandum, Hurley to White, Oct. 8, 1952, NAACP Papers; Aaron Henry, interviewed by John Dittmer and John Jones, April 22, 1981, Clarksdale, Oral History Collection, Mississippi Department of Archives and History, Jackson (hereinafter cited as Mississippi Archives).

34. "The Accomplishments of the Regional Council of Negro Leadership of Mississippi," undated RCNL news release, copy in NAACP Papers.

35. Memorandum, Current to White, Sept. 30, 1952; Hurley to White, Oct. 8, 1952; undated RCNL news release, "No Rest Room, No Gas," NAACP Papers.

36. Lester Velie, "Homemade Boom in Mississippi," *Colliers,* June 19, 1948, 78; "Deep in Dixie: Race Progress," *U.S. News and World Report,* Feb. 26, 1954, 53–54; *Delta Democrat-Times,* April 12, 1954; *Natchez Democrat,* March 23, 1954; Bethany Swearingen, "Mississippi," *New South* 4 (Oct. 1949): 9. See also "Negro Vote in Mississippi," *Ebony,* Nov. 1951, 15–18, 21–22.

37. 1950 Census, vol. 2, 28–29; McMillen, *Dark Journey,* 73; "Our Disgraceful Negro Schools," *JDN* editorial reprinted in *New South* 4 (Feb. 1949): 5.

38. J. Lewis Henderson, "In the Cotton Delta," *Survey Graphic* 36 (Jan. 1947): 110; H. M. Ivey, "Passage of S246 . . . What It Would Mean to Mississippi," *NEA Journal* 39 (Feb. 1950): 97; Leander L. Boykin, "The Status and Trends of Differentials Between White and Negro Teachers' Salaries in the Southern States, 1900–1946," *Journal of Negro Education* 18 (Winter 1949): 47.

39. *Crisis* 55 (April 1948): 123–24; *JDN,* March 28, 1982; Kenneth H. Williams, "Mississippi and Civil Rights, 1945–1954" (Ph.D. diss., Mississippi State University, 1985), 215–19.

40. W. Milan Davis, "There's a Better Day A-Coming," *Mississippi Educational Journal* 26 (April 1950): 123–26; *Jackson Advocate,* March 31, 1951; Williams, "Mississippi and Civil Rights," 229–30; Winter, "New Directions," 150; McComb *Enterprise-Journal,* Dec. 2, 9, 1953.

41. *NYT,* May 2, 1954.

42. "Resolutions Adopted by the 6th Annual Convention of the Mississippi State Conference of Branches," Nov. 3–4, 1951, NAACP Papers; *JDN,* Jan. 22, 1954; Emmett J. Stringer, "The Big Three of First-Class Citizenship," speech delivered at the annual meeting of the Cleveland, Ohio, branch of the NAACP, Dec. 12, 1954, NAACP Papers. Evers was denied admission on technical grounds. He had submitted the two required character recommendations from people in his hometown of Decatur, not from Mound Bayou, where he currently resided. The board of trustees then immediately wrote in a new requirement that in the future applicants must present recommendations from five Ole Miss graduates.

43. Eastland and Carter, quoted in *Delta Democrat-Times,* May 18, 1954; interview with Bishop Duncan Gray, Jan. 31, 1989, Jackson.

44. Gray interview; James P. Coleman to "My Brothers of the State Bar," undated letter in James P. Coleman Papers, Mississippi Archives; *JDN,* July 25, 1954; *NYT,* Sept. 17, 1954.

45. The description of the meeting with Governor White was compiled from the following sources, all of which agree on the essential points of what transpired: Aaron Henry, untitled typescript dated March 1963, Aaron Henry Papers, L. Zenobia Coleman Library, Tougaloo College; interview with Emmett J. Stringer, Aug. 3, 1988, Columbus, Miss.; T. R. M. Howard, "Speech at Governor's Conference," July 30, 1954; Stringer, "The Big Three"; "The Jackson Declaration: Statement Issued by Negro Leaders from Every Area of the State of Mississippi, July 31, 1954," NAACP Papers. See also Memphis *Commercial Appeal,* July 31, 1954; *JDN,* July 31, 1954.

Chapter 3: The Magnolia Jungle

1. "Mississippi, 1954–1955," NAACP Branch Files, NAACP Papers.

2. Ibid.

3. Stringer interview.

4. Ibid.; "Columbus, 1953–1955," NAACP branch files, NAACP Papers.

5. Columbus Branch, "Program for 1955," Feb. 20, 1955; "Biographical Sketch—Dr. E. J. Stringer"; Stringer to Ruby Hurley, Feb. 9, 1953, NAACP Papers.

6. Emmett J. Stringer, "The Big Three of First-Class Citizenship," speech delivered at the annual meeting of the Cleveland, Ohio, branch of the NAACP, Dec. 12, 1954, NAACP Papers; *JDN,* May 29, 1954; "Statement

Issued by NAACP Representatives from Every Area of the State of Mississippi," May 30, 1954, NAACP Papers; *JDN*, Sept. 26, 1954.

7. "Statement Issued by NAACP"; Stringer, "The Big Three"; Clarence Mitchell, "Report on Mississippi for Board and Staff Reference," November 1954, NAACP Papers.

8. Stringer, "The Big Three."

9. J. H. White to E. J. Stringer, Aug. 25, 1964; A. Maurice Mackel to Walter White, Aug. 11, 1954, NAACP Papers.

10. *JDN*, Aug. 24, 31, 1954; Stringer, "The Big Three."

11. Stringer to Marshall, Oct. 7, 1954, NAACP Papers.

12. Neil R. McMillen, *The Citizens' Council: Organized Resistance to the Second Reconstruction, 1954–64* (Urbana: University of Illinois Press, 1971), 18–19. (McMillen's excellent book is the definitive study on that organization.) Hodding Carter II, "A Wave of Terror Threatens the South," *Look*, March 22, 1955, 32; John Barlow Martin, *The Deep South Says "Never"* (New York: Ballantine, 1957), 3–15.

13. McMillen, *Citizens' Council*, 15, 20, 25, 28, 118–24; Carter, "Wave of Terror," 32; Martin, *The Deep South*, 14–15; McMillen, remarks at Freedom Summer Reviewed conference, Jackson and Tougaloo, Mississippi, Oct. 30–Nov. 1, 1979 (transcript in my possession).

14. Mitchell, "Report on Mississippi"; E. J. Stringer to Thurgood Marshall, Oct. 7, 1954, NAACP Papers.

15. Mitchell, "Report on Mississippi"; memorandum, Current to Wilkins, Dec. 13, 1954; E. J. Stringer, "Annual Report by the President of the Mississippi State Conference of NAACP Branches," Nov. 6, 1954, NAACP Papers; Stringer interview.

16. Mitchell, "Report on Mississippi"; Stringer interview.

17. Stringer interview.

18. Current to Wilkins, Dec. 13, 1954; Simeon Booker, *Black Man's America* (Englewood Cliffs, N.J.: Prentice-Hall, 1964), 169; *C-L*, Jan. 2, 1955.

19. Mitchell, "Report on Mississippi"; Current to Wilkins, Dec. 13, 1954; Gus Courts to NAACP, Aug. 30, 1954; Hurley, "Economic Pressures in Mississippi"; A. M. Mackel to Gloster Current, Oct. 12, 1955; Lovie F. Walker to Lucille Black, Nov. 1, 1954, NAACP Papers.

20. NAACP press release, "NAACP Appeals to President to Halt Mississippi Terror," Dec. 22, 1954, NAACP Papers; Mrs. Medgar Evers with William Peters, *For Us, the Living* (New York: Ace, 1970), 125. For more on the NAACP's unsuccessful efforts to get the federal government to intervene in Mississippi, see Denton L. Watson, *Lion in the Lobby: Clarence Mitchell, Jr.'s Struggle for the Passage of Civil Rights Laws* (New York: Morrow, 1990), 277–81.

21. Roy Wilkins to M. Montgomery, Sept. 14, 1955; Wilkins to Morton Grossman, Jan. 21, 1955; "Memorandum to the Board of Directors from Mr. Current," Dec. 13, 1954, NAACP Papers.

22. Evers, *For Us*, 19–21.

23. Ibid., 28, 73–74, 89.

24. Ibid., 82, 87; Ruby Hurley, interviewed by John Britton, Jan. 26, 1968, 28, Howard Civil Rights Documentation Project, Howard University (hereinafter cited as Howard CRDP).

25. McMillen, *Citizens' Council*, 28; Reed Sarrat, *The Ordeal of Desegregation* (New York: Harper & Row, 1966), 200; Richard Kluger, *Simple Justice: The History of* Brown *v.* Board of Education *and Black America's Struggle for Equality* (New York: Vintage, 1975), 744–45.

26. Martin, *The Deep South*, 28–29.

27. Ibid., 28–29; Sarrat, *Ordeal*, 302; James A. Wright to Roy Wilkins, Nov. 18, 1955; memorandum, Ruby Hurley to Roy Wilkins, Oct. 7, 1955, NAACP Papers; David Halberstam, "A County Divided Against Itself," *The Reporter*, Dec. 15, 1955, 30–32. At the outset of the petition drive the Citizens' Council did not have affiliates in Vicksburg, Natchez, and Clarksdale, but it sent representatives into these counties to direct the campaign.

28. Halberstam, "A County Divided," 32. Wilkins had been elected national NAACP executive secretary after the death of Walter White in 1955.

29. Telegram, Medgar Evers to Wilkins, July 19, 1955, NAACP Papers; McMillen, *Citizens' Council*, 29–30.

30. Quoted in Kluger, *Simple Justice*, 753.

31. John Dittmer, "The Politics of the Mississippi Movement, 1954–1964," in Charles Eagles, ed., *The Civil Rights Movement in America* (Jackson: University Press of Mississippi, 1986), 69; Medgar Evers, "Special Report, Mississippi Field Secretary," Dec. 11, 1957, NAACP Papers.

32. United States Commission on Civil Rights, *With Liberty and Justice for All* (Washington: GPO, 1959), 50–51.

33. *NYT*, Nov. 4, 1954; Loewen and Sallis, eds., *Mississippi: Conflict and Change* (New York: Pantheon, 1974), 256.

34. Civil Rights Commission, *With Liberty and Justice*, 50–53.

35. Booker, *Black Man's America*, 161.

36. Lee was not able to speak after he was shot. The account of the killing comes from eyewitnesses interviewed by Ruby Hurley, whose investigation was much more thorough than those undertaken by local and federal authorities. "Memorandum from Mrs. Hurley, Re: Investigation of Death of Reverend G. W. Lee, Belzoni, Mississippi," May 13, 1955, NAACP Papers. See also Jack Mendelsohn, *The Martyrs: Sixteen Who Gave Their Lives for Racial Justice* (New York: Harper & Row, 1966), 5.

37. Undated clipping; A. H. McCoy to President Dwight Eisenhower, May 10, 1955, NAACP Papers; Mendelsohn, *The Martyrs*, 12; Booker, *Black Man's America*, 163, 161. See also Roy Wilkins, *Standing Fast: The Autobiography of Roy Wilkins* (New York: Viking, 1982), 222–24.

38. Mendelsohn, *The Martyrs*, 18–19; "Memorandum from Mrs. Hurley"; *New York Post*, Nov. 30, 1954, clipping in NAACP Papers.

39. *Delta Democrat-Times*, Aug. 16, 1955; NAACP press release, Aug. 18, 1955; "Are You Curious about Mississippi?" undated NAACP press release, NAACP Papers.

40. Curtis Jones, interviewed in *Eyes on the Prize: America's Civil Rights Years* (PBS video, 1986), episode 1· "Awakenings (1954–56)", Stephen J. Whitfield, *A Death in the Delta: The Story of Emmett Till* (New York: Free Press, 1988), 17. Other information on the incident at the store and on the trial of Milam and Bryant comes from testimony at the trial, as reported in the *New York Times*, Sept. 19–24, 1955.

41. Whitfield, *Death in the Delta*, 17–18; Jones, "Eyes" interview.

42. Whitfield, *Death in the Delta*, 19–22. Exactly what took place between the time Till was abducted and his death is problematical. Several months after they had been acquitted, Milam and Bryant admitted to journalist William Bradford Huie that they had killed Till. They told Huie that they had acted alone and that they had intended only to frighten the boy, but when Till continued to act defiantly and boasted again of his white girlfriend, they then decided to kill him. Subsequent accounts of the case have accepted the killers' story as accurate, perhaps in the belief that having confessed to the crime, they would not lie about the details.

However, the Milam-Bryant account contains internal contradictions and is at odds on critical points with the testimony of two trial witnesses, Moses Wright and Willie Reed. Wright said that three white men came to his cabin to abduct Till, and Reed said that he saw *six* men with Till on the Sunday morning of his death. Independent investigations conducted by Medgar Evers, Amzie Moore, and Ruby Hurley also point to a broader conspiracy, with several black men also involved with Milam, Bryant, and the other whites on Sunday morning. Finally, the Milam-Bryant account is self-serving, an effort to justify their actions before their southern white peers. See William Bradford Huie, "Approved Killing in Mississippi," *Look*, Jan. 24, 1956, 46–50; Huie, *Wolf Whistle* (New York: Signet, 1959). Stephen Whitfield, in *A Death in the Delta*, is the first scholar to systematically analyze Huie's accounts (51–60).

43. See trial accounts in the *Jackson Daily News, Clarion-Ledger*, and the *Vicksburg Post*. Hodding Carter's *Delta Democrat-Times* provided the most objective Mississippi coverage. Among the journalists covering the trial was Rob Hall, a native white Mississippian reporting for the communist *Daily Worker*.

44. *Delta Democrat-Times*, Sept. 2, 1965; *JDN*, Sept. 24, 1955.

45. Norma Bradley quoted in NAACP press release, Dec. 18, 1955, NAACP Papers; William Faulkner quoted in *Crisis*, Oct. 1955, 481; *JDN*, Sept. 24, 1955; Huie, "Approved Killing." After the *Look* article hit the stands, Milam and Bryant found themselves ostracized. Mississippi whites who had supported their innocence were angry and embarrassed, while local whites were simply afraid to be around self-confessed cold-blooded killers. Both left the state for a number of years and then returned to Mississippi. Milam died of cancer in 1981. The Bryants divorced, and in the mid-1980s Roy Bryant was again running a small store in the Delta. He was concerned that with all the publicity surrounding the thirtieth anniversary of the Till killing, some blacks might seek him out for revenge; *C-L*, Aug. 25, 1985.

46. Interview with Joyce Ladner, May 9, 1985, Washington, D.C.; Ladner quoted in *NYT,* May 17, 1979; Whitfield, *Death in the Delta,* 91; Anne Moody, *Coming of Age in Mississippi* (New York: Dial, 1968; citations are from Dell edition, 1971), 21–25; Howell Raines, *My Soul Is Rested: Movement Days in the Deep South Remembered* (New York: Putnam's, 1977; citations are from the Penguin edition, 1983), 235.

47. David Halberstam, "Tallahatchie County Acquits a Peckerwood," *The Reporter,* April 19, 1956, 25–30, quote on 28.

48. James W. Silver, *Mississippi: The Closed Society* (New York: Harcourt Brace, 1964; citations are from the 1966 revised edition); David Donald to James W. Silver, Aug. 24, 1963, in James W. Silver Papers, University of Mississippi, Oxford.

49. *NYT,* March 13, 1956; Washington Human Rights Project, "Supplemental Memorandum on Appointment of Former Mississippi Governor J. Coleman to U.S. Fifth Circuit Court of Appeals: Bills Signed into Law by Governor Coleman," June 23, 1963, 2, Southern Christian Leadership Conference Papers, Martin Luther King Center Library, Atlanta; *New York Post,* April 27, 1958, clipping in NAACP Papers; Fred Powledge, *Free at Last? The Civil Rights Movement and the People Who Made It* (Boston: Little, Brown, 1991), 175. The Mississippi legislature did not outlaw the NAACP, as Alabama had done years earlier. At a time when the legislature was acting in blatant disregard for the Bill of Rights, just why it did not go through the motions of banning the NAACP is not entirely clear. Lawmakers did not want to give the NAACP favorable national publicity, and abolishing the organization in Mississippi would have done just that. Moreover, while Governor Coleman was a strong segregationist, his strategy was to avoid needless battles with the federal government and thus opposed taking strong action against the NAACP. Yet talk of passing legislation against the NAACP's right to operate in Mississippi continued well into the administration of Ross Barnett, Coleman's successor; see *C-L,* Jan. 29, 1984.

50. *JDN,* March 1, 1956.

51. New Orleans *Times-Picayune,* April 22, 1973; *C-L,* March 7, 1977. For the point of view of a former director of the Citizens' Council, see Erle Johnston, *Mississippi's Defiant Years: 1953–1973* (Forest, Miss.: Lake Harbor, 1990).

52. *JDN,* March 3, 1956; Sept. 6, 1959; Tom Brady, *Black Monday* (Winona: Association of Citizens' Council of Mississippi, 1955), 12, quoted in McMillen, *Citizens' Council,* 163.

53. Silver, *Closed Society,* 65, 108–9; *JDN,* Sept. 6, 1959; McMillen, *Citizens' Council,* 244; *JDN,* Nov. 15, 1955; Will Campbell, *Brother to a Dragonfly* (New York: Seabury Press, 1977), 113–21; *JDN,* Feb. 21, 1956.

54. Ernst Borinski, interviewed by John Jones, 1981, Tougaloo, Miss., 23, Mississippi Archives; undated newspaper clipping in Edwin King Papers, Zenobia Coleman Library, Tougaloo College (hereinafter cited as Ed King Papers). For a warm, personal portrait of Borinski written by a former colleague, see Rosellen Brown, "Stirring Things Up," *Life,* April 1993, 87.

55. *Jackson State Times,* March 5, 1958; *C-L,* Dec. 2, 1955; news release, Jackson Citizens' Council, March 13, 1958, copy in Hodding and Betty Werlein Carter Papers; *Tupelo Daily Journal,* March 7, 1958; Ellis Finger, Jr., "From the President of Millsaps College," *Mississippi Methodist Advocate,* undated clipping in Ed King Papers; *C-L,* March 19, 28, 1958.

56. *JDN,* June 6, 1954; Cooper quoted in *C-L,* April 4, 1982.

57. Campbell, *Brother,* 131.

58. H. Brent Schaeffer, "The Work for Justice in Mississippi," *New South* 3 (Oct. 1948): 10; Silver, *Closed Society,* 57–58. Lay people who worked for racial advancement were also hounded out of the state. For the story of the controversy surrounding a Holmes County experiment in interracial cooperation run by two white men, Eugene Cox and David Minter, see Will Campbell, *Providence* (Marietta, Ga.: Longstreet, 1992).

59. William H. Crook and Ross Coggins, *Seven Who Fought* (Waco, Texas: World Books, 1971), 10–25; *JDN,* Feb. 21, 1956; interview with Duncan Gray.

60. McMillen, *Citizens' Council,* 25; Joseph Bryant Cumming, Jr., "The Lower Truth of Bill Minor: An Examination of the Role of a Reporter in a Free Society" (master's thesis, Emory University, 1981), 8; Silver, *Closed Society,* 30; McMillen, *Citizens' Council,* 258.

61. Cumming, "The Lower Truth of Bill Minor," 8.

62. *Delta Democrat-Times,* Sept. 13, 1955; undated *Jackson State Times* article, Ed King Papers.

63. Television censorship and biased racial coverage continued throughout the 1960s. As the decade progressed blacks were occasionally able to gain time to present their position on issues important to them, but it was not until the 1970s, after a landmark case in which the federal courts denied the owners of WLBT the renewal of their license because of racial bias, that televison coverage of racial issues in Mississippi began to improve substantially.

64. For an analysis of Minor's contribution written by a fellow journalist, see Cumming, "The Lower Truth of Bill Minor." P. D. East also wrote an autobiography, *The Magnolia Jungle: The Life, Times, and Education of a Southern Editor* (New York: Simon & Schuster, 1960).

65. Betty W. Carter, interviewed by Orley B. Caudill, Aug. 17, 1977, Greenville, 19–20, 44–46, Missisippi OHP; McMillen, *Citizens' Council,* 254–55.

66. Hodding Carter, *Where Main Street Meets the River* (New York: Rhinehart, 1949), 254; Hodding Carter, "Jim Crow's Other Side," in George B. Huszar, ed., *Equality and America: The Issue of Minority Rights* (New York: Wilson, 1949), 102; Anthony Lake Newberry, "Without Urgency or Ardor: The South's Middle-of-the-Road Liberals and Civil Rights, 1945–1960" (Ph.D. diss., Ohio University, 1982), 134.

67. Hodding Carter, "For the Record (A Personal Statement)," letter to the *Clarion-Ledger,* March 19, 1955; Carter's remarks on the NAACP were quoted in Newberry, "Without Urgency," 392.

68. Betty Carter, interviewed by Caudill, 19, 39.

69. Russell Warren Howe, "A Talk with William Faulkner," *The Reporter,* March 22, 1956, 18–20. Faulkner's reply was printed in *The Reporter,* April 19, 1956, 5. Noel Polk, "Faulkner and the Southern White Moderate," in Doreen Fowler and Ann J. Abadie, eds., *Faulkner and Race: Faulkner and Yoknapatawpha, 1986* (Jackson: University Press of Mississippi, 1987), 135–36.

70. Howe, "A Talk with William Faulkner," 18.

71. Faulkner, letter to the editor, *Life,* March 26, 1956, quoted in William Faulkner, "If I Were a Negro," *Ebony,* Sept. 1956, 70.

Chapter 4: Toward a New Beginning

1. Simeon Booker, *Black Man's America* (Englewood Cliffs, N.J.: Prentice-Hall, 1964), 171; *Crisis* 73 (March 1966): 155.

2. Steven Hahn, "Historical Circumstances and Purposes Involved in the Adoption of Dual Registration and the Abolition of Satellite Registration by the State of Mississippi," June 1986, 29. (This report was prepared for the NAACP Legal Defense Fund, Inc. Copy in my possession.) Mississippi voter registration application, copy in Ed King Papers; *C-L,* March 30, 1955.

3. Hahn, "Historical Circumstances," 27–29, 33; *JDN,* March 23, 1958; *Jackson State Times,* April 1, 1958.

4. Newspaper clipping in NAACP Papers, dated "2/57."

5. *Jackson State Times,* April 1, 1958; *JDN,* March 4, 1958; *C-L,* Dec. 8, 1957.

6. Amzie Moore to Roy Wilkins, Oct. 11, 1955, NAACP Papers.

7. Interview with Curtis C. Bryant, Jan. 16, 1984, McComb; Booker, *Black Man's America,* 171.

8. Medgar Evers, "Why I Live in Mississippi," *Ebony,* Sept. 1963, 148; Mrs. Medgar Evers with William Peters, *For Us, the Living* (New York: Ace, 1970), 195. (*Ebony* reprinted the 1957 Evers article shortly after his death.)

9. Julius Eric Thompson, "Mississippi," in Henry L. Suggs, ed., *The Black Press in the South, 1865–1979* (Westport, Conn.: Greenwood, 1983), 188.

10. Ibid., 190; Percy Greene, "More Uncle Toms Greatest Need of Southern Negro," *Jackson Advocate,* Jan. 19, 1957; Stringer interview; Thompson, "Mississippi," 191; Smith interview. See also Julius Thompson, *The Black Press in Mississippi, 1865–1985* (Gainesville: University Press of Florida, 1993), chaps. 2–3.

11. NAACP press release, "Mississippi State Conference of NAACP Branches Meeting, Nov. 4–6, 1960," NAACP Papers, Washington Bureau; interview with Joe Martin, Jan. 13, 1984, McComb; Joyce Ladner interview; Anne Moody, *Coming of Age in Mississippi* (New York: Dell, 1971), 127–28.

12. *The Eagle Eye,* April 9, 1955.

13. Program of the Fourth Annual Meeting of the Mississippi Region-

al Council of Negro Leadership, April 29, 1955; Ruby Hurley to Medgar Evers, Nov. 29, 1954, NAACP Papers; Evers, "Why I Live in Mississippi," 148; Cora B. Britton to Lucille Black, Sept. 8, 1955, NAACP Papers.

14. Benjamin Mays and Joseph Nicholson, *The Negro's Church* (New York: Harper, 1933), 7; John Dollard, *Caste and Class in a Southern Town* (New Haven: Yale University Press, 1937; 3d ed., New York: Doubleday, 1957), 248.

15. "Memorandum from Mr. Wilkins to the Staff: Re: Mississippi and the South," Sept. 27, 1955, NAACP Papers; James Forman, *The Making of Black Revolutionaries* (New York: Macmillan, 1972), 368; Wilkins, interviewed by Robert Wright, May 5, 1970, Howard CRDP, 62.

16. Hurley, "Information Re Killing in Mississippi . . . May 13, 1955," NAACP Papers. After Dr. Howard left the state Aaron Henry became RCNL director, but when Henry took over as NAACP state president in 1960 the RCNL languished, leaving the NAACP as the major black-led protest organization in the state.

17. Adam Fairclough, *To Redeem the Soul of America: The Southern Christian Leadership Conference and Martin Luther King, Jr.* (Athens: University of Georgia Press, 1987), 44–45; Wilkins to Medgar Evers, April 2, 1957, NAACP Papers; Evers, *For Us,* 216; Aaron Henry to Ella Baker, April 5, 1958, SCLC Papers (32:38).

18. William Kunstler, *Deep in My Heart* (New York: Morrow, 1966), 205; Medgar Evers to Ruby Hurley, Jan. 24, 1958, NAACP Papers.

19. Evers, *For Us,* 176, 194; "L. D. Call on Sunday, March 16, to Mr. Medgar Evers re assault on him by taxi driver," NAACP Papers, Washington Bureau.

20. Evers, *For Us,* 183–84; Medgar Evers to William Rogers, Oct. 29, 1959, NAACP Papers.

21. Evers to Rogers, Oct. 29, 1959; Evers, *For Us,* 184.

22. Evers, *For Us,* 186–91; *JDN,* Sept. 16, 1959.

23. "Mississippi State Sovereignty Commission: Report by Zack J. Van Landingham," Dec. 17, 1958, 4, in RG 27, no. 132, Mississippi Department of Archives and History (hereinafter cited as Van Landingham File).

24. Ibid., 1, 28–29.

25. "Memorandum to: Director, State Sovereignty Commission. From: Zack J. Van Landingham," Sept. 3, 1959, 1–2, Van Landingham File. McCain gave three reasons for rejecting Kennard's application. He said that Kennard had not submitted a transcript from the University of Chicago (earlier McCain told Van Landingham that he had lost Kennard's file); that Kennard was not eligible for readmission to the University of Chicago (not true); and that because Kennard apparently had changed the date from an earlier medical application this was evidence of bad "moral character." McCain later told a reporter he had no choice but to deny Kennard's application and that he could accomplish more as president of Mississippi Southern College than he could by losing his job over a "silly martyrdom for one Negro." The Mississippi Southern president later spoke in northern cities under the sponsorship of the Sovereignty Commission.

"Memorandum to: Governor J. Coleman. From: Zack J. Van Landingham. Subject: Clyde Kennard," Sept. 21, 1959, 1, Van Landingham File; Ronald A. Hollander, "One Mississippi Negro Who Didn't Go to College," *The Reporter* 27 (Nov. 8, 1962): 32; Earl Johnston, *Mississippi's Defiant Years* (Forest, Miss.: Lake Harbor, 1990), 116–17.

26. Memorandum, Van Landingham to Coleman, Sept. 21, 1959, 1–4, Van Landingham File; *JDN*, Sept. 16, 1959. When it finally ended funding for the Sovereignty Commission in 1973, the state legislature ordered that commission files be sealed for fifty years. The American Civil Liberties Union sued to have the files released, finally winning the case in 1991, but the files remained closed pending negotiations over the manner in which they would be made available to the public.

27. Evers, *For Us*, 191; Hollander, "One Mississippi Negro," 33–34; R. Jess Brown, interviewed by George S. Burson, April 8, 1972, Jackson, Mississippi OHP, 41. Brown was Kennard's attorney in the original trial.

28. Bradford Daniel and John Howard Griffin, "Why They Can't Wait," *The Progressive* 12 (July 1964): 19; *JDN*, Oct. 9, 1961; Evers, *For Us*, 192; Rabbi Charles Mantiband to James W. Silver, Feb. 22, 1963, Silver Papers.

29. Joyce Ladner interview; Evers, *For Us*, 192; Daniel and Griffin, "Why They Can't Wait," 19; *Memphis Press-Scimitar*, July 5, 1963, clipping in Eugene Cox Papers. Along with her sister, Dorie, Joyce Ladner had transferred to Tougaloo from Jackson State College in the fall of 1961.

30. Daniel and Griffin, "Why They Can't Wait," 19; Evers, *For Us*, 193. Griffin darkened his skin and traveled through Mississippi and other southern states posing as a black man. He wrote of his experiences in his bestseller, *Black Like Me* (Boston: Houghton Mifflin, 1961).

31. Howard Smead, *Blood Justice: The Lynching of Mack Charles Parker* (New York: Oxford University Press, 1986), 12–18, 55–56.

87. June and Jimmy Walters became objects of derision among Poplarville whites, for while the Walterses believed Parker was guilty, they wanted to see him brought to trial and they opposed vigilante justice; ibid., 93–94.

32. Ibid., 199, 175; Wilson F. Minor, "The Citizens' Councils—An Incredible Decade of Defiance," 53, manuscript in Wilson Minor Papers, Mississippi State University; Evers, *For Us*, 177.

33. Medgar Evers to Current, Feb. 24, 1959; Current to Evers, April 7, 1959, NAACP Papers; Evers, *For Us*, 194.

34. Joe Martin interview; Joyce Ladner interview.

35. Martin interview; Medgar Evers to Current, March 14, 1960; "Monthly Report from the Field Secretary," March 22, 1960, NAACP Papers. (Medgar Evers submitted his monthly reports to the NAACP national office under different main headings. They will be cited hereinafter as "Monthly Report.")

36. Medgar Evers, "Monthly Report," April 19, 1960, NAACP Papers.

37. Current, "Annual Report, Department of Branches," 1959, NAACP Papers. An earlier petition submitted by NAACP branch president Dr. Felix Dunn asking Harrison County officials to desegregate the beaches resulted in cross burnings and the loss of jobs for two of the petitioners; ibid.

38. Medgar Evers, "Monthly Report," April 21, 1960; May 23, 1960; affidavit, Dorothy Galloway, May 3, 1960; affidavit, Gilbert Mason, May 3, 1960, NAACP Papers; *JDN*, May 2, 1960; *NYT*, May 18, 1960; Evers, "Monthly Report," July 25, 1961, NAACP Papers. Less than a month later the new Kennedy Justice Department sued the city of Biloxi to desegregate the beaches. The case, eventually won by the Justice Department, dragged on for seven years, by which time the beaches had long since been desegregated. See Johnston, *Defiant Years,* 110–11.

39. "Program Operation Mississippi," notes of April 7, 1961, meeting, NAACP Papers.

40. James C. Bradford, interviewed by Worth Long, April 30, 1983, Jackson, Miss., in Southern Regional Council Archives, Atlanta; "Received via phone from Medgar Evers, March 28, 1961"; Medgar Evers to Wilkins, March 29, 1961, NAACP Papers; *JDN*, March 28, 1961. The nine students arrested were Meredith Anding, Jr., James C. Bradford, Alfred Cook, Jeraldine Edwards, Janice Jackson, Joseph Jackson, Elbert Earl Lassiter, Evelyn Pierce, and Ethel Sawyer; *Jackson State Times,* March 27, 1961. Pierce, who was from Natchez, listed her home address as Buffalo, New York, to prevent her family from suffering harassment.

41. Joyce Ladner interview; "Received via phone"; *JDN*, March 28, 1961; *NYT*, March 29, 1961; Burke Marshall, "Demonstrations in Jackson, Mississippi," March 29, 1961, Burke Marshall Papers, reel 1, John F. Kennedy Library, Boston, Mass.

42. *NYT*, March 30, 31, 1961; *JDN*, March 30, 1961; *Southern Patriot,* May 1961.

43. Evers, *For Us,* 202; *Southern Patriot,* May 1961.

44. Medgar Evers, "Monthly Report," July 28, 1961; Jack Young to Robert L. Carter, Aug. 17, 1961, NAACP Papers.

Chapter 5: Outside Agitators

1. Freedom song, sung to the tune of the old labor anthem "Which Side Are You On?"

2. *NYT*, May 25, 1961; *Washington Post,* May 25, 1961; *JDN*, May 25, 1961.

3. James Farmer, *Lay Bare the Heart: An Autobiography of the Civil Rights Movement* (New York: Arbor House, 1985), 2. For a more detailed account of the freedom rides, see August Meier and Elliott Rudwick, *CORE: A Study in the Civil Rights Movement* (New York: Oxford University Press, 1973), chap. 5, and Taylor Branch, *Parting the Waters: America in the King Years, 1954–63* (New York: Simon & Schuster, 1988), chap. 12.

4. Clayborne Carson, *In Struggle: SNCC and the Black Awakening of the 1960s* (Cambridge: Harvard University Press, 1981), 34–37.

5. Harris Wofford, *Of Kennedys and Kings: Making Sense of the Sixties* (New York: Farrar, Straus & Giroux, 1980), 153.

6. Branch, *Parting the Waters,* 454–77; Carson, *In Struggle,* 35; Howell Raines, *My Soul Is Rested* (New York: Penguin, 1983), 110.

7. New Orleans *Times-Picayune,* June 11, 1961; *Newsweek,* June 26, 1961, 16; Burke Marshall, recorded interview by John Oberdorfer, 1970, 37–41; Robert F. Kennedy, recorded interview by Anthony Lewis, Dec. 4, 1964, 573–74, John F. Kennedy Oral History Program, JFK. Robert Kennedy stated that Eastland's advice was "very, very helpful" during the time he was attorney general and added, "I found it much more pleasant to deal with him than many of the so-called liberals in the House Judiciary Committee or in other parts of Congress or the Senate"; Robert Kennedy, interviewed by Lewis, 527.

8. Marshall, interviewed by Oberdorfer, 37; Robert Kennedy, interviewed by Lewis, 577, 581; interview with Burke Marshall, Dec. 3, 1983, New Haven, Conn.; Marshall, interviewed by Victor Navasky, Nov. 18, 1967, Victor Navasky Papers, JFK.

9. Martin Luther King, quoted in Arthur Schlesinger, Jr., *Robert Kennedy and His Times* (Boston: Houghton Mifflin, 1978), 340; Leslie Dunbar, Howard CRDP interview, 1968, 20.

10. *JDN,* May 28, 1961; *NYT,* May 25, 1961; Wofford, *Of Kennedys and Kings,* 155; Meier and Rudwick, *CORE,* 139; Farmer, interview in Raines, *My Soul Is Rested,* 125–26.

11. *JDN,* May 27, 1961; *NYT,* May 27, 1961; James Farmer, *Freedom—When?* (New York: Random House, 1965), 70; *NYT,* May 29, 30, 1961; Meier and Rudwick, *CORE,* 140.

12. Frank Holloway, "Travel Notes from a Deep South Tourist," *New South* 16 (July-August 1961): 6; Meier and Rudwick, *CORE,* 140–41; Farmer, *Lay Bare the Heart,* 8–21.

13. The account of the freedom riders' stay at Parchman is drawn from the following works: Farmer, *Lay Bare the Heart,* 22–30; William Mahoney, "In Pursuit of Freedom," *Liberation* 6 (Sept. 1961): 7–11; and the previously cited books by Branch, Meier and Rudwick, and Carson. For oral history interviews of freedom riders who were at Parchman, see Dion T. Diamond, interviewed by Kay Shannon, 1967, Washington, D.C., Howard CRDP; John Lewis, interviewed by Robert Wright, 1967, Howard CRDP.

14. "The Movement Remembered: 'Like a Banked Fire,'" interview with Aurelia Norris Young by Worth Long, *Southern Changes,* Dec. 1983, 8; *NYT,* July 23, 1961; *JDN,* May 26, 1961.

15. George Alexander Sewell, *Mississippi Black History Makers* (Jackson: University Press of Mississippi, 1977), 267–75. Clarie Collins Harvey, interviewed by John Dittmer and John Jones, 1981, Jackson, 26–30, Mississippi Archives. Clarie Collins Harvey remained active in the decades following the civil rights movement. In 1964 she was appointed to the Mississippi Advisory Commission to the U.S. Commission on Civil Rights. She was a board member of the Southern Regional Council and active in

the Women's Strike for Peace. In 1971 she was elected national president of Church Women United, and in 1974 she became the first black member of the Millsaps College Board of Trustees.

16. Medgar Evers, "Special Report: Mississippi Field Secretary," Oct. 12, 1961, NAACP Papers; Harvey interview.

17. Farmer, *Lay Bare the Heart,* 14; Medgar Evers, "Monthly Report," June 21, 1961; ibid., July 28; Current to Wilkins and John Morsell, June 6, 1961, NAACP Papers; interview with David Dennis, June 12, 1983, Lafayette, Louisiana; "Minutes of the Student Nonviolent Coordinating Committee Meeting," July 14–16, 1961, Baltimore, copy in Carson Collection; McComb *Enterprise-Journal,* July 20, 1961.

18. Jack Newfield, *A Prophetic Minority* (New York: New American Library, 1966), 73; Moses, remarks at the Mississippi Voices of the Civil Rights Movement conference, McComb, Miss., July 9, 1983, tape transcript in my possession (hereinafter cited as "Mississippi Voices"); *Official Centennial Program, 1872—McComb—1972* (n.p., 1972), copy in McComb Public Library.

19. Nathaniel Lewis, interviewed by Thomas Healy, Oct. 24, 1978, McComb, Mississippi OHP.

20. Carsie Hall to Ella Baker, Oct. 8, 1944; Webb Owens to Lucille Black, June 11, 1955; Black to Owens, June 16, 1955, NAACP Papers; interview with Curtis C. Bryant, Jan. 16, 1984, McComb; interview with Ernest Nobles, Jan. 17, 1984, McComb; interview with Aylene Quin, Jan. 17, 1984, McComb.

21. Bryant interview; Quin interview; interview with Judge Joe Pigott, Jan. 15, 1984, McComb.

22. Carson, *In Struggle,* 46. William Moses submitted the prize-winning design for the Virginia Pavilion in the 1937 World's Fair. When state officials realized that Moses was black, they employed a white architect to design the exhibit. Conversation with William Moses, Nov. 19, 1988, Charlottesville, Va.

23. Howard Zinn, *SNCC: The New Abolitionists* (Boston: Beacon, 1965), 63–64. For the enthusiastic, funny, and flirtatious correspondence between Jane Stembridge and Bob Moses in the summer of 1960, see "Executive Secretary Files, 1959–1972," SNCC Papers, reel 4.

24. Robert Moses, interviewed by Clayborne Carson, March 29, 1982, Cambridge, Mass., 14. I am grateful to Professor Carson for making a copy of this illuminating interview available to me.

25. Ibid., 18.

26. Bob Moses, "Mississippi: 1961–1962," *Liberation* 14 (Jan. 1970): 14. The essay in *Liberation,* a transcript of a tape made in 1963, provides a perceptive look at the McComb movement (for other accounts, see Zinn, *SNCC,* chap. 4; Carson, *In Struggle,* chap. 4; and Branch, *Parting the Waters,* chap. 13). Moses, "Mississippi Voices"; interview with Robert Moses, Aug. 15, 1983, Cambridge, Mass.; Carson interview with Moses, 21–23.

27. Carson interview with Moses, 21–23; interview with Moses.

28. C. C. Bryant, "Mississippi Voices"; interview with Bryant.

29. Moses, "Mississippi," 6; Carson, *In Struggle,* 47; Branch, *Parting the Waters,* 493.

30. Reginald Robinson, "Report on McComb," undated, SNCC Papers, reel 38; Moses, "Mississippi," 6; Moses to Jack Young, Aug. 18, 1961, SNCC Papers, reel 43; McComb *Enterprise-Journal,* Aug. 4, 1961.

31. Charles F. McDew, interviewed by Katherine M. Shannon, 1967, Washington, D.C., 104–5, Howard CRDP; Carolyn Rickert, "Amite Farmer Fought for Something 'Worth Dyin' For,'" McComb *Enterprise-Journal,* Dec. 9, 1984.

32. McComb *Enterprise-Journal,* Sept. 1, 1961; Moses, "Mississippi," 10; Carson, *In Struggle,* 47–48.

33. McComb *Enterprise-Journal,* Aug. 28, 30, 31, 1961; Carson, *In Struggle,* 48; Hollis Watkins, interviewed by John Dittmer and John Jones, July 28, 1981, Jackson, Mississippi Archives.

34. McDew, Howard CRDP interview, 71; Carson, *In Struggle,* 41–42.

35. Moses interview; C. C. Bryant interview.

36. Moses, "Mississippi," 11; Carson, *In Struggle,* 48; Zinn, *SNCC,* 68.

37. Burke Marshall to Byron White, July 14, 1961, Marshall Papers, box 1; "Report of the Attorney General to the President on the Department of Justice's Activities in the Field of Civil Rights," Dec. 29, 1961, 2, Presidential Office Files, box 97, JFK. Three years later Burke Marshall wrote that the Justice Department action here was important "not only because it freed Hardy, but also because it established that, in an extreme case, the Federal Courts . . . will take unusually strong action to protect voting rights." Given this early success, it is curious that the Justice Department did not make extensive use of this tactic. Only one other time, in Greenwood in 1963, did the federal government intervene to protect potential voters from intimidation; Burke Marshall to Allen Markovitz, Dec. 15, 1964, HU2/ST 24, LBJ.

38. McComb *Enterprise–Journal,* Sept. 25, 26, 1961; E. W. Steptoe to Wilkins, Oct.13, 1961, NAACP Papers; Moses, "Mississippi," 12–13; Branch, *Parting the Waters,* 509–11, 520–22; Carson, *In Struggle,* 48–49. According to Taylor Branch, John Doar wanted to pursue the Lee case by bringing a federal suit, but Burke Marshall overruled him; Branch, *Parting the Waters,* 522.

39. McDew, Howard CRDP interview, 102–5.

40. Ibid; Carson, *In Struggle,* 49.

41. Zellner, in Joan Morrison and Robert K. Morrison, eds., *From Camelot to Kent State: The Sixties Experience in the Words of Those Who Lived It* (New York: Times Books, 1987), 48–49; McComb *Enterprise-Journal,* Oct. 5, 6, 1961; "Chronology of Abuses," in *Civil Rights Hearings before Subcommittee No. 5 of the Committee on the Judiciary,* House of Representatives, 88th Congress, First Session, May-August 1963, part II (Washington: GPO, 1963), 1312–13 (hereinafter cited as *Civil Rights Hearings*).

42. Moses, interviewed by Howard Zinn, June 20, 1963, Howard Zinn Papers, SHSW; McComb *Enterprise-Journal,* Oct. 6, 1961.

43. Quin and Nobles interviews; McComb *Enterprise-Journal,* Oct. 6, 1961; Oct. 5, 1961; Lewis, quoted in McComb *Enterprise-Journal,* Dec. 10, 1984.

44. Bryant and Moses interviews.

45. Wilkins to Edward King, Sept. 1, 1961; Medgar Evers, "Monthly Report," Oct. 13, 1961; memorandum, "Mr. Current to Mr. Moon," Oct. 11, 1961, NAACP Papers; Moses interview.

46. McDew, Howard CRDP interview, 96–98; Nobles, quoted in Mc-Comb *Enterprise-Journal,* Dec. 10, 1984.

47. McComb *Enterprise-Journal,* Oct.31, 1961; *Civil Rights Hearings,* 1313; Brumfield interview; Moses, "Mississippi," 14; Robert Talbert, "Mississippi Voices"; Moses letter quoted in Zinn, *SNCC,* 76.

48. McComb *Enterprise-Journal,* Dec. 2, 1961; *NYT,* Nov. 30, 1961.

49. McComb *Enterprise-Journal,* Dec. 6, 1961; James Forman to James Dombrowski, June 30, 1962, SNCC Papers, reel 19; *Southern Patriot,* June 1962; Moses, "Mississippi," 14; McComb *Enterprise-Journal,* Dec. 10, 1984. McDew and Zellner had been bailed out earlier to try to raise bonds for the others.

Chapter 6: Into the Delta

1. *Memphis Press-Scimitar,* Sept. 7, 1961, clipping in Eugene A. Cox Papers; *Voice of the Jackson Movement,* Nov. 14, 1961, clipping in Ed King Papers. Other Nashville students active in the Jackson project included Paul Booth, Marion Barry, and Charles Sherrod.

2. "Minutes of the Student Nonviolent Coordinating Committee Meeting," July 14–16, 1961, copy in Carson Collection; McComb *Enterprise-Journal,* July 20, 1961; *Voice of the Jackson Movement,* undated clipping in Ed King Papers; *Newsweek,* Oct. 30, 1961, 18–19; "Memorandum to Henry Lee Moon from Gloster Current," Oct. 8, 1961, NAACP Papers. The first week of the state fair was for whites only; part of the second week was reserved for black fairgoers. Blacks staged similar protests for the next two years before the fair management dropped the segregated arrangement.

3. Medgar Evers, "Special Report—Mississippi Field Secretary," Oct. 12, 1961; Gloster Current, "Staff Memorandum, Oct. 31, 1961, NAACP Papers.

4. David Dennis, "Field Secretary's Report," July 25, 1962, CORE Papers, Addendum, reel 22.

5. Tom Gaither to Jim McCain, April 12, 1962, CORE Papers, V–249; William Higgs, undated interview, Howard Zinn Papers. Higgs was a white Mississippi attorney who identified with the black struggle and worked with R. L. T. Smith in his 1962 campaign for Congress. In early 1963 the state arrested Higgs on a trumped-up morals charge, and he left Mississippi but continued to work for civil rights as an attorney in Washington; *Meridian Star,* Feb. 7, 1963.

6. Moses interview.

7. Ibid.; Interview with David Dennis, June 12, 1983, Lafayette, Louisiana; *JDN,* May 16, 1961; Aaron Henry, interviewed by Neil McMillen and George Burson, May 1, 1972, Clarksdale, Mississippi OHP, 57; "Mississippi: Structure of the Movement," undated (probably early 1964) COFO report in Ed King Papers; Moses and Dennis interviews.

8. Dennis to James McCain, Nov. 11, 1962, CORE Papers, Addendum, reel 22; Dennis interview.

9. Steven Lawson, *Black Ballots: Voting Rights in the South, 1944–1969* (New York: Columbia University Press, 1976), 261, 265–66; Timothy Jenkins and Lonnie King, interviews in Howell Raines, *My Soul Is Rested* (New York: Penguin, 1983), 227–31; interview with Leslie Dunbar, Pelham, N.Y., June 13, 1985.

10. Clayborne Carson, *In Struggle: SNCC and the Black Awakening of the 1960s* (Cambridge, Mass.: Harvard University Press, 1981), 70–71; Dave Dennis, "Field Report," Aug. 29, 1962, CORE Papers, Addendum, reel 22; see also Wiley Branton, interviewed by James Mosby, Jan. 18, 1968, Washington, D.C., Howard CRDP.

11. Aaron Henry, interviewed by John Dittmer and John Jones, Clarksdale, April 21, 1981, Mississippi Archives, 20; Medgar Evers, "Monthly Report," Nov. 18, 1960, NAACP Papers.

12. Aaron Henry to Gloster Current, Nov. 25, 1961, NAACP Papers.

13. Ibid.; Henry to Ralph Abernathy, June 20, 1962, SCLC Papers, box 35; Coahoma County branch NAACP to board of mayor and commissioners, June 4, 1963, NAACP Papers.

14. Wilkins to Current, Dec. 7, 1961, NAACP Papers; Henry to Abernathy, June 20, 1962; Henry to Martin Luther King, Aug. 3, 1962, King Papers, MLK.

15. Memphis *Commercial Appeal,* April 6, 1962; Tom Gaither, "Field Report," June 23–30, 1963; COFO to W. S. Kincade, undated, CORE Papers, V-249.

16. "Jackson Area Student Movement"; Tom Gaither to Jim McCain, April 12, 1962, CORE Papers, V-249; "Memo to SNCC Executive Committee"; David Lollis to members of the governing board [of the Mississippi Adult Education Program], July 10, 1962, SNCC Papers, reel 12; "Blacks Killed in Civil Rights Related Murders: 1955–65," NAACP Papers.

17. "A MESSAGE FROM: Diane Nash Bevel TO: Individuals and Organizations Working in Civil Rights," April 30, 1962, copy in King Papers, 28:19, MLK; Anne Braden, SCEF news release, May 1, 1962, Carl and Anne Braden Papers, SHSW; *Student Voice,* June 1962; SNCC News release, July 11, 1962, copy in Ed King Papers; *Voice of the Movement,* undated, Ed King Papers.

18. Dennis to Jim McCain, July 3, 1962; Dennis, field secretary's report, July 25, 1962, CORE Papers, Addendum, reel 22. The *Mississippi Free Press* was edited by Charles Butts, a young northern white with labor union backing.

19. Moses interview.

20. Manpower Administrative Representative, "Overview of the Mississippi Delta Concentrated Employment Program (CEP)," Delta Ministry papers, box 24, MLK; "Report on the Delta Submitted to the National Council of Churches," no date, SNCC Papers, reel 38; Roy Wilkins to branch . . . presidents, "RE: Mississippi Relief Pressures," March 14, 1963, NAACP Papers.

21. "The Three Educations," undated, SNCC Papers, reel 68; Mrs. Irene Johnson, "Statement," undated; Eddie LeRoy Jones, affidavit, July 30, 1964; Bettie Jean Doss, "Statement," undated, SNCC Papers, reel 66.

22. Michael Thelwell, "Fish Are Jumpin' an' the Cotton Is High," in *Duties, Pleasures, and Conflicts: Essays in Struggle* (Amherst: University of Massachusetts Press, 1987), 80.

23. Raines, *My Soul Is Rested*, 233.

24. Charles Payne, "'Men Led, But Women Organized': Movement Participation of Women in the Mississippi Delta," in Guida West and Rhoda Blumberg, *Women and Social Protest* (New York: Oxford University Press, 1990), 158. In a list of twenty SNCC organizers in Mississippi submitted to the House Judiciary Committee in May 1963 only two, Diane Nash Bevel and Emma Bell, were women; *Civil Rights Hearings before Subcommittee No. 5 of the Committee on Judiciary,* House of Representatives, 88th Congress, First Session, May–August 1963, part II (Washington: GPO, 1963), 1278 (hereinafter cited as *Civil Rights Hearings*).

Commenting on the relations between black men and women in the movment, the psychiatrist Alvin F. Poussaint has written that "sex-role differentiation was often supported by both black males and females." Such acceptance "was not singularly an issue of male chauvinism but was believed to be the most effective way to function at that particular juncture in history. The black man did not define the black woman and vice versa"; Alvin F. Poussaint, "White Manipulation and Black Oppression," *The Black Scholar,* May–June 1979, 53. For a critical account of discrimination against women in the civil rights movement, see Sara Evans, *Personal Politics: The Roots of Women's Liberation in the Civil Rights Movement and the New Left* (New York: Random House, 1979).

25. Payne, "'Men Led but Women Organized,'" 160–62.

26. See John Dittmer, "The Politics of the Mississippi Movement, 1954–1964," in Charles Eagles, ed., *The Civil Rights Movement in America* (Jackson: University Press of Mississippi, 1986), 73–76.

27. Joseph Sinsheimer, "'Never Turn Back': An Interview with Sam Block," *Southern Exposure,* Summer 1987, 38–39.

28. Howard Zinn, *SNCC: The New Abolitionists* (Boston: Beacon, 1965), 83; Pat Watters and Reece Cleghorn, *Climbing Jacob's Ladder: The Arrival of Negroes in Southern Politics* (New York: Harcourt Brace, 1967), 59; Jack Minnis, "Courage and Terror in Mississippi," *Dissent* 10 (Summer 1963): 228; *NYT,* April 6, 1963; Sinsheimer, "'Never Turn Back,'" 38.

29. Sinsheimer, "'Never Turn Back,'" 42–43.

30. Willie Peacock, interviewed by Tom Dent, Nov. 2, 1979, Jackson, Miss., in Tom Dent Oral History Collection, Amistad Research Center, Tulane University. Dent's extremely valuable collection of interviews with movement activists has not yet been transcribed. Copies of the tapes are also available at the Coleman Library, Tougaloo College. Charles Payne, remarks at *Mississippi Burning* conference, Jackson, Mississippi, April 21, 1989 (tape recording in my possession).

31. Sinsheimer, "'Never Turn Back,'" 43.

32. Thelwell, "Fish Are Jumpin'," 82–83.

33. Moses, "Remarks at McComb Conference."

34. Sinsheimer, "'Never Turn Back,'" 43.

35. "From Samuel Block, Greenwood, Mississippi, July 26, 1962," copy in Amzie Moore Papers.

36. Wiley Branton, VEP report, Aug. 8, 1962; Jack Minnis, VEP report, Aug. 14, 1962, Voter Education Project Papers, reel 175.

37. Luvaughn Brown, quoted in James Forman, *The Making of Black Revolutionaries* (New York: Macmillan, 1972), 284–85; Sam Block, undated statement, VEP Papers, reel 175.

38. Peacock, interviewed by Dent; Willie Peacock, field report, quoted in Forman, *Black Revolutionaries,* 286.

39. Peacock, in Forman, *Black Revolutionaries,* 287; Payne, *Mississippi Burning* conference.

40. Peacock, interviewed by Dent; Block, quoted in Forman, *Black Revolutionaries,* 287; Peacock, quoted in Zinn, *SNCC,* 83.

41. Block, quoted in Forman, *Black Revolutionaries,* 283.

42. Howard Zinn, undated interview by James Marshall, 4, Zinn Papers; Zinn, *SNCC,* 86; Sinsheimer, "'Never Turn Back,'" 44–45; June Johnson, interviewed by Tom Dent, July 22, 1979, Greenwood, Dent Collection; Peacock, interviewed by Dent.

43. Payne, *Mississippi Burning* conference.

44. Robert Moses, "Report to: Voter Education Project of Southern Regional Council," undated, VEP Papers, reel 175.

45. "This Is Sunflower County, Mississippi," undated SNCC fact sheet, SNCC Papers, reel 20; "Sunflower County," undated press release, Lee Bankhead Papers, SHSW.

46. "Memo from Bob Moses: Re: Pressure on the Negro Citizens of Ruleville, Mississippi," Sept. 10, 1962, VEP Papers (copy in collection of Steven F. Lawson); McLaurin, quoted in Kay Mills, *This Little Light of Mine: The Life of Fannie Lou Hamer* (New York: Dutton, 1993), 48; Fannie Lou Hamer, interviewed by Neil McMillen, April 14, 1972, Ruleville, Mississippi OHP, 12.

47. Charles McLaurin, "To Overcome Fear," no date, SNCC Papers, reel 40.

48. Hamer, interviewed by McMillen, 1–8; Zinn, *SNCC,* 93–94; Forman, *Black Revolutionaries,* 291. For the best biography of Fannie Lou Hamer, see Mills, *This Little Light of Mine.*

49. Jack Minnis, "A Chronology of Violence and Intimidation in Mis-

sissippi Since 1961" (Atlanta, 1963), Robert Stone Papers (in my possession); "Memo from Bob Moses . . . Ruleville."

50. Hamer, interviewed by McMillen, 8; "Two Negro Girls Shot in Home of Voter Registration Worker," undated SNCC news release, Carson Collection; Charles Cobb, interviewed by Tom Dent, Feb. 11, 1983, Washington, D.C., Dent Collection; Taylor Branch, *Parting the Waters: America in the King Years, 1954–63* (New York: Simon & Schuster, 1988), 637; Zinn, *SNCC,* 94.

51. Cobb, interviewed by Dent; Branch, *Parting,* 638, quoting Moses.

52. For Meredith's own story, see his *Three Years in Mississippi* (Bloomington: Indiana University Press, 1966).

53. Frank Smith, *Congressman from Mississippi* (New York: Pantheon, 1964), 302–3. A copy of Barnett's speech is in the Godwin Advertising Papers, 3:96, Mitchell Library, Mississippi State University.

54. Smith, *Congressman,* 303; Karl Wiesenburg, "The Oxford Disaster . . . Price of Defiance," copy in National Student Association file, King Papers, 29:12, MLK.

55. John Garner to "Dear Friends," Oct. 1962, copy in my possession. Garner, a white Tougaloo professor, was active in civil rights work. Walter Lord, *The Past That Would Not Die* (New York: Pocket Books, 1967), 152–53, 167, 171–73; Gerald H. Blessey, "The Meredith Incident at the University of Mississippi," interview, Biloxi, July 22, 1975, Mississippi Archives.

56. For the most perceptive analysis of the role of the Kennedy administration during the Ole Miss crisis see Victor Navasky, *Kennedy Justice* (New York: Atheneum, 1977). Carl Brauer is more charitable toward the Kennedys in *John F. Kennedy and the Second Reconstruction* (New York: Columbia University Press, 1977).

57. Robert Kennedy, quoted in *Presidential Recordings Transcripts,* "Integration of the University of Mississippi," Sept. 30, 1962, audiotape 26, Presidential Papers, president's office files, JFK.

58. Chapter 9 of Lord, *The Past That Would Not Die,* remains the best chronological account of what took place on the night of September 30. Taylor Branch's chapter entitled "The Fall of Ole Miss" in *Parting the Waters* is an absorbing narrative that makes excellent use of the presidential recordings. See also Brauer, *John F. Kennedy,* 180–204. Two books by Ole Miss professors on the Meredith crisis are James W. Silver, *Mississippi: The Closed Society* (New York: Harcourt Brace, 1964), and Russell Barrett, *Integration at Ole Miss* (Chicago: Quadrangle, 1965).

59. Branch, *Parting,* 666–69.

60. Lord, *The Past,* 202.

61. Navasky, *Kennedy Justice,* 193, 230; Robert Kennedy, quoted on audiotape 26.

62. *C-L,* April 25, 1963; Silver, *The Closed Society,* 127. In the aftermath of the riot several dissenting voices began to be heard inside the closed society. In January 1963, twenty-eight young white Methodist ministers issued a statement entitled "Born of Conviction" in which they reaffirmed

their church's position that "Our Lord Jesus Christ . . . permits no discrimination because of race, color, or creed." Ira Harkey, editor of the *Pascagoula Chronicle,* had been almost alone in condemning Barnett's policy before Meredith enrolled, and his editorials after the riot won him a Pulitzer Prize. Such hopeful signs were short-lived. The relatively moderate "Born of Conviction" statement created a parishioners' revolt, and by the end of the summer sixteen of the young ministers had been forced from their pulpits. Harkey's courageous stand led to death threats, an advertising boycott, social ostracism, and a shotgun blast through his office window. In July 1963 he sold the *Chronicle* and moved to California. See "Born of Conviction," Summer Walters Papers, copy in my possession. (Walters was pastor of a Methodist church in Natchez and was one of the signers forced to leave the state.) Ira B. Harkey, Jr., *The Smell of Burning Crosses: An Autobiography of a Mississippi Newspaperman* (Jacksonville, Ill.: Harris-Wolfe, 1967), 139–73.

63. Lord, *The Past,* 206; Patrick J. Owens, "Silver of Ole Miss," *The Progressive* 28 (June 1964): 36; *NYT,* Jan. 17, 1963.

Chapter 7: Greenwood and Jackson

1. Berl I. Bernhard, staff director, U.S. Commission on Civil Rights, "Memorandum to Honorable Lee C. White, Subject: Direct Federal Distribution of Surplus Commodities to Needy Mississippi Families," undated, copy in Jane C. Schutt Papers, Coleman Library, Tougaloo College; "Agenda for a Meeting of the Mississippi Advisory Committee to the United States Commission on Civil Rights," Feb. 6, 1963, Schutt Papers.

2. Memorandum, Bernhard to White; Jack Minnis, "Courage and Terror in Mississippi," *Dissent* 10 (Summer 1963): 229.

3. Memorandum, Bernhard to White; "Memorandum from Charles Cobb and Charles Ray McLaurin, Re: Preliminary Survey on the Condition of the Negro Farmers in Ruleville, Mississippi, at the Close of the Cotton Season," Nov. 19, 1963, SNCC Papers, reel 12.

4. Quoted in Howard Zinn, *SNCC: The New Abolitionists* (Boston: Beacon Press, 1965), 86–87.

5. Ibid., 87; Clayborne Carson, *In Struggle: SNCC and the Black Awakening of the 1960s* (Cambridge, Mass.: Harvard University Press, 1981), 80; interview with Ivanhoe Donaldson, Washington, D.C., July 12, 1981; Taylor Branch, *Parting the Waters: America in the King Years, 1954–63* (New York: Simon & Schuster, 1988), 713.

6. Lawrence Guyot, interviewed by Anne and Howard Romaine, 1966, Romaine Papers, SHSW, 6; interview with Wazir Peacock; Randolph T. Blackwell, "A Mississippi Field Report," March 26, 1963, VEP Papers, copy in Steven Lawson files.

7. James Bevel, "Report," Jan., 1963, SCLC Papers, 141:5; Dave Dennis, "Field Report," Jan. 14, 1963, CORE Papers, Addendum, reel 22.

8. Bob Moses to John W. Blyth, undated (probably Feb. 21, 1963),

SNCC Papers, reel 69; Frank Smith, "A Second Beginning of the End," May 11, 1963, VEP Papers, 5, Lawson files; report of Mrs. Monetta A. Hancock, undated, SNCC Papers, reel 38.

9. Moses to Blyth; Jack Minnis, "A Chronology of Violence and Intimidation in Mississippi since 1961," Stone Papers, Atlanta, 12; Sam Block, "Affidavit," July 13, 1964, copy in Margaret Beernick Papers, personal collection, Palo Alto, Calif.; Block, "Affidavit"; Peacock, interviewed by Tom Dent.

10. Peacock interview (with author); "Persons Attempting to Register, 2/26/63," SNCC Papers, reel 38. See also Carson, *In Struggle,* 80; Pat Watters and Reece Cleghorn, *Climbing Jacob's Ladder: The Arrival of Negroes in Southern Politics* (New York: Harcourt Brace, 1967), 59; Branch, *Parting,* 716.

11. Peacock, interviewed by Dent; Branch, *Parting,* 716–17; Carson, *In Struggle,* 81. Three Greenwood whites—a Standard Oil dealer, a service manager for an earthmoving machinery company, and a seventeen-year-old youth—were charged with shooting Travis, but a Leflore County jury acquitted them; *JDN,* March 5, 1963.

12. Zinn, *SNCC,* 90; Watters and Cleghorn, *Climbing Jacob's Ladder,* 60; Dennis to Jack Minnis, March 25, 1963, CORE Papers, Addendum, reel 22; Wiley Branton, "Chronology of Events Following the Shooting of James Travis in Leflore County, Mississippi . . . March 1–4, 1963," VEP Papers, reel 175. Greenwood Leflore was a white millionaire slave-owner, after whom both the city and county were named, who supported the Union in the Civil War; Zinn, *SNCC,* 90.

13. Branton, "Chronology"; Peacock interview.

14. Watters and Cleghorn, *Climbing Jacob's Ladder,* 60, quoting Branton; Branton, "Chronology."

15. Randolph Blackwell, "A Mississippi Field Report," March 26, 1963, VEP Papers, Lawson files.

16. Ibid.; Branton, "Chronology"; Sam Block, Field Report, quoted in *Greenwood Commonwealth,* March 26, 1963; *Mississippi Free Press,* March 16, 1963.

17. Sam Block, "Affidavit," July 13, 1964, SNCC Papers, reel 65; Branch, *Parting,* 718–19.

18. *Greenwood Commonwealth,* June 19, 1963; Zinn, *SNCC,* 91; Branch, *Parting;* SNCC news release, "Nightriders Attack Greenwood Negro's Home," March 27, 1963, SNCC Papers, reel 38; *Greenwood Commonwealth,* March 27, 1963; James Forman, *The Making of Black Revolutionaries* (New York: Macmillan, 1972), 296–97.

19. Branch, *Parting,* 719–20; Peacock, interviewed by Dent; *Newsweek,* April 8, 1963, 25–26.

20. *Greenwood Commonwealth,* March 27, 1963; Carson, *In Struggle,* 86.

21. *Newsweek,* April 8, 1963, 26; Branch, *Parting,* 720.

22. "Greenwood, Mississippi, April 1, 1963," no author, copy in Amzie Moore Papers, SHSW.

23. *Greenwood Commonwealth,* April 2, 1963; *NYT,* April 3, 1963; Branch, *Parting,* 721.

24. Justice Department memorandum, "LEFLORE COUNTY," Aug. 9, 1965, HU2-7: 11/22/63–8/19/65, LBJ.

25. For further discussion of the controversy between the Civil Rights Commission and the Kennedy administration, see 194–98.

26. *NYT,* April 1, 1963.

27. Dorothy Zellner to Anne Braden, April 2, 1963, quoting McDew, SNCC Papers, reel 9; Branton quoted in *Washington Star,* March 30, 1963, clipping in VEP Papers, reel 175; *Robert Moses, Sam Block, Charles McLaurin, Charles Cobb, Jesse Harris, Hollis Watkins, Lafayette Surney, and William Higgs, Plaintiffs, v. Robert F. Kennedy, Attorney General of the United States, and J. Edgar Hoover, Director of the Federal Bureau of Investigation of the United States of America, Defendants,* copy in SCLC Papers, 35:18.

28. *Congressional Record—Senate,* April 2, 1963, 5094–96, copy in VEP Papers, reel 175; Evans, quoted in *NYT,* April 1, 1963.

29. *Greenwood Commonwealth,* April 3, 4, 5, 1963; *NYT,* April 4, 1963; remarks by Charles Payne at *Mississippi Burning* conference, Jackson, Miss., April 21, 1989 (tape recording in my possession).

30. Branton, "Field Report," April 7, 1963, VEP Papers, reel 175.

31. *Mississippi Free Press,* April 13, 1963; Branch, *Parting,* 724–25; *Greenwood Commonwealth,* April 4, 1963; *Birmingham News,* April 28, 1963, clipping in VEP Papers, reel 175.

32. Branton, "Field Report," April 5, 1963, VEP Papers, reel 175; *Greenwood Commonwealth,* April 4, March 29, 1963.

33. Branton, "Field Report," April 4, 1963, VEP Papers, reel 175.

34. Watters and Cleghorn, *Climbing Jacob's Ladder,* 62.

35. John Salter, *Jackson, Mississippi: An American Chronicle of Struggle and Schism* (Hicksville, N.Y.: Exposition, 1979), 57. Salter's book, told from the point of view of the leading strategist, is the most thorough and persuasive account of the Jackson movement. The book is also available as a 1987 Krieger paperback (citations here are from the hardback edition).

36. Ibid., 4–6.

37. Ibid., 58–65. The Gandhi Society for Human Rights was a tax-exempt organization established in New York in 1961 to channel funds into the civil rights movement.

38. Ibid., 64–66; Medgar Evers, "Monthly Report," Jan. 4, 1963, 3, NAACP Papers.

39. Dennis to McCain, Dec. 6, 1962, CORE Papers, V: 126; Dennis, "Field Report," Jan. 14, 1963, CORE Papers, Addendum, reel 22.

40. Joyce Ladner interview; undated letter, John Salter to author.

41. Ibid.; Medgar Evers, "Monthly Reports," 1962, NAACP Papers.

42. Current, memorandum to "Messrs. Wilkins, Carter, Morsell, Moon, and Ashford," Jan. 31, 1963, NAACP Papers.

43. Salter to Kunstler, March 17, 1963, John Salter Papers, Mississippi Archives; Wilkins to Evers, April 16, 1963, NAACP Papers.

44. Current, "Memorandum to Regional Secretaries and Field Secretaries," May 13, 1963, NAACP Papers; Salter, *Jackson,* 111.

45. Salter, *Jackson,* 112–16.

46. Ibid., 122–23; news release, "Background Information on New Desegregation Drive in Jackson, Mississippi," May 28, 1963, NAACP Papers; Memphis *Commercial Appeal,* May 23, 1963; Salter, *Jackson,* 128–31.

47. The account of the Woolworth's sit-in comes from the following sources: Salter, *Jackson,* 132–36; Anne Moody, *Coming of Age in Mississippi* (New York: Dell, 1971), 264–67; *Newsweek,* June 10, 1963, 28–29; Memphis *Commercial Appeal,* May 29, 1963.

48. Salter, *Jackson,* 137–39; *Newsweek,* June 10, 1963, 29.

49. Mrs. Medgar Evers, with William Peters, *For Us, the Living* (New York: Ace, 1970), 217–18, 223, 224–25; Salter, *Jackson,* 152, 154.

50. Evers, *For Us,* 216; Salter, *Jackson,* 164–66, 171–72, 174.

51. Memorandum, John Doar to Burke Marshall, "Demonstrations in Jackson, Mississippi," June 10, 1963, Mississippi File, Burke Marshall Papers, JFK.

52. R. L. T. Smith, a member of the strategy committee who had close contact with national NAACP officers, believes that bail money was the major issue; R. L. T. Smith, interviewed by Robert Wright, July 10, 1969, Howard CRDP, 31. In an October 1, 1983, letter to the author, Gloster Current stated that "the costly mass demonstrations for legal and other reasons had to be reduced." Of Wilkins, Current, and other national NAACP people who came to Jackson, Smith observed that "they were frightened to death and surprised that we somehow weren't afraid of death, to the same degree that they were"; Smith, interviewed by Wright, 28. Smith's grocery store was repeatedly vandalized as a result of his visible participation in the Jackson movement.

53. Current to author, Oct. 1, 1983; Salter, *Jackson,* 183.

54. *NYT,* June 1, 1963; Evers, *For Us,* 241–52. For more on Evers's relations with Clarence Mitchell and other national NAACP officials, see Denton L. Watson, *Lion in the Lobby: Clarence Mitchell, Jr.'s Struggle for the Passage of Civil Rights Laws* (New York: Morrow, 1990), chap. 16.

55. Evers, *For Us,* 253–57; Jack Mendelsohn, *The Martyrs: Sixteen Who Gave Their Lives for Racial Justice* (New York: Harper and Row, 1966), 71–73; Salter, *Jackson,* 183–84; *NYT,* June 13, 14, 1963. Byron De La Beckwith had never attempted to hide his hatred for blacks. Former congressman Frank Smith told Robert Kennedy that several years earlier Beckwith had stopped by Smith's Greenwood office. As he left, Beckwith said, "Let me know if I can kill a nigger for you." Months before Medgar's death, Beckwith wrote the National Rifle Association: "Gentlemen, for the next 15 years, we here in Mississippi are going to have to do a lot of shooting to protect our wives, our children, and ourselves." Frank Smith to Robert Kennedy, June 26, 1963, attorney general's files, PC-9, JFK; *Atlanta Constitution,* June 9, 1983.

Shortly after Beckwith's arrest the Citizens' Council set up a legal defense fund for him, with the presidents of Greenwood's three banks serving as financial advisors. His defense team included a member of Governor Barnett's law firm and Hardy Lott, Greenwood's city attorney. With the establishment behind him, Beckwith survived two trials in which prosecutor (and later governor) William Waller presented persuasive evidence of his guilt. In 1974 FBI agents arrested Beckwith outside of New Orleans with a bomb in his car. The agents had learned that he was on his way to bomb the home of a prominent New Orleans Jewish leader. A jury of five black women found him guilty, and the judge sentenced him to a five-year prison term. On his release from jail, Beckwith returned to live in Mississippi, later moving to Tennessee. In 1990, Beckwith was rearrested and extradited to Mississippi to again stand trial for the murder of Medgar Evers. Memphis *Commercial Appeal,* June 26, July 9, 1963; Jan. 18, 1974; Aug. 2, 1975.

56. "Telephone Call from Thelton Henderson," June 13, 1963, Mississippi File, Burke Marshall Papers; Mendelsohn, *The Martyrs,* 78; *Crisis* 70 (June-July 1963): 330–31; Salter, *Jackson,* 189–92.

57. Mendelsohn, *The Martyrs,* 78–80; Salter, *Jackson,* 213–17; Dennis interview; *NYT,* June 16, 1963; *C-L,* June 16, 1963; Salter, *Jackson,* 220–23; Moody, *Coming of Age,* 283.

58. "Memorandum to the Attorney General from Burke Marshall, July 17, 1963," 4, Marshall Papers, box 321; interview with Burke Marshall, Dec. 3, 1983, New Haven, Conn.

59. Telephone conversation between John Kennedy and Allen Thompson, June 17, 1963, *Presidential Recordings, Logs and Transcripts,* John F. Kennedy Papers, JFK; *C-L,* June 19, 1963.

60. *JDN,* June 19, 1963; Salter, *Jackson,* 232–39; Branch, *Parting,* 831–33.

61. Marshall memorandum to Robert Kennedy, July 17, 1963, 4.

62. Concerning the role of the Kennedy Justice Department in the area of civil rights, Thelton Henderson has said, "At one point, long after I left Mississippi, I became unhappy with an insight I had, that one of the major concerns of the Justice Department was not necessarily how we will go about enforcing the civil rights laws, but how much are the blacks gonna take before they strike back, and then we will have to do something" (interview with Thelton Henderson, May 29, 1981, San Francisco).

Chapter 8: Organizing Mississippi

1. Dennis to McCain, CORE Papers, Addendum, reel 22; June Johnson, interviewed by Dent; Johnson, undated affidavit, copy in Jan Hillegas Collection; Pat Watters and Reece Cleghorn, *Climbing Jacob's Ladder: The Arrival of Negroes in Southern Politics* (New York: Harcourt Brace, 1967), 364–65.

2. Johnson affidavit.

3. Annelle Ponder, telephone conversation with members of the VEP staff, June 13, 1963, quoted in Watters and Cleghorn, *Jacob's Ladder,* 365–

66; Taylor Branch, *Parting the Waters: America in the King Years, 1954–63* (New York: Simon & Schuster, 1988), 819; Howard Zinn, *SNCC: The New Abolitionists* (Boston: Beacon, 1965), 94–95; Kay Mills, *This Little Light of Mine: The Life of Fannie Lou Hamer* (New York: Dutton, 1993), 59.

4. "Verbatim transcript of interview by phone by Jack Minnis with Mrs. Fannie Lou Hamer," June 13, 1963, SNCC Papers, reel 38; Watters and Cleghorn, *Jacob's Ladder,* 371–72.

5. Peacock, interviewed by Dent; Zinn, *SNCC,* 95; interview with Lawrence Guyot, Washington, D.C., May 30, 1989.

6. Johnson, interviewed by Dent; "Federal Jury Frees Five in Mississippi Beating," SNCC press release, Dec. 11, 1963, SNCC Papers, reel 38. For a detailed account of the Winona arrests and the Oxford trial, see Mills, *This Little Light of Mine,* 56–77.

7. Clayborne Carson, *In Struggle: SNCC and the Black Awakening of the 1960s* (Cambridge, Mass.: Harvard University Press, 1981), 90.

8. Mrs. Cora Campbell, affidavit, June 27, 1963, SNCC Papers, reel 38; Anthony Jackson, undated statement, SNCC Papers, reel 65; Zinn, *SNCC,* 98.

9. MacArthur Cotton, undated affidavit; SNCC news releases, June 26, July 30, 1963, SNCC Papers, reel 38; Zinn, *SNCC,* 96.

10. Howard Zinn, "The Battle-Scarred Youngsters," *Nation,* Oct. 5, 1963, 195; "Folk Artists, Local Citizens Attend SNCC Folk Festival in Mississippi Delta," SNCC press release, July 1963, copy in Hillegas Collection; conversation with Wazir Peacock, Jackson, April 23, 1989.

11. "Report from Charles Cobb," July 31, 1963, VEP Papers, Steven Lawson files; Jack Minnis, "A Chronology of Violence and Intimidation in Mississippi since 1961" (Atlanta, 1963), 15, Robert Stone Papers; "Background Information on R. Hunter Morey," Sept. 6, 1963, SNCC Papers, reel 12; "*McLaurin v. the State of Mississippi,*" copy in Hillegas Collection. In January 1967 the U.S. Supreme Court rejected McLaurin's appeal.

12. James and Diane Bevel, "Dear Citizen of Cleveland," May 30, 1963, SCLC Papers, 161:57; Frank Smith, "A Second Beginning of the End," May 11, 1963, 7–12, VEP Papers, Lawson files.

13. "Testimony of Aaron Henry before the House Judiciary Committee in Washington, D.C., Thursday, June 13, 1963," copy in Aaron Henry Papers, Tougaloo College; "Chronology of Violence and Intimidation," 15.

14. "Top NAACP Leaders Fly to Mississippi Trouble Spot," NAACP press release, May 11, 1963; Henry to Wilkins, June 4, 1963, NAACP Papers; Tom Gaither, "Field Report," July 11–22, CORE Papers, V-249.

15. Memphis *Commercial Appeal,* June 13, 1963; Tom Gaither, "Field Report," June 23–30, 1963, CORE Papers, V-249; Henry to Wilkins, July 18, 1963; NAACP press releases, June 22, Aug. 3, 16, and 23, 1963, NAACP Papers; *Crisis* 71 (June-July 1964): 372.

16. Jerry Demuth, "Notes on conversation with Aaron Henry at his Clarksdale home, Monday, August 3, 1964," copy in Henry Papers, Tougaloo College.

17. Charles Evers and Grace Halsell, *Evers* (New York: World, 1971), 96–106, 113.

18. Current to Wilkins, "Memorandum Re: Charles Evers," Sept. 9, 1963, NAACP Papers; *Detroit News,* Aug. 19, 1963, clipping in NAACP Papers; Current to Evers, Aug. 21, 1963, NAACP Papers.

19. "Some Background Notes on Laurel, Mississippi" (no author), Nov. 16, 1965, SNCC Papers, copy in Carson Collection.

20. Zinn, *SNCC,* 102–3; interview with Mrs. Victoria Gray Adams, Petersburg, Va., May 8, 1989.

21. Steven Lawson, *Black Ballots: Voting Rights in the South, 1944–1969* (New York: Columbia University Press, 1976), 273; Charles V. Hamilton, *The Bench and the Ballot: Southern Federal Judges and Black Voters* (New York: Oxford University Press, 1973), 126–130; Wilson F. Minor, undated manuscript, Wilson F. Minor Papers, Mississippi State University.

22. Jack Bass, *Unlikely Heroes* (New York: Simon & Schuster, 1981), 218–20; Hamilton, *Bench and the Ballot,* 135–36.

23. Curtis Hayes, "Report on Forrest County, Mississippi, September, 1962," SNCC Papers, reel 38; Adams interview; Hollis Watkins, interviewed by Dittmer and Jones, 25; Watkins, interviewed by Robert Wright, Jackson, 1968, 17–19, Howard CRDP. Watkins recalled that Dahmer told him that Medgar Evers had advised him against the move and that C. C. Bryant had come over from McComb to warn Hattiesburg NAACP officers that SNCC was up to no good; Watkins, interviewed by Dent.

24. Watkins, interviewed by Dent; Curtis Hayes, "Report on Forrest County"; Adams interview.

25. Adams interview; Victoria Gray Adams, interviewed by Joseph Sinsheimer, Petersburg, Va., Aug. 23, 1987, copy in my possession.

26. Adams, interviewed by Sinsheimer.

27. Hayes, "Report on Forrest County"; "Report from Curtis Hayes, Hattiesburg, Mississippi, Aug. 8, 1962," copy in Amzie Moore Papers; Adams interview.

28. Adams interview.

29. Bob Moses, "Memo to: S.N.C.C. Executive Committee," no date, SNCC Papers, reel 40; Moses, "Memo to: Wiley Branton, Roy Wilkins, Andrew Young, James Forman Re: Hattiesburg Voting Project," Aug. 12, 1963, VEP Papers, Steven Lawson files; *NYT,* July 16, 1963; *United States v. Theron Lynd: Judgment and Order of Civil Contempt,* July 15, 1963, SNCC Papers, reel 38.

30. "Field Report on Voter Registration Activities in Hattiesburg—Forrest County, Mississippi, July 29, 1963," VEP Papers, Lawson files; John O'Neal, "Report on Forrest County, Sept. 23, 1963"; O'Neal to Wiley Branton, Sept. 25, 1963, Zinn Papers.

31. Dennis to McCain, Aug. 8, 1963, CORE Papers, Addendum, reel 22; August Meier and Elliott Rudwick, *CORE: A Study in the Civil Rights Movement* (New York: Oxford University Press, 1973), 269–70.

32. Meier and Rudwick, *CORE,* 269–70.

33. Dennis, "To CORE Groups and Members," Aug. 19, 1963; Dennis to McCain, Aug. 8, 1963, CORE Papers, Addendum, reel 22.

34. SNCC, "Madison County, Mississippi," Oct. 26, 1965, copy in Hillegas Collection; Dennis to McCain, March 25, 1963, CORE Papers, Addendum, reel 22; Dennis, "To CORE Groups."

35. Dennis to McCain, March 25, 1963; Meier and Rudwick, *CORE*, 271. Dennis proved accurate in his prediction that because of its location the Madison County movement would attract media attention. Throughout the mid-1960s reporters and camera crews would fly into Jackson, make the short drive up to Canton, file their stories "from the wilds of Mississippi," and be back in Jackson by early evening, enjoying their poolside drinks at the Sun 'n' Sands Motel.

36. George Raymond, interviewed by Robert Wright, Canton, Sept. 28, 1968, Howard CRDP; Willie Peacock, interviewed by Dent; Charlie Cobb, interviewed by Dent; Tom Dent, "Annie Devine Remembers," *Freedomways* 12 (Second Quarter, 1982): 85–86; Matteo Suarez, interviewed by Tom Dent, New Orleans, July 3, 1977; C. O. Chinn, interviewed by Tom Dent, Canton, March 27, 1983, Dent Collection. In the late 1960s, after all the other outside CORE and SNCC workers had left the state, Raymond remained to work in Canton, but he became both a physical and psychological casualty of the movement, dying of a heart attack in 1970— at age twenty-nine.

37. Debbie Bernstein, "Canton Project History," Feb. 28, 1965, 1–2, CORE Papers, reel 10; Anne Moody, *Coming of Age in Mississippi* (New York: Dell, 1971), 287–88; Dave Dennis, "An Awakening City," Jan. 23, 1964, CORE Papers, Addendum, reel 22.

38. C. O. Chinn, interviewed by Dent; Suarez, interviewed by Dent; Moody, *Coming of Age*, 303–4.

39. Bernstein, "Canton Project," 2; SNCC, "Madison County"; Moody, *Coming of Age*, 292–93; Dennis, "An Awakening City."

40. Dennis to McCain, Oct. 19, 1963; Dennis to McCain, Aug. 6, 8, 1963, CORE Papers, Addendum, reel 22.

41. Dennis to McCain, Aug. 8, 1963.

42. Interview with Annie Devine, Canton, Dec. 11, 1984; Devine, interviewed by Robert Wright, Canton, Sept. 29, 1968, Howard CRDP; Devine, interviewed by Tom Dent, Canton, Sept. 17, 1976, Dent Collection; Dent, "Annie Devine Remembers," 86–88.

43. Suarez, interviewed by Dent; Dent, "Annie Devine Remembers," 87–88.

44. "Canton, Mississippi," 1963 membership list of reorganized branch, NAACP Papers.

45. Susan H. (Lorenzi) Sojourner, "'Got to Thinking . . .': The People of the Holmes County, Mississippi Civil Rights Movement," 1–3, portion of manuscript in my possession. Susan Lorenzi Sojourner and her husband, Henry Lorenzi, were organizers in Holmes County in the mid- and late-1960s. I am indebted to Susan Sojourner for sharing her insights and materials on the Holmes County movement.

46. Sojourner, "'Got to Thinking,'" 1–3; "Facts on Ralthus Hayes, F.D.P. Candidate for U.S. Congress from the Second District," Jan. 3, 1965, SNCC Papers, reel 68; Ben H. Bagdikian, "A Forgotten New Deal Experiment in Mississippi," *I. F. Stone's Weekly,* July 31, 1967.

47. "Facts on Ralthus Hayes"; Hartman Turnbow, interview in Howell Raines, *My Soul Is Rested* (New York: Penguin, 1983), 260–66; Turnbow, interview in Studs Terkel, *American Dreams: Lost & Found* (New York: Pantheon, 1980), 196–97; *Holmes County Herald,* April 11, 1963.

48. *Holmes County Herald,* April 11, 1963; Turnbow, quoted in *My Soul,* 263; Sojourner, "'Got to Thinking,'" 3.

49. James W. Silver, *Mississippi: The Closed Society,* rev. ed. (New York: Harcourt Brace, 1966), 95–96; Turnbow, quoted in *My Soul,* 289; Watters and Cleghorn, *Jacob's Ladder,* 135–36; Branch, *Parting,* 781–82.

Chapter 9: Conflicting Strategies

1. Steven Lawson, *Black Ballots: Voting Rights in the South, 1944–1969* (New York: Columbia University Press, 1976), 213–14; *JDN,* Nov. 14, 1959.

2. *JDN,* Dec. 28, 1959; *Southern Patriot,* March, 1963. The white members of the Mississippi advisory committee were the Reverend Murray Cox, a retired Methodist minister from Gulfport; Admiral Robert Briscoe of Liberty, a retired admiral and Mississippi planter; Mrs. Jane Schutt of Jackson, the president of Mississippi United Church Women; and V. O. Campbell of Collins, a farmer and former president of the Mississippi Rural Carriers Association. The original black members were Dr. James Lucius Allen, a Columbus pharmacist, and Dr. A. Benjamin Britton, a Jackson physician. *JDN,* Dec. 28, 1959.

W. S. Curry, the mayor of Itta Bena, wrote Jane Schutt, "I am sure that your children and grand children will never have cause to be proud that their mother serve [*sic*] with such a subversive group as this." Curry to Schutt, Dec. 8, 1959, Jane Schutt Papers, Coleman Library, Tougaloo College.

3. "Chronology of Events—U.S. Commission on Civil Rights: Mississippi," Marshall Papers, box 31; Robert Kennedy to John A. Hannah, Dec. 15, 1962; Hannah to Kennedy, Jan. 2, 1963, Marshall Papers, box 30, JFK.

4. "Report on Mississippi by the Mississippi Advisory Committee to the United States Commission on Civil Rights," Jan. 1963, 23–27, Schutt Papers.

5. "Chronology of Events"; Robert Kennedy to Hannah, March 26, 1963, Marshall Papers, box 30; Burke Marshall, "Memorandum for the Attorney General," March 29, 1963, Marshall Papers, box 8.

6. "Resolution of the United States Commission on Civil Rights," March 30, 1963, president's office files, John F. Kennedy Papers, box 97, JFK.

7. "Text of Letter from the President to the Chairman, United States

Commission on Civil Rights, Dr. John A. Hannah, April 19, 1963," Marshall Papers, reel 16. The president based his response on a memorandum prepared by Lee C. White, the president's special assistant for civil rights. Concerning the CRC's finding that Mississippi blacks were "beaten and otherwise terrorized because they sought to vote," White wrote, "We are not absolutely certain what incidents are referred to but in 1961 a Negro registration worker was pistol whipped by the registrar of Walthall County. Justice successfully prosecuted the guilty party." White got his facts wrong here (the "guilty party" was never convicted), and he similarly reduced the other CRC charges to individual isolated incidents, thereby enabling the president to assert that the Justice Department had "successfully resolved . . . every case but one." Lee White, "Memorandum for the President. Subject: CRC Resolution," April 10, 1963, Theodore Sorenson Papers, box 30, JFK.

8. Lee White, interviewed by Milton Gwirtzman, May 25, 1964, 130, JFK; Harris Wofford, *Of Kennedys and Kings: Making Sense of the Sixties* (New York: Farrar, Straus & Giroux, 1980), 160–62, 163.

9. Karl Wiesenburg to Peter Sussman, Dec. 27, 1963, Lee White Papers, box 3, JFK.

10. Robert Kennedy, interviewed by Anthony Lewis, Dec. 4, 1964, New York, 854, JFK; "Memorandum for the President from the Attorney General," Oct. 23, 1963; "Memorandum for the President from the Attorney General," Nov. 12, 1963, John F. Kennedy Papers, president's office files, box 97; Burke Marshall, "Memorandum for the Attorney General," Dec. 2, 1963, Marshall Papers, box 8, JFK. The Civil Rights Commission finally held hearings in Mississippi in February 1965.

11. Bob Moses, "Memo to: S.N.C.C. Executive Committee Re: S.N.C.C. Mississippi Project," SNCC Papers, reel 40. (Although this memo is not dated, Moses wrote it after the August 1963 gubernatorial primary and before the October announcement of the freedom vote.)

12. Ibid.

13. Milton Viorst, *Fire in the Streets: America in the 1960s* (New York: Simon and Schuster, 1979), 391; Joan Bowman, "The Freedom Ballot for Governor," Oct. 23, 1963, copy in Hillegas Collection. Lowenstein said that the freedom vote was his idea, a claim SNCC activists dispute. Lowenstein is the subject of an unflattering biography by Richard Cummings, *The Pied Piper: Allard K. Lowenstein and the Liberal Dream* (New York: Grove Press, 1985), and a remembrance by sixties activist David Harris, *Dreams Die Hard* (New York, 1982). By far the best book on Lowenstein is William H. Chafe's new biography, *Never Stop Running: Allard Lowenstein and the Struggle to Save American Liberalism* (New York: Basic Books, 1993).

14. *Mississippi Free Press,* Aug. 10, 31, 1963.

15. David Dennis to National Action Committee, "An Abortion for a Pregnant State," undated, CORE Papers, Addendum, reel 22; Peacock interview; James Forman, *The Making of Black Revolutionaries* (New York: Macmillan, 1972), 354; Clayborne Carson, *In Struggle: SNCC and the*

Black Awakening of the 1960s (Cambridge, Mass.: Harvard University Press, 1981), 97–98. For an informative account of the freeedom vote campaign see Joseph Sinsheimer, "The Freedom Vote of 1963: New Strategies of Racial Protest in Mississippi," *Journal of Southern History* 55 (May 1989): 217–44.

16. Telegram, Charles Evers to Attorney General Robert Kennedy, Aug. 30, 1963, NAACP Papers; *Mississppi Free Press*, Sept. 7, 1963.

17. SNCC press release, "COFO Maps Vote Fight: Henry 'Runs' for Governor in Freedom Ballot Campaign," Oct. 7, 1963, SNCC Papers, reel 38; Forman, *Black Revolutionaries*, 354; Sinsheimer, "Freedom Vote," 227; *Mississippi Free Press*, Oct. 19, 1963.

18. SNCC press release, "COFO Maps"; Sinsheimer, "Freedom Vote," 226; Edwin King, "Freedom Vote" (unpublished manuscript, 1969), 40.

19. King, "Freedom Vote," 41–44.

20. Ronnie Dugger, "History in Mississippi, 1963," *Texas Observer*, Nov. 15, 1963, 3; Forman, *Black Revolutionaries*, 355; Sinsheimer, "Freedom Vote," 230–31. Some estimates of the total number of white students who came to Mississippi run as high as 100. Dugger, who was in the state just after the election, gave the following breakdown of students: Yale, 50; Stanford, 14; College of the Pacific, 4 (Dugger, "History," 3). SNCC was suffering from a shortage of personnel even before the decision to hold the freedom vote. Late in the summer of 1963 the Mississippi SNCC staff sent a memo to the Atlanta office outlining its needs, concluding that "if there are good young people please direct them to Mississippi, the best project around"; memorandum, "Mississippi Staff to SNCC, Re: Operation Mississippi," undated, copy in Hillegas Collection.

21. Forman, *Black Revolutionaries*, 355; Jack Minnis, "A Chronology of Violence and Intimidation in Mississippi since 1961," Stone Papers, Atlanta, 17; "Summary of Events, October 22 through October 28," undated, copy in Hillegas Collection.

22. "Statement on Events in Natchez, Miss.—November 1 and 2, 1963," SNCC Papers, reel 69; "Testimony of Mr. Bruce Lloyd Paine, New Haven, Conn.," *Hearings in Jackson, Miss. before the United States Commission on Civil Rights, Feb. 16–20, 1965*, vol. II (Washington: GPO, 1965), 70–75 (hereinafter cited as *CRC Hearings*).

23. "To: The President of the United States [and] The Attorney General of the United States," undated copy of a telegram signed by Aaron Henry, Edwin King, Robert Moses, David Dennis, Charles Evers, R. L. T. Smith, and Allard Lowenstein, Hillegas Collection; Allard Lowenstein, interviewed by Anne Romaine, New York, 1965, 7, 20–21, Romaine Papers, SHSW.

24. *Mississippi Free Press*, Nov. 16, 1963; Bowman, "Freedom Ballot."

25. King, "Freedom Vote," 65–68; Sinsheimer, "Freedom Vote," 239–40; *Greenwood Commonwealth*, Oct. 23, 1963; Lowenstein, interviewed by Romaine, 20; *Mississippi Free Press*, Nov. 2, 1963.

26. The freedom vote totals and the breakdown by county are found in the *Mississippi Free Press*, Nov. 16, 1963. Ivanhoe Donaldson, "Weekly

Report (30 October thru 5 November 1963)," 5–6, copy in Zinn Papers; Dennis, "Abortion for a Pregnant State."

27. *Mississippi Free Press,* Nov. 16, 1963; Donaldson, "Weekly Report."

28. *Mississippi Free Press,* Nov. 16, 1963; Peacock interview; King, "Freedom Vote," 82–83; Moses quoted in Sinsheimer, "Freedom Vote," 241.

29. King, "Freedom Vote," 141; Dugger, "History in Mississippi," 3, 4–5; Lowenstein, interviewed by Romaine, 7.

30. Howard Zinn, "Notes on Mississippi Staff Meeting, Greenville, Nov. 14–16, 1963," Zinn Papers.

31. *Stanford Daily,* Oct. 29, 1963; "Memo to Mississippi Staff from Bob Moses," undated, copy in Amzie Moore Papers. On November 11 Fred Goff, a white Stanford volunteer, wrote Moses that Stanford would provide "a *good turnout* for civil rights work in Mississippi this *summer*" (Goff to Moses, Nov. 11, 1963, copy in Hillegas Collection; emphasis in the original).

32. Carson, *In Struggle,* 98; Zinn, "Notes on Greenville Meeting," 25. COFO established a WATS line in its Jackson office in 1963 to communicate with its projects around the state. Since a number of the incoming calls were emergencies that required immediate action, the position of WATS line operator was important.

33. Zinn, "Notes," 29, 35, 19; Joan Bowman, undated, unpublished manuscript, 12, copy in Ed King Papers.

34. Zinn, "Notes," 24, 25, 26–28.

35. Quoted in Howard Zinn, *SNCC: The New Abolitionists* (Boston: Beacon, 1965), 188.

36. Willie Peacock, remarks at Freedom Summer Reviewed conference, 18–19.

37. Forman, *Black Revolutionaries,* 374; Peacock, interviewed by Dent.

38. Dennis, quoted in Howell Raines, *My Soul Is Rested* (New York: Penguin, 1983), 274; Forman, *Black Revolutionaries,* 373.

39. Bowman manuscript, 11; Cobb, interviewed by Dent; Zinn, "Notes on Greenville Meeting," 24.

40. Benjamin Muse, "Report on Misissippi," January 1964, 13–14, copy in Hillegas Collection; *Mississippi Free Press,* Dec. 14, 1963.

41. *Mississippi Free Press,* Nov. 30, 1963; Elizabeth Sutherland, "SNCC Takes Stock: Mandate from History," *Nation,* Jan. 6, 1964, 33.

42. "Mississippi Newsletter," Nov. 25, 1963, Hillegas Collection; Sutherland, "SNCC Takes Stock," 33.

43. Wiley Branton to Aaron Henry and Robert Moses, Nov. 12, 1963, copy in Hillegas Collection; *NYT,* Feb. 2, 1964; Marion Barry, interviewed by Robert Wright, 1967, Washington, D.C., 16, Howard CRDP.

44. Lawrence Guyot, report from Hattiesburg, Oct. 2, 1963, Zinn Papers; Mendy Samstein, "On the Hattiesburg Situation," undated, SNCC Papers, reel 38. The Jackson movement also languished. In early December six black women were arrested after defying the court injunction against demonstrations handed down in the spring. They were protesting

the city's failure to live up to its earlier promises. One of the picketers stated that "the city officials promised 12 policemen, and only six were hired. We still don't have enough school crossing guards. . . . Although the mayor was asked five months ago to meet with our ministers, he still hasn't met with them." The protest, however, did not lead to compliance or to renewed demonstrations; *Mississippi Free Press,* Dec. 21, 1963.

45. Bob Moses, interviewed by Anne Romaine, Highlander Folk Center, Sept. 5, 1965, 18, Romaine Papers; Moses, interviewed by Carson, 29; Jane Stembridge to Mary King, Nov. 20, 1963, SNCC Papers, reel 17.

46. Stembridge to King.

Chapter 10: Freedom Days

1. Jack Mendelsohn, *The Martyrs: Sixteen Who Gave Their Lives for Racial Justice* (New York: Harper & Row, 1966), 30–37; *Nation,* March 16, 1964, 254–55; affidavit, Mrs. Elizabeth Allen, May 29, 1964, Hillegas Collection.

2. Arnold Foster and Benjamin R. Epstein, "Report on the Ku Klux Klan," no date, box 26, Eugene Cox Papers; *Student Voice,* Jan. 14, 1964; report to the attorney general from Burke Marshall and John Doar, May 19, 1964, Marshall Papers, reel 3.

3. *Hearings Before the Committee on Un-American Activities, House of Representatives,* 89th Congress, Second Session, Jan. 4–7, 11–14, and 28, 1966 (Washington: GPO, 1966), part 3, 2665; 2799; part 4, 3046–47; part 5, 3872–73 (hereinafter cited as *HUAC Hearings*); Memphis *Commercial Appeal,* Feb. 4, 1966. McDaniel later split away from the White Knights and joined the United Klans of America, whose leader, Robert Shelton, appointed McDaniel Grand Dragon for Mississippi; *HUAC Hearings,* part 4, 3046–47. Another white hate group formed at this time was the Americans for the Preservation of the White Race, which took a harder line than the Citizens' Council but was much less powerful than the Klan.

4. Marshall and Doar report, May 19, 1964; *CRC Hearings,* Jackson, vol. 2, "Testimony of Mr. Archie C. Curtis, Adams County Mississippi," 90–96; *CRC Hearings,* vol. 2, 462–65.

5. *HUAC Hearings,* part 4, 2933–35, 2695; Wilson F. Minor, undated newspaper article, Cox Papers.

6. *HUAC Hearings,* part 4, 2935, 2933; Minor, undated article.

7. The Klan did not make public its membership rolls, but the White Knights' claim in May 1964 of 91,003 members in Mississippi was an obvious exaggeration. The estimate of 5,000 members is that of journalist Bill Minor, a knowledgeable reporter who covered Klan activities closely. Memphis *Commercial Appeal,* May 12, 1964; Minor, undated article, Minor Papers.

8. Memphis *Commercial Appeal,* Nov. 24, 1963; *JDN,* May 8, 1964; United Press International article on Barnett, Sept. 20, 1963; *C–L,* Sept. 20, 1963, newspaper clippings in Cox Papers.

9. *CRC Hearings,* vol. 1, 154.

10. Minutes, SNCC executive committee meeting, Atlanta, Dec. 27–31, 1963, 29, Carson Collection; "Notes on Staff Meeting, January 18 in Hattiesburg," Hillegas Collection; Clayborne Carson, *In Struggle: SNCC and the Black Awakening of the 1960s* (Cambridge, Mass.: Harvard University Press, 1981), 100.

11. Moses interview; Charles Cobb, interviewed by Tom Dent; James Forman, *The Making of Black Revolutionaries* (New York: Macmillan, 1972), 349.

12. James Forman, *The Making of Black Revolutionaries* (New York: Macmillan, 1972), 349; *Mississippi Free Press,* Jan. 18, 1964; Michael Sayer, "Hattiesburg, Mississippi," COFO communication, Jan. 15, 1964, SNCC Papers, reel 38.

13. WATS line transcripts, June 21, 22, 1964, SNCC Papers, reel 15 (unless otherwise indicated, all WATS line transcript citations are from reel 15 in the SNCC Papers); *Mississippi Free Press,* Feb. 1, 1964; Howard Zinn, *SNCC: The New Abolitionists* (Boston: Beacon, 1965), 105, 111. Zinn devotes a chapter of his book to the Hattiesburg Freedom Day (102–22).

14. Zinn, *SNCC,* 112–13, 114–22; WATS line transcript, June 22, 1964, SNCC Papers, reel 15. Moses was charged with obstructing traffic by standing on a sidewalk and refusing to move on when ordered to do so. The following night he was convicted, sentenced to sixty days, and fined $200. He spent more than a week in the Hattiesburg jail before posting bond; see Zinn, *SNCC,* 121; WATS line transcript, Jan. 30, 1964.

15. WATS line transcripts, Jan. 26–Feb. 21, 1964; *Student Voice,* Feb. 3, 1964; *C-L,* Feb. 11, 1964.

16. David Dennis to James McCain, Jan. 15, 1964; Carole E. Merritt, field report, Jan. 11, 1964, CORE Papers, Addendum, reel 22; "Madison County, Mississippi," undated UPI article, Hillegas Collection; "Canton Project History," 1–3; August Meier and Elliott Rudwick, *CORE: A Study in the Civil Rights Movement* (New York: Oxford University Press, 1973), 272; *Mississippi Free Press,* Jan. 25, 1964; *NYT,* March 2, 1964.

17. *Mississippi Free Press,* Jan. 25, 1964; Jack Minnis, "A Chronology of Violence and Intimidation in Mississippi since 1961," Stone Papers, Atlanta; Debbie Bernstein, "Canton Project History," Feb. 28, 1965, CORE Papers, reel 10, 2–5; Ed Hollander, "Report on Canton, Jan. 25–30 incl.," Jan. 31, 1964, CORE Papers, Addendum, reel 23; David Dennis, "An Awakening City," Jan. 23, 1964, CORE Papers, Addendum, reel 22; Meier and Rudwick, *CORE,* 273–74.

18. Robert Gore, "CORE Set for Massive Demonstrations in Mississippi," CORE press release, Feb. 19, 1963; *Madison County Herald,* undated clipping, CORE Papers, Addendum, reel 23; *NYT,* March 2, 1964; *Mississippi Free Press,* March 7, 1964; Meier and Rudwick, *CORE,* 274.

19. *NYT,* March 9, 1964; Meier and Rudwick, *CORE,* 274.

20. *Mississippi Free Press,* March 14, 1964; Meier and Rudwick, *CORE,* 274–75; Dennis, telegram to Lyndon Johnson and Robert Kennedy, Jan. 30, 1964, quoted in "Canton Project History," 7.

21. Mary King, *Freedom Song: A Personal History of the 1960s Civil Rights Movement* (New York: Morrow, 1987), 311, 331; COFO "Confidential Report: Freedom Day—Leflore County, Mississippi—March 25, 1964," SNCC Papers, reel 38; WATS line transcript, March 24, 1964; Marshall and Doar, May 19, 1964, report to the attorney general; *NYT,* March 26, 1964.

22. Fifty-five people were also arrested on April 10, charged with violating the new antipicketing law. *NYT,* April 14, 1964; King, *Freedom Song,* 331; WATS line transcripts, April 19–25, 1964.

23. David Dennis, "Outline for COFO Program, 1964," CORE Papers, reel 25; "Memorandum to Mississippi Field Staff from Dona [Richards] Re: Tougaloo Work-Study Project," undated, copy in personal collection of Margaret Rose Beernink, Palo Alto, Calif.

The Literacy Project resulted from discussions between Moses and his former professor at Hamilton College, John W. Blyth. Working with the Diebold Group, Inc., Blyth was experimenting with a technique that employed the latest technology, particularly computers, to teach literacy skills to adults. More than anyone else in SNCC, Bob Moses was convinced that the movement had a responsibility to provide the opportunity for illiterate Mississippi blacks to learn to read and write, and he saw the Literacy Project as a program that COFO could have adopted once the voting rights act had been passed. See Dr. John W. Blyth to Burke Marshall, Jan. 21, 1963, Marshall Papers, box 19; Moses interview.

24. Dorie Ladner, remarks at the Freedom Summer Reviewed conference, Jackson, Miss., Oct. 31, 1979. (Transcripts of that conference are available in the Mississippi Department of Archives and History.)

25. Interview with Joyce Ladner; Daniel Beittel, interviewed by Gordon Henderson, June 2, 1965, Jackson, copy in Millsaps College Library, Jackson.

26. William Kunstler, *Deep in My Heart* (New York: Morrow, 1966), 245–52; *Mississippi Free Press,* Oct. 12, 1963; Joan Trumpauer to Dear ____ , Dec. 12, 1963, SNCC Papers, reel 38; John and Margrit Garner to "Friends," Nov. 17, 1963. (I am grateful to the Garners for making available their correspondence during the period of the church visits.)

27. *Memphis Press-Scimitar,* June 10, 1963; *C-L,* March 30, 1964; Jan. 15, 1963, clippings in Cox Papers.

28. "Statement on Events in Jackson, Miss.—November 1 and 2, 1963," SNCC Papers, reel 37; *Mississippi Free Press,* March 14, 1964; *Southern Patriot,* Jan. 1964.

29. *Mississippi Free Press,* Jan. 25, 1964; "Impromptu Remarks Relative to TV Program, 'Bonanza,' By Mayor Allen Thompson in Department Head Meeting, January 23, 1964," Zinn Papers; Joan Trumpauer, "Greetings" (mimeographed letter), Jan. 27, 1964, Ed King Papers.

30. *Mississippi Free Press,* March 14, 1964; Eli Hochstadler, affidavit, April 26, 1964, Zinn Papers.

31. Joan Trumpauer, mimeographed letters, March 11, April 29, 1964;

Voice of the Movement, April 23, 1964, Ed King Papers. Of the approximately 500 people attending the Baez concert, about 300 were white. That the concert had to be scheduled during Tougaloo's spring break was the reason for the comparatively low black turnout; Trumpauer letter, March 11, 1964.

32. *Mississippi Free Press,* March 21, 1964; Neil R. McMillen, "Development of Civil Rights, 1956–1970," in Richard Aubrey McLemore, ed., *A History of Mississippi,* vol. 2 (Hattiesburg: University and College Press of Mississippi, 1973), 162–63; James W. Silver, *Mississippi: The Closed Society* (New York: Harcourt Brace, 1966), 252, 314; interview with Mary Ann Henderson, Jackson, Aug. 11, 1980. Judge Mize had previously found against the plaintiffs, but in February the Fifth Circuit Court of Appeals overruled him. Chief attorney for the plaintiffs was Derrick Bell of the NAACP Legal Defense Fund; *Mississippi Free Press,* Feb. 22, 1964.

33. Paul G. Chevigny, "A Busy Spring in the Magnolia State," in Leon Friedman, ed., *Southern Justice* (New York: Random House, 1965), 13–34 (Chevigny quoted, 33–34); SNCC, "Genocide in Mississippi" (Atlanta, n.d.), Carson Collection. In an attempt to be "helpful," the State Sovereignty Commission distributed a summary of the new anti-civil-rights laws to Mississippi police and members of the highway patrol; "From: Mississippi Sovereignty Commission To: Mississippi Law Enforcement Officers," n.d., Cox Papers.

34. Amistad Research Center, "Amistad Symposium on Southern Civil Rights Litigation Records for the 1960s," Dec. 8–9, 1978, 54–56, Amistad Research Center, Tulane University; Forman, *Black Revolutionaries,* 380; Zinn, *SNCC,* 272.

35. Jack Greenberg to Robert Moses, April 7, 1964; Robert W. Spike to Moses, April 27, 1964, Zinn Papers; Carson, *In Struggle,* 107.

36. Anne Braden, "A View from the Fringes," *Southern Exposure,* Spring 1981, 69; Carson, *In Struggle,* 52; Ed Hamlett, "SNCC's Relationship to White Dominated Organizations (exclusive of the NAACP)," Carson Collection. The Bradens were journalists working in Louisville, Kentucky, when in 1954 they were charged with sedition after they had bought a house in a white neighborhood and resold it to a black couple. The two went to work for SCEF in 1957. Although SCEF did not have a policy excluding communists, Anne Braden has written that "by the time Carl and I joined the SCEF staff in 1957, I am sure there was not a real live member of the Communist Party on its board"; Braden, "A View," 70.

On October 4, 1963, New Orleans police raided the SCEF office, confiscating records and arresting Dombrowski, Ben Smith (SCEF's attorney), and Bruce Waltzer, Smith's law partner. They were charged with violating the Louisiana Subversive Activities and Communist Control Law. Not until 1965 did the defendants win vindication from the U.S. Supreme Court. See *Nation,* Nov. 9, 1963, 289; Arthur Kinoy, *Rights on Trial: The Odyssey of a People's Lawyer* (Cambridge, Mass.: Harvard University Press, 1983), 215–33, 283–84.

37. Braden, "A View," 70; Anne Braden, "Those Who Were Not There: The Cold War Against the Civil Rights Movement," *Fellowship* 55 (June 1989): 10; *Washington Post,* Sept. 10, 1962; Bob Moses, comment at SNCC executive committee meeting, Atlanta, Dec. 28, 1963, Zinn Papers.

38. Anne Braden to Wiley Branton, Sept. 26, 1962, Braden Papers; Andrew Young to "Bevel and Diane," Feb. 18, 1963, SCLC Papers, 141:5; Sherrod, remarks at December 1963 SNCC executive committee meeting, Carson Collection.

39. Minutes of COFO convention, Feb. 9, 1964, Carson Collection.

40. Dorothy Zellner to Mendy Samstein, Feb. 27, 1964; Zellner to Lois Chafee and Samstein, March 10, 1964, Hillegas Collection; Forman, *Black Revolutionaries,* 379–80.

41. Ilene Strelitz Melish, unpublished manuscript in her possession, 20, 68; Moses, interviewed by Carson. Ilene Strelitz was the editor of the *Stanford Daily.* She came to Mississippi as a 1964 summer volunteer and returned later to teach at Tougaloo College. I am indebted to Ilene Strelitz Melish for giving me permission to read her manuscript. The other key Stanford students recruited by Lowenstein were Fred Goff, who worked in Mississippi during the freedom vote campaign, and Dennis Sweeney. In 1980 an emotionally disturbed Sweeney shot and killed Lowenstein in New York; see William H. Chafe, *Never Stop Running: Allard Lowenstein and the Struggle to Save American Liberalism* (New York: Basic, 1993), chap. 16.

42. Moses, interviewed by Carson; Melish, unpublished manuscript, 68–73.

43. Moses to Allard Lowenstein, no date, Allard K. Lowenstein Papers, Southern Historical Collection, Wilson Library, University of North Carolina–Chapel Hill, quoted in William Chafe, "Allard K. Lowenstein and the Mississippi Freedom Struggle, 1963–1964: A Case Study of White Liberal Activism," paper presented at the annual meeting of the Organization of American Historians, April 1992, Washington, D.C.

Because Lowenstein had been in Mississippi to speak at the COFO convention on February 7, and Moses in his letter urges Lowenstein to "come to the March . . . meeting," it is likely that Moses wrote the letter sometime after February 7 but before March 1. I am deeply grateful to Professor Chafe, who uncovered this material, for making it available to me. See also Chafe, *Never Stop Running,* chaps. 7 and 8.

44. Moses, interviewed by Carson; Melish, unpublished manuscript, 68–73.

45. Daniel Beittel to James W. Silver, Nov. 17, 1964, Silver Papers; interview with Daniel Beittel, May 25, 1981, San Rafael, Calif.

46. Barnaby Keeney, remarks at the "Inauguration of George A. Owens as President of Tougaloo College, April 21, 1966," copy in Barnaby C. Keeney Papers, Tougaloo file, Brown University Library.

47. Beittel to Keeney, April 5, 1964, Keeney Papers.

48. Keeney to Wilder, April 10, 1964, Keeney Papers. See also Keeney to Beittel, March 9, 1964; Keeney to Lawrence Durgin, March 9, 1964; Keeney to Beittel, March 24, 1964; April 9, 1964, Keeney Papers.

49. Keeney to John W. Blyth, Nov. 10, 1964; Dec. 7, 1964; Keeney to Frank Bowles, April 23, 1965; Keeney, remarks at George Owens's inauguration, Keeney Papers.

50. Dennis to James McCain, Jan. 15, 1964, CORE Papers, Addendum, reel 22; "CORE Staff Reference Sheet," Feb. 1964, SNCC Papers, reel 42; Mendy Samstein, interviewed by Romaine, 20, 30; minutes of SNCC executive committee meeting, Atlanta, June 10, 1964, Zinn Papers; Forman, *Black Revolutionaries,* 377.

51. Moses to Martin Luther King, March 16, 1964, King Papers, 7:25, MLK; *Mississippi Free Press,* April 11, 1964; Leslie Burl McLemore, "The Mississippi Freedom Democratic Party: A Case Study of Grass-Roots Politics" (Ph.D. diss., University of Massachusetts, 1971), 106–8.

52. "Canton Project History," 9; *Mississippi Free Press,* June 13, 1964; Charles Evers to Robert Kennedy, May 19, 1964, NAACP Papers.

53. Lee White to President Lyndon B. Johnson, Dec. 3, 1963, Ex Hu 2, "Equality of Races, 11/22/63–3/25/64," LBJ; Robert Kennedy, "Memorandum for the President," May 21, 1964, Ex Hu 2, PG 135, LBJ; Kennedy, "Memorandum for the President," June 5, 1964, Ex Hu 2 St 24 FG 135, LBJ.

54. Marshall interview; "Memorandum for the Attorney General from Burke Marshall," June 5, 1964, Marshall Papers, reel 3; Victor Navasky, *Kennedy Justice* (New York: Atheneum, 1977), 437. Navasky concludes that the Sheridan unit "had helped to do what the entire civil rights movement couldn't do—put the FBI into Mississippi" (438).

55. *Mississippi Free Press,* Feb. 8, 1964; NAACP press release, Feb. 4, 1964, NAACP Papers.

56. "Memo to: 'Friends of Freedom in Mississippi,' From: Bob Moses," April 6, 1964, copy in Hillegas Collection; "Summary of Major Points in Testimony by Citizens of Mississippi, Public Hearing, Washington, D.C., June 8, 1964," SNCC Papers, reel 20; Aaron Henry, Bob Moses, and David Dennis to President Lyndon B. Johnson, May 25, 1964, Lee White Papers, LBJ; Michael J. Belknap, *Federal Law and Southern Order: Racial Violence and Constitutional Conflict in the Post-Brown South* (Athens: University of Georgia Press, 1987), 140–41.

57. Lee White, "Memorandum for the President," June 17, 1964, Ex Hu 2 St 24, box 39, LBJ; Lee White to Aaron Henry, June 18, 1964, folder "CR MS Summer Volunteer Project," White Papers; Steven Bingham et al. to President Lyndon B. Johnson, June 17, 1964; Lee White to Steven Bingham, Aug. 10, 1964, Ex Hu 2 St 24, box 39, LBJ.

58. "Affidavit IV: Intimidation to Stop Summer Project," statements from Sam Black, James Black, James Jones, Charles McLaurin, and Willie Peacock, CORE Papers, Addendum, reel 23.

Chapter 11: That Summer

1. Bertha Gober, a SNCC activist from Albany, wrote "We'll Never Turn Back" in 1963. See Mary King, *Freedom Song: A Personal History of the*

1960s Civil Rights Movement (New York: Morrow, 1987), 121. Tracy Sugarman, *Stranger at the Gates: A Summer in Mississippi* (New York: Hill and Wang, 1966), 15–18; Elizabeth Sutherland, ed., *Letters From Mississippi* (New York: McGraw-Hill, 1965), 5–7; Mary Aickin Rothschild, *A Case of Black and White: Northern Volunteers and the Southern Freedom Summers* (Westport, Conn.: Greenwood, 1982), 54.

2. Sugarman, *Stranger,* 20–22; Sutherland, *Letters,* 5–7; Rothschild, *Black and White,* 54; Edwin King, unpublished manuscript, 19.

3. COFO press release, "The Mississippi Summer Project," July 15, 1964; Penny Patch to Kathleen Dahl, June 27, 1964, Hillegas Collection; Rothschild, *Black and White,* 48. For more detailed accounts of the summer volunteers see Rothschild, *A Case of Black and White;* Doug McAdam, *Freedom Summer* (New York: Oxford University Press, 1988); and Nicolaus Mills, *Like a Holy Crusade: Mississippi 1964—The Turning Point of the Civil Rights Movement in America* (Chicago: Dee, 1992)

4. McAdam, *Freedom Summer,* 42–43; Rothschild, *Black and White,* 33; Staughton Lynd to "Bob and Donna," March 25, 1964, Hillegas Collection; SNCC executive committee minutes, April 10, 1964, Carson Collection; Clayborne Carson, *In Struggle: SNCC and the Black Awakening of the 1960s* (Cambridge, Mass.: Harvard University Press, 1981), 100.

5. "Minutes, Tougaloo Movement, Fall 1963," Dec. 9, 1963, Ed King Papers; Dave Dennis, Project South interview, 1965, University Archives, Stanford University Libraries, folder 139; conversation with Martha Prescod Norman, Nov. 21, 1992, Greencastle, Ind.; Rothschild, *Black and White,* 33.

6. John Doar, transcript of speech at Oxford, Ohio, June 1964, 8–9, Marshall Papers, box 8; Vincent Harding, "Speech Made at Orientation Session of Student Volunteers in the Mississippi Freedom Summer Project," Oxford, Ohio, June 1964, copy in Mississippi Archives; letter from unnamed volunteer, quoted in McAdam, *Freedom Summer,* 73.

Although invited by COFO organizers, Carl and Anne Braden did not speak at any of the regular orientation sessions. The National Council of Churches, which sponsored and financed the Oxford orientation, denied the Bradens credentials because of their affiliation with SCEF. They did meet off campus with white activists from the Southern Students Organizing Committee (SSOC), a movement support group the Bradens helped organize that spring; Anne Braden, "Those Who Were Not There: The Cold War Against the Civil Rights Movement," *Fellowship* 55 (June 1989): 10–11.

7. Seth Cagin and Philip Dray, *We Are Not Afraid: The Story of Goodman, Schwerner, and Chaney and the Civil Rights Campaign for Mississippi* (New York: Macmillan, 1988), 171; Jack Mendelsohn, *The Martyrs: Sixteen Who Gave Their Lives for Racial Justice* (New York: Harper & Row, 1966), 113; Michael Schwerner, "Report from Meridian, Mississippi," March 28, 1964, CORE Papers, Addendum, reel 23.

8. Mendelsohn, *Martyrs,* 112; Michael Schwerner, field report, April 6, 1964, CORE Papers, Addendum, reel 23.

9. Cagin and Dray, *We Are Not Afraid,* 2–3; *C-L,* 1985, undated clipping in James Brown Collection, Tougaloo, Mississippi.

10. Cagin and Dray, *We Are Not Afraid,* 34–35; Andrew Goodman, Mississippi Summer Project application, original in Hillegas Collection.

11. The most comprehensive account of the Neshoba County lynchings is Cagin and Dray, *We Are Not Afraid,* based in large part on FBI files. Florence Mars, *Witness in Philadelphia* (Baton Rouge: Louisiana State University Press, 1977), is a fascinating and important view of the events from the perspective of a local white woman who spoke out against the murders and cooperated with the FBI investigation.

12. Len Holt, *The Summer That Didn't End* (New York: Morrow, 1965), 23–25; "COFO Contacts with Neshoba County Law Enforcement Officers in the Schwerner-Chaney-Goodman Case," undated copy in Margaret Rose Beernink Papers, Palo Alto, Calif.; *Student Voice,* June 1964; King, *Freedom Song,* 378.

13. Dennis interview; Dennis, interviewed by Tom Dent, Oct. 8, 1963, Dent Collection.

14. Dennis, interviewed by Dent.

15. "COFO Contacts"; Holt, *Summer,* 267; Cleveland Sellers, with Robert Terrell, *The River of No Return: The Autobiography of a Black Militant and the Life and Death of SNCC* (New York: Morrow, 1973), 81–93 (quoted material on 91–92). Sellers's book is available in a 1990 paperback edition from the University Press of Mississippi. Charlie Cobb, interviewed by Dent.

16. Michael Belknap, *Federal Law and Southern Order: Racial Violence and Constitutional Conflict in the Post-Brown South* (Athens: University of Georgia Press, 1987), 146; White House diary, June 23, 1964, LBJ; Bob Zellner, comments, Freedom Summer Reviewed conference, copy in Mississippi Archives.

17. J. Edgar Hoover to Walter Jenkins, July 13, 1964, Hu 26, Ex Hu 2/St 24, LBJ; *New York Daily News,* July 11, 1964, clipping in ibid.; *NYT,* July 11, 1964; Belknap, *Federal Law,* 146.

18. Report on Sovereignty Commission files, undated clipping of *C-L,* Brown Collection; Hoover to Jenkins; Paul B. Johnson, oral history interview in LBJ Library, 30–31; Marshall interview.

19. Pat Watters, *Down to Now: Reflections on the Southern Civil Rights Movement* (New York: Pantheon, 1971), 301.

20. *Mississippi Free Press,* July 25, 1964; *Activities of the Ku Klux Klan Organizations in the United States, Hearings,* 89th Congress, 1st session, part 3 (Washington: GPO, 1966), 2804–7 (hereinafter cited as *Klan Hearings*). Don Whitehead, *Attack on Terror: The FBI Against the Ku Klux Klan in Mississippi* (New York: Funk & Wagnalls, 1970), 98–100.

21. For additional coverage of the Mississippi summer project, see Carson, *In Struggle;* August Meier and Elliott Rudwick, *CORE: A Study in the Civil Rights Movement* (New York: Oxford University Press, 1973); Sugarman, *Stranger at the Gates;* Rothschild, *A Case of Black and White;* Sellers, *River of No Return;* James Forman, *The Making of Black Revolu-*

tionaries (New York: Macmillan, 1972); McAdam, *Freedom Summer;* and Mills, *Like a Holy Crusade.* The "White Folks Project" ran into strong white opposition on the Gulf Coast and did not survive the summer.

22. Sally Belfrage, *Freedom Summer* (New York: Viking, 1965), 39, 76. Written from the point of view of a participant/observer, Belfrage's book is the most perceptive of the first-person accounts of the summer project. The book is also available in a 1992 paperback edition from the University of Viginia Press.

23. Unita Blackwell, interviewed by Tom Dent, Mayersville, Miss., Aug. 19, 1978, Dent Collection; Blackwell, interviewed by Robert Wright, Mayersville, 1968, Howard CRDP; Henry Sias, interviewed by Robert Wright, Mayersville, 1968, Howard CRDP. Both Unita Blackwell and Henry Sias were Freedom Democratic party delegates at the Atlantic City Convention in 1964 and testified at the Civil Rights Commission hearings in Jackson in 1965. Blackwell later became the first black mayor of Mayersville and played an important role in the reconstituted Mississippi Democratic party in the 1970s and 1980s.

24. Susan Lorenzi Sojourner, "The Holmes County Civil Rights Movement Participants: The Mood, Feel, Environment of 1963–1967," 32, 40, unpublished essay in my possession; McAdam, *Freedom Summer,* 255.

25. Margaret Rose, report, Aug. 6, 1964; Rose to "Bruce and Beverly," Aug. 9, 1964; Rose to "Mom and Dad," Aug. 15, 1964; Rose to "Jim and Lois," Sept. 9, 1964, Beernink Papers.

26. "Report of Leonard Edwards, Sunflower County," July-August, 1964, SNCC Papers, reel 66; Sugarman, *Stranger at the Gates,* 127–32.

27. *NYT,* June 7, 9, 15, 1964; "Canton Project History," 9–10.

28. Tom Dent, "Annie Devine Remembers," *Freedomways* 12 (Second Quarter, 1982): 88–89; "Canton Project History," 10; *NYT,* June 15, 1964; Meier and Rudwick, *CORE,* 278.

29. *NYT,* Aug. 16, 1964; Jerome Smith, interviewed by Tom Dent, New Orleans, Sept. 23, 1983, Dent Collection.

30. Mrs. Winson Hudson, interviewed by Dent, Harmony, Miss., Aug. 1, 1979, Dent Collection; Smith, interviewed by Dent; *NYT,* Aug. 16, 1964.

31. *Washington Post,* July 20, 1964; William Jackson, undated testimony; Mrs. Winson Hudson, undated testimony; "Butane Gas Deliveries Stopped for 1 and 1/2 Months," undated report, SNCC Papers, reel 65; *NYT,* Aug. 2, 1964; Dovie Hudson, quoted in Barbara Summers, ed., *I Dream a World: Portraits of Black Women Who Changed America* (New York: Stewart, Tabori, and Chang, 1989), 160.

32. Summers, *I Dream a World,* 160; Citizens and Parents Committee for Equal Schools in Leake County to J. T. Logan, Aug. 10, 1964, SNCC Papers, reel 67; minutes of "Freedom Democratic Party—Leake County Convention—July 26, 1964"; Marvin Batterman to Dorothy Teal, July 15, 1964, SNCC Papers, reel 65.

33. Charles Cobb, "Prospectus for a Summer Freedom School Program," Dec. 1963, 12, SNCC Papers, reel 67; Rothschild, *Black and White,* 99; Featherstone, quoted in *Student Voice,* Aug. 5, 1964.

34. Florence Howe, "Mississippi's Freedom Schools," in Howe, *Myths of Coeducation: Selected Essays, 1964–1983* (Bloomington: Indiana University Press, 1984), 3–4.

35. Cobb, "Prospectus," 1–2; Staughton Lynd, "Mississippi Freedom Schools: Retrospect and Prospect," July 26, 1964, Hillegas Collection; "Freedom Schools—Final Report," undated report in Zinn Papers; McAdam, *Freedom Summer*, 84; Rothschild, *Black and White*, 105.

36. McAdam, *Freedom Summer*, 84–85.

37. Cobb, "Prospectus," 1; "Charles Cobb to SNCC Executive Committee, COFO Summer Program Committee, Re: Summer Freedom Schools in Mississippi, Jan. 14, 1964," copy in Harry Bowie Papers, SHSW.

38. Lynd, "Mississippi Freedom Schools," 2; Carson, *In Struggle*, 120; COFO, "Freedom School Data," undated, Bob Stone Papers; Staughton Lynd, "The Freedom Schools: Concept and Organization," *Freedomways* 5 (Second Quarter, 1965): 305; Lynd, interviewed by Joseph Sinsheimer, Dec. 30, 1981, Akron, Ohio, copy in my possession; Rothschild, *Black and White*, 110, 115; "The 1964 Platform of the Mississippi Freedom Schools Convention, August 6th, 7th, 8th, Meridian, Mississippi," copy in Stone Papers.

39. Carson, *In Struggle*, 120; Jo Ann Ooiman, "Madison County Freedom Schools, Summer Project, 1964," Aug. 25, 1964, Jo Ann Ooiman Papers, SHSW; "Minutes, COFO Executive Committee Meeting," July 10, 1964, 3, Hillegas Collection; Kirsty Powell, "A Report on the Ruleville Freedom School, Summer Project, 1964," SNCC Papers, reel 67; Rothschild, *Black and White*, 104.

40. Howard Zinn, *SNCC: The New Abolitionists* (Boston: Beacon, 1965), 248; Howe, "Mississippi's Freedom Schools," 7, 8; for more information on the Free Southern Theatre, see Thomas Dent, Richard Schechner, and Gilbert Moses, eds., *The Free Southern Theater* (Indianapolis: Bobbs-Merrill, 1969).

41. Walter Saddler, undated statement, Hillegas Collection.

42. Paul Cowan, *The Making of an Un-American: A Dialogue with Experience* (New York: Viking, 1970), 40, 41, 42–43.

43. Ibid., 32, 38, 45–46.

44. McAdam, *Freedom Summer*, 95; Sellers, *River of No Return*, 95–96.

45. Sara Evans, *Personal Politics: The Roots of Women's Liberation in the Civil Rights Movement & the New Left* (New York: Knopf, 1979), 79–80; Sally Belfrage, comments at the Women in the Civil Rights Movement conference, Center for the Study of Civil Rights, Charlottesville, Va., May 31–June 2, 1989, 6; King, *Freedom Song*, 465.

46. King, *Freedom Song*, 464.

47. Interviews with Harry Bowie and Bob Stone.

48. James Findlay, "In Keeping with the Prophets: The Mississippi Summer of 1964," *The Christian Century*, June 8–15, 1988, 574.

49. Alvin F. Poussaint and Joyce Ladner, "Black Power: A Failure for Integration—Within the Civil Rights Movement," *Archives of General Psychiatry* 18 (April 1968): 387; McAdam, *Freedom Summer*, 239.

50. Zinn, *SNCC,* 250; Moses interview; *NYT,* July 6, 1964.

51. Interviews with C. C. Bryant and Aylene Quin; interview with Harry Bowie, Jan. 16, 1984, McComb.

52. John Herbers, "Communique from the Mississippi Front," *New York Times Magazine,* Nov. 8, 1964, 127.

53. Hodding Carter II, *So the Heffners Left McComb* (Garden City, N.Y.: Doubleday, 1965) 61, 65, 69–71; interview with Robert Brumfield. Attorney Brumfield later played a role in bringing an end to the Klan reign of terror in McComb.

54. *Klan Hearings,* part 3, 2836–37; Brumfield interview; *Hearings in Jackson, Miss. before the United States Commission on Civil Rights, Feb. 16–20, 1965,* vol. 2 (Washington: GPO, 1965), 39 (hereinafter cited as *CRC Hearings*); undated COFO press release, Bowie Papers.

55. Myrtle Glascoe, "A Walking Tour," brochure commemorating the Mississippi Voices of the Civil Rights Movement conference, July 8–9, 1983, McComb, copy in my possession; Ed King, "McComb," 3–4, unpublished manuscript, copy in my possession; "Staff Report of Investigation of Incidents of Racial Violence, Pike County, Miss., 1964," in *CRC Hearings,* vol. 2, 458; King, *Freedom Song,* 418.

56. *CRC Hearings,* vol. 2, 450–54.

57. Undated staff field reports from Ralph Featherstone, Dennis Sweeney, Harry Bowie, and Bob Stone, copies in Stone Papers.

58. *Student Voice,* Aug. 5, 1964. On March 9, 1970, Featherstone and another SNCC worker were killed in Maryland by an explosion that tore apart the car in which they were riding. See Carson, *In Struggle,* 297.

59. "Meeting with McComb Businessmen," handwritten notes, Stone Papers; Bowie, Nobles, and Quin interviews.

60. Nobles, Quin, and Bowie interviews.

61. COFO press release, "First Southwest Mississippi Freedom Day Scheduled after Bombings," Aug. 15, 1964; WATS line transcripts, Aug. 1964, SNCC Papers, reel 16; *CRC Hearings,* vol. 2, 454–55.

62. WATS line transcripts, Aug. 18, 19, 1964.

63. Of the white volunteers in McComb, Marshall Ganz became a labor organizer, working for a time with Cesar Chavez in California; Gene Guerrero organized with the Southern Student Organizing Committee (SSOC); and Mario Savio returned to his Berkeley campus and became the catalyst for the Free Speech Movement.

64. Bowie interview.

Chapter 12: The Mississippi Freedom Democratic Party and the Atlantic City Challenge

1. "Emergency Memorandum To: All Field Staff and Voter Registration Volunteers. From: Bob Moses and the FDP Coordinators (Dona, Casey, Dick Jewett)," July 19, 1964, copy in MLK Papers, 16:2.

2. Ibid.

3. Milton Viorst, *Fire in the Streets: America in the 1960s* (New York: Simon & Schuster, 1979), 254–55.

4. "Precinct Meetings: Mississippi," June 17, 1964, SNCC Papers, reel 40; Viorst, *Fire in the Streets,* 255; "Mississippi State Democratic Party in Convention Assembled July 28, 1964," Hillegas Collection; Stokely Carmichael and Charles Hamilton, *Black Power: The Politics of Liberation in America* (New York: Vintage, 1967), 93; *NYT,* July 28, 1964.

5. Gloster Current to Charles Evers, Nov. 5, 1964; Current to Evers, July 1, 1964, NAACP Papers.

6. Edwin King, unpublished manuscript, 46; Current to Charles Evers, July 1, 1964, NAACP Papers.

7. Dr. B. F. Murph to Roy Wilkins, Aug. 26, 1964, NAACP Papers.

8. Margaret Rose to "Mom and Dad," July 2, 1964, Margaret Rose Beernink Papers, copy in my possession.

9. *NYT,* July 6, 1964; *Northside Reporter,* July 9, 1964; *C-L,* July 10, 1964; *JDN,* July 17, 1964. See also the essay on Mississippi by Charles Sallis and John Quincy Adams in Elizabeth Jacoway and David R. Colburn, eds., *Southern Businessmen and Desegregation* (Baton Rouge: Louisiana State University Press, 1982).

10. *NYT,* July 6, 1964.

11. Ibid., July 7, 1964; "Report of the Special Mississippi Investigating Committee to the National Board of Directors for the National Association for the Advancement of Colored People," *Crisis* 71 (Nov. 1964): 585–91; *NYT,* July 7, 1964; *Mississippi Free Press,* July 11, 1964; Current to Evers, July 17, 1964.

12. Silas McGhee, interviewed by Robert Wright, July 2, 1969, Greenwood, Howard CRDP, 18; Sally Belfrage, *Freedom Summer* (New York: Viking, 1965), 125, 170; June Johnson, interviewed by Tom Dent, June 22, 1979, Greenwood, Dent Collection.

13. Silas McGhee, "Affidavit," quoted in Belfrage, *Freedom Summer,* 123–24.

14. Belfrage, *Freedom Summer,* 107–8; Joseph Sinsheimer, "Challenging Myths: White Greenwood and the Community Studies Approach," paper presented at the annual meeting of the American Studies Association, Miami, Fla., Oct. 30, 1988.

15. *NYT,* July 17, 1964; Belfrage, *Freedom Summer,* 124. The FBI arrested a forty-seven-year-old plumber named Willie Belk, his nineteen-year-old son, and another employee and charged them with conspiracy to violate McGhee's civil rights. This was the first arrest made under the new civil rights law. It would also be the only such arrest that summer, despite numerous other assaults on movement workers. *NYT,* July 24, 1964; Belfrage, *Freedom Summer,* 124.

16. Tillinghast, quoted in Clayborne Carson, *In Struggle: SNCC and the Black Awakening of the 1960s* (Cambridge, Mass.: Harvard University Press, 1981), 122; WATS line digest, July 25, 1964, SNCC Papers, reel 15.

17. WATS line digest, July 25, 1964; interview with June Johnson, April 27, 1990, Fillmore, Ind.; Robert Zellner, undated affidavit, copy in Hillegas Collection; Belfrage, *Freedom Summer,* 171–73.

18. Silas McGhee, interviewed by Wright, 20, 21.

19. Ibid., 20; Johnson interview; Belfrage, *Freedom Summer,* 222–23.

20. "Running Summary of Incidents," Greenwood, Aug. 16, 1964; Belfrage, *Freedom Summer,* 224–26.

21. Mississippi Summer Project, "Running Summary of Incidents," Greenwood, Aug. 18, 1964, Ed King Papers; Belfrage, *Freedom Summer,* 234; Johnson interview; Carson, *In Struggle,* 151.

22. "The Independent: The Freedom Voice of Leflore County," July 25, 1964, SNCC Papers, reel 38.

23. "Precinct Meeting, July 27, 1964"; "July 30, 1964: Summit Precinct Meeting, Pike County," SNCC Papers, reel 66.

24. "Joel" to "Dear Folks," in Elizabeth Sutherland, ed., *Letters From Mississippi* (New York: McGraw-Hill, 1965), 211.

25. "Minutes, Madison County Convention," July 26, 1964, SNCC Papers, reel 12; *Mississippi Free Press,* Aug. 1, 1964; "Minutes, Leflore County Convention," July 27, 1964, SNCC Papers, reel 12.

26. Len Holt, *The Summer That Didn't End* (New York: Morrow, 1965), 158; unsigned letter, Aug. 6, 1964, in Sutherland, *Letters,* 213–14; Paul Good, *The Trouble I've Seen: White Journalist/Black Movement* (Washington, D.C.: Howard University Press, 1975), 170.

27. Holt, *Summer,* 157; Sutherland, *Letters,* 213–14; Good, *Trouble,* 212.

28. Good, *Trouble,* 172; conversation with Edwin King, Nov. 5, 1984, Jackson, Miss.; volunteer quoted in Sutherland, *Letters,* 212.

29. Moses interview; Paul Cowan, *The Making of an Un-American: A Dialogue with Experience* (New York: Viking, 1970), 46–47; memorandum, Casey Hayden to Jackson FDP, "Notes on Conversation with Al Lowenstein," July 14, 1964, Hillegas Collection; Edwin King, interviewed by Anne Romaine, 1965, SHSW, 1–10; Leslie Burl McLemore, "The Mississippi Freedom Democratic Party: A Case Study of Grass-Roots Politics" (Ph.D. diss., University of Massachusetts, 1971), 120 (hereinafter cited as "MFDP"); Guyot interview. R. L. T. Smith finally did win election as a delegation alternate. For a list of the FDP delegates and alternates, see *Congressional Record—House,* 88th Congress, Second Session, Aug. 20, 1964, 20753.

30. *NYT,* Aug. 7, 1964; Michael Belknap, *Federal Law and Southern Order: Racial Violence and Constitutional Conflict in the Post-Brown South* (Athens: University of Georgia Press, 1987), 147; A. Belmont to Mr. Rosen, Sept. 16, 1964, MIBURN file, Federal Bureau of Investigation Archives, Washington, D.C. For the starred footnote see Seth Cagin and Philip Dray, *We Are Not Afraid: The Story of Goodman, Schwerner, and Chaney and the Civil Rights Campaign for Mississippi* (New York: Macmillan, 1988), 406–7.

31. Edwin King, unpublished manuscript, 70–72.

32. David Dennis, quoted in Juan Williams, *Eyes on the Prize: America's Civil Rights Years, 1954–1965* (New York: Viking, 1987), 239–40.

33. Cagin and Dray, *We Are Not Afraid*, 407–12; *NYT*, Aug. 21, 1964; King, unpublished manuscript, 75.

34. Mary King, *Freedom Song: A Personal History of the 1960s Civil Rights Movement* (New York: Morrow, 1987), 343; James Forman, *The Making of Black Revolutionaries* (New York: Macmillan, 1972), 387; Joyce Ladner interview.

35. *JDN*, Aug. 13, 1964; Holt, *Summer*, 165; *NYT*, Aug. 22, 1964.

36. Holt, *Summer*, 161; McLemore, "MFDP," 129–31; telegram, Martin Luther King, Jr., to President Lyndon Johnson, Aug. 19, 1964, copy in MLK Papers.

37. King, *Freedom Song*, 345; Dennis and Moses interviews; Ella Baker, interviewed by John Britton, June 19, 1968 Washington, D.C., Howard CRDP, 64.

38. Joseph Rauh, interviewed by Anne Romaine, June 16, 1966, Washington, D.C., 6, Romaine Papers; Watkins quoted in Nicolaus Mills, *Like a Holy Crusade: Mississippi 1964—The Turning Point of the Civil Rights Movement in America* (Chicago: Dee, 1992), 145.

39. *NYT*, Aug. 23, 1964.

40. Ibid. For the text of the brief submitted by the Mississippi Freedom Democratic party to the credentials committee, see *Congressional Record—House*, 88th Congress, Second Session, Aug. 20, 1964, 20742–53.

41. "Partial Proceedings of the Democratic National Convention, 1964, Credentials Committee, Aug. 22, 1964," 43–44, copy in Joseph Rauh Papers, SHSW; *NYT*, Aug. 23, 1964; Kay Mills, *This Little Light of Mine: The Life of Fannie Lou Hamer* (New York: Dutton, 1993), 118–21.

42. *NYT*, Aug. 23, 1964; Carson, *In Struggle*, 125.

43. Rauh, interviewed by Romaine, 17–18; *NYT*, Aug. 24, 1964.

44. Carson, *In Struggle*, 125–26, quoting Charles Sherrod, "Mississippi at Atlantic City," *Grain of Salt* (Union Theological Seminary), Oct. 12, 1964, 6; Sherrod, untitled draft of article, 5, Charles Sherrod Papers, SHSW.

45. Courtland Cox, quoted in Henry Hampton and Steve Fayer, eds., *Voices of Freedom: An Oral History of the Civil Rights Movement from the 1950s through the 1980s* (New York: Bantam, 1990), 199.

46. Lyndon Johnson, *The Vantage Point: Perspectives of the Presidency, 1963–1969* (New York: Holt, Rhinehart and Winston, 1971), 101; Godfrey Hodgson, *America in Our Time: From World War II to Nixon: What Happened and Why* (New York: Vintage, 1978), 213; memorandum, Jack Valenti to President Johnson, July 20, 1964, PL ST 24, box 52; Karl Rolvaag to Walter Jenkins, July 27, 1964, Hu 2/ST 24, 7/17/64–11/30/64, LBJ. To receive convention credentials, Alabama delegates were required to pledge support of the party's nominees in November. All but a handful of the Alabama delegates refused to take the pledge, and most left the convention early; *NYT*, Aug. 26, 1964.

47. Hodgson, *America*, 214.

48. Joseph L. Rauh, interviewed by Paige Mulholland, Aug. 1, 1969, Washington, D.C., 13–14, Oral History Collection, LBJ.

49. President's diary and diary backup, Aug. 15–26, 1964, LBJ; David Garrow, *Bearing the Cross: Martin Luther King, Jr., and the Southern Christian Leadership Conference* (New York: Morrow, 1986), 346; King telegram, Aug. 19, 1964.

50. *Intelligence Activities and the Rights of Americans, Book II: Final Report of the Select Committee to Study Governmental Operations, United States Senate* (Washington: GPO, 1976), 117 (hereinafter cited as *Church Committee Report*).

51. M. A. Jones to DeLoach, "Subject: MFDP Request from White House," July 22, 1964; J. Edgar Hoover to the deputy attorney general, Aug. 21, 1964, Mississippi Freedom Democratic party file, 62–109 555, section 1, FBI Archives; O'Reilly, *"Racial Matters": The FBI's Secret File on Black America, 1960–1972* (New York: Free Press, 1989), 186. O'Reilly did extensive research on the work of the FBI at the 1964 convention (186–90).

52. O'Reilly, *"Racial Matters,"* 186–88; C. D. DeLoach to "Dear Bishop," Sept. 10, 1964, WHCF, name file, box 117, LBJ; presidential diary and diary backup, Aug. 20–27, 1964, LBJ. See also Lee White to president, Aug. 12, 13, 19, 1964; memorandum from Fred Dutton, "Subject: Mississippi Delegation Problem, Aug. 19, 1964, 11/22/63–8/21/64, WHCF, PL1/ST 24, LBJ.

53. DeLoach to "Dear Bishop. For the starred footnote see *Church Committee Report,* 119; O'Reilly, *"Racial Matters,"* 190.

54. Garrow, *Bearing the Cross,* 347.

55. Rauh, interviewed by Romaine, 19–20; Fannie Lou Hamer, interviewed by Anne and Howard Romaine, 1965, 5–6, Romaine Papers.

56. Rauh, interviewed by Romaine, 20–21; presidential diary and diary backup, Aug. 24, 1964.

57. Rauh, interviewed by Romaine, 24–25.

58. Rauh, interview in Hampton and Fayer, *Voices of Freedom,* 200–201; Rauh, interviewed by Romaine, 24–25.

59. Mendy Samstein, interviewed by Anne Romaine, Sept. 1965, 34–35.

60. Rauh, interviewed by Romaine, 22; Garrow, *Bearing the Cross,* 347; presidential diary backup, Aug. 25, 1964; C. D. DeLoach to Mr. Mohr, Aug. 25, 1964, "Subject: Racial Matters, 1964 Democratic Convention," MFDP, file no. 62–10955-7, section 1, FBI Archives.

61. Rauh, interviewed by Romaine, 25–26; *NYT,* Aug. 26, 1964.

62. Rauh, interview in Hampton and Fayer, *Voices of Freedom,* 200–202; Rauh, interviewed by Romaine, 26–27.

63. Edwin King, unpublished manuscript, 126, 122–87 passim; Aaron Henry, interview in Oral History Collection, LBJ, 9.

64. King, unpublished manuscript, 185–86; Joseph Rauh, remarks at Freedom Summer Reviewed conference, Tougaloo, Mississippi, Nov. 1, 1974, Mississippi Archives, 35–36.

65. King, unpublished manuscript, 188; Rauh, interviewed by Romaine, 30–31; Henry, interview in Johnson Library, 8. For the starred footnote see Moses interview; Rauh, interviewed by Romaine, 33.

66. *NYT,* Aug. 26, 1964. Wynn's wife had Texas connections with the Johnson family, and the president was godfather to their daughter.

67. Ibid.; *Indianapolis Star,* Aug. 26, 1964; president's diary, Aug. 25, 1964; Good, *Trouble,* 206–7.

68. Theodore White, *The Making of the President 1964* (New York: Atheneum), 335. White wrote that through its "illegal" sit-in, "the Freedom Democratic party had stained the honor that so much courage and suffering had won it" (335). Hubert Humphrey, *The Education of a Public Man: My Life and Politics* (New York: Doubleday, 1976), 300. Humphrey described his assignment in working out the compromise as "aggravating." Had he failed, would Johnson have chosen someone else as his vice presidential nominee? "It is a question I have never been able to answer" (299).

69. Moses interview; Fannie Lou Hamer, interviewed by Robert Wright, 1968, Ruleville, Miss., 29; Unita Blackwell, interviewed by Robert Wright, Mayersville, Miss., 117, Howard CRDP.

70. Forman, *Black Revolutionaries,* 390–95. Forman states that the quotations were paraphrases of the speeches he heard.

71. Ibid., 395.

72. Henry Sias, interviewed by Robert Wright, 1968, Issaquena County, Miss., Howard CRDP, 20; Victoria Gray Adams interview.

73. Adams interview; Sias, interviewed by Wright, 19–20.

74. Fannie Lou Hamer, interviewed by Anne and Howard Romaine, 12; Carson, *In Struggle,* 126.

75. Joyce Ladner interview; Bob Moses, interview with Clayborne Carson, 38; Cleveland Sellers, with Robert Terrell, *The River of No Return: The Autobiography of a Black Militant and the Life and Death of SNCC* (Jackson: University Press of Mississippi, 1990), 111.

Chapter 13: Aftermath in McComb

1. McComb Project, "Daily Reports and Chronology," Aug. 28–30, 1964, SNCC Papers, reel 16; "Statement by Mrs. Willie Dillon on Bombing," Robert Stone Papers.

2. "Statement by Mrs. Willie Dillon"; "Testimony of Mrs. Willie Dillon, Pike County, Mississippi," *Hearings in Jackson, Miss., Before the United States Commission on Civil Rights, Feb. 16–20, 1965,* vol. 2 (Washington: GPO, 1965), 12–14 (hereinafter cited as *CRC Hearings*); "Staff Report of Incidents of Racial Violence, Pike County, Miss., 1964," in *CRC Hearings,* vol. 2, 455–56; McComb *Enterprise-Journal,* Sept. 29, 1964.

3. Jesse Harris to Burke Marshall, Sept. 9, 1964, SNCC Papers, reel 38; "Testimony of Robert R. Warren, Sheriff, Pike County, Miss.," in *CRC Hearings,* vol. 2, 23. On September 28, 1964, the acting attorney general Nicholas Katzenbach wrote President Johnson that "there have been 17

bombings in McComb since June 22, 1964. . . . The FBI has been directed to investigate each bombing. Thus far they have not reported any significant leads"; Katzenbach, "Memorandum to the President: Re: McComb, Mississippi," Sept. 28, 1964, HU2/ST 24, LG/McComb, PU 2-2, FG 135, LBJ.

4. Quoted in the *Student Voice,* Sept. 23, 1964.

5. Ibid.; "Daily Reports and Chronology," Aug. 30, 1964.

6. Hodding Carter II, *So the Heffners Left McComb* (Garden City, N.Y.: Doubleday, 1965), 30, 105; interview with Harry Bowie; "McComb Incident Summary," Sept. 5, 1964, Stone Papers. The Heffners soon moved to Washington, where Red took a job with the Community Relations Service and Malva worked for a time with Operation Head Start; Carter, *The Heffners,* 142.

7. "McComb Incident Summary," Sept. 2–6, 1964; *CRC Hearings,* vol. 2, 456–57.

8. *CRC Hearings,* vol. 1, 66, 449; interview with C. C. Bryant; *Klan Hearings,* part 4, 2840; interview with Ernest Nobles.

9. "Testimony of Billy Earl Wilson," *Klan Hearings,* part 4, 457–58; interview with Aylene Quin.

10. Quin interview; interview with Joe Martin; Warren, quoted in *CRC Hearings,* vol. 2, 18; McComb *Enterprise-Journal,* Sept. 21, 1964.

11. *CRC Hearings,* vol. 2, 18; "Report on McComb, Mississippi," compiled by Bob Stone, Stone Papers; McComb *Enterprise-Journal,* Sept. 21–23, 1964; Jerry DeMuth, "'Criminal Syndicalism' in Mississippi," *Texas Observer,* Nov. 13, 1964, 13; "McComb Incident Summary," Sept. 23, 1964; copy of affidavit of Jerry Lee Hill, Hillegas Collection.

12. "Review of Conversation with Artis Garner," no author, undated typescript in SNCC Papers, reel 16; *NYT,* Sept. 26, 1964.

13. Lee White to Jack Valenti, Sept. 23, 1964, Lee White Papers, box 6, "Civil Rights—Mississippi" folder, LBJ; Quin interview; *NYT,* Sept. 24, 25, 26, 1964. John F. Kennedy had appointed Louis Martin, the black former editor of the *Chicago Defender,* to the White House staff, a position he continued to hold under Lyndon Johnson. Martin was a major presidential liaison with the civil rights leadership.

14. Carter, *The Heffners,* 135–36; *NYT,* Oct. 6, 1964; interview with Robert Brumfield; interview with Joseph Pigott; Frank Morgan to James W. Silver, Feb. 11, 1965, Silver Papers.

15. McComb *Enterprise-Journal,* Sept. 25, 1964.

16. John A. Griffin to Governor Collins, "Report on McComb, Mississippi," Oct. 2, 1964, Exec. HU 2/ST 24, LG/McComb, LBJ.

17. McComb *Enterprise-Journal,* Sept. 30, Oct. 1, 1964. The information on the reaction in McComb to the threatened federal and state intervention comes from my interview with Judge Joseph Pigott, who had his date book for 1964 in front of him as he spoke.

18. Pigott interview; McComb *Enterprise-Journal,* Sept. 30, Oct. 1, 1964.

19. Pigott interview. For the starred footnote see Oliver Emmerich, *Two*

Faces of Janus (Jackson: University Press of Mississippi, 1971), 141–42; Marshall interview.

20. McComb *Enterprise-Journal,* Oct. 1, 5, 7, 13, 20, 23, 24, 1964; "McComb Incident Summary," Oct. 23, 1964; *NYT,* Oct. 24, 1964. Of the two men not brought to trial on October 23, one was released with all charges dropped. The other, "Bubba" Gillis, had been released on bail raised by his brother, Norman, a prominent McComb attorney. The family then had Bubba committed to the state mental hospital at Whitfield for tests. Brought to trial in February 1965 on the armed robbery charge, Gillis was told to repay the money he stole from the Monticello bank and was given a suspended sentence by Judge Sidney Mize; McComb *Enterprise-Journal,* Oct. 9, 1964; newspaper clipping dated Feb. 24, 1965, in Wilson Minor Papers, Mitchell Library, Mississippi State University.

On January 18, 1965, Willie Dillon paid court costs of $42.60, and the charges against him were dropped. After Matti Dillon had spoken with President Johnson, local authorities lost their enthusiasm for prosecuting his case; *CRC Hearings,* vol. 2, 8.

21. Interviews with Quin, Martin, and Nobles; Dunagin quoted in McComb *Enterprise-Journal,* Oct. 29, 1964; McComb *Enterprise-Journal,* Oct. 26, Nov. 5, 6, 1964; "McComb Incident Summary," Nov. 1964.

22. Emmerich, *Two Faces of Janus,* 135, quoting *Enterprise-Journal* editorial of Oct. 14, 1964; ibid., 136, quoting editorial of Oct. 20, 1964; ibid., 137–38.

23. McComb *Enterprise-Journal,* Nov. 18, 1964; Emmerich, *Two Faces of Janus,* 147–50; Brumfield interview; interview with Newton James, Jan. 15, 1984, McComb.

24. Nobles, quoted in McComb *Enterprise-Journal,* Dec. 11, 1984; Paul Good, "A Bowl of Gumbo for Curtis Bryant," *The Reporter,* 31 (Dec. 31, 1964), 19–22; McComb *Enterprise-Journal,* Nov. 19, 1964; *NYT,* Nov. 19, 1964; "NAACP Desegregates McComb, Mississippi," NAACP press release, Nov. 20, 1964, NAACP Papers.

25. *CRC Hearings,* vol. 2, 63.

26. Good, "A Bowl of Gumbo," 19, 21–22.

Chapter 14: Battle Fatigue

1. "Rough Minutes of a meeting called by the National Council of Churches to discuss the Mississippi Project," Sept. 18, 1964, SNCC memorandum by Mendy Samstein, copy in Hillegas Collection. See also James Forman, *The Making of Black Revolutionaries* (New York: Macmillan, 1972), 399–405. Subsequent quotations are from these minutes, which were not a direct transcription of the meeting conversations. Samstein's minutes are extensive, however, and their accuracy has not been challenged by other participants at the New York meeting.

2. Forman, *Black Revolutionaries,* 405.

3. Interview with Shelton Stromquist, Oct. 5, 1980, Madison, Wisconsin. Stromquist was a Yale graduate student who as a summer vol-

unteer did voter registration work in Vicksburg in 1964. He returned to work with COFO in Mississippi in the summer of 1965. "Memo to: SNCC Staff, From: Dorothy Zellner, Re: Attempts to Change COFO," undated [late January 1965], copy in Tom Levin Papers, box 1, folder 2, MLK.

4. "MEMORANDUM To: Leon Shull, From: Curtis B. Gans, Re: Atlanta Trip and Other Matters," Nov. 20, 1964, Americans for Democratic Action Papers, unprocessed collection. I am indebted to Steven M. Gillon for supplying me with a copy of this document. See also Gillon's *Politics and Vision: The ADA and American Liberalism, 1947–1985* (New York: Oxford University Press, 1987), 161–63.

5. Moses, quoted in Jack Newfield, "The Liberals' Big Stick," *Cavalier,* June 1965, 34.

6. Minutes of SNCC executive committee meeting, Atlanta, Sept. 4–6, 1964, SNCC Papers, reel 3.

7. Minutes of SNCC staff meeting, Atlanta, Oct. 10, 1964, SNCC Papers, reel 13; Forman, *Black Revolutionaries,* 415–20; Moses, interview with Carson, 42.

8. Forman, *Black Revolutionaries,* 417–18; Moses, interview with Carson, 42–43.

9. Minutes of the Sept. 4–6, 1964, SNCC executive committee; minutes of SNCC staff meeting, Atlanta, Oct. 10–14, SNCC Papers, reel 3; Forman, *Black Revolutionaries,* 420–22.

10. Aaron Henry to President Lyndon B. Johnson, Aug. 30, 1964, name file, "Mississippi F-K," LBJ; "Minutes of the Executive Committee of the Mississippi Freedom Democratic Party," Sept. 13, 1964, SNCC Papers, reel 69; FDP, "The Convention Challenge," undated [fall 1964], Robert Stone Papers.

11. Julius Lester, *Look Out, Whitey!: Black Power's Gon' Get Your Mama* (New York: Dial, 1968), 28; Forman, *Black Revolutionaries,* 423.

12. Neil R. McMillen, *The Citizens' Council: Organized Resistance to the Second Reconstruction, 1954–64* (Urbana: University of Illinois Press, 1971), 351. The only member of the Mississippi congressional delegation to endorse Goldwater was Congressman John Bell Williams, who was subsequently stripped of his seniority by the House Democratic caucus.

13. Goldwater-Miller Campaign Headquarters, District of Columbia, "What About—Civil Rights and Barry Goldwater?" pamphlet reprinted by Douglas C. Wynn, chairman, Mississippi Johnson Democratic campaign, copy in Ed King Papers; Paul B. Johnson oral history, LBJ, 47.

14. SNCC news release, "'Freedom Vote' Volunteers Arrive in Mississippi," Oct. 27, 1964, copy in Hillegas Collection. At the urging of the national office of the NAACP, Henry later withdrew from the congressional challenge.

15. List of SNCC staff and Freedom Corps workers in Mississippi, untitled and undated [fall 1964], Hillegas Collection; "Paid CORE staff as of September 21, 1964," CORE Papers, Addendum, reel 22.

16. Leslie Burl McLemore, "The Mississippi Freedom Democratic Par-

ty: A Case Study of Grass-Roots Politics" (Ph.D. diss., University of Massachusetts, 1971), 176–77. Written by a scholar-activist close to the events he describes, this dissertation contains much valuable information.

17. "Running Summary of Incidents During the 'Freedom Vote' Campaign, October 18–November 2, 1964"; "Bombing at the Vicksburg Freedom House," undated statement, Hillegas Collection; *C-L,* Oct. 1, 1964.

18. John Harris, "Report on Sunflower County," undated [late 1964], SNCC Papers, reel 40; Annie Mae King, interviewed by Robert Wright, Sept. 28, 1968, Indianola, Miss, 2, Howard CRDP; "Running Summary."

19. Guyot, interviewed by Anne Romaine, 21; *Southern Patriot,* Nov. 1966.

20. Larry Stevens, "Report, Holmes County Freedom Centers," Sept. 13, 1964, Steve Ewen Papers; Mary Brumder, "Holmes County, Nov. 21, 1964," SHSW.

21. "List of SNCC staff . . . [fall 1964]."

22. "Moses of Mississippi Raises Some Universal Questions," *Pacific Scene,* Feb. 1965, 3–4.

23. Moses, interview with author; Moses, interview with Carson, 51–57.

24. Dennis interview.

25. Ibid.; Dennis, interview with Tom Dent.

26. Robert Coles, "Social Struggles and Weariness," *Psychiatry* 27 (1964): 308, 315.

27. "Minutes, 5th District Meeting, Nov. 25th, 1964," JoAnn Ooiman Robinson Papers, SHSW.

28. Debbie Lewis, untitled manuscript, Civil Rights Movement in the United States Collection, UCLA.

29. Minutes, "Canton–Valley View Staff Meeting," Dec. 3, 4, 1964, Robinson Papers.

30. Ibid., Dec. 3, 4, 12, 1964.

31. Richard Jewett, "Mississippi Field Report," Jan. 19, 1965, Robinson Papers.

32. "Staff Meeting, Jackson COFO," Nov. 23, 1964; "Holly Springs Project—Letters from Cleveland Sellers," Hillegas Collection. See also Mary Aickin Rothschhild, *A Case of Black and White: Northern Volunteers and the Southern Freedom Summers, 1964–1965* (Westport, Conn.: Greenwood, 1982), 72–73; and Clayborne Carson, *In Struggle: SNCC and the Black Awakening of the 1960s* (Cambridge, Mass.: Harvard University Press, 1981), 150.

33. R. Hunter Morey, "Cross Roads in COFO," Dec. 3, 1964, R. Hunter Morey Papers, SHSW.

34. "Staff Meeting, Jackson COFO."

35. Matteo Suarez, interviewed by Robert Wright, 1969, Howard CRDP.

36. "Viki and Martin [Nicklaus] to the Hodeses," Nov. 19, 1964, Braden Papers, box 55; Desmond Callan to Warren McKenna, Dec. 15, 1964, SNCC Papers, reel 68.

37. "Summary of Staff Retreat Minutes," Carson Collection; Carson, *In Struggle,* 138–40; Forman, *Black Revolutionaries,* 424–27. For Forman's views on Waveland, see ibid., 433–37. The best historical treatment is Carson, *In Struggle,* chap. 10, "Waveland Retreat."

38. Mary King, *Freedom Song: A Personal History of the 1960s Civil Rights Movement* (New York: Morrow, 1987), appendix 2, "SNCC Position Paper, November 1964," 567–69.

39. Ibid., 450, 459, 462; Cynthia Washington, "We Started at Different Ends of the Spectrum," *Southern Exposure* 4 (Winter 1977): 14–20. For Sara Evans's interpretation, see her *Personal Politics: The Roots of Women's Liberation in the Civil Rights Movement & the New Left* (New York: Vintage, 1979), chap. 4.

40. "COFO Program (Winter 1964–Spring 1965)," Hillegas Collection; John Harris to Courtland Cox, "Sunflower County Report," Oct. 17, 1964, SNCC Papers, reel 40; Larry Stevens, "Report, Holmes County Freedom Centers," Sept. 13 [1964], Hillegas Collection; Burke Marshall to Helen Gahagan Douglas, Sept. 25, 1964, Marshall Papers, reel 3.

41. "Running Summary"; "COFO Program"; "McComb Report," undated, Harry Bowie Papers, SHSW; "Neshoba Project Report," Sept. 14, 1964, SNCC Papers, reel 66.

42. COFO News, "The Cotton Vote in Mississippi," Dec. 11, 1964, 1–2, Hillegas Collection; Jerry Demuth, "Notes from Mississippi," *The Independent,* Dec. 1964, clipping in Ed King Papers; Rothschild, *A Case of Black and White,* 76–77.

43. "The Cotton Vote," 1–2; Richard Jewett, "Weekly Report, November 9, 1964 through November 15, 1964," CORE Papers, Addendum, Reel 23.

44. "The Cotton Vote," 5; SNCC news release, "Discrimination Charged as Negroes Win Mississippi Farming Elections," Dec. 5, 1964; SNCC news release, Dec. 10, 1964, Hillegas Collection; August Meier and Elliott Rudwick, *CORE: A Study in the Civil Rights Movement* (New York: Oxford University Press, 1973), 342; statement by George Raymond, Jan. 7, 1965, CORE Papers, Addendum, reel 23;

45. COFO News, "ASCS Elections to Be Boycotted by Madison County Negroes," May 2, 1965, Hillegas Collection.

46. Press release, Medical Committee for Human Rights—Mississippi Project, "Nationally Prominent Doctors Form Mississippi Project," July 12, 1964; "Special Report: Medical Committee for Human Rights," undated; Alvin F. Poussaint to James Quigley, Sept. 10, 1965, SNCC Papers, reel 68.

47. R. Hunter Morey, "Proposal for a SNCC Legal Committee," Oct. 9, 1964; Henry Schwarzschild to R. Hunter Morey, Feb. 15, 1965, Morey Papers; Frank R. Parker, *Black Votes Count: Political Empowerment in Mississippi after 1965* (Chapel Hill: University of North Carolina Press, 1990), 80–82. Parker was one of the outstanding attorneys working in Mississippi. His book is the definitive account of the legal history of the movement in Mississippi after 1964.

48. Parker, *Black Votes Count,* 80–82; memorandum, "To: COFO Staff, From: Henry Aronson," undated, Morey Papers.

49. Bruce Hilton, *The Delta Ministry* (New York: Macmillan, 1969), 13–17; "Delta Ministry Fact Sheet," January 1965, Bowie Papers; Owen Brooks, interviewed by Tom Dent, Aug. 18, 1978, Greenville, Miss., Dent Collection. For an excellent scholary treatment of the work of the Delta Ministry, see James F. Findlay, Jr., *Church People in the Struggle: The National Council of Churches and the Black Freedom Movement, 1950–1970* (New York: Oxford University Press, 1993).

Chapter 15: The Collapse of the COFO Coalition

1. Jack Minnis to Bob Moses, July 9, 1964, Carson Collection; J. Francis Polhaus, "Memorandum on the Possibility of Unseating the Mississippi Congressional Delegation," quoted in Denton L. Watson, *Lion in the Lobby: Clarence Mitchell, Jr.'s Struggle for the Passage of Civil Rights Laws* (New York: Morrow, 1990) 280; Richard Rovere, "Letter from Washington," *New Yorker,* Oct. 16, 1965, 240; Steven F. Lawson, *Black Ballots: Voting Rights in the South, 1944–1969* (New York: Columbia University Press, 1976), 641–42. At the urging of the national NAACP office, Aaron Henry, who had also run for Congress in the 1964 freedom vote, withdrew from the congressional challenge.

2. Lawrence Guyot and Michael Thelwell, "Toward Independent Political Power," *Freedomways* 6 (Third Quarter, 1966): 247; statement, Martin Luther King, press conference, Dec. 17, 1964, SCLC Papers, 126: 18; Marvin Rich to Dave Dennis, Jan. 11, 1965, CORE Papers, Addendum, reel 22.

3. Leon Shull, national director, ADA, to national officers, national board, chapter chairmen, Dec. 19, 1964, copy in SNCC Papers, reel 63; "Memorandum to: Presidents of Branches, Youth Councils, College Chapters and State Conferences, from: John Morsell, Assistant Executive Director, re: Challenge to Mississippi Congressmen, March 22, 1965, NAACP Papers; *NYT,* Jan. 1, 1965; Rovere, "Letter from Washington," 240–41. See also Len Holt, *The Summer That Didn't End* (New York: Morrow, 1965), 348–49, and Michael Thelwell to "Fellow Worker for the Challenge," Dec. 24, 1964, copy in Harry Bowie Papers, SHSW.

4. Morton Stavis, "A Century of Struggle for Black Enfranchisement in Mississippi: From the Civil War to the Congressional Challenge of 1965—and Beyond," *Mississippi Law Journal* 57 (1987): 640–45; Guyot and Thelwell, "Toward Independent Political Power," 246–47; *NYT,* Jan. 5, 1965. See also Lawson, *Black Ballots,* 322–28, and Leslie Burl McLemore, "The Mississippi Freedom Democratic Party: A Case Study of Grass-Roots Politics" (Ph.D. diss., University of Massachusetts, 1971), chap. 4.

5. *NYT,* Jan. 6, 1965; *Washington Post,* Jan. 8, 1965; *JDN,* Jan. 14, 1965.

6. Stavis, "Century of Struggle," 647; *NYT,* Feb. 13, 1965; telephone conversation with Marshall Ganz, Aug. 26, 1993.

7. *JDN* , Feb. 10, 1965; *NYT,* Feb. 4, 1965; Stavis, "Century of Struggle," 648–51.

8. Jack Newfield, "The Liberals' Big Stick: Ready for SNCC?" *Cavalier,* June 1965, 33; memorandum, Current to Wilkins, "Problems for Association, Mississippi," Nov. 5, 1964, NAACP Papers.

9. "Remarks of Gloster Current at Mississippi State Conference of NAACP, Nov. 11, 1974; memorandum, Gloster Current to "All Mississippi Branch Presidents," April 19, 1965, NAACP Papers. The national NAACP board finally took up the state NAACP request at its April 1965 meeting, where it decided that since the national board had never formally approved the Mississippi NAACP's affiliation with COFO, it could not officially sanction its withdrawal. The board did state that "the NAACP has had a long established policy against continuing any permanent affiliation of any kind with organizations over which the NAACP exercised no formal control" (ibid.). Perhaps the reason for the delay (and the "neutral" statement at the April meeting) was that, sensitive to charges that it had directed the state NAACP to request the withdrawal, the national office now wanted to appear to be above the fray.

10. "Memorandum, Gloster Current to Roy Wilkins, Bishop Stephen G. Spottswood, Members of the Board Re: NAACP Withdrawal from COFO," Dec. 29, 1964, NAACP Papers.

11. "Minutes of the COFO Convention, March 7, 1965," Archives of Labor and History and Urban Affairs, Wayne State University.

12. "Mr. Current called from New Orleans, March 6," notes on telephone conversation, NAACP Papers.

13. Minutes, SNCC executive committee meeting, Atlanta, March 6, 1965; Holly Springs, April 12–14, 1965, Carson Collection; "Meeting of Civil Rights Workers—Tougaloo College," July 27, 1965, Nick Fischer Papers, SHSW; Gwen Robinson to "Dear Friends," Sept. 1, 1965, Hillegas Collection.

14. Interview with Bob Moses.

15. *NYT,* June 15, 1965.

16. Ibid.

17. Ibid.; John Doar to Senator Daniel Brewster, Aug. 9, 1965, HU2/ST24, general file, LBJ; WATS report, June 16, 1965, SNCC Papers, reel 16.

18. Ed King interview, Howard CRDP, 7; SNCC press release, "Brutality in Jackson," June 18, 1965, Hillegas Collection.

19. *NYT,* June 23, 1965; "ACTION MEMO to: Friends of SCEF, from: Anne Braden," July 1965, Hillegas Collection.

20. SNCC press release, "MFDP Calls for Help," June 18, 1965, UCLA, box 3; *NYT,* June 19, 1965. Among those taken to the stockade that day was five-year-old Anthony Quin, son of Mrs. Aylene Quin, whose home in McComb the Klan had bombed nine months earlier. Part of a small group picketing outside the governor's mansion, Anthony was carrying an American flag. As a squad of police moved in to arrest the demonstrators, police officer Huey Krohn (a driver for Governor Paul Johnson) approached

the boy and demanded the flag. Anthony held on. SNCC photographer Matt Herron was at the scene and took a photograph that captured the essence of the Mississippi freedom struggle: a burly white policeman wrestling with a five-year-old boy for possession of the American flag. Unable to claim his prize, Officer Krohn broke the flagstick and hauled Anthony Quin off to jail, along with his mother and nine-year-old sister; *NYT,* June 19, 1965.

21. Doar to Brewster; WATS report, June 24, 1965; *NYT,* June 30, July 1, 1965.

22. *C-L,* July 19, 1965.

23. Ed King, interviewed by Anne Romaine, August 1965, 9–10, Romaine Papers.

24. *C-L,* July 19, 1965; "The Mississippi Democratic Conference—Naked Grab for Power—Attempt to Kill FDP," in "A Call for Support," Hunter Morey Papers, SHSW; Mississippi Freedom Democratic party *Newsletter,* July 28, 1965, SNCC Papers, reel 69; *New York Herald-Tribune,* Aug. 9, 1965, clipping in Ed King Papers; Rowland Evans and Robert Novak, "Inside Report: The Mississippi Moderates," Aug. 9, 1965, clipping in Ed King Papers; William Simpson, "The Birth of the Mississippi 'Loyalist Democrats' (1965–1968)," *Journal of Mississippi History* 44 (Feb. 1982): 28–29.

25. R. Spencer Oliver to Mrs. Murnett Y. Washington, March 26, 1965; Elmer Cooper, untitled report on the Mississippi Young Democrats' convention, Sept. 6, 1965, Morey Papers; Wilson F. Minor, unedited news story for the New Orleans *Times-Picayune,* Wilson F. Minor Papers; McLemore, "MFDP," 414.

26. McLemore, "MFDP," 414; Minor, unedited news story.

27. Interview with Douglas Wynn, Dec. 4, 1984, Greenville, Miss.

28. MFDP *Newsletter,* July 28, 1965, SNCC Papers, reel 69; Joanne Grant, ed., *Black Protest: History, Documents, and Analyses, 1619 to the Present* (Greenwich, Conn.: Fawcett, 1968), 415–16; McLemore, "MFDP," 234–38.

29. MFDP news release, "MFDP and Vietnam," July 31, 1965, Hillegas Collection; *NYT,* Aug. 4, 1965.

30. *Delta Democrat-Times,* Aug. 8, 1965; Mississippi AFL-CIO news release, "Statement by: Claude Ramsey, President," Aug. 2, 1965, Eugene Cox Papers, box 1.

31. Steven F. Lawson, *In Pursuit of Power: Southern Blacks & Electoral Politics, 1965–1982* (New York: Columbia University Press, 1985), 14–15.

32. *NYT,* Sept. 14–18, 1965; "Contested Elections in the First, Second, Third, Fourth, and Fifth Districts of the State of Mississippi," in *Hearings before the Subcommittee on Elections of the Committee on House Administration, House of Representatives, First Session, September 13 and 14, 1965* (Washington: GPO, 1965).

33. *Southern Patriot,* Nov. 1965.

34. Minutes of SNCC staff meeting, Atlanta, Nov. 24–29, 1964, 13,

Carson Collection; Moses interview; Michael Thelwell, remarks at Civil Rights and Black Power session, Freedom Summer Reviewed conference, Nov. 1, 1979, Jackson, Miss., Mississippi Archives.

35. SNCC press release, "Natchez, Mississippi Background Report," Nov. 8, 1965; statement by Dorie Ladner, SNCC Papers, reel 65.

36. Paul Lauter and Florence Howe, unpublished manuscript, 3–4. Professors Lauter and Howe came to Mississippi in July 1965 to lead discussion groups for summer volunteers. I am grateful to Professor Lauter for making their account of the Natchez movement available to me. Jim Kates to "Dear People," July 21, 1965; SNCC press release, "Negro Ministers Refuse to Open Doors of Church," June 5, 1965, Hillegas Collection; interview with Dorie Ladner, May 10, 1985, Washington, D.C.

37. Interview with Bruce Payne; Charles McDew, Howard CRDP interview, 130; *Hearings in Jackson, Miss. before the United States Commission on Civil Rights, Feb. 16–20, 1965,* vol. 2 (Washington: GPO, 1965), 107 (hereinafter cited as *CRC Hearings*); Penny B. to Jeannette King, Aug. 29, 1965, Ed King Papers; *NYT,* Aug. 28, 29, 1965.

38. *NYT,* Aug. 28, 29, 1965; "Natchez Background Report."

39. "A Declaration of the Negro Citizens of Natchez, Mississippi," undated, SNCC Papers, reel 65; *NYT,* Sept. 3, 1965.

40. Memorandum, Current to Wilkins and John Morsell, Oct. 26, 1964; Current to Morsell, Oct. 5, 1964, NAACP Papers; "Memorandum to: The President From: Lee C. White, Aug. 12, 1965, Exec LE/HU2-7, PU2-2, LBJ; "Memorandum to Mr. Wilkins from Gloster Current," Aug. 13, 1965, NAACP Papers.

41. *NYT,* Sept. 3, 1965; "Natchez Background Report; Ladner interview.

42. Telegram, Charles Evers to Martin Luther King, Sept. 2, 1965, MLK Papers, 10:7; Mark Lundeen, "Excerpts from a Journal with Few Entries, Natchez, 9/16/65–12/10/65," Art Thomas Papers, box 2, MLK.

43. Charles Horwitz, "Natchez, Mississippi—Six Weeks of Crisis," 1–4, SNCC Papers, reel 40; "Natchez Background Report."

44. "Telephone Report from Stoney Cooks, Natchez, Mississippi, September 27, 1965, 11:30 P.M.," SCLC Papers, 146:24; David Garrow, *Bearing the Cross: Martin Luther King, Jr., and the Southern Christian Leadership Conference* (New York: Morrow, 1986), 446; "Mississippi Direct Action Staff," Oct. 13, 1965, SCLC Papers, 146:24.

45. Cooks, "Telephone Report"; Horwitz, "Natchez"; Garrow, *Bearing,* 446.

46. Memorandum, Current to John Morsell, Oct. 5, 1965, NAACP Papers; "Memo to Friends of SNCC," Oct. 6, 1965, SNCC Papers, reel 40; Horwitz, "Natchez," 4–6; statement by Posey Lombard, in Horwitz, "Natchez," 5; *NYT,* Oct. 8, 9, 1965.

47. *CRC Hearings,* 109, 111, 157; *NYT,* Oct. 13, 14, 17, 24, 31, 1965; *Louisville Times,* Nov. 4, 1965, clipping in Ed King Papers; Horwitz, "Natchez," 4–7; NAACP press release, "Natchez Backs Down on Agreement with NAACP," Oct. 16, 1965, NAACP Papers.

48. Memorandum, Gloster Current to Dr. John Morsell, Oct. 5, 1965, NAACP Papers; Garrow, *Bearing,* 450.

49. Jackson WATS report, Oct. 27, 1965; Ladner interview.

50. Jackson WATS report, Oct. 27, 1965; Ladner interview. Evers later admitted that he was part-owner of a Natchez grocery but claimed that "the store is not being used for my personal gain" (Evers to Wilkins, March 28, 1966, NAACP Papers).

51. Memorandum from Current to Wilkins and others, Nov. 30, 1965; NAACP press release, "An Agreement between the City of Natchez, Miss., and the City's Negro Community," undated, NAACP Papers.

52. Lundeen, "Excerpts from a Journal"; Jackson WATS report, Dec. 1, 1965; *NYT,* Dec. 4, 1965; "Boycott Ends, Negroes Call it Victory," undated Associated Press story, clipping in Ed King Papers; "Memorandum from Henry Lee Moon to Editorial Writers and Columnists," Dec. 8, 1965, NAACP Papers.

53. Lundeen "Excerpts from a Journal."

54. Jackson WATS report, Dec. 2, 1965; undated, untitled FDP leaflet, SNCC Papers, reel 65; *NYT,* Dec. 24, 1965; Lundeen, "Excerpts from a Journal."

Chapter 16: CDGM and the Politics of Poverty

1. James T. Patterson, *America's Struggle Against Poverty: 1900–1985* (Cambridge, Mass.: Harvard University Press, 1986), 142–47. For a highly critical evaluation of the Great Society programs, see Allen J. Matusow, *The Unraveling of America: A History of Liberalism in the 1960s* (New York: Harper & Row, 1984), chaps. 8 and 9.

2. SNCC, "Running Summary of Events," undated, Carson Collection; "Shaw, Mississippi: Sounds in the Delta," Carson Collection; *Newsweek,* June 21, 1965, 33–34; Bruce Hilton, *The Delta Ministry* (London: Macmillan, 1969), 68–76; "Mississippi Freedom Labor Union, report from George Shelton, State Chairman," Lisa Vogel Papers, SHSW.

3. Shelton, "Mississippi Freedom Labor Union"; "Minutes of Statewide Meeting-MFLU-September 4," Vogel Papers.

4. Hodding Carter III, "Negro Exodus from the Delta Continues," *New York Times Magazine,* March 10, 1968, 26.

5. "Panola County Okra Co-op," reprint, undated, from *Vicksburg Citizen Appeal,* Hillegas Collection; *Milwaukee Journal,* Dec. 26, 1965, clipping in Hillegas Collection; interview with Owen Brooks; "The North Bolivar County Farm Cooperative," undated report in Lee Bankhead Papers, SHSW; Danny Collum, "Stepping Out into Freedom," *Sojourners,* Dec. 1982, 15.

6. "The Poor People's Corporation," undated fact sheet; "Cooperative Self-Employment Enterprises . . . May 1965 Through July, 1966," Poor People's Corporation Papers, SHSW.

7. PPC, "Reports from Centers," May-June 1966; Jesse Morris to Milton Heimlich, undated, PPC Papers; *Wall Street Journal,* Aug. 19, 1966.

8. SNCC Communications, "Chronology of Events at the Greenville Air Force Base," XI, box 52, UCLA; Hilton, *Delta Ministry,* 87–91; no author, "Why We Are Here at the Greenville Air Force Base," undated, copy in Braden Papers, SHSW.

9. James C. Cobb, "'Somebody Done Nailed Us on the Cross': Federal Agricultural and Welfare Policy and the Civil Rights Movement in the Mississippi Delta," paper delivered at the annual meeting of the Organization of American Historians, April 1991. Cobb's *The Most Southern Place on Earth: The Mississippi Delta and the Roots of Regional Identity* (New York: Oxford University Press, 1992) is a fascinating historical account of the relationship between politics and economics in the Delta. Leon Howell, *Freedom City: The Substance of Things Hoped For* (Richmond, Va.: Knox, 1969), 27–29; Owen Brooks, interviewed by Robert Wright, Sept. 24, 1968, Greenville, Miss., 31, Howard CRDP; Hilton, *Delta Ministry,* 85–87.

10. "Chronology of Events"; Hilton, *Delta Ministry,* 90, 94, 99.

11. "Chronology of Events"; Hilton, *Delta Ministry,* 103.

12. Nicholas Katzenbach, "Memorandum for the President: Civil Rights, Mississippi," Feb. 14, 1966, Ex HU 2/ST 24, AG7, WE 9, LBJ.

13. Harry C. McPherson, memorandum "For the President," McPherson Papers; Wilbur J. Cohen, "Memorandum for the Honorable Jake Jacobsen," July 6, 1966, Ex HU 2/ST 24, WE 9, LBJ; "To: Files. From: Marian E. Wright. Re: Greenville Air Force Base," Aug. 1, 1966, Delta Ministry Papers, box 24, MLK. Two years later the contending parties agreed that the Mississippi Research and Development Center, with support from the Ford Foundation, would operate a program on the base providing a modest job-training program, along with housing for one hundred families. As for the families who had "invaded" the air force base, for five months they drifted from one temporary location to another. Then, after an anonymous donor provided land near Greenville, "Freedom City" became their new home, with houses eventually built for a few of the families.

14. Citizens' Crusade Against Poverty, Board of Inquiry, "Final Report on the Child Development Group of Mississippi," 6, copy in MLK Papers, 6:4; *NYT,* Oct. 19, 1966.

15. Polly Greenberg, *And the Devil Wore Slippery Shoes: A Biased Biography of the Child Development Group of Mississippi* (London: Macmillan, 1969), 3–4, 31 (hereinafter cited as Greenberg, *CDGM*); Office of Economic Opportunity, *Administrative History,* vol.1, part 1, 66–67.

16. Greenberg, *CDGM,* 23–24; Tom Levin to Stokely Carmichael, Dec. 15, 1965, Tom Levin Papers, box 9, MLK; Hollis Watkins, Howard CRDP interview, 42–43; memorandum, Bob Clampitt to Bill Haddad, July 1, 1965, "Records of Agencies for Economic Opportunity and Legal Services, OEO, Inspection Division, Inspection Reports, 1964–67, Head Start: Mississippi," RG 381, box 108, National Archives (hereinafter cited as OEO Archives).

17. Greenberg, *CDGM,* 46; Levin to Carmichael; Southern Reporting

Service, "Mississippi Action for Community Education," July 12, 1965, XI, box 8, UCLA; Andrew Kopkind, "Bureaucracy's Long Arm: Too Heady a Start in Mississippi?" *New Republic,* Aug. 21, 1965, 19–22; memorandum, Gloster Current to Roy Wilkins and Dr. John Morsell, June 15, 1965, NAACP Papers.

18. Citizens' Crusade, "Final Report," 15; *JDN,* May 21, June 26, 1965; "Anguilla: Reported by Jim Dann," Levin Papers, box 1; "Memorandum: Gordon Wilcox to Harassment File," July 25, 1965, OEO Archives, box 108; Kopkind, "Bureaucracy's Long Arm," 20.

19. Memorandum, Ivan Scott to Bill Haddad, June 25, 1965, OEO Archives, box 108; Paul Johnson to Sargent Shriver, June 29, 1965, Gen WE 9-1, 11/22/63–7/16/65, LBJ; no author, "Re: Project Head Start, July 12, 1965"; Erle Johnston, Jr., to William Spell, July 13, 1965, files of the Mississippi State Sovereignty Commission, in the Paul B. Johnson Collection, University of Southern Mississippi Archives (hereinafter cited as Sovereignty Commission files); Erle Johnston, *Mississippi's Defiant Years, 1953–1973: An Interpretive Documentary with Personal Experiences* (Forest, Miss.: Lake Harbor, 1990), 285–86; *JDN,* Aug. 13, 1965; Joann Bowman, "I Am a Budgetary Anachronism," 5, unpublished article, box 5, Levin Papers.

20. *JDN,* July 27, Aug. 13, 1965; Bowman, "I Am," 6, 9; Jule Sugarman, interviewed by Stephen Goodell, March 14, 1969, 29, 30, LBJ.

21. OEO, *Administrative History,* 67–68; Sugarman, interviewed by Goodell, 29; Bowman, "I Am," 9; Greenberg, *CDGM,* 259–75.

22. Greenberg, *CDGM,* 192, 178.

23. Polly Greenberg, "Evaluation of the CDGM Program for Children, Teachers, Parents and Communities," 27, 28, 30, box 3, Levin Papers; Greenberg, *CDGM,* 179, 241.

24. Southern Reporting Service, "Mississippi Action," 2; Unita Blackwell testimony, *Examination of the War on Poverty, Hearings before the Subcommittee on Employment, Manpower, and Poverty of the Committee on Labor and Public Welfare, U.S. Senate,* 90th Congress, First Session, part 2, Jackson, Miss., April 20, 1967 (Washington: GPO, 1967), 585.

25. Greenberg, *CDGM,* 277, 281–88, 329–33; Kopkind, "Bureaucracy's Long Arm," 22. Shortly after his removal Levin told a friend that the CDGM experience was "like a passage out of an undiscovered Kafka manuscript"; Levin to William Haddad, Sept. 7, 1965, Levin Papers, box 3.

26. *C-L,* Oct. 25, 1965; Bowman, "I Am," 9–10.

27. Greenberg, *CDGM,* 367; OEO, *Administrative History,* 70; Sugarman, interviewed by Goodell, 30; Greenberg, *CDGM,* 356–59; Larold K. Schulz, "The CDGM Story," *Christianity and Crisis,* Jan. 23, 1967, 318.

28. Greenberg, *CDGM,* 440; memorandum from Edgar May, "Subject: CDGM," Feb. 9, 1966, OEO Archives, box 109; Greenberg, *CDGM,* 445; *NYT,* Feb. 12, 1966;

29. *NYT,* March 7, 1966; *JDN,* Feb. 24, 1966.

30. Marvin Hoffman and John Mudd, "The New Plantations," *Nation,* Oct. 24, 1966, 411–12; Christopher Jencks, "Accommodating Whites," *New Republic,* April 16, 1966, 21–22.

31. Willie Peacock, Jackson WATS report, Nov. 20, 1965; Freedom Information Service, "Radio News Script," Nov. 13, 1965, Hillegas Collection; Fannie Lou Hamer, quoted in "Notes from Poverty Hearings in Jackson, Miss.," April 10, 1967, author unidentified, Hillegas Collection.

32. Jencks, "Accommodating Whites," 22; Robert Analavage, "Bolivar Head Start Not Funded," *Southern Patriot,* April 1966; telegram, Bolivar County Association of Communities to Sargent Shriver, Frank Sloan, and John Dean, undated, Amzie Moore Papers; *Delta Democrat-Times,* March 7, 1966.

33. Memorandum, Tom Heller to Jack Gonzales, "Re: CDGM and Black Power," undated, OEO Archives, box 107; Douglas Wynn to Harry McPherson, April 2, 1966, Harry McPherson Papers, LBJ.

34. Greenberg, *CDGM,* 584–85; OEO, *Administrative History,* 72–73. By the spring of 1967 CAP agencies were running Head Start programs in thirty-four Mississippi counties *(Examination of the War on Poverty,* 758–59).

35. Paul J. Cotter to Senators Hayden, Stennis, Pastore, Aug. 5, 1966, OEO Archives, box 108.

36. Interview with Hodding Carter III, May 6, 1985, Washington, D.C.

37. Pat Watters, "Mississippi: Children and Politics," *Dissent* 14 (May-June 1967): 299; *JDN,* Sept. 30, 1966; Greenberg, *CDGM,* 601.

38. Mississippi Freedom Democratic party, "What Is M.A.P.?" undated leaflet in Amzie Moore Papers; "Information on Mississippi Action for Progress: Who Are Their Board Members, What Are Their Ties?" undated, unsigned, Levin Papers, box 3.

39. OEO, *Administrative History,* 76–77; Marvin Hoffman, "The Lord, He Works in Mysterious Ways," *New South* 24 (Summer 1969): 9; Mississippi State Sovereignty Commission, "Report on Mississippi State Sovereignty Commission (1964–1967)," 10, copy in Ed King Papers; Johnston, *Defiant Years,* 290.

40. Greenberg, *CDGM,* 635–36; Watters, "Children and Politics," 300–301; Citizens' Crusade, "Final Report," 18; OEO, *Administrative History,* 78; Sugarman, interviewed by Goodell, 34.

41. Watters, "Children and Politics," 301; Citizens' Crusade, "Final Report," 21.

42. *NYT,* Oct. 19, 1966; Sugarman, interviewed by Goodell, 34–35; OEO, *Administrative History,* 85; Greenberg, *CDGM,* 655. Jule Sugarman believed that "there was a call from the White House that was influential in leading us to refund CDGM"; Sugarman, interviewed by Goodell, 35.

43. Hoffman, "The Lord," 17–18; Greenberg, *CDGM,* 665–66; Sugarman, interviewed by Goodell, 36–37; OEO press release, "CDGM to Continue Head Start in Mississippi," Dec. 16, 1966, Ex WE 9 10/13/66–12/13/66, LBJ.

44. Hoffman, "The Lord," 18.

45. Marvin Hoffman, "Negro-White Relations in CDGM," undated, 68–92, copy in John Mudd Papers, Davenport, N.Y. (I am grateful to Professor James Findlay for calling the Hoffman essay to my attention.) Annie Devine, interviewed by Tom Dent.

46. Greenberg, *CDGM,* 632; OEO, "Inspection Evaluation," April 1968, OEO Archives, box 109; *Washington Post,* July 10, 1967. Fannie Lou Hamer, "To Praise Our Bridges," in Dorothy Abbott, ed., *Mississippi Writers: Reflections of Childhood and Youth—vol. II: Nonfiction* (Jackson: University Press of Mississippi, 1986), 327. See also Tony Dunbar, *Our Land Too* (New York: Pantheon, 1971), chap. 7.

47. James Gaither to Harry McPherson, April 22, 1968, McPherson Papers, LBJ; *Washington Post,* July 10, 1967; McPherson to Morris Abram, Feb. 19, 1968, McPherson Papers; *Delta Democrat-Times,* Nov. 15, 1967.

48. New Orleans *Times-Picayune,* April 11, 1967; *NYT,* April 11, 1967.

49. *NYT,* June 16, 1967; "Children in Mississippi: Statement of the United States Subcommittee on Manpower and Development," July 11, 1967, 3–4, copy in Hillegas Collection; testimony of Dr. Raymond M. Wheeler, in *Hearings Before the Subcommittee of Employment, Manpower and Poverty of the Committee on Labor and Public Welfare on Hunger and Malnutrition in America,* U.S. Senate, 90th Congress, First Session, July 11, 12, 1967 (Washington: GPO, 1967), 9 (hereinafter cited as *Hunger and Malnutrition*). Four of the six physicians taught at Harvard, Yale, or MIT. The other two were southerners: Dr. Wheeler and Dr. Cyril Walwyn, a black Mississippian who practiced in Yazoo City.

50. Johnson, quoted in Hilton, *Delta Ministry,* 77; press release, Governor Paul Johnson, Aug. 4, 1967, copy in Wilson Minor Papers; *NYT,* Feb. 18, 1969.

51. Cobb, *The Most Southern Place,* 186–93; U.S. Dept. of Agriculture, Agricultural Stabilization and Conservation Service, *1966 Upland Cotton Domestic Allotment Program, Statistical Summary* (Washington: GPO, 1966), 14; Cobb, "Somebody," 11, 15; *C-L,* June 21, 1967.

52. Cobb, *The Most Southern Place,* 259; Cobb, "Somebody," 11.

53. Cobb, *The Most Southern Place,* 256; Lisle Carter to Lawrence Levison, April 17, 1967, McPherson Papers; Nicholas Lemann, *The Promised Land: The Great Migration and How It Changed America* (New York: Knopf, 1991), 318–19.

54. "Children in Mississippi," 7.

55. "Status Report: Federal Food Assistance Programs in Mississippi," June 1967; Bertrand M. Harding to Thomas Gaither, Aug. 15, 1967, McPherson Papers; Raymond Wheeler to William C. Smith, Aug. 16, 1967, in *Hunger and Malnutrition,* 240–41; Laura M. Engle to J. Francis Polhaus, March 20, 1967, NAACP Papers, Washington branch; Dunbar, *Our Land Too,* chap. 8.

56. Subcommittee on Employment, Manpower and Poverty to the president, April 27, 1967; James Gaither, undated handwritten notes, McPherson Papers; Cobb, "Somebody," 24; "Federal Food Assistance Programs"; Whitten, quoted in Nick Kotz, *Let Them Eat Promises: The*

Politics of Hunger in America (Garden City, N.Y.: Doubleday-Anchor, 1971), 92.

57. Carter to Levinson; Lisle Carter to Thomas Gaither, Aug. 15, 1967, McPherson Papers; Wheeler testimony in *Hunger and Malnutrition,* 10.

58. Dr. Cyril Walwyn, testimony in *Hunger and Malnutrition,* 37; Dr. Raymond Wheeler, ibid., 9; Dr. Joseph Brenner, ibid., 14–15; *NYT,* July 31, 1967; Dr. A. B. Britton, testimony in *Examination of the War on Poverty,* 560.

59. Wheeler, testimony in *Hunger and Malnutrition,* 11; Eastland, ibid., 64.

60. *C-L,* Feb. 25, 1966; New Orleans *Times-Picayune,* April 11, 1967. From 1960 to 1965 more than 60,000 blacks between the ages of fifteen and forty-four left the state. In the year 1967 alone the Delta experienced a net outmigration of about 12,000 people, the vast majority of them black; see *Hunger and Malnutrition,* 280, 339; Cobb, *The Most Southern Place,* 256.

Chapter 17: The Last March

1. *NYT,* June 1, 5, 6, 1966.

2. Interview with Owen Brooks, Jan. 18, 1992, Greenville, Miss.; Gloster Current to Charles Evers, Aug. 5, 1966, NAACP Papers; Douglas Wynn to Hubert Humphrey, Nov. 29, Dec. 7, 1965, name file, Douglas Wynn, LBJ.

3. HEW school desegregation chart, May 2, 1966, EX HU 2-5/ST 24, 4/1/66–5/3/66, box 50, LBJ; Mississippi NAACP annual report, 1966, 7, NAACP Papers; telegram, Constance Curry to President Johnson, Jan. 19, 1966, Gen HU 2-5/ST 24, box 54, LBJ; Lawrence Guyot to President Johnson, Nov. 10, 1965, ibid.

4. Steven F. Lawson, *In Pursuit of Power: Southern Blacks and Electoral Politics, 1965–1982* (New York: Columbia University Press, 1985), 14–15; Lawson, *Black Ballots: Voting Rights in the South, 1944–1969* (New York: Columbia University Press, 1976), 334–35.

5. J. Metz Rollins, Jr., "A Report on CORAR on Dahmer's Death," undated, copy in Arthur Thomas Papers, MLK; Don Whitehead, *Attack on Terror: The FBI Against the Ku Klux Klan in Mississippi* (New York: Funk & Wagnalls, 1970), 235–37; *NYT,* Jan. 11, 1966; *C-L,* March 28, 1968. Two years later sixteen klansmen, all but one from Laurel, were charged with Dahmer's murder, and four were convicted. Klan leader Sam Bowers was tried twice for his role in the attack, but both trials ended in hung juries. *C-L,* March 28, 1968; Erle Johnston, *Mississippi's Defiant Years: 1953–1973* (Forrest, Miss.: Lake Harbor, 1990), 364.

6. Lawson, *Pursuit,* 66.

7. *NYT,* June 7, 1967.

8. Ibid.; *Memphis Press-Scimitar,* June 7, 1966.

9. Clayborne Carson, *In Struggle: SNCC and the Black Awakening of*

the 1960s (Cambridge, Mass.: Harvard University Press, 1981), 203–7; Carmichael, quoted in minutes of SNCC executive committee meeting, Atlanta, June 10, 1968, Carson Collection.

10. Milton Viorst, *Fire in the Streets: America in the 1960s* (New York: Simon & Schuster, 1979), 372.

11. David Garrow, *Bearing the Cross: Martin Luther King, Jr., and the Southern Christian Leadership Conference* (New York: Morrow, 1985), 477–78; Carson, *In Struggle,* 207–8.

12. *NYT,* June 9, 1966; "Mississippi and the NAACP," *Crisis,* July 1966, 315–17; Roy Wilkins, "Memorandum to NAACP Directors on Meredith March," June 10, 1964, NAACP Papers.

13. Interview with Lawrence Guyot, May 22, 1989, Washington, D.C.; interview with Owen Brooks; *NYT,* June 10, 1966; Leslie McLemore, "The Mississippi Freedom Democratic Party: A Case Study in Grass-Roots Politics" (Ph.D. diss., University of Massachusetts, 1971), 311; "Report on a Board meeting of Community Organizers in Mississippi," Oct. 29, 1966, Hillegas Collection; *NYT,* June 8, 1966; McLemore, "MFDP," 312–14.

14. Owen Brooks, Howard CRDP interview, 37; interview with Brooks; *NYT,* June 12, 1966. For documentary coverage of the Canton violence, see "Eyes on the Prize," second series, program 1, "The Time Has Come (1964–1974)," video, Blackside.

15. *NYT,* June 16, 1966; June 6–14, 1966; Lawson, *Pursuit,* 55–56.

16. *NYT,* June 15, 16, 17, 1966; Lawson, *Pursuit,* 56; Garrow, *Bearing,* 480–81.

17. *NYT,* June 17, 1966; *National Observer,* June 20, 1966.

18. Carmichael interview in "The Time Has Come"; SNCC executive committee minutes, June 10, 1966.

19. *NYT,* June 17, 1966.

20. Garrow, *Bearing,* 482; *NYT,* June 21, 1966; Paul Good, *The Trouble I've Seen: White Journalist/Black Movement* (Washington, D.C.: Howard University Press, 1975), 258–59; *Life,* July 22, 1966, 7.

21. *NYT,* June 20, 21, 1966; Good, *Trouble,* 260; Florence Mars, *Witness in Philadelphia* (Baton Rouge: Louisiana State University Press, 1977), 206–10; Garrow, *Bearing,* 483; interview with Owen Brooks.

22. *NYT,* June 21, 1966; telegram, Johnson to King, June 23, 1966, Ex HU 2-7/ST 24, LBJ. On Friday, June 23, King and Carmichael and three hundred other supporters held a successful rally in Philadelphia. This time the Mississippi Highway Patrol was out in force, preventing any major outbreaks of violence; *NYT,* June 24, 1966.

23. *NYT,* June 24, 1966. Chinn was tried and found guilty in October 1966, but he was granted a new trial by the Mississippi Supreme Court in 1968. In September 1970, while he was still under indictment on the earlier charge, a Madison County jury found Chinn guilty of manslaughter in connection with the death of a black man, and he served time in Parchman penitentiary before being released in the late 1970s; *C-L,* Oct. 13, 1966; *Delta Democrat-Times,* Sept. 30, 1970.

24. Good, *Trouble,* 260–61; unidentified CDGM worker, quoted in Polly Greenberg, *And the Devil Wore Slippery Shoes: A Biased Biography of the Child Development Group of Mississippi* (New York: Macmillan, 1969), 650–51; Dr. Alvin Poussaint, interviewed by Peter Kanter, May 11, 1982, Cambridge, Mass., tape copy in my possession; *NYT,* June 24, 1966.

25. Poussaint, interview with Kanter; *NYT,* June 24, 1966; *Bearing,* 486; Lawson, *Pursuit,* 60–61.

26. *NYT,* June 25, 1966; memorandum, McPherson to Johnson, June 25, 1966, McPherson files, box 22; Good, *Trouble,* 261.

27. *NYT,* June 25, 26, 1966.

28. Ibid., June 26, 28, 1966; Garrow, *Bearing,* 487.

29. *NYT,* June 27, 1966.

30. Ibid.; interview with Owen Brooks.

31. Good, *Trouble,* 254–59.

32. Unnamed Sovereignty Commission informant, June 26, 1966, Sovereignty Comission files; *NYT,* June 28, 1966.

33. *C-L,* July 22, 1966; *Southern Patriot,* Aug. 1966; *Newsweek,* July 25, 1966, 29–30; unnamed Sovereignty Commission informant, July 14, 1966, Sovereignty Commission files; *Memphis Press–Scimitar,* July 9, 10, 12, 1966. All published references are clippings from the Grenada file in the Eugene Cox Papers, box 1, Mississippi State University Library.

34. *Southern Patriot,* Aug., 1966; *Newsweek,* July 25, 1966, 29–30; *Memphis Press-Scimitar,* July 11, 12, 13, 1966; Leon Hall to executive committee, SCLC, Aug. 21, 1967, SCLC Papers, 47:15; Garrow, *Bearing,* 531; Memphis *Commercial Appeal,* Sept. 15, 1966.

35. Ibid., Sept. 13, 14, 1966; *Memphis Press-Scimitar,* Sept. 13, 14, 1966; *C-L,* Sept. 13, 14, 1966.

36. *C-L,* Sept. 13, 14, 1966.

37. Memphis *Commercial Appeal,* Sept. 13, 14, 15, 1966; *Memphis Press-Scimitar,* Sept. 13, 14, 1966; *C-L,* Sept. 13, 14, 1966; Goodman quoted in *Press-Scimitar,* Sept. 13, 1966; *Newsweek,* Sept. 26, 1966, 34; "Their Struggle Is Ours Too: The Grenada Story," Operation Freedom fund-raising brochure, copy in Cox Papers.

38. Memphis *Commercial Appeal,* Sept. 13, 14, 15, 1966; *Memphis Press-Scimitar,* Sept. 13, 14, 1966; *C-L,* Sept. 13, 14, 1966; *Newsweek,* Sept. 26, 1966, 34.

39. New Orleans *Times-Picayune,* Sept. 18, 1966; *Memphis Press-Scimitar,* Sept. 13, 1966.

40. *Memphis Press-Scimitar,* Nov. 4, 1966; Garrow, *Bearing,* 531; New Orleans *Times-Picayune,* Sept. 18, 1966; *NYT,* June 7, 1967.

41. *The Christian Century,* editorial, Oct. 5, 1966, clipping in Cox Papers; *C-L,* May 28, 1968.

42. Attorney quoted in Garrow, *Bearing,* 563. In 1968, following the assassination of Dr. Martin Luther King, Congress passed an act providing for federal protection of civil rights workers. The bill also contained an open housing provision, as well as a section providing punishment for agitators who crossed state lines to provoke riots. See Lawson, *Pursuit,* 78–88.

Chapter 18: A New Mississippi?

1. Minutes of SNCC central committee meeting, Knoxville, Tenn., Oct. 22–23, 1966, Carson Collection.

2. Clayborne Carson, *In Struggle: SNCC and the Black Awakening of the 1960s* (Cambridge, Mass.: Harvard University Press, 1981), 239–40; Emily S. Stoper, "The Student Nonviolent Coordinating Committee: The Growth of Radicalism in a Civil Rights Organization" (Ph.D. diss., Harvard University, 1968), 73.

3. Fannie Lou Hamer to Amzie Moore, Oct. 24, 1966; "Report on a Meeting of Community Organizers in Mississippi," Oct. 29, 1966, Amzie Moore Papers, SHSW.

4. Leslie Burl McLemore, "The Mississippi Freedom Democratic Party: A Case Study of Grass-Roots Activism" (Ph.D. diss., University of Massachusetts, 1971) 316–18, 333–34; Freedom Information Service, "Official Vote Tabulation . . . Regular Election, November 8, 1966," quoted in ibid., 335–37. McLemore's dissertation remains the best account of the 1966 elections.

5. "Project Report, Clay County, Mississippi," Nov. 1966, XI, box 24, UCLA.

6. Carson, *In Struggle*, 135; Malcolm X, with the assistance of Alex Haley, *The Autobiography of Malcolm X* (New York: Ballantine, 1973), 426–28; interview with Lawrence Guyot; interview with Owen Brooks. Joyce Ladner's "What Black Power Means to Negroes in Mississippi," in August Meier, ed., *The Transformation of Activism* (Chicago: Aldine, 1970), 131–54, is a persuasive account written by a Mississippi activist-scholar.

7. Brooks interview. For the work of the Delta Ministry in the late 1960s, see James F. Findlay, Jr., *Church People in the Struggle: The National Council of Churches and the Black Freedom Movement, 1950–1970* (New York: Oxford University Press, 1993), chap. 5.

8. Sandra Nystrom and Eleanor Holmes Norton, "Times Changing in Sunflower," undated clipping in Braden Papers, SHSW; *Southern Patriot*, May 1967; McLemore, "MFDP," 353–54, 370.

9. *Southern Patriot*, May 1967.

10. Ibid.; Victor Ullman, "In Darkest America," *Nation*, Sept. 4, 1967, 179–80; Nystrom and Norton, "Times Changing"; McLemore, "MFDP," 369; Freedom Information Service, "Mississippi Newsletter," May 5, 1967, Hillegas Collection (hereinafter cited as "Mississippi Newsletter"). See also Steven F. Lawson, *In Pursuit of Power: Southern Blacks & Electoral Politics, 1965–1982* (New York: Columbia University Press, 1985), 99–102. The federal courts also mandated new elections for the Sunflower County town of Moorhead for the same day. The tactics employed by whites, and the results, were the same as for Sunflower.

11. Delta Ministry report on Ben Brown shooting, May 1967, Moore Papers; *Southern Patriot*, June 1967; *JDN*, May 11, 12, 1967.

12. *JDN*, May 16, 1967; Clarice T. Campbell and Oscar Allan Rog-

ers, Jr., *Mississippi: The View from Tougaloo* (Jackson: University Press of Mississippi, 1979), 228–29. After several tense days of confrontation and negotiation, the Tougaloo Student Judiciary Committee (which was originally denied jurisdiction in the case), determined that Slaughter, a senior, would not be permitted to participate in graduation ceremonies. Thompson was placed on social probation for two semesters. Slaughter went on to become an attorney and assistant secretary of state of Mississippi. Thompson pursued a career in electoral politics, culminating in his 1993 election to the U.S. House of Representatives from Mississippi's second congressional district. The two activists later won recognition from Tougaloo officials as distinguished alumni of the college; Campbell and Rogers, *Mississippi*, 228–29.

13. *Washington Post*, May 18, 1967; *Southern Patriot*, June 1967; "Mississippi Newsletter," May 19, 1967.

14. "Mississippians United to Elect Negro Candidates," undated statement signed by Owen Brooks, Lawrence Guyot, Joseph Harris, Charles McLaurin, and Hollis Watkins, copy in Hillegas Collection.

15. Ibid.

16. U.S. Commission on Civil Rights, *Political Participation* (Washington: GPO, 1968), 222–23, 244–47.

17. Frank Parker, *Black Votes Count: Political Empowerment in Mississippi after 1965* (Chapel Hill: University of North Carolina Press, 1990), 34–37.

18. McLemore, "MFDP," 382, 385; Susan Lorenzi Sojourner, "Holmes County, Mississippi: The Civil Rights Movement—The 1967 Elections," 31–32, 83, work in progress, copy in my possession. While it is not totally clear why Clark won in Holmes County and ten of the eleven other black candidates lost, influential factors included Clark's status in the community and his personal popularity, as well as the fact that his opponent—unlike most other white candidates—made no effort to get black votes.

19. Parker, *Black Votes Count*, 72–75.

20. Ibid.

21. Ibid., 69; "Mississippi Newsletter," July 28, 1967; *Memphis Press-Scimitar*, Sept. 1, 1967; Rubel L. Phillips to Amzie Moore, Oct. 31, 1967, Moore Papers. After the Civil War, General Nathan Bedford Forrest founded the Ku Klux Klan in Pulaski, Tennessee.

22. *C-L*, Dec. 7, 1967; Memphis *Commercial Appeal*, Nov. 16, 1967; Seth Cagin and Philip Dray, *We Are Not Afraid: The Story of Goodman, Schwerner, and Chaney and the Civil Rights Campaign for Mississippi* (New York: Macmillan, 1988), 450. Tarrants's partner, a Jackson schoolteacher named Kathy Ainsworth, was killed in the Meridian shootout. For a fascinating account of the Klan's activities in Mississippi in the late 1960s, see Jack Nelson, *Terror in the Night: The Klan's Campaign against the Jews* (New York: Simon & Schuster, 1993).

23. Six men, including Sheriff Lawrence Rainey, were acquitted in the Meridian trial. The seven convicted men served prison terms, but all were released from jail by the mid-1970s. Tarrants underwent a religious con-

version while serving his sentence in Parchman penitentiary and was released from prison in 1976 after serving eight years of his sentence. See Cagin and Dray, *We Are Not Afraid,* 456; Nelson, *Terror in the Night,* 254–55.

24. "Mississippi Newsletter," Sept. 22, Nov. 3, 1967; *Southern Patriot,* Nov. 1967; McLemore, "MFDP," 415–17.

25. *NYT,* Oct. 1, 1967; "Mississippi Newsletter," Oct. 6, 1967; *Delta Democrat-Times,* Oct. 10, 1967; *JDN,* June 6, 1967; interview with William Silver, May 30, 1981, San Francisco.

26. McLemore, "MFDP," 443–44; Leon Hall to Hosea Williams, Feb. 5, 1968; Hall to Williams, Feb. 21, 1968, SCLC Papers, 178:9; "Meeting of the Mississippi Steering Committee for the Poor People's Campaign," April 20, 1968, SCLC Papers, 178:12; interview with Owen Brooks.

27. McLemore, "MFDP," 399, 397–98; unidentified newspaper clipping, March 6, 1968, Cox Papers; Lawson, *Pursuit,* 103.

28. Simpson, "The Birth of the Mississippi 'Loyalist Democrats,'" 38–42; "Mississippi Newsletter," July 5, 1968; Claude Ramsey to Aaron Henry, June 24, 1968, copy in Amzie Moore Papers; McLemore, "MFDP," 450.

29. Simpson, "The Birth," 41; *Southern Patriot,* Nov. 1968; McLemore, "MFDP," 441.

30. "Mississippi Newsletter," Aug. 16, 1968; *Southern Patriot,* Nov. 1968; McLemore, "MFDP," 452, 441.

31. Lawson, *Pursuit,* 114–17; *NYT,* Aug. 19–21, 29, 1968; McLemore, "MFDP," 475–85; interview with Hodding Carter. The Loyalist vote on the presidential ballot broke down as follows: Humphrey, 9½; McCarthy, 6½; McGovern, 4; and the Reverend Channing Phillips (the first black candidate to be nominated at a convention of the two major parties), 2; *NYT,* Aug. 29, 1968. Since the delegation voted by secret ballot, a policy insisted on by the NAACP–Young Democrats faction to preserve anonymity, no further breakdown of the vote is available; McLemore, "MFDP," 484.

32. William Morris, the late-nineteenth-century English poet, is quoted in Findlay, *Church People in the Struggle,* 224–25.

33. Voter Education Project, *Voter Registration in the South: Summer 1968* (Atlanta, Ga.: Southern Regional Council, 1968), "Mississippi—5."

34. Parker, *Black Votes Count,* 141, 142–43.

35. Office of the Secretary of State of Mississippi, "Mississippi African American Elected Officials, December 1992." I am grateful to Ms. Constance Slaughter-Harvey, assistant secretary of state, for supplying me with a copy of this document.

36. Ibid.

37. *C-L,* April 18, 1991. There is no comprehensive history of the black experience in Mississippi since 1968. Among the books related to the subject are James Findlay, *Church People in the Struggle;* Steven F. Lawson, *In Pursuit of Power;* Jack Nelson, *Terror in the Night;* Frank R. Parker, *Black Votes Count;* and also Kay Mills, *This Little Light of Mine: The*

Life of Fannie Lou Hamer (New York: Dutton, 1993); Minion K. C. Morrison, *Black Political Empowerment* (Albany: State University of New York Press, 1987); Melany Neilson, *Even Mississippi* (Tuscaloosa: University of Alabama Press, 1989); and Tim Spottsford, *Lynch Street: The May 1970 Slayings at Jackson State College* (Kent, Ohio: Kent State University Press, 1989).

38. Francis Fox Piven and Richard A. Cloward, *Poor People's Movements: Why They Succeed, How They Fail* (New York: Vintage, 1979), 32, 36.

39. Vincent Harding, "So Much History, So Much Future: Martin Luther King, Jr., and the Second Coming of America," in William H. Chafe and Harvard Sitkoff, eds., *A History of Our Time: Readings on Postwar America,* 3d ed. (New York: Oxford University Press, 1991), 182.

40. Bob Moses, interviewed by Clayborne Carson, 32.

Afterword

1. Alexis Jetter, "Mississippi Learning," *New York Times Magazine,* Feb. 21, 1993, 29. Jetter's article includes a more detailed description of the Algebra Project.

2. Ibid., 29, 32.

3. Interview with Owen Brooks; interview with June Johnson. See also Kay Mills, *This Little Light of Mine: The Life of Fannie Lou Hamer* (New York: Dutton, 1993), chaps. 16–17.

4. *Washington Post,* March 21, 1977; *NYT,* March 21, 1977; Mills, *This Little Light of Mine,* chap. 17.

5. Fannie Lou Hamer, interviewed by Neil McMillen, April 14, 1972, Ruleville, Miss., Mississippi OHP, 43; Charles McLaurin, "Memories of Fannie Lou Hamer," copy in Fannie Lou Hamer Papers, Amistad Research Center, Tulane University.

Index

Abernathy, Ralph, 76, 398
Abzug, Bella, 21
Agricultural Adjustment Administration (AAA), 384
Agricultural Stabilization and Conservation Service (ASCS), 255, 333–35
Agriculture, black: sharecropping, 10, 14, 19, 124–25, 143–44, 433; farm owners, 30, 187–88, 190–91, 365; decline of old plantation system, 124–25, 364–65, 384–85. *See also* Agricultural Stabilization and Conservation Service; Cooperatives; Mississippi Freedom Labor Union
Aid to Families with Dependent Children (AFDC), 386, 425
Ainsworth, Kathy, 510n
Albert, Carl, 340
Alcorn State College, 225
Alexander v. *Holmes County,* 425
Algebra Project, 432
Alinski, Saul, 357
Allen, James L., 195, 472n
Allen, Louis, 109, 215
American Civil Liberties Union (ACLU), 230, 454n
American Federation of Labor (AFL), 23, 24; AFL-CIO, 346–47, 351, 421
Americans for Democratic Action (ADA), 286, 317, 318, 339
Americans for the Preservation of the White Race (APWR), 266, 476n
Anding, Meredith, Jr., 455n

Andrews, A. L., 364
Anticommunism. *See* Red-baiting
Arnold, Carl, 184
Aronson, Henry, 335–36
Ashmore, Harry, 64
Ashmore, Robert T., 351
Atlanta Declaration, 43
Atlantic City convention. *See* Democratic National Convention, 1964

Baez, Joan, 228
Bailey, Ronald, 432
Bailey, Sam, 161, 211
Baker, Ella, 102, 107, 204, 220, 287, 317, 431; as NAACP director of branches, 29, 30; speech at 1964 MFDP convention, 281–82
Baker, James, 306
Baker, Josephine, 21
Baldwin, James, 211, 239
Ball, John, 191
Banks, E. W., 39
Banks, Fred, 426–27
Barber, Rims, 411
Barnett, Ross, 65, 88, 118, 168, 172, 195, 197, 218, 340, 450n, 468n; and Clyde Kennard, 82–83; and freedom rides, 93, 95–96; and Meredith case, 139–41
Barry, Marion, 106, 107, 110, 459n
Bates, Gladys Noel, 31; and school salary case, 35–36
Battle, Clinton C., 41, 48, 170

Beard, Fred, 65
Beckwith, Byron De La, 166, 277, 467–68n
Beech, Robert, 336
Beittel, Daniel, 225, 369; and Jackson library sit-in, 88; and Woolworth's sit-in, 162; dismissed as Tougaloo's president, 234–36
Belafonte, Harry, 145, 239
Belfrage, Sally, 263, 276
Belhaven College, 61, 228
Bell, Derrick, 139
Bell, Emma, 113, 324, 461n
Bender, William A.: and 1946 election, 2–3, 7, 9; and NAACP work, 30, 31–32
Bennett, Myrtis, 114
Bernstein, Victor, 5, 8
Bevel, Diane Nash. *See* Nash, Diane
Bevel, James, 99, 107, 116, 117, 123, 124, 128, 146, 150, 175, 176, 231
Bikel, Theodore, 174
Bilbo, Theodore, 28, 31, 67, 424, 441n; and 1946 election, 2–9
Biloxi "wade-in," 86–87, 455n
Birdsong, T. B., 33, 310
Birmingham, Ala.: and 1963 demonstrations, 160, 161, 425; and church bombing, 201
Bivins, Mattie, 185
Black, James, 240–41
Black and Tan Republican party, 25, 28
Black Belt Project, 318–19
Black Monday, 60
Black power, 403, 406, 408, 409, 411; and Meredith March, 396–97, 402
Black Votes Count, 415
Blackwell, Randolph, 147, 149
Blackwell, Unita, 253, 347, 367, 373, 484n; on 1964 Democratic National Convention, 300
Blessey, Gerald, 140
Bloch, Emanuel, 4
Block, Sam, 57, 138, 175, 191, 203, 321, 324, 431; and Greenwood movement, 128–35, 145–46, 148, 150, 151; disillusionment of, 213; on being beaten by a highway patrolman, 240–41
Blocker, Dan, 227
Blue, Clyde, 16–17

Blyth, John W., 478n
Bond, Julian, 431, 433
Booker, Simeon, 53, 73
Boone, Richard, 379
Booth, Mary, 174
Booth, Paul, 459n
Borinski, Ernst, 61–62, 202
"Born of Conviction" statement, 463–64n
Bosanquet, Nicolas, 226
Boston Friends of SNCC, 232
Bowers, Sam, 217, 506n; conviction of, 418
Bowie, Harry, 269, 328, 336, 411, 431; on the meaning of the summer project, 271
Bowman, Joann, 371
Boyd, J. D., 38, 39, 44
Boynton v. *Virginia,* 91, 95, 99
Bracey, Charles, 159
Braden, Anne, 317, 482n; on red-baiting of SCEF, 231–32; background of, 479n
Braden, Carl, 231, 482n; background of, 479n
Bradford, James "Sam," 87, 455n
Bradley, Mamie, 55
Bradley, Norma, 57
Brady, Tom: on blacks, 60–61
Branch, A. A., 401
Branch, Taylor, 458n
Brando, Marlon, 239, 401
Branton, Wiley, 147–48, 149, 154, 155, 156, 175, 212; advice to the Bradens, 231
Brenner, Joseph, 387
Brewer, Lenora, 135
Bridges, Styles, 4, 7
Briscoe, Robert, 472n
Britt, Travis, 106
Britton, A. Benjamin, 472n
Britton, Cora, 76
Brooks, Owen, 365, 398, 411, 414, 431, 433; on Poor People's Campaign, 420
Broom, Essie, 150
Brown, Ben, 432; killing of, 413; funeral of, 414
Brown, Bessie, 323
Brown, Ed, 324
Brown, J. W., 181
Brown, Jess, 35–36, 229, 304, 350

Brown, Joyce, 268–69
Brown, Luvaughn, 124, 132–33
Brown, Pat, 295
Brown University: and relationship
  with Tougaloo College, 235–36
Brown v. *Board of Education,* 34, 36,
  41–74 passim, 143, 406, 428; deci-
  sion denounced in Mississippi, 37;
  1955 implementing decision, 50;
  state legislature declares invalid, 59
Brumfield, Robert, 113, 266, 267, 309,
  312, 486*n*
Bryant, Carolyn, 55–56, 449*n*
Bryant, Charles, 268
Bryant, Curtis Conway "C. C.," 42,
  85, 216, 267, 271, 342, 431; on
  black middle class, 73; and Mc-
  Comb movment, 101–14 passim,
  306–7, 313–14
Bryant, Ora, 268, 308
Bryant, Robert, 106
Bryant, Roy, 55–57, 449*n*
Buffington, John, 408, 421, 422; on
  MFDP, 410
Burks, Marylene, 138
Burns, Robert, 132, 134
Burt, Gordon, Jr., 266, 313
Butts, Charles, 460*n*

Campbell, Foote, 188, 221–23
Campbell, Janie, 114
Campbell, V. O., 472n
Campbell, Will, 61, 63
Campbell College, 113–14
Camp Shelby, 16, 17
Camp Van Dorn, 16–17
Canson, Verna, 295
Canton movement. *See* Madison Coun-
  ty movement
CAP. *See* Community Action Program
Carmichael, Stokely, 97, 114, 174,
  249, 253, 264, 280–81, 318, 324,
  411, 433, 507*n;* background of,
  252; and Meredith March, 392–402
  passim; on black power, 396–97,
  403, 406
Carnegie, Alma Mitchell, 191, 192
Carnegie, Charles, 192
Carr, Oscar, 347, 377
Carson, Clayborne, 318
Carter, Betty, 66–67
Carter, Hodding, II, 57, 65, 309; on

Brown decision, 37; background of,
  66–67; racial attitudes of, 67
Carter, Hodding, III, 347, 348–49,
  351, 362, 421, 422, 433; on origins
  of MAP, 377–78
Carter, Jimmy, 433, 434
Carter, Robert, 35
Carver, George Washington, 258
Caste and Class in a Southern Town,
  76
Caston, Billy Jack, 106
CDGM. *See* Child Development Group
  of Mississippi
Central Intelligence Agency (CIA), 236
Chafee, Lois, 162
Chancellor, John, 299
Chandler, Len, 270
Chaney, Ben, 283–84
Chaney, Fannie Lee, 246, 283–84, 333
Chaney, James, 248, 249, 252, 255,
  326, 333, 398, 418, 432; begins
  working with CORE, 246; murder
  of, 247; funeral of, 283–84
Chase, Oscar, 221
Chestnut, Jerry, 132
Child Development Group of Missis-
  sippi (CDGM), 236, 368–82, 387,
  388, 400, 432. *See also* Head Start
Children's Defense Fund, 427
Chinn, C. O., 221–22, 255, 399; back-
  ground of, 188, 190; convicted of
  manslaughter, 507*n*
Chinn, Clarence, 222
Church Committee, 292
Citizens Committee for Human Rights
  in Jackson, 160–61
Citizens' Council: founding of, 45–46;
  and school desegregation, 46–48,
  50–52, 228, 448*n;* opposition to civ-
  il rights in 1950s, 53–89 passim; and
  Ku Klux Klan, 217–18; decline of,
  314; mentioned, passim
Citizens' Crusade Against Poverty
  (CCAP), 379–80
Civil Rights Act of 1957, 194–95
Civil Rights Act of 1964, 260, 273, 309,
  312, 332, 355, 360, 390, 428, 429
Civil Rights Act of 1965, 344, 346,
  351, 352, 390–91, 410, 428, 429
Civil Rights Act of 1968, 508*n*
Civil Rights Commission. *See* United
  States Commission on Civil Rights

Civil Rights Congress, 4, 21

Civil War: in Mississippi, 12

Clark, Alphonso, 75

Clark, Robert, 422; elected to Mississippi legislature, 416, 510n

Clark, Septima, 170

Clark, Thomas, 3

Clayton, Claude F., 404–6

Cleghorn, Reece, 156–57

Clifford, Clark, 291

Clinton, Bill, 426, 433

Cloward, Richard, 429

Coahoma Ministerial Council, 122

Cobb, Charles, 85, 138, 175, 209, 210–11, 249, 253; on local people and white volunteers, 219; and freedom schools, 258–59

Cobb, James C., 384

Cocke, C. E., 6–7

Coffin, William Sloane, 232–33

COFO. See Council of Federated Organizations

Cohen, Wilbur, 368

Cohn, David, 66

Cole, Beatrice, 247

Cole, Bud, 247

Coleman, James P., 38, 59, 72, 93, 189, 450n; and Clyde Kennard case, 80–83

Coles, Robert, 327, 369

Collier, Vernando R., 5

Collins, E. K., 287

Collins, J. D., 6

Collins, LeRoy, 309–10

Collins, M. C., 30

Colmer, William, 371

Commission on Religion and Race, 230, 336

Communist party: and Willie McGee case, 21. See also Red-baiting

Community Action Program (CAP), 363, 375–78, 388

Community Relations Service (CRS), 309–10, 403, 492n

Congressional challenge, 337, 338–41, 351–52, 497n

Congress of Industrial Organizations (CIO): and Operation Dixie, 23–24; AFL-CIO, 346–47, 351, 421

Congress of Racial Equality (CORE): and freedom rides, 90–99; and Madison County project, 186–90, 221–24, 255–56, 328–29, 399–401; and murders of Chaney, Schwerner, and Goodman, 246–48, 283–84; and MFDP (in 1966), 409; mentioned, passim. See also Council of Federated Organizations; Dennis, David; Farmer, James; Mississippi Freedom Democratic party

Connally, John, 290

Connor, Eugene "Bull," 91

Cook, Alfred, 455n

Cooks, Stoney, 357

Cooper, Owen, 63, 377, 378

Cooperatives, 365–66, 433

CORE. See Congress of Racial Equality

Cotter, Paul, 377

Cotton, MacArthur, 105, 116, 173–74, 225, 324

Cotton, Willie Mae, 267

Council of Federated Organizations (COFO): founding of, 118–19; and freedom vote, 200–207; and founding of MFDP, 236–37; attacked by liberals, 315–18; dissolution of, 343–44; mentioned, passim. See also Congress of Racial Equality; National Association for the Advancement of Colored People; Southern Christian Leadership Conference; Student Nonviolent Coordinating Committee

Counter-Intelligence Program (COINTELPRO), 410

Courts, Gus, 48, 53, 70, 135; shooting of, 54

Cowan, Paul, 262–63

Cox, Courtland, 315, 316–17; on LBJ's tactics at 1964 Democratic National Convention, 289–90

Cox, Eugene, 451n

Cox, Harold E., 180, 358, 404; racial epithets by, 223

Cox, Murray, 472n

Crawford, Eartiss, 334

CRC. See United States Commission on Civil Rights

Criswell, John, 293

Cumming, Joseph, 149

Current, Gloster: and Jackson movement, 160–69 passim; and Charles Evers, 178, 355, 359; on summer project, 274; tests 1964 civil rights

law, 275–76; on COFO, 341, 342, 343; mentioned, passim. *See also* National Association for the Advancement of Colored People
Curry, W. J., 472*n*
Curtis, Archie, 216

Dahmer, Vernon, 432, 470*n*, 506*n*; and Clyde Kennard, 81; and Hattiesburg movement, 180–81; murdered by klansmen, 391
Dale, Sebe, 84
Dann, Jim, 370
Darden, Charles R., 42, 43, 86
Dark Journey, 13
Davis, Betty, 184
Davis, Frank, 24
Davis, Sammy, 401
Dawson, William, 33
Deacons for Defense: at the Meredith March, 393, 395
Deas, Geraldine, 184
Dee, Henry, 251
DeLoach, Cartha "Deke," 292–93
Delta Foundation, 427
Delta Ministry, 411, 412, 413, 414; founding of, 336–37; and Natchez movement, 356–59; and poverty program, 369, 372, 373, 376; and Meredith March, 389, 394, 395, 396, 401. *See also* Mississippi Freedom Democratic party
Democratic National Convention
—1964, 271, 285–302, 314; MFDP prepares for, 272–74, 279–83; two-seat compromise proposed, 296; MFDP rejects compromise, 300–302; impact of convention on civil rights movement, 316
—1968, 293, 418–22, 433, 511*n*
—1992, 433
Dennis, David: becomes CORE field secretary, 117–18; and Greenwood movement, 148, 155; and Jackson movement, 159, 161, 164, 167; and Madison County movement, 185–87; on murders of Chaney, Schwerner, and Goodman, 248–49; eulogy at James Chaney's funeral, 284; withdraws from Mississippi, 326–27; at movement reunion, 432; mentioned, passim. *See also* Congress of Racial

Equality; Council of Federated Organizations
Dent, Tom, 256
Derby, Doris, 261
Devine, Annie, 127, 255, 280, 324, 408, 424, 431; becomes active in Canton movement, 189–90; at 1964 Democratic National Convention, 289, 301; and congressional challenge, 322, 338–39; on white organizers in Canton, 328–29. *See also* Madison County movement; Mississippi Freedom Democratic party
Dewey, Thomas E., 28
Diamond, Dion, 112
Diebold Group, Inc., 478*n*
Diggs, Charles, 53, 54, 176, 296, 350
Dillon, Matti, 303–4, 308, 493*n*
Dillon, Willie, 303–4, 493*n*
Dixiecrat movement, 27–28, 291
Dixon, John, 30
Doar, John, 108, 109, 133, 149, 155, 156, 167, 193, 245, 270, 278, 458*n*
Dollard, John, 76
Dombrowski, James, 114, 231, 479*n*
Donaldson, Ivanhoe, 145, 253, 264, 285, 318; on freedom vote, 205, 206; on whites in movement, 209, 210
Dorsey, L. C., 433
Drummond, Doc, 409
Duberman, Martin, 261
Du Bois, W. E. B.: on black troops returning from WWI, 1
Duckworth, Roman, 123
Dugger, Ronnie, 207
Dulles, Allen, 250
Dunagin, Charles, 311
Dunbar, Leslie, 94, 120
Dunn, Felix, 179, 342
Durrough, Charles M., 137, 144, 254
Dylan, Bob, 174

East, P. D., 66, 451*n*
Eastland, James O.: on performance of black troops, 17–18; on *Brown* decision, 37; supports Citizens' Council, 45; and freedom rides, 93, 97; denounces Justice Department suit in Greenwood, 154; on forced migration of blacks, 387; mentioned, passim

Edwards, Don, 267
Edwards, Jeraldine, 455*n*
Einstein, Albert, 21
Eisenhower, Dwight D., 34, 38, 48; on *Brown* decision, 52
Elder, Roy, 240
Elections: of 1946, 1–9; of 1948, 27–28; of 1964, 320–24; of 1966, 389, 394, 409–10; of 1967, 410–13, 415–17; of 1968, 420. *See also* Freedom vote
El Fondren, 395
Ellender, Allen, 4, 5, 8
Else, John, 203
Emmerich, Oliver, 66, 266; and 1964 McComb bombings, 305, 310, 312
Espy, Mike, 426, 427
Ethridge, Tom, 65
Evans, Gray, 154
Evans, Sara, 263, 332
Evers, Charles: background of, 177–78; problems with national NAACP, 178, 355; on blacks and the draft, 350; and the Natchez movement, 354–62; and the Meredith March, 394, 401–3; runs for Congress, 420; at 1968 Loyalist state convention, 422; mentioned, passim. *See also* National Association for the Advancement of Colored People
Evers, Darrell Kenyatta, 49
Evers, Medgar: background of, 49; applies to Ole Miss law school, 49, 446*n*; on black teachers, 73; on black ministers, 75–76; activities in late 1950s, 78–89 passim; and McComb movement, 112; and Jackson movement, 158–69 passim; murder of, 165–66; funeral of, 166–67; mentioned, passim. *See also* National Association for the Advancement of Colored People
Evers, Myrlie, 32, 49, 78, 79, 89, 228, 256; on black teachers, 73; on Jackson movement, 163, 165–66; reservations about Charles Evers, 178. *See also* Evers, Medgar
Ezelle, Robert, 275

Fair Employment Practices Commission (FEPC), 2, 26, 29
Fairlie, J. C., 182, 184

Farmer, James, 98, 150, 223, 291, 315, 338; and freedom rides, 91, 92, 94–95
Farmers Home Administration (FHA), 365
Farm Security Administration, 191
Father Nathaniel, 146
Faulkner, William: on Emmett Till case, 57; attitudes on race, 68–69
FDP. *See* Mississippi Freedom Democratic party
Featherstone, Ralph, 258, 269, 284–85; death of, 486*n*
Federal Bureau of Investigation (FBI), 5, 15, 109, 111, 154, 238, 278, 374, 398, 418, 492*n*; and Mack Parker lynching, 84; and murders of Chaney, Schwerner, and Goodman, 248–51; in Jackson, 250; surveillance of MFDP, 291–93; in McComb, 303–4; in Grenada, 405. *See also* Hoover, J. Edgar
Federalism, doctrine of, 94, 141–42, 156, 212, 391
Fellowship of Reconciliation, 62
Field Foundation, 120, 225, 379, 380
Finger, Ellis, 62
Fletcher, Etoy, 6
Food and Fiber Act of 1965, 384
Food stamp program, 363, 385–86, 425
Ford, Frank, 303–4
Ford Foundation, 235, 502*n*
Forman, James, 149–50, 151, 157, 210, 211, 220, 236, 268, 315, 317, 318, 331; on two-seat compromise, 301; opposes additions to SNCC staff, 319–20; on COFO, 343. *See also* Student Nonviolent Coordinating Committee
Forrest County Voters League, 182, 184
Fortas, Abe, 291, 296
Foster, Isaac, 367
Frank, Barney, 232, 317
Franklin, Marvin, 226
Frazier, Johnny, 349
Freedom corps, 319, 322
Freedom Democratic party. *See* Mississippi Freedom Democratic party
Freedom Farm Cooperative, 365, 433
Freedom rides, 90–99

Freedom schools, 211, 244, 257–61, 268–69, 285, 325, 332
Freedom Summer, 211, 431. *See also* Summer project
Freedom vote, 200–207, 212, 272, 474*n;* in 1964, 322–24
Freeman, Orville, 386
Freeman, Rosemary, 170–71
Free Southern Theatre, 261
Frey, Dick, 174, 208
Friends of Children of Mississippi (FCM), 380–82

Gaither, Tom, 99, 118, 122, 176, 185
Gandhi Society, 158, 466*n*
Gans, Curtis, 317–18
Ganz, Marshall, 331, 486*n*
Garner, Ardis, 308
General Missionary Baptist Convention, 38
Gibson, Jerry, 103
Gilchrist, R. G., 29
Gillian, Marion, 227
Gillis, Norman, 493*n*
Gillis, Sterling "Bubba," 267, 311, 493*n*
Gillon, Gwen, 249, 324
Gober, Bertha, 131, 242
Goff, Fred, 480*n*
Goldwater, Barry, 274, 286, 287, 291, 321–22, 417, 494*n*
Good, Paul, 399, 401
Goodman, Andrew, 240, 252, 255, 284, 326, 398, 418, 432; murder of, 246–47; body recovered, 283
Goodman, Charles, 405
Gore, Al, 433
Gray, Anthony, 182
Gray, Duncan, 63–64, 141; on *Brown* decision, 37–38
Gray, Victoria, 127, 148, 189–90, 283, 321, 324, 424, 432; background of, 181–82; and Hattiesburg movement, 183–84; on two-seat compromise, 301, and congressional challenge, 322, 338–39, 352
Green, Bob, 395
Green, Edith, 293, 298
Green, Ernest, 15
Greenberg, Jack, 230, 315
Greenberg, Polly, 369, 373
Greene, Alma, 151

Greene, Dewey, Jr., 132, 151
Greene, Dewey, Sr., 135, 150–51
Greene, Freddie, 151
Greene, George, 150, 174, 203–4, 324, 353–54
Greene, Lorne, 227
Greene, Percy, 28, 30, 39, 74, 76, 161
Greenville Air Force Base: occupation of, 366–68, 502*n*
Greenwood movement, 128–35, 143–57, 276–79, 396–97
Gregory, Dick, 83, 145, 152, 155, 157, 164, 174
Griffin, Charles, 420
Griffin, John A., 309–10, 312
Griffin, John Howard, 83, 454*n*
Guerrero, Gene, 486*n*
Guy, George, 216, 266, 270, 303, 307
Guyot, Lawrence, 151–52, 174, 184, 212, 220, 221, 236, 282–83, 318; background of, 132–33, 321; in Winona jail, 172; and MFDP, 324, 326, 345, 346, 352, 390, 394, 408–23 passim, 431; on Vietnam war, 350; on black power, 411. *See also* Mississippi Freedom Democratic party

Hall, Carsie, 20, 30, 42, 229
Hall, Rob, 449*n*
Hall, Stanton, 80
Hamer, Fannie Lou, 12, 136, 175, 206, 220, 254, 283, 294, 298, 300, 324, 347, 409, 411, 417, 421, 424; on SNCC workers, 125–26, 127; evicted from plantation, 137–38; beaten in Winona jail, 171–73; on whites in movement, 209; speech at 1964 Democratic National Convention, 288; on two-seat compromise, 302; and congressional challenge, 322, 338–39, 342; on poverty programs, 376, 378, 381–82; resigns from SNCC, 408; death and funeral of, 433–34
Hamer, Perry "Pap," 137
Hamlett, Ed, 231
Hammond, Buff, 277
Hannah, John, 194–96, 198
Harding, Vincent, 245, 249
Hardy, John, 105, 108, 458*n*
Harkey, Ira, 464*n*
Harrington, Evans, 140

Harris, Jesse, 124, 265, 279, 304, 324; on Klan terrorism in McComb, 306
Harris, John, 175, 323, 370
Harris, Joseph, 412
Harvie, Clarie Collins, 31; and Womanpower Unlimited, 98–99; later career of, 456–57n
Hattiesburg movement, 178–84, 219–21
Haughton, G. R., 168
Hawkins, Augustus, 376
Hayden, Sandra "Casey," 207, 331–32
Hayes, Curtis, 135, 209, 264, 280, 313; and McComb movement, 106–7, 113–14, 265–70 passim; and Hattiesburg movement, 180–83
Hays, Ralthus, 191, 192
Head Start, 236, 363, 368, 369, 370, 379, 425. *See also* Child Development Group of Mississippi
Heard, Alexander, 24, 26, 443n
Hearin, Robert, 275
Hederman, Rea, 65
Hederman, Robert, 64–65, 66
Hederman, Thomas, 64–65, 66
Hederman newspapers, 46, 51, 64–65
Heffner, Malva, 305, 492n
Heffner, "Red," 305, 492n
Heilbron, Jerome K., 309–10
Henderson, Gordon, 349
Henderson, J. Lewis, 35
Henderson, Mary Ann, 228
Henderson, Thelton, 164, 166, 468n
Henry, Aaron: background of, 120–21; and Clarksdale movement, 121–23, 176–77; and freedom vote campaign, 202–7; at 1964 Democratic National Convention, 288–301 passim; and MAP, 377–78; mentioned, passim. *See also* Council of Federated Organizations; Mississippi Freedom Democratic party; National Association for the Advancement of Colored People
Henry, Noelle 120, 122
Herbers, John, 256
Hermey, Louise, 248
Herron, Jeannine, 369
Herron, Matt, 499n
Hesburgh, Theodore, 194, 196
Hickenlooper, Burton, 4, 6
Hicks, Fred, 137

Higgins, Commodore Dewey, 110, 111
Higgs, Bill, 229, 459n
High, Arrington, 74, 75
Highlander Folk School, 107, 207
High Wall, The, 61
Hill, Jerry Lee, 307–8
Hill, T. W., 26
Hillet, Vivian, 138
Hirt, Al, 227
Hochstedler, Eli, 227
Hoffman, Marvin, 381
Holland, Ida Mae, 154
Holloway, Frank, 91
Holmes, Mary E., 30
Holmes, Wendell, 7
Holmes County Voters' League, 119
Holt, Len, 230
Honeysucker, Robert, 226
Hoover, J. Edgar, 154, 238, 251, 291–92, 311; on Mack Parker lynching, 84; on protecting civil rights workers, 250. *See also* Federal Bureau of Investigation
Hopson, Clint, 350
Horne, Lena, 174
Horwitz, Charles, 330, 411
House Education and Labor Committee, 375
House Subcommittee on Elections, 351
House Un-American Activities Committee, 230–31
Houston, Charles, 4
Howard, Perry, 25
Howard, T. R. M., 12, 44, 48, 49, 53, 54, 102, 453n; background of, 32–33; and meeting with Governor White, 39; and *Brown* decision, 45; as target of Citizens' Council, 47; leaves Mississippi, 70; speaks at Medgar Evers's funeral, 166. *See also* Regional Council of Negro Leadership
Howard University, students at: impact on SNCC, 324
Howe, Florence, 258, 500n
Hudgins, Douglas, 62–63
Hudson, Dovie, 256–57
Hudson, Winson, 256–57, 283
Hughes, Cephus, 304
Hughes, Matthew, 151
Hughes, Richard, 290
Huie, William Bradford, 57, 449n

Humes, H. H., 38–40, 76
Humphrey, Hubert, 317, 320, 322, 390, 422; and 1964 Democratic National Convention, 288–99 passim; and CDGM, 380; on black power, 397
Hurley, Ruby, 41, 75, 78, 160, 165, 448*n*, 449*n*
Hurst, E. H., 109, 215

Inc. Fund. *See* NAACP Legal Defense Fund
Ingram, Suggs, 404, 405
Interstate Commerce Commission: and freedom rides, 95, 114
In White America, 261

Jackson, Janice, 455*n*
Jackson, Joseph, 455*n*
Jackson, Luther, 79
Jackson, Mahalia, 33
Jackson, Wharlest: murder of, 417
Jackson, Zola, 75
Jackson Chamber of Commerce: calls for compliance with 1964 civil rights law, 275
Jackson movement, 157–69, 475–76*n*
Jackson Nonviolent Movement, 116–17, 123
Jackson Public Library sit-in, 87–89
Jackson State College, 225, 238; and 1967 protests, 413–14
James, Newton, 312, 313
Jencks, Christopher, 376
Jenkins, Walter: and 1964 Democratic National Convention, 290, 291, 292, 296, 299
Jewett, Richard, 329
Job Corps, 363
John Birch Society, 129
Johnson, Aaron, 131, 134, 147, 150
Johnson, Allen, 418
Johnson, Belle, 135
Johnson, June, 135, 431, 433; beaten in Winona jail, 170–71, 173
Johnson, Lyndon B., 211, 224, 237–41, 250, 303, 308, 310, 320–22, 326, 340, 348, 350, 383–401 passim; and 1964 Democratic National Convention, 286–301 passim; and War on Poverty, 363–82 passim
Johnson, Paul, Jr., 189, 195, 199, 250,

275, 286, 310, 314, 321, 344, 346, 355, 356, 392, 417; on poverty program, 371, 375, 377; on hunger in Mississippi, 384; and the Meredith March, 395, 396, 399, 405
Johnston, Erle, Jr.: and State Sovereignty Commission, 60, 371, 378–79
Jones, Charles, 161
Jones, Curtis, 55
Jones, James, 240–41
Jones, Jeffries Bassett, 17
Jordan, Cleveland, 129

Katzenbach, Nicholas, 367–68, 400–401, 491–92*n*
Keeney, Barnaby: and Brown-Tougaloo relationship, 235–36
Kennard, Clyde, 181, 182; attempts to enroll at Mississippi Southern College, 79–83, 453–54*n*
Kennedy, Edward, 419
Kennedy, John F.: and freedom rides, 92–95; civil rights policies of, 94, 120, 153–57, 167–69; and Meredith crisis, 140–42; calls for passage of civil rights law, 165–66; appoints Judge Cox, 180; and CRC hearings, 196–98; assassination of, 211
Kennedy, Robert, 142, 148, 154, 168, 224, 237, 355, 383, 419, 467*n*; and freedom rides, 92–95; and Meredith crisis, 140–42; and CRC hearings, 195–98; assassination of, 419; on James Eastland, 456*n*
Kenyatta, Jomo, 49
Kershaw, Alvin, 61
Key, V. O., 9
Kimball, Elmer, 58
King, Annie Mae, 323, 345
King, Edwin "Ed," 161, 267, 283, 350, 370, 394, 409, 420; and freedom vote campaign, 202–7; on James Chaney's funeral, 284; and 1964 Democratic National Convention, 288, 296, 297, 298, 301; on social class, 347
King, Jeannette, 202, 370
King, Martin Luther, Jr., 94, 98, 122, 152, 160, 165, 338, 344, 356, 357, 406, 429, 434, 507*n*; and 1964 Democratic National Convention, 286–300 passim; and Meredith March,

392–403 passim; on black power, 397; and Poor People's Campaign, 419–20; assassination of, 420. *See also* Southern Christian Leadership Conference

King, Mary, 207, 213, 248, 263, 285, 286, 331–32

Kinoy, Arthur, 336

Kirksey, Henry, 431

Knight, Davis, 20–21

Ku Klux Klan, 24, 214, 224, 238, 240, 248–51, 252, 257, 264, 322, 325, 351, 391, 407, 410, 423, 506*n;* activities of, in early 1964, 215–19; in McComb, 266–68, 270, 303–12, 314; in Natchez, 355, 358–59; decline of, 417–18. *See also* White Knights of the Ku Klux Klan

Kunstler, William, 78, 160, 165, 229

Ladner, Dorie, 57, 75, 86, 116, 225, 324, 332, 431; and Jackson library sit-in, 88; and Jackson movement, 159; and Natchez movement, 353, 359–60; on Charles Evers, 359–60. *See also* Natchez movement

Ladner, Joyce, 57, 75, 85, 225, 431; and Clyde Kennard case, 83; and Jackson library sit-in, 88; on Jackson movement, 159; on Mrs. Turnbow, 285–86; on 1964 Democratic National Convention, 302

Lafayette, Bernard, 99, 116, 117

Lamb, Martha, 132, 153

Lancaster, Burt, 401

Landon, Michael, 227

Lane, Mary, 174

Lang, Charlie, 15

Lanterns on the Levee, 66

Lary, Curtis, 150, 152, 154

Lassiter, Albert Earl, 455*n*

Lauter, Paul, 500*n*

Lawrence, David, 287, 288, 294

Lawrence, Ida Mae, 367

Lawson, James, 90

Lawson, Steven, 391

Lawyers' Committee for Civil Rights Under Law, 229–30, 336

Lawyers' Constitutional Defense Committee (LCDC), 229–30, 335–36

LCDC. *See* Lawyers' Constitutional Defense Committee

Lee, George W., 78, 124; murder of, 53–54, 448*n*

Lee, Herbert, 114, 115, 132, 432, 458*n;* killed by E. H. Hurst, 109–10

Leflore, Greenwood, 148, 465*n*

Leflore County Voters' League, 129

Leigh, Sandy, 221

Levin, Tom: and CDGM, 369, 370, 373–74, 503*n*

Lewis, Anthony, 93

Lewis, David, 180

Lewis, Ike, 107, 110

Lewis, John, 220, 392, 397, 433

Lewis, Nathanael, 7, 25, 100, 104, 111, 265–66

Lewis, Pearlena, 161–62

Lewis, Pete, 270

Lewis, Price, 189

Liddell, Colia, 158

Literacy Project, 225, 478*n*

Lombard, Rudy, 255

Lorenzi, Henri, 416, 471*n*

Lorenzi, Susan. *See* Sojourner, Susan

Lott, Hardy, 468*n*

Love, J. P., 416

Lowe, George, 105

Lowenstein, Allard "Al," 208, 315–17, 480*n;* background of, 200–201; and freedom vote, 203, 204, 207, 473*n;* and summer project, 232–34; attacks COFO, 316; murdered by Dennis Sweeney, 480*n*

Loyal Democrats of Mississippi (Loyalists), 420–22

Lyells, Ruby Stutts, 30

Lynching, 13, 15, 55–56, 83–84, 247, 251–52

Lynd, Staughton, 244, 258, 260

Lynd, Theron, 179–80, 181, 182, 220–21, 243

McAdam, Doug, 265

McCain, James, 159, 170, 185, 186

McCain, William D.: and Clyde Kennard, 80–83, 453–54*n*

McCarthy, Eugene, 422

McCarthyism, 58

McComb movement, 99–115, 266–71, 303–14

McComb "Statement of Principles," 312

McCormack, John, 339

McCoy, A. H., 30, 54
McDaniel, Edward Lenox, 216, 358, 476*n*
McDew, Charles "Chuck," 106, 109, 153–54, 353, 459*n;* and McComb movement, 110–11, 112, 113
McDonald, Joe, 136, 138, 254
McDonald, Rebecca, 136, 138
McGee, Willie: lynching of, 21–22
McGhee, Jake, 135, 276–79
McGhee, Laura, 135, 155, 276–77, 279
McGhee, Silas, 135, 276–79, 487*n*
McGill, Ralph, 64
McGovern, George, 422
McKeigney, Alex, 63
Mackel, A. Maurice, 42, 44, 48, 70
McKinnie, Lester, 116, 179
McKissick, Floyd, 392, 395
McLaurin, Charles, 12, 240–41, 408; background of, 136; and Sunflower County project, 137–38, 175, 254, 324; in Greenwood, 151, 154; and Fannie Lou Hamer, 433–34
McLean, George, 66
McLemore, Leslie, 175, 225, 412
McMillen, Neil R., 13, 46
McNair, Landy, 249
McNease, Mrs. E. H., 129, 131
McPherson, Harry, 376
McRee, James, 381
Madison County Farmers' League, 334–35
Madison County movement (Canton), 186–90, 221–24, 237, 255–56, 328–29, 399–401
Magnolia Mutual Life Insurance Co., 32, 49
Malcolm X, 411, 434
Mangrum, John, 89
Mantiband, Charles, 63
MAP. *See* Mississippi Action for Progress
March on Washington, 198, 201, 217
Marlowe, B. D., 137
Mars, Florence, 483*n*
Marshall, Burke, 93, 108, 120, 167, 168, 196, 238, 306, 308, 310, 458*n*
Marshall, Thurgood, 33, 65, 82; on NAACP's role in Mississippi, 31–32; and Atlanta Declaration, 43
Martin, Joe, 75, 85, 431; and Mc-Comb movement, 112–13, 114, 266, 307, 313; and statement on Vietnam war, 350
Martin, Louis, 308, 492*n*
Marye, Peggy, 150
Mary Holmes Junior College: and Head Start, 369, 372, 382
Mason, Gilbert, 179, 420
Maybank, Burnett, 4
Mays, Benjamin, 76
Medicaid, 363, 425
Medical Committee for Human Rights, 264, 335, 369, 400
Medicare, 425
Melton, Clinton, 58
Meredith, James, 64, 138, 142, 156, 189, 195, 407; background of, 139; desegregates Ole Miss, 139–42; march against fear, 361, 389, 392–403
Meredith March, 361, 389, 392–403
Metcalf, George, 354, 359
MFDP. *See* Mississippi Freedom Democratic party
MFLU. *See* Mississippi Freedom Labor Union
Migration, black, 14, 20, 387–88, 506*n*
Milam, J. W., 55–57, 58, 449*n*
Miles, Robert, 365
Miller, Dorothy. *See* Zellner, Dorothy Miller
Miller, Mike, 174, 207
Millsaps College, 228, 431; Citizens' Council opposition to, 61–62
Mims, Jasper, 51
Minor, Wilson F. "Bill," 60, 66, 476*n*
Minter, David, 451*n*
Mississippi: The Closed Society, 142
Mississippi Action for Community Education (MACE), 427
Mississippi Action for Progress (MAP), 377–82, 388
Mississippians for Public Education, 228
Mississippi Burning, 432
Mississippi College, 61, 228
Mississippi Democratic Conference, 346–48, 378
Mississippi Freedom Democratic party (MFDP; also FDP), 255, 257, 259, 260, 268, 318, 325, 337, 369; founding of, 237; prepares for 1964

convention challenge, 272–74, 279–83; at 1964 Democratic National Convention, 285–302; and 1964 elections, 320–24; and Vietnam war, 350–51, 419; and primary elections, 389, 394; and 1968 Democratic National Convention, 418–22. *See also* Congressional challenge; Natchez movement
Mississippi Freedom Labor Union (MFLU), 364–65, 385
Mississippi Free Press, 124, 460*n*
Mississippi Human Relations Council, 64
"Mississippi Plan," 12, 69
Mississippi Progressive Voters' League, 3, 6, 25–26, 28, 122
Mississippi Southern College, 179; and Clyde Kennard case, 80–82, 453–54*n*
Mississippi State College, 20, 64
Mississippi State Sovereignty Commission, 58, 182, 251, 378–79, 403, 454*n*, 479*n*; creation and work of, 60; and Clyde Kennard case, 80–83; and CDGM, 371
Mississippi Student Union, 260, 332
Mississippi Teachers Association, 421
Mississippi Valley State College, 225
Mitchell, Clarence, 47, 165
Mitchell, Ozell, 191, 192
Mize, Sidney, 35–36, 228, 311, 479*n*, 493*n*
Mondale, Walter, 289, 294, 296
Monsonis, James, 370
Moody, Anne, 58, 75, 188, 189; and Woolworth's sit-in, 161–62
Moon, Henry, 361
Moore, Amzie, 12, 112, 128, 135, 146, 148, 175, 220, 424; opposed by Citizens' Council, 48; on impact of Till case, 58; on black middle class, 72–73; meets Bob Moses, 102–3; organizing strategy of, 124; investigates Till murder, 449*n*
Moore, Austin, 227
Moore, Charles, 251
Moore, Russell, 123–24
Morey, Hunter, 174, 175, 208, 335; on Jackson COFO office, 330
Morris, Jesse, 329–30, 409; and Poor People's Corporation, 365

Morris, John, 175
Morris, William, 423
Morse, Wayne, 300, 317
Morsell, John, 315, 316, 378
Mosely, Jesse, 98
Moses, Gilbert, 261
Moses, Robert: background of, 101–2; meets Amzie Moore, 102–3; and McComb movement, 103–15 passim; and founding of COFO, 118–19; and Greenwood movement, 146–55 passim; on whites in the movement, 209; on burnout, 213; on murder of Louis Allen, 219; on anticommunism, 233; and 1964 Democratic National Convention, 286, 293, 300–302; on liberals, 318; on parallel institutions, 325–26; withdraws from Mississippi, 326; and Algebra Project, 432; mentioned, passim. *See also* Council of Federated Organizations; Mississippi Freedom Democratic party; Student Nonviolent Coordinating Committee
Moses, William, 102, 457*n*
Motley, Constance Baker, 35, 139
Moyers, Bill, 292–93
Mudd, John, 374, 381
Murph, B. E., 42, 179, 275, 342
Murphy, George: on starvation in the Delta, 382–83
Myrdal, Gunnar, 84

NAACP. *See* National Association for the Advancement of Colored People
NAACP Legal Defense Fund (Inc. Fund), 19, 112, 138, 139, 229–30, 335–36, 373
Nash, Diane, 99, 107, 175, 231, 461*n*; and freedom rides, 92; and Jackson Nonviolent Movement, 116–17, 123–24
Natchez Business and Civic League, 34, 216
Natchez Deacons for Defense and Justice, 358
Natchez movement, 353–62
National Association for the Advancement of Colored People (NAACP): history of, in Mississippi, 29–30; Mississippi State Conference of Branches formed, 30–31; and *Brown*

decision, 36–37, 43–45, 50–52; expands in Mississippi in mid-1950s, 41–44; in Mississippi in late 1950s, 77–79; and COFO, 119, 274–75, 498*n;* and Jackson movement, 157–69; tests 1964 civil rights law, 275–76, 312–13; on congressional challenge, 339; mentioned, passim. *See also* Council of Federated Organizations; Evers, Charles; Evers, Medgar; Henry, Aaron; Wilkins, Roy

National Citizens' Committee for the Child Development Program in Mississippi, 380

National Committee for Free Elections in Sunflower, 412

National Council of Churches (NCC), 220, 264, 300, 315–17, 318, 336, 345, 379, 481*n. See also* Delta Ministry

National Lawyers' Guild, 233, 316, 335–36; background of, 230; and congressional challenge, 340–41. *See also* Red-baiting

Navasky, Victor, 141, 481*n*

NCC. *See* National Council of Churches

Neblett, Charles, 353

Negro's Church, The, 76

Negro State Federation of Women's Clubs, 30

Newberry, Anthony, 67

Newfield, Jack, 99

Newspapers, black, 73–74. *See also* Greene, Percy

New World Foundation, 379

Nicholson, Joseph W., 76

Nixon, Richard, 431

Nobles, Billy, 188

Nobles, Ernest, 101, 111, 113, 114, 266, 269, 306, 313, 431

Nobles, Gus, 188, 255

Noel, A. J., 30, 35

Non-Violent Action Group (Tougaloo), 116

Norman, Menphis: and Woolworth's sit-in, 161–62

North Bolivar Farm Cooperative, 365

Northern Student Movement, 232

Norvell, Aubrey James, 392

Nosser, John, 355, 358–59, 361

O'Brien, Larry, 355

Office of Economic Opportunity (OEO), 363, 368–82

Oliver, Bennie, 162

O'Neal, John, 184, 261

Operation Dixie, 23–24

Operation Head Start. *See* Head Start

Osheroff, Abe, 253

Oswald, Robert, 348

Owens, Webb, 101, 103–4, 112, 266, 269, 271

Page, Matthew, 420

Palmer, Hazel, 283

Parchman penitentiary, 82–83, 174, 229, 358; description of, 96; and freedom riders, 96–97

Parker, Frank, 415, 496*n*

Parker, Mack: lynching of, 83–84

Pastore, John, 299

Patterson, Joe, 72, 218

Patterson, Robert "Tut," 45, 47

Payne, Bruce, 204, 207

Payne, Charles, 127

Peacock, Willie, 138, 172, 175, 206, 219, 224, 240–41, 321, 376, 431; and Greenwood movement, 133–34, 145–57 passim; on George Raymond, 187; on impact of white organizers, 209–10

Pearson, Drew, 309, 340

Percy, Leroy, 377–78

Percy, William Alexander, 66

Perkins, Mother, 174

Phillips, Rubel, 417

Pierce, Evelyn, 455*n*

Pierce, M. B., 91

Pigee, Vera, 85, 122, 146, 176, 342

Pigott, Joseph, 101, 310

Pike County Nonviolent Movement, 107, 108. *See also* McComb movement

Pike County Voters' League, 100

Piore, Mike, 255

Piven, Frances Fox, 429

Polhaus, J. Francis, 338

Poll tax, 6, 440*n*, 441*n. See also* Voting laws, Mississippi

Ponder, Annelle, 148, 220; beaten in Winona jail, 170–72

Ponder, L. P., 181

Poole, Betty Anne, 158

Poor People's Campaign, 419–20

Poor People's Corporation, 365–66, 409

Poussaint, Alvin, 335, 400, 461*n*

Pratt, Jack, 300, 315

Price, Cecil, 247, 398; conviction of, 418

Price, Libby, 305

Prince Hall Masons, 421

Professionals, black, 20, 387; and civil rights movement, 30, 44, 72–77, 416

Progressive Voters' League. *See* Mississippi Progressive Voters' League

Puryear, R. W., 367

Quin, Anthony, 306–7, 498–99*n*

Quin, Aylene, 101, 103, 111, 114, 266, 269, 271, 304–5, 313, 354, 431, 498–99*n*; background of, 101; house bombed, 306–7; meets with LBJ, 308

Quin, Jacqueline, 306

Rabinowitz, Victor, 158, 165

Rainey, Lawrence, 79, 247, 251, 333, 398, 510*n*

Ramsay, Tom, 328–29

Ramsey, Claude, 421; and Mississippi Democratic Council, 346–48; on MFDP, 351

Randolph, A. Philip, 261, 291, 379

Rauh, Joseph, 281, 315–17; and 1964 Democratic National Convention, 287–300 passim; speech to MFDP delegation, 295

Raymond, George, 162, 221–22, 237, 246, 249, 255, 334, 381; background of, 187–88; and white organizers, 328–29; death of, 471*n*. *See also* Madison County movement

RCNL. *See* Regional Council of Negro Leadership

Reagan, Ronald, 431

Reagon, Cordell, 110, 270

Reconstruction, 69, 100, 147, 251, 424, 428; history of, in Mississippi, 12–13

Red-baiting, 23, 24, 29, 234, 341, 351, 359; of Lawyers' Guild, 230, 316; of SCEF, 231, 479*n*; of CDGM, 370–71. *See also* Eastland, James; Lowenstein, Allard

Reddix, Jacob L., 88, 116, 161, 225

Reed, Willie, 56, 449*n*

Reese, Arthur, 259

Reese, Carolyn, 259

Regional Council of Negro Leadership (RCNL), 39, 44, 77, 78, 102, 428, 453*n*; program of, 32–33; NAACP opposition to, 32, 77–78; and *Brown* decision, 45. *See also* Howard, T. R. M.

Resnick, Joseph, 376, 388

Reuther, Walter, 291, 294, 296, 297, 317, 401

Rich, Marvin, 334

Richards, Dona, 209, 249

Richardson, Judy, 278

Ricks, Willie, 396

Roberson, David E., 180

Roberts, Johnny Lee, 82

Robinson, Bernice, 148

Robinson, Clarence, 135, 276, 278–79

Robinson, Reginald, 105

Robinson, Ruby Doris, 106, 319

Robinson, Virgie, 181

Rogers, Gertrude, 144

Rogers, Nat, 275

Rogers, William P., 79, 179

Rolvaag, Karl, 290

Roosevelt, Eleanor, 14, 200

Roosevelt, Franklin D., 22

Rose, Margaret, 254

Rosenwald Fund, 256

Rowan, Carl, 63

Rust College, 225, 379

Rustin, Bayard, 297, 298, 300

Ryan, William Fitts, 309, 339, 340

Ryder, Noble, 15

Saddler, Walter, 261

Salter, Eldri, 157

Salter, John, 202; background of, 157–58; and Jackson movement, 158–69 passim

Sampson, Al, 357, 359

Sampson, Charles, 150, 151, 156, 277

Samstein, Mendy, 212–13, 236, 268, 315, 318; on Joe Rauh, 295; on Aylene Quin, 304–5

Sanders, Emma, 409

Sanders, I. S., 161, 323

Sartre, Jean-Paul, 21

Savio, Mario, 486*n*

Sawyer, Ethel, 455n
Scali, John, 299
SCEF. *See* Southern Conference Education Fund
Schools, desegregation of, 228, 360, 390, 425; in Grenada, 404–6. *See also Brown* v. *Board of Education*
Schutt, Jane, 195, 196, 472n
Schwerner, Michael "Mickey," 248, 251, 252, 255, 284, 326, 398, 418, 432; murder of, 246–47; body recovered, 283
Schwerner, Rita, 246, 250, 288
SCLC. *See* Southern Christian Leadership Conference
Seeger, Pete, 174, 261
Segregation, in Mississippi, 62, 67, 417; laws, 13, 20, 59; in WWII, 15–17; examples of, 24, 62, 63, 64, 67, 100; black protests against, 86–89, 106–8, 114, 116–17, 123, 161–64, 170–72, 275–78, 312–13; decline in official practice of, 425–26
Sellers, Cleveland, 324, 329, 392; on search for Chaney, Schwerner, and Goodman, 249–50; on 1964 Democratic National Convention, 302
Selma, Ala.: impact of 1965 demonstrations, 344, 346, 352, 368, 400, 425
Senate Committee to Investigate Campaign Expenditures: 1946 Bilbo hearings, 3–8
Senate Select Committee to Study Governmental Operations, 292
Senate Subcommittee on Employment, Manpower, and Poverty: 1967 hearings, 392–93
Shaeffer, Brent, 63
Shaw, John, 349–50
Shelton, Robert, 476n
Sheridan, Walter: on ineffectiveness of FBI in Mississippi, 481n
Sherrod, Charles, 106, 289, 459n; on Anne Braden, 231–32
Shirah, Sam, 231
Shriver, Sargent, 363, 371, 374, 377, 379–81
Shuttlesworth, Fred, 76
Sias, Henry, 253, 301, 484n
Sigh, Richard, 405
Sillers, Walter, 38, 39–40

Silver, James W., 58–59, 141, 142
Simmons, Eldridge, 15
Simmons, Isaac, 15
Simmons, William J., 195, 321
Simpson, Euvester, 170, 225, 324
Sisson, Hattie, 138, 243
Sisson, Herman, 138, 243
Sitton, Claude, 149, 166, 222
Skates, John Roy, 14
Slaughter, Constance, 413, 510n
Smead, Howard, 84
Smiley, Glenn, 62
Smith, Ben, 230, 336, 479n
Smith, Frank, 146, 318; and Marshall County project, 135, 148, 175, 225; and CDGM, 370, 374
Smith, Frank (congressman), 34, 139, 467n
Smith, Hazel Brannon, 66, 323
Smith, Hattie, 135
Smith, Jerome, 164, 189, 256, 257
Smith, Lamar: murder of, 54
Smith, R. L. T., 30, 77, 118, 204, 222, 282, 316, 488n; on Black and Tan Republican party, 25; on Percy Greene, 74; and Jackson movement, 161, 167–68; appointed to MAP board, 378; runs for Congress, 459n
Smith, Robert, 335, 400
Smith, Ruby Doris. *See* Robinson, Ruby Doris
Smith v. *Allwright*, 2, 4
SNCC. *See* Student Nonviolent Coordinating Committee
Sojourner, Susan Lorenzi, 190, 416, 471n
Southern Christian Leadership Conference (SCLC): rivalry with NAACP, 78; and COFO, 119; and citizenship schools, 170, 183; and Natchez movement, 356–59; and Grenada campaign, 403–7; and Poor People's Campaign, 419–20. *See also* Council of Federated Organizations; King, Martin Luther, Jr.
Southern Conference Education Fund (SCEF), 103, 158, 165, 169, 317, 482n; red-baiting of, 230–32, 479n
Southern Politics in State and Nation, 9
Southern Regional Council, 63, 94, 119, 120, 387

Southern Student Organizing Committee (SSOC), 482*n*, 486*n*
Southern Tenant Farmers Union, 365
Southwest Mississippi Opportunities, 379
Sovereignty Commission. *See* Mississippi State Sovereignty Commission
Spain, David, 283
Spencer, James L., 95
Spike, Robert, 230, 300, 316–17, 379
Spingarn, Arthur B., 176
Spottswood, Stephen Gill, 176
Stanford University, students at: and freedom vote, 203, 206–7; and summer project, 232–34
Starnes, Robert W., 24
Steel, Cornelius, 246–47
Stembridge, Jane, 102, 174, 203, 207, 213
Stennis, John, 156, 218, 322, 348, 368; elected to Senate, 9; on *Brown* decision, 37; denounces Greenwood activists, 154; opposes CDGM, 371, 372, 375, 377
Steptoe, E. W., 109, 112, 114, 188, 283, 331, 347; background of, 106
Stewarts, Nathan, 51
Stone, Bob, 305
Strelitz, Ilene, 480*n*
Strickland, William, 232
Strider, H. C., 57
Stringer, Emmett J., 49, 54, 74, 77, 424; meeting with Governor White, 39; background of, 42; elected president of state NAACP conference, 43; opposed by Citizens' Council, 46–47
Stringer, Flora, 42, 46
Stromquist, Shelton, 493–94*n*
Student Nonviolent Coordinating Committee (SNCC); founding of, 92; and freedom rides, 92–97 passim; and McComb movement, 99–115, 266–71, 303–14; organizing strategies of, 104, 113, 115, 126, 128; and Greenwood movement, 128–35, 143–57; and Hattiesburg movement, 178–84, 219–21; Mississippi staff of (fall 1964), 322; and COFO dissolution, 343–44; and MFDP (in 1966), 408; mentioned, passim. *See also* Council of Federated Organizations;

Freedom vote; Mississippi Freedom Democratic party; Summer project
Suarez, Matt, 188, 189, 190, 246, 249; on Annie Devine, 190; and Jackson COFO office, 330–31
Sugarman, Jule, 372, 374, 379
Sullens, Fred, 23, 26, 34, 35, 39, 65
Sullivan, Joseph, 250
Summer project (1964), 242–85; debate over, 208–11, 218–19; planning for, 232–34, 240; Oxford, Ohio, orientation sessions, 242–46
Sunflower County Progress, Inc., 376
Surney, Lafayette, 137, 154, 176, 225
Swango, Curtis, 57
Sweeney, Dennis, 267, 307; murders Al Lowenstein, 480*n*

Taconic Foundation, 120
Taft, Robert A., 8
Talbert, Bobbie, 107, 113
Tarrants, Thomas Albert, 418, 510*n*, 511*n*
Taylor, Ben, 145
Teacher Corps, 368
Tet offensive, 419
Thelwell, Michael, 125, 338, 431; on movement meeting in the Delta, 131; on congressional challenge, 352
Thomas, Arthur, 316, 336, 369, 373–74
Thomas, Elmer, 4
Thomas, Hattie, 79
Thompson, Allen, 93, 97, 158, 177, 227; and Jackson movement, 161, 163, 167; calls for compliance with 1964 civil rights law, 275
Thompson, Bennie, 413–14, 427, 510*n*
Thompson, Julius, 74
Thornhill, J. E., 266–67
Thurmond, Strom, 27–28
Till, Emmett, 65, 124, 425; murder of, 55–56; trial of Milam and Bryant, 56–57, 449*n*; meaning of his death for Mississippi movement, 57–58
Tillinghast, Muriel, 253, 278, 324, 331, 332, 343
Tobias, Channing, 48
To Secure These Rights, 27
Tougaloo College, 35, 116, 117, 187, 431; history of, 2–3; and Jackson library sit-in, 87–89; and Jackson

movement, 157–69 passim; civil rights activity at, 225–28; and dismissal of President Beittel, 234–36, and Jackson State protests, 413–14, 510n

Tougaloo Cultural and Artistic Committee, 227

Touré, Sekou, 315

Travis, Brenda, 107, 108, 110, 111, 113, 114

Travis, Jimmie, 105, 116, 175, 282, 465n; wounded by gunshot, 147; at Oxford orientation, 243

Trent, Nelson, 192

Truman, Harry S., 21, 27, 28, 441n

Trumpauer, Joan, 116, 162, 228

Tubb, Tom, 50

Tucker, David L., 152, 155

Turnbow, Hartman, 188, 193, 253, 285, 323, 342; background of, 191–92

Turnbow, "Sweets," 285–86

Ullman, Al, 289, 293

United Klans of America, 476n

United States Commission on Civil Rights (CRC), 144, 153, 304, 415; history of, 194–95; Mississippi Advisory Committee to, 195–98, 308, 472n; and Kennedy administration, 196–98, 473n; 1965 hearings in Jackson, 484n

United States Department of Agriculture, 156, 386; and ASCS election, 333–35

United States v. *Lynd,* 180

University of Mississippi, 10, 211; and Meredith case, 138–42

University of Southern Mississippi. *See* Mississippi Southern College

Valenti, Jack, 290

Van Landingham, Zack: and Clyde Kennard case, 80–82, 453n

VEP. *See* Voter Education Project

Vietnam war, 419, 422, 433; MFDP opposition to, 349–50

Viorst, Milton, 393

Vivian, C. T., 95–96

Voter Education Project (VEP), 119–20, 147, 148; cuts off COFO funding, 212

Voting laws, Mississippi: in 1890 constitution, 6–7; of 1954–55, 52–53, 70–72, of 1966–67, 415. *See also* Poll tax

Voting rights act. *See* Civil Rights Act of 1965

Wagner, Robert, 18

Walker, Clinton, 216

Walker, Edwin, 141

Walker, Lovie, 48

Walker, Prentiss, 410

Walker, Wyatt T., 102

Wallace, George, 290

Wallace, Henry, 28

Waller, William, 468n

Walt, Thatcher, 277

Walters, Jimmy, 84, 454n

Walters, June, 83–84, 454n

Walters, Summer, 464n

Waltzer, Bruce, 479n

Walwyn, Cyril, 505n

Ward, Jimmy, 65

Ware, Bill, 353, 356

War on Poverty, 362, 363–88 passim, 425

Warren, Earl, 37

Warren, R. R., 266, 303–4, 307, 308

Warren County Improvement League, 282

Warrick, Odessa, 399

Wash, Howard, 15

Washington, Booker T., 258

Washington, Cynthia, 332

Watkins, Burt, 353

Watkins, Hollis, 135, 174, 209, 219, 225, 253, 264, 313, 324, 408, 431, 432, 470n; and McComb movement, 106–7, 113–14; and Hattiesburg movement, 180–83; on 1964 Democratic National Convention, 287

Watkins, W. H., 311

Watkins, Wes, 347

Watson, Marvin, 293

Watters, Pat, 156–57

Waveland retreat, 331–32

Webb, J. W., 24

Welch, Claude, 24

Wells, A. W., 30

Wesley, John D., 192

West, James, 170, 172

Wheeler, Jean, 174

Wheeler, Raymond, 387, 505*n*
White, Byron, 108
White, Hugh L., 36, 44, 47; and meeting with black leaders, 38–40
White, J. H., 38, 39, 44, 81
White, Lee, 237, 239, 292, 308, 473*n*
White, Walter, 32, 33
White Folks Project, 252
White Knights of the Ku Klux Klan, 216–18, 247, 476*n. See also* Ku Klux Klan
Whitley, Alfred, 216
Whitley, Clifton, 394, 409–10
Whitten, Jamie, 57, 384, 386
Whitten, John C., 57
Wiesenburg, Karl, 139, 197–98
Wilder, Robert, 235
Wilkins, Roy: opposes SCLC, 78; on freedom rides, 99; and Jackson movement, 160, 163–65, 169; on COFO, 274; on Charles Evers, 355; and Meredith March, 393–94, 402; on black power, 397; mentioned, passim. *See also* Current, Gloster; National Association for the Advancement of Colored People
William Carey College, 179
Williams, Helen Bass, 382
Williams, Hosea, 403–4, 406–7
Williams, John Bell, 142, 195, 371, 471, 494*n*
Williams, Otha, 237, 334–35
Williams, Walter, 162
Wilson, T. B., 25, 26–27
Winter, William, 417, 419
Wise, Stanley, 392
WLBT, 65, 451*n*
Wofford, Harris, 92
Wolf, Melvin, 229–30
Womanpower Unlimited, 98–99
Women: and the civil rights movement, 126–27, 263–64, 330–32, 461*n*

Wood, John Q., 108
Woods, Mrs. L. E., 181
Woolworth's sit-in (Jackson), 161–63
Work-Study Project (Tougaloo), 225, 324
World War II: impact on Mississippi, 13–18
Woullard, R. W., 81, 182
Wright, Ellis, 51
Wright, Fielding, 21, 27, 36
Wright, James H., 50
Wright, Lowry, 16
Wright, Marian, 336, 373–74; on poverty program, 382
Wright, Moses, 55, 56, 449*n*
Wright, Richard, 54
Wroten, Joe, 139
Wynn, Douglas, 299, 322, 347, 348–49, 376, 390, 491*n*

Yale University, students at, 232; and freedom vote, 203, 204, 206–7
Yarborough, George, 140
Young, Andrew, 173, 231, 315, 356, 403; eulogy at Fannie Lou Hamer's funeral, 433–34
Young, Aurelia, 31, 97, 98
Young, Charles, 347
Young, Jack, 30, 95, 97, 229
Young, Whitney, 393–94, 401
Young Democrats—Mississippi, 378, 390, 419–20; founding of, 348–49; and 1968 Democratic National Convention, 420–22

Zeeck, Ernest, 306–7
Zellner, Dorothy, 207, 232, 317
Zellner, Robert, 207, 231, 431, 459*n;* and McComb movement, 110–11, 113; and summer project, 250, 252, 278
Zinn, Howard, 135, 220, 261

Books in the Series Blacks in the New World

Before the Ghetto: Black Detroit in the Nineteenth Century
David M. Katzman

Black Business in the New South: A Social History of the North
Carolina Mutual Life Insurance Company
Walter B. Weare

The Search for a Black Nationality: Black Colonization and Emigration,
1787–1863
Floyd J. Miller

Black Americans and the White Man's Burden, 1898–1903
Willard B. Gatewood, Jr.

Slavery and the Numbers Game: A Critique of Time on the Cross
Herbert G. Gutman

A Ghetto Takes Shape: Black Cleveland, 1870–1930
Kenneth L. Kusmer

Freedmen, Philanthropy, and Fraud: A History of the Freedman's Savings
Bank
Carl R. Osthaus

The Democratic Party and the Negro: Northern and National Politics,
1868–92
Lawrence Grossman

Black Ohio and the Color Line, 1860–1915
David A. Gerber

Along the Color Line: Explorations in the Black Experience
August Meier and Elliott Rudwick

Black over White: Negro Political Leadership in South Carolina during
Reconstruction
Thomas Holt

Keeping the Faith: A. Philip Randolph, Milton P. Webster, and the
Brotherhood of Sleeping Car Porters, 1925–37
William H. Harris

Abolitionism: The Brazilian Antislavery Struggle
Joaquim Nabuco; translated and edited by Robert Conrad

Black Georgia in the Progressive Era, 1900–1920
John Dittmer

Medicine and Slavery: Health Care of Blacks in Antebellum Virginia
Todd L. Savitt

Alley Life in Washington: Family, Community, Religion, and Folklife in the City, 1850–1970
James Borchert

Human Cargoes: The British Slave Trade to Spanish America, 1700–1739
Colin A. Palmer

Southern Black Leaders of the Reconstruction Era
Edited by Howard N. Rabinowitz

Black Leaders of the Twentieth Century
Edited by John Hope Franklin and August Meier

Slaves and Missionaries: The Disintegration of Jamaican Slave Society, 1787–1834
Mary Turner

Father Divine and the Struggle for Racial Equality
Robert Weisbrot

Communists in Harlem during the Depression
Mark Naison

Down from Equality: Black Chicagoans and the Public Schools, 1920–41
Michael W. Homel

Race and Kinship in a Midwestern Town: The Black Experience in Monroe, Michigan, 1900–1915
James E. DeVries

Down by the Riverside: A South Carolina Slave Community
Charles Joyner

Black Milwaukee: The Making of an Industrial Proletariat, 1915–45
Joe William Trotter, Jr.

Religious Philanthropy and Colonial Slavery: The American Correspondence of the Associates of Dr. Bray, 1717–77
Edited by John C. Van Horne

Black History and the Historical Profession, 1915–80
August Meier and Elliott Rudwick

Paul Cuffe: Black Entrepreneur and Pan-Africanist (formerly Rise to Be a People: A Biography of Paul Cuffe)
Lamont D. Thomas

Making Their Own Way: Southern Blacks' Migration to Pittsburgh, 1916–30
Peter Gottlieb

My Bondage and My Freedom
Frederick Douglass; edited by William L. Andrews

Black Leaders of the Nineteenth Century
Edited by Leon Litwack and August Meier

Charles Richard Drew: The Man and the Myth
Charles E. Wynes

John Mercer Langston and the Fight for Black Freedom, 1829–65
William Cheek and Aimee Lee Cheek

The Old Village and the Great House: An Archaeological and Historical Examination of Drax Hall Plantation, St. Ann's Bay, Jamaica
Douglas V. Armstrong

Black Property Owners in the South, 1790–1915
Loren Schweninger

The Sociogenesis of a Race Riot: Springfield, Illinois, in 1908
Roberta Senechal

Coal, Class, and Color: Blacks in Southern West Virginia, 1915–32
Joe William Trotter, Jr.

No Crooked Death: Coatesville, Pennsylvania, and the Lynching of Zachariah Walker
Dennis B. Downey and Raymond M. Hyser

Black Towns and Profit: Promotion and Development in the Trans-Appalachian West, 1877–1915
Kenneth Marvin Hamilton

Slaves, Peasants, and Rebels: Reconsidering Brazilian Slavery
Stuart B. Schwartz

Africa in America: Slave Acculturation and Resistance in the American South and the British Caribbean, 1736–1831
Michael Mullin

The Creation of Jazz: Music, Race, and Culture in Urban America
Burton W. Peretti

Kenneth and John B. Rayner and the Limits of Southern Dissent
Gregg Cantrell

Lynching in the New South: Georgia and Virginia, 1880–1930
W. Fitzhugh Brundage

Local People: The Struggle for Civil Rights in Mississippi
John Dittmer

REPRINT EDITIONS

King: A Biography
Second Edition
David Levering Lewis

The Death and Life of Malcolm X
Second Edition
Peter Goldman

Race Relations in the Urban South, 1865–1890
Howard N. Rabinowitz; foreword by C. Vann Woodward

Race Riot at East St. Louis, July 2, 1917
Elliott Rudwick

W. E. B. Du Bois: Voice of the Black Protest Movement
Elliott Rudwick

The Negro's Civil War: How American Negroes Felt and Acted during
the War for the Union
James M. McPherson

Lincoln and Black Freedom: A Study in Presidential Leadership
LaWanda Cox

Slavery and Freedom in the Age of the American Revolution
Edited by Ira Berlin and Ronald Hoffman

Diary of a Sit-In
Second Edition
Merrill Proudfoot; introduction by Michael S. Mayer

They Who Would Be Free: Blacks' Search for Freedom, 1830–61
Jane H. Pease and William H. Pease

The Reshaping of Plantation Society: The Natchez District, 1860–80
Michael Wayne

Rice and Slaves: Ethnicity and the Slave Trade in Colonial South
Carolina
Daniel C. Littlefield